Public Speaking

SIXTH EDITION

Public Speaking

INSTRUCTOR'S ANNOTATED EDITION

Michael Osborn
University of Memphis

Suzanne Osborn
University of Memphis

Houghton Mifflin Company
Boston New York

Sponsoring Editor: Adam Forrand
Associate Editor: Kristen Desmond LeFevre
Editorial Associate: Brigitte Maser
Associate Project Editor: Claudine Bellanton
Editorial Assistant: Shelley Dickerson
Senior Production/Design Coordinator: Jodi O'Rourke
Senior Manufacturing Coordinator: Priscilla Bailey
Marketing Manager: Barbara LeBuhn

Cover Image: © Pedro Lobo—Photonica

Printed in the U.S.A.

Library of Congress Catalog Card Number: 2001098676
Student Edition ISBN: 0-618-22351-7
Instructor's Annotated Edition ISBN: 0-618-22352-5

1 2 3 4 5 6 7 8 9 — DOW— 06 05 04 03 02

We dedicate this edition of Public Speaking to Nader Darehshori, president of Houghton Mifflin Company. Nader believed in us from the beginning. He motivated and promoted this book, and we have celebrated its success together. Authors everywhere and in all fields appreciate his contribution to international book publishing.

Contents

15 Ceremonial Speaking 403

Appendix A Communicating in Small Groups 429

Appendix B Handling Communication Apprehension 443

Appendix C Speeches for Analysis 453

Preface

This sixth edition of *Public Speaking* continues to follow our philosophy of revision. We have consistently refused to do "tear-sheet revisions," an approach that invites writers simply to make superficial changes on pages from the previous edition, and to offer these as a new edition of their book. Instead, we follow a concept we call "zero-based revision." Put simply, this means that everything in the book—every photograph, every graphic, every sentence—must rejustify itself. The result is that our revisions take a good deal of time and are often extensive. A textbook must constantly adapt to the changing times and needs of students. Moreover, even though our book has been well received, we know that it can always be better, and we are in constant pursuit of that standard.

"**Better**," therefore, is the theme of this new revision. This edition is better in four major ways: (1) it contains new learning aids—*Ethics Alert!* and *InterConnections.LearnMore*—that highlight ethical concerns and Internet-enriched learning opportunities, (2) it places greater emphasis on dealing with communication apprehension, including an appendix for students who need additional counseling, (3) it incorporates new material on preparing PowerPoint presentations, and (4) it offers extensive revisions in the opening chapter and in later chapters on persuasion and language. We are confident that users will be pleased with these large areas of improvement, so we wish to describe them more fully.

New Learning Aids

We are especially pleased with two pedagogical innovations. We have always discussed ethical issues as they arise in the context of topics, rather than confining the subject to a chapter on its own. We believe that isolating ethics in a separate chapter diminishes its importance. The new *Ethics Alert!* feature helps us to highlight even more of these concerns as they develop within various chapters so that attention is drawn to their importance.

The *InterConnections.LearnMore* feature connects the student with sources of additional information on the Internet. In addition, Chapter 5 offers guidelines for the evaluation of Internet research to help students assess the quality of what they find. It also offers a research plan in which the Internet might play a substantial role, and provides a master list of web sites for Internet research carefully selected with the speaker's needs in mind.

Greater Emphasis on Communication Apprehension

Every teacher of public speaking is aware of the corrosive effect of fear on student presentations. Some students need special help with this problem. In addition to our usual consideration of this problem in Chapters 2 and 11, we now provide an appendix that offers extended counseling to those suffering from acute communication apprehension.

PowerPoint Presentations

Many students will be expected to have mastered the basic skills of PowerPoint presentations as they move into work situations. The sixth edition offers simple, user-friendly instructions on how to develop such presentations. As a matter of fact, we have put this new section to the ultimate test. One of your co-authors has said that if her colleague, who is technologically challenged, could follow them successfully, anyone could. And he can!

Intense Revisions of Challenging Chapters

Writing on public speaking in a way that is simple, clear, and useful offers special challenges. Chapter 1 is as crucial to a book as an introduction is to a speech. The new chapter blends the best elements of previous editions to provide a fresh approach to public speaking as a dynamic, interactive process that can have important consequences for participants and the society in which they live. The chapter reverses the order of discussion so that we define our subject before discussing the benefits of studying it. The result is that the chapter develops more logically.

Another challenge is that of writing usefully about the oral uses of language. We have shortened and restructured Chapter 10 so that it places more emphasis on standards of language use and how to apply them. The new chapter also offers more selective treatment of certain techniques that can magnify the natural power of language at strategic moments in a speech.

A challenge that confronts all public-speaking-textbook writers is how to compress the rich and extensive subject of persuasive speaking into a few brief chapters. We have restructured Chapter 13 so that it develops in a more orderly way. In the process, we have also developed a clearer account of the impact of persuasive speaking on attitudes, beliefs, and values. This account discovers a deep, therapeutic and ethical role for persuasive speaking that has not previously been discussed in public speaking textbooks.

In our revision of Chapter 14, we have concentrated on reducing jargon, clarifying and simplifying discussion, and making it more useful to students. We have also expanded and sharpened our discussion of fallacies, while adding a major new figure, the Gallery of Fallacies.

Throughout the book, new student and professional speaker examples enliven the discussion.

Distinctive Features of Public Speaking

Long-term users of our text know that the belief that "public speaking texts are all the same" does not apply to this book. *Public Speaking* is an innovative textbook that contains a number of distinctive features, in addition to those introduced in this edition. Many of these features have received the ultimate compliment—they have been imitated.

Speaker's Notes

Our book was the first to introduce a special feature to help students focus on the essentials of the discussion as they are reading. *Speaker's Notes* are highlighted boxes that summarize major points to help students apply what they are reading. Now augmented by *Ethics Alert!* and *InterConnections.LearnMore*, this feature, more than ever, will bring focus to the learning experience.

Special Preparation for the First Speech

As teachers, we all realize the importance of the first speaking experience to a student's ultimate success in the course. Yet so much useful advice must be delayed until later chapters as the subject of public speaking develops systematically over a semester. Having experienced this frustration ourselves while teaching the course, we decided to include an overview of practical advice early in the book to preview later chapters and to prepare students more effectively for their first experiences. This overview is provided in Chapter 2 of our book.

Enriched Treatment of Listening

We have enriched the discussion of listening in three important ways. First, we introduced the concept of listener apprehension, which is presently receiving considerable attention in listening research. This new concept identifies an important challenge that both speakers and listeners must overcome to achieve authentic communication. Second, we created the idea of the *ladder of listening* as a graphic device to help students understand the various kinds of listening and the relationships among them. Third, we have enlarged the focus on listening in order to emphasize its constructive and critical dimensions.

Improved Account of Motivation

Appealing to motives is a major technique in successful speechmaking, yet much of the information concerning motivation in speech textbooks has been general and derivative, gleaned mainly from textbooks in psychology. *Public Speaking* innovates by grounding its discussion of motivation in a direct examination of over a hundred student speeches. This empirical grounding lends considerable authority to the advice we offer.

Selected Directory of Web Sites

We were the first to offer a directory of web sites selected specifically for their application to the needs of student speakers. The *InterConnections.LearnMore* feature, offered within various chapters, represents a further evolution of this sensitivity to the needs of students.

Responsible Knowledge as a Standard for Student Speakers

In order to develop a standard for the quality and depth of information that should be reflected in student speeches, we developed the concept of *responsible knowledge*. This concept is developed in detail in Chapter 5, where we discuss the foundation of research that should support speeches.

The Importance of Narrative in Public Speaking

We were the first to elevate narrative to an important form of supporting material. We were also the first to identify appeals to cultural traditions, heroic symbols and their opposites, and patriotic legends—all built upon narrative—as an important emerging form of proof (*mythos*) in persuasive speaking.

Innovations in Outlining

We innovated by developing a process approach to outlining, and by developing the first software for self-directed learning in outlining speeches.

Improving Listening Skills

We developed a novel approach to teaching language skills that emphasizes understanding the power of language, applying standards so that this power is not diminished, and learning special techniques that can magnify this power at important moments in speeches. Among the standards is learning how to avoid grammatical errors that make listeners cringe.

Enhanced Understanding of Informative Speaking

We were the first to ground informative speaking in psychological learning theories so that student speakers can understand how and why successful informative speeches work.

Enhanced Understanding of Persuasive Speaking

We were the first to successfully adapt McGuire's psychological theory of persuasion to the needs of the student speaker. This adaptation allows students to understand successful persuasion as a process that moves through distinct stages, and to develop their strategies accordingly.

Enhanced Understanding of Argument

We were the first to develop an integrated, systematic approach to argument that indicates how thoughtful persuasion begets effective relationships among evidence, proof, and forms of argument.

Enhanced Understanding of Ceremonial Speaking

The study of ceremonial speaking has been treated too often as a collection of "occasional speech" assignments, combined without explanation or reason into a chapter that sometimes seemed tacked on at the end of a book. We gave this subject coherence and dignity by pointing out the importance of ceremonial speaking in society, and by indicating how two powerful ideas, one offered by Aristotle and the other developed by Kenneth Burke, can be combined to generate successful ceremonial speeches, especially speeches of tribute and inspiration.

Continuing Themes in Public Speaking

Our book continues to reflect the enduring values of the public speaking course. One such value is the role of public speaking in a diverse society. The ancient writers on rhetoric never had to contend with a diverse audience. The increasing cultural diversity of our society adds to the importance of public speaking as a force that can counter division. For this reason, the theme of cultural diversity remains embedded throughout the book. We have also renewed our emphasis on ethics: a diverse society heightens the importance of values that can join people of different backgrounds.

We continue to believe that a major ethical obligation of textbooks about public speaking is to make students sensitive to the potential impact of public speaking on the lives of others. Because of the pervasive importance of values and ethics, we discuss ethical considerations throughout the book. For example, we direct the attention of students to ethical concerns as we consider listening, audience analysis and adaptation, cultural variations, topic selection, research, ways of structuring speeches, presentation aids, use of language, and the consequences of informing and persuading others.

We honor a study that ancient educators believed was the core of a liberal arts education. What other discipline requires students to think clearly, organize their thoughts, select and combine words artfully and judiciously, and express themselves with power and conviction, all while under the direct scrutiny of listeners? The study of public speaking should empower students in social, economic, and political situations that require open discussion. Not only personal success but also the fate of communities may depend upon such discussions.

For these reasons, we believe that a college or university course in public speaking should offer both practical advice and an understanding of why such advice works. We emphasize both the *how* and the *why* of public speaking—*how* so that beginners can achieve success as quickly as possible, and *why* so that they can manage their new skills wisely. Consistent with this philosophy, we base our practical advice on underlying principles of human communication. As we offer advice on structuring speeches, we show how various speech designs connect with basic psychological concepts of "good form," explaining why some speeches succeed and others fail. We ground our advice for informative speaking in the principles of learning theory, and our suggestions for persuasive speaking on research from social psychology and the communication discipline. Our approach is eclectic; we draw from the past and present, and from the social sciences and humanities to help students understand and manage their public speaking experiences.

The Roman educator, Quintilian, held forth the ideal of "the good person speaking well" as a goal of education, and we join him in stressing the value of speech training in the development of the whole person. We also emphasize that successful public speaking is excellent training for leadership. In addition, understanding the basics of public communication can make students more resistant to unethical speakers and more critical of the mass-mediated communication to which they are exposed. The class should help students become both better consumers as well as producers of public communication.

We have continued throughout the book to follow the metaphorical themes of the student as climber, builder, and weaver to represent the important dimensions of personal growth and development that the public speaking class makes possible. The student learns to climb barriers of personal and cultural interference, and grows in the process. The student also learns how to build ideas by mastering the arts of practical logic and organization, and learning how and when to utilize various forms of supporting materials. Finally, the student learns how to weave words into a clear, colorful fabric of communication and how to fashion a tapestry of argument out of evidence and proof. Mastering these central metaphors is the key not only to effective communication, but also to successful living.

Plan of the Book

Overview

Public Speaking is designed to help beginners build knowledge and skills step by step. Positive initial speaking experiences are especially important. For this reason, Chapter 2 offers an overview to help students design and present successful first speeches.

In the chapters that follow, students learn how to listen critically and constructively; analyze their audiences; select, refine, and research speech topics; develop supporting materials; arrange these materials in appropriate structures; outline their thinking; and create effective presentation aids. They also learn how to manage words and present their messages. Students become acquainted with the nature of information and how to present it, the process of persuasion and how to engage it, and the importance of ceremonial speaking in its various forms. Appendix A, "Communicating in Small Groups," describes how to participate effectively in small group interactions. Teachers may adapt the sequence of chapters to any course plan, because each chapter covers a topic thoroughly and completely.

Detailed Plan of the Book

Part One, "The Foundations of Public Speaking," provides basic information that students need for their first speaking and listening experiences. Chapter 1 defines public speaking as communication; highlights the personal, social, and cultural benefits of being able to speak effectively in public; and emphasizes the ethical responsibilities of speakers. Chapter 2 offers students practical advice for organizing, practicing, and presenting their first speeches. The chapter also helps them handle communication apprehension. Chapter 3 identifies common listening problems and ways to overcome them, helps students sharpen critical-thinking skills, and presents criteria for the constructive evaluation of speeches.

Part Two, "Preparation for Public Speaking," introduces the basic skills needed to develop effective speeches—audience analysis, topic selection, research, development of supporting materials, and structuring and outlining procedures. Chapter 4 emphasizes the importance of the audience as it considers how to adapt a message and how to adjust to factors in the speaking situation. Chapter 5 provides a systematic way to select, refine and research speech topics. We emphasize the importance of acquiring *responsible knowledge* based upon personal experience, library and computerized resources, and interviewing. Chapter 6 covers the major types of supporting materials including facts and statistics, examples, testimony, and narratives. This chapter shows students how to select the most appropriate supporting materials and bring them to life through comparison, contrast, and analogy. Chapter 7 shows students how to develop simple, balanced, and orderly speech designs, how to select and shape their main points, how to use transitions, and how to prepare effective introductions and conclusions. Chapter 8 explains how to develop working outlines, refine them into formal outlines, and derive a key-word outline to use during presentation. An extended example in Chapters 6, 7, and 8 illustrates how a speech on an environmental topic might develop from its initial conception to its final presentation. Chapter 8 ends with the annotated text of this speech.

Part Three, "Developing Presentation Skills," brings the speaker to the point of presentation. Chapter 9 explains the preparation of presentation aids including PowerPoint presentations. Chapter 10 provides an understanding of the role of language in communication and offers practical suggestions for using words effectively. Chapter 11 offers exercises for the improvement of voice and body language and helps students develop an extemporaneous style that is adaptable to most speaking situations.

Part Four, "Functions of Public Speaking," discusses informative, persuasive, and ceremonial speaking. Chapter 12 covers speeches designed to share information and increase understanding. The chapter discusses the different types of informative speeches and presents the major designs that can be used. Chapter 13 describes the persuasive process, focusing on how to meet the many challenges of persuasion. The chapter also discusses designs that are appropriate for persuasive speeches. In Chapter 14, we explain the use of evidence, proof, and argument to help students develop strong, reasoned cases to support their positions. The chapter also identifies the major forms of fallacies so students can avoid them in their speeches and detect them in the messages of others. Chapter 15 describes how the classical technique of magnification can combine productively with the contemporary technique of identification to generate effective ceremonial speaking, especially speeches of tribute and inspiration. The chapter features interesting, annotated speech excerpts by and about Olympic track-and-field legends Jesse Owens and Wilma Rudolph, and concludes with two striking student speeches.

Appendix A, "Communicating in Small Groups," introduces students to the problem-solving process and the responsibilities of group participants. This appendix also provides guidelines for managing informal and formal meetings, and explains the basic concepts of parliamentary procedure. Appendix B offers advice to those who suffer from acute speaking anxiety. Appendix C provides a number of student and professional speeches for additional analysis.

Learning Tools

To help students master the material, we developed a number of special learning tools:

- We open each chapter with an outline and learning objectives that prepare students for efficient and productive reading.
- The epigrams and vignettes that start each chapter help highlight the topic's significance and motivate readers.
- We use contemporary artwork and photographs to illustrate ideas, engage student interest, and add visual appeal to the book.
- Examples illustrate and apply the content in a clear, lively, often entertaining way.
- *Speaker's Notes*, *Ethics Alert!*, and *InterConnections.LearnMore* features help students learn the essentials, apply what they are learning to ethical issues, and pursue additional information using the Internet.
- We end each chapter with *In Summary* and *Terms to Know* sections that further reinforce learning.
- Sample classroom speeches illustrate important concepts. The book contains many annotated speech texts so that students can see how the concepts apply in actual speeches. These speeches are found at the ends of chapters. Appendix C contains additional speeches for analysis. These speeches cover an interesting array of topics, contexts, and speakers. They illustrate the major functions of self-introductory, informative, persuasive, and ceremonial speeches.
- A glossary at the end of the book defines *Terms to Know* in an accessible format.

Supplementary Materials

The following materials are available to adopters of *Public Speaking*:

For Instructors

- An **Instructor's Annotated Edition** that includes general and ESL teaching tips for every chapter.
- The **Instructor's Resource Manual (IRM),** written by Suzanne Osborn and Randall Parrish Osborn. Part I of the manual includes a section on the purpose and philosophy of the course, a section on syllabus preparation, various sample syllabi, an assortment of speech assignment options, a discussion of evaluating and grading speeches, a troubleshooting guide with teaching strategies for new instructors, and an extensive bibliography of resource readings. Part II offers a chapter-by-chapter guide to teaching *Public Speaking*, including learning objectives, suggestions for teaching, lecture/discussion outlines, classroom activities, transparency/handout masters, and a bibliography of readings for enrichment. This comprehensive manual can be used as a text for training teaching assistants.
- A printed **Test Bank** separate from the IRM to provide test security.
- A **PowerPoint Presentation Program** available on the Houghton Mifflin web site (http://college.hmco.com/instructors).
- The **HMClassPrep™ Instructor's CD-ROM,** which contains digital versions of the IRM, Test Bank Items (in MS Word), the sixth edition Power-

Point slides, as well as Instructor Professional Development modules such as the Speech Assessment Videos and Guide for training in speech evaluation.

- **Student Speeches Videos—**a compilation of student speeches accompanied by a guide that contains the text of each speech, an evaluation of the presentation, discussion items, and commentary.
- ***Contemporary Great Speeches* Videos**—the latest compilation in the series from the Educational Video Group.
- The ***Using Presentation Aids* Video** illustrating class lectures on presentation aids.
- **Speech Assessment Video and Guide** with training in speech evaluation.
- An **ESL Teaching Guide** available online.
- **Blackboard & WebCT courseware** that offers content from the sixth edition, as well as classroom management functionality for every level of online coursework.
- **Instructor companion web site** including updated links, research sites, exercises, and other ancillary material for both instructor and student use.

For Students

- **Real Deal Upgrade CD-ROM,** which offers digital student speech videos with commentary, an electronic glossary, emailable discussion and application exercises, and a chapter-by-chapter preparation checklist. In addition, the student CD-ROM will include valuable study-skills assessments and strategies promoting student success in their coursework.
- The **Speech Designer** computer software program that offers students a self-directed, step-by-step electronic process for outlining speeches and includes formats for each major speech design discussed in the text.
- The **Speech Preparation Workbook** developed by Suzanne Osborn that contains materials for activities mentioned in the text and skeleton outline formats for the major speech designs.
- ***Multicultural Activities Workbook for the Public Speaking Classroom***
- The ***Classical Origins of Public Speaking*** supplement, written by Michael Osborn, offers a concise overview of the ideas developed by early Greek theorists on the nature and importance of public speaking.
- **Student companion web site** including chapter-specific comprehension tests known as **ACE** (A Cyber Evaluation), vocabulary and topic flashcards, updated links to relevant web sites and additional communication career resources.
- **Blackboard & WebCT courseware** that offers content from the sixth edition.

Acknowledgements

Public Speaking has been a labor of love for many people. For this edition, we especially wish to thank Adam Forrand, our sponsoring editor, and Barbara LeBuhn, marketing manager, for their commitment and encouragement. Kristen Desmond LeFevre, associate editor for Communication at Houghton Mifflin, has coordinated the work that makes a revision possible with a deft touch. Brigitte Maser, editorial associate for Communication, has risen to the challenge of maintaining and extending what we think is the finest ancillary program available. Claudine Bellanton, our associate project editor, has guided us through the final processes of the revision with good humor and a fine professional hand. Special appreciation goes to George Hoffman, our outgoing editor and friend, whose contribution to this and to previous editions has been outstanding.

We thank our colleagues listed below, whose helpful critical readings guided our revisions for the sixth edition.

Kenneth Broda-Bahm
Towson University

John Gore
Indiana University–South Bend

Cathy Mester
Pennsylvania State University–Behrend

Glynis Strause
Coastal Bend College

Donna Thomson
Johnson & Wales University

Dr. Elaine VanderClute
Wor-Wic Community College

Our applause for all these people.

List of Speeches

Self-Introductory

Informative

Persuasive

Ceremonial

Public Speaking

PART ONE

The Foundations of Public Speaking

1

You as a Public Speaker

OUTLINE

Public Speaking as Communication

Public Speaking as Expanded Conversation

Public Speaking Preserves Conversational Directness and Spontaneity

Public Speaking Is Colorful and Compelling

Public Speaking Is Tuned to Listeners

Distinctive Features of Public Speaking

Speaker

Purpose

Message

Medium

Setting

Listener

Response

Interference

Consequences

How a Public Speaking Course Can Help You

Personal Benefits

Social Benefits

Cultural Benefits

Ethical Public Speaking

Respect for the Integrity of Ideas

Responsible Knowledge

Communication Techniques

Avoiding Plagiarism

Concern for Listeners

Developing an "Other" Orientation

Applying Universal Values

THIS CHAPTER WILL HELP YOU

- understand public speaking as communication
- realize how a public speaking course can help you
- appreciate the social and cultural benefits of the course
- recognize your responsibilities as an ethical speaker

ary was worried about taking public speaking. She had put off the course as long as she could but finally had to take it to graduate. At the first class meeting she saw about twenty other stone-faced students who looked as uncomfortable as she felt. Realizing that dropping the course was not an option, she steeled herself to stick it out.

Mary's first oral assignment was a speech of self-introduction. As she prepared her speech, it dawned on her why she found marine biology so fascinating. When she spoke, her enthusiasm for the topic helped relieve her nervousness. Although her speech was not perfect, she did some things very well. Listeners could now relate to her as an individual. She had also built up credibility for her later informative and persuasive speeches on the fate of the oceans.

As she listened to others speak, Mary began to enjoy the class. Many of the speeches were interesting, and she joined in the discussion of what worked well and how the speeches might be improved. The "great stone faces" of her classmates began to chip away and reveal the real human beings they had masked.

As Mary gave her speeches, she found that her audience took her seriously. She began to care about her classmates and to take joy in their successes. As she researched her speeches, she kept her audience in mind. She sought out facts, opinions, examples, and stories her listeners would find useful and interesting. Toward the end of the term it dawned on her: *she had become a competent speaker!* She also could recognize the strategies and techniques of others. She believed she could meet the challenges of public speaking and critical listening whenever she needed to do so.

Ask students how they became proficient at some skill (i.e., music or sports). Discuss the important phases and stages involved, and trace possible connections to the acquisition of public speaking skills.

The ability to make a good speech is a great gift to the people from their Maker, Owner of all things.

— Oglala Sioux

The "Mary" in our example represents the many successful students we have known in our years of teaching public speaking. You too may wonder why you are taking this course, even whether you can make it through the semester, let alone be successful. To make yourself into a "Mary," you must commit yourself to the work required to be successful. You must decide that you want to learn the art of public speaking, that you will select worthwhile topics, that you will treat listeners ethically, and that you will listen constructively to others. In this chapter, we explain more about this art you will be learning, why it deserves your commitment, and why it requires your utmost ethical sensitivity.

Public Speaking as Communication

Seeing yourself as public speaker may at first seem difficult, especially if you think of public speaking as a mysterious skill possessed only by a privileged few. But you have been preparing for public speaking for a long time. As an infant, you developed the most essential tool of the speaker—language. When your grandfather explained how to catch a fish and why you must stay away from fire, you were introduced to two of the great functions of human communication, *informing* and *persuading*. Later, as you developed friendships, you began practicing interaction skills that are vital to communication: how to listen as well as speak.

Public speaking only expands the conversational skills we have been practicing all of our lives. On the other hand, some distinctive features make public speaking a unique form of communication.

Public Speaking as Expanded Conversation

Public speaking retains three important characteristics of good conversation. First, it preserves the natural directness and spontaneity of informal talk. Second, it is colorful. And third, it is tuned to the reactions of listeners.

Ask students to describe an ideal conversationalist. Which of these traits might also describe an ideal public speaker?

Public Speaking Preserves Conversational Directness and Spontaneity. Even though a speech has been carefully researched, thoughtfully prepared, and well rehearsed, it should sound conversational and spontaneous as it comes to life before an audience. Those words bear repeating: *a speech comes to life before an audience.* Consider the following opening to a self-introductory speech:

> **It may seem hot here today, but it's not near as hot as Plainview, Texas, where I was born and reared. I almost said "roasted." John has just told us about the joys of urban living. Now you're going to hear about what you might call a "country-fried" lifestyle.**

Compare that opening with

> **My name is Sam Johnson, and I come from Plainview, Texas.**

The first version seems fresh and spontaneous. The "us" and "you," along with the casual humorous remarks, suggest that the speaker is reaching out to his audience. The second, unless presented with a great deal of oomph, will sound quite ordinary. The first opening invites listening; the second invites yawning.

Public Speaking Is Colorful and Compelling. We enjoy talking with good conversationalists often because their speech is colorful. Consider the following development of the "heat" theme from the above example:

ESL: ESL students may have special problems both understanding and using informal speech. After each round of speeches, ask them if there were any words they didn't understand and help them translate colloquial language. Have them begin a "language log" in which they record unfamiliar words, phrases, or pronunciations.

> **That place was so hot it would make an armadillo sweat! It was so hot that rattlesnakes would rattle just to fan themselves!**

Compare those words with the following:

> **The average summer day in Plainview was often over a hundred degrees.**

The literal meaning of both statements is not that different, but the first contains the kind of vivid conversational qualities that listeners usually enjoy.

Ask a student to observe the audience during the introductory speeches and to report these observations at the end of the speeches. The report should focus on verbal and nonverbal cues that signal attentiveness and interest. This activity should help ESL students who may not know how listeners express active and engaged listening in the United States.

Public Speaking Is Tuned to Listeners. Like a good conversation, a good public speech is tuned to listeners. As you converse with people in social situations, you learn to monitor their reactions. If they look confused, you try to explain yourself more clearly. You may even give an example or tell a story. If they frown, you may rephrase an idea or present evidence that supports your views. If they smile or nod, you may feel you have the green light to develop your thoughts.

If good conversations are interactive and audience centered, effective speeches are even more so. Speakers must be constantly aware of the reactions of listeners and make on-the-spot adjustments. But from the very beginning, a speech must be planned with the audience in mind. (For more on audience analysis see Chapter 4.) Your entire speech should be designed to answer the questions that audiences will instinctively ask:

- Why should I be interested in this topic?
- What do you mean?
- How do I know this is true?
- What can I do about it?

You must give listeners a reason to be interested in the introduction of your speech or you will lose them before you ever get started. Your speech must be clearly organized and your language simple and direct so listeners can understand what you mean. You must provide facts and figures, examples, and expert testimony to demonstrate the truth of your statements. If your speech is persuasive, you must give listeners clear directions concerning what they should believe or do.

It seems clear that public speaking—far from being a mysterious skill—is a natural expansion and application of abilities we develop from our earliest years. On the other hand, some features make public speaking distinctive (see Figure 1.1).

Distinctive Features of Public Speaking

What makes public speaking distinctive as a form of communication are the relationships among a set of nine elements: speaker, purpose, message, medium, setting, listener, response, interference, and consequences. These elements interact with one another in ways that can affect those who participate and the world around them. They constitute a dynamic, interactive communication process.

Speaker. In public speaking, speaker and listener roles are clearly defined. There is little doubt as to who the speaker and listeners are. Public speaking spotlights the role of the **speaker**, but whether speakers can take advantage of

FIGURE 1.1
Talking or Speaking?

Conversations	Public Speaking
1. Audience-centered	1. More audience-centered
2. Loosely organized	2. Organized and planned
3. Off the top of your head	3. Grounded in responsible knowledge
4. Often no clear purpose	4. Has a clear purpose
5. Informal language	5. More formal language
6. Speaker/listener change roles	6. Speaker/listener roles clearly defined
7. Informal environment/small groups	7. More formal environment/larger groups

this attention depends on their ability to reward listeners with interesting and useful messages. As Aristotle pointed out more than two thousand years ago, our impressions of speakers themselves affect how we respond to what they say. We are far more inclined, he noted, to react favorably when we think speakers know what they're talking about and when we trust them. These qualities of competence and integrity form the basis of **credibility**. Aristotle also noted that audiences respond more favorably when speakers seem likeable—when they seem to be people of good will. Modern researchers have uncovered still another important speaker characteristic, forcefulness (or dynamism).[1] Some speakers strike us as vital, action-oriented people. When important interests are at stake and action seems called for, we may turn to such people to lead the way. These qualities of likeableness and forcefulness combine to form the basis of **charisma**.[2] Taken together, credibility and charisma provide an updated account of what Aristotle called the *ethos* of the speaker.[3] We consider ethos at greater detail in Chapter 2.

Ask students to identify a speaker they regard as credible and charismatic. Discuss what factors or behaviors contributed to this perception. Note any differences in responses between ESL and native students.

Purpose. People seldom speak in public unless they have some **purpose** in mind, something they wish to accomplish. A purpose can be complex, private, and psychological: speakers may speak because they like the sound of their own voices or because they like attention—they like being listened to. Or they may speak out of a need to define themselves and to establish their presence—to have some impact on the course of events. What makes public speaking a useful art is that people may also speak because they have ideas to offer and share. They know something other people may find valuable. They have the good of others at heart and want to contribute to it. It does not diminish the importance of their contribution if public speaking also satisfies inner psychological needs.

With respect to the public work performed by public speaking, scholars called *rhetoricians* have been working to identify major types of purposes for over two thousand years. Aristotle, who lived about 2,400 years ago, near the end of a great era of civilization called the Golden Age of Greece, divided purposes into three forms: forensic, deliberative, and ceremonial. The **forensic** purpose, enacted in speeches before the Athenian courts, satisfied the needs of the justice system. These speeches were concerned largely with past events and with the guilt and innocence of individuals. The **deliberative** purpose was fulfilled in speeches before the assembly dealing with the formation of public policy. How the future might be shaped and controlled was the business of such speeches. The **ceremonial** purpose was satisfied by speeches that celebrated what it meant to be an Athenian—an equivalent modern form might be a Fourth of July oration.

In this book we update these ancient accounts by identifying three basic forms of purpose: speeches that *inform* listeners, speeches that *persuade* them, and *ceremonial* speeches given on special occasions. We shall address these forms of purpose in Chapter 12 (informative), Chapters 13 and 14 (persuasive), and Chapter 15 (ceremonial). To help you form your purpose—to find and develop an appropriate topic and theme for your speech—we offer suggestions in Chapter 5.

Message. Successful public speaking offers a **message** that is designed to serve the speaker's purpose. It is based on responsible research and careful thought and should be internally consistent and complete. Its aim is to coax an audience to give sympathetic attention to the speaker's ideas. It has been carefully worded and rehearsed so that it achieves maximum impact. The message is the product of the speaker's **encoding** processes—the effort to convey through words, tones, and gestures how the speaker thinks and feels about the subject. Audience members respond by **decoding** the message, deciding what the speaker intended and determining the value of the message for their lives.

Shaping a message is a basic public speaking skill. It begins with a search for supporting material—facts, examples, testimony, and stories—that will help convey your purpose. The discussion in Chapters 5 and 6 will help you find such material. Next you build a message structure—we discuss the arts of developing speech structure in Chapter 7, "Structuring Your Speech," and in Chapter 8, "Outlining Your Speech." To clarify your points and add variety, you may decide to use illustrative maps, models, or charts. We discuss how to develop such materials in Chapter 9, "Presentation Aids."

Have students generate a list of memorable words or phrases they have heard in speeches. Discuss how such language can help embed a message in the minds of listeners.

How you word your message can determine its fate. In the 2000 presidential election, George W. Bush used the term *compassionate conservatism* to describe his philosophy of government. This term quickly became the central theme of his campaign, made it seem focused and coherent, and helped many people relate to him. On the other hand, the wrong words can destroy a speaker's ethos. One senator, speaking in support of a balanced federal budget, did not help the cause when he declared: "We're finally going to wrassle to the ground this gigantic orgasm that is just out of control."[4] We discuss how to use words effectively in Chapter 10, "Using Language Effectively."

Finally, you convey your message by the way you use your voice, facial expressions, and gestures. We cover these topics in Chapter 11, "Presenting Your Speech." Becoming a master of the message is a goal you can achieve through practice and constructive advice from your teacher and classmates.

Medium. The **medium** transmits a speaker's message. When public speaking takes place in a direct, face-to-face encounter, the medium is the air through which the sound travels. When a speech is presented outside or in a large auditorium, a microphone and amplifiers may be part of the medium. We tend to take the medium for granted until we discover something wrong with it, like poor acoustics. Public speeches can also be transmitted through the electronic media of radio, television, and video- or audiotapes.

The electronic media have major effects on the entire communication process. For example, radio emphasizes the attractiveness, clarity, and expressiveness of a speaker's voice. Television brings a speaker into a close relationship with viewers, so personality and physical appearance take on added importance. When speakers want news coverage, they must compress important ideas into twenty-second sound bites, and the language must be immediately clear and

Transformational speakers inspire audiences to see new possibilities in themselves and their worlds.

colorful. Any change in the medium can complicate the speaker's job. We cover media presentations in Chapter 11.

To develop their flexibility, arrange for students to speak in different settings during the term.

Setting. A speech occurs within a physical and psychological **setting** that can determine how well it succeeds. The physical setting in which a speech is presented can include such factors as the time the speech is given, the time allotted for the presentation, the place of the presentation, and the size and arrangement of the audience. For example, when speaking outside, a speaker may need a more forceful presentation than when speaking in a small room. A larger audience may require a more formal manner of presentation than a smaller audience. The very quality of the physical setting can affect the speech. For example, one of the most profound discussions of the ethics of communication, Plato's *Phaedrus*, written in ancient Greece some 2,400 years ago, takes place in a woodland setting that frames and colors its message appropriately.[5] In this setting, Socrates envisions an ideal communication that promotes spiritual growth for both listeners and speakers.

One classroom setting in which we taught recently required us to open windows and doors because both heating and air conditioning were inadequate. Speakers often had to contend with unpredictable distractions from outside. The room had an oblong shape, shallow in depth but wide, so that listeners were spread out in front of the speaker. This required the speaker to shift attention from side to side to maintain eye contact. Most of our students eventually learned to adapt to this setting.

The psychological setting for a speech includes such factors as the occasion for the speech and the context of recent events. The occasion for a speech sets the stage for what listeners expect. If they anticipate an informative presentation on investing in the stock market but instead hear a sales pitch for mutual funds, they may feel exploited. Recent events can change the climate of communication overnight. If you have planned a speech attacking oppressive campus security and a major crime occurs on campus shortly before your presentation, you may need to adapt your message to fit the changed situation. We cover adaptations to setting in Chapter 4.

Listener. A constructive **listener** is supportive yet listens carefully and critically. As we shall see in Chapter 3, such listeners seek the value in all messages. Because the fate of a message depends on how listeners respond to it, the audience must be at the center of your thinking as you plan, prepare, and present your speeches. What needs or problems concern them? What subjects interest them? What biases could distort their reception of messages? Such questions are crucial to the selection of your topic and to the way you frame your message. Moreover, you should be sensitive to the fact that your words could affect the lives of listeners and even their perception of themselves.

Listeners do not come to a speech with a blank slate. Their minds are filled with past experiences, information or misinformation about a topic or speaker, attitudes and values, aspirations and fears. All of these factors form the *frame of reference* that a listener brings to a speech. The better you understand these audience factors, the more effective your speech will be. We cover audience analysis and adaptation in Chapter 4.

Response. The **response** to a speech is what happens during and as a result of the speech. Of course you hope that your speeches are well received and that they will affect the lives of your listeners favorably. But whether they achieve that result depends a great deal on what happens during the speech. One of the things that makes public speaking dynamic is its interactive quality. While you are speaking, listeners are responding. As they respond, so should you. This makes a speech an interaction in which listeners and speakers constantly adjust to each other. These on-the-spot adjustments lend an unpredictable quality to

Constructive listeners encourage speakers, listen to speeches with open minds, and emphasize the positive values of messages.

public speaking that can make it an interesting and exciting form of communication. Note the adjustment that one of our speakers made during a speech on the dangers of global warming:

> **Some of you are frowning, and I can hardly blame you. This is really hard to believe. But let me quote to you the words of *Time* magazine in a recent survey of all these scientific discoveries: "Except for nuclear war or a collision with an asteroid, no force has more potential to damage our planet's web of life than global warming." Yeah, I know. Tough words. Maybe an exaggeration. But I don't think so. And I don't think we can afford to ignore the threat, hoping it will be untrue or that it might just go away.**

Although somewhat unpredictable, public speaking is also prepared, and this student was ready for such a possible response to his speech.

The technical term for the response listeners make during a speech is **feedback**. Feedback is important because it can improve the quality of communication. It can alert you to problems, signaling that some listeners failed to understand the point you just made, or that others are drifting away, or that still others may want more proof before they are willing to grant your point. Therefore, a good speaker will constantly monitor feedback so that she or he can make adaptations to make the speech more effective. Specific ways to adapt to feedback when making a presentation are covered in Chapter 11.

Interference. **Interference** can enter at any point in the process to disrupt the effectiveness of communication. Interference, which we discuss further in Chapter 3, can range from physical noise that impedes the hearing of a speech, such as a plane flying over the building, to psychological "noise" within speakers and listeners that prevents them from connecting.

Try to get student fears about public speaking out in the open. Discuss your own experience with such apprehension and how you cope with it. Advise students to read the relevant discussion in Chapter 2 and Appendix B.

Three forms of interference are especially troubling. The first is *speaker apprehension*. Fear is an understandable reaction to public speaking experiences. The situation may seem strange, and speakers may feel exposed and vulnerable. Listeners may seem distant, unfriendly, or threatening. Beginning speakers will learn to control their fears and to convert them into positive energy that adds sparkle and power to a speech. But at the outset, these feelings can interfere with effective communication. Communication apprehension is covered in more detail in Chapter 2 and Appendix B.

A second form of interference is *listener distraction*, which imposes a barrier between an audience and a message. Listeners may decide that a topic really doesn't concern them and lapse into daydreams. They may be distracted by worries over an upcoming test or dreams about the weekend ahead. Limitations in the physical setting, such as poor acoustics or a noisy environment, can add to the distraction. Listener apprehension, the counterpart of speaker apprehension, can further compound the problem. We discuss such fear of listening in Chapter 3. The result of all these factors is psychological drift away from the speech. The message never really reaches the listener, and there is no true response to the speech.

A third important form of interference is *cultural barriers*. People from different backgrounds can view each other suspiciously. Speakers may prejudge how certain listeners will respond to their words and as a result make poor adaptations that listeners resent. Listeners may fear hidden agendas and close their minds to the speaker's words. Stereotypes about race, gender, lifestyle, religion, nationality, and so forth can clutter our heads with prejudice that blocks the fair reception and interpretation of messages. The result is psychological distance and misunderstanding—the opposite of what speakers hope to achieve.

ESL: Prejudices about people from different cultures may sometimes betray and defeat even well-intentioned speakers. Ask ESL students to discuss common assumptions about their cultures that they resent.

Fortunately, what you learn in this class can help you overcome the problems of interference. *The art of public speaking is to overcome interference so that genuine communication can occur.*

Consequences. Successful speeches obviously have impact. As a result of them, listeners learn, decide to change their minds or to take action, or join in celebrating the meaning of exemplary lives. Moreover, if we could *see* the communication process at work in a speech, we might note a constant play of interactions among the elements we have identified. We might also *see* the identities of speakers and listeners coming into or out of focus as a result of communication or show those same people growing larger or smaller. These effects would all represent the **consequences** of public speaking, especially the ethical impact of public speaking as transactional and transformational communication.

Transactional communication suggests that successful communication goes beyond personal achievement and the sharing of vital information, ideas, and advice. It implies the shaping and sharing of selves. In the introduction to *Bridges Not Walls*, John Stewart, an interpersonal communication scholar, notes: "Every time persons communicate, they are continually offering definitions of themselves and responding to definitions of the other(s). . . ." Therefore, Stewart suggests, communication is an ongoing transaction "in which *who we are* . . . emerges out of the event itself."[6] We agree: *public speaking is often a self-creative event in which we discover ourselves as we communicate with others.*

Ask students to keep a record of changes they notice in themselves while they are in the public speaking course. Are they more willing to speak out in other classes? Do they participate more freely in groups?

This may seem like a mystical idea, but in large social movements when many speeches work together over time to create the identities of speakers and audiences, the transactional effects can be quite obvious. Consider what happened during the civil rights movement from 1956 to 1968, when it was led by Martin Luther King Jr. During those years, King repeatedly identified himself with the biblical Moses. He spoke as though he had been destined and commanded by God to lead his followers out of semislavery. His followers, accordingly, many of whom had suffered from the degrading identities assigned to them in the land of segregation, were redefined by his rhetoric as the "Children of Israel."[7] Through the many battlefields of the civil rights movement, where they would be beaten, jailed, and a few of them even killed, these people were moving toward a Promised Land. King was still offering visions of that land on the night before he was assassinated.

This example illustrates not only transactional but **transformational communication** as well.[8] The figure of King grew and expanded into epic proportions as his leadership emerged. His followers were transformed into heroic figures as they marched through one ordeal after another. These transformations indicate how people can grow and develop when they interact in ethical communication. On the other hand, deceitful and dishonest communication will thwart the process of spiritual growth.

This is no more than what Plato told us long ago in the *Phaedrus*. Plato realized that ethical communication that respects the humanity of listeners and

FIGURE 1.2
Public Speaking as Dynamic Process

Speaker	One who initiates the communication process
Purpose	What the speaker wishes to accomplish
Message	Fabric of words, presentation aids, gestures, and vocal cues meant to achieve the purpose
Medium	Channel (air, electronic media) through which the message is transmitted
Setting	Physical and psychological contexts in which the message is presented
Listener(s)	Receiver(s) of the message who can realize the purpose and make the message effective
Response	What happens during and after the speech as a result of hearing it, evident in listener feedback
Interference	Factors that can disrupt the communication process and defeat its purpose
Consequences	Impact of communication both in terms of immediate effect and of long-range ethical influence on speaker and listener identity

nourishes it with responsible knowledge encourages the spiritual growth of both speaker and listeners. As you develop in your public speaking class, you may notice the growth in yourself. You may also see your classmates change in response to good speeches throughout the term.

Finally, as rhetorical scholar Lloyd Bitzer has noted, successful communication builds **public knowledge**, what we as a community decide is worth knowing.[9] Public speaking expands and builds this knowledge base. It develops the scope and accuracy of our public awareness. In these fundamental ways, then, for the speaker, listener, and public knowledge, public speaking can be both transactional and transformative. These consequences make participating in public speaking and public listening both ethical and significant. They suggest why you are in this class and how you might benefit from it.

How a Public Speaking Course Can Help You

Where do you fit into the communication process we have described? Why should you be concerned about it? For one thing, the principles you learn in this class can make you a more astute consumer of public messages. They will help you sort through the barrage of informative and persuasive messages that bombards you on a daily basis, and they will alert you to the ways that messages can be distorted or disguised. For another thing, learning to prepare and make effective public presentations can equip you to handle some of the more important moments in your life—times when a grade may be decided, a public problem you care about needs action, or the chance for a job you want hangs in the balance. In such situations, family, spiritual, and material values may all depend on your ability to speak effectively. Developing public speaking and listening skills can result in personal, social, and cultural benefits.

Personal Benefits

The skills you develop in this course should help you feel more confident about yourself, project your best self to others, justify your points of view, and use language more effectively. During the preparation of a speech you learn more about yourself. To select a promising topic you must explore your own interests and positions on issues. To prepare a substantive message you must expand your knowledge. Preparing an effective speech involves creative self-expression as you combine ideas and information in new ways. As you learn to manage your normal anxiety about speaking in public, you will develop more self-confidence.

ESL: Ask ESL students how they would define for themselves success in this course. Discuss how their goals might differ from those of native speakers.

During the preparation for your speech, you also learn about others. To tailor your message to your audience you must become sensitive to their needs and interests. We hear a lot these days about "multiculturalism" and "cultural diversity." In your public speaking classroom you will encounter many diverse voices. Public speaking experiences allow us to listen to each other directly, to savor what makes each of us unique and valuable, and to develop an appreciation of the different ways people live. Your experiences in this class should bring you closer to meeting one of the major goals of higher education: "to expand the mind and heart beyond fear of the unknown, opening them to the whole range of human experience."[10]

You will also learn to be a more effective listener. Listening is a part of communication that is often neglected, even though we listen far more than we speak. Education in public speaking can help you critically evaluate what you hear. You will also learn how to become a constructive listener who plays an essential role in the creation of meaning. We examine listening in more detail in Chapter 3.

The personal growth you experience in a public speaking class also makes possible a number of other benefits. The skills you develop can help you in other classes, in campus activities, and in whatever career you undertake. On a practical level, the ability to communicate ideas effectively is vital to getting a good job and advancing professionally. Each year the National Association of Colleges and Employers (NACE) surveys hundreds of corporate recruiting specialists. On the basis of a recent survey of 294 employers in various fields, NACE isolated eleven fundamental skills that recruiters seek in job candidates. The most important of these skills—at the top of the list—was oral communication! NACE concluded: "Learn to speak clearly, confidently, and concisely."[11] In a similar study, 250 companies surveyed by the Center for Public Resources rated speaking and listening as among the most critical areas in need of improvement for people entering the work force. Martin Ives, vice chair of the Governmental Accounting Standards Board, commented, "The difference between an average career and a 'special' career is the ability to communicate orally and in writing."[12] Finally, an American Council on Education report, *Employment Prospects for College Graduates*, advises readers that "good oral and written skills can be your most prized asset" in getting and holding a desirable position.[13]

Ask students whether they think speaking skill is innate, something that can be learned, or a combination. Try to dissuade students from the idea that speakers are born and that no amount of training can help someone who does not have the innate ability.

The abilities you develop in this class also can help you be a more effective citizen. If you think you may never have to speak in public, picture the following scenarios:

> **The local school board has announced that it plans to remove *A Catcher in the Rye, Huckleberry Finn, Of Mice and Men,* and *To Kill a Mockingbird* from the high school library. It will hold a public hearing on this issue at its next regular meeting. Because you feel strongly about this issue, you decide to speak out for your principles and your children.**
>
> **You just rented an off-campus apartment. It isn't until after you move in that you discover the faucets leak, the wiring is dangerous, and you're about to be run out of the place by roaches. You think that the city's rental properties department either has or should have some regulations that might help you,**

but you don't know where to start or how to speak out for yourself and other students in similar situations.

Anna Aley, a student at Kansas State University, was living in such substandard off-campus housing. She brought that problem to the attention of her classmates in a persuasive speech. Her persuasive speech (see Appendix C) was selected by her classmates for presentation in a public forum on campus. During that presentation, she made such an impression that the local newspaper printed the text of her speech and launched an investigation of the off-campus housing problem. The paper then followed up with a strong editorial, and the mayor established a rental inspection program in the community. Anna's experience is a dramatic example of a student speech making a difference.

Ask students to provide examples of times when they needed to use good public communication in work, social or civic activities. Have ESL students compare these incidents with experiences in their own culture.

A final personal bonus of your public speaking class is that it makes you an active participant in the learning process. You don't just sit in a class, absorbing lectures. You put communication to work. The speeches you give illustrate the strategies, the possibilities, and the problems of human communication. As you join in the discussions that follow these speeches, you learn to identify elements that can promote or block communication. In short, you become a vital member of a learning community. It is no accident that the words *communication* and *community* have a close relationship: they are both derived from the Latin word for "common," meaning "belonging to many" or "shared equally."

Social Benefits

The political system of the United States is built on faith in public communication. Without open and responsible communication there could be no freedom of choice, no informed decision making, no representative law making. The effectiveness of a democracy depends on our ability to deliberate and make wise judgments on public policy. At the very least, we must be able to listen critically to those who represent us in government, advise them concerning our positions, and evaluate their performance at election time. We should be able to take part in public discussions in which we learn from others, develop responsible convictions on important issues, and speak our minds for the benefit of others.

Public speaking is vital to the maintenance of a free society. The right to assemble and speak on public issues is guaranteed by the Bill of Rights.

InterConnections.LearnMore 1.1

FREEDOM OF SPEECH

American Library Association Office for Intellectual Freedom **http://www.ala.org/alaorg/oif/quickoif.html**
A quick guide to intellectual freedom resources on the Internet, with links for easy access.

First Amendment Cyber-Tribune **http://w3.trib.com/FACT/index.html**
An excellent resource for anyone wanting to learn more about the First Amendment. Contains links to recent news stories and other web sites of interest.

The Freedom Forum **http://www.freedomforum.org**
A nonpartisan international foundation dedicated to free press, free speech, and free spirit for all people.

Justice on Campus **http://joc.mit.edu/**
A free-speech advocacy web site dedicated to preserving freedom and due process rights at universities and colleges.

Philosophers and Freedom of Speech
http://www.sjsu.edu/faculty/Brent/190/speechlinks.html
A San Jose State University web site with a variety of links to sites relevant to freedom of speech, including sites containing texts of many historical documents in this area.

Discuss what personal and social benefits may be lost in societies that do not encourage the free and open exchange of ideas. Have ESL students discuss this in relation to their own culture.

To be able to speak without fear and to hear all sides of an issue are rights basic to our social system. Our nation's founders realized the crucial importance of freedom of speech when they wrote the First Amendment to the Constitution:

> **Congress shall make no law respecting an establishment of religion, or prohibiting the free exercise thereof; or abridging the freedom of speech, or of the press; or the right of people peaceably to assemble, and to petition the government for a redress of grievances.**

Why is freedom of speech so important? The answer is simple. To submit public decisions to open discussion is to distribute power. Those in power often don't like to give it up.

The importance of public speaking in democratic societies has a long and rich history. The study of public speaking as we know it today had its origins in the ancient Greek academies, where the curriculum included mathematics, music, gymnastics, and **rhetoric**, or public speaking. During the Golden Age of Greek civilization, approximately 350 years B.C., Aristotle and other leading intellectuals were teaching rhetoric to the citizens of Athens. Public speaking was especially important in that society because there were no professional lawyers or judges. Juries of over two hundred citizens decided legal cases, and the contending parties had to speak for themselves. Rhetorical skills also were needed because all citizens were expected to participate in the assembly that established the laws of the land. Finally, rhetorical skills were an important component of their rituals.

Aristotle organized and systematized the study of rhetoric.[14] He described the three major forms of discourse we covered earlier: forensic, deliberative, and epideictic (ceremonial). He also discussed three major types of appeals: **logos**, appeals based on reasoned demonstrations; **pathos**, appeals based on emotional arousal; and **ethos**, appeals based on the character of the speaker. Aristotle stressed the importance of using examples and narratives to illustrate points. He further suggested that all speeches should have an introduction that gains attention, predisposes hearers positively toward the speaker, and makes clear the purpose of the speech; a body composed of claims and proofs; and a conclusion that amplifies the subject and reminds the audience of the main points of the message.

Aristotle's *Rhetoric* laid the groundwork for later Roman rhetoricians. Cicero described rhetoric as "an art made up of five great arts." He identified these

InterConnections.LearnMore 1.2

CLASSICAL ORIGINS OF PUBLIC SPEAKING

Aristotle's *Rhetoric* **http://classics.mit.edu/Aristotle/rhetoric.html**
The W. Rhys Roberts translation of the full text of this document, made available through the Massachusetts Institute of Technology.

Forest of Rhetoric [Silva Rhetoricae] **http://humanities.byu.edu/rhetoric/silva.htm**
A guide to the terms of classical and Renaissance rhetoric, with sample rhetorical analyses or extended examples for each major entry. Developed by Professor Gideon O. Burton of the Department of English, Brigham Young University.

History of Rhetoric **http://www.uta.edu/english/V/histrhet.html**
A site developed by Professor Victor Vitanza of the University of Texas at Arlington, with links to many documents and other materials relevant to the history of rhetoric.

Plato's *Gorgias* **http://www.dfw.net/~sherrin/plato.html**
An interactive web site in which you can assume the role of one of the discussants in the dialogue. Developed by Sherrin Roberts, Robert Sanderson, and Chun-yuan Tseng as a class project at the University of Texas at Arlington.

Plato's *Phaedrus* **http://ccat.sas.upenn.edu/jod/texts/phaedrus.html**
The B. Jowett translation, made available through the University of Pennsylvania.

arts as (1) **invention**, the discovery and selection of ideas, themes, and lines of argument for a speech; (2) **arrangement**, the placing of these ideas in an appropriate order; (3) **style**, the expressing of these ideas in effective language; (4) **memory**, the storing of these ideas in the mind for recall; and (5) **delivery**, the presenting of the ideas to an audience. Quintilian later elaborated on the five great arts and stressed the importance of ethics, defining an ideal orator as a "good person speaking well."

Many of the topics covered in this text are based on the work of these classical theorists. For example, in Chapter 6 we discuss the importance of examples and narratives as supporting materials. In Chapter 7 we discuss the three major parts of a speech (the introduction, body, and conclusion). In our chapters on persuasive speaking we consider the three types of appeals proposed by Aristotle (*logos*, *pathos*, and *ethos*) and add to them appeals based on cultural traditions, or *mythos*. We also present material relevant to rhetoric's five great arts. The art of invention is covered in Chapter 5, where we provide a system for selecting and focusing a topic; in Chapter 6, where we discuss the selection of supporting materials; and in Chapter 14, where we cover the development of arguments. The arts of style and delivery are considered in Chapters 10 and 11. Finally, like Quintilian, we stress the ethical imperatives of public communication. We begin our treatment of communication ethics in this chapter and continue this emphasis throughout the text.

Although more than two thousand years have passed and the media of public communication have changed dramatically, much of what these classical theorists said still holds true today.

Cultural Benefits

Several generations ago, if you listened to the radio (in those prehistoric days before television) or read magazines, you would find one striking assumption: America was the best of all possible worlds. This attitude typified our **ethnocentrism**, the tendency of any nation, race, or religion to believe that its way of seeing and doing things is right and proper, and that other perspectives and behaviors are incorrect. Ethnocentrism can touch everything from the clothes we wear and the food we eat to the values we affirm and the God we worship.

In the first half of the twentieth century, the idea of America as a "melting pot" suggested that as various groups of immigrants came to this country, they would be melted down in some vast cultural cauldron into a superior alloy called "the American character." This metaphor reinforced ethnocentrism and cultural arrogance. It created a stereotype, a generalized picture of a race, gender, or nationality that supposedly represented the essential character of the group.

We may have stereotypes of Latinos, or of athletes, or of "rednecks." If we look inside ourselves honestly, we may discover many such stereotypes. They become habits of thinking. We may use them because they simplify human interactions or because they are endorsed by our social group. Unfortunately, stereotypes can be quite damaging. They may involve harsh prejudgments of others and may keep us from seeing the true value of a person who just happens to be a Latino, or an athlete, or a southerner. Stereotypes also can impede our ability to communicate with others.

Ask students to identify film or TV characters that stereotype their race, ethnicity, or gender. Ask ESL students how Americans are stereotyped in their native cultures.

The stereotype accompanying the "melting pot" seemed harmless on the surface: it offered an image of the ideal American citizen. However, that citizen always had a white male face. Asians, Native Americans, and African Americans did not mix readily into a common pot. Moreover, often these people did not wish to lose their ethnic identities. Within the melting pot, women simply disappeared. It was hard to champion the economic and political rights of women when the ideal citizen was always a man. Elizabeth Lozano summarizes the shortcomings of the melting pot stereotype and proposes an alternative view of American character:

> **The "melting pot" is not an adequate metaphor for a country which is comprised of a multiplicity of cultural backgrounds. . . . [W]e might better think of the United States in terms of a "cultural [stew]" in which all ingredients conserve their unique flavor, while also transforming and being transformed by the adjacent textures and scents.[15]**

A public speaking class is an ideal place to savor this rich broth of cultures. As we hear others speak, we often discover the many flavors of the American experience. If you examine your own identity, you may discover that you yourself are "multicultural." One of your authors describes herself as "part Swedish, part Welsh, part German, and all hillbilly." The other is Scots, Irish, and English with a dollop of Creek Indian. As we strive to understand our own and others' unfolding identities, we must guard against the subtle intrusion of stereotypes into our thinking. Perhaps the best protection against stereotyping is to remember that we are, in the final analysis, talking to individuals.

To help appreciate the uniqueness of each student's heritage, consider asking students to do a self-introductory speech (see Chapter 2) on how their gender, race, or ethnicity helped shape who they are today.

One of our favorite metaphors for the complex culture of the United States was introduced in the conclusion of Abraham Lincoln's first inaugural address, as Lincoln sought to hold the nation together on the eve of the Civil War:

> **The mystic chords of memory, stretching from every battlefield, and patriot grave, to every living heart and hearthstone, all over this broad land, will yet swell the chorus of the Union, when again touched, as surely they will be, by the better angels of our nature.[16]**

Lincoln's image of America as a harmonious chorus implied that the individual voices of Americans will not only survive but will create a more beautiful music than that of any one voice alone. Lincoln's vision holds forth a continuing dream of a society in which individualism and the common good can not only survive but enhance each other.

In your class and within these pages you will hear many voices: Native Americans and new Americans, women and men, conservatives and liberals,

Americans of all different colors and lifestyles. Sometimes these voices may seem bitter, alienated, or dispossessed, but all of them are a part of the vital chorus of our nation. The public speaking class gives you an opportunity to hear these voices and to add yours to them.

Ethical Public Speaking

In this time of spin doctors, misleading advertising, and cynical disinformation campaigns, communication ethics has become a vital concern. **Ethics** is the moral dimension of human conduct—the way we treat others and want to be treated by them in return.

Because it is so important, ethics is covered in many places in this book. You will find these places highlighted as an "Ethics Alert!" throughout the text. In addition, the code of ethics of the National Communication Association, the *Credo for Ethical Communication,* is reprinted at the end of this chapter. Here we discuss the two major considerations that underlie ethical communication: *respect for the integrity of ideas and concern for listeners.*

Respect for the Integrity of Ideas

Respect for the integrity of ideas involves speaking from responsible knowledge, using communication techniques carefully, and avoiding plagiarism.

Responsible Knowledge. Over 2,500 years ago, Plato complained that political speakers were ignorant of their subjects but that they shamelessly paraded their ignorance before the public anyway. He also accused speakers of pandering to public tastes, making listeners feel satisfied with themselves when actually they should have felt the need for improvement. The continual cynicism of Americans concerning public affairs and politicians suggests that things haven't improved all that much in the last two thousand years.

No one expects you to be an expert on a topic as you speak in class. You should, however, make a strong effort to acquire **responsible knowledge** of your subject. As we describe in greater detail in Chapter 5, responsible knowledge of a topic includes

- knowing the main points of concern.
- understanding what experts believe about them.
- being aware of the most recent events or discoveries concerning them.
- realizing how these points affect the lives of listeners.

Responsible knowledge requires that you know more about a topic than your audience does so your speech has something useful to give them.

Consider how one of our students, Stephen Huff, a student at the University of Memphis, acquired responsible knowledge for an informative speech. Stephen knew little about earthquakes before his speech, but he knew that Memphis was on the New Madrid fault and that this meant trouble. He also knew that a major earthquake research center was located on campus. Stephen arranged for an interview with the center's director. During the interview, he asked a series of well-planned questions: Where was the New Madrid fault, and what was the history of its activity? What was the probability of a major quake in the near future in the area? How prepared was Memphis for a major quake? What kind of damage could result? How could his listeners prepare for it? What readings would the director recommend? All these questions were designed to gain knowledge that would interest and benefit his listeners. Armed with knowledge from the interview, Stephen went to the library and found the readings suggested by the director. He was well on his way to giving the good speech reprinted in Appendix C. Acquiring responsible knowledge requires time and effort, but it is well worth the effort to be able to speak from such knowledge.

Communication Techniques. You should also use speaking techniques carefully. For example, you may wish to quote authorities in support of your position. When used ethically, this technique helps establish the credibility of ideas by demonstrating that they are not simply your ideas but are verified by experts. You must be careful, however, to avoid abusing this technique by **quoting out of context**. This unethical use of a quotation distorts its meaning. In effect, it lies to the audience. Harper Barnes, movie critic for the *St. Louis Post-Dispatch*, describes a typical case of quoting out of context:

> Jan Boyar of the *Orlando Sentinel* recently reported a fairly egregious example. . . . An ad for the Richard Gere–Sharon Stone stinker "Intersection" attributed this line to Boyar: "Sizzling! Hot stars, steamy sex." He replied, "What I actually wrote was that the premise of "Intersection" is 'considerably less sizzling' than those of other movies . . . and those sex scenes, which I called only 'ostensibly steamy,' are, I noted, 'presented in a deliberately unsexual way.' As for the ad's suggestion that I had characterized Richard Gere, Sharon Stone, and Lolita Davidovich as 'hot stars,' that much is correct. But I would now add that they're not quite so hot after appearing in "Intersection."[17]

Have students apply the idea of ethical communication to advertising. Ask them to bring in an example of an advertisement that they think is unethical to share with their classmates. Ask ESL students to share insights on the ethics of advertising in their native cultures.

In more serious situations, quoting out of context can produce disastrous effects. A high point of Dr. Martin Luther King Jr.'s famed "I Have a Dream" speech came when he said that he wanted his children to be judged "not by the color of their skin but by the content of their character." Tom Teepen of the *Minneapolis Star Tribune* argues that when you hear that quote "being piously invoked these days, you can be sure black folks are about to get nailed again":

> Gov. Pete Wilson flew the quote like air cover over his political turnaround when he supported the referendum that killed affirmative action in California. A man whose lawsuit has all but cleared the University of Texas law school of black students crowed, "It's kind of finishing Dr. King's dream. . . ." Colorado Attorney General Gale Norton cited King, too, in her effort to end scholarships to the state's colleges and universities targeted for black students. Mississippi Gov. Kirk Fordice used the quote to explain why he was appointing only white men to the board that runs the university system. Robert Brustein, theater critic and artistic director of the American Repertory Theater, cited King in condemning the formation of black theatrical companies. And on and on goes this political grave robbery.[18]

Teepen's point is that King's words were quoted not only out of the context of his speech but out of the context of his life. Such citations subverted all that King had fought and died for as a civil rights activist. Be sure to quote people carefully and to reflect the true spirit of their meaning.

As we discuss the use of supporting materials in Chapter 6 and developing evidence and proofs in Chapter 14, we will be especially attentive to the potential for ethical abuse.

Avoiding Plagiarism. A speech must be original and must acknowledge major sources of information and ideas. *If you present the ideas or words of others as though they were your own, and don't acknowledge their contribution—you are guilty of* **plagiarism**.

Distribute your school's guidelines on plagiarism to use as a basis of discussion on this issue. Impress students with the need for oral documentation in their speeches.

Most colleges consider plagiarism a major infraction of the student code and impose penalties ranging from grade reduction to suspension. Because this is such a serious problem in any classes that involve creating original work, we will treat it in some detail in this section. You should, however, become very knowledgeable of the policies established at your school. Ignorance of the policies will not excuse you from not complying with them. These can usually be found in the student handbook or on your college web site. Your communication department or your individual instructor may have even more specific definitions and examples of plagiarism with which you should become familiar.

Plagiarism comes in various degrees and forms. Plagiarism is *blatant* when a speaker intentionally steals the work from another source. Examples of blatant plagiarism might include using a speech or outline offered by a friend or found in fraternity files, on the Internet, or in another public speaking text. One truly reckless student once memorized the text of a student speech from an earlier edition of this book and presented it in class as his own effort. Unfortunately for him, the instructor had taught from that earlier edition and recognized the material.

Remember, if you can find the material to copy, your instructor can usually find it as well. Many departments maintain files of speech outlines, instructors discuss speeches with each other, and there are even software programs that uncover Internet plagiarism.

A similar type of blatant plagiarism involves simply parroting a magazine article or an essay written for another class. Related to this practice is what we call "cut and paste" plagiarism because it involves lifting passages verbatim from more than one source, then splicing them together into a "speech." You must not just rearrange the order of ideas or change a few words, then claim the material as your own.

Beyond the ethical considerations involved in plagiarism, there are also some very practical limitations. Speeches that are blatantly plagiarized are usually not very effective because they don't have your stamp of commitment in them or your own personal touch. They may also be dated in terms of their information and examples or may be irrelevant to your particular audience. Speeches plagiarized from magazine articles or essays will usually lack the conversational style that is a part of oral language. Finally, when you plagiarize a speech you are cheating yourself. It's like "sending a friend to practice tennis for you—you'll never score an ace yourself!"[19]

You must also guard against more subtle forms of plagiarism, many involving the use of citations or oral credits. You must always credit the sources when you are using a direct quotation from either a published or an unpublished work. You should also provide citations if you are paraphrasing someone's ideas or opinions. You should credit any especially colorful or striking language that you pick up from someone else and use in your speech. For example, had we started this paragraph on citations by asserting, "A citation is not a traffic ticket," but neglected to say that we found this quotation in a document published by the Georgetown University Honor Council, we would have been guilty of plagiarism.[20]

How can you avoid any hint of plagiarism? We suggest that you adhere strictly to the following rules of conduct:

Never simply summarize a newspaper or magazine article and present it as your speech. Such a speech will probably not be appropriate for your particular audience. It will not reflect your own thinking and feeling, so it will not seem authentic. If the speech is not really a part of you, it will be hard for you to present it effectively. You should also be careful about relying too much on any single source of information. Gather facts and ideas from a variety of sources, develop your own thinking about what they mean to you and your listeners, and present them in your own words.

Credit the sources of ideas in your speech. When you quote someone, let your listeners know. Also give credit to the sources of ideas and information in your speech. Rather than simply saying:

Ethics Alert! 1.1

AVOIDING PLAGIARISM

1. Don't memorize a speech, article, or essay and use it for your presentation.
2. Don't summarize an article or articles and present this as your speech.
3. Don't parrot other people's language and ideas as though they are your own.
4. Draw information and ideas from a variety of sources; then interpret it to create your personal approach.
5. Always provide oral citations for direct quotes, paraphrased material, or especially colorful or striking language.
6. Credit those who originate ideas: "John Sheets, director of secondary curriculum and instruction at Duke University, suggests that there are three criteria we should apply in evaluating our high school."
7. Identify your sources of information: "According to *The 1998 Information Please Almanac,* tin cans were first used as a means of preserving food in 1811"; or "The latest issue of *Time* magazine notes that . . ."
8. Introduce your sources as lead-ins to direct quotations: "Studs Terkel has said that a book about work 'is, by its very nature, about violence—to the spirit as well as the body.'"
9. Allow yourself enough time to research and prepare your presentation.
10. Take careful notes as you do your research.

> **The Dean of the College of Communication at Boston University resigned after he presented a commencement address that was plagiarized.**

say instead:

> **According to the *Boston Globe* of July 2, 1991, the Dean of the College of Communication at Boston University presented a plagiarized speech at the University's commencement ceremonies that year. Then on July 15, the *Washington Times* confirmed that the president of the University had accepted the dean's resignation, saying, "It's the duty of all responsible scholars and writers to credit their sources."**

It doesn't make sense not to credit the sources of your information and ideas. Citing your sources strengthens your speech. It shows that you have prepared carefully. It also associates your thinking with that of respected experts, publications, or opinion leaders.

Finally, allow enough time to prepare thoroughly for your presentation. Not only will this allow you to acquire responsible knowledge, it may reduce the temptation to take the easy way out by copying from someone else's work. As you do your research, take careful notes. Be sure to put any quotations or striking words you might want to use in quotation marks so you will know what they are when you are ready to compose your speech. Keep your own ideas about what you read separate from quotations or paraphrasing in your notes.

Concern for Listeners

Recognizing the power of communication leads ethical speakers to a genuine concern for how words affect the lives of their listeners. We end this chapter by introducing two related ideas: how the "other" orientation of public speaking requires us to be more ethically sensitive, and how applying universal values may help us overcome the challenge of audience diversity.

Developing an "Other" Orientation. In our opening vignette, Mary began her public speaking class with a great deal of concern about her own fate. During the class, however, as she came to know and like her classmates, she prepared her speeches more with them in mind. In so doing, Mary developed an "other" orientation and grew away from **egocentrism**, the tendency to believe that our thoughts, dreams, interests, and desires are or should be shared by others. In their book *Communication Ethics*, Jaksa and Pritchard give this example: "After offering a lengthy explanation of the importance of egocentricity in Kohlberg's theory of moral development, [one of the authors of this text] . . . was greeted with this response from a student. 'I think I understand what egocentric thinking is. Here's an example. You're interested in Kohlberg. So you assume we are, too.'"[21] The discipline of the public speaking class encourages an "other" orientation and the expansion of the self that this implies.

Have students list five values that are important to them in order of importance. Tally the results. Look for similiarities and differences between the values of ESL students and native students.

Applying Universal Values. We have already noted that the public speaking class encourages us to counter ethnocentrism, which holds up our own culture as the most desirable model. We learn to respect one another's backgrounds and to look on the world through different cultural windows. But this also presents a problem. If the members of your class represent many cultures, each offering a different outlook, how can you frame a speech that will communicate and appeal across these many different audiences-within-an-audience?

One answer to this dilemma has been offered by Rushworth M. Kidder, former senior columnist for the *Christian Science Monitor* and president of the Institute for Global Ethics. In his book *Shared Values for a Troubled World*, Kidder reports interviews with leading moral representatives of many cultures that indicate the existence of a **global code of ethical conduct**, centering on the deeply and widely shared values of *love, truthfulness, fairness, freedom, unity, tolerance, responsibility, and respect for life.*[22] If Kidder is correct, appeals to these fundamental values should resonate in any culture and should be well received by the diverse members of your public speaking class. We shall say more about how to effectively engage such values in Chapter 4.

In Summary

Public Speaking as Communication. Public speaking builds on the basic communication skills we originally develop as we acquire language and learn how to converse with others. As expanded conversation, public speaking preserves the natural directness and spontaneity, and the colorful and compelling qualities, of good conversation. Like conversation, public speaking is tuned to the reactions of listeners. Speeches are also designed with the anticipated reactions of listeners in mind.

What makes public speaking distinctive are the relationships among nine elements. *Speakers* themselves are the first element. Audiences respond to them in terms of their *credibility* and *charisma*, which together make up their *ethos*. The second element, *purpose*, recognizes that people speak out of some intention or need. The book identifies three major categories of purpose: speeches to *inform*, speeches to *persuade*, and *ceremonial* speeches. The third element, *message*, is the speech itself, which represents the speaker's *encoding* process and the listener's *decoding* process. The fourth element, *medium*, transmits the message to listeners. The physical and psychological *setting* in which the speech is presented represents the fifth element. *Listeners* themselves form the sixth element, and their *response*, called *feedback*, provides the seventh element. *Interference*, the eighth element, recognizes the possibility of distortion and misunderstanding at any point in the communication process. Major forms of it are speaker apprehension, audience distraction, and cultural barriers. The ninth element, *consequences*, measures the immediate effect of speeches and their ethical impact in terms of their transactional and transformational effects. As they interact with each other, these nine elements constitute public speaking as a dynamic process.

How a Course in Public Speaking Can Help You. This class deserves your commitment because of the significant benefits it offers. Personally, you should benefit from the opportunity to grow as a sensitive, skilled communicator and from the practical advantages such growth makes possible. You should also become a more effective member of society. Self-government cannot work without responsible and effective

The more comfortable you are when speaking to an audience, the more effective you will be.

public communication, and public speaking is the basic form of such communication. The public speaking class can expose you to different cultures as you hear others express their lifestyles, values, and concerns. Such exposure can counter *ethnocentrism*, the tendency to feel that our way to live is the only right way.

Ethical Public Speaking. Ethical considerations in public speaking are inescapable. Ethical public speaking respects the integrity of ideas and focuses on the impact of communication on listeners. Respect for the integrity of ideas means meeting the demands of *responsible knowledge*, carefully using communication techniques, and avoiding such practices as *quoting out of context* and *plagiarism*. Responsible knowledge is useful knowledge. It requires having up-to-date information on the major points of a topic, what the most respected experts have to say about them, and how these points affect your immediate audience. Quoting out of context deceives listeners concerning the original intent of a quotation. Plagiarism is intellectual theft. Being convicted or even suspected of such a crime can damage your ethos beyond repair.

Concern for listeners comes as you develop an "other" orientation in your public speaking class to balance the *egocentrism*, or excessive preoccupation with the self, that you may bring to such a class. You can solve the problem of adapting to the many cultures that may be represented in your class if you base your appeals in a *global code of ethics* based on deep and widely shared values.

Terms to Know

speaker
credibility
charisma
purpose
forensic
deliberative
ceremonial
message
encoding
decoding
medium
setting
listener
response
feedback
interference
consequences
transactional communication
transformational communication
public knowledge
rhetoric
logos
pathos
ethos
invention
arrangement
style
memory
delivery
ethnocentrism
ethics
responsible knowledge

quoting out of context
plagiarism
egocentrism
global code of ethical conduct

Notes

1. See the discussion summarizing ethos-related research in James C. McCroskey, *An Introduction to Rhetorical Communication* (Englewood Cliffs, N.J.: Prentice Hall, 1993), pp. 78–98, and a critique of such research in Gary Cronkhite and Jo Liska, "A Critique of Factor Analytic Approaches to the Study of Credibility," *Communication Monographs* 43 (1976): 91–107.
2. *Fortune* magazine offers an interesting discussion of the importance of charisma in American business in Patricia Sellers, Shaifali Puri, and David Kaufman, "What Exactly Is Charisma?" *Fortune*, 15 Jan. 1996. http://www.pathfinder.com/fortune/magazine/1996/960115/charisma.html (15 May 1998).
3. Book 2.1 of the *Rhetoric*, trans. Lane Cooper (New York: Appleton-Century-Crofts, 1960), 92.
4. Cited in *Newsweek*, 25 May 1992, p. 21.
5. *The Dialogues of Plato*, trans. Benjamin Jowett, in Great Books of the Western World, vol. 7 (Chicago: Encyclopaedia Britannica, Inc., 1952), p. 116. See also the analysis by Richard M. Weaver, "The *Phaedrus* and the Nature of Rhetoric," in *Language Is Sermonic*, ed. Richard L. Johannesen, Rennard Strickland, and Ralph T. Eubanks (Baton Rouge: Louisiana State University Press, 1970), pp. 57–83.
6. John Stewart, ed., *Bridges Not Walls: A Book About Interpersonal Communication*, 5th ed. (New York: McGraw-Hill, 1990), p. 22.
7. Malinda Snow argues that the flight of the children of Israel from Egypt has been a suggestive comparative theme for African Americans since the days of slavery. See her "Martin Luther King's 'Letter from Birmingham Jail' as Pauline Epistle," *Quarterly Journal of Speech* 71 (1985): 318–334.
8. This concept may be closely related to an idea developed by famed historian James MacGregor Burns. Burns describes "transformation leaders" as those who "elevate, motivate, define values, offer vision, and creatively produce reform and at times revolutionary developments in the face of unusual opportunities and challenges" (as summarized in David M. Abshire, "A Call for Transformational Leadership," *Vital Speeches of the Day*, 1 May 2001, p. 432). Among the American presidents, Abraham Lincoln and Franklin Delano Roosevelt clearly exemplify transformational leaders. Presumably, transformational leadership is enabled by transformational communication, such as one sees in Lincoln's "Gettysburg Address" and in Roosevelt's "First Inaugural."
9. Lloyd F. Bitzer, "Rhetoric and Public Knowledge," in *Rhetoric, Philosophy, and Literature: An Exploration*, ed. Don M. Burks (West Lafayette, Ind.: Purdue University Press, 1978), pp. 67–93.
10. Arati R. Korwar, *War of Words: Speech Codes at Public Colleges and Universities* (Nashville: The Freedom Forum First Amendment Center at Vanderbilt University, 1944).
11. "Be the Person Employers Want to Hire," *Job Web and Job Choices Online*. http//www.jobweb.org/jconline/Tips/tips4.shtml (5 July 1998).
12. Sandy Hock, "Communication Skills Top List of Student Advice," *Accounting Today* 8, no. 5 (1994): 27.
13. From Kathleen Peterson, ed., *Statements Supporting Speech Communication* (Annandale, Va.: Speech Communication Association, 1986).
14. Aristotle, *On Rhetoric*, trans. George A. Kennedy (New York: Oxford, 1991).
15. Elizabeth Lozano, "The Cultural Experience of Space and Body: A Reading of Latin American and Anglo American Comportment in Public," in *Our Voices: Essays in Culture, Ethnicity, and Communication*, ed. Alberto Gonzalez, Marsha Houston, and Victoria Chen (Los Angeles: Roxbury Publishing, 1994), p. 141.
16. T. Harry Williams, ed., *Abraham Lincoln: Selected Speeches, Messages, and Letters* (New York: Holt, Rinehart and Winston, 1964), p. 148.
17. Harper Barnes, "'Distorted!' 'Pretentious!' 'Arrogant!'" *St. Louis Post-Dispatch*, 28 July, 1994, p. 1G. Reprinted with permission of the *St. Louis Post-Dispatch*, copyright © 1994.
18. Tom Teepen, "Twisting King's Words to Give His Antagonists Comfort," *Minneapolis Star Tribune*, 14 July 1997, p. 9A.
19. "Avoiding Plagiarism: Mastering the Art of Scholarship," Student Judicial Affairs, University of California, Davis, October 1999. http://sja.ucdavis.edu/sja/plagiarism.html.
20. Georgetown University Honor Council, "What Is Plagiarism?" (1999). http://www.georgetown.edu/honor/plagiarism.html.
21. James A. Jaksa and Michael S. Pritchard, *Communication Ethics: Methods of Analysis*, 2nd ed. (Belmont, Calif.: Wadsworth, 1994), p. 94.
22. Rushworth M. Kidder, *Shared Values for a Troubled World: Conversations with Men and Women of Conscience* (San Francisco: Jossey-Bass, 1994).

CREDO FOR ETHICAL COMMUNICATION

The National Communication Association has adopted the following code of ethics concerning free expression:

Questions of right and wrong arise whenever people communicate. Ethical communication is fundamental to responsible thinking, decision making, and the development of relationships and communities within and across contexts, cultures, channels, and media. Moreover, ethical communication enhances human worth and dignity by fostering truthfulness, fairness, responsibility, personal integrity, and respect for self and others. We believe that unethical communication threatens the quality of all communication and consequently the well-being of individuals and the society in which we live. Therefore we, the members of the National Communication Association, endorse and are committed to practicing the following principles of ethical communication.

- We advocate truthfulness, accuracy, honesty, and reason as essential to the integrity of communication.
- We endorse freedom of expression, diversity of perspective, and tolerance of dissent to achieve the informed and responsible decision making fundamental to a civil society.
- We strive to understand and respect other communicators before evaluating and responding to their messages.
- We promote access to communication resources and opportunities as necessary to fulfill human potential and contribute to the well-being of families, communities, and society.
- We promote communication climates of caring and mutual understanding that respect the unique needs and characteristics of individual communicators.
- We condemn communication that degrades individuals and humanity through distortion, intimidation, coercion, and violence and through the expression of intolerance and hatred.
- We are committed to the courageous expression of personal convictions in pursuit of fairness and justice.
- We advocate sharing information, opinions, and feelings when facing significant choices while also respecting privacy and confidentiality.
- We accept responsibility for the short- and long-term consequences for our own communication and expect the same of others.

Credo of Ethical Communication; National Communication Association. Used by permission of the National Communication Association.

2

Your First Speech

OUTLINE

THIS CHAPTER WILL HELP YOU

- control communication apprehension
- manage the first impressions you make on others
- prepare and present your first speech

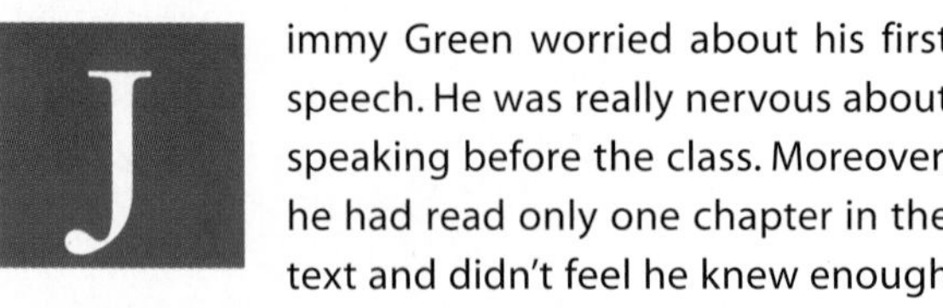

Jimmy Green worried about his first speech. He was really nervous about speaking before the class. Moreover, he had read only one chapter in the text and didn't feel he knew enough to get up and speak without making a fool of himself. To top that off, his instructor had assigned a speech of self-introduction. Jimmy felt that nothing exciting had ever happened to him. What could he talk about? After working through the self-awareness inventory discussed later in this chapter, Jimmy decided to talk about growing up in rural Decatur County. He opened his speech by referring to a popular country song, "A Country Boy Can Survive." Then he captivated his urban audience with delightful descriptions of jug fishing for catfish and night-long barbecues where "more than the pig got sauced."

Many of us just can't see ourselves as "public speakers." We worry about showing our fears and inadequacies in front of the class. We're not sure we really know how to go about putting together a speech that won't make us look bad. We don't appreciate our own experiences and doubt whether others will find us interesting. We are amazed (and relieved) when we make it through our first oral assignment without coming apart at the seams. We are surprised to discover that we can organize our ideas and get them across to the audience. We are pleased when listeners get caught up with what we are saying and seem truly interested in us.

The first speeches in a class can help build a communication climate that nurtures effective speaking and listening. No matter what the exact nature of your assignment, your first speech serves three useful purposes. First, it gets you speaking early in the course so that you don't build up an unhealthy level of communication apprehension. In this chapter we provide some guidelines for managing your anxiety. Second, your first speech provides you with an opportunity to present yourself as a credible source of ideas. As we noted in Chapter 1, people are more likely to respond favorably to those whom they respect and like. In this chapter we show you how to get off on the right foot by managing the all-important first impression you make as a speaker. Third, your first speech allows you to try out some of the basic skills needed to develop a speech and present it effectively. Much of what is in this chapter will be covered in more depth in later chapters of the text. Here, we simply want to provide you with a preview of materials that will enable you to speak with a reasonable amount of confidence the first time you address the class. We conclude this chapter with some special advice on developing a speech in which you introduce yourself or a classmate.

Before the opening round of speeches, you and your classmates are usually strangers. These speeches are often called "icebreakers," because they give members of the class a chance to know each other better. You will probably discover that your classmates are both diverse and interesting. What you learn about them will help you prepare later speeches, giving you insights into their knowledge, interests, attitudes, and motivations. Because it is easier to communicate with people you know, you should also feel more comfortable about speaking before the class.

> ***Without speech there would be no community.... Language, taken as a whole, becomes the gateway to a new world.***
>
> —*Ernst Cassirer*

Controlling Communication Apprehension

When people are asked what they fear the most, public speaking is usually at or near the top of the list.[1] Many speakers have some degree of anxiety when they have to appear before a group. Barbra Streisand and Carly Simon—among countless other professional entertainers and communicators—have described their struggles to control this **communication apprehension**.[2] International students and students from marginalized cultural groups often have a great deal of it.[3] As you give your first speech, you may experience some communication apprehension as well. In fact, there might be something wrong if you didn't have feelings of anxiety. The absence of any nervousness could suggest that you do not care enough about the audience or your message. We once attended a banquet where an award was presented to the "Communicator of the Year." Before sitting down to eat, this recipient confessed privately to us, "I dread having to make this speech!" We were not surprised when this person, a former governor of Tennessee, made an effective presentation.

There are many reasons why public speaking is frightening. Speaking before large groups of people and being the center of attention are not everyday occurrences for most of us. Moreover, public speaking often takes place on important occasions when much seems to depend on how well we speak. This element of risk, combined with the feelings of strangeness, can explain why many people dread public speaking. They are afraid they will make mistakes "and look bad to other people."[4] We have had students anguish over not having said exactly what they had planned: they worry that others were aware of their "mistake." Apparently, they think listeners are clairvoyant!

The truth is, listeners simply don't know what you've planned to say and therefore have no way of knowing that you haven't said something exactly as you had planned it. Furthermore, what you say on the spur of the moment may be *better* than the exact wording you had planned. That's why extemporaneous presentations are usually superior to memorized or read speeches. They are prompted by the moment, and by the interaction of speaker and listener. Finally,

FIGURE 2.1
Public Speaking Fears

Type of Fear	Percent Reporting
Trembling or shaking	*80%*
Mind going blank	*74%*
Doing or saying something embarrassing	*64%*
Unable to continue talking	*63%*
Not making sense	*59%*
Sounding foolish	*59%*

Source: Adapted from M. B. Stein, J. R. Walker, and D. R. Forde, "Public Speaking Fears in a Community Sample: Prevalence, Impact on Functioning, and Diagnostic Classification," *Archives of General Psychiatry* (February 1996): 169–174. *Thrive Online Health Library.* http://www.thriveonline.com/@@14vdSwUA@G5s2ojN/thrive/health/Library/CAD/abstract25252.html (July 1997).

Have students discuss communication apprehension in small groups to elicit suggestions on how to handle it. Have one person in each group report their findings to the class.

even if listeners are aware of a mistake, they really don't care that much about it. You will probably brood about an error much longer than your listeners will remember it.

So keep communication apprehension in perspective. Above all, don't be anxious about your anxiety. Accept it as natural, and be assured that the general effect of the public speaking class is to reduce it.[5] Even more significant, you will learn how to convert these feelings into positive energy. *One of the biggest myths about public speaking classes is that they can or should rid you of any natural fears*. Instead, you should learn how to harness the energy generated by anxiety so that your speaking is more dynamic. No anxiety often means a flat, dull presentation. Transformed anxiety can make your speech sparkle. The late Edward R. Murrow, prize-winning radio and television commentator, once said: "The best speakers know enough to be scared. . . . The only difference between the pros and the novices is that the pros have trained the butterflies to fly in formation."

How can you train your butterflies to fly for you? If you find yourself building to an uncomfortable state of nervousness before a speech, don't stand around and discuss with your classmates how frightened you feel, especially with other speakers scheduled that day. You will only increase your own anxiety and make theirs worse as well.[6] Instead, go off by yourself and practice relaxation exercises. While breathing deeply and slowly, concentrate on tensing and then relaxing your muscles, starting with your neck and working down to your feet. These relaxation techniques will help you control the physical symptoms of anxiety.[7] While you are relaxed, identify any negative thoughts you may harbor about yourself as a speaker, such as "Everybody will think I'm stupid" or "Nobody wants to listen to me." Replace them with positive messages that focus on your ideas and your audience, such as "These ideas are important and useful" or "Listeners will really enjoy this story." This approach to controlling communication anxiety by deliberately replacing negative thoughts with positive, constructive statements is called **cognitive restructuring**.[8]

Still another technique to help you control communication anxiety is **visualization**, in which you systematically picture yourself succeeding as a speaker, then practice with that image in mind. Athletes often employ visualization to improve their performance.[9] A memorable example occurred when Mark McGuire hit his sixty-second home run, breaking baseball's long-standing record. In the moments before McGuire came to bat, television caught him in the on-deck circle with his eyes closed. The announcer noted, "He's visualizing what will happen at the plate." Using this same technique, you picture a day of success, from the moment you get up to the moment you enjoy the congratulations of classmates and teacher for an excellent speech.[10] To make visualization work best, you should develop and enact a script like the one at the end of this chapter.[11] You must have a vivid sense of your successful day for visualization to be effective.[12]

There are other things you can do to control communication anxiety, which go under the general heading of **skills training**.[13] Actually, just about everything you learn in a speech class can help you harness your feelings of fear. First, select a topic that interests and excites you, so that you will get so involved with it that there is little room in your mind for worry about yourself. Second, choose a topic that you already know something about so that you will be more confident. Then build on that foundation of knowledge. Visit the library. Access the Internet. Interview local experts. The better prepared you are, the more confident you will be that you have something worthwhile to say. Third, consider whether you might use a presentation aid—a chart, a graph, an object, or a model. Referring to a presentation aid during your speech encourages gesturing, and gesturing helps release excess energy in constructive ways. (For advice on preparing a presentation aid, see Chapter 9.) Fourth, practice, practice, and then practice some more. The more you master your message, the more comfortable you will be, and the more successful you can expect to be.[14] Fifth, develop a positive attitude toward your listeners. Don't think of them as "the enemy." Expect them to be helpful and attentive.

Finally as we stated earlier, act confident, even if you don't feel that way. When it is your turn, walk briskly to the front of the room, look at your audience, and establish eye contact. If appropriate to your subject, smile before you begin your presentation. Whatever happens during your speech, remember that listeners cannot see and hear inside you. They know only what you show them. Show them a controlled speaker communicating well-researched and carefully thought-out ideas. *Never place on your listeners the additional burden of sympathy for you as a speaker*—their job is to listen to what you are saying. Don't say anything like, "Gee, am I scared!" Such behavior may make the audience uncomfortable. If your mind should go blank during a presentation, don't panic. Go back over what you have just said, as though you are giving your audience a reminder. They will appreciate the help, and you'll be giving your mind a chance to get back on track. Above all, keep talking. You will find your way. If you put your listeners at ease with your confident appearance, they can relax and provide the positive feedback that will make you a more assured and better speaker.

When you reach your conclusion, pause, and present your summary and concluding remarks with special emphasis. Maintain eye contact for a moment before you move confidently back to your seat. This final impression is very important. *You should keep the focus on your message, not on yourself.* Even though you may feel relieved that the speech is over, don't say, "Whew!" or "I made it!" and never shake your head to show disappointment over your presentation. You probably did better than you thought, and at the very least, you don't want to encourage negative reactions to your message.

Do these techniques really work, and is such advice helpful? Research on communication apprehension has established the following conclusions: *(1) such techniques do work, and (2) they work best in combination.*[15] Keep in mind that controlling anxiety takes time. As you become more experienced at giving speeches and at practicing the suggestions in Speaker's Notes 2.1, you will find your fears abating, and you should improve your ability to convert communication apprehension into positive, constructive energy.[16] If you think you still need more help with this problem, work through the material in Appendix B, "Handling Communication Apprehension," and check out the web sites in InterConnections.LearnMore 2.1.

One way to control apprehension is to objectify it. Ask students to keep a diary in which they describe any related problems they may experience before and during the first speech. After the speech, ask them to develop a plan to control these problems, and meet with the more troubled students to discuss the plans. Continue through the term until communication apprehension is no longer a serious difficulty.

Thus far, we have discussed controlling speech anxiety in terms of what the speaker can do, but the audience also can help speakers by creating a positive communication climate.[17] As an audience member, you should listen attentively

The character and personality of a speaker can influence how well a message is received. Likeableness is an important component of speaker ethos.

InterConnections.LearnMore 2.1

COMMUNICATION ANXIETY

Overcoming Speaking Anxiety **http://www.selfgrowth.com/articles/laskowski.html**
Useful advice from a professional speaker on coping with communication apprehension.

Speech Anxiety **http://de.cstcc.cc.tn.us/anxiety**
An online resource for working through communication anxiety prepared as a class project under the direction of Debra Jones, Chattanooga State Community College.

Stage Fright **http://www.selfgrowth.com/articles/zimmer5.html**
A self-help article, "Transforming Stage Fright into Magnetic Presence," prepared by Sandra Zimmer, presentation, voice, and communication consultant and director of the Self-Expression Center, University of Houston.

and look for something in the speech that interests you. Even if you are not excited about the topic, you might pick up some techniques that will be useful when it is your time to speak. When you discuss or evaluate the speeches of others, be constructive and helpful. That's an attitude you will appreciate when others comment on your speech.

Managing the Impressions You Make

When you stand before others to offer information or advice, you are acting as a leader. You may never have thought of yourself that way, but as you develop your speaking ability, you will also grow in leadership potential.

Write the names of two or three public figures on the board. Ask students to rate them in terms of their competence, integrity, likeableness, and forcefulness.

Both leading and communicating begin with listeners forming favorable impressions of you, based on their perceptions of your competence, integrity, likeableness, and dynamism. In this section we explore ways you can encourage these impressions.

Speaker's Notes 2.1

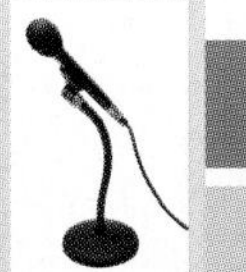

TEN WAYS TO CONTROL COMMUNICATION APPREHENSION

1. Develop your speech skills to strengthen your confidence.
2. Practice relaxation exercises to control tension.
3. Replace negative, self-defeating statements with positive ones.
4. Visualize yourself being successful.
5. Select a topic that interests and excites you.
6. Speak only on topics you can address competently.
7. Use a presentation aid to release energy.
8. Practice, practice, practice!
9. Expect your audience to be helpful and attentive.
10. Act confident, even if you are not.

InterConnections.LearnMore 2.2

ETHOS

"Analysis: Likeability and Its Effects in Politics and Entertainment" **http://www.elibrary.com.**
Talk of the Nation (NPR) transcript, Michael Krasny, 10 August 2000, available through eLibrary.

Credibility **http://www.cios.org/concept$$TARGET=credibility&MIN=1&MAX=20**
A directory of links related to credibility in scholarly literature online, compiled by the Communication Institute for Online Scholarship: Communication Concept Explorer.

Credibility in Campaign 2000: "A Long Strange Journey" by Roger Simon
http://www.usnews.com/usnews/issue/001120/campaigns.htm
U.S. News & World Report cover story analyzing the impact of ethos on the 2000 Bush/Gore presidential campaign.

Establishing Ethos Online **http://lor.trincoll.edu/~writcent/warriner.html**
An interesting article, "Email Debate and the Importance of Ethos," on developing ethos in online interactions, prepared by Professor Allison Warriner, Department of English, California State University, Hayward, as part of the Electronic Democracy Project.

Competence

Competent speakers seem informed, intelligent, and well prepared. You can build a perception of **competence** by selecting topics that you already know something about and by doing the research necessary to qualify yourself as a responsible speaker. You can further enhance your competence by quoting experts and authoritative sources who support your position. For example, if you are speaking on the link between nutrition and heart disease, you might quote a prominent medical specialist or a publication of the American Heart Association: "Dr. Milas Peterson heads the Heart Institute at Harvard University. During his visit to our campus last week, I spoke with him about this point. He told me . . ." Note the competence-related elements here:

ESL: Ask ESL students what the perceived qualities of a good leader are in their countries. Discuss the similarities and differences between perceptions of ethos by ESL and native students.

- The speaker cited the qualifications of the expert, noting his connection to a prestigious institution.
- The quotation contains recent information.
- The connection between the expert and the speaker is direct and personal, suggesting a favorable association.
- The speaker shows that he or she has prepared carefully for the speech by interviewing a visiting expert.

When you cite authoritative sources in this way, you are "borrowing" their ethos to enhance your own as you strengthen the points you make in the speech. Remember, though, that borrowed ethos enhances but does not replace *your own*. Personal experience related as stories or examples can also help a speech seem authentic, bring it to life, and make you seem more competent. "Been there, done that" can be a very effective technique. Your competence will be further enhanced if your speech is well organized, if you use language ably and correctly, and if you make a polished presentation.

Have students make a list of subjects on which they feel most competent as they select topics for their speeches.

Integrity

A speaker with **integrity** seems ethical, honest, and dependable. Listeners are more receptive when speakers are straightforward and concerned about the

Ethics Alert! 2.1

THE ETHICS OF ETHOS

1. Do the research necessary to make you a responsible speaker.
2. Be sensitive to the impact of your words on others.
3. Present all sides of an issue fairly before explaining your position.
4. Be honest about where you stand in relation to your topic.
5. Acknowledge possible differences between your listeners' beliefs, values, and attitudes and your own.
6. Point out how these differences might be bridged.
7. Demonstrate that you are willing to follow your own advice.
8. Trust your listeners if you would have them trust you.

Ask students to write a short character sketch of someone they know who exemplifies integrity. Discuss in class what contributes to these perceptions.

consequences of their words. You can enhance your integrity by presenting all sides of an issue and then explaining why you have chosen your position. You should also demonstrate that you are willing to follow your own advice. In a speech that calls for commitment or action, it should be clear to listeners that you are not asking more of them than you would of yourself. The more you ask of the audience, the more important your integrity becomes.

Let us look at how integrity can be conveyed in a speech. Mona Goldberg was preparing a speech on welfare reform. The more she learned about the subject, the more convinced she became that budget cuts for welfare programs were unwise. In her speech, Mona showed that she took her assignment seriously by citing many authorities and statistics. She reviewed arguments both for and against cutting the budget and then showed her audience why she was against reducing aid to such programs. Finally, Mona revealed that her own family had had to live on unemployment benefits at one time. "I know the hurt, the loss of pride, the sense of growing frustration. I didn't have to see them on the evening news." Her openness showed that she was willing to trust her listeners to react fairly to this sensitive information. The audience responded in kind by trusting her and what she had to say. She had built an impression of herself as a person of integrity.

This example also shows how a "halo effect" can cause competence and integrity to be linked in judgments of credibility.[18] Speakers who rank high in one quality may get positive evaluations in the other.

Likeableness

ESL: Likeableness may be especially valued in the American culture. Ask ESL students if this trait is valued for leadership in their cultures and how it is defined.

Speakers who rate high on **likeableness** radiate goodness and goodwill, which inspire audience affection in return. Audiences are more willing to accept ideas and suggestions from speakers they like.[19] A smile and direct eye contact can signal listeners that you want to communicate. Likeable speakers share their feelings as well as their thoughts. They enjoy laughter at appropriate moments, especially laughter at themselves. Being able to talk openly and engagingly about your mistakes can make you seem more human and appealing as well as more confident.

The more likeable speakers seem, the more audiences want to identify with them.[20] **Identification** is the feeling of sharing or closeness that can develop between speakers and listeners. Identification typically occurs when you believe someone is like you—that you have the same outlook on life or that you share similar backgrounds or situations. Identification is more difficult to establish when the speaker and listener have different cultural backgrounds. In such situations, speakers can invite identification by telling stories or by using examples that

When speakers are likeable, we feel closer to them and are more inclined to give favorable attention to their ideas.

help listeners focus on the experiences, values, or beliefs that they share. Despite speaking before a class that included students from all sections of the United States, Marie D'Aniello encouraged identification in her self-introductory speech by developing a theme everyone could share, family pride. At one moment in her speech, Marie pointed out how she had drawn inspiration from her brother's athletic accomplishments:

> **When I think of glory, I have to think of my brother Chris. I'll never forget his championship basketball game. It's the typical buzzer beater story: five seconds to go, down by one, Chris gets the ball and he drives down the court, he shoots, he scores! . . . I'll never forget the headline, "D'Aniello saves the game!" D'Aniello, hey wait, that's me. I'm a D'Aniello. I could do this too. Maybe I can't play basketball like Chris, but I can do other things.**

After this speech, which appears at the end of this chapter, it was hard not to like Marie. This impression, combined with other favorable impressions of her competence, integrity, and confidence, created respect for her point of view.

Select a prominent public figure and analyze his or her ethos. Focus on how that person fosters identification in public settings.

Likeableness can also be enhanced by appropriate touches of humor. Marcos White, a point guard for the University of New Mexico basketball team, endeared himself to listeners during his first speech. Marcos introduced himself as the son of an African-American father and a Mexican mother: "I guess," he said, "that makes me a blaxican."

Audiences often identify with speakers who talk or dress the way they do. Audiences prefer speakers who use gestures, language, and facial expressions that are natural and unaffected. You should speak a little more formally than you do in everyday conversation. Similarly, you should dress nicely for your speech, but not extravagantly. You don't want to create distance between yourself and listeners by language or dress that seems either too formal or too casual.

Dynamism

James Norton, who introduced Rosamond Wolford as an accomplished violinist, later confessed that he was scared before he gave his speech. He was not sure how his speech would be received and worried that he might make a mistake. But when James walked in front of the room to speak, he seemed confident, decisive, and enthusiastic. In short, he conveyed the qualities of **dynamism**. Whatever he might have secretly felt, his audience responded only to what they saw and gave him high marks for his commanding presence.

At first you may not feel confident about public speaking, but you should act as though you are. If you appear self-assured, listeners will respond as though you are, and you may find yourself becoming what you seem to be. In other words, you can trick yourself into developing a very desirable trait! When you appear to be in control, you also put listeners at ease. This feeling comes back to you as positive feedback and further reinforces your confidence. One of our students, John Scipio, was at first intimidated by the public speaking situation, but John was blessed with two natural virtues: he was a large, imposing person and he had a powerful voice. And then he found a subject he truly believed in. When John presented his classroom tribute to the final speech of Dr. Martin Luther King Jr., he radiated dynamism, in addition to competence, likeableness, and integrity:

Show a videotape of Dr. Martin Luther King speaking. To demonstrate how nonverbal language contributes to the perception of forcefulness, plays a portion of the tape with the sound turned off having students concentrate on facial expressiveness and gestures.

> **When I asked him during a telephone interview why he thought Dr. King was such an effective leader, Ralph Abernathy said, "He possessed a power never before seen in a man of color." What was this power that he spoke of? It was the power to persuade audiences and change opinions with his words. It was the power of speech. . . . In this speech, Dr. King had to give these people hope and motivate them to go on. . . . He spoke to all of us, but especially to those of us in the black community, when he said, "Only when it is dark enough can you see the stars." And when he talked of standing up to the fire hoses in Birmingham, he said, "There's a certain kind of fire that no water can put out." And on the last night of his life, with less than twenty-four hours to live, he was still thinking—not of himself, but of our nation: "Let us move on," he said, "in these powerful days, these days of challenge, to make America what it ought to be."**

FIGURE 2.2
Components of Ethos

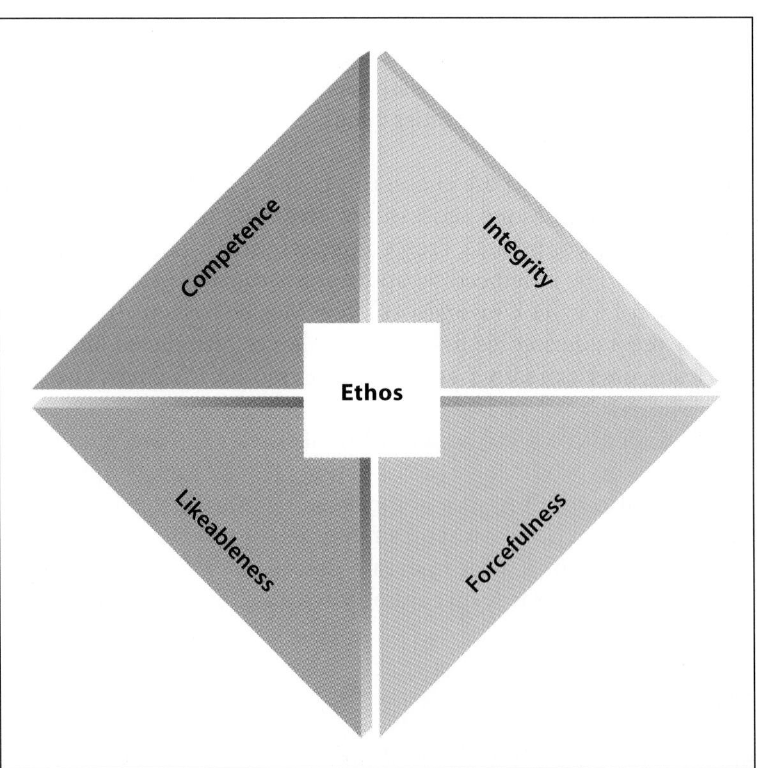

To appear dynamic, you must also be decisive. In persuasive speeches, you should cover the important options available to your audience, but by the end of the speech there should be no doubt where you stand and why. Your commitment to your position must be strong.

Finally, you gain dynamism from the enthusiasm you bring to your speech. Your face, voice, and gestures should indicate that you care about your subject and about the audience. Your enthusiasm endorses your message. We discuss more specific ways of developing confidence, decisiveness, and enthusiasm later in this chapter and in Chapter 11.

Putting Together Your First Speech

So now you have your first speech assignment. Whatever it may require, the planning, thought, creativity, and excitement of presentation are all up to you. One thing we can count on—you will have a limited time to speak. You'll have to plan and rehearse carefully—*and time yourself as you practice*—to be sure you fit within the time limits. In this section we will preview material that is covered in greater detail in later chapters. Our objective is to give you the basics you will need in order to have a successful first speech. How well you prepare will largely determine how well you succeed.[21]

Many students learn through modeling. Show videotapes of students presenting the type of speech you require for the first presentation. Discuss the strengths and weaknesses of these speeches.

As you prepare, you should follow an orderly process that includes

1. selecting and focusing your topic.
2. finding material to make your speech clear and interesting.
3. designing your speech so that it fits together.
4. practicing your presentation.

Selecting and Focusing Your Topic

Your topic should be appropriate to you, your listeners, and the assignment. The best topic for your first speech will help you build positive ethos for later speeches. The more you know already about a topic, the easier it will be to appear competent as you speak on it. Ask yourself:

- What am I most interested in? Can I make it interesting to listeners as well?
- What are they most interested in? Can I add anything to their knowledge on any of these topics?
- Might this speech help me give later, related speeches?

As we have noted, Jimmy Green's first speech, "My Life as a River Rat," created favorable ethos for him and aroused interest for his later speeches on environmental policy.

If the general nature of your topic is assigned by your instructor, you still must select your particular slant on it so that you can handle it within the limited time available. In the final section of this chapter we have more to say about selecting topics for speeches in which you introduce yourself or a classmate.

Finding Material for Your Speech

A well-developed speech will have facts and statistics, testimony, examples, and/or stories to support its major points.

Facts and Statistics. **Facts and statistics** help turn claims into well-documented arguments. For example, to support her idea that American business has a legal as well as a moral obligation to reach out to disabled persons, Karen Lovelace cited the Americans with Disabilities Act.

> **The ADA said that "privately owned businesses that serve the public such as restaurants, hotels, retail stores, taxi cabs, theaters, concert halls, and sports facilities are prohibited from discriminating against individuals with disabilities." The ADA went on to say that "companies have an ongoing responsibility to remove barriers to access for peoples with disabilities if it is readily achievable."**

Karen's factual information strengthened her speech urging reform.

Testimony. **Testimony** in support of your ideas provided by experts or other respected persons can strengthen the authority of your speech. As she developed her speech, Karen cited Sandy Blondino, director of sales at Embassy Suites Hotels, who confirmed that the lodging industry is now more receptive to disabled travelers. She concluded with Ms. Blondino's exact words: "But that's just hospitality, right?" She followed up this *expert testimony* with *prestige testimony* by quoting President Clinton: "When I injured my knee and used a wheelchair for a short time, I understood even more deeply that the ADA isn't just a good law, it's the right thing to do." When you quote expert testimony, be sure to mention the expert's credentials, and when and where she or he made the statement you are quoting.

Have students find examples of expert and prestige testimony in advertisements. Discuss the differences between these types of testimony, as well as when and why each might be effective.

Examples. **Examples** illustrate points and make them seem authentic. An example says, in effect, "This really happened." To illustrate her point that it is good business to serve the needs of disabled people, Karen Lovelace described a group called Opening Doors, which encourages companies to improve travel for the disabled. "One hotel chain that has used this program is Embassy Suites. Their staff are taught by Opening Doors to problem-solve based on guests' needs. And you'd better believe that the word gets around to disabled travelers!" Her example made her claim seem realistic.

Stories. **Stories** in which the characters come to life make a speech more interesting, authentic, and convincing. To illustrate her points, Karen spoke of a day she spent with a disabled person, describing all the barriers he had to overcome to achieve simple, everyday needs that most of us take for granted.

ESL: Ask ESL students to share with the class examples of bedtime stories or fairy tales from their culture. Discuss the similarities and differences between these and those told in America.

For the first speeches in a class, examples and narratives are especially useful. They help develop a feeling of closeness between the audience and the speaker that creates a positive learning community. They also enhance a speaker's ethos, making him or her more likeable. Stories hold the interest of the audience while revealing some important truth about the speaker or the topic. They should be short and to the point, moving in natural sequence from the beginning to the end. The language of stories should be colorful, concrete, and active; the presentation should be lively and interesting.

Taken as a whole, facts and statistics, testimony, examples, and stories provide the substance that makes us take a speech seriously. Karen's classmates at Vanderbilt felt that her speech was one of the most effective that they heard that semester.

Stories of real-life experiences can make speeches more interesting, authentic, and convincing.

Designing Your Speech

You should design your speech so that your points fit together in a way that is easy to follow and understand. Your design provides the pattern into which you fit your supporting materials to achieve your purpose.

If you wanted to introduce yourself by explaining how you were shaped by the neighborhood in which you grew up, you might select a *categorical* design in which you develop a series of related points. You could begin with the setting, a description of a street scene in which you capture sights, sounds, and smells: "I can always tell a Swedish neighborhood by the smell of *lutefisk* on Friday afternoons." Next you might describe the people, focusing on a certain neighbor who influenced you—perhaps the local grocer, who loved America with a passion, helped those in need, and always voted stubbornly for the Socialist Party. Finally, you might talk about the street games you played as a child and what they taught you about people and yourself. This "setting-people-games" categorical design structures your speech in an orderly manner.

Have students read one of the self-introductory speeches in this text (see the end of this chapter or Appendix C) and develop a key word outline of that speech showing the main points and supporting materials. Discuss the types of designs that are used in these speeches.

The example also suggests how the introduction, body, and conclusion of your speech must be closely related. Your **introduction**, in which you arouse interest and set the mood for what will follow, could be the opening street scene. In the **body** of the speech, you might describe the people of your neighborhood, using the grocer as an example. You might also describe the childhood games that reinforced the lessons of sharing. Your **conclusion** should make clear the point of the speech:

> **I hope you have enjoyed this "tour" of my neighborhood, this "tour" of my past. If you drove down this street tomorrow, you might think it was just another crowded, gray, urban neighborhood. But for me it is filled with memories of colorful people who cared for each other and who dreamed great dreams of a better tomorrow. That street runs right down the center of my life.**

Other topics and purposes might suggest other designs. If you select an experience that influenced you, such as "An Unforgettable Adventure," your

Speaker's Notes 2.2

PUTTING TOGETHER YOUR FIRST SPEECH

1. Select a topic that fits you, your audience, and the assignment.
2. Choose a topic that will help you build ethos for later speeches.
3. Design your speech so that your thoughts develop in a coherent pattern.
4. Develop an introduction that arouses attention as it leads into your topic.
5. Limit yourself to two or three main points.
6. Use examples or stories to clarify ideas and make your speech interesting.
7. Prepare a conclusion that reflects on your meaning.
8. Time yourself as you practice.

speech might follow a *sequential* pattern as you tell the story of what happened. You would talk about events in the time sequence in which they occurred. Should you decide to tell about a condition that had a great impact on you, a *causation* design might be most appropriate. Maria One Feather, a Native American student, used such a design in her speech "Growing Up Red—and Feeling Blue—in White America." In this instance she treated the condition as the cause and its impact on her as the effect. The various designs available to you are discussed in Chapters 12 and 13, and you may wish to refer to these chapters as you plan your first speech.

Just a bit more on introductions, bodies, and conclusions: In addition to arousing interest and preparing listeners for the rest of the speech, your introduction should also build a good relationship between you and your audience. That, of course, fits in with the idea of developing ethos in the first speech. The best introductions are framed *after* the body of the speech has been planned—after all, it is difficult to draw a map if you don't yet know where you are going. We provide other suggestions for preparing introductions in Chapter 7.

Caution students not to write out their speeches as though they were essays. Introduce some of the differences between good writing and good speaking covered in Chapter 10.

The body is where you develop your main points, the most important ideas in your message. For a three- to five-minute assignment, limit yourself to two or three main points so that you can develop them in depth. Determining and wording main points is covered in more detail in Chapter 7.

The conclusion often summarizes your main points and ends with reflections on the meaning of the speech. Good conclusions are easily remembered—even eloquent. Sometimes they quote well-known people who state the point very well. They may tie back to the introduction, completing a symbolic circle in a way that the audience finds satisfying. More information on developing conclusions may be found in Chapter 7.

Outlining Your Speech

ESL: Ask ESL students to submit their formal and key-word outlines before they present their speeches. Go over these with them in an office conference.

To ensure that your design will work for your speech, prepare an outline using complete sentences. The outline should contain your introduction, your purpose (the **thesis statement**), your main ideas and their subpoints and subsubpoints, and your conclusion. In addition, your outline should contain planned **transitions** to help you move from one point to another. Marie D'Aniello's first speech, "Family Gifts," which appears at the end of this chapter, illustrates especially skillful, subtle use of transitions.

You should also prepare a **key-word outline**, a shorter version of your full-sentence outline, to use as you practice and present your speech. As its name suggests, this outline contains only key words and phrases to prompt your memory. It can also contain presentation cues, such as "pause here" or "talk slowly." Although the full outline may require several pages to complete, the key-word outline should fit on one or two index cards. We say more about outlining in Chapter 8.

In the following outline for a self-introductory speech, several critical parts of the speech—the introduction, thesis statement, and conclusion—are written out word for word. They set forth the meaning of your message and make your entrance into and exit from the speech smooth and effective. Thus, it is important to plan them carefully, even though you may make changes during presentation to adjust to the immediate situation. Note, however, that the body of the speech is not written out to encourage spontaneity in your presentation.

"Free at Last"

by Rod Nishikawa

Introduction

Attention-arousing and orienting material: Three years ago I presented the valedictory speech at my high school graduation. As I concluded, I borrowed a line from Dr. Martin Luther King's "I Have a Dream" speech: "Free at last, free at last, thank God almighty we're free at last!" The words had a joyful, humorous place in that speech, but for me personally, they were a lie.

Thesis statement: I was not yet free, and would not be free until I had conquered an ancient enemy, both outside me and within me—that enemy was racial prejudice.

Body

I. When I was eight years old I was exposed to anti-Japanese prejudice.
  A. I was a "Jap" who didn't belong in America.
  B. The bully's words burned into my soul.
    1. I was ashamed of my heritage.
    2. I hated having to live in this country.
      [Transition: "So I obviously needed some help."]

II. My parents helped me put this in perspective.
  A. They survived terrible prejudice in their youth during World War II.
  B. They taught me to accept the reality of prejudice.
  C. They taught me the meaning of *gaman:* how to bear the burden within and not show anger.
      [Transition: "Now, how has *gaman* helped me?"]

III. Practicing *gaman* has helped me develop inner strength.
  A. I rarely experience fear or anger.
  B. I have learned to accept myself.
  C. I have learned to be proud of my heritage.

■ ***Rod's three main points are each supported with facts, examples, or narratives. The outline uses Roman numerals to indicate main points, capital letters to indicate subpoints, and Arabic numbers to indicate sub-subpoints. These numerals and letters are indented to show the structure of the ideas in the speech.***

Conclusion

Summary Statement: Practicing *gaman,* a gift from my Japanese roots, has helped me conquer prejudice.

Concluding Remarks: Although my Japanese ancestors might not have spoken as boldly as I have today, I am basically an American, which makes me a little outspoken. Therefore, I can talk to you about racial prejudice and of what it has meant to my life. And because I can talk about it, and share it with you, I am finally, truly, "free at last."

Preparing for Presentation

Show videotapes of students presenting speeches that illustrate both good and poor presentation styles. Discuss these differences in class.

Once you have developed and outlined your first speech, you are ready to practice your presentation. *An effective presentation spotlights the ideas, not the speaker, and is offered as though you were talking with the audience, not reading to them or reciting from memory.*

Spotlight the Ideas. The presentation of a speech is the climax of planning and preparation—the time you have earned to stand in the spotlight. Though presentation is important, it should never overshadow the substance of the speech. Have you ever had this kind of exchange?

> **"She's a wonderful speaker—what a beautiful voice, what eloquent diction, what a smooth delivery!"**
> **"What did she say?"**
> **"I don't remember, but she sure sounded good!"**

Unfortunately, there are times when speakers do use presentation skills to cover up a lack of substance or to disguise unethical speaking. In such moments the basic purpose of public speaking—communicating ideas—is lost.

As you practice speaking from your outline and when you present your speech, concentrate on the ideas you have to offer. *You should have a vivid realization of these ideas during the moments of actual presentation.*[22] The thoughts should come alive as you speak.

ESL: Work with ESL students to help them overcome the tendency to speak in word units rather than thought units.

Speak Naturally. An effective presentation, we noted in Chapter 1, preserves many of the best qualities of conversation. It sounds natural and spontaneous yet has a depth, coherence, and quality not normally found in social conversation. The best way to approach this ideal of improved conversation is to present your speech extemporaneously. An **extemporaneous presentation** is carefully prepared and practiced but not written out or memorized. If you write out your speech, you will be tempted either to memorize it or read it to your audience. Reading or memorizing almost always results in a stilted presentation. DO NOT READ YOUR SPEECH! *Audience contact is more important than exact wording.* The only parts of a speech that should be memorized are the introduction, the conclusion, and a few other critical phrases or sentences, such as the wording of main points or the punch lines of humorous stories.

Prepare a Key-Word Outline. To sound conversational and spontaneous, use a key-word outline while speaking. *Do not make the mistake of using your full outline as you present your speech.* You may lapse into reading it. Instead, go through your full-sentence outline and highlight the key words in each section. Transfer these to a single sheet of paper or index cards to use as prompts as you speak. You can also include on this outline reminders to yourself as to how you want to present the speech. The following key-word outline is based on the outline presented earlier.

■ ***Note that Rod's key-word outline reminds him not only of the flow of ideas, but of his presentation plan as well. It is the "game plan" of his speech.***

"Free at Last"

Introduction

"Free at last"—high school valedictory speech
Not free—enemy both outside and within was racial prejudice

Body

I. Encounter with bully when I was 8

A. "Jap," didn't belong here [Mime bully]

B. Words burned in soul
1. Ashamed of heritage
2. Hated living in America [Pause, smile]
II. Parents help
A. Survived much worse
B. Taught me to accept reality
C. Taught me *GAMAN* [Pause and write word on board]
III. *Gaman*—inner strength
A. No fear or anger [Stress]
B. Accepted self
C. Proud of heritage [Pause]

Conclusion

Gaman from my Japanese roots helps conquer prejudice.
Also an American. Can talk about it: therefore, "free at last."

Rehearse Your Speech. Speech classrooms often have a speaker's lectern mounted on a table at the front of the room. Lecterns can seem very formal and can create a barrier between you and listeners. Also, short people can seem to almost disappear behind a lectern. If their gestures are hidden from view, their messages may lose much of the power of body language. For these reasons, you may wish to speak either to the side or in front of the lectern.

Provide an opportunity for students to present their speeches in small groups prior to their graded presentations. Encourage constructive criticism in the groups.

If you plan to use the lectern, place your outline high on its slanted surface so that your notes are easy to see without having to lower your head abruptly to refer to them. This reduces the loss of eye contact with your listeners. Print your key-word outline in large letters. If you decide to hold your outline and note cards, don't try to hide them or look embarrassed if you need to refer to them. Most listeners probably won't even notice when you use them. Remember, your audience is far more interested in what you have to say than in any awkwardness you may feel.

Imagine your audience in front of you as you practice. Start with your full outline, then move to your key-word outline as the ideas become imprinted in

Practice speaking from your key-word outline until the main points of your speech are fully embedded in your mind.

your mind. Maintain eye contact with your imaginary listeners, just as you will during the actual presentation. Look around the room so that everyone feels included in your message. Be enthusiastic! Let your voice suggest confidence. Avoid speaking in a monotone, which never changes pace or pitch; instead, strive for variety and color in your vocal presentation. Pause to let important ideas sink in. Let your face, body, and voice respond to your ideas as you utter them.

Introducing Yourself or a Classmate: An Extended Application

Show videotapes of self-introductory speeches from the Houghton Mifflin ancillary package. Ask your students to critique and grade the speeches, then discuss how you would critique and grade the speeches.

A speech of introduction is sometimes the first assignment in a public speaking class because it helps warm the atmosphere, creates a sense of community, and provides an opportunity to develop credibility. Outside of the classroom you may be called on to introduce yourself or an organization to which you belong. Typically this will be part of a longer speech. When she spoke to the Republican National Convention in the summer of 2000, Condoleezza Rice in effect introduced herself as a future leader in the Bush administration as she praised the party's candidates. When he spoke before the National Press Club, the commandant of the Coast Guard introduced that less well known branch of the military:

> **If the Coast Guard were a topic on the TV game show "Family Feud" and Richard Dawson surveyed a hundred Americans to ask them what the Coast Guard does for a living, the first contestant trying to match the survey would recall seeing us on "Baywatch" and would confidently declare that we "save lives." Richard Dawson would thoughtfully repeat the answer, turn to the display board, and say, "Show me 'Saves lives!'" The bell would ring, the top panel would roll over to reveal the words "Search and Rescue," and the crowd would go wild when they saw that saving lives had been named by 85 of the 100 respondents. High fives all around, and Dawson kisses the contestant's mother-in-law, who's next in line.**
>
> **After a minute or so, the excitement would die down, Mr. Dawson would approach the mother-in-law, and suddenly the sound stage would get tense as the contestants scratched their heads and tried to imagine what else could possibly be involved in the business of guarding the coast. Maybe one of the family members would hesitantly mumble something about law enforcement and pick up a few more points—but pretty soon we'd be hearing the harsh buzzing sound that means no match—you lose!**
>
> **My purpose today is twofold: first, to raise the visibility of the national relevance of current and future Coast Guard service to America; and second, to offer two reasons why the members of the National Press Club should care about the direction and effectiveness of this fifth armed service, housed in the Department of Transportation and consuming about one quarter of one percent of the federal budget.[23]**

A classroom speech of introduction is usually quite short. Since there is no way to tell an entire life story in a short speech, you have to be selective. What you should avoid is relating a few superficial facts, such as where you went to high school or what your major is. Such information reveals very little about a person and is usually not very interesting.

One way to introduce yourself or others is to answer this question: *What is the one thing that best describes me or the person I am introducing as a unique person?* You should then develop a speech around the answer that will build positive ethos for later speeches.

To help stimulate your creativity, what the ancient, classical writers on public speaking called your "inventional processes," conduct a **self-awareness inventory** in which you consider the following possibilities:

1. *Is your cultural background the most important thing about you?* How has it shaped you? How might you explain this influence to others? In her self-introductory speech, reprinted in Appendix C, Sandra Baltz described herself as a unique product of three cultures. She felt that this rich cultural background had widened her horizons. Note how she focused on food to represent the convergence of these different ways of life:

> **In all, I must say that being exposed to three very different cultures—Latin, Arabic, American—has been rewarding for me and has made a difference even in the music I enjoy and the food I eat. It is not unusual in my house to sit down to a meal made up of stuffed grape leaves and refried beans and all topped off with apple pie for dessert.**

The speech by Sandra Baltz in Appendix C and on videotape illustrates the use of cultural background from the self-awareness inventory. Suggest to ESL students that this could be a very rich source of ideas for their speeches.

2. *Is the most important thing about you the environment in which you grew up?* How were you shaped by it? What stories or examples demonstrate this influence? How do you feel about its effect on your life? Are you pleased by it, or do you feel that it limited you? If the latter, what new horizons would you like to explore? In his self-introductory speech, "My Life as a River Rat," Jimmy Green concluded by saying:

> **To share my world, come up to the Tennessee River some fall afternoon. We'll take a boat ride north to New Johnsonville, where Civil War gunboats still lie on the bottom of the river, and you will see how the sun makes the water sparkle. You will see the green hills sloping down to the river, and the rocky walls, and I will tell you some Indian legends about them. We'll "bump the bottom" fishing for catfish, just drifting with the current. And if we're lucky, we might see a doe and her fawn along the shoreline, or perhaps some Great Blue Herons or an eagle high overhead.**

Jimmy's descriptions of nature conveyed his feelings about his home without his having to tell us about them.

3. *Was there some particular person—a friend, relative, or childhood hero—who had a major impact on your life?* Why do you think this person had such influence? Often you will find that some particular person was a great inspiration to you. Here is a chance to share that inspiration, honor that person, and in the process, tell us much about you. In her speech to the Republican Convention, Condoleezza Rice spoke of her grandfather's influence on her:

> **Granddaddy Rice . . . was a poor farmer's son in rural Alabama—but he recognized the importance of education. Around 1918, he decided it was time to get book learning, so he asked, in the language of the day, where a colored man could go to college. He was told about little Stillman College, a school about 50 miles away. So Granddaddy saved his cotton for tuition and went off to Tuscaloosa.**
>
> **After the first year, he ran out of cotton and needed a way to pay for college. Praise be—God gave him one. Grandfather asked how the other boys were staying in school. "They have what's called a scholarship," he was told, "and if you wanted to be a Presbyterian minister, then you could have one, too." Granddaddy Rice said, "That's just what I had in mind." And my family has been Presbyterian and college-educated ever since.[24]**

4. *Have you been marked by some unusual experience?* Why was it important? How did it affect you? What does this tell us about you as a person? Ashley

Caution students to avoid talk-show- or tabloid-like revelations. You might wish to discuss the idea of propriety in communication at this time.

Smith decided to speak on what she had learned from her experiences as an exchange student in Costa Rica and Botswana. After she told stories to illustrate how peoples' lives were controlled and limited in those countries, Ashley confided—in a speech that is reprinted at the end of this chapter—that her travel experiences had made her want to return as an educator:

> **I want to teach people to succeed on their merits despite the social and economic inequalities that they're faced with. And I want to learn from them as well. I want to teach the boy who never mastered welding that he could own the factory. And I want him to teach me how to use a rice cooker. I want to teach the girl who is exhausted each afternoon after walking to the river with a jar on her head to gather water that she could design an irrigation system. But I also want her to teach me how to weave a thatched roof. I want to travel and teach and learn.**

Experiences need not be dramatic to be meaningful. Rod Nishikawa related how an encounter with prejudice at an early age changed his life and helped him develop personal inner strength. His self-introductory speech, outlined earlier in this chapter, is reprinted in Appendix C.

5. *Are you best characterized by an activity that brings meaning to your life?* Remember, what is important is not the activity itself but how and why it affects you. The person being introduced must remain the focus of the speech. When you finish, the audience should have an interesting picture of you. As she reflected on her identity, Julie Cunningham decided that the most meaningful thing in her life was her participation in a weekly off-campus ritual:

> **Every Sunday morning before sunrise I arrive out at Shelby Forest State Park with a few friends of mine. My responsibilities are to gather wood and sweep the area for our sweat lodge. The sweat lodge is a Native American ceremony of spirituality and purification, and the lodge itself represents the womb of mother earth. You crawl in for the sweat ceremony, and when you crawl out you are reborn to this world. This is a time of respect and prayer, of singing and remembering our ancestors, of sharing our feelings. . . . It is a time for me to slow down and relax and remember things that are important to me in the past, present, and future. It's a time for me to exist as one part of a whole, to reflect on my ties to mother earth and to all of her children, to realize my kinship with my tree brothers, the four-leggeds, and the winged creatures as well as with my human brothers and sisters who sit with me in the sweat lodge. I listen to the wind and feel the warm sun on my face. And I feel so immune and so distant from the world outside, even though I know that I will return there.**

6. *Is the work you do a major factor in making you who you are?* If you select this approach, focus on how your job has shaped you rather than simply describing what you do. What have you learned from your work that has changed you or made you feel differently about others? In introducing Mike Peterson, Carol Solomon told how his work as a bartender had influenced him. She explained that his job involved more than just mixing drinks—that it had made him an observer of people.

> **He sees them in their times of happiness, when they are celebrating a promotion or a grandson or an anniversary. He sees the sadness of lonely people, trying to make a connection, and he sees the other people, the predators, who try to take advantage of them. He hears lots of good stories, and he thinks he may become a writer so that he can tell these stories. Maybe, if we're lucky, he'll tell us sometime about the land shark who got hooked by the hooker.**

After her speech the audience saw both Mike and his work in a new light. Carol's introduction also communicated an impression of her as a thoughtful, sensitive person.

7. *Are you best characterized by your goals or purpose in life?* Listeners are usually fascinated by those whose lives are dedicated to some purpose. If you choose to describe some personal goal, be sure to emphasize why you have it and how it affects you. Tom McDonald had returned to school after dropping out for eleven years. In his self-introductory speech he described his goal:

> **Finishing college means a lot to me now. The first time I enrolled, right out of high school, I "blew it." All I cared about was sports, girls, and partying. Even though I have a responsible job that pays well, I feel bad about not having a degree. My wife's diploma hangs on our den wall. All I have hanging there is a stuffed duck!**

As he spoke, many of the younger students began to identify with Tom; they saw a similarity between what caused him to drop out of school and their own feelings at times. Although he wasn't "preachy," Tom's description of the rigors of working forty hours a week and carrying nine hours a semester in night school carried its own clear message.

8. *Are you best described by some value that you hold dear?* How did it come to have such meaning for you? Why is it important to you? Values are abstract, so you must rely on concrete applications to make them meaningful to others. As she described her commitment to the value of justice, Valessa Johnson also established her goal, to become an attorney, and paid tribute to her personal role model:

> **If you go down to 201 Poplar at nine o'clock in the morning on any weekday, you will find yourself faced with hundreds of individuals and their quest for justice. Many of these will be convicted, and rightly so. Unfortunately, while they're incarcerated, the illiterate and unlearned will remain so, as will the unskilled and the uncrafted. Who's going to stand for these so that they have an alternative to standing in the revolving doors of the criminal justice complex? Or better yet, how about the ones that are truly innocent? Oh yes, that's right, not everyone in the court system, not everyone institutionalized, is guilty. Who is going to stand for these? I will.**
>
> **You know, we were once blessed with a true advocate for justice, attorney Barbara Jordan. She fought a long, hard battle to ensure that we all abided by the constitutional creed "All men are created equal" and "justice for all." Someone has to continue to beat the path of justice for all men. That includes black men, white men, yellow men, brown men, and *women*. Someone has got to continue to fight the good fight. And I submit to you that I am that someone.**

When Valessa concluded, no one questioned the sincerity of her commitment to justice.

As you explore your own background or that of a classmate, we suggest that you ask all the probe questions within the self-awareness inventory. Don't be satisfied with the first idea that comes to you. You should find this thorough examination of yourself and others to be quite rewarding. Just remember: You are not on a tabloid talk show. You don't want to embarrass listeners with personal disclosures they would just as soon not hear. If you are uncertain about whether to include personal material, you should discuss it with your instructor. The general rule to follow is, *When in doubt, leave it out!*

Speaker's Notes 2.3

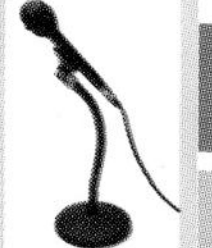

SELF-AWARENESS INVENTORY

1. Was your cultural background important in shaping you?
2. Was your environment a major influence?
3. Did some person have an impact on you?
4. Were you shaped by an unusual experience?
5. Is there an activity that molds you?
6. Has your work had a major impact on who you are?
7. Does some special goal or purpose guide the way you live?
8. Does a value have great meaning for you?

In Summary

Many of us underrate our potential for public speaking. Starting with your first speech, you can help build a positive communication environment for yourself and others. You can also develop your ethos as a speaker.

Controlling Communication Apprehension. Use your nervousness as a source of energy. Cope with communication apprehension by using relaxation exercises before you speak. Use *cognitive restructuring* to replace negative messages with positive ones. Use *visualization* techniques to build in your mind a vivid image of success as you address your audience. Select a topic that interests you and that you already know something about so that you can build on this foundation of confidence. Use presentation aids to give your nervous energy a constructive outlet. Practice until your outline is imprinted on your mind. During actual presentation, you should appear confident and avoid expressions of personal discomfort.

Managing the Impressions You Make. Listeners acquire positive impressions of you based on your ability to convey competence, integrity, likeableness, and dynamism. You can build your perceived *competence* by citing examples from your own experience, by quoting authorities, and by organizing and presenting your message effectively. You can earn an image of *integrity* by being accurate and complete in your presentation of information. You can promote *likeableness* by being a warm and open person with whom your listeners can easily identify. *Dynamism* arises from listeners' perceptions of you as a confident, enthusiastic, and decisive speaker.

Putting Together Your First Speech. Select a topic that is appropriate to you, your listeners, and the assignment. Seek *facts and statistics*, *testimony*, *examples*, and *stories* that will support your points and make them interesting to listeners. Find a design for your speech so that your ideas fit together in a cohesive pattern. Develop an *introduction*, *body*, and *conclusion* so that your speech forms a satisfying whole. Prepare a full-sentence outline of your speech that contains your main points and *transitions* to help you move from one point to another. As you practice and present the speech, use a *key-word outline* to jog your memory. When presenting your first speech, keep the spotlight on the message and strive for a conversational presentation. Never let presentation skills overshadow your ideas.

Introducing Yourself or a Classmate. A speech of introduction helps establish you or the person you introduce as a unique person. Prompted by your *self-awareness inventory*, it may focus on cultural background, environmental influences, a person who inspired you, an experience that affected you, an activity that reveals your character, the work you do, your purpose in life, or some value you cherish.

Terms to Know

communication apprehension
cognitive restructuring
visualization
skills training
competence
integrity
likeableness
identification

dynamism
facts and statistics
testimony
examples
stories
introduction
body
conclusion
thesis statement
transitions
key-word outline
extemporaneous presentation
self-awareness inventory

Application

To help in visualizing yourself succeeding as a speaker, write a script in which you describe specific details of an ideal experience of speaking. Start with getting up in the morning on the day of your speech, and continue to the moments after you have concluded. Once you have completed your script, relax, concentrate on it, and bring it to life in your mind. As a guide, follow the script and instructions for an informative speech developed by Professors Joe Ayres and Theodore S. Hopf:

> **Close your eyes and allow your body to get comfortable in the chair in which you are sitting. Move around until you feel that you are in a position that will continue to be relaxing for you for the next ten to fifteen minutes. Take a deep, comfortable breath and hold it . . . now slowly release it through your nose (if possible). That is right . . . now take another deep breath and make certain that you are breathing from the diaphragm (from your belly) . . . hold it . . . now slowly release it and note how you feel while doing this . . . feel the relaxation fluidly flow throughout your body. And now, one more REALLY deep breath . . . hold it . . . and now release it slowly . . . and begin your normal breathing pattern. Shift around, if you need to get comfortable again.**
>
> **Now begin to visualize the beginning of a day in which you are going to give an informative speech. See yourself getting up in the morning, full of energy, full of confidence, looking forward to the day's challenges. You are putting on just the right clothes for the task at hand that day. Dressing well makes you look and feel good about yourself, so you have on JUST what you want to wear, which clearly expresses your sense of inner well-being. As you are driving, riding, or walking to the speech setting, note how clear and confident you feel, and how others around you—as you arrive—comment positively regarding your fine appearance and general demeanor. You feel thoroughly prepared for the task at hand. Your preparation has been exceptionally thorough, and you have really researched the target issue you will be presenting today. Now you see yourself standing or sitting in the room where you will present your speech, talking very comfortably and confidentially with others in the room. The people to whom you will be presenting your speech appear to be quite friendly, and are very cordial in their greetings and conversations prior to the presentation. You feel ABSOLUTELY sure of your material and of your ability to present the information in a forceful, convincing, positive manner. Now you see yourself approaching the area from which you will present. You are feeling very good about this presentation and see yourself move eagerly forward. All of your audiovisual materials are well organized, well planned, and clearly aid your presentation.**
>
> **Now you see yourself presenting your talk. You are really quite brilliant and have all the finesse of a polished, professional speaker. You are also aware that your audience is giving head nods, smiles, and other positive responses, conveying the message that you are truly "on target." The introduction of the speech goes the way you have planned. In fact, it works better than you had expected. The transition from the introductory material to the body of the speech is extremely smooth. As you approach the body of the speech, you are aware of the first major point. It emerges as you expected. The evidence supporting the point is relevant and evokes an understanding response from the audience. In fact, all the main points flow in this fashion. As you wrap up your main points, your concluding remarks seem to be a natural outgrowth of everything you have done. All concluding remarks are on target. When your final utterance is concluded, you have the feeling that it could not have gone better. The introduction worked, the main points were to the point, your evidence was supportive, and your conclusion formed a fitting capstone. In addition, your vocal variety added interest value. Your pauses punctuated important ideas, and your gestures and body movements were purposeful. You now see yourself fielding audience questions with brilliance, confidence, and energy equal to what you exhibited in the presentation itself. You see yourself receiving**

the congratulations of your classmates. You see yourself as relaxed, pleased with your talk, and ready for the next task to be accomplished that day. You are filled with energy, purpose, and a sense of general well-being. Congratulate yourself on a job well done!

Now—we want you to begin to return to this time and place in which we are working today. Take a deep breath . . . hold it . . . and let it go. Do this several times and move slowly back into the room. Take as much time as you need to make the transition back.[25]

Notes

1. Geoffrey Brewer, "Snakes Top List of American's Fears," Gallup press release, 19 Mar. 2001. http://www.gallup.com/poll/Releases/pr010319.asp.
2. Robert Hilburn, "Barbra on Tour: The Private Streisand," *Newsday*, 23 May 1994, p. BO3; and Edna Gundersen, "Carly Conquers Grand Central, Stage Fright," *USA Today*, 17 May 1995, p. 12D.
3. Marianne Martini, Ralph R. Behnke, and Paul E. King, "The Communication of Public Speaking Anxiety: Perceptions of Asian and American Speakers," *Communication Quarterly* 40 (1992): 280.
4. Laura J. Toler, "Scared of the Spotlight? You're Not Alone," Gannett news service, 1995.
5. Heidi M. Rose, Andrew S. Rancer, and Kenneth C. Crannell, "The Impact of Basic Courses in Oral Interpretation and Public Speaking on Communication Apprehension," *Communication Reports* 6 (1993): 54–60. The physiological and neurological bases of communication apprehension are summarized in Terri Freeman, Chris R. Sawyer, and Ralph R. Behnke, "Behavioral Inhibition and the Attribution of Public Speaking State Anxiety," *Communication Education* 43 (1997): 175–187.
6. Ralph R. Behnke, Chris R. Sawyer, and Paul E. King, "Contagion Theory and the Communication of Public Speaking State Anxiety," *Communication Education* 43 (1994): 246–251.
7. Gustav Friedrich and Blaine Goss, "Systematic Desensitization," in *Avoiding Communication: Shyness, Reticence, and Communication Apprehension*, ed. John A. Daly and James C. McCroskey (Beverly Hills: Sage, 1984), pp. 173–188.
8. William J. Fremouw and Michael D. Scott, "Cognitive Restructuring: An Alternative Method for the Treatment of Communication Apprehension," *Communication Education* 28 (1979): 129–133.
9. Joe Ayres and Theodore S. Hopf, "Visualization: Is It More Than Extra-Attention?" *Communication Education* 38 (1989): 1–5.
10. Tim Hopf and Joe Ayres, "Coping with Public Speaking Anxiety: An Examination of Various Combinations of Systematic Desensitization, Skills Training, and Visualization," *Journal of Applied Communication Research* 20 (1992): 183–198. Also see Joe Ayres and Brian L. Hewett, "The Relationship Between Visual Imagery and Public Speaking Apprehension," *Communication Reports* 10 (1997): 87–94.
11. The effectiveness of self-devised and enacted scripts has been demonstrated in Joe Ayres, "Comparing Self-constructed Visualization Scripts with Guided Visualization," *Communication Reports* 8 (1995): 193–199.
12. Joe Ayres, Tim Hopf, and Debbie M. Ayres, "An Examination of Whether Imaging Ability Enhances the Effectiveness of an Intervention Designed to Reduce Speech Anxiety," *Communication Education* 43 (1994): 252–258.
13. These techniques are summarized in Thomas E. Robinson II, "Communication Apprehension and the Basic Public Speaking Course: A National Survey of In-Class Treatment Techniques," *Communication Education* 46 (1997): 179–197.
14. Kent E. Menzel and Lori J. Carrell, "The Relationship Between Preparation and Performance in Public Speaking," *Communication Education* 43 (1994): 17–26; and Joe Ayres, "Speech Preparation Processes and Speech Apprehension," *Communication Education* 45 (1996): 228–235.
15. Randolph H. Whitworth and Claudia Cochran, "Evaluation of Integrated Versus Unitary Treatments for Reducing Public Speaking Anxiety," *Communication Education* 45 (1996): 306–314.
16. Mike Allen, John E. Hunter, and William A. Donohue, "Meta-Analysis of Self-Report Data on the Effectiveness of Public Speaking Anxiety Treatment Techniques," *Communication Education* 38 (1989): 54–76.
17. Peter D. MacIntyre, Kimly A. Thivierge, and J. Renee MacDonald, "The Effects of Audience Interest, Responsiveness, and Evaluation on Public Speaking Anxiety and Related Variables," *Communication Research Reports* 14 (1997): 157–168.
18. W. H. Cooper, "Ubiquitous Halo," *Psychological Bulletin* 90 (1981): 218–224.
19. James C. McCroskey and Mason J. Teven, "Goodwill: A Reexamination of the Construct and Its Measurement," *Communication Monographs* 66 (1999): 90–103.
20. Kenneth Burke, *A Rhetoric of Motives* (Berkeley and Los Angeles: University of California Press, 1969), pp. 20–23.
21. John A. Daly, Anita L. Vangelisti, and David J. Weber, "Speech Anxiety Affects How People Prepare Speeches: A Protocol Analysis of the Preparation Processes of Speakers," *Communication Monographs* 62 (1995): 383–397.

22. Donald C. Bryant and Karl R. Wallace, *Fundamentals of Public Speaking*, 4th ed. (New York: Appleton-Century-Crofts, 1969), p. 233.

23. James M. Loy, speech to the National Press Club, Washington, D.C., 24 Feb. 2000, “Proud of What We Do for America,” in *Vital Speeches of the Day*, 15 June 2000, pp. 517–520.

24. Condoleezza Rice, “American Dream for All of Us,” address to the Republican National Convention, Philadelphia, 1 Aug. 2000, in *Vital Speeches of the Day*, 15 Aug. 2000, pp. 653–655.

25. Joe Ayres and Theodore S. Hopf, “Visualization: Is It More Than Extra Attention?” *Communication Education*, 38 (1989): 2–3. Used by permission of the National Communication Association.

SAMPLE SPEECHES OF SELF-INTRODUCTION

Three Photographs

Ashley Smith

■ *The three photographs are an ingenious way to structure this speech. Each photograph stands for a main point. Ashley's use of Spanish and her colorful language reinforce her competence. The contrast between the types of education in Costa Rica is dramatic and her on-the-scene report of life there makes her account both authentic and authoritative. In effect she provides her own expert testimony that is adequate for this brief speech. In an informative or persuasive speech, more supporting material would be needed.*

Photographs often tell stories that only a few can hear. I would like to tell you the story told me by three snapshots that hang in my room in quiet, suburban Jacksonville, Florida. If you saw them, you might think them totally unrelated; together, they tell a powerful tale.

"Ashley, *levantete*!" I heard each morning for the month that I spent in Costa Rica as an exchange student. I would wake up at 5:30 to get ready for school and would stumble off to the one shower that the family of five shared. I had to wash myself in cold water because there was no warm water—that usually woke me up pretty fast! I then got dressed and breakfast would be waiting on the table. Predictably it would be fruit, coffee, and *gallo pinto*, a black bean and rice dish usually served at every meal. We would then walk to school and begin the day with an hour and a half of shop class. After shop we would have about 15- to 20-minute classes in what you and I might call "regular" academic subjects: math and Spanish, for example. Those classes had frequent interruptions and were not taken very seriously. The socialization process was quite clear: These children were being prepared for jobs in the labor force instead of for higher education. Each afternoon as we walked home we passed the elite school where students were still busy working and studying. The picture in my room of my Costa Rican classmates painting picnic tables in the schoolyard reminds me of their narrow opportunities.

■ *Ashley uses examples as her major form of supporting material. Again stronger support would be needed for informative or persuasive speeches to support her assertion of European exploitation.*

The second photograph on my wall is of a little girl in Botswana who is not much younger than I. She's nearing the end of her education and has finished up to the equivalent of the sixth grade. She will now return to a rural setting because her family cannot afford to continue her schooling. To add to the problem, the family goat was eaten by a lion, so she had to return to help them over this crisis. But she didn't miss out on much—most likely, she would have gone on into the city and ended up in one of the shantytowns, one more victim of the unemployment, poverty, even starvation endured by the people. Her lack of opportunity is due not so much to class inequalities as in Costa Rica, but more to the cultural tradition of several hundred years of European exploitation. Recently there has been extensive growth there, but the natives have been left far behind.

■ *The scene she depicts of life in Jacksonville provides a vivid contrast with the other lifestyles she has sketched.*

The third photograph in my room is of four high school students, taken where I went to school in Jacksonville, Florida. We're all sitting on the lawn outside school, overlooking the parking lot full of new cars that will take us home to warm dinners and comfortable beds and large homes and privileged lives. Many of us—including myself for most of my life—took this world for granted. But now, for me, no more. I may have gained a lot on my travels, but I lost my political innocence.

■ *Here Ashley draws out the meaning of the three photographs for her life. The goal she describes confirms her integrity as well as her competence. Her conclusion ties in skillfully with her introduction, completing the circle of the speech.*

One thing I gained is an intense desire to become an educator. I want to teach people to succeed on their merits despite the social and economic inequalities that they're faced with. And I want to learn from them as well. I want to teach the boy who never mastered welding that he could own the factory. And I want him to teach me how to use a rice cooker. I want to teach the girl who is exhausted each afternoon after walking to the river with a jar on her head to gather water that she could design an irrigation system. But I also want her to teach me how to weave a thatched roof. I want to travel and teach and learn.

Three photographs, hanging on my wall. They are silent, mute, and the photographer was not very skilled. But together they tell a powerful story in my life.

Family Gifts

Marie D'Aniello

Lorraine, John, John Victor, Christopher, Michael, and Anthony. That's my family. My mom, my dad, and my four brothers—that's my life. Together these people have shaped me as an individual. Growing up in a small town with a large family teaches you a lot, especially if you grow up like I did, with a lot of love, a little money, and a whole lot of gifts. Not tangible gifts like clothes and jewelry (although those are nice, too), but gifts like strength, and glory, and pride, pride not only in myself, but also in them and in my family name. I am Marie D'Aniello . . . a D'Aniello. I belong to them like they belong to me. I'm a little bit like my Mom and a little bit like my Dad. I can work like my brother John and play like Chris. I can dream like Michael and love like Anthony. I'm Marie, exactly like no one but a little bit like everyone.

■ *This speech records one student's appreciation of her family's meaning to her life. Even from the printed transcript, one can sense Marie's command of oral rhythm. Her sentences flow in a pleasing way that reinforces the meaning of her words. The speech is woven around three themes, each connected with a member of her family. This strategy seems casual because like most good art, it conceals itself. As a result, we don't think of Marie's technique, we think of her message.*

Every now and then I hear people say things like, "You know, my family just doesn't understand me." Well, yeah, I feel that way too at times. My family's not perfect. We have our hard times and disagreements. But I always walk away from these spats with a little more knowledge about myself. Maybe I learn that I'm stronger than I thought. That strength comes from my Mom.

It takes a strong woman to work a full-time job, hold together a family, and raise five children. But my mom does it all. I can remember when I was little waking up at night and listening to the sound of the vacuum cleaner. My Mom would stay up all night, cleaning the house and making sure everything was ready for the next day. She never complained about the hard work. She just did it because she loved us.

I never realized the influence my mother had on me until I went away. Now that I'm here, a thousand miles away from her, I sometimes see her smiling and working the night away. And when I get a grade and I don't think it reflects my effort, I can hear my Mom saying, "You're worth more than this, Marie. You'll get it next time." My Mom's strength has given me my own strength and my own perseverance. I know these qualities are the keys to glory.

When I think of glory, I have to think of my brother Chris. I'll never forget his championship basketball game. It's the typical buzzer beater story: five seconds to go, down by one, Chris gets the ball and he drives down the court, he shoots, he scores! We all rush the floor, everyone. But Chris doesn't care about anyone else. All he looks for is us, his family. He wanted to share his glory with us. I'll never forget the headline, "D'Aniello saves the game!" D'Aniello, hey, wait, that's me. I'm a D'Aniello. I could do this too. Maybe I can't play basketball like Chris, but I can do other things.

■ *Marie uses a story to describe her brother's glorious moment. Note how she re-creates the excitement of the situation and how she focuses on his gift of inspiration to her.*

So I started trying harder in school, "applying myself," as they say. And I had my own taste of glory. I became a valedictorian, won a scholarship, and now I'm here at Vanderbilt. Unbelievable. After I watched Chris drive toward the hoop to score the winning basket, I wanted to "drive" toward my future. And you know what? I just might make it!

And even if I don't make it, at least I'll try and I'll have my pride. At least, that's what my Dad always says. He knows about pride. He knows what it's like to be scorned because you don't make as much money as other people or because you don't have an impressive job. My Dad is a small-town mechanic. He couldn't go to school, so he taught himself everything he knows. And he knows a whole lot, not just about cars, but about honor. I hear my Dad all the time, saying, "Marie, whatever you do, just try to put your whole heart into it. Make it count. Take pride in it." Not a day goes by that I don't hear those words. Because of him, I take pride in my work and I take pride in myself.

■ *Marie's praise of her father's pride and sense of honor was presented to an audience of students from mainly affluent families. The story reminded listeners that the most valuable gifts may not be material, and that you can't always measure the worth of a person by wealth or formal education.*

I practiced my speech in front of one of my friends, and she said, "Marie, are you sure you're really talking about yourself?" Yeah, I am. When I talk about my family, I'm talking about the main sources of myself. They've given me a

■ *In her conclusion Marie counters an impression that her identity relies too much on her family. She affirms that because of their influence she can be the individual that she is.*

world, but it's not like I'm trapped in it. I can go anywhere and do anything because of the gifts they've given me. Strength, glory, pride—thank you, John, Chris, Michael, Anthony, Mom, and Dad. You've made me an individual, Marie D'Aniello, a little bit different from each one of you, and a little bit like all of you.

OUTLINE

3

Becoming a Better Listener

THIS CHAPTER WILL HELP YOU

- appreciate the importance of effective listening
- overcome barriers to effective listening
- improve your critical thinking skills
- evaluate messages constructively
- become aware of the ethical responsibilities of listeners

You walk to the front of the room, ready to make your first presentation. You pause and make eye contact with your audience. This is what you see:

In a far corner of the room a student is frantically trying to finish her accounting homework. A ledger is open on her desk, and a textbook is open on her lap. Her eyes move from the book to the ledger. She never stops writing, and she never looks up.

In the other far corner, a student is sleeping off last night's party. His eyes are closed most of the time. Occasionally his chin drops down onto his chest, and he jerks himself up and tries to look alert, but alas, within twenty seconds he has wandered off again.

Finally, you spot a friendly face—someone who actually looks as though he's ready to listen. His desk is empty except for a notebook. He is sitting alert, a pencil poised in his hand. His eyes are on you. He looks interested in what you have to say.

Legend has it that President Franklin Delano Roosevelt was bemused by the poor listening behavior of people who attended social functions at the White House. To test his contention that people didn't really listen, he once greeted guests in a receiving line by murmuring, "I murdered my grandmother this morning." Typical responses ran along the lines of "Thank you," "How good of you," or other platitudes of polite approval. Finally he met someone who had actually listened and responded, "I'm sure she had it coming to her."[1]

Easy listening exists only on the radio.

—David Barkan

Poor listening exacts a large price. As the eminent psychologist Carl Rogers once observed, "Man's inability to communicate is a result of his failure to listen effectively, skillfully, and with understanding to another person." The consequences can be enormous, both globally and personally. Nations may misunderstand one another's motives, and go to war over the misunderstanding. When people in a group don't listen well, they may make poor decisions. When juries don't attend to the evidence presented, they cannot render a just verdict. If you don't listen well to another person, you may lose his or her respect and affection. If you are not listening effectively in a classroom lecture or at a new-employee orientation at work, you may miss important information. At the very least, poor listening skills can create negative impressions of your competence that can hurt your ethos when you decide to speak.

The most encouraging thing is that better listening is a teachable and learnable skill.[2] You can improve as a listener if you work at it. In this chapter we consider the nature of effective listening and its benefits to both listener and speaker. We also discuss the external and internal sources of interference that impede effective listening and suggest ways to cope with these problems. Next, we relate effective listening to the analysis and evaluation of speeches. Finally, we consider what it means to be an ethical listener.

The Nature and Importance of Effective Listening

Although we spend the greatest amount of our communication time listening, we receive less formal training in listening than we do in speaking, writing, or reading.[3] Why is this so? Perhaps educators assume that we know by nature how to listen well, despite a good deal of evidence to the contrary. They may undervalue listening because they associate it with following, at the same time that they associate speaking with leading. In the dominant American culture, leadership is admired more than "followership," even though being a judicious follower is one definition of a good citizen. As S. I. Hayakawa once commented, "Living in a competitive culture, most of us are . . . chiefly concerned with getting our own view across, and we . . . find other people's speeches a tedious interruption of our own ideas." Perhaps this is why we frequently emphasize speaking while neglecting the obvious fact that listening is essential to any communication transaction. Finally, in a society that admires being "on the move," we may think of speaking as an active and listening as a passive behavior. This ignores the fact that effective listening is a dynamic activity that

- seeks out the meaning intended in messages.
- considers apparent and not-so-apparent motivations.
- evaluates the soundness of reasoning and the reliability of supporting materials.
- calculates the value and risk of accepting recommendations.
- integrates all this creatively into the world of the listener.

Other cultures place a higher premium on good listening behaviors. Some Native American tribes, for example, have a far better appreciation for their importance. The council system of the Ojai Foundation has three main rules for conducting business derived from tribal custom: "Speak honestly, be brief, and listen from the heart."[4] The Lakota also recognize the value of listening. In their culture:

> **Conversation was never begun at once, nor in a hurried manner. No one was quick with a question, no matter how important, and no one was pressed for an answer. A pause giving time for thought was the truly courteous way of beginning and conducting a conversation. Silence was meaningful with the Lakota, and his granting a space of silence to the speech-maker and his own moment of silence before talking was done in the practice of true politeness and regard for the rule that, "thought comes before speech."[5]**

For the people of the Blackfeet tribe, listening is a way of opening themselves to the sacredness of their surroundings.[6] We shall apply these lessons from the Ojai, Lakota, and Blackfeet people and regard listening as vital to successful communication.

The Ladder of Listening

When people are strangers to each other, or when they see each other as threats or possible enemies, they often erect invisible walls to protect or separate themselves. Communication may be pictured as an effort to climb these walls, using the ladders of speaking and listening. This section concerns the ladder of listening.

* * Develop a videotape which illustrates effective and ineffective listening behaviors in classroom settings. Use this tape to spark class discussion as to what constitutes effective listening.

ESL: Ask ESL students to describe what is good listening in their cultures. Concentrate on specific traits—eye contact, facial expression, interruptions, deference to speaker, etc. Will they have to adapt these expectations to become good listeners in the public speaking class? How can they make these changes?

InterConnections.LearnMore 3.1

LISTENING

Assessing Listening and Speaking Skills
http://ericae.net/ericdb/ED263626.htm
General information and bibliography on listening from the ERIC (Educational Resources Information Center) database.

Improving Your Listening **http://www.scs.tamu.edu/selfhelp/elibrary/listening_skills.htm**
Techniques and principles from the Student Counseling Service, Texas A&M University.

International Listening Association
http://www.listen.org
The official web site of the International Listening Association, dedicated to improving listening skills, with links to exercises and resources, including ILA's quarterly publication, *Listening Post*.

Listening and Negotiation Skills **http://www.healthyplace.com/communities/depression/wilkerson/listening_skills.html**
An article on the role of listening in successful negotiating.

The Power of Listening (LearningResource Network)
http://www.speaking.com/articles_html/TonyAlessandra,Ph.D.,CSP,CPAE_107.html
An interesting essay on the importance of listening skills, written by a professional speaker and applied behavioral scientist.

Have students discuss the Chinese symbol for listening. Especially, what does it mean to listen from the eyes and heart? To spark the discussion, show videotapes of student speakers and ask, respectively, how would an effective audience member listen to each speaker with the ears, the eyes, and the heart?

The Chinese symbol for the verb "to listen" has four basic elements: undivided attention, ears, eyes, and heart.[7] This symbol suggests some of the basic differences between simply hearing and actually listening. *Hearing* is an automatic process in which sound waves stimulate nerve impulses to the brain. We may call it the **discriminative phase**, in which we detect the vital sounds of spoken communication. Although it is a necessary condition to the listening experience, it is only the first step up the ladder. *Listening* is a voluntary activity that goes beyond the mere physical reaction to sounds. At the very least, listening involves focusing, understanding, and interpreting:

- You must focus on the message and block out factors that compete for attention.
- You must understand the speaker's verbal and nonverbal language.
- You must interpret what you hear in light of your own knowledge and experience.

These elements make up the **comprehensive phase**, the next rung of the ladder we must climb if we are to participate fully in communication. Beyond these basic processes is the **empathic phase**, which emphasizes the heart in the Chinese symbol. When we are empathic, we encourage speakers by suspending judgment and allowing them to be heard.[8] We try to see things from their point of view, even though we may not agree with them. Our next step up the ladder of listening is to the **appreciative phase**, in which we respond to beauty in the message. For example, we may enjoy the simplicity, balance, and proportion of a speech structure or the eloquence of a speaker's words.

Have students consider what it means to listen as though you were participating in a dialogue with the speaker.

Critical listening represents another step up the ladder. Critical listeners analyze and evaluate the content of a message. They factor into the analysis their assessment of the speaker's motives and feelings. This step adds the element of "mind" to the Chinese symbol for listening. Critical listeners also provide appropriate feedback to the speaker. As you evaluate, you may offer visual cues, such as smiles or frowns, puzzled looks, or nods of agreement, that let a speaker know how you are responding.

The final rung on the ladder of listening is **constructive listening**. Constructive listening involves seeking in messages their value for our lives. We of-

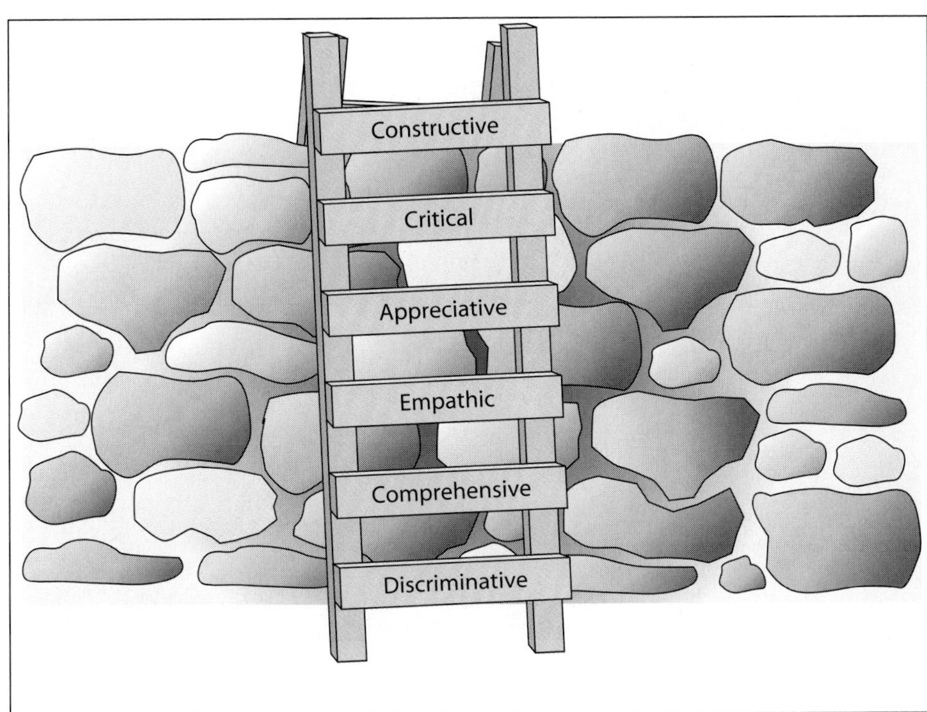

FIGURE 3.1
The Ladder of Listening

ten think of listeners as merely the "unpackers" of meaning in messages. Constructive listeners *add* to a message, finding in it special applications useful to them. As they listen to a speech on the importance of air bags in automobiles, they may question whether there are differences in the quality of air bags from one automobile to another. They may wonder if there are any drawbacks to air bags and, if so, how they might avoid them. If they don't hear the answers they seek in the speech itself, these listeners may question the speaker afterward, creating a dialogue that *extends the meaning of the speech*. Such dialogues often produce discoveries, better realizations of shared values, and better answers to public questions. As described by Stewart and Logan, dialogue "is an event where meaning emerges *through* all the participants."[9]

Climbing the ladder of listening allows an audience to join with the speaker in creating meaning.[10] As speakers offer messages and listeners respond, their worlds interact to produce the transactional and transformative effects of communication (described in Chapter 1), in which speaker, listener, and the state of public knowledge can be enlarged or diminished by the communication experience.

After a classroom speech, have students reflect upon the "ladder of listening" and how they climbed each rung of the ladder as they listened.

Benefits of Effective Listening

Effective listening benefits both listeners and speakers.

Benefits to the Listener. Sharing successful communication transactions can be both emotionally and intellectually rewarding. As you develop better listening skills, you also develop resistance to persuasive exploiters, especially to those charlatans who may try to cover up a lack of substance or of reasoned appeals with a glib presentation or irrelevant appeals.[11]

Have students bring to class copies of print advertisements. As they analyze these ads, ask them to illustrate critical listening skills.

Better listening skills have broad application in your academic and professional life. Those who listen effectively earn better grades and achieve beyond expectation.[12] The reasons would seem obvious: effective listeners learn to concentrate on what is being said and to identify what is important. They motivate themselves to learn by exploring the value of information for their lives. The most effective student listeners read assignments ahead of time to familiarize

The ability to listen effectively can help you in your other classes.

themselves with the language and to provide a foundation for understanding. By listening well to the speeches presented in your class, you can discover the kinds of subjects that interest your classmates. You can also learn from their experience what techniques work best and the mistakes you should avoid. By observing how they structure, support, and present their speeches, you can tell why one presentation works better than another.

At work, improved listening skills can mean the difference between success and failure—both for individuals and for companies. A Department of Labor report emphasizes the value of learning how to listen effectively.[13] A survey of over four hundred top-level personnel directors suggests that the two most important factors in helping graduates find jobs are speaking and listening ability.[14] Another survey of major American corporations reports that poor listening is "one of the [companies'] most important problems" and that "ineffective listening leads to ineffective performance."[15] If you listen effectively on the job, you will improve your chances for advancement.[16] This is especially true in organizations that provide services rather than goods. Companies that encourage people at every level to develop effective listening skills enjoy many dividends. Employees are more innovative when they sense that management will listen to new ideas. Morale improves, and the work environment becomes more pleasant and productive. For these reasons many Fortune 500 corporations provide listening training programs for their employees.[17]

Ask students to reflect upon moments in which they realized others were not listening to them. What cued them to this realization? How did it make them feel?

Benefits to the Speaker. Speakers obviously benefit from an audience of good listeners. When audiences don't listen well, they can't provide useful feedback. Moreover, a good audience can help alleviate communication apprehension by creating a supportive classroom environment.[18] Speakers need to realize that listeners want them to succeed. You can convey your support by being a pleasant and responsive listener rather than dour and inattentive.[19] Give speakers your undivided attention. Take an occasional note at appropriate moments—this suggests to them that you think their ideas are important.[20] Nod occasionally in response to what they say. Show respect for them as people, even when you may disagree with their ideas. Look for value in what they say.

An audience of effective listeners also can boost a speaker's self-esteem and can make speaking an exhilarating experience. A congenial audience can help reduce a speaker's communication apprehension.[21] How many times have you had people *really listen* to you? How often have you had an opportunity to educate others? How frequently have your ideas and recommendations been taken seriously? If your answer is "seldom" or "never," you may be in for a pleasant surprise when you make your presentations. You will soon discover that there are few things quite as rewarding as having people really listen to you and respect what you say. As Henry David Thoreau once commented, "The greatest compliment that was ever paid me was when one asked me what I thought, and attended to my answer."

Negative evidence of the importance of this factor is indicated by the difficulty many women executives have in American business.[22] Often they hold an organizational title, but are not regarded as company "insiders." Consequently, they are sometimes not taken seriously when they speak. They suffer, and the company suffers from the loss of their ideas.

Overcoming Barriers to Effective Listening

Some barriers to good listening arise from external sources of interference, such as a noisy room. But the most formidable barriers to effective listening are internal, based in the listener's own attitudes. At best, these barriers present a challenge; at worst, they may completely block communication.

Once we understand what our listening problems are, we can begin to correct them. Figure 3.2 should help you identify areas you will need to work on. Look through the list and place a check next to items that describe your listening attitudes and behaviors.

FIGURE 3.2
Listening Problems Checklist

- ☐ *1.* I believe listening is automatic, not learned behavior.
- ☐ *2.* I stop listening when a speech is uninteresting.
- ☐ *3.* I find it hard to listen to ideas about which I feel strongly.
- ☐ *4.* I react emotionally to some words.
- ☐ *5.* I am easily distracted by noises when someone is speaking.
- ☐ *6.* I don't like to listen to speakers who are not experts.
- ☐ *7.* I find some people too objectionable to listen to.
- ☐ *8.* I nod off when someone talks in a monotone.
- ☐ *9.* I can be so dazzled by a glib presentation that I don't listen critically.
- ☐ *10.* I don't like to listen to messages that contradict my values.
- ☐ *11.* I think of counterarguments during the speech when I disagree with a speaker.
- ☐ *12.* I know so much on some topics that I don't need to hear more.
- ☐ *13.* I believe a speaker—not the listener—is responsible for effective communication.
- ☐ *14.* I find it hard to listen when I have a lot on my mind.
- ☐ *15.* I stop listening when a subject is difficult.
- ☐ *16.* I can look like I'm listening when I am not.
- ☐ *17.* I listen only for facts and ignore the rest of a message.
- ☐ *18.* I try to write down everything a lecturer says.
- ☐ *19.* I let a speaker's appearance determine how well I listen.
- ☐ *20.* I often jump to conclusions before I have listened to all of a message.

External Sources of Interference

External sources of interference may arise from the environment, from the message, or from the presentation. Most of the time, these sources of interference are relatively minor contributors to poor listening, and often they are better addressed by speakers than by listeners. For example, if a helicopter passes overhead, the speaker may need to talk louder to be heard. We cover how speakers can make such adjustments during their presentations in Chapter 11. Keep in mind, however, that communication is a joint enterprise. As a listener, you should provide feedback to let the speaker know that there is a problem. If you can't hear, give the speaker a signal, or move to a seat closer to the front of the room.

Environmental Problems. The most obvious source of environmental interference is noise. If the general noise level is high, you need to sit close enough to the speaker to hear comfortably. If the noise is intermittent or comes from outside the room, you may need to close a window or a door. Obviously it is best to do this before speakers start their presentations. If you must do so while someone is speaking, be as unobtrusive as possible.

Message Problems. Messages that are full of jargon or unfamiliar words, or that are poorly organized, make it difficult for people to listen effectively. We provide suggestions to speakers on using language effectively in Chapter 10, and on how to organize a message clearly in Chapters 7 and 8. As a listener, you have to put forth some effort to help overcome these problems. If you know that there may be unfamiliar words in a presentation, such as a lecture in one of your courses, try to acquaint yourself with that vocabulary ahead of time. If a message is poorly organized, taking notes can help. Often you can find a pattern in the speaker's thoughts that will make them easier to remember and evaluate. Try to identify the main points or claims the speaker makes. Differentiate these from supporting materials such as examples or narratives. Figure 3.3 provides some helpful suggestions for taking notes.[23]

Show videotapes of speakers with the sound turned off. Have students identify particular points of interest in the body language. Now view the speeches again, this time with sound. Does the body language add to or subtract from the listening experience? Try the same exercise in reverse: First listen to the speech without the picture, noting especially such vocal factors as emphasis, pitch, rate, variety, and loudness. Then both listen to and view the speech. Do all these presentational factors work together to facilitate listening?

Presentation Problems. Speakers who talk too fast may be difficult to follow. On the other hand, speakers who talk too slowly or too softly may lull you to sleep. Speakers may also have habits that are distracting. They may sway to

Elie Wiesel, recipient of the 1986 Nobel Peace Prize, had to overcome many distractions when speaking at this Holocaust memorial service. A compelling message and forceful presentation can help speakers cope with problems of traffic noise and inclement weather.

FIGURE 3.3
Guidelines for Taking Notes

1. Study background material ahead of time in preparation for a lecture.
2. Come prepared with a notebook and pen or pencil (have a backup available).
3. Leave a large margin on the left and take notes in outline form. Align the main points with the left-hand margin and indent supporting material. Leave spaces between main points.
4. Don't try to write down everything you hear. Omit nonessential words.
5. Be alert for signal words such as:
   a. *for example or case in point,* which suggest that supporting material will follow.
   b. *the three causes or the four steps,* which suggest a list that you should number.
   c. *before* or *after,* which suggest that the order is important.
   d. *therefore* or *consequently,* which suggest a casual relationship.
   e. *similarly* or *on the other hand,* which suggest that a comparison or contrast will follow.
   f. *above all* or *keep in mind,* which mean that this is an important idea.
6. As you listen, silently summarize what you are hearing and note questions in the large left-hand margin for clarification after the speech.
7. After the speech, review, correct, and complete your notes.

and fro or fiddle with their hair while they are talking. Occasionally, you may even encounter speakers whose dress or hairstyle is so unusual that you find yourself concentrating more on them than on what they are saying. We advise speakers on how to minimize such distractions in Chapter 11. As a listener, sometimes just being aware that you are responding to such cues may be enough to help you listen more attentively. If you find yourself drifting away because of such problems, remind yourself that what speakers say is the most important part of their message.

Internal Sources of Interference

Internal listening problems may be caused by reactions to words, personal concerns, attitudes, cultural differences, bad listening habits, and listener apprehension. Fortunately, some of these problems can be anticipated by the speaker, and most are under the listener's control. Figure 3.4 shows how good and poor listeners respond differently to such problems.

One of the most common barriers to effective listening is simply not paying attention. How many times have you found yourself daydreaming, even when you know you should be listening to what is said? One reason for this problem is that our minds can process information far faster than people usually speak. Most people speak at about 125 words per minute in public, but can process information at about 500 words per minute.[24] This time lapse provides an opportunity for listeners to drift away to more delightful or difficult personal concerns. All too often daydreamers smile and nod encouragingly even though they haven't heard a word the speaker has said. This deceptive feedback is a major cause of failed communication. Both personal reactions to words and distractions can set off such responses.

ESL students may be especially tempted to feign attention for the sake of politeness or to avoid admitting that they have not understood. Ask students to discuss moments in which they pretended to be listening without actually doing so. Were they successful? What were the consequences? Let students know that it is permissible to ask clarifying questions. How might one ask such questions?

Reactions to Words. As you listen to a message, you react to more than just the objective meanings of words. You respond to their emotional meanings as

FIGURE 3.4
Differences Between Good and Poor Listeners

Good Listeners	Poor Listeners
1. focus attention on the message.	1. allow their minds to wander.
2. control reactions to trigger words.	2. respond emotionally to trigger words.
3. set aside personal problems when listening.	3. let personal problems interfere when listening.
4. work to overcome distractions.	4. succumb easily to distractions.
5. don't let their biases interfere with listening.	5. let their biases interfere with listening.
6. don't let speaker mannerisms interfere with listening.	6. allow speaker mannerisms to interfere with listening.
7. listen for things they can use.	7. tune out dry topics.
8. recognize the role of the listener in communication.	8. hold the speaker responsible for communication.
9. listen actively.	9. listen passively.
10. reserve judgement until a speaker is finished.	10. jump to conclusions before a speaker is finished.
11. provide honest feedback to speakers.	11. feign attention, giving false feedback.
12. become familiar with difficult material ahead of time.	12. avoid listening to difficult material.
13. listen for main ideas.	13. listen only for facts.
14. don't demand that all messages be entertaining.	14. want all messages to be entertaining.

Have students identify their personal trigger words. Have they worked out ways to cope with such words? Trigger words can also be culture-wide in the form of "god and devil" terms. Have ESL students report on words that are especially potent positive or negative terms in their cultures.

well. Some **trigger words** may set off such powerful emotional reactions that they dominate the meaning of the discourse. Although some words deserve condemnation whenever they are used, people should control words and not the other way around. We should not let trigger words prevent us from hearing and evaluating the entire message in which they are embedded.

Let's consider a hypothetical case. Assume that you find the use of the word *girls* to refer to adult females demeaning and disrespectful. Now suppose a recruiter visiting your campus is describing opportunities for advancement in his company. He tells about "one of the girls from the office" who was recently promoted to a management position. His use of the term *girls* makes you think this may be a sexist organization. As you sit there stewing over his word choice, you miss his later statement that two-thirds of all recent promotions into management have gone to women and that an aggressive program aimed at promoting more females and minority employees is in effect.

How can you demystify such language and lessen its power over your reactions? Train yourself to look at the total message and analyze the particular case. For example, would it make any difference if the recruiter were a woman rather than a man? Ask yourself: Why is this person using such language? Is he personally insensitive, or is he testing me? Is this an attitude that is widespread in the company? By concentrating on such questions, you can reduce the power of trigger words and distance yourself somewhat from your own emotions. You can then decide whether you wish to confront the recruiter to clarify these questions. For example, you might tactfully say, "I'm impressed by what you have told me. But I'm troubled by your use of the term *girls*. As a woman, would I really be respected in your company?" There is an obvious risk in this strategy: you might offend the recruiter and not get a highly desirable position. But there is also a risk in committing to a job situation that might not be good for you.

Trigger words can be positive as well as negative. Positive trigger words can blind us to flawed or dangerous messages. How many times have people been deceived by such trigger words as *freedom*, *democracy*, or *progress* to justify courses of action?[25] Such techniques are related to *mythos*, a form of persuasion that appeals to people on the basis of traditions they hold dear. We discuss this more fully in Chapter 14. To gain control over your trigger words, Professor Richard Halley of Weber State University suggests that you observe your own behavior over a period of time and make a list of words that cause you to react emotionally.[26] You might then ask yourself the following questions:

- Did these words shape my responses to the messages?
- Were others trying to manipulate me?
- Should I have reacted differently?
- How can I gain more control over my reactions to words?

Chance associations with words can also derail your attention. For example, a speaker mentions the word *desk*—which reminds you that you need a better place to study in your room—which reminds you that you have to buy a new lamp—which starts you thinking about going shopping—which gets you thinking about the fried mushrooms at the restaurant in the mall—which reminds you that you didn't eat breakfast and you're hungry. By the time your attention drifts back to the speaker, you have lost the gist of what is being said. To prevent this kind of woolgathering, remind yourself of what is at stake in listening and commit yourself to do your part to make communication work.

Personal Concerns. If you are tired, hungry, angry, worried, or pressed for time, you may find it difficult to concentrate. Your mood may be a distraction,[27] or personal problems may take precedence over listening to a speaker. Perhaps your ears are tired from too much listening—what Barker and Watson call "listening burnout."[28]

Be assured that you can control inattention caused by internal distractions. Come to your classes well rested and well fed. Remind yourself that you can't really do your homework for another class when someone is talking. Decide to do your worrying later. Clear your mind and your desk of everything except paper on which to take notes. Sit erect, leaning forward slightly, establish eye contact with the speaker, and commit to listening!

Attitudes. You may have strong positive or negative attitudes toward the speaker or the topic that can diminish your listening ability. All of us have biases of one kind or another. Listening problems arise when our biases prevent us from receiving messages accurately. Some of the ways in which bias can distort messages are through filtering, assimilation, and contrast effects.[29]

Filtering means that you simply don't process all incoming information. You hear what you want to hear. You unconsciously screen the speaker's words so that only some of them reach your brain. Listeners who filter will hear only one side of "good news, bad news" speeches—the side that confirms their preconceived notions. **Assimilation** means that you see positions similar to your own as being closer to it than they actually are. Assimilation most often occurs when listeners have a strong positive attitude toward a speaker or topic. For example, if you believe that President Bush can do no wrong, you may be tempted to assimilate everything he says so that it seems consistent with all your beliefs. A **contrast effect** occurs when you see positions that differ from yours as being more distant than they actually are. For example, if you are a staunch Democrat, you may think anything Republicans say will differ from what you believe, even

Have students observe some important speech, such as the presidential State of the Union address. Which of the reactions to this speech by prominent politicians of both parties might illustrate assimilation and contrast effects?

To become effective listeners, we may have to overcome boredom and fatigue, change some basic listening habits, and play a more positive part in the communication process.

if that is not true. Biases can make you put words in a speaker's mouth, take them away, or distort them.

The attitudes that cause most listening problems are those related to the speaker or the topic. If you know a speaker or have heard something about him or her, you may have developed attitudes that cause listening problems. The more competent, interesting, and attractive you expect a speaker to be, the more attentive you will be and the more likely you are to accept what the speaker has to say. If your positive feelings are extremely strong, you may accept anything you hear from the speaker without considering the merits of the message. But if you anticipate an incompetent, uninteresting, or unattractive speaker, you may be less attentive and less likely to respect his or her ideas. You may dislike speakers because of positions they have previously defended or groups with which they are associated. Such biases may impair your listening ability.

Your attitudes toward certain topics also can affect how well you listen. If you believe that a topic is relevant to your life, you may listen more carefully than if you are indifferent. Speeches about retirement planning may fall on deaf ears with younger audiences. You may listen more attentively, although less critically, to speeches that support positions you already hold. If you feel strongly about a subject and oppose the speaker's position, you may find yourself rehashing counterarguments instead of listening. For example, if you have strong feelings against gun control, you may find yourself silently reciting the Second Amendment to the U.S. Constitution instead of listening to a speaker's arguments in favor of gun control. When you engage in such behaviors, you may miss much of what the speaker actually has to say. Finally, you may think that you already know enough about a topic. In such cases, you are not likely to listen effectively and may miss out on new, potentially useful information.

Attitudes are not easy to control. The first step in overcoming biases is to admit you have them. Next, decide that you will listen as objectively as you can, and that you will delay judgment until you have heard the entire message. Being objective does not mean that you must agree with a message—it only means that you believe a speech deserves to be heard on its own terms. What you hear may help you see clearly the faults or the virtues of an opposing position. As a result, you may feel confirmed in what you already believe, or you may decide to reevaluate your position. Finally, determine that you will find value in listening. Even if you are not interested in a topic, look for something in the speech that will benefit you personally.

Habits. Many listening problems are simply the result of bad habits. You may have watched so much television that you expect all messages to be fast moving and entertaining. You may have learned how to pretend you are listening to avoid dull or difficult materials. Your experiences as a student may have conditioned you to listen just for facts. You may jump to conclusions before hearing a complete message. Such habits can interfere with effective listening.

William F. Buckley Jr. has commented that "the television audience . . . is not trained to listen . . . to 15 uninterrupted minutes."[30] Our television-watching experiences may also lead us into "the entertainment syndrome," in which we demand that speakers be lively, interesting, funny, and charismatic to hold our attention.[31] Unfortunately, not all subjects lend themselves to such treatment.

Although honest feedback is important to speech effectiveness, we all have learned how to pretend to pay attention. We sit erect, gaze at the speaker, nod or smile from time to time (although not always at the most appropriate times), and do not listen to one word that is being said! You are most likely to feign attention when a message is difficult. If the speaker asks, "Do you understand?" you may nod brightly, sending false feedback just to be polite or to avoid seeming dimwitted.

Our fear of failure may cause us to avoid listening to difficult material. If we are asked questions later, we can always say "I wasn't really listening" instead of "I didn't understand." Additionally, our desire to have things simplified so that we can understand them without much effort makes us susceptible to oversimplified remedies for everything from fallen arches to failing government policies.

Your experiences as a student may contribute to another bad habit: listening only for facts. If you do this, you may miss the forest because you are so busy counting leaves. Placing too much emphasis on facts can keep you from attending to the nonverbal aspects of a message. Effective listening includes integrating what you hear and what you see. Gestures, facial expressions, and tone of voice communicate nuances that are vital to understanding a message.

Overcoming bad habits requires effort. When you find yourself feigning attention, remember that honest feedback helps speakers, but that inappropriate feedback deceives them. Don't try to remember everything or write down all that you hear. Instead, listen to the main ideas and identify supporting materials. Paraphrase what you hear so that it makes sense to you. Try to build an overall picture of the meaning in your mind. Attend to the nonverbal cues as well. Does the speaker's tone of voice change the meaning of the words? Are the gestures and facial expressions consistent with the words? If not, what does this tell you?

Listening Apprehension. Listening apprehension is the counterpart to the communication apprehension experienced by speakers that we discussed in Chapter 2. At first, this may surprise you: do listeners really suffer from anxiety? The answer is, they can, and like speaker apprehension, this can be positive as well as negative.

Listener fear, which goes by the technical name **receiver apprehension** (RA), is a relatively new research area in communication. As defined initially by Wheeless, it is "the fear of misinterpreting, inadequately processing and/or not being able to adjust psychologically to messages sent by others."[32] A later research team has connected it with motivation, evaluation, and message complexity.[33] To put the matter simply, we are apt to experience listener apprehension when we perceive that a message will be vital to our lives, when we expect to be judged on how well we respond to it, and when it challenges our ability to understand things.

ESL students can be especially susceptible to receiver apprehension. Advise speakers in classes where there are many such students to slow the rate of speaking, to pause more often, to avoid idioms, to clarify the connections among points with careful transitions, and to restate points more often than they otherwise might.

Assume for the moment that the first speaker of the day announces that her speech will argue that government student loans are unnecessary. You are attending school with the help of such a program, so you feel threatened by her message. The fear and resentment you initially feel cause you to listen to the message with some apprehension.

Now let's take this hypothetical situation a step further. Your teacher announces he wants to designate a respondent for each speech to demonstrate the importance of constructive listening. In an impromptu critique after the speech, the respondent must demonstrate a grasp of the meaning of the speech, appreciation of its qualities, and sensitivity to the speaker's aims. The respondent also must be able to discuss possible shortcomings of content and presentation, and suggest a constructive application for the speech. Congratulations! You have just been designated the respondent for the speech on government loan programs. How can you meet the challenge of listening constructively on a subject on which you have strong initial bias? As you contemplate this challenge, you may experience an acute case of listener apprehension.

Take the case one more step. As you listen to the speech, it is presented with an incredible array of examples and statistics. The message is highly complex. As you attempt to follow the meaning of the speech, you feel your anxiety growing.

We hope we have made our point. Listener apprehension can be an important factor in communication. In the workplace, those who suffer from acute RA tend to receive lower salaries. They are also likely to suffer from high communication apprehension. Thus it is easy for them to slip into the background, because they often avoid crisis situations in which communication interactions are vital to an organization's well-being. Generally speaking, victims of high RA are not highly motivated to succeed, perceive themselves as not especially competent in communication interactions, and fear negative evaluations.[34]

Until social scientists can tell us more about RA, and what to do about it, we may assume the following: Listener apprehension can be positive if it makes us *want* to listen to messages; nothing is worse than a bored audience.[35] But this same anxiety can distract us and even cause us to distort what we hear. If our discomfort is obvious, we may give speakers negative feedback and trigger communication anxiety in them!

To control your own RA, and put it to work for you, we suggest that you experiment with procedures already demonstrated to work for speaker anxiety. That is, practice deep muscle relaxation, rewrite negative messages you may be giving yourself about the listening experience, and visualize successful outcomes.[36] Instead of telling yourself, "I don't understand this at all," say, "I can grasp the overall meaning here." Picture yourself giving a response that helps both speaker and other listeners see the virtues as well as the problems in the message. Then, just as an anxious speaker can create confidence by acting confident, act as though you are interested and motivated by the speaker's message. After a time, you may discover that you actually *are* interested! Such techniques might help you put a positive spin on your experience as listener.

Speaker's Notes 3.1 summarize how you might listen more effectively to messages.

Developing Critical Thinking and Listening Skills

Developing your critical thinking and listening skills will further increase your effectiveness as a listener. *Critical thinking and listening* is an integrated process of examining information, ideas, and proposals. It involves

- questioning what you hear, accepting nothing at face value.
- developing your own position on issues by examining competing ideas.
- being receptive to new thoughts and new perspectives.

Speaker's Notes 3.1

IMPROVING YOUR LISTENING SKILLS

1. Identify your listening problems and work to correct them.
2. Motivate yourself to get everything you can out of messages.
3. Put problems and biases aside so that you listen more effectively.
4. Control your reactions to trigger words and other distractions.
5. Postpone judgments until you have heard all a speaker has to say.
6. Don't try to write down everything a speaker says.
7. Listen for the main ideas.

- evaluating evidence and reasoning.
- discussing with others the meanings of events.[37]

Throughout this course the skills and knowledge you acquire as you learn to prepare speeches will also be useful in analyzing and evaluating the messages you receive. You will learn how to use and evaluate supporting materials and language resources in speeches. As you learn to prepare responsible arguments, you will also be learning how to evaluate the arguments of others. Although these topics will be covered in more depth in later chapters, here we will preview some questions important to critical listening.

Have students listen to some prominent speech—perhaps the presidential State of the Union address mentioned earlier—and apply the critical listening questions that follow. Have students report their answers in class discussion following the speech.

Does the speaker support ideas or claims with facts and figures, testimony, and examples or narratives? Whenever speakers claim, "This statement is beyond dispute!" it is a good time to start a dispute. Listen for what is *not* said, as well as what is said. *No supporting material equals no proof. No proof should equal no acceptance.* Don't hesitate to ask such speakers challenging questions.

Does the speaker use supporting materials that are relevant, representative, recent, and reliable? Supporting materials should relate directly to the issue in question. They should be representative of the situation as it exists rather than exceptions to the rule. The speaker who shouts, "Television is destroying family values!"

The ability to listen effectively is valued in the workplace.

and then offers statistics that demonstrate a rising national divorce rate has not demonstrated a causal relationship between television and family values. Facts and figures should be the most recent ones available. This is particularly important when knowledge about a topic is changing rapidly. Supporting materials should come from sources that are trustworthy and competent in the subject area. Controversial material, especially, should be verified by more than one source, and the sources should represent different perspectives on the issue.

Does the speaker cite credible sources? Ethical speakers specify the credentials of their sources. When credentials are left out or described in vague terms, the testimony may be questionable. We recently found an advertisement for a health food product that contained "statements by doctors." A quick check of the current directory of the American Medical Association revealed that only one of the six "doctors" cited was a member of AMA and that his credentials were misrepresented. Always ask yourself: Where does this information come from? Are these sources qualified to speak on the topic? We cover the use of supporting materials in greater detail in Chapters 6 and 14.

Does the speaker clearly distinguish among facts, inferences, and opinions? Facts are verifiable units of information that can be confirmed by independent observations. Inferences are projections based on facts. Opinions add personal judgments to inferences: they tell us what someone thinks about a subject. For example, "Mary was late for class today" is a fact. "Mary will probably be late for class again tomorrow" is an inference. "Mary is an irresponsible student" is an opinion. It may sound easy to make these distinctions among facts, inferences, and opinions, but you must be constantly alert to detect confusions of them in the messages you hear.

At the height of the media frenzy during the impeachment investigation of President Clinton, White House Press Secretary Mike McCurry charged that "in our political culture now, opinion often is pronounced as judgment before there are facts to support opinion." Walter Isaacson, managing editor of *Time* magazine, and Kathleen Hall Jamieson, dean of the Annenberg School of Communication, supported his charge by pointing out a kind of "echo chamber" effect in modern journalism. The echo chamber works this way: an unconfirmed rumor is initially published by one news source and then is repeated by others as though it had been substantiated. Of one such rumor Isaacson said: "Within one day, it had spun around the city of Washington as if it were fact, and it had gotten embellished."[38]

Facts, inferences, and opinions all have a legitimate place in public discourse, but they also can be misused. Evaluating supporting material is covered in more detail in Chapter 6. Inferences are discussed as part of the reasoning process in Chapter 14.

Does the speaker use language that is concrete and understandable or purposely vague? When speakers have something to hide, they often use incomprehensible or vague language. Introducing people who are not physicians as "doctors" to enhance their testimony on health subjects is one form of such vagueness. Another trick is to use pseudoscientific jargon, such as "This supplement contains a gonadotropic hormone similar to pituitary extract in terms of its complex B vitamin–methionine ratio." If it sounds impressive, but you don't know what it means, be careful. We cover other problems relating to language use in Chapter 10.

Does the speaker ask you to ignore reason? Vivid examples and stories often express the speaker's deep passion for a subject and invite the listener to share this feeling. An ethical speaker will also include sound information and good reasons to justify such a feeling. In politics, those who try to inflame feelings to promote their own agendas, without regard to the accuracy or adequacy of their claims, are called **demagogues**. We should always ask, *What are these speakers asking us to ignore?* Republican leaders recently charged that their Democratic opponents were asking voters to ignore the fact that without significant change, the entire

InterConnections.LearnMore 3.2

CRITICAL THINKING

Critical Thinking Across Cultures: What We Think We Know About Critical Thinking **http://www.asia-u.ac.jp/english/cele/articles/Connolly_Critical_Thinking.htm**
An article discussing Eastern and Western perspectives on critical thinking, prepared by Professor Mark Connolly, Center for English Language Education, Asia University, Tokyo, Japan.

The Critical Thinking Consortium **http://www.criticalthinking.org**
The official web site of the Critical Thinking Consortium, an organization dedicated to promoting change in education and society through critical thinking. Affiliated with Sonoma State University, California.

Critical Thinking on the Web
http://www.philosophy.unimelb.edu.au/reason/critical
A comprehensive directory of online resources on critical thinking, prepared by Dr. Tim van Gelder, Department of Philosophy, University of Melbourne, Australia.

Critical Thinking: What It Is and Why It Counts
http://www.calpress.com/critical.html
An essay on the importance of critical thinking, prepared by Professor Peter A. Facione, dean of the College of Arts and Sciences at Santa Clara University, and director of Critical Thinking Assessment and Consulting Services, California Academic Press.

Medicare program would collapse. Democratic leaders countered that the Republicans were asking voters to ignore the fate of the poor and elderly who would be affected by their reforms. In the face of such conflicting claims, the critical thinker will investigate carefully before coming to a conclusion.

Does the speaker rely too much on facts and figures? Although we have just cautioned you to be wary of speakers who rely solely on emotional appeals, you also should be wary of speakers who exclude emotional appeals. You can never fully understand an issue unless you understand how it affects others, how it makes them feel, how it colors the way they view the world. Suppose you were listening to a speech on environmental pollution that contained the following information: "The United States has 5 percent of the world's population but produces 22 percent of the world's carbon dioxide emissions, releases 26 percent of the world's nitrogen oxides, and disposes of 290 million tons of toxic waste."[39] Although these numbers are impressive, what do they really tell you about the human problem of pollution? Consider how much more meaningful this material might be if accompanied by the story of Colette Chuda, a five-year-old California girl who died recently from cancer caused—some feel—by her direct exposure to a polluted environment.[40]

Does the speaker use plausible reasoning? When reasoning is plausible, conclusions appear to follow from the points and supporting materials that precede them. In other words, they make good sense. The basic assumptions that support arguments should be those on which most rational people agree. Whenever reasoning doesn't seem plausible, ask yourself why, and then question the speaker or consult with independent authorities before you commit yourself. We cover the use of appeals and reasoning in more detail in Chapter 14.

Does the message promise too much? If an offer sounds too good to be true, it probably is. The health food advertisement previously described contained the following claims: "The healing, rejuvenating and disease-fighting effects of this total nutrient are hard to believe, yet are fully documented. Aging, digestive upsets, prostrate [*sic*] diseases, sore throats, acne, fatigue, sexual problems, allergies, and a host of other problems have been successfully treated. . . . [It] is the only super perfect food on this earth. This statement has been proven so many times in the laboratories around the world by a chemical analyst that it is not subject to debate nor [*sic*] challenge." Maybe the product is also useful as a paint remover and gasoline additive.

Does this message fit with what I already know? Although we have stressed the importance of being open to new knowledge, inconsistent information should set off an alarm in your mind. You should always evaluate information that is inconsistent with your beliefs very carefully before you accept it. Yet keep in mind that what you think you know might not necessarily be so. Ask the speaker tough questions suggested by the considerations summarized in Speaker's Notes 3.2. Use the library to further verify information.

What other perspectives might there be on this issue? How would people from a different cultural background perceive the problem? How would someone older see it? How might someone of the other gender see it? Why might these people see it differently from you? Would their solutions or suggestions be different? Whenever a message addresses a serious topic, try to examine the issue from several points of view. New and better ideas often emerge when we look at the world from a different angle.

These questions provide a framework for critical thinking. When we add these skills to the improved listening behavior that comes when we confront our listening problems, we are on the way to becoming effective listeners.

Evaluating Speeches

Your overall improvement as a listener should enhance the quality of the feedback you offer to speakers. Up to now, we have been emphasizing immediate feedback, your body language as a listener. Alert attention and cues such as nods of agreement or puzzled looks can be important *during* a speech. But you may also have an opportunity to give oral feedback *after* speakers have made their presentations. You may ask questions, comment on effective techniques, or offer suggestions for improvement.

To participate in this oral feedback, you must understand one important distinction: there is a difference between criticizing a speaker and giving a

Speaker's Notes 3.2

GUIDES FOR CRITICAL THINKING AND LISTENING

1. Require all claims to be supported with facts and figures, testimony, examples, or narratives.
2. Evaluate supporting materials in terms of relevance, representativeness, recency, and reliability.
3. Assess the sources' competence and trustworthiness.
4. Distinguish among facts, inferences, and opinions.
5. Be wary of language that is vague or incomprehensible.
6. Look for a balance between rational and emotional appeals.
7. Be on guard against claims that promise too much.
8. Check what you hear against what you know.
9. Consider alternate perspectives.
10. Ask questions whenever you have problems understanding or accepting a message.

The critical listener gives close attention to the evidence and reasoning in a speech and is wary of proposals that promise too much.

critique, or evaluation, of a speech. Criticism suggests emphasizing what someone did wrong. It can create a negative communication environment. In contrast, when you give a critique, your manner should be helpful and supportive. Point out strengths as well as weaknesses. Whenever you point out a problem, do so tactfully and try to suggest remedies or solutions. This type of interaction stresses the willingness of students to help one another.

To provide constructive oral feedback, you need a set of standards to help you answer the question *What is a good speech?* These standards can vary in importance according to the assignment; for example, the critique of an informative speech might focus on the adequacy of information and examples, and that of a persuasive speech might emphasize evidence and reasoning. Nevertheless, there are four general categories of guidelines you can use to evaluate all speeches: overall considerations, substance, structure, and presentation.

Overall Considerations

Considerations about commitment, adaptation, purpose, freshness, and ethics apply to the speech as a whole.

Ask students to evaluate some prominent speech—perhaps the presidential State of the Union address assigned for critical listening—in terms of overall considerations, substance, structure, and presentation. If the speech were given in class, what grade would they assign it? What kind of critique would they offer the speaker? Does it qualify as an ethical speech?

Commitment. Commitment means caring. You must feel that the speaker cares deeply about the subject and also about your welfare as a listener. Committed speakers will have invested the time and effort needed to gain responsible knowledge of their subject. Commitment also shows up in how well a speech is structured. A good speech cannot be prepared at ten-thirty the night before a presentation. It takes time to analyze an audience, select a topic and research it adequately, organize a message, and practice its presentation. Finally, commitment shows up in the energy, enthusiasm, and sincerity the speaker projects. Commitment is the spark in the speaker that can touch off fire in the audience.

Karen Lovelace became a model of commitment in her class at Vanderbilt University by developing a series of informative, persuasive, and ceremonial speeches on the fate of disabled people in our society. By the end of her class, no one doubted the passion of Karen's commitment, and many of us were ready to join her crusade for reform of laws and customs.

Adaptation. For a speech to be effective, it must meet the particular requirements of the assignment and be adapted to listeners' needs. An assignment will typically specify the **general purpose** of the speech: an **informative speech** that aims at extending your understanding of a topic, a **persuasive speech** that attempts to influence your attitudes or actions, or a **ceremonial speech** that celebrates shared values on special occasions. The assignment may also specify time limits, the number of references required, and the manner of presentation (such as a required presentation aid or extemporaneous mode of speech).

Effective speakers are listener centered. This means that as speakers plan and prepare their messages, they should weigh each technique and each piece of supporting material in terms of its appropriateness for the particular audience. Will this example interest listeners? Is this information important for them to know? How can the speaker best involve the audience with the topic? The close involvement of subject, speaker, and listener, called **identification** (which we discussed in Chapter 2), is vital for effective speaking. One way in which speakers can invite identification is to ask involving questions at the beginning of a speech: "Have you ever thought about what it would mean not to have electricity?" Also, the pronoun *we* used artfully throughout a speech may draw audience, speaker, and subject closer together.

Purpose. Beyond a general purpose, speeches should also have a specific purpose. For example, an informative speech may have the specific purpose of increasing listeners' knowledge of the causes of the greenhouse effect. The specific purpose of a speech will typically be evident by the time the speaker finishes the introduction and must be unmistakably clear by the time the speaker begins the conclusion.

A speech that lacks a clear sense of purpose will seem to drift and wander as though it were a boat without a rudder, blown this way and that by whatever thought occurs to the speaker. Developing a clear purpose begins with the speaker considering audience needs. Speakers must determine precisely what they want to accomplish: what they want listeners to learn, think, or do as a result of their speeches.

Freshness. Any speech worth listening to will bring something new to you. The topic should be fresh and involving. If the topic has been overused, then the speech must be innovative to sustain attention. One frequently overused topic for persuasive speeches is drinking and driving. When speakers choose such a topic, they can't simply reiterate the common advice "If you drink, don't drive" and expect to be effective. The audience will have heard that message hundreds of times. To get through to listeners on such a subject, speakers have to find a fresh way to present the material. One student of ours gave a speech on "responsible drinking and driving" that stressed the importance of understanding the effects of alcohol and of knowing your own tolerance limits. Her fresh approach and important information gave us a new perspective on an old problem.

Ethics. Perhaps the most important measure of a speech is whether it is good or bad for you. *An ethical speech demonstrates respect for the audience, responsible knowledge, and concern for the consequences of exposure to the message.*

Respect for the audience means that speakers are sensitive to the cultural composition of their audience and are aware that well-meaning people often hold varying positions on an issue. Ethical speakers are considerate of others even as they dispute their arguments or question their information. We discuss additional audience considerations in Chapter 4.

Ethical speakers base their messages on responsible knowledge of their subject. They assess the accuracy and objectivity of their sources of information, and watch for potential bias. They are sensitive to their own prejudices and try to be accurate and objective in their presentation of information. Ethical speak-

Ethics Alert! 3.1

ETHICS QUOTIENT OF A SPEECH

To determine the EQ (ethics quotient) of a speech, ask the following questions:

1. Does the speaker have responsible knowledge of the topic?
2. Does the speaker show respect for the audience's intelligence?
3. Does the speaker show concern about the impact of ideas on the audience?
4. Does the speaker document sources of information?
5. Does the speaker avoid inflammatory language that might impair the audience's judgment?

ers try not to pass off opinions and inferences as facts. An ethical speaker will report the sources of factual data and ideas, especially if this information runs counter to what is generally believed. Ethical speakers do not fabricate data or present the ideas or words of others without acknowledging their contributions.

Finally, ethical speakers are aware that words have consequences. Inflammatory language can arouse strong feelings in audience members that sometimes block constructive deliberation. Ethical speakers think through the possible ramifications of their messages before they present them. The greater the possible consequences, the more carefully speakers must assess the potential effects of their messages, support what they say with credible evidence, and temper their conclusions with regard for listener sensitivities.

Evaluating Substance

A speech has **substance** when it has a worthwhile message that is supported by facts and figures, testimony, examples, and/or narratives. The starting point for a substantive presentation is a well-chosen topic that interests both speaker and listeners, once they are shown how it affects their lives. It is desirable for speakers to already know something about the topics they select. This knowledge serves as the foundation for further research that enables them to speak responsibly and authoritatively. Although personal experiences are a valuable source of information, speakers should always validate, update, and broaden such experience with research or interviews with knowledgeable people. We discuss selecting and researching topics in more detail in Chapter 5.

Speakers add substance by weaving reliable information into the fabric of their messages. *Facts and figures* give precise focus to a speaker's points. *Testimony* adds the authority and prestige of knowledgeable or respected others to the speaker's claims. Such testimony can contribute expert opinions or eloquent quotations to the speech. At other times, speakers may rely on lay testimony from ordinary people with whom listeners might identify. For example, the opinions of other students might be meaningful on issues that pertain to campus life. *Examples* can help you understand better what speakers are talking about. *Narratives* can engage you by telling some colorful story that illustrates the speaker's message.

Skillful speakers often combine different types of supporting material to make their points more accessible to listeners. Combining statistical data with an example can make ideas clearer and more compelling. For instance, a speaker might say, "The base of the Great Pyramid at Giza measures 756 feet on each side." Although precise, this may be difficult for you to visualize. But what if the speaker adds, "More than eleven football fields could fit in its base"? Aha! This example gives you a concrete point of reference by comparing the unfamiliar or hard to understand with something you can relate to. We discuss the use of supporting materials in greater detail in Chapter 6.

Evaluating Structure

A good speech is carefully planned so that it carries you through an orderly progression of ideas, making it easy for you to follow. Without a good design, a speech may seem to consist of random ideas that have been thrown together willy-nilly. A worthwhile message can get lost in the confusion. There are three main parts to every message: an introduction, the body of the speech, and a conclusion. The introduction should arouse interest in the topic and preview the message to follow. The body of the speech presents the speaker's main ideas and the supporting material needed to develop them. The conclusion should summarize the main points, reflect on the meaning of the message, and provide a sense of closure.

The introduction may begin with an example, a quotation, or a question that draws you into the topic, such as "So you think there's no need to worry about California's energy crisis?" Once speakers gain attention, they will usually prepare listeners for what is to come by focusing on their purpose and previewing the main points. More suggestions for developing introductions can be found in Chapter 7.

The organization of the body of the speech will vary according to the subject and purpose. If a speech tells you how to do something—for instance, how to plan a budget—its main points should follow the order of the process that it describes. If the subject breaks naturally into parts, such as the three major causes of California's energy crisis, speakers can use a categorical design to present them. Chapters 12 and 13 discuss these and other designs for speeches.

A variety of concluding techniques can be used to end a speech. If speakers have covered several main points in the body, they should summarize them and then make a final statement that will help you remember the essence of the message. Chapter 7 provides additional information on developing conclusions.

Effective speeches also contain transitions that link together the various parts of the speech. Transitions bridge ideas and aid understanding. They signal that something different is coming and help the speech flow better. Transitions should be used between the introduction and body of a speech, between the body and conclusion, and between the main points within the body. You will learn more about them in Chapter 7.

Evaluating Presentation Skills

No speech can be effective unless it is presented well. Both the actual words speakers use and the way they convey these words are important factors in presentation. The oral language of speeches must be instantly intelligible. This means that speakers' sentences should be simple and direct. They should avoid complex chains of dependent clauses. Compare the following examples:

> **Working for a temporary employment service is a good way to put yourself through school because there are always jobs to be found and the places you get to work are interesting—besides, the people you work for treat you well, and you don't have to do the same thing day after day—plus, you can tailor the hours to fit your free time.**
>
> **Working for a temporary employment service is a good way to put yourself through school. Jobs are readily available. You can schedule your work to fit**

in with your classes. You don't stay at any one place long enough to get bored. And you meet a lot of interesting people who are glad to have your services.

Which is easier to follow? The first example rambles on; the information is presented in no particular order, and the speaker pauses only to catch a breath. In the second example, the sentences are short, inviting the effective use of pauses to separate ideas. As a result, the meaning is more clear.

Concrete words are generally preferable to abstract ones because they create vivid pictures for you and enhance the speaker's meaning. Consider the following levels of abstraction:

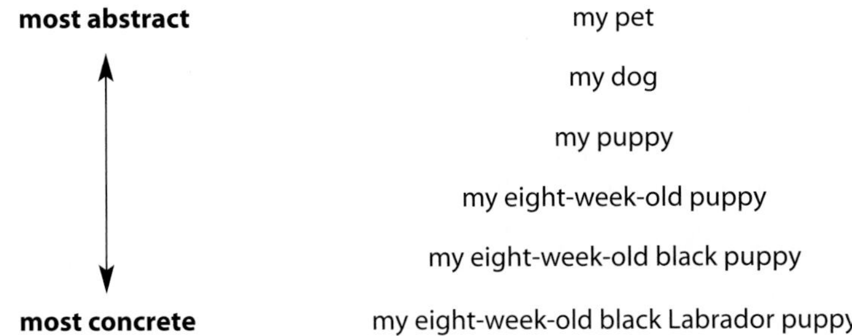

As the language becomes more concrete, you can better visualize what is being talked about, and there is less chance of misunderstanding. We discuss other language factors that help improve communication in Chapter 10.

An effective presentation sounds natural and enthusiastic. Speakers draw attention to their ideas, rather than to themselves, and avoid distracting mannerisms. To achieve these qualities, most class assignments call for an **extemporaneous presentation**. In this style of speaking, the speech is carefully prepared and practiced but *not* written out or memorized. Extemporaneous speaking allows speakers to adapt to the audience during a presentation. If listeners look confused, speakers can rephrase what they have said or provide another example. This kind of speaking does require practice, however. Extemporaneous does *not* mean "off the top of the speaker's head."

Practice may not make perfect, but it certainly improves a speaker's chances of doing a good job. While rehearsing, a speaker may discover that a technique that looked good on paper sounds stilted or silly when spoken. It often helps if speakers can tape-record their speeches, leave them overnight, then play them back the next day. Supportive roommates or friends can listen to the speech before presentation and offer suggestions for further improving it. They should be able to identify the purpose and the main points of the speech. Speakers should imagine their audiences before them as they practice. If possible, they should find a time when the classroom is not being used so that they can try out the speech where it actually will be presented. The more they can practice under these conditions, the better the speech should flow when the class actually hears it. As we saw in Chapter 2, practice can also help speakers reduce communication anxiety.

During actual presentations, speakers should talk loud enough to be heard easily in the back of the room. Body language is also an important part of effective presentation. The speaker's posture should be relaxed. Movements should seem natural and spontaneous. Speakers who point to their heads every time they say "think" or who spread their arms wide every time they say "big" will seem artificial and contrived. Gestures should complement what a speaker has to say, not compete with it for attention. Additional suggestions for effective presentation can be found in Chapter 11.

Keep these points in mind as you prepare to offer constructive feedback. Figure 3.5 summarizes these categories of guidelines. You may use it as a checklist for critiquing the speeches that you hear in class and in everyday life.

FIGURE 3.5
Guidelines for Evaluating Speeches

Overall Considerations

- [ ] Was the speaker committed to the topic?
- [ ] Did the speech meet the requirements of the assignment?
- [ ] Was the speech adapted to the audience?
- [ ] Did the speech promote identification among topic, audience, and speaker?
- [ ] Was the purpose of the speech clear?
- [ ] Was the topic handled with imagination and freshness?
- [ ] Did the speech meet high ethical standards?

Substance

- [ ] Was the topic worthwhile?
- [ ] Had the speaker done sufficient research?
- [ ] Were the main ideas supported with information?
- [ ] Was testimony used appropriately?
- [ ] Were the sources documented adequately?
- [ ] Were examples or narratives used effectively?
- [ ] Was the reasoning clear and correct?

Structure

- [ ] Did the introduction arouse interest?
- [ ] Did the introduction preview the message?
- [ ] Was the speech easy to follow?
- [ ] Were the main points of the speech evident?
- [ ] Were transitions used to tie the speech together?
- [ ] Did the conclusion summarize the message?
- [ ] Did the conclusion help you remember the speech?

Presentation

- [ ] Was the language clear, simple, and direct?
- [ ] Was the language colorful?
- [ ] Were grammar and pronunciations correct?
- [ ] Was the speech presented extemporaneously?
- [ ] Were notes used unobtrusively?
- [ ] Was the speaker appropriately enthusiastic?
- [ ] Did the speaker maintain good eye contact?
- [ ] Did body language complement ideas?
- [ ] Was the speaker expressive?
- [ ] Were the rate and loudness appropriate?
- [ ] Did the speaker use pauses?
- [ ] Did presentation aids enhance the message?
- [ ] Were presentation aids integrated into the speech?
- [ ] Was the presentation free from distracting mannerisms?

Ethical Responsibilities of a Listener

Listeners as well as speakers bear ethical responsibilities. Ethical listeners do not prejudge a speech, but keep an open mind. John Milton, a great English poet and intellectual of the seventeenth century, observed in *Areopagitica*, his treatise on freedom of communication, that listening to our opponents can be beneficial. We may learn something from them and gain a new and better perspective

Ethics Alert! 3.2

ETHICAL LISTENING

1. Give the speaker your undivided attention.
2. Keep your mind open to new ideas.
3. Park your biases outside the classroom door.
4. Provide honest feedback to the speaker.
5. Seek out what is good or useful in the message.
6. Consider how the speech might affect others.
7. Listen to others as you would have them listen to you.

on an issue. Or, as we question and argue with them, we may discover *why* we believe as we do. When we protect ourselves from opposing ideas, we deprive ourselves of the chance to engage, apply, and strengthen our own convictions.

Just as we should be open to ideas, we should also remain open to people of different lifestyles and cultural backgrounds. We should not deprive ourselves of the chance to explore other worlds. In comparing and contrasting our life-ways with those of others, we learn more about ourselves.

Although ethical listeners should remain open to ideas that may at first seem strange or even hostile, we do not suggest that you lower your guard entirely. Some ideas, after fair consideration, prove to be faulty, risky, or even evil. Not every speaker has our good at heart. Perhaps our best advice to you is to be an open but cautious listener, combining the best traits of ethical and critical listening.

Finally, keep in mind the impact of your listening on others. Good listeners help develop good speakers. Good listeners seek out the value in ideas, often finding unexpected worth in a speech. Good listeners are also concerned about the ethical impact of messages on others who may not be present. Good listeners not only practice their own version of the Golden Rule—"Listen to others as you would have them listen to you"—they also learn the communication values of other people so that they can apply what Bennett has called the Platinum Rule: "Listen to others as *they* would have you listen to them."[41] All sides benefit when speakers and listeners take their ethical roles seriously.

Ask the class to discuss the meaning of the "Platinum Rule." What specific behaviors would they like to see in *their* listeners? How can they develop these behaviors in themselves?

In Summary

Listening is as important to communication as speaking. Bad listening can devastate both nations and individuals. To climb the ladder of effective listening, we must first be able to hear a message, the *discriminative phase*. Thereafter, we must master the skills of focusing, understanding, and interpreting, the *comprehensive phase*. In the *empathic phase*, we share the speaker's point of view, and in the *appreciative phase* we enjoy the speaker's ability to structure messages skillfully and to word ideas attractively. *Critical listening* requires that we evaluate messages, and *constructive listening*, the final rung of the ladder, challenges us to find the value in messages for our lives.

Benefits of Effective Listening. Effective listening benefits both listeners and speakers. Listeners become less vulnerable to unethical advertising or to dishonest public communication. Improved listening skills can enhance both your academic performance and your chances for a successful career. Feedback from good listeners can help communication work better. Supportive listeners help relieve communication apprehension and can boost a speaker's self-esteem.

Overcoming Listening Problems. Some listening problems may arise from external sources, such as noisy surroundings. They may also result from a poorly organized message, unfamiliar language, or a speaker whose presentation is distracting. Most serious listening problems arise from factors internal to the listener, such as personal reactions to words, worries, attitudes, bad listening habits, or listener apprehension. Personal reactions to *trigger words* may set off strong emotions that block effective listening. Biased attitudes toward the speaker or topic can interfere with listening. For example, *filtering* is a form of message distortion in which you hear only what you want to. *Assimilation* occurs when you interpret some favored person's views as identical with your own when there is actually a significant distance between the two positions. A *contrast effect* occurs when you see a position only slightly different from yours as quite different because you have a negative bias toward the source.

Bad habits, such as pretending we are listening when we are not or listening only for facts, can also impair listening behavior. Fear of listening is a major form of *receiver apprehension*. We are often fearful listeners when we know that a message will be important for us personally, when we will be held responsible for it, and when it is difficult to understand.

Effective listening skills can be developed. The first step is to identify your listening problems. Concentrate on the main ideas and the overall pattern of meaning in the speech. Strive to be as objective as you can, and withhold judgment until you are certain you understand the message.

Developing Critical Thinking Skills. Critical thinking skills help you analyze and evaluate messages more effectively. Critical listeners question what they hear, require support for assertions and claims, and evaluate the credentials of sources. Critical listeners differentiate among facts, inferences, and opinions. They become wary when language seems overly vague or incomprehensible, when inflammatory speech takes the place of cool reason, or when a message promises too much. When what they hear does not fit with what they know, critical listeners start asking the tough questions.

Evaluating Speeches. Speech evaluation in the classroom takes the form of a *critique*, a positive and constructive effort to help speakers improve. Criteria for speech evaluation include overall considerations, substance, structure, and presentation skills. Overall considerations encompass the speaker's commitment, adaptation to the audience and occasion, clarity of purpose, freshness of perspective, and ethical standards. Substance involves the value of the topic, the sufficiency of research, the adequacy of supporting material, and the speaker's ability to reason. Structural criteria include the presence of an effective introduction, a clearly organized body that includes the main points and supporting materials, and a conclusion that provides closure. Presentation questions touch on how well speakers use words and their ability to convey their messages through voice and gesture.

Listeners have ethical responsibilities. Ethical listeners do not prejudge a speech but are open to ideas and receptive to different perspectives. Ethical listeners test what they hear and are sensitive to the impact of ideas on others. They represent all who might be affected by the message.

Terms to Know

discriminative phase
comprehensive phase
empathic phase
appreciative phase
critical listening
constructive listening
trigger words
filtering
assimilation
contrast effect
receiver apprehension
demagogues
critique
general purpose
informative speech
persuasive speech
ceremonial speech
identification
substance
extemporaneous presentation

Notes

1. Cited in Clifton Fadiman, ed. *The Little, Brown Book of Anecdotes* (Boston: Little, Brown, 1985), pp. 475–476.

2. Thomas L. Means and Gary S. Klein, "A Short Classroom Unit, but a Significant Improvement, in Listen-

ing Ability," *Bulletin of the Association for Business Communication* 57 (1994): 13.

3. L. Barker et al., "An Investigation of Proportional Time Spent in Various Communication Activities by College Students," *Journal of Applied Communication Research* 8 (1980): 101–109; and Walter Pauk, *How to Study in College*, 4th ed. (Boston: Houghton Mifflin, 1989), pp. 121–133.

4. Richard Bruce Hyde, "Council: Using a Talking Stick to Teach Listening," *Speech Communication Teacher* (Winter 1993): 1–2.

5. Luther Standing Bear, Oglala Sioux chief, cited in *Native American Wisdom: Photographs by Edward S. Curtis* (Philadelphia: Running Press, 1993), pp. 58–59.

6. Donal Carbaugh, "'Just Listen': 'Listening' and Landscape Among the Blackfeet," *Western Journal of Communication* 63 (1999): 250–270.

7. Ronald B. Adler and George Rodman, *Understanding Human Communication*, 5th ed. (Fort Worth, Tex.: Harcourt Brace, 1994), p. 130.

8. C. Glenn Pearce, "Learning How to Listen Empathically," *Supervisory Management* 36 (1991): 11.

9. John Stewart and Carole Logan, "Empathic and Dialogic Listening," in *Bridges Not Walls: A Book About Interpersonal Communication*, 7th ed., ed. John Stewart (New York: McGraw-Hill, 1999), p. 227.

10. We describe this concept further in Michael Osborn and Suzanne Osborn, *Alliance for a Better Public Voice: The Communication Discipline and the National Issues Forums* (Dayton, Ohio: National Issues Forums Institute, 1991).

11. Waldo Braden, "The Available Means of Persuasion: What Shall We Do About the Demand for Snake Oil?" in *The Rhetoric of Our Times*, ed. J. Jeffry Auer (New York: Appleton-Century-Crofts, 1969), pp. 178–184.

12. W. B. Legge, "Listening, Intelligence, and School Achievement," in *Listening: Readings*, ed. S. Duker (Metuchen, N.J.: Scarecrow Press, 1971), pp. 121–133.

13. U.S. Department of Labor, "What Work Requires of Schools" (Washington, D.C.: U.S. Government Printing Office), 1991.

14. Dan B. Curtis, Jerry L. Winsor, and Ronald D. Stephens, "National Preferences in Business and Communication Education," *Communication Education* 38 (1989): 7–14.

15. Gary T. Hunt and Louis P. Cusella, "A Field Study of Listening Needs in Organizations," *Communication Education* 32 (1983): 399.

16. B. D. Sypher, R. N. Bostrom, and J. H Seibert, "Listening Communication Abilities and Success at Work," *Journal of Business Communication* (Fall 1989): 293–303.

17. Andrew D. Wolvin and Carolyn Gwynn Coakley, "A Survey of the Status of Listening Training in Some Fortune 500 Corporations," *Communication Education* 40 (1991): 152–164.

18. Lou Davidson Tillson, "Building Community and Reducing Communication Apprehension: A Case Study Approach," *Speech Communication Teacher* (Summer 1995): 4–5.

19. Some material for this section was synthesized from William B. Gudykunst, Stella Ting-Toomey, Sandra Sudweeks, and Lea P. Stewart, *Building Bridges: Interpersonal Skills for a Changing World* (Boston: Houghton Mifflin, 1995), pp. 228–229.

20. Hank Trisler, "Now Hear This," *American Salesman* 39 (July 1994): 8.

21. Peter D. MacIntyre and J. Renée MacDonald, "Public Speaking Anxiety: Perceived Competence and Audience Congeniality," *Communication Education* 47 (1998): 359–365.

22. Patricia O'Brien, "Why Men Don't Listen . . . and What It Costs Women at Work," *Working Woman* 18 (1993): 56.

23. Adapted from Dave Ellis, *Becoming a Master Student*, 7th ed. (Boston: Houghton Mifflin, 1994), pp. 136–150; and Pauk, pp. 136–161.

24. Andrew D. Wolvin and Carolyn Gwynn Coakley, *Listening*, 2nd ed. (Dubuque, Iowa: William C. Brown, 1985), p. 177.

25. Richard M. Weaver, "Ultimate Terms in Contemporary Rhetoric," *Language Is Sermonic: Richard M. Weaver on the Nature of Rhetoric*, ed. Richard L. Johannesen, Rennard Strickland, and Ralph T. Eubanks (Baton Rouge: Louisiana State University Press, 1970), p. 95.

26. Professor Halley discussed this "Triggering Stimuli Assignment" on the web site of the International Listening Association, http://www.listen.org (4 Aug. 1998).

27. D. M. Mackie and L. T. Worth, "Processing Deficits and the Mediation of Positive Affect in Persuasion," *Journal of Personality and Social Psychology* 57 (1989): 27–40.

28. Larry Barker and Kittie Watson, *Listen Up* (New York: St. Martin's Press, 2000), p. 33.

29. J. J. Makay and W. R. Brown, *The Rhetorical Dialogue: Contemporary Concepts and Cases* (Dubuque, Iowa: William C. Brown, 1972), pp. 125–145.

30. William F. Buckley Jr., "Has TV Killed Off Great Oratory?" *TV Guide*, 12 February 1983, p. 38.

31. James J. Floyd, *Listening: A Practical Approach* (Glencoe, Ill.: Scott, Foresman, 1985), pp. 23–25.

32. L. R. Wheeless, "An Investigation of Receiver Apprehension and Social Context Dimensions of Communication Apprehension," *Speech Teacher* 24 (1975): 263.

33. Joe Ayres, A. Kathleen Wilcox, and Debbie M. Ayres, "Receiver Apprehension: An Explanatory Model and Accompanying Research," *Communication Education* 44 (1995): 223–235. Also see Michael J. Beatty, "Receiver Apprehension as a Function of Cognitive Backlog," *Western Journal of Speech Communication* 45 (1981):

277–281; Michael J. Beatty and Steven K. Payne, "Receiver Apprehension and Cognitive Complexity," *Western Journal of Speech Communication* 45 (1981): 363–369; and Raymond W. Preiss, Lawrence R. Wheeless, and Mike Allen, "Potential Cognitive Processes and Consequences of Receiver Apprehension: A Meta-analytic Review," *Journal of Social Behavior and Personality* 5 (1990): 155–172.

34. Kaidren Leigh Winiecki and Joe Ayres, "Communication Apprehension and Receiver Apprehension in the Workplace," *Communication Quarterly* 47 (1999): 430–440.

35. C. V. Roberts, "A Validation of the Watson-Barker Listening Test," *Communication Research Reports* 3 (1986): 115–119.

36. Anthony J. Clark may have indicated indirectly the value of such exercises when he demonstrated a positive relationship between communication confidence and listening comprehension in "Communication Confidence and Listening Competence: An Investigation of the Relationships of Willingness to Communicate, Communication Apprehension, and Receiver Apprehension to Comprehension of Content and Emotional Meaning in Spoken Messages," *Communication Education* 38 (1989): 237–248.

37. John Chaffee, *Thinking Critically*, 2d ed. (Boston: Houghton Mifflin, 1988), p. 59.

38. See their discussion in "Investigating the President: Media Madness?" transcript of a special report on CNN, 28 Jan. 1998.

39. *Time*, 18 Dec. 1989, cover.

40. Jim Motavalli, "In Memory of Colette," *E: The Environmental Magazine*, May/June 1994, pp. 30–31.

41. Milton J. Bennett, "Overcoming the Golden Rule: Sympathy and Empathy," in *Communication Yearbook 3*, ed. Dan Nimmo (New Brunswick, N.J.: Transaction Books, 1979), pp. 407–422.

PART TWO

Preparation for Public Speaking

4

Adapting to Your Audience and Situation

OUTLINE

THIS CHAPTER WILL HELP YOU

- understand audience dynamics
- adapt your message to fit your audience
- meet the challenges of audience diversity
- adjust your message to the speaking situation

It's the beginning of the fall term, and the president of Students for Environmental Action (SEA) has a busy day ahead. At eight o'clock in the morning she will recruit new members from the students assembled in the field house. Later that day she will address the County Industrial Development Board to tell them about SEA's plans for the year. She wants to reassure them that the group's work will help and not hurt business in the area.

The general topic of this student's speeches will not change, but the two audiences and situations will require quite different approaches. Her listeners must be at the center of her thinking as she plans and develops her speeches. Moreover, the setting for these speeches can make a big difference in how she presents them. Her manner of presentation, as well as the language she chooses, may vary from the field house to the boardroom.

This chapter begins with a basic assumption: *the more you know about your audience and speaking situation, the more effective your speech will be.* A good audience analysis will help you determine what your listeners may already know about your topic, what they need to know, and how they feel about it. Your audience analysis can also help you select the most effective supporting materials, decide on the design and structure of your speech, and choose the best techniques to help listeners understand and relate to your topic.

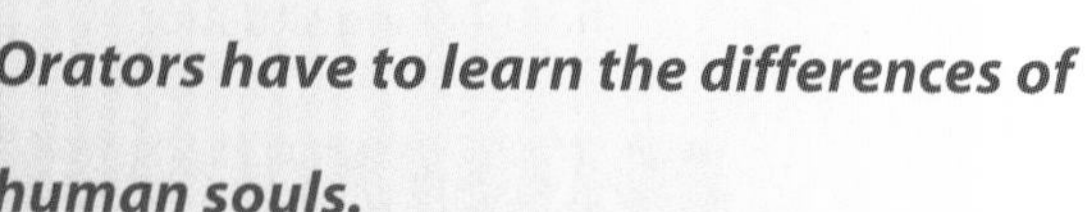

Orators have to learn the differences of human souls.

—Plato

You may question the ethics of adapting a message to fit a particular audience. Many of us have encountered speakers who "waffled"—taking one position with one audience and a different position with another. Such maneuvering is clearly unethical. But you can adapt to your audience without changing the essence of your message or surrendering your convictions. You can ethically adapt your message to a given audience in terms of the language you use, the examples you provide, the stories you tell, the authorities you cite, and your manner of presentation. Ask yourself: How can I tailor my message so that I can reach my audience without compromising my convictions?

In this chapter we open with *audience dynamics*, the motivations, attitudes, and values of listeners. Second, we consider *demographic factors*, such as age, political and religious preferences, and gender. Next, we discuss some of the major challenges of *audience diversity*. Finally, we focus on features of the *communication situation* that may call for adaptations.

Adapting to Audience Dynamics

Audience dynamics are the motivations, attitudes, beliefs, and values that affect how listeners receive a message. An understanding of how these dynamics work is central to understanding your audience. The more you understand what makes people tick, the better you can tailor your message so that it serves their interests and needs.

Motivation

Our needs and wants make up our **motivation**, the force that draws our attention to certain things and makes us act in certain ways. Motivation helps explain *why* people behave as they do.[1] Therefore, motivation is important to both persuasive and informative speeches. *People will listen, learn, and remember a message only if it relates to their needs, wants, or wishes.* Understanding motivation can also help a speaker appeal to the common humanity in listeners that crosses cultural boundaries.

Motives can vary in importance according to the person, situation, and culture. *People are motivated by what they don't have that they need or want.* If you have recently moved to a new town, your need to make friends may attract you to places where you can meet others. Even when needs are satisfied, people respond to wants. Suppose you have just eaten a very filling meal. You're not hungry, but if someone enters the room with a tray of freshly baked cookies, the sight and smell can make you want some.

Develop transparency masters of print ads that illustrate the various types of motivation. Show these in class and ask students to identify the predominant motive in each ad. Discuss what other motivational appeals might have been used. Ask ESL students to bring in advertisements from their native cultures to enrich the discussion.

The study of human motivation had an interesting history in twentieth-century psychology. Social scientists first concentrated on identifying different types of human motivation. In a pioneering study published during the 1930s, Henry A. Murray and his associates at the Harvard Psychological Clinic identified more than twenty-five different human needs.[2] Perhaps the best-known motivational theorist was the late psychologist Abraham Maslow, who described human needs in terms of a hierarchy of potency (see Figure 4.1). The lower-

People will listen to a speech when it relates to their interests and needs.

FIGURE 4.1
Maslow's Hierarchy of Needs

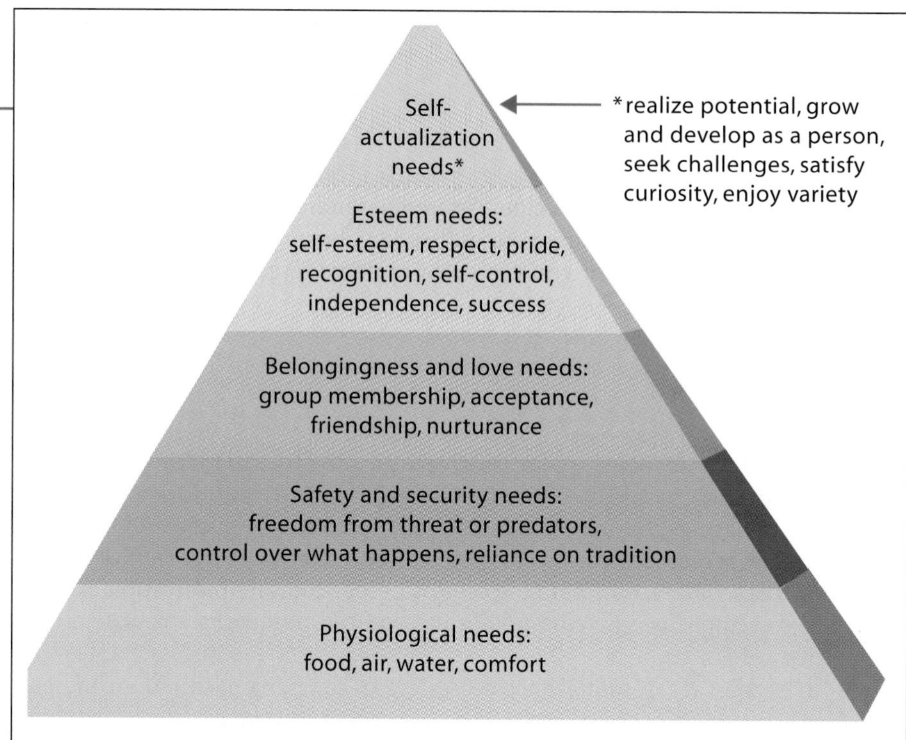

Show several videotaped speeches in class. Ask students to analyze them applying Maslow's Hierarchy of Needs.

level needs in Maslow's hierarchy include our physiological requirements for food, water, air, and comfort and our basic desires for safety and security. When these needs are not satisfied, they can dominate behavior. If you can arouse a sense of lower-level needs, then you will surely have your listeners' attention. According to Maslow, these needs must be satisfied to some degree before higher level needs can come into play.

The higher levels in Maslow's hierarchy encompass our needs for belongingness, esteem, and self-actualization. Showing listeners how they can be liked and respected and how they can realize their full potential may help you reach many of them. Maslow also suggested that freedom of inquiry and expression was necessary for need satisfaction and that people had an innate desire to know and understand that served both lower- and higher-level needs.

To get an idea of how motivation is used in classroom speeches, we inspected tapes and transcripts of more than a hundred speeches presented in recent years by our students at the University of California at Davis and at Indiana, Memphis, and Vanderbilt Universities. We identified seven motives that were often used in those speeches: understanding, control, health and safety, nurturance and altruism, friends and family, self-actualization, and the desire for fairness (see Figure 4.2 on page 91).

Understanding. Speakers attempted to help their listeners understand a wide range of topics, explaining such matters as cloning, genetic testing, and the legal and moral issues involved in sexual harassment. We all need to understand the world and the people around us, so we look for the causes of events and seek explanations for why people act as they do. This curiosity may also help explain the appeal of foreign travel and cross-cultural comparisons. One student talked about what she had learned in a cultural exchange visit to China. Another compared holiday customs in Mexico and the United States. You can make almost any topic interesting to listeners if you can show them how understanding might empower them. Speeches that emphasize the need for understanding are typically informative.

Control. Control closely connects with understanding. We need to understand things, or at least think that we understand them, because this makes us feel less vulnerable. Understanding gives us a sense of having some control over our lives—of being able to influence events and people—of shaping our own destiny. Our desire for control may place us in competition with others. Speeches that show listeners how they can gain control over their environment, themselves, or others typically hold an audience's attention. In the student speeches, this theme often came through as a warning about controllers. Cloning and genetic testing, as well as other forms of technology, could have dire as well as favorable consequences for the human species. The powerful forces of advertising could turn control against us. Thus the fear of control is often a powerful motivational appeal. Speeches that satisfy our need to gain, regain, or resist control over the forces around us are typically persuasive in nature.

Health and Safety. All of us need to feel free from threats to both health and safety. Speeches describing the endangered ozone layer and the warning signs of deadly diseases obviously involve both kinds of threat. Our student speakers warned of the dangers of smoking and obesity and of the need for clean air and water, and they expounded on the advantages of exercise. They described rising crime rates, discussed the potential dangers of earthquakes, and urged classmates to be organ donors. Appeals to our safety needs often arouse fear in the audience. Fear appeals, if too obvious or frightening, can give listeners the impression that you are manipulating them. Therefore, use this technique with caution. If you develop fear appeals, be sure to show listeners how they can protect themselves from the dangers you describe.[3]

Nurturance and Altruism. Although we may seem concerned primarily with ourselves, we also have strong needs to care for others. Protecting and comforting the helpless or those in need can make us feel good. We heard moving student speeches describing the plight of the disabled and homeless, urging listeners to become volunteers in the community, and exhorting them to support programs and laws ensuring the rights of marginalized groups. Helping others is a basic tenet of most religious groups—as reflected, for example, in the story of the good Samaritan.

People will be attentive when a speech addresses matters they care deeply about.

InterConnections.LearnMore 4.1

AUDIENCE DYNAMICS

Attitudes **http://www.epsychlopedia.net/concepts/socialPsychology/?id=bAttitudesP1**
A basic discussion of how attitudes are formed and how they function.

Motivation **http://psychclassics.yorku.ca/Maslow/motivation.htm**
A reprint of Maslow's original article "A Theory of Human Motivation," setting forth his theory of human motivation, originally published in *Psychology Review* in 1943.

Values **http://www.valuescope.com/Theory/frames21.htm**
"The Study of Values," an article that covers a variety of approaches to the study of human values, by Professor Hans L. Zetterberg, sociologist and director of the Social Research Consulting Group in Stockholm, Sweden. The seminar on values, available on the ValueScope web site (http://www.valuescope.com) is especially interesting.

Appeals to this motive can be especially strong when speakers discuss the problems of children. We had powerful speeches describing child abuse and the plight of "children at risk." Speakers engaged this need positively when they advocated educational reform, promoted arts education, or debated bilingual education. The central issue was always "Would this program help children develop?"

Divide the class into homogeneous groups based on culture, i.e., gender, age, ethnicity, etc. Ask the groups to consider the importance of family and family values and present their findings to the class. Focus discussion on the similarities and differences in the meaning of family among the groups.

Friends and Family. People value friendship and family ties. Friends and family help define who we are, warm us with affection, and make the world a less lonely place. The importance of these needs is demonstrated by the intense feelings of homesickness many people develop when they move away from the support of family and friends. They may feel isolated, diminished, or uprooted, and may even develop physical illnesses.

In an era that advocates strengthening "family values," it is not surprising that we had many speeches like Marie D'Aniello's tribute to her family, seen at the end of Chapter 2. Other speakers praised the importance of both traditional and nontraditional families. The importance of family can express itself in traditions and rituals. Our families can give us a sense of roots, of cultural and personal history. It can be comforting to know that some things don't change. In many families, Thanksgiving dinner is always turkey and dressing, cranberries, and pumpkin pie. Such holiday rituals convey the meaning of family.

The need for friendship may explain our desire to join with others and take pride in our group memberships. We like being with those who share similar backgrounds and values. Friendship is probably the most prevalent appeal in contemporary American advertising. How many ads have you seen that suggest that if you don't use the "right" deodorant, drink the "right" beverages, or drive the "right" car, you risk losing friends?

Self-Actualization. One of the most powerful and persistent motive appeals in the student speeches we reviewed was the need for self-actualization. When we self-actualize, we realize our potential for growth and success, and we strive to become the better selves we can imagine. Perhaps it is not surprising to find that self-actualization is so important for college students. They are part of a privileged population, among the most able and promising. They are prime candidates for self-actualization.

This complex motive can express itself in a number of ways. There is, for example, an important "play instinct" in humans that may explain our needs for *enjoyment* and *variety*. All work and no play will make Jill about as dull as Jack and may retard the full expression of our humanity. College students, who find themselves inundated with tests and papers and speeches to prepare, not to mention full- or part-time jobs, are not exempt from this need. If you can show listeners how to put some fun into their lives, you can be sure of their attention.

As for variety, too much of anything—even a good thing—can be dull. The need for variety can include a longing for adventure, a desire to do something different or exciting, or a yen to travel to exotic places. Offer listeners something different, a topic out of the ordinary, or a different point of view on a familiar subject, and you will be rewarded with their attention. Self-actualization also ties together a number of other personal needs, including those for self-esteem, independence, success, and recognition.

Healthy *self-esteem* is a condition for self-actualization. Before we can hope to grow and develop, we must have some degree of confidence in our own abilities. Marie D'Aniello expressed her personal sense of self-esteem as she paid tribute to her father: "Because of him, I take pride in my work and I take pride in myself." As you achieve success in this class and begin to develop more confidence, you should notice an increase in your own self-esteem. This increased sense of self-esteem can become a key to greater self-actualization, both in class and outside the classroom. This is why the public speaking class is valued by so many people. As Professor Rod Hart of the University of Texas has put it, "Communication is the ultimate people-making discipline."[4]

Although family and friends are important, we also need to learn that we can stand on our own two feet. The quest for *independence* allows young people to mature into productive adults, making decisions on their own and taking responsibility for their lives. For this reason, college audiences may be especially responsive to the need for freedom from arbitrary constraints on their ideas, actions, or lifestyles. One speech in our sample attacked censorship of books in the public schools on the grounds that it places restrictions on self-actualization by young people, who must be free to explore ideas. Also, speeches that show listeners how to "do it yourself" often appeal to this need for independence.

The need for *success* or achievement is one of the most thoroughly studied human motives.[5] A sense of success provides assurance that self-actualization is going forward. There were numerous outstanding speeches in our sample on

FIGURE 4.2
Seven Motives Often Used in Classroom Speeches

Motive	Description
Understanding	Satisfying your curiosity, understanding yourself, determining the causes of events, knowing why people act as they do, exploring the unusual
Control	Having a hand in your own destiny, developing plans of action, fixing things, influencing others, resisting control and manipulation
Health and Safety	Feeling secure in your surroundings, protected from crime, pollution, accidents, and natural disasters; doing things and avoiding dangers that promote or menace physical well-being
Nurturance and Altruism	Caring for others, especially marginalized people and children, and promoting their well-being
Friends and Family	Establishing warm relations with others, being a member of a group or organization, feeling secure and accepted within your family, having someone to love and be loved by
Self-Actualization	Seeking to fulfill your potential for growth, satisfying your needs for self-esteem, independence, success, and recognition
Fairness	Seeking to establish and restore moral balance in the world so that people receive the treatment they deserve

the theme of success. Ashlie McMillan inspired her Vanderbilt classmates by her tribute to her cousin Tina, who is a dwarf (the text of her speech can be found at the end of Chapter 15). Ashlie painted a picture of her cousin as a very short person with a very large personality. Tina, she said, is fiercely independent and had received undergraduate and graduate degrees from Texas Christian University. Now she was planning marriage and entrance into the University of Texas law school. And if Tina, against all odds, can self-actualize, so could members of Ashlie's audience. Ceremonial speeches often establish models for emulation as they praise achievers in public life. They challenge audiences to set high goals for themselves, to work hard to achieve them, and to enjoy success as well. Speeches that show how to be successful or how to master a difficult skill will have an attentive audience.

If we harbor any doubts about our quest for self-actualization, *recognition* from others can reassure us. The need for recognition may lead to our placing great value on trophies or awards as tangible symbols of success. Speakers who recognize the accomplishments of listeners and the institutions or groups they represent may also satisfy this need. This can be especially helpful when speakers are not well known or are uncertain of acceptance.

Fairness. Fairness is one of the "universal values" (see Chapter 1) that can help bridge cultural differences. Fairness is also such a constant theme in student speeches that it may qualify as a motive. It envisions an ideal moral balance in the world, in which we deserve whatever happens to us, both good and bad. For college audiences, especially those who are idealistic, fairness is a compelling theme in speeches. Thus our students argued that homosexuals are treated unfairly in our society, that the disabled don't get a fair break, and that affirmative action ensures (or denies) fairness. They expressed outrage over human rights abuses in China, over sexism in America, and over the past and present treatment of Native Americans. They pled for justice, the legal form of fairness, in our courts. The conclusion one draws from these speeches is that fairness is a dream that is sometimes denied, abused, and repudiated in our society. The students sought ways, especially in their persuasive speeches, to restore it. The quest for fairness might enter into your speeches as well.

Have students read a persuasive speech in Appendix C and determine its major motivational appeal. What other types of motivational appeal might have been used? Could there have been ethical problems with any of these options?

Attitude Systems

As you plan and prepare presentations, you should also consider the attitude systems of your listeners. A person's attitude system is composed of attitudes, beliefs, and values. **Attitudes** refer to our feelings—whether we like or dislike, approve or disapprove of people, events, or ideas—and how we are inclined to act toward them.[6] **Beliefs** are what we know or think we know about subjects. Our more important attitudes and beliefs are anchored by our **values**, how we think we should behave or what we regard as an ideal state of being. Our values influence the attitudes we form and the beliefs we develop. If you can point out that listeners' attitudes and beliefs are *inconsistent* with their values, you may be able to help them change.

Information about your audience's attitudes, beliefs, and values is important in planning your speech. If your listeners' beliefs are based on incomplete information or a lack of understanding, you may be able to provide new information or improve their understanding. Being aware of audience attitudes can suggest strategies you might use to get a fair hearing. For example, suppose you are preparing a speech favoring capital punishment, and you know that most members of your audience strongly oppose this policy. An audience that disagrees with you may distort your message, discredit you, or even refuse to listen. Given these conditions, how can you reach your listeners? One way of dealing with a negative audience includes establishing identification between yourself and your

Ask students to read the "Letters to the Editor" in a Sunday paper. Have them note the major issues and the types of attitude expressed. Discuss whether these attitudes seem representative of the community as a whole.

listeners, avoiding emotional appeals, limiting what you hope to accomplish, and acknowledging that others may disagree with you.[7] You should consider such strategies as you plan your presentation. These and other techniques for handling reluctant audiences are discussed in detail in Chapter 13.

How can you find out in advance about your audience's values, beliefs, and attitudes? In the classroom this is not difficult because people reveal this kind of information constantly as they take part in class discussions. Outside the classroom you might question the person who invites you to speak about those aspects of the audience's attitude system that are related to your topic.

To understand more fully how your audience's attitude system may relate to your presentation, you could conduct a survey to explore what your listeners know about your topic, how they feel about it, and how they might respond to different sources of information. Figure 4.3 shows a sample audience survey

FIGURE 4.3
Sample Attitude Questionnaire

For each question, please circle the number that most clearly represents your position.

1. How interested are you in the topic of capital punishment?

Very Interested			Unconcerned			Not Interested
7	**6**	**5**	**4**	**3**	**2**	**1**

2. How important do you think the issue of capital punishment is?

Very Important			No Opinion			Very Unimportant
7	**6**	**5**	**4**	**3**	**2**	**1**

3. How much do you know about capital punishment?

Very Little			Average Amount			Very Much
7	**6**	**5**	**4**	**3**	**2**	**1**

4. How would you describe your attitude toward capital punishment?

Total Opposition			"On the Fence"			Total Support
7	**6**	**5**	**4**	**3**	**2**	**1**

5. Please place a check beside the sources of information on capital punishment that you would find the most acceptable.

_____ Attorney general's office
_____ FBI
_____ Local police department
_____ Criminal justice department of the university
_____ American Civil Liberties Union
_____ Local religious leaders
_____ Conference of Christians and Jews
_____ NAACP
_____ Other (please specify) ______________________

Comments:

questionnaire on the subject of capital punishment that may be used as a guide to developing a questionnaire on your subject.

Classroom surveys can yield helpful results if you use the following guidelines to prepare your questionnaire:

- Use simple, concrete, clear language.
- Keep questions short.
- Avoid words such as *all*, *always*, *none*, and *never*.
- Keep your own biases out of the questions.
- Provide room for comments.
- Keep the questionnaire short.

Finally, you should keep in mind that any questionnaire results you get, either from one you conduct yourself or one that is professionally administered, provide only a general idea of where your audience stands on a topic.[8] Compare what you learn from a questionnaire with what you hear as you listen to others talking about the issue in question.

Adjusting to Audience Demographics

Audience demographics include the age, gender, education, group affiliations, and sociocultural background of your listeners. If you are not familiar with the group you will be addressing, ask the person who invited you about these factors. Demographic analyses are often used in marketing and political campaigns to identify important attitudes, preferences, or concerns. In the classroom, demographic information can help you estimate interest in your topic and how much listeners may already know about it. When you combine this information with an understanding of audience dynamics, you can better understand how they feel about your subject and how you can best motivate them.

Select several controversial issues and ask students to look for public opinion polls regarding them either online (see InterConnections. LearnMore 4.2) or in print. Ask students to report their findings in class.

ESL: Ask ESL students if public opinion polling is common in their cultures, and if so, how the results are reported. Encourage them to comment on how they feel about such reporting in the U.S. culture.

The insights you can get from classroom demographics and published public opinion surveys can help you tailor an effective message. The richest source of information on current public opinion is the Internet. InterConnections. LearnMore 4.2 contains a list of public opinion web sites that may be helpful as you plan your speeches. Most of these sites contain complete data from recent surveys across a wide variety of topics. Many of them include searchable archives of previous surveys, useful for tracing trends and drawing comparisons across time. Public opinion information is also available in many popular print periodicals: *Harper's* magazine regularly includes "Harper's Index," a compilation of unusual and interesting statistics; *USA Today* provides tidbits of poll results on a daily basis. *U.S. News & World Report* publishes a page of vital statistics in each issue. Each winter the Higher Education Research Institute at UCLA releases the results of a national survey of college freshmen attitudes, available on the Internet at http://www.gseis.ucla.edu/heri/heri.html. During political campaigns, the network news shows mention poll results on a regular basis. With a little effort and ingenuity, you can usually find the complete text of the poll either in hard copy or on the Internet.

A word of caution is needed when interpreting demographic data. Most information on audience demographics—as well as on attitudes and values—is gathered through surveys that rely on self-reports. In such surveys people tend

Knowing the group affiliations of your listeners could help you adapt your message to their interests, concerns, and needs.

their religious convictions. As a speaker, you should be aware of this sensitivity and be attuned to the religious makeup of your anticipated audience. Appealing to "Christian" values before an audience that includes members of other religious groups may offend listeners and diminish the effectiveness of your message. The classroom audience of today is likely be made up of students from different religious backgrounds. Since religious affiliation may be a strong indicator of values, it is wise not to ignore its potential importance.

Social Groups. Membership in social groups can be as important to people as any other kind of affiliation. Typically, we are born into a religious group, raised in a certain political environment, and end up in an occupation as much by chance as by design. But we choose our social groups on the basis of our interests. Photographers join the Film Club, businesspeople become involved with the Chamber of Commerce, and environmentalists may be members of the Sierra Club.

Knowing which social groups are represented in your audience and what they stand for is important for effective audience adaptation. A speech favoring pollution control measures might take a different focus depending on whether it is presented to the Chamber of Commerce or to the Audubon Society. With the Chamber of Commerce, you might stress the importance of a clean environment in inducing businesses to relocate in your community; with the Audubon Society, you might emphasize the effects of pollution on wildlife. People tend to make their important group memberships known to others around them. Be alert to such information from your classmates and consider it in planning and preparing your speeches.

Sociocultural Background. People often are grouped by sociocultural background, a broad category that can include everything from the section of the country in which they live to their racial or ethnic identity. There is a wealth of information available on such groups. The web sites listed at the end of this chapter provide access to a wide array of resources and information relevant to a variety of sociocultural groups. Although such material may be fascinating,

ESL: ESL students may not understand the mainstream American culture. Use class discussions to highlight similarities and differences between cultures.

take the findings with a grain of salt. Remember, it is *your* audience for *your* speech that is important.

People from different sociocultural backgrounds often have different experiences, interests, and ways of looking at things. Consider, for example, the different perspectives that urban and rural audiences may have on gun control. Urban audiences may associate guns with crime and violence in the streets, and rural audiences may associate guns with hunting and recreation. A white, middle-class audience might have difficulty understanding what it means to grow up as a member of a minority. Midwesterners and Southerners may have misconceptions about each other.

Since most college classes represent a variety of backgrounds, you must strive to reach the majority without ignoring or offending the minority. With diverse audiences, your appeals and examples should relate to those experiences, feelings, values, and motivations that people hold in common. It also may be helpful to envision smaller audiences within the larger group. You may even want to direct specific remarks to these smaller groups. You might say, for example, "Those of you majoring in the liberal arts will find computer skills just as important in your work as they are for business majors" or "Those of you majoring in business may discover that large corporations are looking for employees with the breadth of perspective that comes from a liberal arts education." Direct references to specific subgroups within the audience can keep your speech from seeming too general.

If your classmates gave introductory speeches or responded to one another in class, you should have a good idea of the diversity of their backgrounds and interests. This specific information will be much more valuable than anything you can learn from reading about college students in magazines or books. Your *classmates* are the listeners you will address. The more information you have about them, the better you should be able to adapt your message and the better it should be received.

Meeting the Challenges of Audience Diversity

Some thirty years ago Marshall McLuhan, an English professor at the University of Toronto, suggested that technological changes in the media of communication were turning the world into a "global village."[31] Today we live in the village that McLuhan envisioned. Satellite transmissions bring news into our living rooms as it happens. The Internet provides access to information that was previously available only in the libraries of colleges and universities. Speeches that once were dusty relics in the pages of anthologies come to life on videotape and CD-ROM. Computer conferencing makes it possible for executives in Singapore to "meet" with executives in New York without having to travel. Time and space no longer impede the flow of information and ideas.

As we move into this twenty-first century, we must adapt to our diverse world. Although speaking to a diverse audience is a challenge, it is also an opportunity. Learning to communicate with others from different backgrounds and cultures can be one of the most rewarding experiences of your public speaking class. To find out more about your own sociocultural background, or about those of others, consult the relevant web sites listed at the end of this chapter. Again, keep in mind that the information you access relates to groups in general and not necessarily to your particular classmates. Try to integrate and reconcile such information with the information you derive about them firsthand.

To make the most of the opportunities of addressing varied audiences, you must be able to avoid some pitfalls. You must understand the power of stereotypes and bias and of the problematic "isms"—ethnocentrism, sexism, and racism. Finally, you should know how to find and build common ground with your listeners.

Stereotypes and Bias

We all use our past experiences to make sense of new information and to guide our interactions with others. To use our past experience efficiently, we react in terms of categories.[32] For example, having heard many stories about poisonous reptiles, we may be leery of all snakes. Severe problems can arise, however, when we start categorizing people. The categories can harden into stereotypes. **Stereotypes** are rigid sets of beliefs and expectations about people in a certain group. They reflect our attitudes or biases toward the group.[33] When stereotypes dominate our thinking, we react more to them than to the people within those groups. Wilma Mankiller, who served as principal chief of the Cherokee nation, offers a good idea of the practical problems posed by stereotypes:

Provide students with a list of cultural groups (men, women, Caucasians, African Americans, Latinos, Asians, etc.). Ask them to circle the group(s) with which they identify, then list five adjectives describing each group. They should not identify themselves by name. Tabulate the results and use them to discuss stereotypes and biases.

> **Sometimes in Oklahoma, it's really discouraging to sit down with a group of people from different backgrounds and cultures and try to work on a common problem, whether it's education or economic development or whatever the problem is, because everybody's sitting around this table, and they're all looking at each other with stereotypes, and they can't get past that. It's like everybody's sitting there and they have some kind of veil over their face, and they look at each other through this veil that makes them see each other through some stereotypical kind of viewpoint. If we're ever gonna collectively begin to grapple with the problems that we have collectively, we're gonna have to move back the veil and deal with each other on a more human level.[34]**

People often form stereotypes based on easily visible characteristics, such as gender, race, or age.[35] Stereotypes also may be related to ethnic identity, religion, occupation, or place of residence. We can form them from direct experiences with a few individuals who we assume are representative of a group. Most stereotypes, however, are learned indirectly from our families and friends, schools and churches, or media exposure. For example, our stereotype of Native Americans may come from exposure to Western movies, or our stereotype of West Virginians may be shaped by TV shows like *The Beverly Hillbillies.*

Whatever their origin, stereotypes can have a powerful influence on our thinking. We may judge people on the basis of stereotypes rather than on their merits as individuals. Stereotypes are also persistent: we are reluctant to give them up, especially when they agree with the stereotypes held by our friends and families. When we encounter people who do not fit our stereotypes, we may simply discount them as "exceptions to the rule." Beyond their obvious unfairness, stereotypes can also lead to disastrous behaviors. In their most extreme form they can justify the genocide that took place in Hitler's Germany or the more recent cases of "ethnic cleansing" in places like Bosnia.

Ethnocentrism, Sexism, and Racism

Ethnocentrism, sexism, and racism represent the most common types of problems that impede effective communication with a diverse audience.

Ethnocentrism. As we noted in Chapter 1, **ethnocentrism** is the belief that our way of life is the "right" and superior way. Actually, ethnocentrism is not always bad. In its milder form, ethnocentrism expresses itself in patriotism and national pride. It helps people unite and work toward common goals. It encourages immigrants to assimilate into a new national identity that provides common ground for living and getting along with one another.

But ethnocentrism has a darker side. Charles De Gaulle, who led the French people during the mid-twentieth century, once noted: "Patriotism is when love of your own people comes first; nationalism, when hate for people other than your own comes first."[36] When ethnocentrism goes beyond pride in one's own group and comes to include the rejection or derogation of others, it becomes a real problem in human relations and a barrier to cross-cultural communication.

The first step in controlling ethnocentrism is to recognize any tendencies you may have to undervalue other cultures. *We must learn to respect the humanity in all people, and to recognize that this humanity transcends race and culture.* As part of this respect, you should avoid using offensive language that denigrates others on the basis of their race or group affiliation.

Sexism. **Sexism** occurs when we allow gender stereotypes to control our interactions with members of the opposite sex. **Gender stereotyping** involves making broad generalizations about men or women based on outmoded assumptions, such as "Men don't know how to take care of children" or "Women don't understand business." Such beliefs transcend national boundaries and have been reported in over thirty countries in North and South America, Europe, Africa, Asia, and Australia.[37] Gender stereotyping is especially problematic when it implies that the differences between men and women *justify* discrimination. As you plan and prepare your message, try to be aware of any gender stereotypes you might have that could interfere with effective communication. Be careful not to portray gender roles in ways suggesting superiority or inferiority. For instance, when you use examples or stories to illustrate a point, don't make all your authority figures male.

Administer the exercise "Avoiding Sexist Language" found in Chapter 4 of the IRM. Discuss the choices and alternatives provided by your students.

Gender stereotyping often reveals itself in the use of sexist language. **Sexist language** involves making gender references in situations in which the gender is unknown or irrelevant. It may involve the generic use of masculine nouns or pronouns, such as referring to "man's advances in science" or using *he* when the intended reference is to both sexes. You can avoid this problem simply by saying "she or he" or by using the plural *they*. Some people have criticized this practice, saying that it makes the wording of messages awkward. They scoff at the seriousness of the problem. In her book on gender and communication, Julia Wood quotes the experience of a skeptical male student who suddenly found the situation reversed:

> **For a long time I thought all this stuff about generic *he* was a bunch of junk. I mean it seemed really clear to me that a word like *mankind* obviously includes women or that *chairman* can refer to a girl or a guy who chairs something. I thought it was pretty stupid to hassle about this. Then last semester, I had a woman teacher who taught the whole class using *she* or *her* or *woman* whenever she was referring to people as well as when she meant just women. I realized how confusing it is. I had to figure out each time whether she meant women only or women and men. And when she meant women to be general, I guess you'd say generic for all people, it still made me feel left out. A lot of the guys in the class got pretty hostile about what she was doing, but I kind of think it was a good way to make the point.**[38]

Racism. Just as gender stereotyping and sexist language can block communication, so can racism. Although blatant racism and discrimination are no longer socially acceptable in most circles, a subtle form of such prejudice can still infect our thinking. Although we may pay lip service to the principles of racial equality, we may still engage in **symbolic racism**, which is expressed subtly or covertly.[39] For example, if we say, "In our [white] neighborhood we believe in family values," the unspoken message may be "You don't, and therefore we are superior." Or we might say, "We believe in hard work and earning our way," when we really mean, "Why don't you [blacks] get off welfare!" Thus we may excuse the vestiges of racial stereotypes by appeals to values like family stability or the Protestant work ethic. In such cases our underlying message may be, "We honor such values and you don't."

It may be helpful to view the impact that symbolic racism can have from the perspective of someone on the receiving end. Television commentator Bryant Gumbel described how it feels:

> **It is very hard for any white person to appreciate the depth of what it means to be black in America. . . . Racism isn't only being called a nigger and spit on. It's being flipped the bird when you're driving, or walking into a store and being asked to check your bag, or being ignored at the checkout counter, or entering a fine restaurant and being stared at.[40]**

As you take the factor of race into consideration in your audience analysis, examine your thinking for biases and stereotypes that you may rationalize as value or lifestyle differences. Be sensitive about the language you use. When you are referring to a different racial or ethnic group, use the terms members of that group prefer. Stay away from examples that cast members of a particular ethnic group into stereotypical roles that imply inferiority. And of course, avoid racist humor.

One language problem that relates to all three of these negative "isms" is **marking**, adding an irrelevant reference to gender, ethnicity, race, or sexual preference when none is needed. For example, if you referred to "Thompson, the African American engineer," you might be trivializing her contribution by drawing attention to her race when it is irrelevant. Some audience members may interpret your remarks as suggesting that "Thompson is a pretty good engineer *for a person of color*," whether you intend that or not. The following excerpt from a speech by Martina Navratilova, who was named the world's top-rated female tennis player for seven years, shows how marking affects people:

> **Labels, labels, labels—now, I don't know about you, but I hate labels. Martina Navratilova, the lesbian tennis player. They don't say Joe Montana, the heterosexual football player. One's sexuality should not be an issue. . . . I did not spend over 30 years of my life working my butt off trying to become the very best tennis player that I can be, to then be called Martina, the lesbian tennis player. Labels are for filing. Labels are for bookkeeping. Labels are for clothing. Labels are not for people.[41]**

Speaker's Notes 4.1

AVOIDING RACIST AND SEXIST LANGUAGE

1. Do not use slang terms to refer to racial, ethnic, religious, or gender groups.
2. Avoid using the generic *he* and gender-specific titles such as chair*man*.
3. Avoid "markers" that introduce irrelevant references to race, gender, or ethnicity.
4. Avoid stereotypic references that imply inferiority or superiority.
5. Do not use sexist, racist, ethnic, or religious humor.

InterConnections.LearnMore 4.3

SEEKING COMMON GROUND

Anti-Defamation League http://www.adl.org
Founded in 1913, this organization has been in the forefront in fighting anti-Semitism and other forms of bigotry and discrimination against any body of citizens.

Center for the Study of Hate and Extremism
http://www.hatemonitor.org
Affiliated with the University of California, San Bernadino, this site provides resources for examining how bigotry, prejudice, and terrorism threaten human rights on the basis of race, ethnicity, religion, gender, sexual orientation, and disability.

National Conference for Community and Justice http://www.nccj.org
Formerly known as the National Conference for Christians and Jews, this organization promotes understanding among all races religions, and cultures.

Stop the Hate http://www.stopthehate.org
An antiviolence initiative created by students for students in high schools, colleges, and communities.

Finding Common Ground

Preliminary results from an ongoing study sponsored by the National Conference of Community and Justice demonstrated that stereotypes and prejudice are present in all groups in our culture. The survey revealed that people of color see whites as "bigoted, bossy, and unwilling to share power."[42] Although each of the minority groups surveyed also demonstrated negative stereotypes of and feelings toward other people of color, they were united by a sense of being victims of discrimination. Some 80 percent of African Americans, 60 percent of Latino Americans, and 57 percent of Asian Americans are convinced that their opportunities in work, housing, and education are not equal to those enjoyed by whites. On the other hand, over 50 percent of all whites believe that people of color enjoy equal opportunities. The survey concluded that "most whites simply do not acknowledge the tangible effects that discrimination has on the daily lives of minorities."

Lest you think the situation is hopeless, we should also point out that there were some positive results in this research. More than 80 percent of all groups polled expressed admiration of Asian Americans for the value they presumably place on intellectual and professional achievement and for having strong family ties and respecting their elders. Similarly large majorities felt that Latino Americans take pride in their culture, work hard to attain a better life, and have deep religious and family ties. Equally sizable majorities agreed that African Americans work hard when given a chance, believe strongly in American ideals and the American Dream, are deeply religious, and have made valuable contributions to American society. Over 90 percent of all groups surveyed also agreed that learning to understand and appreciate the lifestyles, tastes, and contributions of other groups was either "very important" or "important." *The most heartening finding of the study was the indication that nine out of ten Americans from all groups would be willing to work with one another to try to solve the most pressing problems in their neighborhoods and communities.* They expressed a willingness to work together to help protect each other's children from gangs and violence; to help improve schools, including teaching understanding and respect for the cultural heritage of all groups; and to look for ways to ease racial, religious, and ethnic tensions.

Ask students to rank in order of importance the universal values listed in Figure 4.4. Discuss the similarities and differences between the various cultural groups represented in the class. Note especially how ESL students respond. Discuss the role that universal values may play in smoothing relationships between groups.

In Chapter 1 we noted that Rushworth Kidder of the Institute for Global Ethics has identified eight **universal human values** that transcend cultural differences: love, truthfulness, fairness, freedom, unity, tolerance, responsibility, and respect for life.[43] Contemporary social scientific research has also demonstrated the existence of transcendent social values. Shalom Schwartz and his

FIGURE 4.4
Universal Values

Value	Description
Power	Social power, authority, recognition from others, wealth
Achievement	Success, ambition, influence
Tradition	Acceptance of one's fate, devoutness, humility, respect for cultural heritage
Enjoyment	Pleasure
Self-Direction	Freedom, independence, choice of own goals, self-respect, curiosity, creativity
Security	National security, social order, family security, sense of belonging, personal health and cleanliness, reciprocity in personal relationships
Unity	Unity with nature, protecting the environment, inner harmony, social justice, equality, tolerance, a world at peace
Benevolence	Honesty, helpfulness, forgiveness, loyalty, responsibility, friendship, love, spiritual life, meaning in life
Conformity	Politeness, obedience, self-discipline, honoring parents and elders
Stimulation	Variety, excitement, daring

associates at the Hebrew University of Jerusalem conducted a study of values in twenty different countries. They identified ten universal values: power, achievement, tradition, enjoyment, self-direction, security, unity, benevolence, conformity, and stimulation.[44] Figure 4.4 lists these universal values and shows how they appear to come together.

If you can appeal to these common values in your speeches to a diverse audience, you can often unite your listeners behind your ideas or suggestions.

Adjusting to the Communication Situation

Finally, we come to the setting for your speech. You must consider the time, place, occasion, size of the audience, and overall context of recent topic-related events to make final adjustments in your presentation.

Time

The time of day, day of the week, time of the year, and amount of time allotted for speaking must be taken into account. If you are speaking early in the morning, you may need to be more forceful to awaken listeners. The vigor of your voice must assert the importance of your message. Since we tend to grow drowsy after we eat, after-dinner speeches (discussed in detail in Chapter 15)

Ethics Alert! 4.1

THE ETHICS OF AUDIENCE ADAPTATION

1. When speaking before diverse audiences, change your tactics, *not your convictions.*
2. Appealing to shared needs helps to cross cultural boundaries that divide listeners.
3. Do not disguise problems simply by appealing to common needs.
4. Adapting to your audience helps you understand the importance of your message for a wider range of humanity.
5. Remember: Demographic similarities do not mean members of your audience are all alike.
6. Adapting your presentation to the immediate situation gives your message a better chance for a fair hearing.

need lively examples and humor. Speeches presented in the evening also present a problem. Most listeners will have completed a day's work and will have left the comforts of home to hear you. You must justify their attendance with good ideas well presented.

If your speech is scheduled for a Monday, when people have not yet adjusted to the weekend's being over, or a Friday, when they are thinking of the weekend ahead, you need especially interesting material to hold attention. Similarly, gloomy winter days or balmy spring weather can put people in a different frame of mind, and their mood can color how they receive your speech.[45] Your materials and presentation style will have to be bright and engaging to overcome the blahs or to forestall daydreaming.

The amount of time allotted for your presentation is also critical. *A short speech does not necessarily mean shorter preparation time.* Short speeches require you to focus and streamline your topic so that it can be handled in the time allotted. You must limit the number of main points and use supporting materials selectively. Choose the most relevant and impressive facts, statistics, and testimony, the most striking examples and stories. Plan your speech so that you begin with a burst and end with a bang.

Place

Ask students to identify any possible sources of distraction or interference in the immediate classroom setting. Discuss how a speaker might adjust to these conditions.

The place where you will be speaking should also be considered in your planning. When speaking outside, you may have to cope with unpredictable distractions. When speaking inside, you need to know the size and layout of the room and whether a lectern or electronic equipment you may need is available.

Even in the classroom, speakers must learn to cope with distractions—noises may filter in from outside, or people in the hall may start talking loudly. How can you handle such problems? If the noise is temporary, you should pause and wait until it stops; then repeat your last words and go on with your message. If the noise is constant, you may have to step up your own volume to be heard. You may even have to pause and close a window or door. The important thing is to take such problems in stride and not let them distract you or your audience from your message.

Occasion

As you plan your message, you need to take into account *why* people have gathered to listen. When an audience is required to attend a presentation, such as a

Speaker's Notes 4.2

CHECKLIST FOR ANALYZING THE COMMUNICATION SITUATION

1. Will the time or timing of my speech present any challenges?
2. Will room arrangements be adequate? Will I have the equipment I need for presentation aids?
3. What does the audience expect on this occasion?
4. Is there any late-breaking news on my topic?
5. Will I possibly have to adjust to previous speakers?
6. How large will the audience be?

mandatory employee meeting, you may have to work hard to arouse interest and sustain attention. When audience members voluntarily attend a presentation, they usually are more motivated to listen. But you need to know why they are there and what they expect from your speech. When a speaker does not offer the kind of message listeners expect, they may be annoyed. For example, if they are expecting an informative presentation on investment strategies and instead get a sales pitch for a mutual fund, they may feel exploited. This could result more in irritation than in persuasion.

Have students recall a time when a presentation they heard seemed inappropriate for the occasion. Discuss how they felt at that time and what the speaker might have done differently.

Size of Audience

The size of your audience can affect how you speak. A small audience provides feedback and an opportunity for interaction. Generally, a small group of listeners invites a more casual presentation. You could easily overwhelm them with a formal oratorical style, too loud a voice, or exaggerated gestures.

On the other hand, large audiences offer less feedback. Because you cannot make or sustain eye contact with everyone, you should choose representative listeners in various sections of the audience and change your visual focus from

The size of your audience can affect the structure, style, and presentation of your message.

time to time. Establishing eye contact with listeners in all sections of the room helps more people feel included. With large audiences you also should speak more deliberately and distinctly. Your gestures should be more emphatic so that everyone can see them, and any presentation aids used must be large enough for those in the back of the audience to see without strain.

Context

Anything that happens near the time of your presentation becomes part of the context of your speech. Both recent speeches and recent events can influence how the audience responds to you.

The Context of Recent Speeches. Any speeches presented immediately before yours create an atmosphere in which you must work. This atmosphere has a **preliminary tuning effect** on listeners, preparing them to respond in certain ways to you and your message.[46] At political rallies, patriotic music and introductions prepare the audience for the appearance of the featured speaker. At concerts, warm-up groups put listeners in the mood for the star.

Preliminary tuning may also affect classroom presentations. Earlier speeches may affect the mood of the audience. If the speech right before yours aroused strong emotions, you may need to ease the tension in the introduction to your speech. You can do this by acknowledging listeners' feelings and using them as a springboard into your own speech:

> **Obviously, many of us feel very strongly about the legalization of same-sex marriages. What I'm going to talk about is also very important—but it is something I think we can all agree on—the challenge of finding a way to stop children from killing other children in our community.**

Another technique might be to begin with a story that involves listeners and refocuses their attention. At times, humor can help relieve tension, but people who are upset may be in no mood for laughter. Your decision on whether to use humor must be based on your reading of the situation: the mood of listeners, the subject under discussion, and your own ability to use the technique effectively.

In addition to dealing with the mood created by earlier speeches, you may also have to adapt to their content. Suppose you have spent the past week preparing a speech on the *importance* of extending endangered species legislation. Then the speaker before you makes a convincing presentation on the *problems* of extending endangered species legislation. What can you do? Try to turn this to your advantage. Point out that the earlier speech established the importance of the topic but that—as good as that effort was—it did not give the total picture: "Now you will hear the *other* side of the story."

The Context of Recent Events. When listeners enter the room the day of your speech, they bring with them information about recent events. They will use this knowledge to evaluate what you say. If you are not up on the latest news on your topic, your credibility can suffer. A student in one of our classes once presented an interesting and well-documented speech comparing public housing in Germany with that in the United States. Unfortunately, she was unaware of a local scandal involving public housing. For three days before her presentation, the story had made the front page of the local paper and had been the lead story in area newscasts. Everyone expected her to mention it. Her failure to discuss this important local problem weakened her credibility.

At times the context of events to which you must adjust your speech may be totally unexpected. When that happens, you must make on-the-spot adjustments so that things work in your favor. During a graduation ceremony at Loyola Marymount University, the school's president fell off the platform immediately before the commencement address. Although the only thing injured was his dignity, the

FIGURE 4.5
Audience Analysis Worksheet

Topic: ______________________________

Audience: ______________________________

	Factor Description	**Adaptations Needed**
Audience Dynamics	Audience Attitude: ________	________
	Relevant Values: ________	________
	Motivational Appeals: ________	________
Audience Demographics	Age: ________	________
	Gender: ________	________
	Education: ________	________
	Group Affiliations: ________	________
	Sociocultural Background: ________	________
	Interest in Topic: ________	________
	Knowledge of Topic: ________	________
Speaking Situation	Time: ________	________
	Place: ________	________
	Occasion: ________	________
	Audience Size: ________	________
	Context: ________	________

fall certainly distracted the audience. The speaker, Peter Ueberroth, organizer of the 1984 Los Angeles Summer Olympic Games, recaptured their attention and brought down the house by awarding the president a 4.5 in gymnastics.[47]

Figure 4.5 provides an Audience Analysis Worksheet that will help you consider all the factors we have discussed in this chapter as you plan for the audience and situation of your speech.

In Summary

Both the audience you anticipate and the setting of your speech are critical to your planning. Successful audience adaptation requires that you understand *audience dynamics*, have relevant information concerning audience demographics, be sensitive to the challenges of audience diversity, and be able to adjust to situational factors.

Adapting to Audience Dynamics. *Motivation* explains why people behave as they do. People will listen, learn, and retain your message only if you can relate it to their needs, wants, or wishes. Some motives you may call on include understanding, control, health and safety, nurturance and altruism, friends and family, self-actualization, and the desire for fairness.

Your audience's *attitudes*, *beliefs*, and *values* will also affect the way they receive and interpret your message. If your listeners are initially negative toward your topic, you will have to adjust your presentation to receive a fair hearing.

Adjusting to Audience Demographics. *Audience demographics* include information about more specific characteristics of your listeners, such as their age, gender, educational level, group membership, and sociocultural makeup (race, social class, and so forth). The more you know about such factors, the better you can tailor your speech so that it serves your listeners' interests and needs.

Meeting the Challenges of Audience Diversity. Today we live in a global village composed of many diverse groups. Learning to understand and adapt to diversity will help you prepare more effective messages. Examine your thinking to identify any *stereotypes* that might categorize people inflexibly and attribute positive or negative traits to them. Be on guard against *ethnocentrism*, *sexism*, and *racism* as you plan and prepare your presentations. When speaking to a diverse audience, search for common ground based on *universal human values.*

Adjusting to the Communication Situation. You must be flexible enough to adjust to particular features of the speaking situation. The time at which you speak, the place of your speech, the constraints of the occasion, and the size of your audience can all pose challenges. In addition, you will be speaking in a context of other speeches and recent events which can serve a *preliminary tuning effect* to which you must adjust as you make your presentation.

Terms to Know

audience dynamics
motivation
attitudes
beliefs
values
audience demographics
stereotypes
ethnocentrism
sexism
gender stereotyping
sexist language
symbolic racism
marking
universal human values
preliminary tuning effect

Notes

1. Barbara Engler, *Personality Theories: An Introduction*, 4th ed. (Boston: Houghton Mifflin, 1995), pp. 273–280, 340–363; and Thane S. Pittman, "Motivation," in *The Handbook of Social Psychology*, 4th ed., ed. Daniel T. Gilbert, Susan T. Fiske, and Gardener Lindzey (Boston: McGraw-Hill, 1998), vol. 1, pp. 549–590.

2. Henry A. Murray, *Explorations in Personality* (New York: Oxford University Press, 1938). Interest in Murray's research continues, and Radcliffe Institute for Advanced Study maintains a web site for the Murray Research Center at http://www.radcliffe.edu/.

3. Richard E. Petty and Duane T. Wegener, "Attitude Change: Multiple Roles for Persuasion Variables," in *Handbook of Social Psychology*, vol. 1, pp. 353–354.

4. Roderick P. Hart, "Why Communication? Why Education? Toward a Politics of Teaching," *Communication Education* 42 (1993): 101.

5. The study of achievement motivation began with the work of the Murray group, op. cit., and was extended by D. C. McClelland, *Human Motivation* (Glenview, Ill.: Scott, Foresman, 1985). Research in this area continues with the investigation of such elements as the influence of situation on achievement motivation. See Minette A. Bumpus, Sharon Olbeter, and Saundra H. Glover, "Influences of Situational Characteristics on Intrinsic Motivation," *Journal of Psychology* (July 1998): 451–453. *eLibrary*, http://www.elibrary.com (7 Aug. 1998); and Edward A. Ward, "Multidimensionality of Achievement Motivation Among Employed Adults," *Journal of Social Psychology* (August 1997): 542–544, accessed at *eLibrary* (www.elibrary.com), 7 Aug. 1998.

6. Alice A. Eagly and Shelly Chaiken, "Attitude Structure and Function," in *The Handbook of Social Psychology*, vol. 1, pp. 323–390; and James M. Olson and Mark P. Zanna, "Attitudes and Attitude Change," *Annual Review of Psychology* 44 (1993): 117–154.

7. Herbert W. Simons, *Persuasion: Understanding, Practice, and Analysis*, 2nd ed. (Reading, Mass.: Addison-Wesley, 1986), pp. 121–139.

8. J. Michael Hogan, "George Gallup and the Rhetoric of Scientific Democracy," *Communication Monographs* 64 (1997): 161–179.

9. *The Rhetoric of Aristotle*, trans. George Kennedy (New York: Oxford University Press, 1992), pp. 163–169 (Book 2, Chs. 11–14).

10. S. J. Ceci and M. Bruck, "Suggestibility of the Child Witness: A Historical Review and Synthesis," *Psychological Bulletin* 113 (1993): 403–439; J. A. Krosnick and D. F. Alwin, "Aging and Susceptibility to Attitude Change," *Journal of Personality and Social Psychology* 57 (1989): 416–425; Petty and Wegener, "Attitude Change," p. 358; Milton Rokeach, *The Open and Closed Mind* (New York: Basic Books, 1960); and T. R. Tyler and R. A. Schuller, "Aging and Attitude Change," *Journal of Personality and Social Psychology* 61 (1991): 689–697.

11. J. Walker Smith and Ann Clurman, *Rocking the Ages: The Yankelovich Report on Generational Marketing* (New York: HarperCollins, 1997), p. 89.

12. "Measuring Diversity: How Does Your State Rate?" *National Education Association Today* (September 1992): 8.

13. "Total Fall Enrollment in Institutions of Higher Education, by Attendance Status, Sex, and Age: Fall 1970 to Fall 2010," *Digest of Education Statistics 2000* (September 2000), table 175. http://nces.ed.gov/pubs2001/digest/dt175.html (30 May 2001).

14. Ibid.

15. "An Overview of the 2000 Freshman Norms" (January 2001). http://www.gseis.ucla.edu/heri/heri.html (30 May 2001).

16. Smith and Clurman, pp. 88–90.

17. Northwestern Mutual Life, "Generation 2001 Survey Results–Executive Summary." http://www.northwesternmutual.com/contentassets/pdfs/gen_2001_executive_summary.pdf (10 Sept. 2001).

18. Smith and Clurman, p. 88.

19. Cited in Allison Adato and Melissa G. Stanton, "If Women Ran America," *Life*, June 1992, p. 40.

20. James R. Gaines, "A Note from the Editor," *Life*, June 1992, p. 6.

21. "High School and College Graduates" (©2000, 2001 The Learning Network Inc.) http://www.infoplease.com/ipa/A0112596.html (10 June 2001).

22. "Women in the Civilian Labor Force, 1900–2000" (© 2000, 2001 The Learning Network Inc.). http://www.infoplease.com/ipa/A0104673.html (10 June 2001).

23. John Gettings and David Johnson, "Wonder Women: Profiles of Leading Female CEOs and Business Executives" (©2000, 2001 The Learning Network Inc.). http://www.infoplease.com/spot/womenceo1.html (10 June 2001).

24. Russell L. Kent and Sherry E. Moss, "Effects of Sex and Gender Role on Leader Emergence," Academy of Management Journal (October 1994): 1335–1346.

25. Hester Lacy, "Girls Behaving Affluently . . . ," *Independent on Sunday*, 23 March 1997, pp. 1, 2. *eLibrary*, http://www.elibrary.com (18 Aug. 1998).

26. "New Wheels," *U.S. News & World Report*, 5 June 1995, p. 70.

27. Daniel J. Canary and Kimberley S. Hause, "Is There Any Reason to Research Sex Differences in Communication?" *Communication Quarterly* 41 (1993): 129–144.

28. James Atlas, "Beyond Demographics," *Atlantic Monthly*, October 1984, pp. 49–58; Arnold Mitchell, *The Nine American Lifestyles: Who We Are and Where We're Going* (New York: Macmillan, 1983); Rokeach, *Open and Closed Mind;* and P. Schonback, *Education and Intergroup Attitudes* (London: Academic Press, 1981).

29. William McGuire, "Attitudes and Attitude Change," in *Handbook of Social Psychology*, vol. 2, ed. Gardner Lindzey and Eliot Aronson (New York: Random House, 1985), pp. 271–272.

30. For a detailed analysis of this topic, see Donald R. Kinder, "Opinion and Action in the Realm of Politics," in *Handbook of Social Psychology*, vol. 2, pp. 778–867.

31. Marshall McLuhan, *Understanding Media: The Extensions of Man* (New York: McGraw Hill, 1964).

32. Sharon S. Brehm and Saul M. Kassin, *Social Psychology*, 3rd ed. (Boston: Houghton Mifflin, 1996), pp. 120–161; Susan T. Fiske, "Stereotyping, Prejudice, and Discrimination," in *Handbook of Social Psychology*, vol. 2, pp. 357–414; and Annie Murphy Paul, "Where Bias Begins: The Truth About Stereotypes," *Psychology Today*, May/June 1998, pp. 52–55, 82.

33. R. C. Gardner, "Stereotypes as Consensual Beliefs," in Mark P. Zanna and James M. Olson, *The Psychology of Prejudice: The Ontario Symposium*, vol. 7, (Hillsdale, N.J.: Erlbaum, 1994), pp. 1–32.

34. Wilma Mankiller, "Rebuilding the Cherokee Nation," paper presented at Sweet Briar College, 2 Apr. 1993. http://gos.sbc.edu/index.html (18 Sept. 1998). Reprinted by permission of the author.

35. Susan T. Fiske, "Social Cognition and Social Perception," *Annual Review of Psychology* 44 (1993): 155–194.

36. Cited in *The Merriam-Webster Dictionary of Quotations* (Springfield, Mass: Merriam-Webster Inc., 1992), p. 309.

37. Brehm and Kassin, p. 164.

38. Julia T. Wood, *Gendered Lives: Communication, Gender, and Culture* (Belmont, Calif.: Wadsworth, 1994), p. 126.

39. Fiske, "Stereotyping, Prejudice, and Discrimination," pp. 357–414.

40. G. Plaskin, "Bryant Gumbel," *Us*, 5 Sept. 1988, pp. 29–35.

41. From a speech presented 4 April 1993; reprinted in DiMona and Herndon, pp. 344–345.

42. The data in this section come from The National Conference of Christians and Jews, "Taking America's Pulse: A Summary Report of the National Conference Survey on Inter-Group Relations," undated, available from The National Conference, 71 Fifth Avenue, New York, NY 10003.

43. Rushworth M. Kidder, *Shared Values for a Troubled World* (San Francisco: Jossey-Bass, 1994), pp. 1–19.

44. Shalom H. Schwartz, Sonia Roccas and Lilach Sagiv, "Universals in the Content and Structure of Values: Theoretical Advances and Empirical Tests in Twenty Countries," *Advances in Experimental Social Psychology* 25 (1992): 1–65.

45. N. Schwarz, H. Bless, and G. Bohner, "Mood and Persuasion: Affective States Influence the Processing of Persuasive Communications," *Advances in Experimental Social Psychology* 24 (1991): 161–199.

46. For more about preliminary tuning, see Theodore Clevenger Jr., *Audience Analysis* (Indianapolis: Bobbs-Merrill, 1966), pp. 11–12.

47. Reported in *Time*, 17 June 1985, p. 68.

DIVERSITY RESOURCES ON THE INTERNET

General

Diversity Web **http://www.diversityweb.org** An Association of American Colleges and Universities web site providing materials relevant to diversity in higher education.

ESL Magazine **http://www.eslmag.com** An online magazine for educators and others interested in understanding the challenges of learning English as a second language.

In Motion **http://www.inmotionmagazine.com** A multicultural online U.S. publication covering a variety of topics relevant to cultural diversity. Also available in Spanish.

Race and Ethnicity Database **http://eserver.org/race/** A University of Washington web site containing a compilation of reference materials, essays, and literary collections pertinent to race and ethnicity in the United States.

Human Rights

Amnesty International **http://amnestyusa.org** The official web site of Amnesty International, a humanitarian advocacy group concerned with promoting human rights throughout the world.

Civil Liberties and Civil Rights **http://www.priweb.com/internetlawlib/93.htm** An Internet Law Library directory to legal documents from a variety of sources.

Human Rights Interactive Network **http://www.webcom.com/hrin/** An extensive directory of web sites related to human rights organizations and activities around the world.

Human Rights Watch **http://www.hrw.org/** The official web site of Human Rights Watch, a nonprofit nongovernmental organization dedicated to protecting the human rights of people around the world.

Humanitarian Affairs **http://www.reliefweb.int/ocha_ol/index.html** The web site of the United Nations Office for the Coordination of Humanitarian Affairs, which deals with humanitarian policies, advocacy, and action worldwide.

Racial/Ethnic Diversity Web Sites

African American

Afro-American Newspapers **http://www.afroam.org** African-American Newspaper Association web site containing sections on history, culture, current news, and information relevant to the African American community.

Black History **http://www.blackhistory.com** A web site offering articles on the contributions and problems of African Americans.

NAACP **http://www.naacp.org** The official web site of the National Association for the Advancement of Colored People, containing current information on problems relating to justice for African Americans.

National Civil Rights Museum **http://www.civilrightsmuseum.org** This site features an interactive tour documenting the struggle for civil rights in America.

Latino/Chicano/Hispanic

Cuba Free Press **http://www.cubafreepress.org/** The web site of a nonprofit organization offering news and feature articles published in English, Spanish, and Russian.

Hispanic.com **http://www.hispanic.com/** A web site containing information, services, and technology access to the Hispanic community in the United States.

HispanicOnline.com **http://www.hispaniconline.com/** A web site covering arts and entertainment, politics, lifestyles, and news of importance to the Hispanic community.

Latino Web **http://www.latinoweb.com/** Primarily a comprehensive search tool covering major areas of Latino culture, such as history, politics, culture, and art.

Mexico Connect **http://www.mexconnect.com/** An online magazine with news and feature articles, plus a directory of web sites.

Asian American

China Today **http://www.chinatoday.com** A web site containing general information on the culture, history, and traditions of China.

Hmong Homepage **http://www.hmongnet.org/** A web site offering links of interest on the history, culture, and traditions of the Hmong people in Vietnam, Laos, and Thailand.

India Culture **http://www.indiaculture.net** A source of articles and links on the arts, culture, religion, and history of India.

Japan Window **http://www.jwindow.net** An information source for businesses and consumers, offering information on business practices, culture, and education.

Korean Historical Connection **http://www.hongik.ac.kr/~khc/khc-eng.htm** A web site from the Department of History Education at Hong-Ik University, Seoul, Korea, that maintains an extensive database of articles on history, arts, and culture.

Orientation Asia **http://as.orientation.com/en/home.html** A source of information on current news, travel, and social issues relevant to Asia.

Native American

Indian Country Today **http://www.indiancountry.com** The online version of a Native American newspaper distributed across the United States, containing current news and perspectives.

National Museum of the American Indian **http://www.si.edu/nmai** The web site of a branch of the Smithsonian Institution, containing material and information documenting the arts and culture of Native Americans.

Native American Nations **http://www.nativeculture.com/lisamitten/nations.html** A directory of links to the major American tribes.

Native Peoples **http://www.nativepeoples.com/** The online version of *Native Peoples* magazine, with current issues and archives.

Native Web **http://www.nativeweb.com** A web site containing news and an extensive directory of over 3,000 links to other sources of information relevant to indigenous cultures around the world.

Middle-Eastern

Arab Internet Directory **http://www.1001sites.com/home.htm** A directory with links to major sites in the Arab world covering news, art, culture, and travel.

Jewish/Israel Link Launcher **http://ucsu.colorado.edu/~jsu/launcher.html** A directory of links to Israeli politics, culture, arts, and history.

Middle-Eastern Orientation **http://me.orientation.com/en/home.html** A source of information on current news, travel, and social issues relevant to the Middle East.

European American

The following web sites contain information on the history and culture of the designated country plus links to other relevant web sites.

France **http://www.france.com**
Germany **http://www.germany-info.org/**
Greece **http://www.greekvillage.com**
Ireland **http://www.local.ie/**
Italy **http://www.italian-american.com/main.htm**
Poland **http://www.polish.org/**
Russia **http://www.amherst.edu/~acrc/**
Scotland **http://www.geo.ed.ac.uk/home/scotland/scotland.html**
Spain **http://www.cyberspain.com**

Gender

Women's Resources

Advancing Women **http://www.advancingwomen.com** Information and links to sites relevant to women in the work force.

NOW **http://63.111.42.146/home** The official web site of the National Organization for Women.

Women Leaders Online **http://www.wlo.org/** A networking web site for women in politics, the media, the work force, and cyberspace.

Women's Studies Database **http://www.inform.umd.edu/EdRes/Topic/Women'sStudies/** A large directory of links to web sites for and about women.

Men's Resources

Backlash **http://www.backlash.com** An equalitarian web site with articles and links on gender issues, parenting, divorce and employment from the male perspective.

Menstuff **http://www.menstuff.org** The web site of the National Men's Resource Center, with information for men on fatherhood, health, and relationships.

MenWeb **http://www.vix.com/menmag** An online magazine with articles about battered men, male sex abuse survivors, friendship, and male health and employment issues.

National Coalition of Free Men **http://www.ncfm.org** A web site devoted to examining how sexual discrimination affects men and boys.

Alternative Life Styles

The Advocate **http://www.advocate.com** An online magazine focusing on news, health, family, and homophobia issues.

Lifestyle Resources **http://www.inform.umd.edu/EdRes/Topic/Diversity/Specific/Sexual_Orientation/Bibliographies** An online directory and bibliographies pertaining to alternative lifestyles.

National Gay and Lesbian Taskforce **http://www.ngltf.org** The official web site of the National Gay and Lesbian Taskforce, an activist organization working to extend civil rights to those with alternative lifestyles.

OUT.com **http://www.out.com** An online magazine with an emphasis on media, arts, and fashion.

Political Diversity

General

Campaign Finance **http://www.opensecrets.org** A Center for Responsive Politics web site containing information on who's giving and who's getting political contributions.

Political Information **http://www.politicalinformation.com** A directory and specialized search engine with over 5,000 links to web sites on campaigns, grassroots movements, political issues, and political organizations.

Politics1 **http://www.politics1.com** A nonpartisan web site with directories for parties and issues.

Political Parties

Democratic **http://www.democrats.org** News and information on the official Democratic National Committee web site.

Green Parties **http://www.greens.org/** News and information about the Green Parties worldwide.

Libertarian **http://www.lp.org/** News and information on the official Libertarian Party web site.

Republican **http://www.rnc.org/** News and information on the official Republican National Committee web site.

Young Democrats **http://www.yda.org/yda/** News and information of interest to Democrats under thirty-six.

Young Republicans **http://www.yrock.com/home/** News and information of interest to Republicans between the ages of eighteen and forty.

Conservative

Media Research Center **http://www.mediaresearch.org** An exposé of the "liberal" media bias in American politics.

Town Hall **http://www.townhall.com** Conservative news, information, and issues with a library categorized by topics.

Young Americans for Freedom **http://www.yaf.com** News and information about issues of interest to young conservatives.

Liberal

Brookings Institution **http://www.brookings.org** Foreign policy and domestic issues presented from a liberal viewpoint.

People for the American Way **http://www.pfaw.org** Political news and issues from the liberal perspective.

TurnLeft **http://www.turnleft.com/liberal.html** The home of liberalism on the Web: information and links.

Religious Diversity

General

American Religious Experience **http://are.as.wvu.edu** Articles and images of American religious history on the Web.

Finding God in Cyberspace **http://www.fontbonne.edu/libserv/fgic/fgic.htm** A directory of print and Internet resources on religious traditions.

Theology and Religion **http://www.wabashcenter.wabash.edu/Internet/front.htm** An annotated guide to sources relevant to religious education.

Religious Traditions

The following web sites contain information on some of the major religious organizations active in the United States.

Anglicans **http://www.anglican.org**
Baptist **http://www.baptist.org**
Buddhism **http://www.dharmanet.org/**

Christian Scientist **http://www.tfccs.com**
Church of Christ **http://www.church-of-christ.org**
Church of God in Christ **http://www.cogic.org**
Episcopal **http://ecusa.anglican.org/**
Friends **http://www.quaker.org**
Hinduism **http://www.hindunet.org**
Islam **http://www.usc.edu/dept/MSA/introduction/woi_toc.html**
Judaism **http://www.shirhadash.org/**
Latter Day Saints **http://www.lds.org**
Lutheran **http://www.lcms.org**
Methodist **http://www.umc.org**
Presbyterian **http://www.pcusa.org**
Roman Catholic **http://www.catholic.net**
Unitarian **http://www.uua.org**
United Church of Christ **http://www.ucc.org**

5

Selecting and Researching Your Topic

OUTLINE

THIS CHAPTER WILL HELP YOU

- select a topic
- focus your topic
- determine your purpose
- develop a clear thesis statement
- obtain responsible knowledge

"I have to speak for five whole minutes? Why, I don't know that much about anything!" Your instructor has just given you your assignment. You are to prepare an informative speech on a subject of your choice. Your stomach starts to tighten as you worry. "Speech about what? How do I begin?"

Preparing to speak before an audience can seem overwhelming, especially if you've never done it before. Simply getting started may be the most difficult part of speech preparation. If the task before you seems to be too much, take it in small steps, advises Robert J. Kriegel, a performance psychologist who has counseled many professional athletes. While working as a ski instructor, Kriegel found that beginners would look all the way to the bottom of a slope. The hill would seem too steep and the challenge too difficult, and the skiers would back away. However, if he told them to think only of making the first turn, this would change their focus to something they knew they could do.[1]

On the "first turn" in speech preparation, you will decide on a topic that fits both you and your audience. Fortunately, there are some good ways to help you meet this challenge. On the "second turn," you will develop a clear sense of purpose for your speech. On the "third turn," you will expand your knowledge so that you can make a responsible presentation. This chapter will help you negotiate these turns.

Selecting your topic, determining your purpose, and acquiring responsible knowledge are part of the first phase of speech preparation shown in the flow chart in Figure 5.1, "Major Steps in the Preparation of a Speech." As the chart indicates, you will work back and forth between these steps, always keeping your audience in mind. In later chapters, we will deal with the second phase, structuring and outlining your speech, and with the third phase, preparing for presentation.

But for now, back to that first turn. What is a good topic? It is one that involves you, that allows you to express something that is important to you, and/or that explores something that fascinates you. It should also enrich the lives of your listeners by providing them with useful information or advice. Finally, a good topic is one that you can speak about responsibly, given the time allowed for your speech and the preparation time available.

A good topic involves you. Imagine yourself speaking successfully:

> You're excited about what you're saying. Your face shows your interest in your topic. Your voice expresses your feelings. Your gestures reinforce your meaning. Everything about you says, "This is important!" "You're going to love this!" or "This will make a real difference in your lives!"

Now, let's work backward from this image. What subject might make you feel or act this way? That's the topic you want! If you don't care about your topic, you will find it hard to spend the time and effort needed to speak responsibly and effectively. The enthusiasm you generate when you speak on topics to which you are committed is contagious. It gets listeners involved as well.

A good topic involves your listeners. Now imagine an audience of ideal listeners:

I use not only all the brains I have, but all I can borrow.

—President Woodrow Wilson

> Their faces are alive with interest. They lean forward in their seats, intent on hearing you. They nod or smile appropriately. You enjoy their attention. At the end of your speech, they break out in applause. They want to ask you questions about your ideas or to voice their own reactions. They really don't want you to sit down!

What topic will help you reach this audience ideal? By now, you probably have heard the first speeches in your class, and you are already learning about your listeners. Ask yourself, "What are their interests? What do they care about? What do they need to know more about?"

Ask students to develop a list of promising topics based on audience reactions to the first speeches presented in class.

Perhaps one of your classmates gave a speech honoring his family doctor. It sparked a lively classroom discussion and got you thinking about your less pleasant experiences with doctors. The lights come on in your mind. You could present an informative speech on the relationship between physician skills and malpractice complaints or a persuasive speech encouraging training in interpersonal communication skills for doctors. Although these topics may seem intrinsically interesting, you still can't take audience involvement for granted. Your introduction must arouse their interest. You must show your audience how the topic affects *them* and what *they* stand to gain from hearing your message. For a topic to be really effective, it also must fit the time, place, and occasion for the speech, as we noted in Chapter 4. For example, a celebration in honor of a friend is not an occasion for a political tirade.

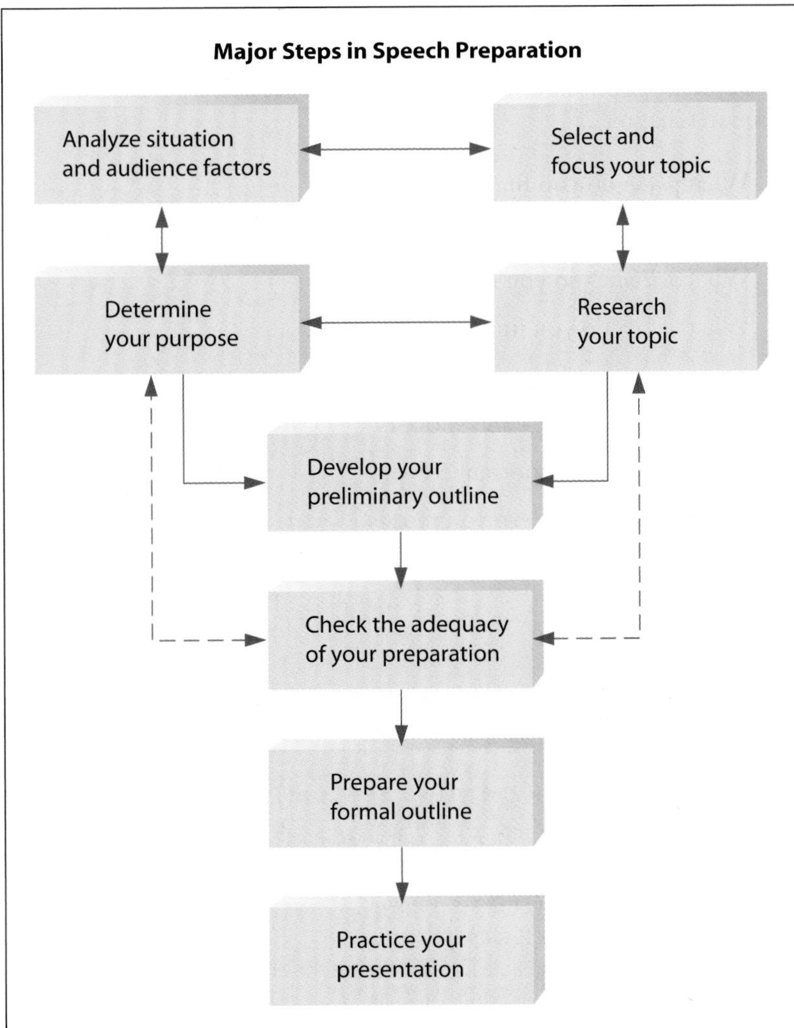

FIGURE 5.1
Major Steps in the Preparation of a Speech

Assign the topic briefing exercise described in Chapter 5 of the IRM. Have students compile a list of reference materials available on the topic. Discuss ways the topic might be limited to something manageable in a short classroom speech.

The final test of a good topic is whether you can acquire the knowledge you need to speak responsibly on it. The time you have for the preparation and presentation of your speech is limited. Consequently, you should select a topic area you already know something about, then concentrate on developing a *manageable part* of that topic area for your presentation. Instead of trying to cover all the problems involved in the disposal of nuclear waste, it would be better to limit yourself to discussing your state's role in nuclear waste disposal or to focus on whether your community has an adequate plan to cope with the problem. The limited topic would be more manageable, could be better adapted to your audience, and should allow for responsible preparation.

Finding a Good Topic

One way to go about finding a good topic is to chart your personal interests and then those of your listeners so that you can analyze topic ideas in terms of their appropriateness and practicality.

Charting Interests

Ask students to email you their interest inventories. Compile a list of potential informative and persuasive speech topics based on these reports. Distribute these lists to the class to help students become more aware of their classmates' interests.

Begin your search for a good topic by listing your interests and those of your listeners to determine points of convergence. To develop these interests charts, use a system of prompt questions similar to the self-awareness inventory introduced in Chapter 2:

1. What *places* do you find interesting?
2. What *people* do you find fascinating?
3. What *activities* do you enjoy?
4. What *objects* do you find interesting?
5. What *events* are foremost in your mind?
6. What are your long- and short-range *goals*?
7. What *values* are important to you?
8. What *problems* concern you most?
9. What *campus concerns* do you have?

Speaker's Notes 5.1

QUESTIONS TO ASK ON YOUR SPEECH TOPIC

1. Have I selected a topic that has value for my listeners?
2. Do I really care about this topic?
3. Does the topic satisfy the assignment?
4. Have I narrowed the topic sufficiently?
5. Can I develop responsible knowledge on this topic?

Browsing through current periodicals can give you ideas for speech topics.

Write out brief responses to these prompt questions. Try to come up with at least five alternatives for each question. Your interests chart might look like that in Figure 5.2.

Getting Ideas from the Media. Sometimes it is hard to come up with a list of topics. If your mind goes blank, try using newspapers or magazines to generate ideas. Go through the Sunday paper, scan *Time*, *Newsweek*, or *People*. Study the headlines, titles, advertisements, and pictures. What catches your attention? Add these topics to your interests chart.

One student developed an idea for a topic after seeing an advertisement for bank services. The ad stirred some unpleasant memories of having written a bad check. This suggested an informative speech on keeping better personal financial records. His problem was getting listeners to see the importance of this

Places	People	Activities
Livingston, MT	Cesar Chavez	hiking
Yellowstone Park	Sammy Sosa	fly fishing
New Orleans	Wilma Mankiller	basketball
Route 66	Charles Lindbergh	wood working
Manhattan	Sojourner Truth	traveling
Objects	**Events**	**Goals**
Kachinas	Olympics	starting own business
movie posters	hurricanes	work in NYC
antique fishing lures	canoeing the Colorado	visit Australia
political cartoons	Mardi Gras	physical fitness
graffiti	Cody Rodeo	have a family
Values	**Problems**	**Campus Concerns**
close family ties	air and water pollution	race relations
tolerance	yellow journalism	off-campus housing
physical fitness	substance abuse	date rape
respect	Internet censorship	campus security
world peace	prayer in schools	parking

FIGURE 5.2
Your Interests Chart

topic to their lives. His solution was to develop an introduction that startled the audience into attention.

> **Last month I committed a crime! I wrote a bad check, and it bounced. The check was for $4.67 to a local grocery store where I bought the makings of a spaghetti supper. The bank charged me $25.00 for the overdraft, and the store charged me $10.00 to retrieve my bad check. That was the most expensive spaghetti I've ever eaten!**

Consider an assignment in which students become "cultural ambassadors" presenting speeches to bring about an increased appreciation and understanding of another culture. The web sites at the end of Chapter 4 can be a good starting point for research on this topic. Encourage ESL students to represent their home cultures in their presentations. Be sure they research their topics in addition to using personal experience.

Similarly, the headline "Travel Money Tips Offered" might inspire you to speak on "Champagne Travel on a Beer Budget." Or the personals section in the classified ads might prompt a speech on "The Dangers of Computer Dating Services."

Be careful not to misuse media sources. The media can suggest ideas for speeches, but you can't simply summarize an article and use it as a speech. The article should be only a starting point for your thinking. *Your* speech must be *your* message, designed to appeal to *your* specific audience. You should always bring something new to your topic—a fresh insight or a special application for your listeners.

Matching Your Interests to Your Audience. Once you have completed your personal interests chart, make a similar chart of audience interests as revealed by class discussion and your audience analysis. What places, people, events, activities, objects, goals, values, problems, and campus concerns seem to spark discussions in class? Study the two charts together, looking for shared interests to pinpoint your best topic possibilities. To do this systematically, make a three-column **topic area inventory chart**. In the first column (your interests), list the subjects you find most appealing. In the second column (audience interests), list the subjects that seem uppermost in the minds of your listeners. In the third column, match columns one and two to find the most promising areas of speech topics. Figure 5.3 shows a sample topic area inventory chart.

Use the chalkboard to demonstrate use of the topic area inventory chart. Imagining yourself as speaker, complete the first column of personal interests. For the second column, construct a profile of audience interests as revealed by the interest charts previously elicited from students. During class discussion, ask class members to suggest possible speech topics in the third column as suggested by points of convergence between these columns.

In this example, your interests in travel and hiking are matched with the audience's interest in unusual places and developed into a possible speech topic area: "Weekend Adventures Close to Campus." Similarly, your concern for physical fitness is paired with the audience's interest in deceptive advertising to

Personal experiences, such as building houses for Habitat for Humanity, can be a useful source of examples or narratives for use in speeches.

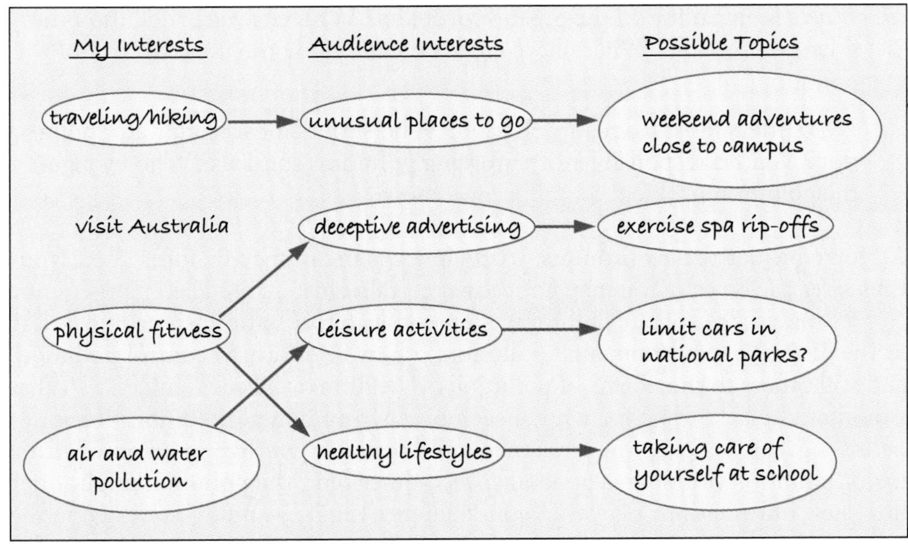

FIGURE 5.3
Topic Area Inventory Chart

generate another possible topic area: "Exercise Spa Rip-offs." Your interest in air and water pollution could combine with audience interests in leisure activities to lead to another topic area: "Should Cars Be Limited in Our National Parks?"

Focusing Your Topic

The problem with these topic areas is that they are areas, not actual topics for speeches. They may be too broad for a short classroom speech. You must narrow and focus them so they are more specific and more concrete. The importance of focusing your topic cannot be underestimated. As Winston Churchill once noted, "A speech is like a spotlight; the more focused it is, the more intense the light with a smaller area covered."[2]

To focus your topic properly, you need a system of analysis. You might ask the questions beginning reporters are taught to assure that they investigate a story thoroughly: what, why, when, how, where, and who. Not all these questions will apply to every topic area, but by working through the list systematically, you should be able to develop a number of possible topics. Let's take "Environmental Pollution" as a topic area and see where these questions can lead us:

1. *What* is environmental pollution? What are the major airborne pollutants? What are the major water pollutants? What causes environmental pollution? What are the effects of environmental pollution? What can we do to control environmental pollution? What can individuals do to reduce environmental pollution? What is the greatest pollution problem in our area?
2. *Why* do we have environmental pollution? Why are some companies reluctant to stop polluting? Why are some rural areas polluted? Why do some cities have more environmental pollution than others?
3. *When* did environmental pollution first become a problem? When did people first become concerned about environmental pollution? When was the first important book about environmental pollution published? When were the first laws protecting the environment passed?
4. *How* can air pollution be reduced? How can water pollution be reduced? How can companies be brought into compliance with pollution laws? How can individuals help reduce pollution?

5. *Where* is air pollution the greatest problem? Where is water pollution the greatest problem? Where have cities or states done the most to control pollution?
6. *Who* suffers most from air pollution? Who suffers most from water pollution? Who is responsible for enforcing pollution controls? Who brought the pollution problem to public awareness?

Using the topic analysis prompts, ask students to brainstorm a topic area and post their ideas on the chalkboard. What ideas for specific speech topics emerge from this analysis?

As you consider the six prompts, write down as many specific ideas about your topic area as you can. You may notice that certain clusters of ideas emerge: some entries may center on air pollution, some on water pollution; some may relate to the history of environmental pollution, others to efforts to control pollution, and still others to the effects of pollution on wildlife or business interests. What would be the best topic for your speech on environmental pollution? That depends a great deal on your audience and locale. If you live in an area with a major pollution problem, a general speech describing the pollution might offer little new information. However, your audience might be quite interested in the history of environmental legislation or in local efforts to solve the problems. On the other hand, if you live in an area where pollution is not an immediate or apparent problem, you may need to work hard to convince listeners that they should be concerned about the situation.

Your final choice of a topic should be made in light of your purpose: what you hope to accomplish in your speech for the benefit of your listeners. We shall discuss purpose in the next section and defer discussion of the final selection process until then.

Our example of topic analysis has related to an informative speech topic. The same type of analysis also can be used to find topics for persuasive speeches. Because persuasion often addresses problems, you simply change the focus of the questions and add a few that are specific to persuasive situations:

1. *Who* is affected by this problem?
2. *What* are the most important issues?
3. *Why* did the problem arise?
4. *Where* is this problem happening?
5. *When* did the problem begin?
6. *How* is this problem like or unlike previous problems?
7. *How* extensive is the problem?
8. *What* options are available for dealing with the problem?

Selecting Your Topic

After you have completed the interests charts and analyzed the topic areas they suggest, two or three specific topics should emerge as important and appealing possibilities. Now you should ask of each:

- Does this topic fit the assignment?
- Could I give a speech on this topic in the time available?
- Can I learn enough about this topic to give a responsible speech?
- Why would I want to speak on this topic?

As you consider your options in light of these questions, a final choice should become clear.

Determining Your Purpose

As you lay the foundations for your speech, you must consider its general function, determine your specific purpose, and develop a clearly worded thesis statement and preview.

General Function

Invitations to speak outside class will usually indicate the **general function** for your speech. In class, the general function is usually assigned. The three general functions of speeches are to inform, to persuade, or to celebrate. The general function of a speech to inform is to share knowledge with listeners. If your general function is to persuade, you will advise listeners how to believe or act and give them sound reasons to accept your advice. A speech of celebration emphasizes the importance of an occasion, event, or person. Speeches of celebration include tributes, eulogies, toasts, after-dinner speeches, and inspirational messages. Although it is easy to separate these functions on paper, they often overlap in practice. For example, Marge Anderson, chief executive of the Mille Lacs Band of the Ojibwe, informed her mainstream Minnesota audience of her people's contributions to the larger community, extolled the values of her culture, and urged listeners to begin a dialogue of learning, understanding, and appreciation—all in the same speech (reprinted in Appendix C).

As we noted earlier, people who invite you to speak outside the classroom will usually suggest the general function for your speech. One of your authors was recently invited to speak to the county historical society on his work with Humanities Tennessee. He knows that this audience will be most interested in the council's grants for local activities in the humanities. His speech will be largely informative, but he will also introduce himself and try to create good feelings toward the organization. Were he to use the occasion to launch an attack on senators who want to reduce financial support for the arts and humanities, he would violate the audience's expectations by presenting a persuasive speech. That would be his last invitation to address the Decatur County Historical Society!

Specific Purpose

Your **specific purpose** helps focus your topic. It spells out what you want your listeners to understand, believe, feel, or do. Having a specific purpose clearly in mind helps direct your research toward relevant information so that you don't waste valuable time. You should be able to state your specific purpose clearly as a single sentence. Let's look at how a specific purpose statement gives focus to your speech:

Topic:	National parks
General function:	To inform
Specific purpose:	To inform my audience about hiking trails in Shenandoah National Park
Topic:	Greenhouse effect
General function:	To persuade

Specific purpose:	To persuade my audience that the greenhouse effect poses a serious threat to our environment

Ask students to frame a specific purpose for a topic of their choice. Write these statements on the board and see if the class can improve them. Impress upon students the need to have clear goals for what they wish to accomplish.

How can you tell if you have a good specific purpose? Your specific purpose should ensure that you provide listeners with new or useful information or advice. When you tell listeners something they already know, you simply bore them and waste their time. Your specific purpose also should be manageable in the time allotted to you. In a five-minute speech you have only about seven hundred words to get your message across. If you can't cover the material in the time allowed, then you must narrow your focus to something you can handle. Let's look at some examples of poor specific purpose statements and see how they might be improved:

Poor:	To inform my audience about our national parks
Improved:	To inform my audience of three lesser-known attractions in Yellowstone Park
Poor:	To persuade my audience that driving while distracted is dangerous
Improved:	To persuade my audience not to talk on a cell phone while driving

In the first example, the specific purpose is too general. It does not narrow the topic sufficiently. With this *nonspecific* purpose you could prepare a speech on the fate of grizzly bears in Yellowstone Park, on the differences between national parks and national forests, on national parks in urban areas, or on a multitude of other related subjects. The *improved* version limits the topic so that it can be handled within the time permitted. This helps you concentrate your research on those materials most useful to your speech.

The second *poor* specific purpose is also too vague and general, and tells the audience nothing new. Who would argue that driving while distracted is not dangerous? The *improved* version focuses more precisely on a contemporary problem.

Thesis Statement and Preview

Most of the time your specific purpose will be reflected in the **thesis statement** of your speech. The thesis statement condenses your message into a single declarative sentence. It is often offered as you introduce your speech so that listeners will understand your intentions from the outset. Notice how the following speaker presents his thesis statement:

> **Today I want to discuss a moral blight on our campus—the problem of date rape—and what we can do about it.**

ESL: ESL students may have special problems developing speeches in a linear fashion. Show them that the preview statement is a key step toward developing and structuring their speeches.

The thesis statement will often be followed by a **preview**. The preview signals the main points that will be developed in the body of the speech. In effect, it presents an agenda for the speech:

> **I will define date rape, show its causes and consequences, and end with some advice on how to prevent it.**

By foreshadowing the three main points of the speech, the preview helps audience members listen effectively, thereby reducing misunderstandings.

In ethical speaking, the thesis statement will reveal the speaker's specific purpose. *But let the listener beware!* Not all speakers will be totally candid. Although a speaker's specific purpose may be to sell listeners an encyclopedia, the thesis statement may suggest a different intention altogether:

> **I want to help you improve the quality of your lives by offering you—free of charge—this wonderful encyclopedia set [thesis statement]. Your only obligation is to let us mention you as a satisfied customer when we are selling encyclopedias in this community. And of course we ask that you do keep your set up to date for the next ten years by purchasing the annual supplements at a special discount rate.**

Such disguised intentions may seem fairly trivial (unless you find yourself responsible for purchasing the set in ten installments!). But if you substitute a political philosophy or a religious cause for an encyclopedia, you can see how serious the problem can become. The greater the distance between the hidden specific purpose and the thesis statement actually expressed in the speech, the larger the ethical problem.

At times ethical speakers may omit the thesis statement from their presentations, leaving it to be constructed by listeners from cues within the speech. Note how Cecile Larson left the thesis statement implicit in her speech "The 'Monument' at Wounded Knee," which appears in Appendix C. Speakers may leave the thesis statement unstated to create a dramatic effect as listeners discover it for themselves. Although it has some artistic merit, this technique also entails considerable risk. Listeners may miss the point! In most cases, speakers should integrate the thesis statement into the introduction of their speeches.

Within a speech, the thesis statement should adapt your specific purpose to listeners in a way calculated to gain their attention. In like manner, the preview should raise curiosity and motivate listening. Note how the language grows more colorful and personal as one moves from specific purpose to preview in the following examples:

Have students read a speech from Appendix C and write out the specific purpose, thesis statement, and preview of the speech. If any of these elements are missing, have them comment on how this affects the speech.

Specific purpose:	To inform my audience about three less famous attractions in Yellowstone Park
Thesis statement:	Today I want to introduce you to three remarkable features of Yellowstone Park that are often missing from your guidebook.
Preview:	I will take you on a brief tour of the Fountain Paint Pots, the Grand Canyon of the Yellowstone, and the Firehole River.

Specific purpose:	To persuade listeners to lobby state representatives to support the bill limiting cell phone use by drivers
Thesis statement:	Limiting cell phone use by drivers could help you avoid a serious accident and might even save your life.
Preview:	I want to show you, first, how "driving while distracted" by the cell phone causes many serious accidents; second, how a bill now pending before the legislature could reduce this hazard; and third, how you as a citizen can help make this bill a reality.

Let us now look at the entire process of moving from general topic area to preview to see how these steps may evolve in speech preparation:

Topic area:	Vacations in the United States
Topic:	Camping in the Rockies
General function:	To inform

Specific purpose:	To inform my audience that there are beautiful, uncrowded places to camp in the Rockies
Thesis statement:	You can get off the beaten path and find some wild and wonderful places to camp in the Rockies.
Preview:	Three beautiful yet uncrowded camping areas in the Rockies are Bridger-Teton National Forest in Wyoming, St. Charles Canyon in Idaho, and Dinosaur National Monument in Utah.

A speech titled "Camping in the Rockies: Getting Off the Beaten Path" might then take the following form:

Introduction:	Page 43 of the tour guide to Grand Teton National Park reveals this idyllic picture of camping. [Show enlarged photo] As you can see, the area is beautiful and uncrowded. With this picture in mind, I went on my first camping trip to the Rockies two summers ago. Was I ever disappointed! After a long drive I arrived at Jenny Lake campground about two in the afternoon—early enough to set up camp, take a hike, and prepare a leisurely dinner. But, no! All the campsites had been taken since eight-thirty that morning. Not only were no sites available, but after driving through the campground, I realized I wouldn't have wanted to camp there anyway. Hundreds of tents were crowded on top of one another. It looked like a refugee relocation center after a disaster. And it wasn't only the crowding that was bad, but the noise! Radios and television sets blasted you with an unholy mixture of music and game shows and soap operas. I might just as well have been back in our freshman dorm.
Transition:	Not every camping area in the Rockies is like this.
Thesis statement:	You can get off the beaten path and find some wild and wonderful places to camp in the Rockies.
Preview:	Three of the most interesting, beautiful, and uncrowded are Bridger-Teton National Forest in Wyoming, St. Charles Canyon in Idaho, and the Dinosaur National Monument in Utah.
Main points:	1. Bridger-Teton National Forest at Slide Lake has a magnificent view of the Tetons. [Show enlarged photo] 2. St. Charles Canyon, on a whitewater stream, offers the ultimate in seclusion. [Show enlarged photo] 3. At Dinosaur National Monument you can watch the excavation of gigantic skeletons that are millions of years old. [Photo]
Transition and conclusion:	There are interesting, beautiful, and uncrowded places to camp if you know where to look. Try the National Forest Service campgrounds or national monuments rather than the overcrowded national parks. Last summer I enjoyed the peace and serenity of Slide Lake while reveling in its view of the

> Tetons. I caught native cutthroat trout in secluded St. Charles Canyon and studied the ancient petroglyphs at Dinosaur National Monument. I can't wait to get back!

Although the thesis statement appears in the foregoing example, you will note that the speaker *does not* begin with "My thesis statement is . . ." Rather, it appears naturally in the introduction as a lead into the preview. Both thesis statement and preview suggest that this speech should give us interesting information, vivid examples, and engaging stories. The thesis statement indicates what kind of informative speech we will hear (descriptive), and the preview implies the overall design or pattern the speech will follow (categorical).

With a clear thesis statement in mind, speakers can focus their research to acquire responsible knowledge of the topic. In this case the speaker might use materials obtained at the sites, attendance figures from almanacs or newspaper articles, and materials available in the government documents section of the library or on the Internet.

Acquiring Responsible Knowledge

Although we have discussed selecting and focusing your topic before taking up research, your background reading for a speech often begins before you form your thesis statement. To determine your approach and the main points you will develop, you will probably have to find out more about your topic. Once you have your specific purpose in mind, you can begin a quest for responsible knowledge. **Responsible knowledge** is the most comprehensive understanding of your topic that you can acquire in the time available for preparation. It includes information on

This is a good time to discuss the differences between information and opinions. Direct students to the strategic research worksheet (Figure 5.6); have them use it as a guide for acquiring responsible knowledge.

- the main issues concerning your topic.
- what respected authorities say about it.
- the latest developments relevant to it.
- related local applications of special interest to your audience.

When you ask an audience for their time and attention, you must give them something of value in return. Having responsible knowledge earns you the right to speak.[3] It allows you to enrich the lives of listeners with good information or advice. Whenever you speak, you put your mind and character on display. If you haven't made an effort to acquire responsible knowledge, you are saying, in effect, "I haven't much to offer, and I really don't care." On the other hand, having responsible knowledge should enhance your perceived ethos in terms of both competence and character.[4]

Although you cannot become an authority on most topics with ten hours or even ten days of research, you can certainly learn enough to speak responsibly. The major sources of information available to you are your own knowledge and experience, Internet and library resources, and interviews. Each of these sources can supply facts, testimony, examples, or narratives to use as supporting materials in your speech.

As you pursue your quest for responsible knowledge, keep in mind the checklist offered in Figure 5.4, "Quest for Responsible Knowledge." It offers an

FIGURE 5.4
Quest for Responsible Knowledge

- [ ] I have explored my personal knowledge of my topic.
- [ ] I have expanded my knowledge of the topic by consulting general and/or specialized dictionaries or encyclopedias.
- [ ] I have checked newspaper indexes and recent news magazines to assure that my information is up-to-date.
- [ ] I have used Internet and library search services to identify books and articles on my subject.
- [ ] I have looked for materials in periodicals to enrich my speech.
- [ ] I have considered the usefulness of the following sources:
    - [ ] atlases
    - [ ] biographical resources
    - [ ] books of quotations
    - [ ] almanacs
    - [ ] government documents
- [ ] I have looked for local applications of my topic using the indexing services and searching local newspaper indexes and abstracts.
- [ ] I have interviewed experts about my topic.

overview of possible resources. Not every source will be appropriate for every speech, and for any given speech, some sources will be much more appropriate than others. By checking off the items one by one as they apply in your situation, you can be assured that you have conducted the research phase of your speech preparation thoroughly and systematically.

Because your preparation time will be limited, you should begin by developing a research strategy. Having a strategy will help you make more efficient use of your time and enable you to locate and evaluate the materials you need. You should begin by assessing your personal knowledge and experience to determine what additional information you might need to make a responsible presentation. Next, you should develop a strategy for obtaining this information by accessing library resources, using the Internet, and/or interviewing for information and opinions. Finally, you should conduct your research and make note cards to use as you organize your speech.

Personal Knowledge and Experience

Personal knowledge and experience add credibility, authenticity, and interest to a speech. You may not be an acknowledged authority on a subject, but personal stories may suggest that you have a special kind of intimate knowledge of it. They may make it easier for an audience to identify with you and the topic.[5]

If you lack direct experience with a topic, you can always try to arrange some. Suppose you are planning a speech on how local television stations prepare newscasts. You have gathered information from books and periodicals, but it seems rather dry and lifeless. Call a local television station and ask the news director if it would be possible for you to spend an afternoon in the newsroom of the station so that you can get a feel for what goes on during that hectic time right before a broadcast. Take in the noise, the action, and the excitement that occurs before and during a show. All of this can help enrich your speech. You might also try to schedule an interview with the news director while you are at the station (see the "Interviewing for Information" section later in this chapter).

As valuable as it is, experience is rarely sufficient to provide all the information, facts and figures, and testimony that you will need for your speech. Your personal knowledge may be limited, the sources from which you learned may have been biased, or your experiences may not have been typical. Even people who are acknowledged authorities on a subject look to other experts to give credence to their messages. Use personal knowledge and experience as a starting point and expand it through research. Prepare a personal knowledge and experience summary sheet similar to the one shown in Figure 5.5. Include on your summary sheet what you know (or think you know) about the topic, where or how you learned it, and what additional information you might need to find. Also jot down any examples or narratives based on your experience so that you can remember them as you put your speech together. Use your summary sheet to give direction to your research.

The Internet as a Research Tool

The Internet offers a wealth of information that is easily accessible to students, either through their own personal computers or through those provided by the campus library.

Chances are you have already used the Internet. Over 98 percent of all secondary schools were using the Internet in 1999, and at least three out of every four teens have been online.[6] If you are a beginner, the following books and web sites might be helpful:

John R. Levine, Carol Baroudi, and Margaret Levine Young, *The Internet for Dummies* (IDG Books, latest edition).

Joe Kraynak, *The Absolute Beginners Guide to Computers and the Internet* (Que Corp., 2001).

The Complete Internet Guide and Web Tutorial. http://www.microsoft.com/insider/internet/default.htm

Internet Tutorial for Internet Explorer. http://www.kokomo.lib.in.us/it/class/int/intintro.htm

FIGURE 5.5
Personal Knowledge Summary

What I Know (or Think I Know)	Where/How I Learned It	What I Need to Find Out
Not many grizzly bears in park	Worked there 2 summers. Heard rangers talk about it, only saw 1 and I was looking	Approximately how many bears are in the park
Go to back country to see the grizzlies	Same as above/personal experience	Where in park they are most likely to be seen; specify trails and areas
Grizzly attacks are rare	Same as above	When was first attack recorded? Last? # of attacks relative to # of tourists; relative to other types of injuries
Camping precautions	See above, brochure, personal experience	Information probably sufficient

Examples/Narratives I Might Use in Speech:

For the past two summers I've worked waiting tables at Mammoth Springs Lodge in Yellowstone Park. We got two days a week off, and I spent nearly all my free time hiking and camping in the back country, far away from the tourists and crowds in the park. I counted up the number of hours I spent that way and discovered that I had logged in more than 350 hours in these remote locations—in the grizzly bear habitat of the park—hoping to see one. Only once, in all those hours, did I see a grizzly bear, and that was from a distance of about half a mile. If I hadn't been sitting quietly with my binoculars focused on a watering area, I probably would have missed seeing that one!

To ensure responsible knowledge in your speeches, carefully evaluate materials you find on the Internet.

Even if you have been online, your experience may not have prepared you to do college-level research on the Internet. A recent report in *USA Today* noted that over half of the school-based Internet traffic went to one hundred popular sites. By far, students spent more time on entertainment and consumer-oriented sites than on educational or news sites.[7] Moreover, observed the report, "Students are just flailing around the Web. They're wasting time using ineffective techniques for finding information." Some of these problems result from the way we have been trained to do library research, which doesn't always transfer easily into doing research on the Internet. According to a recent article in *USA Today*:

> **We expect the Internet to be a nice, tidy library staffed by helpful reference librarians. It more resembles a giant refrigerator covered with old cartoons. . . . Somewhere on that refrigerator, under the dry-cleaning receipts and photo Christmas cards of babies who are entering college, is an article from a respected, peer-reviewed medical journal evaluating ultrasound as a valid follow-up diagnostic technique after an abnormal mammogram. It's that article that you need now—but after you type in "ultrasound," you have to sift through the "7,235 matches found" to get it.[8]**

To make your web-based research efficient, you have to learn how to use the Internet search engines. There are many different search engines available. You have probably used one of the more popular ones such as Yahoo! (http://www.yahoo.com), but you may not know that there are a variety of more advanced search sites on the Net. Because there is often little overlap among engines, it is best to run more than one search using more than one search engine. InterConnections.LearnMore 5.1 provides information on some search engines that may be of use to you. You also need to learn how to conduct a Boolean search to limit or expand the information you retrieve (see Speaker's Notes 5.2, "Tips for Conducting a Boolean Search").

Some final suggestions on using the Internet to search for material: When you access an article, be sure to jot down the specific information you will need to document the source before you save the information on your computer. Note the author's name and credentials if stated, the sponsoring source, the date of publication, date of access, and the URL or web address, which may be lost once you download. Better still, save the link with your favorites or bookmark command so that you can easily revisit all of this information. One final caution: Be very careful when typing in the web address of an Internet site you wish to reach. Once, when trying to access a popular computer magazine online, one of

InterConnections.LearnMore 5.1

INTERNET SEARCH ENGINES

All Academic **http://www.allacademic.com**
Provides a search of free academic resources and journals online.

Ixquick **http://www.ixquick.com**
Searches many prominent search engines simultaneously and eliminates duplicates

Northern Light **http://www.northernlight.com**
Organizes hits into category folders to help you focus your search.

Oingo **http://www.oingo.com**
Has drop-down boxes that ask you how you want to limit your hunt for sites.

Raging Search (from AltaVista)
http://www.altavista.com/sites/search/text?raging=1
Provides one of the fastest searches available.

your authors inadvertently typed in ".net" rather than ".com," and she ended up at a porn site! To see what this minor difference in a web address can mean, access and compare the following sites:

http://www.whitehouse.net
and
http://www.whitehouse.gov

Evaluating Internet Research

It has been said—and it certainly is true!—that anyone can put anything on the Internet. This being the case, how can you be sure that the information you find satisfies the requirements of responsible knowledge? One way to approach this problem is to apply the critical thinking skills discussed in Chapter 3. In addition to using these basic skills, you should consider the following guidelines that are applicable to Internet materials. Begin by evaluating the source of the material:

Speaker's Notes 5.2

TIPS FOR CONDUCTING A BOOLEAN SEARCH

1. Use AND or a plus sign to focus your search:
   mammogram AND ultrasound or mammogram+ultrasound.
2. Use OR or a slash mark to broaden your search:
   mammogram OR ultrasound or mammogram/ultrasound.
3. Use NOT or a minus sign to restrict or narrow your search:
   Lions NOT NFL or Lions-NFL.
4. Use NEAR when words should be close to each other in the document:
   moon NEAR river.
5. Use quotation marks to be more specific in your search:
   Baltimore Preparatory School gives 2,765 hits.
   "Baltimore Preparatory School" gives 275 hits.
6. When all else fails, read the instructions under "Advanced Search Tips" on the search engine home page.

Have students download and print out an Internet article on a topic they are considering for a speech. Have them use these guidelines to evaluate the source and information in the article.

- Is the author of the document identified?
- Is a URL or email address provided?
- Are the credentials of the source listed?
- Is the source an authority on the specific subject?
- Does he or she list a professional affiliation? occupation? educational background?
- Can you verify the credentials of the source?
- Check the home page of the web site (to find the home page, delete all information in the source URL after the server name).
- Run a search with the author's name in quotation marks.
- Check organizations/associations via the Scholarly Societies Project at http://www.lib.uwaterloo.ca/society/overview.html.
- Run a search with the name of the organization/association in quotation marks.

Evaluate the information provided:

- Is the source of statistical information identified?
- Are dates of information within the document provided? Is the information recent?
- When was the document last updated?
- Is the information linked to other sources you can check?
- Is a bibliography provided?
- How does this compare with other information in the field?
- Are differing points of view presented?
- Is there more sizzle than substance in the document?
- Are the spelling and grammar correct?
- Is the writing clear or obscure?

If the material satisfies these tests, it probably can be relied on as a source of responsible knowledge. You can find a list of useful web sites in the "Guide to Library and Internet Resources" following this chapter.

Using Library and Internet Resources

Arrange a library tour for your students that focuses on how to find materials that will be useful for speeches.

Begin your adventure into research by developing a research strategy. The "Research Strategy Worksheet" shown in Figure 5.6 (page 138) should help you plan your research efficiently. Have your topic and specific purpose clearly in mind before you begin. Work back and forth between your strategy worksheet and the major resources for preparing speeches until you are satisfied that you have gained responsible knowledge.

The major resources available for speakers include (1) sources of background information, (2) sources of access to information, (3) sources of in-depth information, (4) sources of current information, and (5) sources of local information. You should use all of these resources to acquire responsible knowledge of your subject. In this section we explore the types of resources available and show you how to prepare a research strategy that will help you use your time efficiently.

Sources of Background Information. Even if you feel you know almost everything you need to know about your topic, you should begin by reading

Sources for Current Information

Facts on File: A Weekly Digest of World Events with Cumulative Index
Recent issues of newspapers
Recent issues of periodicals, especially newsweeklies

Sources for Local Applications

City or state magazines from your area
Index to major local or area newspapers
Vertical File Index

Search Engines, Directories, and Libraries

Internet Resources

Argus Clearing House **http://www.clearinghouse.net** Topical guides to web sites.

Ask Eric **http://ericir.syr.edu/** The online search engine of the Educational Resources Information Center (ERIC); large collection of resources on educational issues.

Internet Public Library **http://www.ipl.org/** An easy-to-access cyberlibrary maintained as a public service by the University of Michigan School of Information.

Libraries Online **http://library.usask.ca/hytelnet/usa/usall.html** A directory of links to libraries in the United States.

New York Times Navigator **http://www.nytimes.com/library/tech/reference/cynavi.html** Annotated links to interesting web sites; frequently updated.

Research It **http://www.itools.com/research-it/** Tools for tracking down quotations; retrieving biographical, geographical, and financial information; translating terms from language to language; etc.

Scoop **http://scoop.evansville.net** Designed for journalists; links to an interesting assortment of web sites, classified by topic.

Health Issues

Centers for Disease Control and Prevention **http://www.cdc.gov** An online digest of information on current public health issues, including news, statistics, and reports.

Merck **http://www.merck.com/** A guide to diseases, disorders, and prescription medications.

National Library of Medicine **http://www.nlm.nih.gov/** Health information, publications, research reports, and news in medicine; maintained by the National Institutes of Health.

Prevention **http://www.prevention.com/** The online version of the popular medical magazine.

World Health Organization **http://www.who.int/home-page/** News, information, and updates on humanitarian relief by a consortium of medical personnel from around the world.

Museums and Art Galleries

American Museum of Natural History **http://www.amnh.org/home/index.html** Information on exhibits, history, and an online edition of this New York City museum's magazine.

Louvre **http://www.louvre.fr** The official web site of the Louvre; information on collections, special exhibits, and virtual tours.

Museum Computer Network **http://www.mcn.edu/sitesonline.htm** Special interest forums and links to over 1,000 museum and museum-related sites.

Smithsonian **http://www.si.edu/i+d** The web site of *Increase and Diffusion*, a Smithsonian web magazine; articles and information on the various museums in the system.

Environmental Concerns

EnviroLink Network **http://envirolink.netforchange.com** An environmental and animal concerns web site with news and links to educational and government resources. Network for Change is currently developing this web site in partnership with the EnviroLink Network and the Animal Concerns Community as a comprehensive resource for individuals, organizations, and businesses working for social and environmental change.

Greenpeace **http://www.greenpeace.org/** An activist environmental web site; news on ongoing campaigns involving climate, toxics, nuclear power, oceans, genetic engineering, and forests.

National Environmental Information Service **http://www.eco-web.com** Information on environmental organizations, conferences, publications, products, and services; indexed by problem area.

Sierra Club **http://www.sierraclub.org/** The official web site of the Sierra Club; news, feature articles, and an energy saving guide.

Books and Literature

Complete Works of Shakespeare **http://tech-two.mit.edu/Shakespeare/works.html** Links to full-text versions of the works of William Shakespeare.

Online Books Page **http://digital.library.upenn.edu/books/** Over 14,000 links to full-text manuscripts of classics and other titles that are not under copyright or that have been given reprint permission; hosted by the University of Pennsylvania. This site was founded, and is edited, by John Mark Ockerbloom. He is a digital library planner and researcher at the University of Pennsylvania. He is solely responsible for the content of the site.

Project Gutenberg **http://www.promo.net/pg/** A large full-text book repository of material no longer under copyright, including major classics; searchable by author or title.

News

AJR Newslink **http://ajr.newslink.org** The official web site of the *American Journalism Review;* articles about journalism and journalists, plus links to newspapers, magazines, radio and television stations, and news services.

College News Online **http://www.collegenews.com/campusnews.htm** A directory of links to student-run, college and university newspapers; indexed by campus.

News Directory **http://www.newsdirectory.com** A directory of worldwide links to more than 14,500 newspapers and TV stations searchable by country, state, and region; magazine database of links searchable by type and topic. "NewsDirectory is your guide to all online English-language media . . . newspapers, magazines, television stations, colleges, visitor bureaus, governmental agencies and more . . ."

TV News Archive **http://tvnews.vanderbilt.edu/** A searchable database of newscasts from ABC, CBS, and NBC, plus news specials; online abstracts/transcripts back to 1968; videotapes of newscasts available; maintained by Vanderbilt University.

MAJOR U.S. NEWSMAGAZINES AND NEWSPAPERS

Los Angeles Times **http://www.latimes.com/**
New York Times **http://www.nytimes.com**
Newsweek **http://www.newsweek.com**
Time **http://www.time.com/time/index.html**
U.S. News & World Report **http://www.usnews.com**
USA Today **http://www.usatoday.com**
Washington Post **http://www.washingtonpost.com/**

Communication—General

Archives of American Public Address **http://douglass.speech.nwu.edu/** An electronic archive of American oratory; maintained by Northwestern University.

Gifts of Speech **http://ripley.wo.sbc.edu/departmental/library/gos/** Texts of women's speeches presented from around the world, including texts of lectures given by female Nobel laureates; maintained by Sweet Briar College.

Historical Speeches Archive **http://www.webcorp.com/sounds/index.htm** An audio archive of clips from famous, contemporary speeches.

National Communication Association **http://www.natcom.org** The official web site of a professional association serving communication instructors and students.

Science—General

Discovery **http://www.discovery.com** The online accompaniment to the TV channel; interactive, in-depth coverage of topics from current programs.

Science Frontiers **http://www.knowledge.co.uk/frontiers/** Articles on scientific anomalies that challenge prevailing scientific thinking.

Science News **http://www.sciencenews.org** The online version of the weekly magazine; some articles from the print edition, plus a searchable archive.

Scientific American **http://www.sciam.com/** The online edition; science news, articles, and archives of past issues.

Humanities—General

Biography Find **http://www.biography.com** Biographical information and articles on contemporary celebrities and people in the news.

EDSITEment **http://edsitement.neh.fed.us** Learning activities in literature and language arts, foreign languages, art and culture, history and social studies.

HistoryNet **http://www.thehistorynet.com/** Online articles and information on World and American history, the Civil War, and World War II; archived with a site search tool.

H-Net **http://h-net2.msu.edu/** Articles and discussions on the humanities and social sciences; maintained by Michigan State University.

Philanthropies and Charities

International Service Agencies **http://www.charity.org** A directory of U.S.-based, international service agencies offering humanitarian and disaster relief for families and children.

Nonprofit Organizations on the Internet **http://www.fiu.edu/~time4chg/non-profit.html** A directory with links to nonprofit organizations; sponsored and maintained by Florida International University.

United Way **http://www.unitedway.org** A gateway with links to local chapters and information on health and human services activities and issues.

Government and Politics

Central Intelligence Agency **http://www.cia.gov** Interesting unclassified information about the workings of this agency; detailed, almanac-type information on the countries of the world available in site's *World Fact Book.*

Great American Web Site **http://www.uncle-sam.com** A citizen's guide to government web sites.

Library of Congress **http://www.loc.gov** Online catalogues with special sections on legislative information, exhibits, collections, and services; excellent "American Memory" archive of words, sounds, and pictures of American history.

U.S. Census Bureau **http://www.census.gov** Immediate online access to the latest census information as it becomes available.

U.S. House of Representatives **http://www.house.gov** The official web site of the U.S. House of Representatives; information on legislation and a source of contact with your representative.

U.S. Senate **http://www.senate.gov** The official web site of the U.S. Senate; information on legislation and a source of contact with your senators.

White House **http://www.whitehouse.gov** The official web site of the presidency; links to full texts of speeches and press conferences.

Business and Commerce

Business Connections **http://www.nytimes.com/library/cyber/reference/busconn.html** An extensive directory to business links on the Internet. This *New York Times* web site describes itself as "a selective guide to Internet business, financial, and investing resources."

Business Week **http://www.businessweek.com** The online version of the magazine; continuously updated with business news from Reuters and stock market reports.

Business Women's Network **http://www.bwni.com** An interactive web site with news and articles of interest to women in the workplace.

Forbes **http://www.forbes.com** The online version of the financial magazine; articles on investing and other financial topics.

Fortune **http://www.fortune.com** The online version of the magazine; articles of interest on financial and investment topics.

Inc. **http://www.inc.com** An extensive assortment of articles and advice on starting up and running a business.

Language

AmeriSpeak **http://www.rootsweb.com/~genepool/amerispeak.htm** Phrases and idioms no longer in use, with their contemporary equivalents.

Jack Lynch's Grammar Notes **http://andromeda.rutgers.edu/~jlynch/Writing** A guide to grammar and style with rules, explanations, common errors, and usage suggestions.

Language Trivia **http://www.bluerider.com/english/trivia.htm** Interesting tidbits on unusual aspects of English usage.

Slanguage **http://www.slanguage.com** A fun site cataloging regional and foreign slang.

Legal Concerns

Decisions of U.S. Supreme Court **http://supct.law.cornell.edu/supct/index.html** Supreme Court Collection maintained by the Legal Information Institute. Information on current decisions and pending cases, with links to historical documents.

Findlaw **http://www.findlaw.com** A directory of online, legal resources for professionals, students, and the public, with daily news updates and a site search tool.

Internet Legal Resource Guide **http://www.law.utexas.edu/research** A directory with guides to state, federal, and international legal resources online; sponsored by the University of Texas School of Law.

Law.Com **http://www.law.com** News and articles of interest, updated daily.

6

Using Supporting Materials in Your Speech

OUTLINE

THIS CHAPTER WILL HELP YOU

- understand the importance of supporting materials
- select the best supporting materials for your speeches
- learn how to use supporting materials to best advantage

Our home stands atop a ridgeline several hundred feet above the Tennessee River. The terrain slopes at about a 45-degree angle, so that while the front of the home rests on solid earth, the back of it rises on posts some thirty feet above the ground. You might think that the structure is flimsy, but actually it is quite strong. Our builders selected quality wood, concrete, plastics, and steel and formed these materials into powerful supports.

In the next several chapters we will think of you as a builder—a builder of ideas. We will think of your speeches as thought structures raised up on solid pillars of supporting materials. Like our builders, you must know your materials and what they can support. You need to know how to select them and how to use them wisely. Just as our home is built to withstand storms and high winds, your speech must withstand doubt and even controversy. When you stand to present it, you must be confident of its structural integrity.

Facts and statistics, testimony, examples, and narratives are the major forms of **supporting materials** used in the building of speeches. *Their essential functions are to arouse and sustain interest, to explain the meaning of your ideas, to make your interpretations credible, to point out their importance to listeners, and to verify controversial statements.*

Your personal experience, Internet and library research, and interviews with experts, described in Chapter 5, should have provided you with a good stockpile of these materials. We will discuss each type of supporting material, how to identify good and defective forms of it, how to know when it can be most useful, and how to put it to work in your speeches.

The universe is made up of stories, not of atoms.

—Muriel Rukeyser

Facts and Statistics

Facts and statistics are the most objective forms of supporting material. They do not depend on the experience of one person or group but rather are confirmed consistently in human experience. This means that you can count on them to add credibility to your ideas. If "the facts are in your favor," this creates a presumption that what you are saying is true. Therefore, facts and statistics are especially important when your topic is unfamiliar or your ideas are controversial.

Have students select one of the student speeches reprinted in this text and identify the forms of support. Ask them to remove the forms, one by one. As they take away each, what does the speech lose? When all forms of support are removed, what is left?

Facts

The factual test of a speech is the extent to which it is grounded in reality or feeds on illusion. The more an issue means to us, the more concerned we are that the speech be grounded in reality. Richard Weaver, a prominent communication critic writing in the 1950s, suggested that Americans honor **facts** and numbers as the highest form of knowledge, much as some other societies respect divine revelation.[1] A 1994 Gallup survey confirmed that 86 percent of those polled agree that "references to scientific research in a story increased its credibility."[2] We still worship at the altar of science.

ESL students and some non-ESL students may come from backgrounds in which facts are relatively unimportant, or even suspect, as a form of support. In some cultures, prestige testimony by revered elders and religious narratives may be more prized. See if any of these backgrounds are represented among your students. Ask these students to explain how messages are supported in their culture.

The following statements are factual because they can be shown to be either true or false:

Chevrolet Tahoe is an American-made utility vehicle.

Most students at our school earn their degree in five years.

Television ads often rely on emotional appeals.

Relate the discussion of facts to the first speeches presented in class. In what instances might more facts have improved or strengthened the speeches?

Although factual statements can stand by themselves, speakers rarely use them without interpreting them. Interpretations usually add a few judgmental or value terms that transform factual statements into **claims**:

Chevrolet Tahoe is a *superior* American-made utility vehicle.

Most *hard-working* students at our school earn their degree in five years.

Television ads often rely on *unethical* emotional appeals.

There is nothing wrong with making interpretations or claims. We often need to shape factual statements so that they reflect our point of view. The problem comes when speakers and audiences forget that these are no longer simply factual statements that require only minimal demonstration. The addition of such words as *superior*, *hard-working*, or *unethical* means that these speakers have assumed another burden of support. They now must produce other facts or statistics, examples, testimony, or stories to prove that the claims are justified—that they are more than just expressions of personal feeling or **opinions**.

We usually cannot verify directly the accuracy of such claims. We have no idea how we might proceed on our own to verify that Chevrolet Tahoes actually are "superior." We therefore have to look to independent authorities who have the reputation of competence and who claim to have no economic ax to grind. So we might say in a speech, "According to the latest issue of *Consumer Reports*, which did extensive tests with many utility vehicles, the Chevrolet Tahoe is superior." If our reading of *Consumer Reports* is correct, we have introduced additional support for our claim. This support comes in the form of expert testimony, which we discuss later in this chapter. Incidentally, note also how we

ESL students may not be familiar with print sources of political opinion in this country. Bring several periodicals and newspapers to class and discuss their appropriateness as sources of information. Compare and contrast how they report the same story.

Students may have difficulty separating fact from opinion. Hold a discussion on a controversial topic and ask students to offer factual statements about it. After collecting a number of such statements, pose the question, "Fact or opinion?". Point out the qualities that make a given statement one or the other.

further reassure listeners: our source is the "latest," and *Consumer Reports* was responsible in its work ("did extensive tests").

Sources of information have ethos just as speakers do. For example, *Consumer Reports* enjoys a reputation for responsible, objective testing of products. On social or political issues, the ideological position of the source may be important. For example, if you cited William F. Buckley's *National Review* in support of a claim, skeptical listeners might respond, "Well, that's a conservative magazine. Of course Buckley will support this right-wing claim!" On the other hand, if you also cite the *New Republic*, a more liberal publication, then skeptical listeners might think, "Well, if both left and right agree, then maybe what she's saying is true."[3]

Even seemingly neutral sources present "factual" information that is colored by its cultural environment. Compare the following excerpts from the same encyclopedia in its 1960 and 1990 editions:

> **1960: Kiowa Indians hunted buffalo on the southwestern plains of the United States. The Kiowa and their allies, the Comanche, raided many Texas ranches. They probably killed more whites than any other Indian tribe. . . . By [a] treaty signed in 1868, the Kiowa agreed to go with the Comanche to a reservation in Indian territory (now Oklahoma). But only the Kiowa chiefs had signed the treaty, and no chiefs could force their young men to make such a sacrifice. Many struggles and arrests occurred before the Kiowa finally went to live on the reservation. When trouble broke out in 1874, Satanta, one of the most daring Kiowa leaders, was arrested and sentenced to prison. There he committed suicide. The Kiowa then "put their hands to the plow." They now live peacefully as farmers. Several have become well-known artists.**
>
> **1990: Kiowa Indians are a tribe that lives largely in Oklahoma and elsewhere in the Southwestern United States. The tribe has about 8,000 members, most of whom live in rural communities near Anadarko, Carnegie, and Mountain View, Oklahoma. Other tribal members live in urban areas and work in law, medicine, teaching, and other professions. . . . [In] 1970 the Kiowa adopted their own tribal constitution. The tribe is governed by the Kiowa Indian Council, which consists of all members who are at least 18 years old. The Kiowa Business Committee, an elected group, manages tribal programs in such fields as business, education, and health.[4]**

Both of these accounts are "factual," but the first dwells upon past conflict, defining the Kiowas as adversaries of the dominant culture, and the second emphasizes their present assimilation. The contrast reminds us that even relatively objective descriptions are selective and incomplete. We should always ask ourselves what any given description leaves out, and whether that omission might be critical. In short, we should try to determine what is information and what is **disinformation**, "misplaced, fragmented, irrelevant, or superficial information . . . that creates the illusion of knowing something but which, in fact, leads one away from knowing."[5]

Statistics

Statistics are numerical facts that can describe the size of something, make predictions, illustrate trends, or show relationships. They are *precise* factual statements, used to verify claims, comparisons, and contrasts. Americans are almost as much in awe of numbers as they are of science. In the same Gallup study cited earlier in this chapter, 82 percent of those surveyed said that statistics increased a story's credibility.[6] These figures confirm that statistics can be one of the most powerful forms of supporting material. Indeed, scientific research itself confirms the utility of statistical evidence in persuasive speaking.[7]

The following example from a student speech demonstrates how statistical information can appear in speeches:

> **The Environmental Protection Agency is saying that secondhand smoke causes 3,000 lung cancer deaths a year and 35,000 heart disease deaths a year and contributes to 150,000 to 300,000 respiratory infections in babies, mainly bronchitis and pneumonia, resulting in 7,500 to 15,000 hospitalizations. It triggers 8,000 to 26,000 new cases of asthma in previously unaffected children and exacerbates symptoms in 400,000 to 1 million asthmatic children.**

When presented orally, statistics can be overwhelming. By using a brief explanation, example, or presentation aid (see Chapter 9), you can make numerical information more understandable. Compare the example cited above with the way a physician used similar figures to help his listeners understand the extent of medical problems caused by smoking:

Ask students to search through a recent issue of *Vital Speeches of the Day* to find examples of statistics used as supporting materials. Were the students convinced by the statistics? Did speakers use definitions, explanations, or descriptions to increase the effectiveness of the support? Ask students to apply the tests of relevance, recency, credibility, and reliability to evaluate their findings.

> **I ask you to check your watches. Because in this hour, by the time I'm done speaking, 50 Americans will die from smoke-related diseases. By the time you sit down to breakfast in the morning, 600 more will have joined them: 8,400 by the end of the week—every week, every month, every year—until it kills nearly half-a-million Americans, year in, year out. That's more than all the other preventable causes of death combined. Alcohol, illegal drugs, AIDS, suicide, car accidents, fires, guns—all are killers. But tobacco kills more than all of them put together.**
>
> **These are hard, cold realities, defined by hard, cold statistics. But I'd ask you to remember this most important fact. Every statistic is an encoded memorial to what was once a living, breathing—loving and loved—mother, father, sister, brother. Not numbers, real people, and the toll is as terrible as the most horrific war.[8]**

The contrast provided by these two examples is revealing. The first speaker almost drowns the listener with numbers. The second uses fewer numbers, but connects them into a clearer pattern. Moreover, by comparing smoking to other forms of preventable death, he builds its importance in our minds. Finally, he increases the emotional impact by describing the people his numbers represent. We shall discuss these techniques of comparison and description in more detail later in this chapter.

Evaluating Facts and Statistics

For almost any topic you select, your research notes should contain a wide assortment of facts and statistics. Before you decide which of these materials you will actually use in your speech, apply the critical thinking skills we discussed in Chapter 3. Ask yourself:

Have students look in newspapers or magazines for recent pronouncements by public officials that purport to be objective statements of fact but may actually distort the truth. What tips students off to this possible distortion?

- Is this information relevant?
- Is this information the most recent available?
- Are the sources of this information credible?
- Is this information reliable?

As you review your research notes, you may discover much interesting information about your topic that does not relate directly to your specific purpose. No matter how fascinating it seems, if the information does not fit, don't use it. A speech that is cluttered with interesting digressions is hard for listeners to follow. You should also be certain that any statistics you cite are relevant to your locale. If you talk about the "crisis of unemployment" in your area, basing your claim on a national average of 7 percent, you could have a problem if someone points out that the local rate is only 4 percent.

You must also consider how current the information is, especially when your topic is one on which information changes rapidly. On certain fast-breaking subjects, yesterday's news is already obsolete. When you speak on such topics, be sure you are up to date. Save yourself the embarrassment of having a listener point out that your claims are invalid because of what happened this morning!

It is also important that you evaluate the sources of your information. Test even "factual" material for potential bias, distortions, or omissions. Don't be taken in by "scientific sounding" names, especially if the information contradicts common sense. Cynthia Crossen, a reporter and editor with the *Wall Street Journal*, exposes many instances of such deception in her book *Tainted Truth*. For example, she points to a claim made by "the Cooper Institute for Aerobic Research" that "white bread will not make you gain weight." It turns out that the study that produced this amazing conclusion was funded by the makers of Wonder Bread.[9]

To guard against deceptive information, do not rely too heavily on any one source. Compare what different expert sources have to say. The more controversial your topic, the more important it is that your information be sound. In your speech, tell listeners how you have tested vital pieces of information. They will appreciate your efforts to offer them the truth.

ESL students are often interested in immigration issues. Ask students to read recent newspaper and magazine articles to compile a statistical picture of numbers of immigrants, the conditions of their lives, and their impact on the country's economy. Discuss how adequately the numbers portray reality and whether the numbers ever seem misused for political purposes.

As you weigh the use of facts and statistics, be careful not to read into information what you want to find or to exaggerate the results. Be on guard against the tendency to distort facts and statistics by the way you word them. Don't ignore information that contradicts your claims by rejecting it out of hand as atypical or irrelevant.

Be especially careful when using statistics. Keep in mind that statistical predictions are based on probability, not certainty, and that they are subject to misuse and abuse. Peter Francese, founder and president of *American Demographics*, has pointed out that although statistics are supposed to represent reality, they may also be used to *create* reality:

> **Politicians and lobbyists carefully select the numbers they use to talk about crime (it's always rampant) or immigration (it's always out of control). The numbers are typically used to prove there is a "big" problem. It's like rounding up vicious dogs to prove that all dogs bite. . . . No number can represent truth perfectly. Every survey has some error or bias. Data from public records, such as crime reports, can be underreported or misclassified. And even perfectly collected data are open to different interpretations.[10]**

Chapter 14's discussion of other misuses of facts and statistics as evidence in persuasive speaking will give you additional help in evaluating information and using it ethically.

Using Facts and Statistics

Three techniques for framing facts and statistics into powerful supporting materials are definitions, explanations, and descriptions.

Definitions. A **definition** translates technical terms into words your listeners will understand. It helps to ensure that speaker and listeners will be talking and thinking about the same things. Audience analysis should help you determine the need for definitions in your speech. As a general rule, you should provide definitions for any terms that are unfamiliar to listeners as you first use them. In her informative speech at Vanderbilt on genetic testing, Ashlie McMillan first offered a technical definition: "According to 'The Genetic Revolution,' an article in *Scientific* magazine, genetic testing 'is co-relating the inheritance of a distinctive segment of DNA, a marker localizing the mutant gene on a DNA strand which composes our chromosomes.'" Noting the puzzled look on her listeners' faces, Ashlie then said, "I found that a little confusing too, so I tried to put it in my own words: genetic testing looks at people's DNA to see if they have a genetic condition or disease or are likely to get the disease. That's basically what it is."

Definitions can be persuasive as well as informative. A persuasive definition reflects your way of looking at a controversial subject. It presents your perspective in such a way that your listeners will want to share it. A persuasive definition usually puts the subject in an emotional context. In a speech on domestic violence against women, Donna Shalala, then secretary of health and human services, provided the following persuasive definition of domestic violence: "Domestic violence is terrorism. Terrorism in the home. And that is what we should call it."[11]

Explanations. Longer and more detailed than definitions, **explanations** clarify a topic or demonstrate how it works. John F. Smith Jr., chairman of the board of General Motors Corporation, used an explanation to both define and clarify the OnStar system:

Explain to your students why a diverse audience may require more definitions and explanations than a homogeneous audience.

> **Basically, the OnStar system combines the Global Positioning System (GPS) satellite network with wireless technology to link the driver and vehicle to the OnStar Center. There are currently two centers, in Michigan and North Carolina. Each is staffed by real human beings, 24 hours a day, 7 days a week, 365 days a year. . . . They are there to offer immediate, real-time, personalized help to any query.**
>
> **OnStar has been used to assist subscribers in everything from emergency services to tracking stolen vehicles; getting the doors opened when the keys are accidentally locked inside; finding the nearest ATM machine; guiding the driver to the local zoo or gasoline station; and arranging dinner reservations and theater ticket purchases. If an OnStar-equipped vehicle is in a crash that deploys an airbag, the car itself automatically "calls" the Center and an advisor immediately calls the vehicle to see what kind of assistance is needed.**[12]

It is important to offer such explanations early in your speech to help listeners grasp your meaning.

Descriptions. **Descriptions** are "word pictures" that help listeners visualize information. The best descriptions evoke vivid images in the minds of the audience. The great Roman rhetorician Longinus once said that images occur when, "carried away by enthusiasm and passion, you think you see what you describe, and you place it before the eyes of your hearers."[13] Images color information with the speaker's feelings: they establish a mood in addition to increasing understanding. Note how the following description of the monument at Wounded Knee, which commemorates the massacre of hundreds of Sioux men, women, and children, both paints a picture and establishes a mood (the complete text of this speech is in Appendix C):

> **Two red-brick columns topped with a wrought-iron arch and a small metal cross form the entrance to the grave site. The column to the right is in bad shape: Cinder blocks from the base are missing; the brickwork near the top has deteriorated and tumbled to the ground; graffiti on the columns proclaim an attitude we found repeatedly expressed about the Bureau of Indian Affairs: "The BIA sucks!" Crumbling concrete steps lead you to the mass grave.**

> **The top of the grave is covered with gravel, interrupted by unruly patches of chickweed and crabgrass. . . .**

Ask students to describe a photograph to the class, using vivid, concrete, active language. Listeners should draw what they hear. To measure the effectiveness of the descriptions, compare these drawings with the original, and discuss how the descriptions might have been more effective.

Such descriptions help bring information to life before an audience. But a word of caution is in order. The description above works well because it is *understated*. All too often beginning speakers indulge in emotional overkill. They add too many adjectives, too much emotional coloration. If "grave site" here were "lonely grave site," if "attitude" were "angry attitude," if "mass grave" were "abandoned mass grave," we would begin to think more about the speaker's feelings than about the subject being portrayed. *Let listeners supply the adjectives in their minds*. That way, they will *participate* in creating the image. They will feel engaged by the speech rather than manipulated by it.

Descriptions can provide some of the most artful moments in speeches. Note how Thabo Mbeki, president of South Africa, described his nation's condition in the early summer of 1999:

> **Our country is in that period of time which the seTswana-speaking people of Southern Africa graphically describe as "mahube a naka tsa kgomo"—the dawning of the dawn, when only the tips of the horn of the cattle can be seen etched against the morning sky.**
>
> **As the sun continues to rise to banish the darkness of the long years of colonialism and apartheid, what the new light over our land must show is a nation diligently at work to create a better life for itself.[14]**

Testimony

You use **testimony** when you cite the words and ideas of others in support of your message. When you repeat the exact words of others, you are using a **direct quotation**. Direct quotations are useful when the material is brief, the exact wording is important, or the language is especially eloquent. When points are controversial, a direct quotation can seem especially authoritative and conclusive. Note, for example, how former senator Sam Nunn underscored the threat of the

Speaker's Notes 6.1

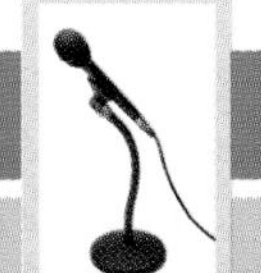

USING FACTS AND STATISTICS

1. Use the most recent, reliable facts and statistics.
2. Don't overrely on one source; check several sources to verify important information.
3. Use information from unbiased sources with no vested interest in what they report.
4. Interpret information accurately. Do not stretch or twist its meaning.
5. When using statistics in speeches, round off numbers whenever you can do so without distorting results.
6. Make statistics understandable by amplifying them with examples or visual aids.
7. Don't overwhelm your audience with a barrage of facts and statistics.

spread of nuclear and biological weapons by citing the exact words of an archenemy of the West: "In 1999, terrorist Osama bin Laden said: 'To seek to possess the weapons that could counter those of the infidels is a religious duty.'"[15]

You also may **paraphrase**, or restate in your own words, what others have said, especially when to repeat the exact words would be too long for your speech. When you paraphrase testimony, you must cite the source: who said it, why we should respect that person, where it was said, and when it was said.

Three types of testimony are useful as supporting material. Expert testimony comes from sources who are authorities on the topic. Lay testimony involves citing ordinary citizens, who may have firsthand experience with the topic. Prestige testimony comes from someone who is highly regarded but not necessarily an expert on the topic.

Have students find a speech that makes extensive use of testimony in a recent *Vital Speeches of the Day*. Ask them to consider the following questions: Does the speaker establish the credentials of sources cited? Has the speaker used appropriate forms of testimony? Might other forms have worked better?

Expert Testimony

Expert testimony comes from people who are qualified by training or experience to serve as authorities on a subject. As you review your research notes, you will probably discover statements by experts offering opinions, information, or simply interesting quotations. When you cite experts in your speeches, you are calling on them as qualified witnesses to support your case. Using expert testimony allows you to borrow their credibility to make your own message more convincing. Expert testimony is especially important when your topic is innovative, unfamiliar, highly technical, or controversial.

When you use expert testimony, remember that competence is area-specific. That means that your experts can speak *as experts* only within their area of expertise. For example, emergency room physicians who could provide expert testimony on the physical effects of gunshot wounds may not qualify as experts on gun control legislation. As you introduce expert testimony, be sure to establish that your source *is* an expert on the specific topic of the speech. If the testimony is recent, emphasize that fact. When the testimony appears in a prestigious journal, book, or newspaper, emphasize that as well.

> **Dr. Lee Gonzales, chair of our Criminal Justice Department and former member of the Presidential Task Force on Inner-City Violence, said last week in the *Washington Post* that a law requiring the licensing of handguns would . . .**

Expert testimony from people qualified by training or experience can make your message more credible.

Obviously, knowing the exact source of information is vital for critical listening. This sometimes presents a dilemma in contemporary journalism, when information is important but sources wish to remain anonymous. As Kathleen Hall Jamieson, dean of the Annenberg School at the University of Pennsylvania, has said:

> **Journalists, in many cases, aren't telling us anything about the source to let us judge whether or not there might be a bias. . . . Where [for example] did *Newsweek* get the [secret] tape? Is it a reliable source or a biased source? Can we trust that this wasn't a selective leak for partisan advantage?[16]**

Both speakers and listeners need to be cautious about such information. Ethical speakers should warn listeners when sources are not disclosed, and careful listeners should factor this into their critical reception of messages.

Bias, as Jamieson indicates, is a major consideration in assessing expert testimony. Sources who have an ax to grind put critical listeners on guard. But there is one situation in which bias works *for* the usefulness of a source. This occurs in the case of **reluctant testimony**, in which sources speak *against* their apparent self-interest. Listeners give high marks for character and honesty to those who feel compelled to tell the truth *despite* their own agendas.[17] Therefore, reluctant testimony is highly valued by persuaders. Benoit and Kennedy describe an incident from the first presidential debate of 1996 in which President Clinton—on at least three occasions—attacked Senator Bob Dole's proposed tax cut by citing Dole's campaign manager:

> **And now with this risky $550 billion tax scheme of Senator Dole's, even his own friends, his campaign co-chair, Senator D'Amato, says that they can't possibly pay for it without cutting Medicare more and cutting Social Security as well, according to him. . . . But it won't be possible to do if his tax scheme passes, because even his own campaign co-chair, Senator D'Amato, says he'll have to cut Medicare even more than was cut in the bill that I vetoed. . . . Now, remember, folks, even Senator Dole's campaign co-chair, Senator D'Amato, says he's got to cut Medicare to pay for this.[18]**

Clinton obviously ground this reluctant testimony into Dole's face by repeating the charge at strategic moments during the debate. For knowledgeable listeners, the effect was even more dramatic. They would have known that D'Amato was not only Dole's campaign co-chair—he was also chair of the senatorial committee investigating Clinton's Whitewater real estate dealings. As Benoit and Kennedy conclude, "No one would expect Senator D'Amato to give evidence supporting Clinton and his policies."[19] Therefore, this was a classic instance of the use of reluctant testimony.

Lay Testimony

Lay testimony representing the wisdom of ordinary people is highly regarded, especially in societies in which popular elections are the source of political power. In these societies "the people" often become a symbol of almost mystical power, frequently invoked to justify policy.[20] Why should we have (or not have) gun control, or educational reform, or lower taxation? Because "the people" demand (or reject) it. Therefore, public opinion polls that purport to tell us what "the people" actually think or feel about issues and candidates enjoy great respect, especially during political campaigns.[21] Newspapers keep us informed on a daily basis of the state of the public mind. *USA Today* even features lay testimony along with that of experts on its editorial page.

Well-known, respected people qualify as both expert and prestigious. They can provide testimony that is authentic and moving.

Moreover, speakers often use lay testimony to provide an understanding of the real-life consequences of issues. As he addressed the annual meeting of the Public Broadcasting System, Bill Moyers used lay testimony to point up the value of public radio and television:

> **There was a cabbie [in New York City] named Youssef Jada. He came here from Morocco six years ago. . . . Youssef kept his car radio tuned to National Public Radio all day and his television set at home on Channel Thirteen. He said—and this is a direct quote—"I am blessed by these stations." He pointed me to a picture on the dashboard of his 13-month-old son, and he said: "My son was born in this country. I will let him watch Channel Thirteen so he can learn how to be an American."[22]**
>
> **Think about that. . . . Why shouldn't public television be the core curriculum of the American experience?**

Lay testimony that is used in support of a person, practice, product, or institution is called a **testimonial**. However, lay testimony cannot be used to establish the objective validity of ideas. That is the job of expert testimony, which provides dispassionate facts and carefully considered interpretations based on them. In contrast, lay testimony often reflects personal experience and appeals to feelings. Use such testimony when it is appropriate to point up the relevance of your topic to the lives of ordinary people.

Ask students to think of circumstances in which lay testimony might be misused. How serious is this problem in contemporary society?

Prestige Testimony

Prestige testimony associates your message with the words of a respected public figure. This person is usually an eloquent writer or cultural hero or heroine who, although not necessarily an expert on your particular topic, has voiced some timeless truth that supports, illuminates, and elevates your ideas. Citing such testimony can add distinction to your speech. It allows you to associate your cause with the ethos of the revered person. Because of these qualities, prestige testimony is often the source of inspiration in ceremonial speaking. Note

InterConnections.LearnMore 6.1

SOURCES OF PRESTIGE TESTIMONY

Bartleby.com http://www.bartleby.com/quotations/
A collection of quotations from contemporary and classic sources with a search tool.

Dictionary of Scientific Quotations http://www.naturalscience.com/dsqhome.html
A short collection of interesting quotations from scientists.

PhilosophyQuotes http://www.philosophyquotes.com
A free daily ezine, plus archives, with an assortment of quotations by philosophers.

Quoteland.com http://www.quoteland.com
A compilation of quotations from literature accessible by topic or author.

how Colin Powell used prestige testimony to dramatize his inspirational speech at the National Volunteer Summit in Philadelphia:

> The great American poet Langston Hughes talked about a dream deferred, and he said, "What happens to a dream deferred? Does it dry up like a raisin in the sun, or fester like a sore and then run? Does it stink like rotten meat or crust and sugar over like a syrupy sweet? Maybe it just sags, like a heavy load. Or, does it explode?"
>
> For too many young Americans, that dream deferred does sag like a heavy load that's pushing them down into the ground. . . . As we see too often, it does explode in violence, in youngsters falling dead, shot by other youngsters. . . . And it has the potential to explode our society.
>
> So today, we . . . pledge that the dream must no longer be deferred, and [that] it will never, as long as we can do anything about it, become a dream denied.[23]

Prestige testimony is also one source of *mythos*, a form of proof discussed in Chapter 14 that summons the power of tradition in support of your message. In a speech on the "giveaway of our public lands," Brock Evans, vice president of the Audubon Society, used prestige testimony to emphasize the depth of the problem and to place it in cultural perspective:

> If there ever was a crisis for all our public lands and wildlife heritage, it is now. The words that keep running through my head, over and over again these terrible times, come from President Abraham Lincoln who in another time of crisis, 130 years ago, said:
>
> > "Fellow countrymen, we cannot escape history. . . . The dogmas of the quiet past will no longer suffice for the stormy present. . . . As the occasion now before us is piled high with difficulties, so we must rise to that occasion. . . . History will judge us if we fail."
>
> And that is how I feel about these times now. . . . These are frightening times for anyone who loves the American land and its biological treasures, for anyone who believes in that great tradition of public lands ownership, for anyone who shares the opinion of our forefathers that some lands should belong to all the people.[24]

In this example, Evans used Lincoln's exact words so that he would not lose the elegance and force of the language. If you must paraphrase a lengthy passage, be sure that you reflect fairly the spirit and meaning of the words you summarize.

Evaluating and Using Testimony

Like facts and statistics, testimony must meet the test of *relevance*. And like facts and statistics, testimony must seem *free from bias*. For example, a doctor who promotes vitamin therapy may be the part owner of a company that sells vitamins. Her expert advice to "start taking Nature Blessed vitamins today" may be somewhat suspect because of self-interest. The test of *recency* takes a strange twist when applied to testimony. If you are using expert or lay testimony, the conventional rule applies: *Latest is best*. But if you are using prestige testimony, often *the older the better*. Wisdom ages well, and heroes and heroines frequently glow brighter with the passage of time.

In addition to these basic tests, you must also consider whether the type of testimony is appropriate for your purpose. Lay testimony can humanize a speech and promote identification among listeners, your message, and yourself. Prestige testimony can enhance the attractiveness of both speech and speaker, but only expert testimony can demonstrate that a statement is factually true.

As you use testimony, be sure that the quotation you select reflects the overall meaning and intent of its author. Never twist the meaning of testimony to make it fit your purposes—this unethical practice is called "quoting out of context." Political advertising, as candidates try to put a positive spin on their image, is often rife with it. For example, during a political campaign in Illinois, one state representative sent out a fundraising letter that claimed he'd been singled out for "special recognition" by *Chicago* magazine—and, indeed, he had. He had been cited as "one of the state's ten worst legislators."[25]

To ensure accuracy, have quotations written out on note cards so that you can read them, rather than relying on your memory. A transition, such as "According to . . ." or "In the latest issue of . . . ," leads gracefully into such material. To discover useful information about the credentials of your sources, check the biographical resources mentioned in the list following Chapter 5.

Finally, don't simply accept what experts say uncritically. Experts have been known to be wrong. In 1903, the president of the Michigan Savings Bank advised Henry Ford's lawyer not to invest in the Ford Motor Company, saying, "The horse is here to stay, but the automobile is only a novelty—a fad." In 1943 Thomas Watson, chair of IBM, reached the following brilliant conclusion: "I think there is a world market for maybe five computers."[26] And in 1946 Darryl F. Zanuck, head of 20th Century Fox studios, predicted: "Television won't be able to hold on to any market it captures after the first six months. People will soon get tired of staring at a plywood box every night."[27]

Speaker's Notes 6.2

USING TESTIMONY

1. Select sources your audience will respect.
2. Be careful to quote or paraphrase material accurately.
3. Point out the qualifications of sources you are citing as experts.
4. Use only expert testimony to validate information.
5. Use lay testimony to build identification and add authenticity.
6. Use prestige testimony to enhance the general credibility of your message.

Examples

Ask students to develop examples that illustrate abstract concepts such as love, compassion, peace, pain, justice, etc. How and why are such examples important to communication?

Examples bring a speech to life. Just as pictures serve as graphic illustrations for a printed text, **examples** serve as verbal illustrations for an oral message. In fact, some scholars prefer the term *illustration* to *example*. This term derives from the Latin *illustrare*, which means "to shed light" or "to make bright." Good examples illuminate the message of your speech, making it clearer and more vivid for your audience.

In addition to clarifying ideas, examples can also arouse attention and sustain interest. A speech without examples is often boring. Examples make ideas seem real by providing concrete applications. They demonstrate that what you have said either has happened or could happen. Speakers acknowledge these functions when they say, "Let me give you an example." Similarly, examples may be used to personalize your topic and to humanize both you and your message. Sue Suter, speaking before the Dallas conference of the National Industries for the Severely Handicapped, used a series of brief examples to point up the challenges she had experienced as a disabled person:

> I contracted polio when I was two years old. I don't remember it. But I do remember my parents telling me about the advice the doctor gave when it was time for me to leave the hospital. He told them, "Just put her in bed, she's going to be staying there the rest of her life." I had a college counselor who advised me that going after more education might hurt me. He warned that it was hard enough for a woman with a disability to get married; a master's degree would only intimidate a man more.
>
> And I remember when I went after my first job as a secretary. The boss nearly didn't hire me because he worried that I couldn't carry coffee to him every morning. Talk about a double barrel insult—being doubted whether you could do something that you really shouldn't have to do in the first place! . . . I never spilled coffee on the boss's lap, although the temptation was real.[28]

Examples about people give the audience someone with whom they can identify, thus involving them in the speech. Personalized examples help the audience to *experience* the meaning of your ideas, not simply to *understand* them. Examples that point out common experiences, beliefs, or values also help to bridge gaps in cultural understanding. When Hillary Rodham Clinton spoke at the United Nations Fourth World Conference on Women in Beijing, China, she used many brief examples to demonstrate that all women share common problems and face a common destiny:

> Over the past two-and-a-half years, I have had the opportunity to learn more about the challenges facing women in my own country and around the world. I have met new mothers in Jojakarta, Indonesia, who come together regularly in the village to discuss nutrition, family planning, and baby care. . . . I have met women in South Africa who helped lead the struggle to end apartheid and are now helping build a new democracy. . . . I have met women in India and Bangladesh who are taking out small loans to buy milk cows, rickshaws, thread and other materials to create a livelihood for themselves and their families. I have met doctors and nurses in Belarus and Ukraine who are trying to keep children alive in the aftermath of Chernobyl. The great challenge of this conference is to give voice to women everywhere whose experiences go unnoticed, whose words go unheard.[29]

Examples also provide emphasis. When you make a statement and follow it with an example, you are pointing out that what you have just said is IMPOR-

TANT. Examples amplify your ideas. They say to the audience, "This bears repeating." Examples are especially helpful when you introduce new, complex, or abstract material. Not only can they make such information clearer, they also allow time for the audience to process what you have said before you move on to your next point.

Types of Examples

Examples take different forms, and these forms have different functions. An example may be brief or extended and may be based either on an actual event or on something that might have happened.

Brief Examples. A **brief example** mentions a specific instance to demonstrate a more general statement. Brief examples are concise and to the point. To open the speech cited above on effective marketing for people with disabilities, Sue Suter, former president of the World Institute on Disabilities, used the following brief example:

> You do vital work. And much of it deals with marketing. That reminded me of a message found on an old tombstone in Springdale, Ohio. It reads: "Here lies Jane Smith, wife of Thomas Smith, marble cutter. This monument was erected by her husband as a tribute to her memory and a specimen of his work. Monuments of the same style $350."[30]

Extended Examples. An **extended example** contains more detail and allows you to dwell more fully on an illustration. In her speech on disabilities, Suter used two extended examples, one contained within the other, to allow her audience to focus on her theme. The wider, inclusive example was her tribute to Franklin Delano Roosevelt, who was also disabled by polio. The extended example contained within this tribute was her own experience:

> Back in 1990, I became the first person with a disability to be nominated by a major party to run for a statewide office in Illinois. That was tough. Wondering how people would accept me. Having to crawl into small planes (they were free rides) so that I could make the next engagement. Riding in parades and waving while other candidates walked and shook hands along the route. And being hoisted onto hay stacks to address crowds. These were accommodations I accepted. Just as Roosevelt had done years before.
>
> We lost a close race. Yet looking back on it all, one impression especially touched me. Most people, I'm convinced, saw the real Sue Suter. A major party candidate fighting in a tough election. Not a cripple to pity. And I'm convinced that is the way people would see FDR today.[31]

Extended examples give us more detailed information. They allow speakers to develop the message of their speeches as they develop the examples.

Factual Examples. A **factual example** is based on an actual event or a real person. Factual examples provide strong support for your ideas because they actually did happen. University of Memphis student Mark Thompson used the following factual example to define the meaning of generosity:

> Generosity? I'll tell you what it means. Last week, tennis champion Arthur Ashe died—one more innocent victim of AIDS. Yesterday, a retired secretary and grandmother who is dying of lung cancer in Brooklyn gave $400,000 to St. Jude Children's Research Hospital to help create the Arthur Ashe Chair for Pediatric AIDS Research. She wanted his name remembered, not hers. We

know only that she is a person "of very modest means" who received the money in a malpractice suit when doctors failed to recognize her symptoms of cancer. She wanted to reach out to children who, like her, are fighting terminal illness.

While she remains anonymous, this obscure woman is a champion too—a champion of the human spirit. She has given us a gift far more precious than her money.

Hypothetical Examples. Examples need not be real to be effective. A **hypothetical example** is a composite of actual people, situations, or events. Although created by the speaker, it claims to represent reality and therefore must be plausible. The following hypothetical example was used by University of New Mexico student Susan Romero to illustrate the meaning of "cabin fever":

Picture the following: you're in a room with five other people—four of them under ten years old, brimming with energy. It's been raining for six days—a cold, heavy rain. No one can go outside. The kids run in circles and fight with one another. The other adult nags at you when awake and snores when asleep. Would you feel the walls closing in on you? Would you have an irresistible impulse to go somewhere, anywhere, to escape? That, my friends, is cabin fever.

You should use hypothetical examples when the factual examples you find don't adequately represent the *truth* of a situation, or when a factual example might embarrass actual, living people. Be especially careful that your hypothetical examples are truly representative, and that they don't distort the truth just to make your point. Always alert your listeners to the hypothetical nature of your example: such introductory phrases as "Imagine yourself . . . ," "Picture the following . . . ," or "Let's pretend that . . ." should caution audiences that they will be hearing a hypothetical example that nevertheless purports to represent the truth. The standards of ethical speech require that you never present a hypothetical example as though it were factual.

Evaluating and Using Examples

Evaluate examples in terms of their relevance, representativeness, and believability. No matter how interesting an example may seem, if it does not advance your specific purpose, leave it out. Examples must also fairly represent situations as they actually exist. Remember, what works well with one audience may seem

ESL students may have trouble understanding some of the examples that are specific to life in the United States. In like manner, examples that ESL students take for granted may draw blank looks from others. Remind speakers that they should consider carefully whether their examples will be readily understood by diverse audiences.

Speaker's Notes 6.3

USING EXAMPLES

1. Use examples to arouse and sustain attention, clarify abstract or technical ideas, and emphasize major points.
2. Make your examples specific by naming the people and places in them.
3. Use factual examples whenever possible.
4. Use examples that are believable and representative of a situation.
5. Keep examples brief and to the point; do not ramble.
6. Be selective in your use of examples. Save them for points of major importance.

out of place with another. Examples must meet the tests of taste and propriety. They should fit the mood and spirit of the occasion. Risk offending listeners only when they must be shocked into attention before they can be informed or persuaded.

Examples often make the difference between a speech that is humdrum and one that is successful. Highlight their authenticity by providing concrete details—the names of the people, places, times, and institutions involved in them. It is much easier for a listener to relate to Matt Dunn of the local General Motors plant than to some anonymous worker in an unnamed company. Use transitions to move smoothly from statement to example and from example to statement. Phrases such as "For instance . . ." or "As you can see . . ." work nicely.

Narratives

A **narrative** goes beyond an extended example by *telling a story* within the speech, relating a sequence of actions that have a beginning, middle, and end. Humans have been storytellers from the dawn of time. Most children are brought up on narratives—stories that entertain, fables that warn of dangers, and parables that teach virtues. People organize their experiences and memories in terms of the stories they tell.[32] Moreover, when information seems odd (for example, a Harvard-educated plumber), people look for the stories that will explain the phenomenon and satisfy their curiosity.[33]

Ask students to find ads that tell stories in order to sell products. What qualities make these stories effective or ineffective?

Narratives are especially effective in speeches because they draw listeners into the action. Because listeners can often "see" themselves enacting certain roles within the stories, narratives can encourage desirable transformations of identity and behavior. As listeners, we may wish to imitate the models of good and bad behavior presented in the stories. Moreover, narratives stimulate the process of constructive listening that we discussed in Chapter 3. Because stories prompt listeners to create meaning from what they hear, the audience becomes involved in the creation of the message. It becomes *their* discovery, *their* truth. Such involvement enhances the impact of the message.

Personal narratives also increase identification between speakers and audiences. They can help bridge the cultural differences that separate people of diverse backgrounds. According to Al Gore, storytelling can even help old enemies make peace. On one occasion, when Palestinian, Israeli, Jordanian, and Syrian leaders met to discuss a peace treaty, Gore saw the negotiations coming to a standstill. The situation looked unpromising until, in Gore's words, "The breakthroughs came when they told stories about their families. I have seen time and time again how storytelling brings people together."[34]

Many ESL students come from oral cultures with strong traditions of storytelling. Ask students to tell a story authentic to their culture and explain what purposes it serves. As they tell the story ask them to use dialogue.

Successful narratives serve many of the same functions as examples. They make a speech livelier and help sustain attention. They clarify abstract or technical ideas. They emphasize a point by telling a dramatic story that illustrates it. A narrative functions as a speech within a speech—it begins with an attention-getting introduction, continues with a body in which the story develops, and ends with a conclusion that points up the message. Facts and statistics fade with time, but narratives leave the audience with something to remember.

For all these good reasons, the ability to tell stories effectively has become one of the most sought-after skills among candidates for top entry-level positions in American business. More than fifty corporate recruiters surveyed by the Owen Graduate School of Management at Vanderbilt University identified

Narratives create interest and make us think about the lessons they illustrate.

communication skills in general, and storytelling ability in particular, as key to successful interviewing for top positions. Peter Veruki, director of career planning at Owen, concluded:

> **It is becoming increasingly important for candidates to be adept at the art of storytelling. The more the candidate can make his or her experience vivid and memorable for the recruiter, the greater the odds are of advancing to the next stage of the interview process. M.B.A.s should engage the interviewer by adding rich, visual detail to what they relate about their work and personal histories.[35]**

Because they can be so effective at involving the audience, narratives are often used in the introductions of speeches. Heather Rouston Ettinger, principal of the Roulston Company, told a story to illustrate the emerging status of women:

> **Last summer, Buffalo Bills quarterback, Doug Flutie, was watching the final game of the Women's World Cup soccer match on TV with his 12-year-old soccer-playing daughter, Alexa. During the soccer match between the USA and China teams, the hugely successful advertisement for Gatorade featuring Michael Jordan and Mia Hamm came on. As most of you well know, Michael Jordan, formerly of NBA fame, is the most influential athlete of the last century. Mia Hamm was the star forward of the USA national team. You might remember the theme to this was "Anything you can do I can do better." As Doug Flutie tells the story, when the ad came on, Alexa asked, "Dad, who's the guy with Mia?"[36]**

Narratives that are humorous also help make the audience comfortable.[37] Bob Newhart opened his 1997 commencement speech at Catholic University of America with the following story:

> **When I was asked to be the commencement speaker I was reminded of a story about Jascha Heifetz, the famed violinist, who was asked to play in Grange Hall in Minot, North Dakota. He agreed to do it sometime in December. As December came around the weather turned terrible in New York and he called up and said, "I'm sorry, I won't be able to make it." The man who arranged for him to appear there said, "We have 3,000 people in Grange Hall here in Minot, could you try to?" And he said, "I will." So he finally got out of New York and flew to Denver, caught a small plane, and finally got into Minot at about 11 o'clock at night and walked into Grange Hall and there were 12 people waiting.**
>
> **He said, "I'm sorry, I can't appear in front of such a small audience. You said there were 3,000 people here." And he said, "Well there were, but they were afraid you wouldn't show up." He said, "I've never appeared in front of such a small audience." And the man who had arranged for him to be there said, "Jascha, if you could just sing one or two songs, that would be . . ."**
>
> **So I feel somewhat like that. . . . I'm not sure you have the right man, but I'm very honored.**[38]

Concluding narratives leave the audience with something to remember and extend the impact of a message. They can establish a mood that will last long after the closing words have been spoken. In a speech presented in April 1997 to the Economic Club in Chicago, Newton Minow, former chair of the Federal Communications Commission, concluded his plea for campaign finance reform with the following:

> **I leave you with a story President Kennedy told a week before he was killed. The story was about French Marshal Louis Lyautey, who walked one morning through his garden with his gardener. He stopped at a certain point and asked the gardener to plant a tree there the next morning. The gardener said, "But the tree will not bloom for one hundred years!" The Marshal looked at the gardener and replied, "In that case, you had better plant it this afternoon."**[39]

In a narrative, dialogue is usually preferable to paraphrase. When speakers use dialogue, they reproduce conversation directly. Paraphrasing can save time, but it can also rob a narrative of power and a sense of immediacy. Let people speak for themselves in your narratives. The late senator Sam Ervin of North Carolina was a master storyteller. Note how he used dialogue in the following narrative, which opened a speech on the Constitution and our judicial system:

Speaker's Notes 6.4

USING HUMOR

1. Use humor to put the audience at ease.
2. Remember that the kind of humor you use reflects on your character. Avoid religious, ethnic, racist, or sexist humor.
3. Don't be funny at the expense of others. If you poke fun at anyone, let it be yourself.
4. Keep humor to a minimum in informative and persuasive speeches.
5. Avoid irrelevant humor: be sure that humorous stories fit into and complement the flow of meaning.

> **Jim's administrator was suing the railroad for his wrongful death. The first witness he called to the stand testified as follows: "I saw Jim walking up the track. A fast train passed, going up the track. After it passed, I didn't see Jim. I walked up the track a little way and discovered Jim's severed head lying on one side of the track, and the rest of his body on the other." The witness was asked how he reacted to his gruesome discovery. He responded: "I said to myself, 'Something serious must have happened to Jim.'"**
>
> **Something serious has been happening to constitutional government in America. I want to talk to you about it.[40]**

Had "Mr. Sam" paraphrased this story as "The witness reported that he knew instantly that the victim had had a serious accident," he would have destroyed its effect. Dialogue makes a narrative come alive by bringing listeners close to the action. Paraphrase distances the audience.

Evaluating Narratives

Speakers sometimes "borrow" a narrative from an anthology of stories or jokes and then strain to connect it with their topic. Narratives should never be used simply to amuse listeners. They must also help you make your point. An irrelevant narrative distracts listeners. Audiences can also be turned off by stories that foster negative stereotypes or that contain offensive language. Finally, ask yourself whether the narrative will seem fresh and original. If listeners have already heard your story, they may decide you have nothing new to say in the rest of your speech.

Storytelling is an important folk art. Set off the story from the rest of your speech by pausing as you begin and end the story. Slow down! Tales are to be savored, and pause is essential to add to the unfolding drama. Your language should be colorful and active, and you can use voice and dialect changes to signal listeners that a "character" is speaking. Create a sense of anticipation and suspense as you build to the punch line or conclusion. If your story evokes laughter, wait for it to subside before going on. Since storytelling is an intimate form of communication, reduce the distance between yourself and your listeners—either by actually moving toward them or by being less formal. Finally, you should practice telling your story to get the wording and timing just right.

Avoid stories that are funny at the expense of others. If you poke fun at anyone, let it be yourself. Speakers who tell amusing stories about themselves sometimes rise in the esteem of listeners. When this technique is effective, the stories that seem to put the speakers down are actually building them up.[41] Note how former president Jimmy Carter used this type of humor as he acknowledged his introduction as a speaker at commencement exercises at Rice University:

> **I didn't know what Charles [the person who introduced him] was going to say. For those who have been in politics and who are introduced, you never know what to expect. There was a time when I was introduced very simply. "Ladies and gentlemen, the President of the United States," period. But then when I left office I was quite often invited by lowly Democrats who were in charge of a program at an event. Then when I got there with two or three TV cameras, the leaders of the organization—almost invariably Republicans—would take over the introduction of me, and quite often the introduction would be a very negative one derived primarily from President Reagan's campaign notes. I had to do something to heal my relationship with the audience before I could speak so I always would tell them after that, "Ladies and gentlemen, of all the introductions I've ever had in my life, that is the most recent."[42]**

A well-told narrative can add much to a speech, but too many stories can turn a speech into a rambling string of tales without a clear focus. Use narratives to arouse or sustain attention, to create a special mood for your message, or to demonstrate some important truth.

Three Techniques for Using Supporting Materials

The best materials for building homes on hilltops are only as good as the builders who use them. Similarly, the best supporting materials for speeches depend for their effectiveness on the skill of speechmakers. Much of the art of building speeches depends on the wise use of three major techniques—comparison, contrast, and analogy.

Comparison

A **comparison** helps an audience grasp a subject by pointing out its similarities to something else. These similarities provide a context or frame in which the subject can be understood. In this way comparison can make an unfamiliar or controversial idea seem more clear or acceptable by connecting it with something the audience already understands or accepts. Comparisons can also help the audience see the significance of supporting materials. Consider how Maurice Johnson used comparison in a classroom speech to point up the meaning of a statistic:

> **Let's suppose that you have a job offer here in Memphis that pays $35,000 per year. You're not really sure you want to stay in Memphis, and you know salaries are higher in other cities. But how do these salaries really compare? Will that higher salary in Boston, or New York City, or Chicago actually be higher than what you could earn in Memphis? *Money Magazine*'s web site has a "Salary Comparator" that let's you see how things stack up. For example, in 2001, to equal the Memphis $35,000 salary, you'd have to make $63,000 in Chicago; in Boston, you'd have to make $69,000; and, in New York City you'd have to make a whopping $104,000.**

Here the background of similarities really makes the meaning of the hypothetical salary offer stand out in bold relief. Before you decide to use a comparison, ask yourself these questions:

- *Are there enough similarities to justify the comparison?* The similarities among four places that are all large urban cities in the United States might be enough to justify a comparison.
- *Are the similarities significant to the idea you wish to support?* The fact that crime statistics are higher (or lower) in New York City than in the other cities cited would not be especially pertinent to the point of the comparison.
- *Are there important differences that might invalidate the comparison?* Here you must imagine yourself as an unfriendly critic of the comparison. An unfriendly critic might argue that while the dollar has more purchasing power in Memphis, it might well have less to purchase. You will have to decide whether the comparison is strong enough to overcome such objections.

Contrast

A **contrast** emphasizes the differences among things. Just as a red cross stands out more vividly against a white background than against an orange one, contrasts make facts and statistics, examples, testimony, and narratives stand out. Note how Marge Anderson, chief executive of the Mille Lacs band of Ojibwe, used contrast in prestige testimony to illustrate fundamental cultural differences:

> In Genesis, the first book of the Old Testament, God creates man in his own image. Then God says, "Be fruitful, multiply, fill the earth and conquer it. Be masters of the fish of the sea, the birds of the heaven, and all living animals on the earth."
>
> Masters. Conquer. Nothing, nothing could be further from the way Indian people view the world and our place in it. Here are the words of the great nineteenth-century Chief Seattle:
>
> "You are a part of the earth, and the earth is a part of you. You did not weave the web of life, you are merely a strand in it. Whatever you do to the web, you do to yourself."
>
> In our tradition, there is no mastery. There is no conquering. Instead, there is kinship among all creation—humans, animals, birds, plants, even rocks. We are all part of the sacred hoop of the world, and we must all live in harmony with each other if that hoop is to remain unbroken.[43]

In his previously cited speech on campaign finance reform, Newton Minow used contrast in his introduction to heighten the effects of both example and statistics:

> Campaign spending is as old as the republic. When George Washington ran for the Virginia House of Burgesses in 1757, his total campaign expenditures, in the form of "good cheer," came to "28 gallons of rum, 50 gallons of rum punch, 34 gallons of wine, 36 gallons of beer, and 2 gallons of cider royal."
>
> Today, the era of good cheer is gone. For four decades now, campaign expenditures have been driven relentlessly upward by one thing: television. In 1960, in what would be the first presidential campaign to make wide use of television, Democrats and Republicans together spent $14.2 million on radio and television commercials. In 1996, candidates for federal office spent more than 128 times that amount on television and radio commercials, an estimated $1.8 billion.[44]

As you consider whether to use a particular contrast, ask yourself the following:

- *Is the sense of contrast dramatic enough to help my case?* The contrasts between 1757, 1960, and 1996 are quite striking.
- *Is the difference relevant to the point I wish to make?* The point that per capita consumption of alcoholic beverages also differed during these three eras would hardly serve the point of the contrast.
- *Are there other points of difference that might invalidate the point?* Again, take the point of view of an unfriendly critic. Such a person might point out that George Washington had to appeal to a highly elite electorate, all of whom lived in one small area of a state. The costs of federal elections with a national electorate are the price, such a critic might argue, of modern democracy.

Analogy

An **analogy** combines the principles of both comparison and contrast: *It points out the similarities between things or concepts that are essentially dissimilar.* Analogies come in two forms. The first, literal analogies, are much the same as comparison in that they tie together subjects from the same realm of experience, such as foot-

Ethics Alert! 6.1

SELECTING SUPPORTING MATERIALS

1. Provide details of the time, source, and context of information.
2. Don't present a claim or opinion as though it were a fact.
3. Remember that statistics are open to different interpretations.
4. Protect your listeners from biased information.
5. Inform listeners when the sources of information are not identifiable.
6. Avoid "quoting out of context" to misrepresent a person's position.
7. Be sure examples are representative of reality.
8. Never present hypothetical examples as though they were actual.
9. Avoid racist, ethnic, or gender-based humor that belittles others.

ball and soccer, to reinforce a point. The second form, **figurative analogy**, combines subjects from different realms of experience. Our opening to this chapter uses a figurative analogy between building homes and building speeches. We will return to this analogy over the next several chapters. Successful analogies make ideas that are remote or abstract seem more immediate and comprehensible—they are productive ways of thinking. They are especially useful near the beginnings of speeches, where they establish a frame of thinking in which the speech can develop. M. George Allen, senior vice president of research and development for the 3M Company, combined comparison, contrast, and analogy as he established a perspective for his speech, "Succeeding in Japan":

> **I think of doing business in Japan as being like a game of football. But first, you need to know which game of football it is you are playing. Is it the American gridiron sport—or what the rest of the world calls football and what we call soccer?**
>
> **American football is a bruising battle. The players are huge and strong. They have nicknames like "Refrigerator." And the game is played in short bursts of intense energy. In soccer football, the players are smaller, but faster. Play is continuous. And a soccer fullback weighs less than lunch for a gridiron fullback.**
>
> **In a nutshell, gridiron football is trench warfare: soccer football is the cavalry. Likewise, when it comes to business, the Japanese play a different game than we do.[45]**

In this example Mr. Allen first draws a *comparison* with football, perhaps to emphasize the aggressive, competitive qualities of international business. He next proceeds to develop a *contrast* between the sports of football and soccer to establish the basis for a *figurative analogy:* just as similar forms of sport can be quite different, so can styles of business reflect the fundamentally different lifestyles of nations.

As you weigh the use of an analogy, ask yourself the following:

- *Will the analogy help me make some fundamental point about my subject?*
- *Will the analogy distract my listeners?* In the above example, Mr. Allen risked losing some listeners who would prefer to think more about soccer and football than about international business practices.
- *Does the analogy establish a beneficial association for my subject?* Some critics complain that the analogy between sports and politics, so popular among American journalists who describe the "horserace" of political campaigning, both trivializes politics and dehumanizes politicians. The above example could illustrate a similar problem in talking about international business.

Deciding What Supporting Material You Should Use

In addition to the outlines students submit for their next speeches, ask them to write an attachment explaining and defending their selection of supporting materials. What do they hope to accomplish with each instance of supporting material?

The following general guidelines may help you make wise choices as you select supporting materials for your speech and ways to combine them:

1. If an idea is *controversial*, rely primarily on facts, statistics, factual examples, or expert testimony from sources the audience will respect and accept.
2. If your ideas or concepts are *abstract*, use examples and narratives to bring them to life. Use comparisons, contrasts, or analogies so that your listeners grasp your ideas and develop appropriate feelings about them.
3. If an idea is highly *technical*, supplement facts and statistics with expert testimony. Use definitions, explanations, and descriptions to aid understanding. Use examples, comparisons, contrasts, and analogies to help listeners integrate information.
4. If you need to *arouse emotions*, use lay and prestige testimony, examples, or narratives. Excite listeners by using contrast and analogy.
5. If you need to *defuse emotions*, emphasize facts and statistics and expert testimony. Keep the focus on definitions and explanations.
6. If your topic is *distant* from the lives of listeners, draw it closer to them through information, examples, and narratives, activated by descriptions, comparisons, and analogies.

Although the need for particular types of supporting material may vary with different topics and audiences, a good rule of thumb is to *support each main point with the most important and relevant facts and statistics available*. To clarify each point, use testimony, and provide sufficient definitions, explanations, and descriptions. Additionally, *support each main point with at least one interesting example or narrative*. To make your presentation more dramatic or memorable, emphasize examples and narratives, brought to life through striking comparisons, contrasts, or analogies.

In Summary

Facts and statistics, testimony, examples, and narratives are the major forms of *supporting materials*. They provide the substance, strength, credibility, and appeal a speech must have before listeners will place their faith in it.

Facts and Statistics. Information in the form of facts and statistics is the most objective form of supporting material, especially useful for unfamiliar or controversial topics. *Facts* are verifiable, which means that independent observers see and report them consistently. *Statistics* are numerical facts that describe the size of something, make predictions, illustrate trends, or show relationships. Be careful not to confuse factual statements with interpretations and claims. Be sure that your information meets the tests of relevance, recency, credibility, and reliability.

Use definitions, explanations, and descriptions to frame facts and statistics into powerful supports. A *definition* states the meaning of an unfamiliar term concisely in words the audience can understand. An *explanation* more fully expands on what something is or how it works. *Descriptions* are word pictures that help the audience visualize what you are talking about.

Testimony. *Testimony* cites the ideas or words of others in support of your message. When you repeat the exact words of others, you make use of *direct quotation*. When you summarize what others say, you *paraphrase* them. *Expert testimony* comes from recognized authorities who support the validity of your claims. *Lay testimony* represents "the voice of the people" on a topic; sometimes it takes the form of a *testi-*

monial. *Prestige testimony* connects your message with the general wisdom of some revered figure.

Be sure that the sources you cite are free from bias. State their credentials as you introduce their testimony, and never quote them out of context.

Examples. *Examples* serve as verbal illustrations. They help arouse interest, clarify ideas, sustain attention, personalize a topic, emphasize your major points, demonstrate how your ideas can be applied, and make it easier for listeners to remember your message. *Brief examples* mention specific instances. *Extended examples* contain more detail and give the speaker more time to build impressions. *Factual examples* are based on actual events and persons. *Hypothetical examples* are invented by the speaker to represent reality. Use people's names to personalize examples and magnify their power.

Narratives. A *narrative* tells a story that illustrates some truth about the topic. Good narratives draw listeners into the action and help establish a mood. They should be told in colorful, concrete language, using dialogue and characterization. A lively and informal style of presentation can enhance narration. Avoid narratives that demean others or reinforce negative stereotypes.

Three Techniques for Using Supporting Materials. Comparison, contrast, and analogy are general techniques used to make the most of supporting materials. *Comparison* points out the similarities of an unfamiliar or controversial topic to something the audience already understands or accepts. *Contrast* emphasizes the differences among things to make some important point. *Analogy* combines the principles of comparison and contrast to heighten awareness. *Figurative analogy* especially can help listeners see a topic in a new way by pointing out previously unexpected relationships.

Terms to Know

supporting materials
facts
claims
opinions
disinformation
statistics
definition
explanation
description
testimony
direct quotation
paraphrase
expert testimony
reluctant testimony
lay testimony
testimonial
prestige testimony
examples
brief example
extended example
factual example
hypothetical example
narrative
comparison
contrast
analogy
figurative analogy

Notes

1. Richard Weaver, "Ultimate Terms in Contemporary Rhetoric," in *The Ethics of Rhetoric* (Chicago: Henry Regnery, 1953), pp. 211–232.
2. Cynthia Crossen, *Tainted Truth: The Manipulation of Fact in America* (New York: Simon & Schuster, 1994), p. 36.
3. For similar commentary on other periodicals, see Howard Kahane, *Logic and Contemporary Rhetoric: The Use of Reason in Everyday Life* (Belmont, Calif.: Wadsworth, 1984), pp. 337–338.
4. Reprinted by permission of *World Book Encyclopedia*. This material was brought to our attention by Professor Gray Matthews of the University of Memphis.
5. Neil Postman, "Critical Thinking in the Electronic Era," *Phi Kappa Phi Journal* 65 (1985): 7.
6. Crossen, p. 36.
7. Franklin J. Boster, Kenzie A. Cameron, Shelly Campo, et al., "The Persuasive Effects of Statistical Evidence in the Presence of Exemplars," *Communication Studies* 51 (2000): 296–306.

8. Lonnie R. Bristow, "Protecting Youth from the Tobacco Industry," in *Vital Speeches of the Day*, 15 Mar. 1994, pp. 333–334.

9. Crossen, p. 42.

10. Peter Francese, "Editorial: Lies, Damned Lies . . . ," *American Demographics*, November 1994, p. 2.

11. Donna E. Shalala, "Domestic Terrorism: An Unacknowledged Epidemic," in *Vital Speeches of the Day*, 15 May 1994, p. 451.

12. John F. Smith Jr., "Eyes on the Road, Hands on the Wheel," *Vital Speeches of the Day*, 15 Nov. 2000, pp. 67–68.

13. Longinus, *On the Sublime*, trans. W. Rhys Roberts, in *The Great Critics: An Anthology of Literary Criticism*, 3rd ed., ed. James Harry Smith and Edd Winfield Parks (New York: W. W. Norton, 1951), p. 82.

14. Thabo Mbeki, "South Africa: Looking Towards the Future," *Vital Speeches of the Day*, 15 July 1999, p. 580.

15. Sam Nunn, "A New Way of Thinking," *Vital Speeches of the Day*, 1 May 2001, p. 425.

16. Kathleen Hall Jamieson appeared as a panelist on the CNN special report "Investigating the President: Media Madness?" aired on 28 Jan. 1998.

17. William L. Benoit and Kimberly A. Kennedy, "On Reluctant Testimony," *Communication Quarterly* 47 (1999): 376–387.

18. Bill Clinton, "First 1996 Presidential Debate," 6 Oct. 1996. http://www.cnn.com/ALLPOLITICS/1996/debates/transcripts/index.shtml (Accessed 10 Oct. 1996).

19. Benoit and Kennedy, p. 377.

20. The power of lay testimony is one possible implication of Michael Calvin McGee's "In Search of the People: A Rhetorical Alternative," *Quarterly Journal of Speech* 61 (1975): 235–249.

21. For a critique of such faith in political polling, see J. Michael Hogan, "George Gallup and the Rhetoric of Scientific Democracy," *Communication Monographs* 64 (1997): 161–179.

22. Bill Moyers, "Best of Jobs: To Have and Serve the Public's Trust," keynote address at the PBS Annual Meeting, 23 June 1996, reprinted in *Current*, 8 July 1996.

23. Colin Powell, "Sharing in the American Dream," in *Vital Speeches of the Day*, 1 June, 1997, p. 484. Excerpt from "Harlem (A Dream Deferred)" by Langston Hughes. From *Collected Poems of Langston Hughes* by Langston Hughes, copyright © 1994 by the Estate of Langston Hughes. Used by permission of Alfred A. Knopf, a division of Random House, Inc.

24. Brock Evans, "A Time of Crisis: The Giveaway of our Public Lands," in *Vital Speeches of the Day*, 1 Sept. 1995, p. 691.

25. "On the Campaign Trail," *Reader's Digest*, March 1992, p. 116.

26. Chester Burger, "Sooner Than You Think: Technology Pulling the World Together," *Vital Speeches of the Day*, 15 Sept. 2000, p. 715.

27. *Newsweek*, 27 Jan. 1997, p. 86.

28. Sue Suter, "Disability Is No Big Deal: Seeing People as They Really Are," in *Vital Speeches of the Day*, 15 Aug. 1997, pp. 650–651.

29. Hillary Rodham Clinton, "Women's Rights are Human Rights," in *Vital Speeches of the Day*, 1 Oct. 1995, p. 739.

30. Suter, p. 649.

31. Suter, p. 650.

32. Jerome S. Bruner, *Acts of Meaning* (Cambridge: Harvard University Press, 1990), and "The Narrative Construction of Reality," *Critical Inquiry* 18 (1991): 1–21.

33. Z. Kunda, D. T. Miller, and T. Claire, "Combining Social Concepts: The Role of Causal Reasoning," *Cognitive Science* 14 (1990): 551–577.

34. Associated Press, "Gore Promotes Benefits of Good Storytelling," *Memphis Commercial Appeal*, 8 Oct. 1995, p. B2.

35. "M.B.A.s Who Tell Stories Get a Jump on the Job Search," excerpted from *Spotlight*, 15 Sept. 1995.

36. Heather Rouston Ettinger, "Shattering the Glass Floor: Women Donors as Leaders of Fundamental Change," *Vital Speeches of the Day*, 15 Sept. 2000, p. 727.

37. Roger Ailes, *You Are the Message* (New York: Doubleday, 1988), pp. 70–74.

38. Bob Newhart, "Humor Makes Us Free: Laughter Gives Us Distance," in *Vital Speeches of the Day*, 15 July 1997, p. 607.

39. Newton Minow, "Campaign Finance Reform: We Have Failed to Solve the Problem," in *Vital Speeches of the Day*, 1 July 1997, p. 558.

40. Sam J. Ervin Jr., "Judicial Verbicide: An Affront to the Constitution," presented at Herbert Law Center, Louisiana State University, Baton Rouge, 22 Oct. 1980, in *Representative American Speeches 1980–1981*, ed. Owen Peterson (New York: H. W. Wilson, 1981), p. 62.

41. Charles R. Gruner, "Advice to the Beginning Speaker on Using Humor—What the Research Tells Us," *Communication Education* 34 (1985): 142–147; and Christie McGuffee Smith and Larry Powell, "The Use of Disparaging Humor by Group Leaders," *Southern Speech Communication Journal* 53 (1988): 279–292.

42. Jimmy Carter, "Excellence Comes from a Repository That Doesn't Change: The True Meaning of Success," in *Vital Speeches of the Day*, 1 July 1993, p. 546.

43. Marge Anderson, "Looking Through Our Window: The Value of Indian Culture," *Vital Speeches of the Day*, 1 Aug. 1999, p. 633.

44. Minow, pp. 555–556.

45. M. George Allen, "Succeeding in Japan: One Company's Perspective," in *Vital Speeches of the Day*, 1 May 1994, p. 430.

7

Structuring Your Speech

OUTLINE

THIS CHAPTER WILL HELP YOU

- develop a simple, balanced, and orderly speech design
- select and arrange your main points
- plan transitions to make your speech flow smoothly
- prepare effective introductions for your speeches
- design memorable conclusions for your speeches

Global warming is a gradual warming of the earth caused by human activities that dump carbon dioxide and other gases into the atmosphere. August 1998 was the hottest month since weather records have been kept. Fossil fuel use has more than doubled since 1950. One cause of global warming is industrial emissions. The ten hottest years in recorded history have occurred since 1970. Skin cancers could increase as much as 26 percent if the ozone level drops another 10 percent. El Niño seems to be related to global warming. Global warming endangers our world.

How much of this randomly scrambled information would you remember if you heard it presented this way? There seems to be important news here, but it gets lost because it is poorly organized. A well-organized presentation makes it easier for listeners to learn and remember your message.[1]

Suppose you must take basic physics next semester and you get the following material from Students for Better Teaching about the instructors who teach the course:

> JOHNSON, DENNIS Professor Johnson is very entertaining. He tells a lot of funny stories and puts on demonstrations that seem like a "magic show." But he doesn't explain difficult material in any systematic fashion, so it's hard to take notes. When it's time for departmental examinations, you often don't know how or what to study.
>
> MARTINEZ, MARIA Professor Martinez is very businesslike. She starts each lecture by reviewing the material covered in the last session and asks if anyone has questions. Her lectures are easy to follow. She points out what is most important for students to know and uses clear examples that make difficult ideas easier to understand and apply.

Which instructor would you choose? When a message is important, most of us would choose the well-organized person over the entertainer. In fact, a recent study indicated that students dislike instructors who go off on tangents, jump from one idea to another, ramble, or are generally disorganized.[2]

How well your presentation is organized affects your ethos.[3] As we noted in Chapter 2, "competence" is an important part of credibility. It is hard for listeners to think of you as competent when your speech is poorly organized. They may conclude either that you lack the capacity to organize or that you did not care enough to prepare carefully.

In this chapter we look at the principles that underlie well-organized messages to explain how to structure the body of your speech. Next, we consider the important role of transitions in making a speech flow smoothly. Finally, we discuss how to prepare effective introductions and conclusions.

Every discourse ought to be a living creature; having a body of its own and head and feet; there should be a middle, beginning, and end, adapted to one another and to the whole.

—Plato

Ask students to identify two instructors they have had: one who was well-organized and one who was poorly organized. Ask them how they responded to these instructors—the one whom they found it easiest to learn from, and the one whose class they enjoyed the most. Relate being organized to a speaker's credibility.

Principles of Good Form

The structure of a speech should follow the ways people naturally arrange things in their minds. People rarely store information in individual bits. Instead they "chunk" material for easy recall. For example, people recall telephone numbers as two or three chunks of numbers such as 219-647-2830, not 2-1-9-6-4-7-2-8-3-0.[4] Information is organized according to a few simple principles of **good form**.[5] To develop good form, you should keep your presentation simple, balance the parts of your speech, and arrange your main points so that they flow smoothly. In other words, good form depends on simplicity, balance, and order.

Simplicity

A simple design makes it easy for listeners to follow, understand, and remember your message.[6] Simplicity is important because listeners usually do not have manuscripts to refer to if material is confusing. To achieve **simplicity**, you should limit the number of your main ideas and keep your design direct and to the point.

Number of Main Points. The fewer main points in a speech, the better because each main point must be developed.[7] It takes time to present information, examples, narratives, and testimony effectively. Short classroom speeches usually should have no more than four main points. Look at what happens when a speech becomes overburdened with main points:

Thesis statement: Government welfare programs aren't working.

Main points:
I. There are too many programs.
II. The programs often duplicate coverage.
III. Some people who need help are left out.
IV. The programs are poorly funded.
V. The programs waste money.
VI. Recipients have no input into what is needed.
VII. The programs create dependence.
VIII. The programs stifle initiative.
IX. They rob the poor of self-respect.

Each of these points may be important, but presented this way they could be confusing. It would be hard for listeners to remember them. They are not organized into a meaningful pattern of "chunks." Let's see how these ideas might be clustered into a simpler structural pattern:

Make a poster containing pictures of fifteen randomly-displayed objects. Let the students view the poster for thirty seconds, then ask them to list all of the objects they saw. Display a second poster containing three groups of five related objects, i.e. man's shoe, woman's shoe, baby's shoe, cowboy boot, snow boot. After thirty seconds, ask students to list the objects on that poster. Discuss the effects of organization upon recall.

Thesis statement: Our approach to welfare in America is inadequate, inefficient, and insensitive.

Main point: I. Our approach is inadequate.
Subpoints:
A. We don't fund it sufficiently.
B. Some people who need help get left out.

Main point: II. Our approach is inefficient.
Subpoints:
A. There are too many programs.
B. There is too much duplication.
C. There is too much waste of money.

Main point:	III.	Our approach is insensitive.
Subpoints:		A. It creates dependence.
		B. It stifles initiative.
		C. It robs people of self-respect.

This simpler structure makes the speech easy to follow. Each main point has subpoints that extend its meaning. Overlapping points have been combined, and unnecessary ideas have been omitted. The result is a design that helps listeners remember.[8]

Phrasing Main Points. You should state your main points simply. In our example, the new wording of main points is clear and direct. The repeated phrase ("Our approach is . . .") suggests that these are *main* points and helps listeners remember them. It allows the speaker to refer to the "Three I's" of welfare (Inadequate, Inefficient, and Insensitive) in the introduction and conclusion, a strategy that ties the speech together.

Balance

Have students watch a local, television news broadcast and observe how the producer achieves balance in terms of international, national, and local news.

Balance means that the major parts of your speech—the introduction, the body, and the conclusion—receive appropriate development. Instructors typically specify time limits for speeches, so keep these in mind as you plan your message. It can be very upsetting to finish the first point of your speech and find that you have only one minute left and two more points plus your conclusion to present. Time yourself as you practice your speech to be sure it fits within the time limits. The following suggestions will help you plan a balanced presentation:

1. *The body should be the longest part of your speech.* It contains your major ideas. If you spend three minutes on your introduction, a minute and a half on the body, and thirty seconds on the conclusion, your speech will be out of balance.

2. *Consider the development of each main point.* If your main points seem equally important, you should give each point *equal emphasis*. This strategy might be appropriate for the speech on the "Three I's" of welfare policy, in which each point merits equal attention.

   If your main points vary in importance, however, you must adjust your strategy. You might start with the most important point, spending more of your time on it, then present the other points in a *descending order* of emphasis, according to their importance. For example, in a problem-solution speech, you may need to convince listeners that there actually is a problem. Thus you would devote most of your time to meeting the challenge of establishing this first main point. Such a speech appears at the end of Chapter 13.

   Alternatively, you might wish to develop your main points in an *ascending order* of emphasis. If listeners agree there is a problem, but don't know what to do about it, then you should devote most of your time to your solution, the second main point. Such a speech appears at the end of Chapter 14. Figure 7.1 illustrates how these orders of emphasis can work.

3. *The introduction and conclusion should be about equal in length.* The total amount of time spent on your introduction and conclusion should be less than the amount spent on the body of your speech. As a general rule, in a five-minute presentation, the combined length of the introduction and conclusion should be about a minute. This leaves four minutes to develop the main points of the message.

Equal Emphasis	Descending Order	Ascending Order
Introduction	Introduction	Introduction
1	1	1
2	2	2
3	3	3
Conclusion	Conclusion	Conclusion

FIGURE 7.1
Balanced Speeches

Order

A speech that meets the requirement of **order** follows a consistent pattern of development from beginning to end. It starts by introducing its subject and purpose, continues by developing ideas in the body of the speech, and ends by summarizing and reflecting on the meaning of what it has accomplished. To build an orderly speech, you should design the body of the speech first because that is where you will do the hard work of demonstrating, proving, and illustrating your message. Once you have organized the body, you can prepare an introduction and conclusion tailored to your purpose.

Order also applies to the way you arrange your main points. If you propose a solution, you should first present the problem. Why? Because that is how our minds work. We don't normally come up with solutions, then look for problems to fit them. An orderly arrangement is also important when you are presenting the steps in a process. Begin with the first step, then cover the rest in the order in which they occur. If you jump around, the audience may get lost, decide that you are unprepared, or conclude that the disorderly speech reflects a disorderly mind.

Have students read a speech from Appendix C and write a critique in terms of how well the speech satisfied the principles of good form. Was the structure simple, balanced, and easy to follow? Was each part of the speech the proper length in relation to the whole? Were transitions used to make the speech flow smoothly?

Structuring the Body of Your Speech

In developing the body of your speech, you have three major tasks to accomplish:

1. You must select your main points.
2. You must arrange your main points effectively.
3. You must decide on supporting materials.

Selecting Your Main Points

Copy a short newspaper or magazine article on a topic such as global warming. Distribute this to the class and have them identify the main points and the principle by which these points are arranged. Discuss whether any other designs might have been more appropriate.

Use the "Impromptu Structuring" exercise in Chapter 7 of the IRM.

Your **main points** are the most important ideas of your message, the points you wish to emphasize. How do you identify and construct them? As you research your topic, you should discover some repeated themes. These are the most important issues connected with your topic. Consider how they relate to your specific purpose, your thesis statement, and the needs and interests of your listeners. From them will come the main points of your speech.

Let's look at how you might select the main points for a speech on global warming. Begin with a **research overview**, listing your main sources of information and a summary of the major ideas from each. Figure 7.2 presents a research overview based on four sources of information: a *Time* magazine special issue, summary reports from the Intergovernmental Panel on Climate Change, an article from *U.S. News & World Report*, and research reports from the Environment News Service. Scanning the overview, you might come up with the following themes:

- Increased temperatures are evidence of global warming.
- Human activities cause global warming.
- Global warming will cause climate changes.
- Global warming will cause health, environmental, and economic problems.

ESL: Distribute copies of several short newspaper articles on the same subject. Ask students to read these and prepare a research overview as shown in Figure 7.2. Their task is to identify the main themes of the articles and to show how these might become the main points of a presentation.

Once you have identified the major themes from the research, you need to determine how these relate to your specific purpose and your audience. In this example, your specific purpose is "to inform my audience about the problem of global warming." You anticipate that the audience's knowledge of the subject may be limited and even confused. Therefore, you decide that your first major challenge will be to define global warming in terms these listeners can understand, using simple, everyday comparisons and explanations. Thereafter, to deepen audience understanding, you decide that you must describe the consequences and causes of the problem. In light of the major themes revealed by your research overview, you might proceed to fashion the following main points:

1. Global warming is a gradual warming of the earth's surface.
2. Global warming may cause climate changes and health problems.
3. The major causes of global warming are industrial emissions, deforestation, and personal energy use.

FIGURE 7.2
Sample Research Overview

Environment News Service	Time	U.S. News	Intergovernmental Panel on Climate Change
1. Increase in Earth's temperature 2. Build-up of greenhouse gases 3. Flooding and climate changes 4. Attributed to human influences	1. Use less energy 2. Drive efficient vehicles 3. Go with solar or gas energy 4. Geoengineering ideas	1. CO_2 problems 2. Climate changes 3. What we can do A. Learn more about it B. Save energy C. Drive less	1. Climate changes 2. U.S. largest polluter 3. Energy and global warming 4. Transportation and global warming

Arranging Your Main Points

Once you have determined your main points, you must decide how to arrange them. You need to come up with a way of ordering them that is appropriate for your audience, fits your material, and serves your specific purpose. For example, in the above case, the first main point will provide needed definitions and heighten interest. The next point will establish the possible negative effects of global warming. The final main point will cover the major causes of global warming.

As we noted earlier in this chapter, people mentally organize information into patterns that are easy to remember. These patterns set up expectations that are used to process further experiences. They function like mental templates into which we fit new information. We see and experience the world through them. The way we arrange our speeches must be in harmony with these expectations. *These templates are based on the principles of similarity, proximity, and closure.* In this section we discuss some basic speech designs that relate to these principles. More detailed examples of speech designs are provided in Chapters 12 and 13, which cover informative and persuasive speaking.

Similarity. The **principle of similarity** leads people to group things together that seem alike. This tendency underlies the *categorical design* for speeches. Speakers use categories when they discuss "three major causes of global warming" or "the four basic components of a good stereo system." Categories can be based on the actual divisions of a topic, such as the symptoms of a disease. They also may represent customary ways of thinking about a subject, such as the four basic food groups. Such factors go together because they seem alike in some important way.

Have students visualize the way things are arranged in a grocery or department store. Ask them to identify the principles by which items are arranged.

Proximity. The **principle of proximity** suggests that things that usually occur together in time or space should be presented in the order in which they naturally occur. For example, a how-to speech should have a *sequential design* that presents the steps in the order in which they should be taken. If you want to discuss the events that led to a present-day problem, you might use the sequential design to present a historical perspective on the situation. Your research may show

Ask students to name the four time zones in the United States. If they live in the eastern United States, they will probably say, "Eastern, Central, Mountain, and Pacific." If they live in the western United States, they will probably say "Pacific, Mountain, Central, and Eastern." Ask them to identify the principle by which they arranged their response.

Speeches that use sequential design follow a step-by-step pattern of development.

that the major events occurred in 1955, 1970, and 1987. If you follow this chronological pattern, your speech will be easy to understand. But if you start talking about 1970, then jump back to 1955, then leap ahead to the present before doubling back to 1987, you will probably lose most of your listeners by violating the principle of proximity.

If you were preparing a speech on the wineries in California's Napa Valley, you might well use a *spatial design*. Such a design is based on physical relationships, such as east-west, up-down, or points around a circle. You might begin at Domaine Chandon at the southernmost end of the valley, take listeners next to the wineries along the Silverado Trail, and end up with the cable ride to the top of the hill at the Sterling Winery. This way your audience gets a verbal map to follow as well as a picture of the major wineries in the valley.

Closure. The **principle of closure** is based on people's natural tendency to seek completion.[9] We like to have patterns carried through so that we feel we have the "whole story." Have you ever started reading a magazine article in a waiting room, only to find that someone had torn out the last page of the story? Do you remember how frustrated you felt? Your need for closure had been violated.

The principle of closure applies to several speech designs. For example, if you omit an important category when developing your topic, listeners may notice its omission. If you leave out a necessary step in a sequence, audiences may sense the flaw. Although all speeches should satisfy this need, there are two speech patterns for which closure is absolutely essential. These are *cause-effect* and *problem-solution designs*. Because we want the world to seem purposeful and controllable, we want all events to have clear causes and all problems to have satisfactory solutions.

A cause-effect speech can go in two directions: it can begin by focusing on some present situation as an effect and then seek its causes, or it can look at the present as a potential cause of future effects. Sometimes these variations can be combined. You might take a current situation, such as a budget deficit on campus, and develop a speech tracing its origins. If you had enough time, you might continue by predicting the future effects of the deficit, such as tuition increases. Understanding the causes could help your listeners see what needs to be done to reduce the deficit. Predicting future effects might make them want to reduce it.

The problem-solution design focuses attention on a problem and then provides a solution for it. Such speeches often must arouse strong feelings to motivate listeners. Once you have aroused emotions, your solutions must show listeners a way out of the problem, or they will feel frustrated.

Use the principles of similarity, proximity, and closure to develop the most effective design for your speech.

Speaker's Notes 7.1

DETERMINING AND ARRANGING YOUR MAIN POINTS

1. Prepare a research overview to identify repeated ideas.
2. Create main points in light of your purpose and the needs of your audience.
3. Limit your main points to four or fewer for a short speech.
4. Apply the principle of similarity as you develop categories.
5. Apply the principle of proximity as you arrange main points in sequential or spatial patterns.
6. Apply the principle of closure as you provide completeness in cause-effect and problem-solution designs.

Adding Supporting Materials

Once you have selected and arranged your main points, you must support them with facts and figures, testimony, examples, or narratives. As you develop your main points, also consider whether you need to divide them into subpoints. The subpoints should contain information or ideas that listeners need to understand or accept the main point. For example, let us assume that you are presenting a speech on the topic "New Weapons in the War on Cancer." As you design the speech, you frame the following main point: "Scientists have developed productive new ways of thinking in cancer research." To develop this main point, you realize that you must establish two subpoints: "Scientists no longer seek to *cure* cancer" and "Scientists now seek to *control* cancer."

You strengthen both main points and subpoints by providing supporting materials. In the instance just mentioned, you could support your first subpoint by presenting facts, testimony, and narratives that show how scientists were at first frustrated by their inability to find a magic bullet—the master cure for cancer. To support your second subpoint, you might explain how scientists now approach the research problem of controlling cancer. You might use examples to show how powerful new drugs successfully stop the growth of cancer cells in specific forms of the disease. Notice that you have also used two of the special techniques discussed in Chapter 6. The first is *contrast*, drawn between past and present, cure and control. These dramatic contrasts should interest listeners and help them to see your point clearly. The second technique is *analogy*, especially the figurative analogy between scientific research and war (new "weapons," "war on cancer," the researcher as heroic "warrior," and so forth). This technique heightens the drama and can also aid understanding, especially when subjects are complex and abstract. Note, for example, how Dr. Leonard Saltz, a colon cancer specialist at Memorial Sloan-Kettering, used another figurative analogy (often called *metaphor*) to illustrate the significance of this contrast in research approaches: "I don't think we're going to hit home runs, but if we can get a series of line-drive singles going and put enough singles back to back, we can score runs."[10] The example shows how both contrast and analogy can make supporting materials more effective.

In Chapter 6 we provided general guidelines for selecting supporting materials. Here we show how to work supporting materials into the structure of your speech. Supporting materials help to fortify a message against the doubts or disagreements of reasonable listeners. They answer the basic questions that listeners often ask:

Ask students to read a speech from Appendix C and identify the supporting materials in terms of how well they were integrated into the structure of the speech. Note especially whether the source was cited and identified.

1. *What is the basis of that idea?* (You answer with facts or statistics.)
2. *How do you know? Who else says so?* (You supply testimony.)
3. *How does it work? Where is it true?* (You offer an example.)
4. *So what? Why should I care?* (You develop a narrative that explains why.)

Although the situation will vary from topic to topic, speaker to speaker, and audience to audience, it is possible to set up an ideal model for the support of any main point or important subpoint. This model includes the point plus the following supporting materials:

- The most important relevant facts and statistics
- The most authoritative testimony offered by respected sources
- At least one story or example that clarifies the idea or brings it to life

Figure 7.3 provides a format for applying this model to support a point. Assume that you want to demonstrate the main point that suntans are not a sign of good health. Here is another way you could follow this format to support the point:

FIGURE 7.3
Outline Format for Supporting a Point

Statement: ____
____

Transition into facts or statistics: ______________________________

1. Factual information or statistics that support statement: ________
____
____

Transition into testimony: ______________________________

2. Testimony that supports statement: ______________________
____
____

Transition into example or narrative: ______________________

3. Example or narrative that supports statement: ______________
____
____
____

Transition into restatement: ______________________________

Restatement of original assertion: ________________________
____

Have students make a short, one-point presentation that illustrates the outline format for supporting a point as described in Figure 7.3.

Statement:	Suntans are not as good for you as they look on you.
Transition:	Let's examine some of the evidence.
Facts/statistics:	According to a 1995 report by the American Cancer Society, prolonged exposure without protection is responsible for about 90 percent of all skin cancers.
Transition:	Moreover, exposure without protection also accelerates the aging process.
Expert testimony:	According to Dr. John M. Knox, head of dermatology at the Baylor University College of Medicine, "If you do biopsies on the buttocks of people ages seventy-five and thirty-five, you won't see any differences under the microscope. . . . Protected skin stays youthful much longer."
Transition:	Let's look at one person who suffered from overexposure.
Example:	Jane was a fair-skinned blond-haired girl who loved swimming and sunbathing. She often sunburned but didn't think there would be any effects other than the short-term pain. Having a good tan seemed so healthy, she didn't dream it could harm her. Now at forty-five, she knows better. She couldn't believe it when her doctor told her she had skin cancer. Now she can't go out into the sun, even for a few minutes, without using a sunscreen and wearing a hat, a long-sleeved shirt, and long pants.
Transition:	What does all this mean?

InterConnections.LearnMore 7.1

PRINCIPLES OF PERCEPTION

Gestalt and the Principles of Design in Art
http://daphne.palomar.edu/design/gestalt.html
An article covering the concepts of closure, continuance, similarity, proximity, and alignment, including how they apply to the graphic arts; prepared by Professor James T. Saw of the Art Department at Palomar College, San Marcos, California.

The Gestalt Archive **http://www.enabling.org/ia/gestalt/gerhards/archive.html**
Links to some of the classic writings in gestalt psychology, including the first chapter of Koffka's 1935 *Principles of Gestalt Psychology* (http://www.enabling.org/ia/gestalt/gerhards/Koffka.html) and Luchins and Luchins's 1959 "Comments on the Concept of Closure" (http://www.enabling.org/ia/gestalt/gerhards/closure.html).

Gestalt Laws of Organization
http://www.epsychlopedia.net/concepts/sensationAndPerception/sensandperc6.html
A resource for introductory psychology students and educators; provides a basic understanding of psychological terms and concepts.

Restatement: A suntan may make you look healthy, but it is not healthy. Overexposure to the sun causes cancer and premature aging. Are you willing to take that risk just to look good for a brief time?

In this example, three forms of supporting material—statistical information, expert testimony, and example—work together to establish the main point. Each contributes its special strength. If each of your main points is well supported, your message should stand up even if challenged.

Using Transitions

Our example of using supporting materials also illustrates the way **transitions** work in a speech. Transitions show your listeners how your ideas connect with one another. They help your listeners focus on the meaning of what you have already discussed and prepare them for what is still to come. They serve as signposts that help listeners see the overall pattern of your message. Transitions connect your main points and tie the body of a speech to its introduction and conclusion.

Some transitions are simple, short phrases such as "Another point that must be made is . . ." More often, however, transitions are worded as phrases that link ideas. For example, the sentence "Having looked at why people don't pay compliments more often, let's consider some ways to give them" summarizes what you have just said and directs listeners to your next point.

ESL: Show ESL students how to emphasize transitions through the use of stress, rate, pitch, volume, energy, and pauses.

Certain stock words or phrases can be used to signal changes in a speech. For example, words and phrases like *until now* or *only last week* point out time changes. Transitions such as *in addition* show that you are expanding on what you have already said. The use of the word *similarly* indicates that a comparison will follow. Phrases such as *on the other hand* cue listeners to a contrast. Cause-and-effect relationships can be suggested with words like *as a result* or *consequently*. Introductory phrases like *traveling north* can indicate spatial relationships. Phrases or words like *in short*, *finally*, or *in conclusion* signal that the speech is coming to its end. Figure 7.4 contains a list of some commonly used transitions.

FIGURE 7.4
Common Transitions

To Indicate	Use
Time Changes	until, now, since, previously, later, earlier, in the past, in the future, meanwhile, five years ago, just last month, tomorrow, following, before, at present, eventually
Additions	moreover, in addition, furthermore, besides
Comparison	compared with, both are, likewise, in comparison, similarly, of equal importance, another type of, like, alike, just as
Contrast	but, yet, however, on the other hand, conversely, still, otherwise, in contrast, unfortunately, despite, rather than, on the contrary
Cause-Effect	therefore, consequently, thus, accordingly, so, as a result, hence, since, because of, due to, for this reason
Numerical Order	first, second, third, in the first place, to begin with, initially, next, eventually, finally
Spatial Relations	to the north, alongside, to the left, above, moving eastward, in front of, in back of, behind, next to, below, nearby, in the distance
Explanation	to illustrate, for example, for instance, case in point, in other words, to simplify, to clarify
Importance	most importantly, above all, keep this in mind, remember, listen carefully, take note of, indeed
The Speech is Ending	in short, finally, in conclusion, to summarize

An **internal summary** is a special type of transition that reminds listeners of the points you have covered before you move on to the next part of your message. Internal summaries are especially useful in cause-effect and problem-solution speeches where they signal that you have finished your discussion of the causes or problem and are now going to describe the effects or solution. In addition, an internal summary condenses and repeats your ideas, which can help your listeners remember your message. If listeners have somehow missed the point, the transition helps get them back on track. Consider the following example:

> **So now we see what the problem is. We know the cost in human suffering. We know the terrible political consequences and the enormous economic burden. The question is, What are we going to do about it? Let me tell you about a plan that experts agree may turn things around.**

Internal summaries should be brief and to the point so that they highlight the major features of your message.

A lack of planned transitions may cause beginning speakers to overuse words and vocalized pauses such as *well*, *you know*, *okay*, or "*er*." Plan a variety of transitions to help your speech flow smoothly. If you have trouble developing effective transitions, rethink the structure of your message. Outline your thoughts to be sure that they move in a clear direction and an orderly sequence. We cover outlining in Chapter 8.

Once you have identified and arranged your main points, decided how to develop them with supporting materials, and planned how to connect them with transitions, you can prepare an introduction and conclusion that will begin and end your speech effectively. Introductions and conclusions are very important because listeners tend to be most affected by what they hear at the beginning and end of a message.[11] The introduction allows you to make a good first impression and to set the stage for how your audience will respond. The conclusion gives you a final opportunity to make a lasting impression.

Introducing Your Message

The introduction to your speech is the invitation you give your audience to listen. When you first begin to speak, the audience will have two basic concerns in mind: *Why should I listen to this speech?* and *Why should I listen to this speaker?* These questions relate to two of the three basic functions of an introduction. First, it should capture attention and arouse interest so that your audience wants to listen to your message. Second, it should help establish your ethos as a competent, trustworthy, and likeable person with whom the audience can identify. Finally, your introduction should focus and preview your message to make it easier for the audience to follow.

A successful introduction also helps prepare you to present the rest of your speech. When you get off to a good start, you have less performance anxiety. Therefore, you should prepare your introduction carefully. Practice until you are confident and comfortable with your opening words. Establish good eye contact with listeners. *Do not read your introduction!*

Use the "Optional Introductions and Conclusions" exercise in Chapter 7 of the IRM.

Capturing Attention

All too often, speakers open their presentations with something like "Good evening. My speech tonight is on . . . ," then jump right into their message. Needless to say, this is not a good way to begin a speech. It does not make the audience want to listen.

There are several ways to attract, build, and hold the interest of your audience. You may:

Tape several television commercials to show in class. Have your students identify the techniques used to attract, build, and hold interest and attention in these ads.

- Involve the audience.
- Ask questions.
- Relate a personal experience.
- Tell a story.
- Use humor.
- Develop suspense.
- Begin with a quotation.
- Use a presentation aid.
- Startle listeners.

Involve the Audience. You involve listeners when you connect them with your message. One of the most frequently used involvement techniques is to offer sincere, well-deserved compliments. Does the group, the location, the occasion, or an audience member merit praise? People like to hear good things about themselves and their community. This technique is often used in formal speeches when custom requires a speaker to make such acknowledgments before moving

The introduction of your speech must immediately engage your audience. If you don't get their attention within the first minute of speaking, they may be lost to you forever.

into the actual presentation. These introductory remarks can be very brief, as illustrated by the opening words of President John F. Kennedy in a speech given at a White House dinner honoring Nobel Prize winners:

> **I think this is the most extraordinary collection of talent, of human knowledge, that has ever been gathered together at the White House, with the possible exception of when Thomas Jefferson dined alone.[12]**

With this elegant tribute, Kennedy was able to honor his guests without embarrassing them or going overboard with praise. His witty reference to the genius of Thomas Jefferson also paid tribute to the past.

Involvement is especially important if your topic seems distant from the audience's immediate concerns or experiences. A student at Kutztown University wanted to give an informative speech on the Black Plague of the Middle Ages. He knew that he had to do something dramatic to involve his audience from the outset to make the topic interesting and relevant. Here is how he handled it:[13]

> **As the students entered the classroom, a confederate gave each a card containing the name of a profession, such as clergyman, sailor, farmer, or merchant. The number of cards for each profession was proportional to its representation in European society at the time of the plague. When the student's name was called to speak, he entered from the back of the room wearing an oversized black sweatshirt, hood up, cinched around the waist with a length of sash cord. He opened with a rhetorical question, "If the Black Plague were to strike Kutztown today, given the same medical limitations, how many do you think would survive?" He then asked everyone to stand, and after a pause, continued as follows: "Will all of you with a card reading 'physician' please sit down. In tending the sick, you have come in contact with the disease and have become one of its victims." A student took her seat. He followed with "Will all of those identified as 'sailor' or 'merchant' please be seated. You have traveled about the country or the world and so have also**

come close to other victims and have sealed your fate." Five more students sat down. He then called out the clergy, city dwellers, dock workers, soldiers, and others who would have been exposed to the disease.

By the time he finished reading the list of those most susceptible to the disease, only three of his twenty-five classmates were left standing. He then explained that if the plague were to strike Kutztown the way it did many cities during the Middle Ages, those three would have the awesome task of rebuilding society.

Your introduction need not be this dramatic to involve the audience. If you can demonstrate that what you are talking about matters to listeners, your speech will be more effective.[14] You also can involve them by relating your topic to their motivations or attitudes and by using inclusive pronouns such as *we* and *our*.

Ask Questions. Speakers will often open a presentation with a question or series of questions. Questions start the audience thinking about a topic and also get them actively involved. Sometimes the questions will call for a direct answer. For example, Holly Carlson, a student at Vanderbilt, opened a speech on censorship by reading a list of banned books. As she read off the title of each book, she asked listeners to raise their hands if they had read it.

Caution students that when asking questions they must be careful not to let the speech get away from them and evolve into a dialogue with the audience.

Not all questions used in speeches call for direct answers, however. **Rhetorical questions** (such as "Have you ever thought about what your life would be like if you were a different color?") arouse curiosity and start listeners thinking about the topic. Wendy Liebmann, president of WSL Strategic Retailers, opened a speech to the Non-Prescription Drug Manufacturers Association with the following series of rhetorical questions:

Have you ever wondered of late what's going on with consumers? Why they are so full of contradictions when it comes to spending money? Why they will buy a $500 leather jacket at full price but wait for a $50 sweater to go on sale? Will buy a top-of-the-line sports utility vehicle then go to Costco to buy new tires? Will eagerly pay $3.50 for a cup of coffee but think $1.29 is too expensive for a hamburger? Will spend $2.00 for a strawberry-smelling bath soap but wait for a coupon to buy a 99-cent twin pack of toilet soap?

The economy is booming. Unemployment is at a 25-year low. Real income has increased. Why isn't everyone out spending like they did in the 1980s—shopping everywhere, buying everything? Why are so many companies struggling? What is this paradox? Is there a paradox? Well, that's what we are going to talk about today. This apparent consumer paradox: what it is, what it means, and how to make sense of it.[15]

Relate a Personal Experience. An old adage suggests that people are interested first in themselves, next in other people, then in things, and finally in ideas. This may explain why relating a topic to personal experience heightens audience interest. When speakers have been personally involved with a topic, they gain credibility. We are more willing to listen to others and take their advice if we know they have traveled the road themselves. Jason Shafer, a Dean's List student at Vanderbilt University, related the following personal experience as he began his self-introductory speech:

With a lot of hard work, your son will hopefully make it through a trade school. That heart-gripping statement was what my parents heard when I was in third grade. You see, I was a terrible student in grade school. I was the worst. I'm sure most of you just flew through grade school, getting A's and B's. No problem whatsoever. Me, on the other hand, not at all. I got C's and D's. And I had to work for them. All of my teachers tried. They didn't know what was wrong. They tried different techniques, but nothing really seemed to

Calling on personal experience at the beginning of a speech can gain interest and create high credibility for the message.

work. I guess the point of crisis came in third grade when my teacher realized that I couldn't even read yet. It just about killed my parents. They wanted the best for me. So they had some testing done and found out I had a learning disability.

Relating your subject to personal experience can be very important if you face an unfriendly audience. Brock Evans, vice president of the Audubon Society, once addressed the Seattle Rotary Club on the Endangered Species Act amid controversy over logging restrictions in the Northwest. Because of the possible hostility of this group to some of his ideas, the introduction to his speech would be especially critical. Note how in his introduction Evans combined the techniques of involving the audience and relating the topic to personal experience:

It is always a distinct honor to be invited to speak before a prestigious group like the Rotary Club of Seattle. I thank you for inviting me to be here today, and not just because of the opportunity to share a few thoughts about this very important subject. Those of you who know me know that my roots here run very deep. It was 30 years ago that I moved here from the Midwest, because I wanted to live in what I thought then—and still do now— was the most beautiful part of the country.

And those of you who know me know that my passion for this special Northwest land, its unique blend of mountain and forest and sea, goes even deeper. It caused me to leave a law practice here, in order to devote my life to fight to help keep our way of life, to keep the Northwest the special place it is. It has now become a life's work that has taken me many places, first all across the Northwest, and finally into "exile" as I now believe—in the nation's capital—that other Washington, where for better or worse, so many of the great issues of our time are finally resolved.[16]

In this example, the love of the area and its beauty unites the speaker and his listeners. The fact that the speaker "adopted" the area lends special credence to his passion for it.

Tell a Story. We humans began our love affair with stories around the campfires of ancient times. It is through stories that we remember the past and pass on our heritage to future generations. Stories also entertain and educate us—they depict abstract problems in human terms. In introductions, stories help capture audience attention and involve listeners in creating the meaning of the message. Marie D'Aniello opened a speech on the nature of friendship with the following story:

Ask students to tell a story that might be told to children. Encourage ESL students to share the fairy tales and bedtime stories of their culture.

> **It's nine o'clock at night. I'm curled up in the back seat of a new truck and my friends, Cammy and Joe, are in the front singing along with the radio. As I listen to them sing, and I'm lying there, I start to think about my life and all the changes that have occurred in the past year. A year ago I didn't even know who Cammy and Joe were. And now they're two of my dearest friends. It made me think about friendship and its meaning.**

Narratives are also good at establishing a mood for your message. In a self-introductory speech, Ashlie McMillan began with the following sensory narrative:

> **Imagine you're sitting aboard a dive boat. It's rocking back and forth, you can feel the sun beating down on you. You can feel the wind blowing on you. You smell the ocean, the salt water. You can hear the waves crashing up against the boat. You put on your dive pack with your heavy oxygen tank and you walk unsteadily across the deck of the rocking boat. And all of a sudden you plunge into a completely different environment. All around you is vast blueness and infinite space, a world completely different from the one you left above. But all you have to do is turn on your back and look above you and you see the sunlight streaming in through the top of the water. And you can see the world that you left behind.**

An opening narrative may also be based on a historical event. Sandra Baltz, a premed major, opened a speech on setting priorities for organ transplants with the following narrative:

> **On a cold and stormy night in 1841 the ship *William Brown* struck an iceberg in the North Atlantic. Passengers and crew members frantically scrambled into the lifeboats. To make a bad disaster even worse, one of the lifeboats began to sink because it was overcrowded. Fourteen men were thrown overboard that horrible night. After the survivors were rescued, a crew member was tried for the murders of those thrown overboard.**
>
> **Fortunately, situations like this have been few in history, but today we face a similar problem in the medical establishment: deciding who will live as we allocate scarce medical resources for transplants. Someday, your fate—or the fate of someone you love—could depend on how we resolve this dilemma.**

In the preceding example, the story sets a somber mood for the serious message that follows. Stories can also be used to establish a lighter mood through the use of humor.

Use Humor. Humor can enliven an introduction and, when used appropriately, can put your audience in a receptive mood for your message. But humor may also be the most misused technique for introducing speeches. Because someone once told them that starting with a joke will ensure success, beginning speakers often search through anthologies of humor to find something that will make people laugh. Unless it is carefully adapted, however, such material often sounds canned, inappropriate, or only remotely relevant to the topic or occasion. If you wish to use humor in your introduction, be certain the material is fresh and pertinent.

Advise students that opening a speech with a joke is a risky proposition. Discuss the advantages and disadvantages of using humor in speeches. Stress the importance of relevance and propriety.

Be especially careful when using humor to open a speech. It can be grossly inappropriate for some topics and occasions. Also, don't let a humorous introduction "upstage" the rest of your speech. We once heard a student open a speech with a rather risqué quotation from Mae West, "Is that a gun in your pocket, or are you happy to see me?" It drew an initial gasp followed by some hearty laughter. Unfortunately, as the speech continued, one student would chuckle over the remembered joke; then the audience would start laughing all over again even when nothing funny had been said. After the speaker finished, we questioned the audience about their "inappropriate" responses. Their reply? "We kept remembering that Mae West line. We just couldn't help it." And to this day, neither of your authors can remember the topic of the speech, just the opening humor.

Develop Suspense. You can attract and hold your listeners' attention by arousing their curiosity, then making them wait before you satisfy it. The following introduction creates curiosity and anticipation:

> **Getting knocked down is no disgrace. Champions are made by getting up just one more time than the opponent! The results are a matter of record about a man who suffered many defeats: Lost his job in 1832, defeated for legislature in 1832, failed in business in 1833, defeated for legislature in 1834, sweetheart died in 1835, had nervous breakdown in 1836, defeated for nomination for Congress in 1843, elected to Congress in 1846, lost renomination in 1848, rejected for land officer in 1849, defeated for Senate in 1854, defeated for nomination for Vice-President in 1856, defeated for Senate in 1858. In 1860 Abraham Lincoln was elected President of the United States. Lincoln proved that a big shot is just a little shot who keeps shooting. The greatest failures in the world are those who fail by not doing anything.**[17]

The list of failures aroused the audience's curiosity. Who was this loser? Many were surprised when they discovered his identity. This effective introduction set the stage for the speaker's message that perseverance is the key to success.

Have students find five quotations that are applicable to the subject of their next presentation. Have them identify the originator of the quotation, present his or her credentials, and note where and how they found the material in the library or on the Internet.

Begin with a Quotation. Starting your speech with a striking quotation or paraphrase from a well-known person or respected authority, with the possible exception of one from Mae West, can both arouse interest and give you borrowed ethos. The person you cite should be someone the audience knows, respects, or can identify with. Historical figures are especially apt, particularly in ceremonial speeches, where they evoke a sense of cultural heritage. Elissa Scadron opened her speech celebrating the United States as a sanctuary of human rights by saying: "We are, in the words of Abraham Lincoln, 'the last best hope of earth.'"

Most effective opening quotations are short and to the point. They are used to lead into the message. One student used a very brief quote from folklore as a lead-in to an informative speech on cystic fibrosis:

> **"Woe to the child who when kissed on the forehead tastes salty. He is bewitched and he soon will die." This northern European folk adage is a reference to the genetic disorder cystic fibrosis. Well, we know today that children with cystic fibrosis aren't bewitched. And we have a lot better ways to test for cystic fibrosis than to kiss them on the forehead.**

Most books of quotations (see Chapter 5) are indexed by key words and subjects as well as by authors. Collections of quotations are also available on the Internet. They are an excellent source of statements you might use to introduce your topic.

Use a Presentation Aid. Sometimes using a presentation aid at the beginning of a speech can help to establish a mood or set a theme that carries on throughout the message. One of our students placed a photograph face down on each seat in the audience. At the beginning of her speech she had listeners turn over the photos, then asked them, "Do you think the girl in the photo is at risk?" Her speech on volunteer services for at-risk teenagers presented the stories of the girls pictured in the photos.

The use of presentation aids is not confined to the classroom. Let's look at how Carol Quinn, director of human resources for Argonne National Laboratory, integrated a novel visual aid into a speech presented at a Secretary's Day breakfast in Chicago:

> **Good morning, everyone. I am delighted to be here and am honored that you have selected me as your keynote speaker for Secretary's Day. Most of you have coffee or juice, or perhaps tea. What I have here in this glass is Kool-Aid. But I'm not going to drink it.**
>
> **Why I have this Kool-Aid and why I'm not going to drink it are in a sense what I want to talk about this Secretary's Day. What I would like to share with you today are six suggestions for maximizing your career success by playing to your strengths.**
>
> **This glass of Kool-Aid represents the worst job I've ever had. Yes, you are looking at a former "Kool-Aid tester" for General Foods. There really is—or at least "was"—such a job. When we weren't testing Kool-Aid, we were expected to taste daiquiri mixes, or nibble potato chips, or smell soap, or otherwise play the role of "average consumer." I came away from that with a long-standing aversion to Kool-Aid, which is why I'm not going to drink this.[18]**

Additional references to the Kool-Aid were artfully woven into the speech.

Startle the Audience. Anything truly unusual draws attention to itself and arouses curiosity. Consider the headlines from the sensationalist tabloids: "BIGFOOT SPOTTED IN NORTHWEST ARKANSAS!" "WOMAN PREDICTS EARTHQUAKES WITH HER TOES!"

Ask students to find two startling statistics that apply to the topic of their next presentation. Have them demonstrate how they might work this information into the introduction or conclusion of their speech.

One of our students at Vanderbilt opened with the following narrative:

> **Imagine a warm, sunny June day. A bride stands at the back of the church. It is beautifully decorated with fresh flowers, and the music of a pipe organ fills the sanctuary. There is not a dry eye as the father gives the bride away. The couple recites their vows, and upon pronouncing the couple married, the minister proclaims, "Katie, you may kiss the bride."**
>
> **The surprise that many of you just experienced is the reaction gay rights activists have been trying to eliminate since 1969. This fight simply to be accepted as part of everyday life is one that continues today.**

The startle technique must always be used with care. You don't want your introduction to arouse more interest than the body of your speech can satisfy. If your opening is too sensational, it will upstage the rest of your speech. Similarly, be careful not to go beyond the bounds of propriety. You want to startle your listeners, not offend them.

Establishing Your Credibility

The second major function of an effective introduction is to establish yourself as a competent, trustworthy, likable, and strong person. People tend to form first impressions of speakers that color their later perceptions.[19] In Chapter 2 we discussed the importance of the impressions you make on listeners in terms of your competence, integrity, likableness, and dynamism—your ethos. As you make later presentations, you will carry over some of the initial ethos you established with your first presentation and with your interactions in class. You must confirm or strengthen this initial ethos in the introduction of each speech.

Speaker's Notes 7.2

CAPTURING ATTENTION

1. Involve listeners.
2. Call on personal experience.
3. Ask questions.
4. Create suspense and anticipation.
5. Open with a story.
6. Engage listeners with humor.
7. Begin with a quotation.
8. Startle the audience.

ESL: Advise ESL students that they will find it easier to establish credibility if their topic involves something related to their culture or experience.

Establishing their qualifications to speak on a subject is often difficult for beginning speakers. As we noted in Chapter 2, you can seem competent only if you know what you are talking about. People listen more respectfully to those who speak both from knowledge and from personal experience.[20] As we noted in Chapter 5, the perception of competence can be fortified by selecting topics you already know something about and by doing research to qualify yourself as a responsible speaker. In your introduction you can allude to your research to reinforce your credibility:

> **I was amazed to learn in psychology class that research does not support a strong link between exposure to persuasive communications and behavior. This discovery led me to do more reading on the relationship between advertising and consumer activity. What I found was even more surprising, especially when you consider that, according to *American Demographics*, advertisers routinely paid over $550,000 for a half minute of air time on *ER*.**

Here the specific reference to a respected source of information suggests that you have done the research needed to make a responsible speech. It would not be effective, however, to simply announce at the beginning of your speech:

> **The information for my speech comes from my psychology textbook, two articles from the *Journal of Applied Psychology*, and an article in *American Demographics*.**

That would seem forced, awkward, and artificial. It would interrupt the natural flow of your introduction. Your perceived competence will be further strengthened if your speech is well organized, if you use language ably and correctly, and if you have practiced so that your presentation flows smoothly.

To create a perception of integrity you must seem ethical and honest. Audiences are more receptive to speakers who are straightforward, sincere, and concerned about the consequences of their words.[21] You can enhance your integrity by showing respect for those who hold different opinions while still maintaining your personal commitment to your topic and position.

You should also present yourself as a likable and confident speaker. Likeable speakers are pleasant and tactful. They treat listeners as friends, inspiring affection in return.[22] Likeable speakers share their feelings and are able to laugh at themselves. To come across as a confident speaker, you must appear in control of the situation from the outset. Your introduction should show your enthusiasm for your message. A smile and direct eye contact signals listeners that you want to communicate. These qualities build an overall impression of dynamism that should make you more effective.

When you establish favorable ethos at the outset, you also lay the foundation for one of the most powerful effects of communication: identification between yourself and listeners. **Identification** occurs when people overcome the personal and cultural differences that separate them and share thoughts and feelings as though they were one.[23] When you seem likable, sincere, competent, and forceful, your listeners want to identify with you, and your effectiveness as a communicator is magnified.

Previewing Your Message

The final function of an introduction is to preview the body of your speech. The **preview** indicates the main points you will cover and offers your listeners an overview of the speech to come.

Martha Radner offered the following preview for her speech on campus security problems.

> **This campus will be a much safer place if we adopt my plan to improve campus security. First, I want to show you how dangerous our situation has become. Second, I'll explore the reasons why current security measures on our campus are ineffective. And third, I'll present my plan for a safer campus environment.**

By informing her listeners of her intentions and her speech design, Martha helped her audience listen intelligently.

Have students be on the alert for examples of previews to lectures in their other classes. Ask them how the presence or absence of a preview affects their listening ability in those classes.

Selecting and Using Introductory Techniques

There are no hard and fast rules for determining exactly how you should open a speech. As you review your research notes, look for material that would make an effective introduction. The following guidelines may help you make a wise selection:

- *Consider your audience.* Use your introduction to tie your topic to their needs, interests, or well-being.
- *Consider the mood you want to establish.* Some topics will mandate a light touch, and others may call for more solemnity.
- *Consider your time constraints.* If you are to speak for seven minutes, you can't get bogged down in a five-minute introduction.
- *Consider what you do best.* Some people are effective storytellers, and others are better using striking statistics or quotations. Go with your strength!

Ask students to develop an alternative introduction for one of the student speeches in Appendix C. Have them explain their rationale for using that type of introduction.

Developing an Effective Conclusion

Many beginning speakers end their presentations awkwardly. The conclusion of your speech should not be that moment when you just got tired of talking or ran out of time. "That's all, folks!" may be an effective ending for a film cartoon, but in a speech such a conclusion violates the audience's need for closure. Saying "That's it, I guess" or "Well, I'm done," accompanied by a sigh of relief,

Many persuasive speeches end with a call for action.

To impress upon students the importance of an effective conclusion, have them submit the conclusion they plan for their next presentation and what they hope to accomplish with it. Help them develop an ending that provides closure and leaves the audience with something to remember.

suggests that you have not planned your speech carefully. The final words of your speech should stay with listeners, remind them of your message, and, when appropriate, move them to action.

Summarizing Your Message

Your conclusion will normally include a summary and final remarks. Most often, you should begin the conclusion with a brief **summary statement** of the main points made in your speech. The more complicated your topic, the more important this summary becomes. The summary statement then may function as a transition between the body and your final remarks. It signals the audience that you are about to finish.

Concluding Remarks

Although a summary statement can offer listeners a sense of closure, to seal that effect you need to provide some concluding remarks that stay with your listeners. Many of the techniques that create effective introductions can also be used to develop memorable conclusions.

Echo the Introduction. A conclusion that echoes the introduction can provide a nice sense of closure for the audience. Note that we have said "echoes," not "repeats." A conclusion that echoes the introduction may use the same technique as you used in the introduction. For example, if you began with a story, you might end with a different story that reinforces the meaning. You could also finish a story that you started in the introduction. The speaker who recited the long list of Lincoln's failures might have waited until the end before satisfying audience curiosity as to who this "loser" actually was. Carol Quinn came back to her glass of Kool-Aid for the conclusion of her speech:

> **If I really wanted to end this speech with flair, I would now drink this glass of Kool-Aid. But there being no power on the planet which could force me to drink another glass of Kool-Aid, I will instead wish you health, happiness, a**

wonderful day, and—you know what?—strawberry Kool-Aid is really the best. Thanks for inviting me.[24]

Involve the Audience. At the beginning of a speech, you involve the audience by showing them how your message relates directly to their lives. At the conclusion of your speech, you should remind them of what they personally have at stake. In the speech on global warming mentioned earlier, the summary statement was followed immediately by remarks that brought the message close to the lives of listeners:

> **Global warming is a monster we are making. If we don't stop now, we, our children, and our children's children will have to pay the price: sky-high temperatures, rising seas, violent storms, and a host of dangerous health problems that will make future generations wonder why we sacrificed the quality of their lives.**

In persuasive speeches, concluding remarks also often urge listeners to take the first step to confirm their commitment to action and change.

Ask Rhetorical Questions. When used in an introduction, rhetorical questions help arouse attention and curiosity. When used in a conclusion, such questions give your audience something to think about after you have finished. Annette Berrington opened a speech attacking the use of cell phones while driving in the following way: "How many of you had a nice little cell phone chat while driving to class this morning?" After a speech that proved the danger of such behavior in graphic terms, her final words were: "Now that you know the risk you are running, are you going to talk again on the way home? If so, tell me so I can travel in a different direction."

Play videos of the conclusions of student speeches; see if your students can identify the techniques that were used.

When used at the end of a persuasive speech, concluding questions may be more than rhetorical. They may actually call for a response from the audience. During political campaigns, Jesse Jackson often used this technique to register voters. He would end a speech by asking:

> **How many of you are not registered to vote? Raise your hands. No, stand up so we can see you! Is that all of you who aren't registered? Stand up! Let me see you!**

Such questioning and cajoling would be followed by on-site voter registration. Evangelists who issue an invitation to salvation at the end of their sermons often use concluding questions in a similar way. To be effective, this technique must be the climax of a speech that has prepared its audience for action.

End with a Story. Stories are remembered long after facts and figures are forgotten. A concluding narrative can help your audience *experience* the meaning of your message. To end a speech on "domestic terrorism," which she opened with a narrative, Donna E. Shalala, then secretary of health and human services, told the following story:

> **Let me conclude by telling you about a child psychologist named Sandra Graham-Berman who took responsibility for doing even more [about the problem of domestic abuse]. Several years ago she became aware of a support group for battered women. But she heard that there was no professional support for their children. On her own time and with her own money she began a support group for the children of these battered women. She began to see the girls and boys act out, talk out, and draw out their fears and their frustrations. She helped them learn they are not alone in their pain. And she taught them that when mommy is in trouble—when she is being hurt by daddy—it's possible to get help by dialing 9-1-1.**

> **A few years later, a shy 8-year-old girl walked in on a fight. Her father—if you can believe it, a child psychiatrist—was beating her mother on the head with a hammer. Try to imagine that. Try to imagine what you would do. Well, that little girl knew what to do. She remembered the lesson taught to her by a caring adult. And so she went to that phone, picked it up, pressed 9-1-1, and saved her mother's life. The father is in prison now and the family's trying its best to build a new life. If that little girl can have the courage to pick up the telephone, surely we can have the courage to prevent such stories from happening.[25]**

Close with a Quotation. Brief quotations that capture the essence of your message make effective conclusions. For example, if one historic quotation opens a speech, another on the same theme or from the same person can provide an elegant sense of closure. Elissa Scadron closed her ceremonial speech honoring America as a sanctuary of human rights by completing the quotation from Abraham Lincoln she had cited in her opening:

> **The best way to complete this speech is to fill in what Lincoln said about our responsibilities a century and a half ago: "Fellow citizens, we cannot escape history. . . . In giving freedom to the slave, we assure freedom to the free . . . honorable alike in what we give and what we preserve. We shall nobly save, or meanly lose, the last best hope of earth."**

More information on developing and using metaphors can be found in Chapter 10.

End with a Metaphor. A striking **metaphor** can end your speech effectively.[26] As we will discuss at greater length in Chapter 10, metaphors combine things that are apparently unlike so that we see unexpected relationships. As a conclusion to a speech, an effective metaphor reveals a hidden truth about the speaker's subject in a memorable way. Melodie Lancaster, president of Lancaster Resources, used such a metaphor, combined with a narrative, as she concluded a speech to the Houston Council of the American Business Women's Association:

> **We recall the story of the three stonemasons who were asked what they were doing. The first said, "I am laying brick." The second replied, "I am making a foundation." And the third said: "I am building a cathedral." Let's you and I set our sights that high. Let's build cathedrals of success today, tomorrow, and the day after tomorrow.[27]**

Consider the many meanings this metaphor might evoke in the minds of listeners. First, the speaker suggests listeners must work hard. Second, she suggests they must work with specific goals in mind. Third, she suggests they must work with a vision that gives significance to what they do. All these meanings are packed into the metaphor, making it memorable for her audience.

Whatever closing technique you select should satisfy your audience that what was promised in the beginning has now been delivered. Plan your summary statement and concluding remarks carefully, just as you did with your introduction. Practice them until you are confident you will end your speech impressively. After your final words, pause a moment to let them sink in; then take your seat.

In Summary

A carefully structured speech helps the audience understand the message and enhances the speaker's ethos.

Good Form. A well-structured speech has *good form*: it is simple, balanced, and orderly. *Simplicity* occurs when you limit the number of main points and use clear, direct language. A speech has *balance* when the major parts receive proper emphasis and work together. The requirement of *order* means that a speech follows a consistent pattern of development.

Structuring the Body of Your Speech. You should structure the body first so that you can build an introduction and conclusion that fit your message. To develop the body, determine your *main points*, decide how to arrange them, then select effective supporting materials. To discover your main points, prepare a *research overview* of the information you have collected. This summary can help you spot major themes that can develop into main points.

Arrange your main points so that they follow natural mental patterns based on the principles of similarity, proximity, and closure. The *similarity* of objects or events may suggest a categorical design for structuring main points. *Proximity* suggests that things should be discussed as they happen together in space or time. If they occur in a time sequence, use a sequential design for your speech. If they occur in physical relationship to one another, a spatial design might be appropriate. The structure of the body satisfies the principle of *closure* when it completes the design it begins. Cause-effect and problem-solution designs require closure to be effective.

Supporting materials fill out the speech and buttress ideas. In an ideal arrangement, you should support each point with information, testimony, and an example or story that emphasizes its human aspects.

Using Transitions. Effective *transitions* point up the relationships among ideas in your speech and tie the speech together. *Internal summaries* remind listeners of the points you have made in one part of your speech before you move on to another.

Preparing an Effective Introduction. The introduction to a speech should arouse your listeners' interest, establish your credibility, and focus and *preview* your message. Some useful ways to introduce a speech include involving the audience, relating your subject to personal experience, asking *rhetorical questions*, creating suspense, telling a story, using humor, beginning with a quotation, using a presentation aid, or startling the audience. As you build credibility, you also make possible *identification* between yourself and the audience.

Developing an Effective Conclusion. An effective conclusion should review the meaning of your speech in a *summary statement*, provide a sense of closure, leave the audience with final reflections on the significance of the speech, and, if appropriate, motivate listeners to act. Techniques that are useful for conclusions include echoing the introduction, involving the audience, asking questions, closing with a quotation, telling a story, and ending with a *metaphor*. Your speech will seem more symmetrical and satisfying if your conclusion ties into your introduction.

Terms to Know

good form
simplicity
balance
order
main points
research overview
principle of similarity
principle of proximity
principle of closure
transitions
internal summary
rhetorical question
identification
preview
summary statement
metaphor

Notes

1. Patricia R. Palmerton, "Teaching Skills or Teaching Thinking," *Journal of Applied Communication Research* 20 (1992): 335–341; and Robert G. Powell, "Critical Thinking and Speech Communication: Our Teaching Strategies Are Warranted—Not!" *Journal of Applied Communication Research* 20 (1992): 342–347. Most of the research on the effects of structure was conducted in the 1960s and 1970s. Notable among these studies are Christopher Spicer and Ronald E. Bassett, "The Effect of Organization on Learning from an Informative Message," *Southern Speech Communication Journal* 41 (1976): 290–299; Ernest Thompson, "Some Effects of Message Structure on Listeners' Comprehension," *Speech Monographs* 34 (1967): 51–57; and Arlee Johnson, "A Preliminary Investigation of the Relationship Between Organization and Listener Comprehension," *Central States Speech Journal* 21 (1970): 104–107.
2. Patricia Kearney, Timothy G. Plax, Ellis R. Hayes, and Marily J. Ivey, "College Teacher Misbehaviors: What Students Don't Like About What Teachers Say and Do," *Communication Quarterly* 39 (1991): 309–324.
3. J. C. McCroskey and R. S. Mehrley, "The Effects of Disorganization and Nonfluency on Attitude Change and Source Credibility," *Communication Monographs* 36 (1969): 13–21.
4. Saul Kassin, *Psychology* (Boston: Houghton Mifflin, 1995), pp. 208–251.
5. Material in this section is based on the work of the Gestalt psychologists as summarized in Kassin, pp. 78–129.
6. Scott E. Caplan and John O. Green, "Acquisition of Message-Production Skill by Younger and Older Adults: Effects of Age, Task Complexity, and Practice," *Communication Monographs* 66 (1999): 31–48.
7. Charles Hulme, Steven Roodenrys, Gordon Brown, and Robin Mercer, "The Role of Long-Term Memory Mechanisms in Memory Span," *British Journal of Psychology* 86 (1995): 527–536.
8. Douglas A. Bernstein, Edward J. Roy, Thomas K. Srull, and Christopher D. Wickens, *Psychology*, 2nd ed. (Boston: Houghton Mifflin, 1991), p. 308.
9. Kassin, p. 111.
10. Michael D. Lemonick and Alice Park, "New Hope for Cancer," *Time*, 28 May 2001, p. 65.
11. Loren J. Anderson, "A Summary of Research on Order Effects in Communication," *Concepts in Communication*, ed. Jimmie D. Trent, Judith S. Trent, and Daniel J. O'Neill (Boston: Allyn and Bacon, 1973), pp. 129–130.
12. Cited in Arthur M. Schlesinger Jr., *A Thousand Days: John F. Kennedy in the White House* (Boston: Houghton Mifflin, 1965), p. 733.
13. Our thanks for this example go to Professor Reno Unger, Kutztown University.
14. James Price Dillard, "Persuasion Past and Present: Attitudes Aren't What They Used to Be," *Communication Monographs* 60 (1993): 91.
15. Wendy Liebmann, "How America Shops: The Consumer Paradox," *Vital Speeches of the Day*, 15 July 1998, p. 595.
16. Brock Evans, "The Endangered Species Act: Implications for the Future," *Vital Speeches of the Day*, 15 Mar. 1993, p. 339.
17. Bob Lannom, "Patience, Persistence, and Perspiration," *Parsons (Tenn.) News Leader*, 20 Sept. 1989, p. 9.
18. Carol Quinn, "Playing to Your Strengths," *Vital Speeches of the Day*, 1 June 1998, p. 508. Reprinted by permission.
19. Sharon S. Brehm and Saul M. Kassin, *Social Psychology*, 2nd ed. (Boston: Houghton Mifflin, 1993), pp. 127–128.
20. R. G. Hass, "Effects of Source Characteristics on the Cognitive Processing of Persuasive Messages and Attitude Change," in *Cognitive Responses in Persuasion*, ed. R. Petty, T. Ostrom, and T. Brock (Hillsdale, N.J.: Erlbaum, 1981), pp. 141–172; M. Heesacker, R. E. Petty, and J. T. Cacioppo, "Field Dependence and Attitude Change: Source Credibility Can Alter Persuasion by Affecting Message-Relevant Thinking," *Journal of Personality* 51 (1983): 653–666; and J. E. Maddux and R. W. Rogers, "Effects of Source Expertness, Physical Attractiveness, and Supporting Arguments on Persuasion: A Case of Brains over Beauty," *Journal of Personality and Social Psychology* 39 (1980): 235–244.
21. H. Eagly, W. Wood, and S. Chaiken, "An Attribution Analysis of Persuasion," in *New Directions in Attribution Research*, ed. J. Harvey, W. Ickes, and R. Kidd (Hillsdale, N.J.: Erlbaum, 1981), pp. 37–62.
22. Brehm and Kassin, pp. 220–221.
23. Kenneth Burke, *A Rhetoric of Motives* (Berkeley and Los Angeles: University of California Press, 1969), pp. 20–23.
24. Quinn, p. 510.
25. Donna E. Shalala, "Domestic Terrorism: An Unacknowledged Epidemic," *Vital Speeches of the Day*, 15 May 1994, p. 453.
26. John Waite Bowers and Michael Osborn, "Attitudinal Effects of Selected Types of Concluding Metaphors in Persuasive Speeches," *Speech Monographs* 33 (1966): 148–155.
27. Melodie Lancaster, "The Future We Predict Isn't Inevitable: Refraining Our Success in the Modern World," *Vital Speeches of the Day*, 1 Aug. 1992, p. 638.

8

Outlining Your Speech

OUTLINE

THIS CHAPTER WILL HELP YOU

- understand why outlining is important
- learn how to develop a working outline
- prepare a formal outline
- condense your formal outline to a key-word outline

As we planned our home on the Tennessee River, we often met with our builders to make decisions. We knew what materials we had to work with, and we knew our options for constructing the home. But before the construction could begin, we had to make commitments. As we made our choices, the builders would revise their projections. Eventually, they emerged with a set of blueprints that represented the final detailed plans of the home that would rise on the hilltop above the river.

In like manner, as you plan your speeches, you will become acquainted through research (Chapter 5) with supporting materials available to you (Chapter 6). As you weigh the options available to you, you will consider various ways of structuring your speech (Chapter 7) before a plan for it begins to emerge in your mind. As the form of the speech emerges, you will record this process in a series of working outlines. Finally, as the plan becomes complete, you will have before you a formal outline, the final product of the commitments you have made, the blueprints of the speech you will present.

Outlining is an instrumental process that helps the structuring phase of a speech proceed to an effective conclusion. It is also a parallel process: as you structure your speech, you will also be outlining it.

Ask students to use the Speech Designer computer software as they prepare the outline for their next speech. If computer access for your students is limited, have them use the related hard copy materials in the IRM or the Speech Preparation Workbook.

Our plans miscarry because they have no aim. When a man does not know what harbor he is making for, no wind is the right wind.

—Seneca

The reasons for outlining are clear. Outlining objectifies your thinking: It takes ideas out of your head, where they can get all tangled up, and puts them down on paper, where you can see them and work with them.[1] It is both a creative and a corrective process: as you think about the relationships among your ideas, you may come up with new ones. You can see where you need more research, whether a point is really relevant, and whether the overall structure is well balanced.[2] You may need to add something here, subtract something there. Outlining helps you find and correct problems *before* they become mistakes. Finally, an outline points out where you need transitions and helps you see whether your introduction and conclusion really fit your speech.

To assist you in developing outline skills, we have developed Speech Designer software, available with this text. In this chapter we also provide you with sample outline formats for the general structure of any speech. In Chapter 12 we offer sample outlines for informative speech designs: spatial, sequential, chronological, categorical, comparative, and causation. In Chapter 13 we provide sample outlines for the major persuasive speech designs: problem-solution, motivated sequence, and refutative.

As you prepare your speech, you will probably develop several working outlines, a formal outline, and a key-word outline to use as a prompt during presentation.

Developing a Working Outline

A **working outline** is a *tentative* plan of your speech. It is a work in process in which you display the relationships among ideas and identify potential trouble spots. Why should you start with a working outline? Assume that you plan to present an informative speech on "the greenhouse effect." You have done some research but you are not completely sure how your speech should develop. Your working outline is a tool that can help reduce your uncertainty. It is also a discipline: merely following the format of an outline helps you think productively about the design of your speech. Figure 8.1 provides you with a format for developing a working outline.

Use the exercise "Idea Maps" in Chapter 8 of the IRM to introduce an alternate method of organizing material. ESL students may find this format easier to use.

You should not think of this format as a rigid structure. Adapt it so that it works for you. In this early stage of developing your speech, don't worry about the formalities of outlining.[3] Your working outline is a disposable tool to help you arrange your ideas. You will probably prepare and discard several working outlines before you find the right approach.

A good starting point for your working outline is to write out your specific purpose and thesis statement. You need to have these clearly in mind so that you can check how well your main points fit them. Your specific purpose and thesis statement form the foundation for your speech.

FIGURE 8.1
Format for a Working Outline

Topic: ____________________
Specific purpose: ____________________
Thesis statement: ____________________

INTRODUCTION

Attention material: ____________________
Credibility material: ____________________
Thesis statement: ____________________
Preview: ____________________

(**Transition** to body of speech)

BODY

First main point: ____________________
  Subpoint: ____________________
    Sub-subpoint: ____________________
    Sub-subpoint: ____________________
  Subpoint: ____________________

(**Transition** to second main point)

Second main point: ____________________
  Subpoint: ____________________
  Subpoint: ____________________
    Sub-subpoint: ____________________
    Sub-subpoint: ____________________

(**Transition** to third main point)

Third main point: ____________________
  Subpoint: ____________________
  Subpoint: ____________________

(**Transition** to conclusion)

CONCLUSION

Summary: ____________________
Concluding remarks: ____________________

Specific purpose:	To inform my audience of the significance of the greenhouse effect.
Thesis statement:	We must understand the greenhouse effect before we can hope to counter global warming.

Developing Your Main Points

The second step in preparing a working outline is to sketch the body of your speech. Following the process discussed in Chapter 7, write out your main points. You may recall that in selecting main points, you work from a research overview. Consider the major themes from this overview in light of the purpose of your speech, your audience's needs, and the amount of time available for you to speak. In the hypothetical example of preparing a speech on the greenhouse effect, the first working outline contained the following main points:

First main point:	Harmful agricultural and industrial emissions accelerate the greenhouse effect.
Second main point:	Personal energy consumption magnifies the greenhouse effect.
Third main point:	The loss of woodlands adds to the greenhouse effect.

Once you have the main points written out, ask the following questions:

- Will these points make my message clear to my audience?
- Is this the right order in which to develop them?
- Have I left out anything important?

Check your students' working outlines to see if they have done enough research to develop a substantive speech. Arrange conferences with those who may need additional help in preparation.

As you consider these questions, you realize that you have indeed left something out. You remember that all of your sources explained what the greenhouse effect was before discussing its causes. You note that your original list of main points neither explains the greenhouse effect nor gives the audience a reason to be interested in it. You also see another potential trouble spot: there is no clear, logical order in your arrangement of main points. But if you developed a motivating explanation in your first main point, then reordered the remaining points so that you would discuss, in order, lost woodlands, agricultural and industrial emissions, and personal consumption, then you would both involve and inform listeners and establish an order of increasing importance among the remaining points. Your speech could build toward its conclusion. You decide to toss out your first working outline and to revise the main points as follows:

First main point:	The greenhouse effect is a process by which certain gases in the atmosphere retain the heat of the sun.
Second main point:	The loss of woodlands adds to the greenhouse effect.
Third main point:	Agricultural and industrial emissions accelerate the greenhouse effect.
Fourth main point:	Personal energy consumption magnifies the greenhouse effect.

Developing Subpoints

Once you have determined and arranged your main points, you can break them down into more specific statements that explain and support them. These more specific statements belong at the **subpoint** level of your outline. Usually each main point will be buttressed by two or more subpoints that substantiate and clarify it. Each subpoint must relate directly to the main point it follows and should make that point more understandable, believable, or compelling.[4]

To identify the subpoints for each of your main points, imagine a critical listener in front of you. When you state the main point, this listener will want to know:

- What do you mean?
- Why should I care?
- How do I know this is true?

The subpoints of each main point should answer these questions. If the main points are columns built on the foundation of your purpose and thesis statement, the subpoints reinforce these columns so that they will stand up under critical scrutiny. For example, as you develop your working outline, you might list the following subpoints for your first main point:

First main point:	The greenhouse effect is a process by which certain gases in the atmosphere retain the heat of the sun.
Subpoints:	A. Among these gases are carbon dioxide and methane.
	B. They form a window that holds the heat.
	C. Natural process has been unbalanced by human activities.
	D. Too many gases are holding too much heat.
	E. Artificial heat wave is breaking all records.
	F. This situation is causing climate and health problems.

You notice that you have listed six subpoints. Recalling the principles of good form learned in Chapter 7, you conclude rightly that you have *too many* subpoints for your speech to remain simple, balanced, and orderly.

At this point, you examine how your subpoints relate to one another. Can you combine any of them? Do you need to break out the material to a more detailed level of **sub-subpoints**? Just as subpoints reinforce and clarify main points, sub-subpoints strengthen and specify subpoints. You should also include supporting material as you work out the sub-subpoints. For example, you might expand the first main point in this working outline as follows:

First main point:	The greenhouse effect is a process by which certain gases in the atmosphere retain the heat of the sun.
Subpoint A:	This natural process makes the Earth livable.
Subpoint B:	Process now unbalanced by human activities.
Sub-subpoints:	1. High concentrations of carbon dioxide and methane in the atmosphere.
	2. Artificial heat wave is breaking all temperature records.
	3. This threatens Earth's climate and many living things.

Follow this same procedure as you develop each main point. When you finish, review the working outline of the body of your speech and ask yourself:

- Will a speech based on this outline satisfy my thesis statement?
- Will I be able to do all of this in the time available?

Be honest with yourself. It's better to be frustrated now than disappointed later during your presentation. In addition, be sure your ideas are arranged in an orderly manner that is easy to follow. Make certain that each subpoint relates directly to the main point above it and that you have enough supporting material to build a strong, responsible structure of ideas. If you are lacking in any of these respects, now is the time to discover and correct the problem.

FIGURE 8.2
Sample Working Outline

■ *Begin by writing down your topic, specific purpose, and thesis statement so that you have them clearly in mind as you work.*

■ *Sketch your introduction, including short notes on attention materials. Notice that this tentative plan omits any direct effort to build credibility. A credibility strategy should emerge by the formal outline. As planning proceeds, revise any of these elements as needed.*

■ *Labeling the body of the speech points out its importance. Remember to develop the body of the speech* before *you develop the introduction or conclusion.*

■ *Include transitions to remind yourself to tie material together and make it flow smoothly.*

■ *Note that the working outline does not follow the numbering and lettering system of a formal outline. The purpose of the working outline is to allow you to organize ideas and see how they work together.*

Topic: The Greenhouse Effect
Specific purpose: To inform my audience of the significance of the greenhouse effect.
Thesis statement: We must understand the greenhouse effect before we can hope to counter global warming.

INTRODUCTION

Attention material: Antarctic icebergs breaking loose: ominous signs of global warming. Nero fiddled while Rome burned: we're fiddling while the Earth burns.
Thesis statement: We must understand the greenhouse effect before we can hope to counter global warming.
Preview: We need to be concerned especially about the loss of woodlands, harmful agricultural and industrial emissions, and our own energy consumption.
(**Transition** to body of speech: "Let's begin by understanding the greenhouse effect.")

BODY

First main point: The greenhouse effect is a process by which certain gases in the atmosphere retain the heat of the sun.
Subpoint A: This natural process makes the Earth livable.
Subpoint B: Process now unbalanced by human activities.
Sub-subpoints:
1. High concentrations of carbon dioxide and methane in the atmosphere.
2. Artificial heat wave is breaking all temperature records.
3. This threatens Earth's climate and many living things.

(**Transition** to second main point: "Let's examine the causes, one by one.")

Second main point: The loss of woodlands adds to the greenhouse effect.
Subpoint A: Loss from cutting.
Subpoint B: Loss from clearing.
Subpoint C: Loss from burning.
(**Transition** to third main point: "An even greater cause is harmful agricultural and industrial emissions.")

Third main point: Agricultural and industrial emissions accelerate the greenhouse effect.
Subpoint A: Farming an important part of problem.
Sub-subpoints:
1. Frequent tilling and massive CO_2.
2. Rice farms and methane.
3. Cattle ranches and more methane.

Subpoint B: Industrial emissions from burning fossil fuels another big source of problem.

(continued)

(**Transition** to fourth main point: "Finally, let's consider the most important cause of the runaway greenhouse effect—ourselves.")

Fourth main point: Our personal energy consumption magnifies the greenhouse effect

Subpoint A: Both population and prosperity fuel the problem.

Sub-subpoints: 1. More people = more energy consumption.

2. Improved living standards add to the problem.

Subpoint B: Personal energy consumption single largest cause of greenhouse effect.

Sub-subpoints: 1. Fossil fuels account for 90% of U.S. personal energy consumption.

2. Personal cars tripled since 1950.

(**Transition:** "In conclusion . . .")

CONCLUSION

Summary statement: The greenhouse effect is the key to understanding global warming. Major causes are loss of woodlands, agricultural and industrial emissions, and increased personal consumption.

Concluding remarks: Future generations will ask why we did this to the quality of their lives.

■ ***The working outline serves as your guide and provides a check on the structure of the speech and the adequacy of your preparation.***

■ ***Like the introduction, the conclusion is merely sketched in the working outline. Specific techniques are worked out as planning proceeds.***

Completing Your Working Outline

To complete your working outline (see Figure 8.2), prepare an introduction that gains attention, establishes your credibility, and previews your speech, as we discussed in Chapter 7. Next, prepare a conclusion that includes a summary and concluding remarks. Finally, add transitions to tie your speech together. Remember that your transitions should connect the introduction to the body, connect each main point to the next main point, and move the speech from the body to the conclusion.

Now, take a final look at your working outline. Figure 8.2 is a sample working outline for a speech on the greenhouse effect.

Review the outline using the "Checklist for a Working Outline" in Speaker's Notes 8.1. Go over the outline with someone whose judgment you respect. Another person sometimes can see problems you might miss because you are too close to the material.

As you review your working outline, keep the audience at the center of your thinking. Remember the advice given to beginning journalists: *Never overestimate your audience's information, and never underestimate their intelligence!* Ask yourself the following questions:

- Are my main points arranged so they are easy to understand and remember?
- Do I have enough supporting material for each main point?
- Do I have different types of supporting materials for each main point?

Speech preparation often proceeds in fits and starts, periods of frustration followed by moments of inspiration and revision. You may find yourself making and revising several working outlines before you are satisfied.

Speaker's Notes 8.1

CHECKLIST FOR A WORKING OUTLINE

____ 1. My topic, specific purpose, and thesis statement are clearly stated.
____ 2. My introduction contains attention-getting material, establishes my credibility, and focuses and previews my message.
____ 3. My main points represent the most important ideas on my topic.
____ 4. I have an appropriate number of main points to cover my material in the time allotted.
____ 5. Each subpoint breaks its main point into more specific detail.
____ 6. My conclusion contains a summary statement and concluding remarks that reinforce and reflect on the meaning of my speech.
____ 7. I have planned transitions to use between the introduction and body, between each of my main points, and between the body and conclusion of my speech.

Developing a Formal Outline

Have students use the "Sample Formal Outline" in Figure 8.4 as a model for developing formal outlines. Refer ESL students or those having problems to additional sample, formal outlines in the Speech Designer software or the Speech Preparation Workbook.

Once you are pleased with your working outline, you can prepare a formal outline. The **formal outline** is the final step you take in planning the substance of your speech. It imposes a helpful discipline on your preparation and indicates to your instructor that the research and planning phase of your work is completed. The formal outline for a speech follows many of the established conventions of outlining. Figure 8.3 shows a formal speech outline format illustrating these conventions:

1. Identification of speech topic, specific purpose, and thesis statement
2. Separation of speech parts: introduction, body, and conclusion
3. Use of numbering and lettering to display coordination and subordination
4. Wording of main points and subpoints as simple declarative sentences
5. A title
6. A list of major sources consulted

Topic, Specific Purpose, and Thesis Statement

Some student speakers recite their topic, specific purpose, and thesis statement at the beginnings of each speech as though they had been programmed: "My topic is . . . , My specific purpose is . . . , My thesis statement is . . ." This is not a good way to begin a speech! Nevertheless, you should write these headings out at the top of your outline. The headings help you focus your message.

Separation of Speech Parts

The introduction, body, and conclusion of the speech should be separated in the outline. Separating the major parts of your speech helps ensure that you give each section the careful attention it requires.

FIGURE 8.3
Format for a Formal Outline

TITLE

Topic: ______________________
Specific purpose: ______________________
Thesis statement: ______________________

INTRODUCTION

Attention material: ______________________

Credibility material: ______________________

Thesis statement: ______________________

Preview: ______________________

(**Transition** into body of speech)

BODY

I. First main point:
- **A.** Subpoint or supporting material: ______________________
- **B.** Subpoint or supporting material: ______________________
  - **1.** Sub-subpoint or supporting material: ______________________
  - **2.** Sub-subpoint or supporting material: ______________________

(**Transition** into next main point)

II. Second main point:
- **A.** Subpoint or supporting material: ______________________
  - **1.** Sub-subpoint or supporting material: ______________________
  - **2.** Sub-subpoint or supporting material: ______________________
- **B.** Subpoint or supporting material: ______________________

(**Transition** into next main point)

III. Third main point:
- **A.** Subpoint or supporting material: ______________________
- **B.** Subpoint or supporting material: ______________________
  - **1.** Sub-subpoint or supporting material: ______________________
  - **2.** Sub-subpoint or supporting material: ______________________
    - **a.** Sub-sub-subpoint or supporting material: ______________________
    - **b.** Sub-sub-subpoint or supporting material: ______________________

(**Transition** into conclusion)

CONCLUSION

Summary statement: ______________________

Concluding remarks: ______________________

WORKS CONSULTED

Tell students that the indentation system provides a visual map of their thinking and helps them see where there may be a lack of balance or a need for more material.

Note that in Figure 8.3, only the body of the speech follows an outlining format.[5] As we suggested in Chapters 2 and 7, it is best to plan your introduction and conclusion verbatim to ensure that you get into and out of your speech gracefully and effectively. Although there may be times when you must change your introduction (we discussed these under "Context" in Chapter 4), as a general rule a carefully worded beginning works best. Knowing *exactly* what you want to say and how you want to say it gets you off to a good start and helps build the confidence you need to make your presentation effective. At the end of your speech, the exact wording of your concluding remarks can determine whether you make a lasting impression.

Numbering and Lettering Your Outline

ESL: Urge ESL students to take advantage of available campus resources (ESL Resource Center, Student Writing Center, etc.) for help in outlining their presentations.

Figure 8.3 shows you how to use letters, numbers, and indentation to set up a formal outline that follows the principles of coordination and subordination. The actual number of main points and levels of subpoints may vary, but the basic format remains the same. Roman numerals (I, II, III) identify the main points of your speech. Capital letters (A, B, C) identify the subpoints under each main point. Arabic numbers (1, 2, 3) identify the sub-subpoints under any subpoint. Lowercase letters (a, b, c) identify any sub-sub-subpoints in your outline.

The principle of **coordination** requires that all statements at a given level (your *I*'s and *II*'s, *A*'s and *B*'s, and so forth) be of similar importance. In the sample formal outline shown later in this chapter the main points include an explanation of the greenhouse effect and its three major causes, arranged in ascending order of importance. Think how strange it would seem if a fifth main point, "The greenhouse effect will decrease our recreational opportunities," were added to this outline. That statement would not be coordinate with the other main points. It would not equal them in importance, nor would it fit within the pattern of relationships. Adding such a main point would violate the principle of coordination.

The principle of **subordination** requires that material descend in importance from the general and abstract main points to the concrete and specific subpoints, and sub-subpoints related to them, as shown below:

more important	I. Main point	**more general**
	A. Subpoint	
	1. Sub-subpoint	
less important	a. Sub-sub-subpoint	**more specific**

The more important a statement is, the farther to the left it is positioned. If you rotate an outline so that it rests on its right margin, the "peaks" will represent the main points, the most important ideas in your speech, with the height of the other points representing their relative significance.

The easiest way to demonstrate the importance of coordination and subordination is to look at an abbreviated sample outline that violates these principles:

Use the "Scrambled Outline" exercise in Chapter 8 of the IRM to emphasize the importance of subordination and coordination. This activity also helps students see the importance of a clear speech design.

I. Computers can help you develop writing skills.
   A. Using PCs can improve your schoolwork.
   B. PCs can be useful for organizing class notes.

II. Computers can help you keep better financial records.
   A. They can help you plan personal time more effectively.
   B. They can be useful in your personal life.
   C. They can help organize your research notes for class projects.

This collection of ideas may look like an outline, but it isn't. It violates the principles of coordination and subordination. The points at each level are not equal in importance, nor are they logically related to one another. To straighten out this problem, look at the points I and II. They are neither the most important nor the most general statements. The main points are actually I-A and II-B: the ideas that PCs can improve your schoolwork and can be useful in your personal life. Once we put the main points where they belong, we can see where the subpoints go:

I. Computers can improve your schoolwork.
   A. PCs can help you develop writing skills.
   B. PCs can be useful for organizing class notes.
   C. PCs can help organize your research notes for class projects.

II. Computers can be useful in your personal life.
  A. PCs can help you keep better financial records.
  B. PCs can help you plan personal time more effectively.

Wording Your Outline

Each main point and subpoint in your outline should be worded as a simple declarative sentence. As the name suggests, such a sentence makes a simple declaration, such as "Computers can be useful in your personal life." It is not weighted down with qualifying, dependent clauses, such as "*Even though they are expensive*, computers can be useful in your personal life." If the points in your outline start sprouting such clauses, you should simplify the structure of your speech. You may need to break down complex main points into subpoints or complex subpoints into sub-subpoints. For example, the following does not make a good main point sentence: "Bad eating habits endanger health and lower feelings of self-worth, reducing life span and causing personal anguish." The sentence works better in an outline if it is simplified in the following way:

I. Bad eating habits are a threat to our well-being.
  A. Bad eating habits endanger health.
    1. They can result in increased heart disease.
    2. They can shorten the life span.
  B. Bad eating habits can damage self-image.
    1. Obese people sometimes dislike themselves.
    2. They can feel that they have nothing to offer others.

Breaking the complex sentence down into outline form helps you to focus what you are going to say. It simplifies and clarifies both the structure and the logic of your speech.

Try to use **parallel construction** when wording the main points of your speech. If you were developing a speech on the need for reforms in political campaign financing, you might word your main points as follows:

Have students work in pairs and critique each other's formal outlines. Often an outside eye can spot problems in wording that the originator of the material cannot see.

I. We need reform at the national level.
II. We need reform at the state level.
III. We need reform at the local level.
IV. But first, we need to reform ourselves.

You could use these words in the introduction of your speech. The parallel construction would give listeners a guide to the structure of your speech. You could also repeat the parallel pattern as you summarize your speech, further imprinting its message on the minds of your listeners.

Parallel construction has many advantages. Because each sentence has the same basic structure, any variations stand out sharply. Thus parallel construction emphasizes important points. In this example, the parallel structure helps the speech narrow its focus like a zoom lens as it moves from a national to an individual perspective.

Using parallel construction for your main points can also help you sharpen internal summaries: "Having looked at reform at the national, state, and local levels, we come to the most important part of the problem—ourselves." Since it involves repetition, it makes your message easy to remember. It satisfies the principles of good form and closure discussed in Chapter 7. Not all material lends itself readily to parallel construction, but look for opportunities to use it.

ANNOTATED SAMPLE SPEECH

Life in the Greenhouse

■ ***Since you have watched the development of the "greenhouse effect" speech from its beginnings, we thought you might like to see the final product. Note how the outlined body of the speech transforms into text that reaches out to its listeners.***

Almost twenty years ago, environmentalists urged scientists to look to Antarctica for signs of what they called the runaway "greenhouse effect"—the rapid warming of the earth because of human activity. Right on cue, during the winter of 1995, *Time* magazine reported that a gigantic iceberg—23 miles wide and 48 miles long, almost as large as the state of Rhode Island—broke off the Larsen Ice Shelf in the Antarctic Peninsula. More than this, the whole Ice Shelf is crumbling. Rudolfo Del Valle, director of geoscience at the Argentine Antarctic Institute, told *Newsweek* that it "looked liked polystyrene that had been broken by a little boy." The elephant seals that once thrived nearby have now vanished, reports *U.S. News & World Report* in its February 2000 issue.

■ ***Note also how the source citations become "oral footnotes" woven into the message. These oral footnotes make the speech authoritative and strengthen the speaker's ethos, especially important when the topic is so technical. The oral footnotes are especially numerous near the beginning of the speech, where they help establish credibility for the speech yet to come.***

These are ominous signs for our future. They are symptoms of global warming—that great calamity that now threatens to turn the whole Earth into one gigantic hothouse. According to the authoritative *Summary for Policymakers*, provided by the United Nations Intergovernmental Panel on Climate Change, the 1990s were the warmest decade of the past thousand years, and 1998 in particular was the hottest year of the millennium. Reporting the views of hundreds of the world's foremost environmental scientists, the IPCC warns of a world in which rising temperatures will transform green places into deserts, displace great masses of people, destroy coastal areas with rising seas, cause massive epidemics of disease, eliminate many species of plants and animals—and generally raise hell with all living things.

■ ***Note that this text omits a formal statement of the preview, a risky strategy at best. To keep the speech from becoming too technical and too far removed from everyday experience, the speaker uses a number of brief comparisons to help listeners understand and to create vivid word-pictures. "Like a huge iceball suspended in space" illustrates this technique.***

If we want to rein in global warming—and I can't imagine us not wanting to—we must first understand this runaway "greenhouse effect." That's my purpose today—I want to pass along what I've learned about "life in the greenhouse," and hopefully add to your knowledge of how we might cope with it.

So what is this greenhouse effect? First of all, there's nothing wrong with a healthy dose of it. As a matter of fact, it makes our planet livable. Certain gases that collect naturally in the atmosphere trap the sun's heat: This natural "greenhouse effect" helps keep the Earth's average temperature at a comfortable average of 59° Fahrenheit. Without these natural greenhouse gases, the Earth would be about 0° Fahrenheit—like a huge iceball suspended in space.

So how did the greenhouse effect become such a problem? That's where *we* enter the picture. So much of what we do, especially those of us in the highly industrialized nations, changes the order of nature. We are responsible for adding enormous amounts of carbon dioxide, methane, and nitrous oxides to this natural canopy of gases. Each year, according to *Science News*, five tons of carbon are pumped into the atmosphere for each man, woman, and child in the United States. You heard me right: *that's five tons for each and every one of us!* It's no accident that the 1990s were the hottest decade on record!

■ ***Note how the speech uses repetition to emphasize the importance of a critical fact. In actual presentation, a skillful speaker might also vary the vocal pattern to present the italicized statement slowly and forcefully, and also use pause, gesture, and body language to drive the point home dramatically.***

So just what has thrown nature out of balance? Let's examine the major causes, one by one. The first is the loss of woodlands that convert carbon dioxide into oxygen. One football field-sized area of forest is lost every second from cutting, clearing, or burning. Significant forest loss occurs in the rain forests in Central and South America, where teak and mahogany are logged for furniture and houses. But it also occurs in this country and elsewhere as developers clear more and more land for more and more people. The wide-scale burning of these forests in places like Indonesia to clear land for farming and housing further compounds the problem. From these vast burning fields huge clouds of smoke choked with carbon dioxide rise into our atmosphere. Altogether, according to *Time*'s "Earth Day 2000" special edition, deforestation accounts for about 20 percent of the problem we face with runaway greenhouse gases.

■ *The use of stylistic touches as heightening devices are important here: the comparison to a "football field" helps bring the magnitude of the problem into focus. "Vast burning fields," and descriptions of cattle as "living, belching methane factories" touch off ugly pictures in listeners' minds.*

An even greater cause of the greenhouse effect—according to *Time*'s 2001 special report on global warming—are agricultural and industrial emissions. They occur on the farm, where frequent tilling of the earth releases carbon dioxide into the atmosphere. They occur on vast rice farms, where frequent flooding and the wrong uses of fertilizer add methane to the noxious mix. They occur on cattle ranches, where feeding cows the wrong food can transform them into living, belching methane factories.

The picture for industrial emissions is just as ugly. The smokestack has become the icon of our times. As we burn more and more fossil fuels in our desperate quest for energy, we release larger and larger amounts of carbon dioxide into the atmosphere. Fleets of trucks and flocks of airplanes swell the canopy of gas and magnify the heat.

And the greenhouse effect continues to grow! Every day, more and more third world nations become more and more industrialized and use more and more fuel. But, guess what? We Americans are the worst offenders. We have only 5 percent of the world's population, but we use 26 percent of the world's oil, release 26 percent of the world's nitrogen oxide, and produce 22 percent of the world's carbon dioxide emissions. We are the world's greatest energy hogs!

■ *Here the speech uses striking statistics leading to an even more striking conclusion. Better documentation of these facts would make them more effective.*

The good news in all this is that we could do much better. Better agricultural and industrial practices are available to us, if only we have the will—personally and as a nation.

All of which leads us to the last and greatest cause of the runaway greenhouse effect—ourselves! *Personal energy consumption is the single most important cause of the greenhouse effect.* The more of us there are, especially in industrialized countries, the more energy we consume. And here's another point: as populations grow and as living standards rise around the world, more people develop greater expectations—they want to live the good life. If you multiply more people times rising expectations, you can see what this means for energy consumption—and for the greenhouse effect!

■ *The struggle to make this technical subject understandable makes this speech interesting to analyze for its use of style. The wording of a speech can determine whether it engages listeners and holds their interest. We shall discuss stylistic techniques in detail in Chapter 10.*

According to the U.S. Department of Energy, 90 percent of America's personal energy consumption comes from fossil fuels. In 1950 there were 40 million cars in the United States. Today there are more than three times that many cars on our roads. Too many gas guzzlers, too many energy hogs! We are paying a considerable environmental price by driving too much and keeping our houses too hot in the winter and too cold in the summer.

■ *The conclusion uses a number of artful techniques. Instead of a bare summary, the speaker invites the audience to "listen," "watch," and "smell," challenging them to use their own senses to verify the problem. To make the imagery of the speech even more effective, the speaker adds irony, asking listeners to "smell the rich bouquet of exhaust fumes." Finally, the speech concludes by combining rhetorical questions with parallel structure to leave listeners contemplating the large question, "Why?"*

In conclusion, if you want to understand why global warming has become one of the great crises of our time, you've simply got to step outside into the greenhouse. Listen for the falling trees, watch the industrial smokestacks darkening the sky, and smell that rich bouquet of exhaust fumes that we are constantly pumping into the air. The greenhouse effect is a monster we all are creating. And if we don't stop, we, our children, and their children face an ominous future. Generations to come may well ask of us: "Why did they carelessly, willfully, ignorantly allow this to happen to our world? Why did they poison planet Earth?"

PART THREE

Developing Presentation Skills

9

Presentation Aids

OUTLINE

THIS CHAPTER WILL HELP YOU

- appreciate how presentation aids can help you
- understand which presentation aids work best in different situations
- plan, design, and prepare presentation aids
- make PowerPoint presentations

During your summer vacations, you run a small landscaping business. Most of your work has come from neighbors who want you to mow their grass and carry off trash. To attract new business, you posted notices on a community bulletin board. You have just gotten a call from a small company asking you to present a landscaping plan for its property next week. You will be competing against other, better-established landscaping companies.

If you want to have a shot at the contract, you will need some well-designed presentation aids to use as you introduce your plan. You could construct a model that shows the building and proposed landscaping. If that isn't feasible, you could draw sketches that show your plan. You could have these made into slides or transparencies. If the proper equipment is available, you could make a computer-assisted presentation. Regardless of the method you choose, without presentation aids you won't stand a chance against the competition.

With the advent of computerized technology in the 1990s, the types and uses of presentation aids are multiplying rapidly. In this chapter we describe both traditional and new kinds of presentation aids, identify the ways they can be used in speeches, offer suggestions for preparing them, and present guidelines for their use.

You should employ presentation aids only when they increase the clearness and effectiveness of your speech. As you read this chapter, you will notice that certain suggestions are repeated time and again: keep things simple and be consistent! These considerations are primary to whatever type of presentation aid you use.

Seeing . . . , most of all the senses, makes us know and brings to light many differences between things.

—*Aristotle*

How Presentation Aids Can Help You

It is sometimes difficult to translate words into mental images. **Presentation aids** can give your audience more direct sensory contact with your message. They can help speeches in the following ways:

1. *Presentation aids can enhance understanding.* It is easier to give directions when you have a map in front of you.
2. *Presentation aids help establish authenticity.* When you show listeners what you are talking about, you demonstrate that it actually exists.
3. *Presentation aids add variety.* Variety helps sustain audience interest and attention.
4. *Presentation aids may improve delivery.* Presentation aids encourage movement (as you point out specific features of an aid), and movement energizes a speech.
5. *Presentation aids help reduce anxiety.* Purposeful movement, such as pointing to something on an aid, provides a constructive outlet for nervous energy and directs your attention away from your anxiety.
6. *Presentation aids make a speech more memorable.* They are easy to remember because they are concrete.
7. *Presentation aids can enhance credibility.* Speakers who use well-prepared presentation aids are judged more professional, clearer, more credible, more interesting, and more persuasive than speakers who do not use such aids.[1]
8. *Presentation aids are expected in business and professional settings.* If you don't have them, you may disappoint listeners.[2]

Although there are many advantages to using presentation aids, there can also be some drawbacks.

1. *Presentation aids can distract listeners.* If you use aids when they are not appropriate or if you use too many aids, they can divert attention from your message.
2. *Presentation aids can distract a speaker.* If you are not confident about using the equipment needed to display your aid, your uneasiness may show up in your presentation.
3. *Presentation aids can damage your credibility.* If the aid is ill prepared, sloppy, or inaccurate, your ethos will suffer.
4. *Presentation aids take time to prepare.* You must plan and prepare your aids carefully and practice integrating them into your message.
5. *Presentation aids can reduce eye contact with the audience.* Novice speakers sometimes address the presentation aid and not the listeners.

Keep all these factors in mind as you consider whether to use a presentation aid.

ESL: Visual presentation aids can help ESL students better understand lecture material. Use the chalkboard, transparencies, slides, or computerized materials to provide more variety and interest in your lectures.

Ask students to scan an issue of *USA Today* and consider whether the graphics help or impede understanding. Ask them to consider how the graphics might be transformed into presentation aids that would be useful in speeches.

Living things used as presentation aids can present certain problems.

Kinds of Presentation Aids

The number and kinds of presentation aids are limited only by your imagination. We examine some of the more frequently used types and the situations in which they are most helpful.

People

As a speaker, you are your own unavoidable presentation aid. Your body, grooming, actions, gestures, voice, facial expressions, and demeanor provide an added dimension to your speech. What you wear for a presentation can be important. If you will be speaking about camping and wilderness adventures, blue jeans and a flannel shirt might be appropriate attire. If you are a nurse discussing a medical topic, your uniform might enhance your credibility. If you are talking about how to dress for an employment interview, your clothes should illustrate your recommendations. We discuss the importance of personal appearance in more detail in Chapter 11.

You can also use other people as presentation aids. Neomal Abyskera used two of his classmates to illustrate the lineup positions in the game of rugger as played in his native Sri Lanka. At the appropriate moment, Neomal said, "Pete and Jeff will show you how the opposing players line up." While his classmates demonstrated the shoulder grip position, Neomal explained when and why the position was assumed. This demonstration was more understandable than if he had tried to describe the position verbally.

The people you ask to function as a presentation aid should be willing to do so. They should understand that their role is to illustrate your message, not draw attention away from it. They should agree to meet with you to rehearse the presentation. They should sit in the front row as you stand to speak so they can come forward at the right moment and then sit down quickly.

Objects and Models

Nothing is better than using exactly what you are talking about. However, if the objects are very large or small or valuable, models may be a better option.

Objects. If you are speaking about something portable that all listeners can see without straining, then you can use the object itself as a presentation aid. You should also be able to keep the object out of sight until it is time to use it. If you display the object throughout your speech, listeners may focus on it rather than on your message. If you plan to use more than one object, display them one at a time.

Have students make a brief presentation describing an object that they find interesting. Then have them repeat the presentation, using the object as a visual aid. What are the advantages and disadvantages of using the visual aid?

Inanimate objects work better than living things. One of our students once brought a puppy for a speech on caring for animals. As she began, she spread some newspapers on the table, and placed the puppy on them. The first thing the puppy did was to wet the papers (including her note cards). From there it was all downhill.

Other problems can arise when presentation aids are used to shock the audience into attention. Objects that are dangerous, illegal, or possibly offensive, such as guns, drugs, or pornography, present special difficulties. One of our students brandished a realistic "toy" weapon during a speech on gun control. Several audience members became so upset that they could not listen effectively to his message. Another student was more successful at shocking the audience into attention with a presentation aid. At the beginning of a speech on regulating the sale of tobacco products to minors, Allison McIntyre held up a gallon jar of cigarette butts that she had collected on the Vanderbilt campus right before her speech. Be careful when using dramatic presentation aids. If you have questions about the propriety of an object, check with your instructor.

Models. When an object is too large to carry, too small to be easily seen, very rare, expensive, or fragile, or simply unavailable, a replica of the object can work well as a presentation aid. When using a model, be sure it is constructed to scale and maintains the proper proportions between parts.

Models are useful when your subject is too small to be seen in its natural state or too large to be brought to the scene of the speech.

Graphics

Graphics include sketches, maps, graphs, charts, and textual materials. Because graphics will be displayed for only a short time during your speech, they must be instantly clear. They must be simpler than graphics designed for print, which readers can study at their leisure. Each graphic should focus on one idea. Because they will be viewed from a distance, the colors should be intense and should contrast sharply with the background. We will cover such considerations more fully under "Preparing Presentation Aids" later in this chapter.

Sketches. Sketches are simplified representations of what you are talking about. If you don't draw well, search children's coloring books for drawings that you can trace. Make the sketch first on paper; then enlarge it or transfer it onto a transparency with a copier. You can also make sketches using clip art or the drawing program on a computer. Mark Peterson used a sketch that he had transferred to a transparency to illustrate the measurements one should take before buying a bicycle. In talking about making bar-to-pedal and seat-to-handlebar measurements, he pointed to his presentation aid as he said, "Let me show you how to take some basic measurements."

Maps. Commercially prepared maps contain too much detail to use as presentation aids. The best maps are those that you make specifically for your speech so that they are simple, relevant to your purpose, and uncluttered. Maps are particularly useful for speeches based on spatial relationships.

The map in Figure 9.1 was used to show the route between major attractions at Yellowstone National Park. Seeing such a map helps the audience put locations into perspective.

Whether a map works as a presentation aid depends on how well you integrate it into your presentation. Elizabeth Walling used a map of the wilderness canoe area in northern Minnesota to familiarize her Memphis audience with that area. She made a double-sided poster that she was able to keep hidden behind the speaker's table until she was ready for it. On one side she highlighted the wilderness canoe area on an outline map of northern Minnesota, pointing

FIGURE 9.1
Map of Yellowstone Park

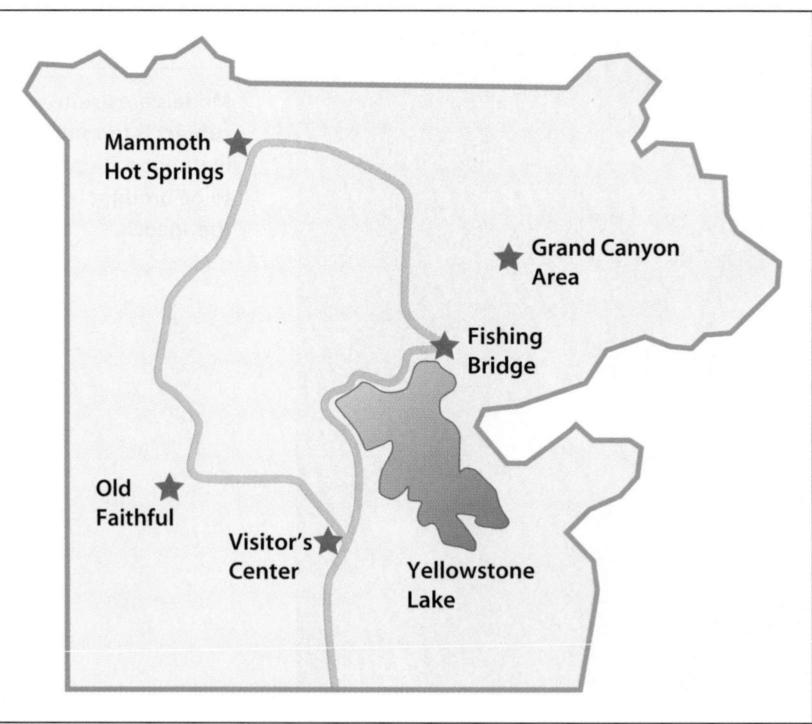

out various places of interest. To illustrate how large the area is, Elizabeth said, "Let me put this in a more familiar context for you." She then turned the poster over, revealing an outline map of western Tennessee on which she had superimposed the wilderness area. At a glance we could see that the area would extend from Memphis to past Jackson, Tennessee, some eighty miles away. Elizabeth's artful use of the two maps had created a striking visual comparison. The same type of effect can be obtained by overlaying transparencies.

Graphs. Mrs. Robert A. Taft once commented, "I always find that statistics are hard to swallow and impossible to digest. The only one I can ever remember is that if all the people who go to sleep in church were laid end to end, they would be a lot more comfortable."[3] Many people share Mrs. Taft's feelings about statistics. As we noted in Chapter 6, masses of numbers presented orally can be overwhelming. A well-designed graph can make statistical information easier for listeners to understand.

A **pie graph** shows the size of a subject's parts in relation to one another and to the whole. The "pie" represents the whole, and the "slices" represent the parts. The most effective pie graphs have six or less segments. Too many segments make the graph difficult to read. The pie graph in Figure 9.2 shows how creative such graphs can be.

A **bar graph** shows comparisons and contrasts between two or more items or groups. Bar graphs are easy to understand because each item can be readily compared with every other item on the graph. Bar graphs can also have a dramatic visual impact, especially when they make use of **pictographs** (symbolic representations) in place of the bars. Figure 9.3 is such a bar graph. It presents the results of a Gallup poll comparing how confident Americans are in law enforcement agencies, ranging from local police to the CIA.

A **line graph** demonstrates changes across time and is especially useful for indicating trends in growth or decline. Figure 9.4 shows the number of college graduates by gender from 1950 through 2000. The upward-sloping lines confirm the dramatic increases in the numbers of both male and female graduates

Have students prepare a pie graph, a bar graph, and a line graph using the same set of statistical data. Ask them to discuss which type of graph would make the information most clear and striking.

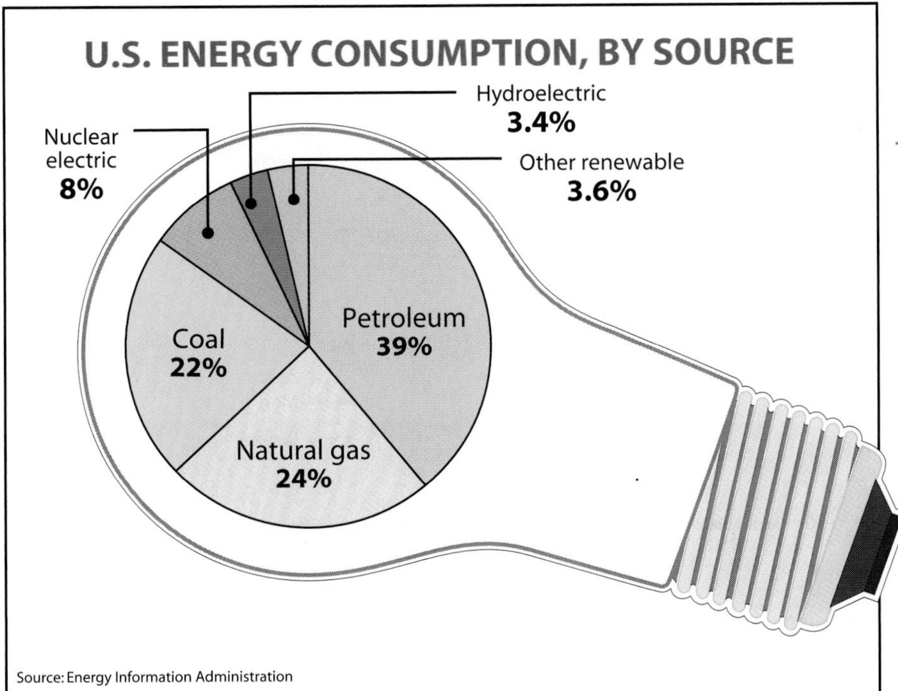

FIGURE 9.2
Sample Pie Graph: U.S. Energy Consumption, by Source

Source: Kid's Almanac for the 21st Century (Scholastic Press: NY, 1999), p. 119.

FIGURE 9.3
Sample Bar Graph: Confidence in U.S. Law Enforcement Agents

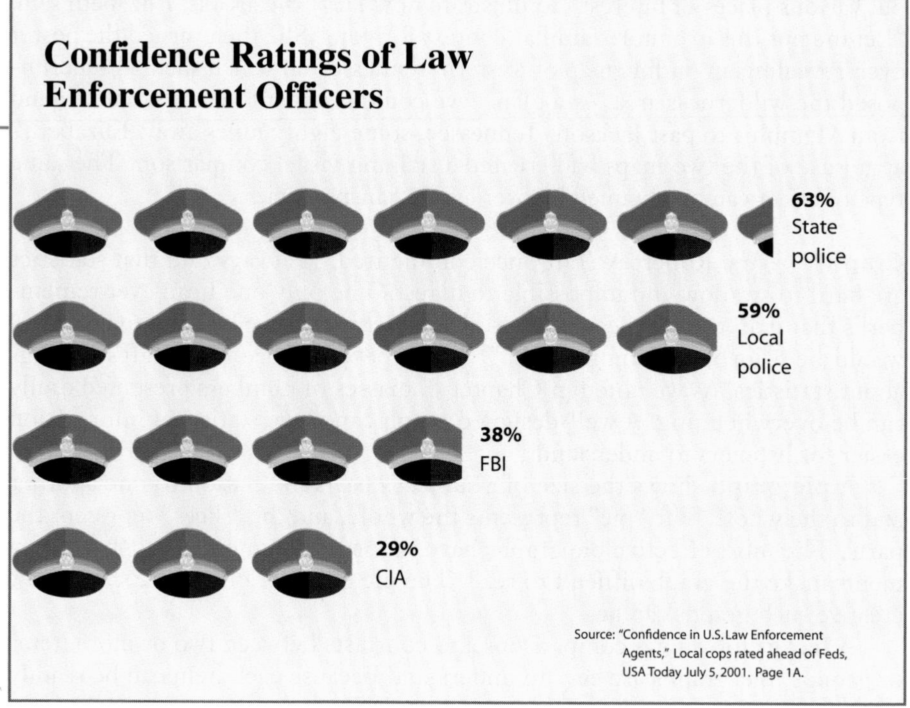

Source: Local Cops Rated Ahead of Feds, from "Confidence in U.S. Law Enforcement Agents," *USA Today,* July 5, 2001. Page 1A. Copyright 2001, USA TODAY. Reprinted with permission.

FIGURE 9.4
Sample Line Graph: College Graduation by Gender, 1950–2000

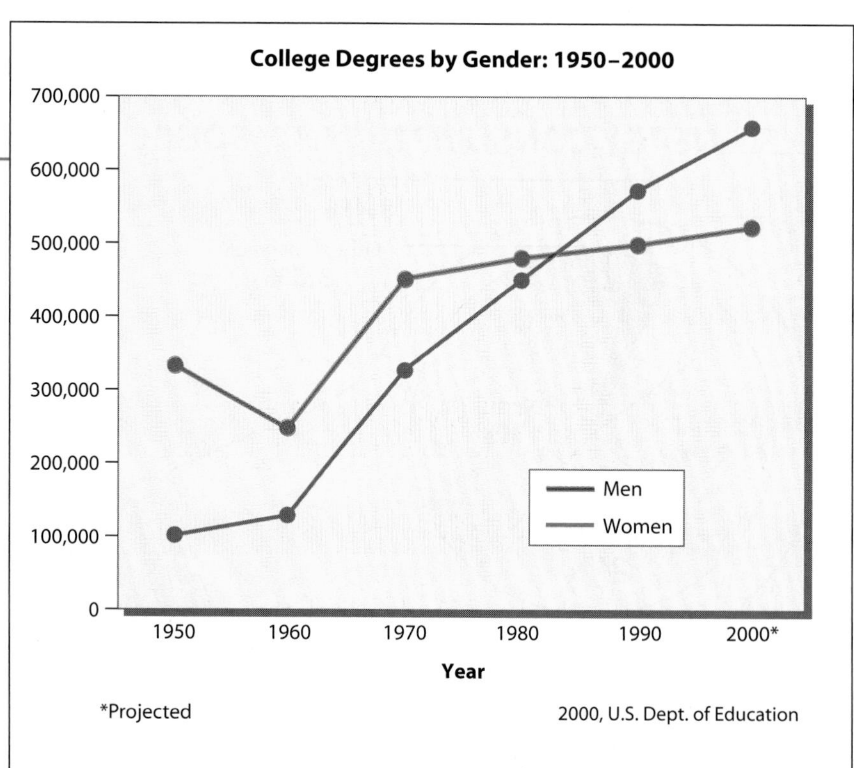

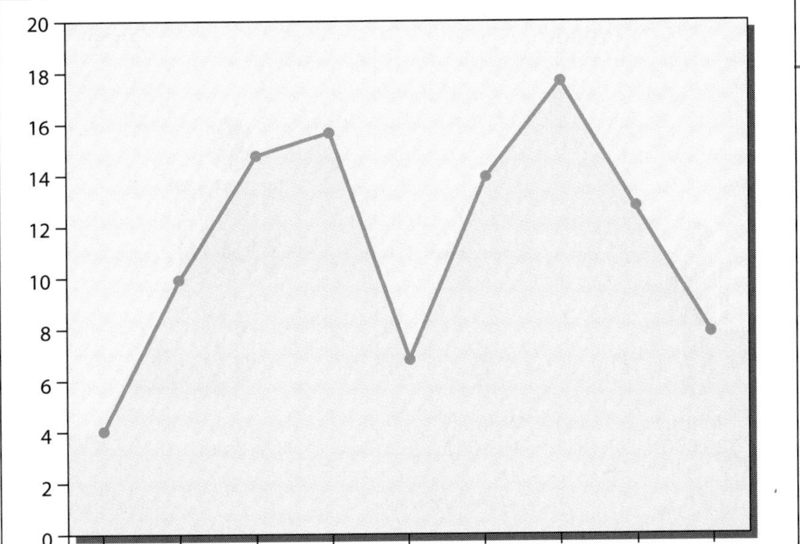

FIGURE 9.5
Sample Mountain Graph

across this span of time. When you plot more than one line on a graph, use different colors. Never try to plot more than three lines on a graph.

A **mountain graph** is a variation of the line graph that works to heighten the impact of simple graphs in which only a single line is drawn. It uses different colors to fill in the areas on either side of the line. Mountain graphs are especially effective when there are extreme variations in the data. Figure 9.5 is a mountain graph charting the amount of snowfall in an area from 1980 through 1996.

Charts. Charts provide visual summaries of processes and relationships that are not in themselves visible. In print communication they can be quite complex: The challenge to the speaker is to simplify them without distorting their meaning so that they meet the needs of oral communication. The listener must be able to understand them instantly and to read them from a distance. One frequently used type of chart is a flow chart.

A **flow chart** shows the steps in a process. The lines and arrows in a flow chart indicate what steps occur simultaneously and what steps occur sequentially. In Chapter 5 we used a flow chart to illustrate the major steps in the preparation of a speech (see Figure 5.1 on page 121). Flow charts are also used to show power and responsibility relationships, such as who reports to whom in an organization.

A problem that often arises when charts are used in oral communication is that speakers may be tempted to load them with too much information. If they are complicated, they may confuse rather than enlighten listeners. One way around this problem is to use **sequence charts**, which are presented in succession. For example, you might choose to illustrate information on the awarding of college degrees by gender in a series of charts. Figure 9.6 reveals the first and last charts in a series showing degrees by gender across the years. In the first chart, the pictograph of a man is three times larger than that of a woman, representing the 3:1 ratio in earned degrees during 1950. The second chart uses the pictographs to underscore the dramatic reversal of this ratio, such that by 2000 women actually received more degrees than did men. Intermediate charts for decade years could show the more gradual changes in the relative sizes of these figures as the trend developed.

Have students generate a list of speech topics for you to write on the chalkboard. Ask students to suggest the types of presentation aids that might be most appropriate for each of the topics.

FIGURE 9.6
Sample Sequence Charts

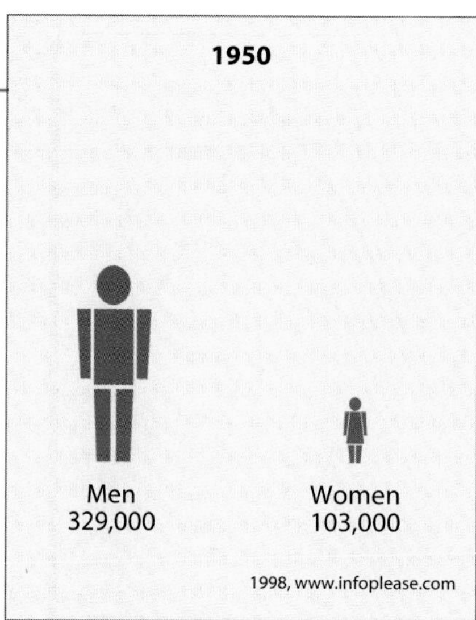

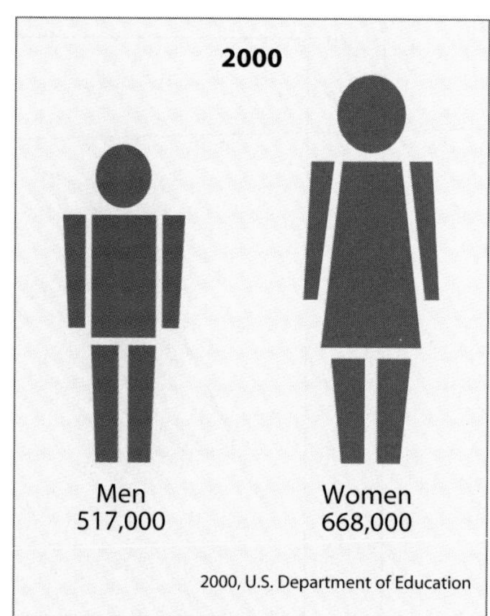

Textual Graphics. **Textual graphics** are lists of phrases, words, or numbers. Unfamiliar material is clearer and easier for listeners to remember when they can both hear and see the message. Presenting the key words in a message visually can help an audience follow complicated ideas more easily. For example, in an informative speech that describes a process, you might show a sequence of slides that identify each step in the process. That way you could guide your audience through the main points of your speech.

The most frequently used textual graphics contain **bulleted lists** of information such as that shown in the computer-generated slide in Figure 9.7. When you make a bulleted list, begin with a title, then place the material under it. Keep the graphic simple. Use intense colors for contrast. Have no more than six lines of information and no more than six words to a line.

Another frequently used type of textual graphic presents an **acronym** composed of the initial letters of words to help your audience remember your message. The transparency in Figure 9.8 used the acronym EMILY in a persuasive speech urging students to begin saving early for retirement. When preparing such a graphic, use the acronym as a title; then list the words under it. Use size and/or color to make the first letters of the words stand out.

FIGURE 9.7
Sample Bulleted List

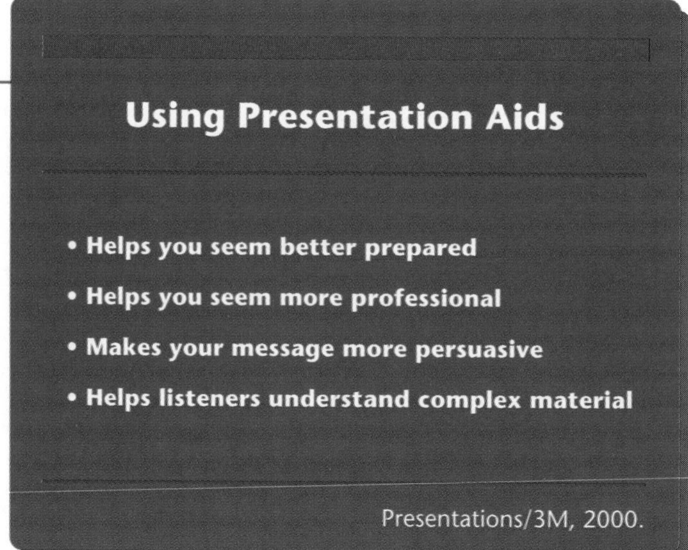

EMILY

EARLY
MONEY
IS
LIKE
YEAST

IT MAKES
DOUGH GROW!

FIGURE 9.8
Acronym Graphic

Textual graphics may also be used to present numerical information. When you use a textual graphic to present numbers, you should keep it very simple. Have no more than three columns and five rows. Textual graphics designed for handouts can contain more information, but not so much that they compete with your words for attention. Figure 9.9 illustrates a simple numerical graphic.

Pictures

An old Chinese proverb suggests that a picture is worth a thousand words. Although this may be true in some situations, it is also true that pictures and photographs are difficult to use effectively in speeches unless you have the proper projection equipment. Small photographs will be difficult for anyone beyond

INVESTMENT GROWTH
$1,000 – 8%

5 years	$1,469
10 years	$2,159
15 years	$3,172
20 years	$4,666

Berger, *Feathering Your Nest*, 1995.

FIGURE 9.9
Numerical Graphic

FIGURE 9.10
Photos of Glacier National Park

These two photos illustrate the dramatic reduction in size of the glacier at Glacier National Park between 1910 and 1997.

Use the exercise "Presentation Aid Adaptations" in the IRM to get students thinking about how they can overcome problems with using a variety of presentation aids.

the first row to see, and passing them around during a presentation can be a major distraction. Moreover, speakers may rely too heavily on the pictures, forgetting that words are the primary means of communication in a speech. Pictures that are disturbing can be distracting. One student who was a paramedic showed pictures of child abuse victims taken in a local emergency room. Some members of the audience became so upset that they were not able to concentrate on her message.

Despite these problems, a good photograph can authenticate a point in a way that words alone cannot. It can make a situation seem more vivid and realistic. For instance, suppose a speaker said, "If present climate conditions continue, the glaciers in Glacier National Park will be gone in thirty years." Would this not be more dramatic and impressive if the speaker showed the photographs in Figure 9.10 to reveal the changes that have already taken place?

Pictures should be selected for their relevance to your speech. They should be controlled just as you control charts and graphs—revealed only to illustrate a point and then put out of sight. Color copiers can make inexpensive eleven-by-seventeen-inch enlargements from snapshots. This is probably the minimally acceptable size for most classroom speeches. Mount pictures on poster board for ease of presentation. Photographs can also be scanned into a computer for use in multimedia presentations or to make transparencies.

Museum prints and commercial posters are made to be seen from a distance and are usually large enough to use as presentation aids in a classroom setting. In his speech describing an extended camping trip, Michael McDonald used a print of Thomas Moran's painting of the Green River in the American West to convey his feelings about the landscape and to give context to his words. Paintings can invoke a mood, especially when used as a backdrop to eloquent language.

Presentation Media

There are many different types of presentation media. Traditional media include flip charts, posters, handouts, chalk or marker boards, transparencies, videotapes, and audiotapes. Newer presentation media use computer programs, such as PowerPoint, that can incorporate slides, videotapes, and sound. These are rapidly becoming the standard for presentations in organizational and educational settings.

Flip Charts

A flip chart is a large, unlined tablet. Most flip charts are newsprint pads that measure about two feet wide by three feet high. They are placed on an easel so that each page can be flipped over the top when you are done with it. Flip charts are convenient, inexpensive, and adaptable to many settings. Business meetings, decision-making groups, and organizational training sessions often use flip charts in addition to more sophisticated types of presentation tools.

Bring a flip chart, easel, and broad-tipped felt markers for your next lecture to demonstrate the use of the chart technique. After the lecture, ask students how well they felt the flip chart worked as a presentation aid.

Flip charts are designed to be used spontaneously. This makes them especially useful when subjects come up in a meeting that should be written out so that they can be analyzed and understood. When using flip charts, keep each page as simple as possible. Use wide-point felt markers in strong colors, and print or write legibly in large letters.

Although flip charts can be effective in some group communication settings, they seldom work as well in classroom speeches. They often look sloppy and suggest that the speaker did not care enough to prepare a more polished presentation aid. Writing on a flip chart also forces the speaker to either stop speaking or speak with his or her back to the audience. This loss of direct audience contact can offset any gain from using the charts.

Posters

Posters can be used to display sketches, maps, charts, graphs, or textual graphics. In an average-size room with a small audience, posters about fourteen by seventeen inches may work best because they are so easy to handle. They can be used for sequence charts with one idea or graphic per board. You can place them face down on the lectern or table and display them as you refer to them. You can also use the back as a "cheat sheet" that cues you to the next point in your presentation. Be sure to number the posters on the back so that they don't get out of sequence. Keep your posters simple and neat. Use large letters in strong colors so that they are easy to read. Have a lot of white space. Rehearse your speech using the posters, so you can integrate them smoothly into your presentation.

Handouts

Handouts are useful when your subject is complex or your message contains much statistical information. When the speech is over, listeners have something to remind them of your message.

Have students prepare a handout that could be distributed after their informative speeches. Not only will this exercise give them the experience of preparing a handout, but it may also help them focus their ideas more effectively.

There is one serious drawback to using handouts: they can distract listeners from what you are saying. If you distribute a handout before you speak, it will compete with you for attention. The audience may decide to read the handout instead of listening to you. Therefore, you should distribute handouts before your speech *only* when it is necessary for listeners to refer to them as you speak and you are confident of your ability to command attention. Never distribute handouts during your speech; this is a sure-fire way to divert, confuse, and lose listeners. Multipaged handouts are multidistracting.

Dwight Davidson distributed a one-page handout at the beginning of his speech on job trends. His audience was able to follow along with him as he explained the statistical table in the handout. Without this material his listeners would have been lost. George Stacey distributed a handout listing the steps required for administering CPR *after* his speech on that subject. By waiting until he was finished, he avoided distracting listeners but still helped his audience remember the procedure. Your decision on whether to distribute a handout before or after a speech should be based on the nature of the subject, how confident you are in your ability to control attention, and what you would like your handout to accomplish.

Chalk and Marker Boards

ESL: Writing key words or unfamiliar terms on the chalkboard can aid the understanding of ESL students.

A chalk or marker board is a presentation medium available in almost every corporate conference room or classroom. Like flip charts, boards are best used for spontaneous, unpredictable illustrations and demonstrations. Despite careful preparation, there may be times when you look at your listeners and realize that some of them have not understood what you have just said. One way you can respond to such feedback is by writing a few words on the board or by drawing a simple diagram to help reduce audience confusion.

Mumble part of your lecture with your back to the class as you scribble words hastily on a cluttered chalkboard. After a few moments, turn around and ask the students to critique this use of a presentation aid.

When you write on a board, use large letters so that people in the back of the room can read them without straining. Write or print legibly. Clear the board before you begin and, as a courtesy to later speakers, erase the board when you are finished. Because you inevitably lose contact with listeners while writing on a board, do not use this medium for any illustration that will take more than a few seconds to write or draw. Never use chalk or marker boards simply because you did not want to take the time to prepare a polished presentation aid.

Transparencies and Slides

If your college has an audiovisual resources center, ask a center representative to speak to your class about the help that is available or arrange a tour of the facility.

Transparencies and slides allow audiences to see graphics or photographs more easily, especially when audiences are large or spread out over a large room. Business speakers often prefer them to posters or flip charts because they look more professional.

Transparencies are easier to use than slides because you don't have to darken the room when you show them. They are simple to make, inexpensive, and adaptable. Another advantage is that you can revise a transparency while it is being shown, thereby adding flexibility and spontaneity to your presentation. You can also use a pencil as a pointer to direct listeners' attention to features you want to emphasize.

When using slides and a traditional carousel projector, the room usually has to be darkened. Unfortunately, this means that the illuminated screen becomes the center of attention instead of you. The major disadvantage of using either transparencies or slides is that often you must speak from where your equipment is located. You may have to stand behind or in the middle of the audience to run the projector. This means you will be talking to someone's back. If you do not have remote-control equipment, your best solution may be to have a classmate change the projections or slides on cue. You will need to practice with your assistant to coordinate the slides with your words.

Most transparencies and slides are now prepared on personal computers. You can purchase transparency sheets for use with most printers. You also can draw or print your material onto plain paper and convert it to a transparency on a copying machine. If you only have access to a black-and-white copier or printer, you can add color with opaque markers.

To prepare materials for use as transparencies, you should follow the general guidelines presented earlier for the use of graphics. You should frame your transparencies to avoid glare from light showing around the outside edges of the projection. Frames can be purchased at most copy shops or made from construction paper.

When you arrange slides in a carousel, be sure they are in the proper order and that none of them are upside down. Today, many personal computers are packaged with software that allows you to prepare and present slides. We will discuss this in greater detail as we discuss computer-assisted presentations.

If you decide to use transparencies or slides, check the equipment ahead of time and become familiar with its operation. You may need a long extension cord to position the equipment where you want it. Practice using the equipment as you rehearse your speech. One final caution: Don't use too many slides or transparencies in a short speech. A presentation aid should do just that—*aid* your speech, not compete with or replace it.

Videotapes and Audiotapes

Videotapes and audiotapes can authenticate and add variety to your presentation. Videos are especially useful for transporting the audience to distant, dangerous, or otherwise unavailable locations. Although you could verbally describe the beauty of the Montana Rockies, your word-pictures might come to life if reinforced with scenes from a videotape.

Using a videotape, however, can present some special problems. Moving images attract more attention than the spoken word, so they can easily upstage you. Moreover, a videotape segment must be edited so that splices blend without annoying static. Such editing takes special skill and equipment. Finally, videotapes can be difficult to work into a short speech without consuming all of your time. In a short speech, a video clip should be no more than thirty seconds long. Unless they are carefully managed, properly cued, and artistically edited, videotapes can become more of a handicap than an aid.

For certain topics, however, carefully prepared videos can be more effective than any other type of presentation aid. One student at Northwest Mississippi Community College, who was a firefighter, used videotape in an informative speech on fire hazards in the home. By customizing the videotape to fit the precise needs of his speech, he was able to show long shots of a room and then zoom in on various hazards.[4] He prepared the videotape without sound so that his speech provided the commentary needed to interpret and explain the pictures seen by the audience. Using this technique, he made his subject much more meaningful for listeners.

Audiotapes may also be useful as presentation aids and are not as difficult for most students to handle and integrate into their speech. If you wanted to describe the alarm cries of various animals or the songs of different birds, an audiotape could be essential. When in doubt about the wisdom or practicality of using such aids, consult your instructor.

Computer-Assisted Presentations

Most personal computers can generate a wide variety of presentation aids, including sketches, maps, graphs, charts, and textual graphics for handouts, slides, and transparencies. The materials produced on computers are usually much neater and more accurate than those drawn by hand. Presentation software programs, such as PowerPoint, are readily available. You can also find shareware

Computerized slide presentations and flip charts are frequently used as presentation aids in business meetings.

on the Internet. Freeserve (http://5star.freeserve.com/Business/Presentations/Presentations1.html) provides links, ratings, and demos for multimedia shareware available online. These programs are either free or reasonably priced. Specialized publications sponsored by computer and software manufacturers, such as *Presentations* (http://www.presentations.com/) are available both online and in hard-copy versions. Your campus computer lab may have training programs to help you learn how to access and use these materials.

Computer-assisted presentations can bring together text, numbers, pictures, and artwork made into slides, videos, animations, and audio materials. Materials such as graphs and charts that are generated with the computer can be changed at any time, even during a presentation. The programs come with a variety of templates to assist you in designing your presentation aids. The templates can be adapted to suit your particular needs.

When using a computer for developing presentation aids, be careful not to get so caught up with the glitz and glitter that you lose sight of the fact that *it is your message that is most important*. In cautioning against the misuse or overuse of such technology, Rebecca Ganzel in *Presentations* magazine pictured the following scenario:

> **It's that nightmare again—the one in which you're trapped in the Electronic Presentation from Hell. The familiar darkness presses in, periodically sliced in half by a fiendish light. Bullet points, about 18 to a slide, careen in all directions. You cringe, but the slides keep coming, too fast to read, each with a new template you half-remember seeing a hundred times before: Dad's Tie! Sixties Swirls! Infinite Double-Helixes! A typewriter clatters; brakes squeal. Somewhere in the shadows, a voice drones on. Strange stick people shake hands and dance around a flowchart. Typefaces morph into Word Art.**
>
> **But the worst is yet to come. As though you're watching a train wreck in slow motion, you look down at your hand—and *you're holding the remote.*[5]**

Using sophisticated technology in your presentation does not excuse you from the usual requirements for speaking. In fact, if your presentation aids draw more attention than your ideas, they may be a hindrance more than a help. Be especially careful not to get caught up with swirling backgrounds and flashy transitions. Remember, it is better to be subtle than sensational. Follow the guidelines for developing and using presentation aids put forth in this chapter. See the "PowerPoint Presentations" section later in this chapter.

Speaker's Notes 9.1

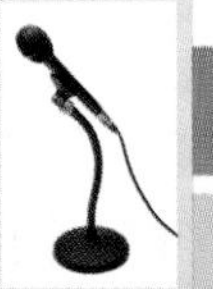

WHAT PRESENTATION MEDIA TO USE

1. Use flip charts, chalk, and marker boards only as an audience adaptation tool.
2. Use posters to display maps, charts, graphs, or textual graphics to a small audience.
3. Use handouts to present complex information or statistical data.
4. Use transparencies or slides to show graphics or photos to a large audience.
5. Use audiotapes and videotapes to authenticate a point.
6. Use computerized materials to make your presentation seem more professional.

Ethical Considerations

Presentation aids can enlighten, but they can also mislead. Tempted by their power, speakers can use them to deceive listeners. Thus, presentation aids can raise challenging ethical questions.[6]

ESL: Ask ESL students to bring in photos, ads, or graphics from magazines or newspapers that show a distorted image of their culture. Use these materials to discuss ethical considerations regarding the use of presentation aids.

Graphs and charts, for example, can be rigged so that they misrepresent reality. Figure 9.11 shows how a recent decade's growth in percentage of women partners in major accounting firms might be misrepresented in bar graph A to make nothing look like something—the advances go from pitiful to sorry. Bar graph B in the same figure puts these slight gains into the proper perspective.[7] Be careful to prepare graphs so that they honestly represent a situation.

You must also remember to credit your sources on your presentation aids. Be sure to include this information in smaller, but still visible, letters at the bottom of any material you plan to display (see how this is done in Figure 9.7). Citing your source in this fashion both verifies the data presented and reminds you to mention the source in your oral presentation.

Probably the most interesting ethical questions involve the use of film and tape materials. For example, the most famous photographer of the Civil War, Matthew Brady, rearranged bodies on the battlefield to enhance the impact of his pictures. Eighty years later, another American war photographer carefully staged the now celebrated photograph of marines planting the flag at Iwo Jima.[8] Fifty years after that, *Time* magazine electronically manipulated a cover photograph of O. J. Simpson to "darken it and achieve a brooding, menacing quality."[9] On the one hand, these famous images are fabrications: they pretend to be

Women Partners in Accounting Firms

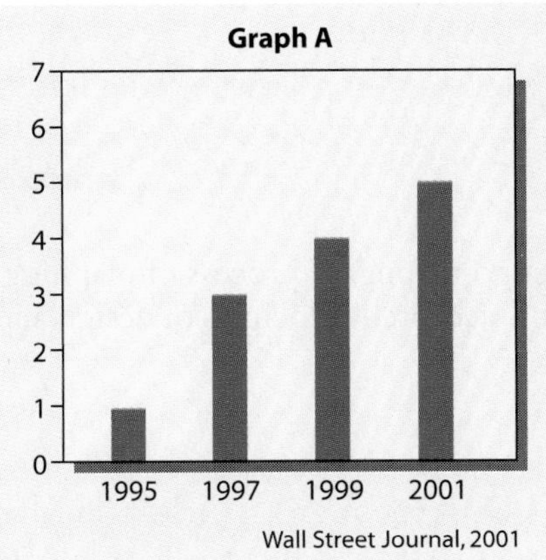

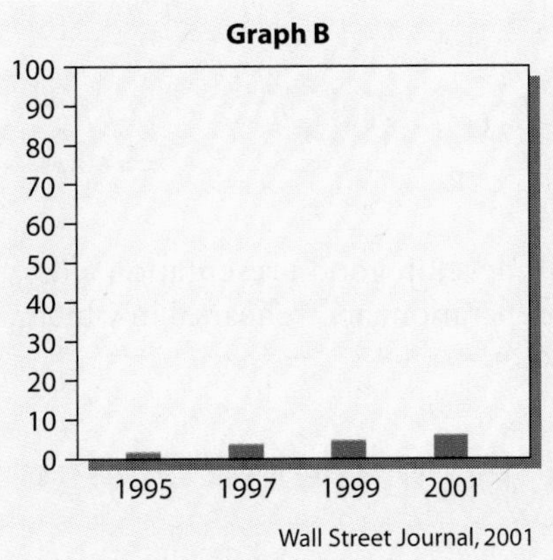

FIGURE 9.11
Misleading Bar Graph and Same Material Presented So It Is Not Misleading

Ethics Alert! 9.1

THE ETHICAL USE OF PRESENTATION AIDS

1. Be certain charts or graphs do not distort information.
2. Never manipulate visual images to deceive your audience.
3. If you alter an image to reveal some deeper truth, let the audience know you have done so.
4. Cite the source of any data you present in a graph.
5. As a listener, be on guard against the power of presentation aids to trick you.

what they are not. On the other, they bring home reality more forcefully. In other words, the form of the photos may be a lie, but the lie may reveal a deeper truth. So are these photographs unethical, or are they simply artistic?

With today's technology, the potential for abuse looms ever larger. Video and audio editing easily produces illusions of reality. Consider how moviemakers depicted Forrest Gump shaking hands with Presidents Kennedy, Johnson, and Nixon. Call to mind the image of the late Fred Astaire dancing with a vacuum cleaner in a television commercial. In movies and ads, such distortions can be amusing. In real life, they can be dangerous. When they purportedly convey actual objects or events, as when television networks or newspapers "stage" crashes to make their stories more dramatic without letting us in on the artifice, they can be quite deceptive.[10]

Consider the dark industry of deception that has developed around the misuse of audiotapes. Tapes that purportedly reveal personal or business crimes, or that confess to crimes against humanity when offered by prisoners of war, are occasionally revealed on close inspection to be nothing more than total fabrications, the artful splicing together of pieces of taped conversations that may have been illegally or wrongfully recorded to begin with. All these practices may relate to the ancient adage "Seeing (or hearing) is believing." We have been conditioned by experience and taught by tradition to trust the "reality" revealed by our eyes and ears.

To be an ethical communicator, you should alert your listeners to the illusion whenever you manipulate sounds and images so that they reveal your message more forcefully. You should also be prepared to defend your creation as a "better representation" of the truth. As a listener, you should develop a skeptical attitude about images and recordings and seek additional evidence if there is any question concerning their validity.

Preparing Presentation Aids

To develop good presentation aids, you must go through a process of planning, preparation, and rehearsal in which you follow accepted principles of design and color.

Principles of Design

The basic principles of design are visibility, emphasis, and balance. To apply them effectively to presentation aids, you should always consider how the aids will function before an audience. Keep in mind one rule: *Simplicity is the golden virtue of presentation aids.*

Collect examples of presentation aids to illustrate good and poor design practice.

Visibility. The size of any presentation aid must be appropriate to the setting in which it is used. An overly large aid may be cumbersome and overwhelm listeners in a small room. Similarly, a small aid will not be effective in a large room. Listeners in the back of the room must be able to see your presentation aid without straining. Otherwise, the aid will *not* be an aid.

When preparing a poster board presentation aid for speeches in standard classrooms, follow these minimum size guidelines: your titles should be about three inches high and other text at least an inch and a half high. If you generate slides or transparencies on a computer, use a large font. Computer print is typically sized in terms of points (pt). Such presentation aids should use the following sizes of letters:

	Transparencies	Slides	Handouts
Title	36 pt	24 pt	18 pt
Subtitles	24 pt	18 pt	14 pt
Other text	18 pt	14 pt	12 pt

Use a plain font that is easy to read. For example, which of the following styles do you think would work better?

How Easy Is This to Read?

compared with

How Easy Is This to Read?

Emphasis. Focus your presentation aids so that they emphasize only what your speech emphasizes. Each aid should make only one point. Your listeners' eyes should be drawn immediately to what you want to illustrate. The map of Yellowstone Park (Figure 9.1) eliminates all information except what the speaker wishes to stress. Had the speaker added pictures of bears to indicate grizzly habitats and drawings of fish to show trout streams, the presentation aid would have been decorative but distracting. Avoid cuteness! Graphics prepared for handouts may be more detailed than those used for posters, slides, or transparencies, but they should not contain extraneous material. When in doubt, leave the details out. Let your words provide the elaboration.

Balance. Presentation aids that are balanced are pleasing to the eye. The focal point of the aid can be the center of the chart or poster, or it can be deliberately placed off-center for the sake of variety. You should have a margin of about two inches at the top and bottom of a poster board. On computer-generated graphics, you should leave blank space at both the top and bottom and have equal side margins. For poster boards, side margins should be about one and a half inches wide. On computer-generated graphics they should be at least an inch wide.

Principles of Color

As many of the illustrations in this chapter show, color adds impact to presentation aids. Most colored presentation aids attract and hold attention better than black-and-white ones. Color also can convey or enhance meaning. For example, a speech about crop damage from a drought might use an enlarged outline map showing the least affected areas in green, moderately damaged areas in orange, and severely affected areas in brown. The natural colors would reinforce the message.

Bring in construction paper in a variety of colors and ask students to write down the first words that come to mind as you display them. Discuss the different reactions of students to different colors. Note whether any cultural differences show up in the meanings.

Color can also be used to create moods and impressions. Blue suggests power, authority, and stability (blue chip, blue ribbon, royal blue). Using blue in your graphics can invest them with these qualities. Red signals excitement and may be used to indicate the presence of crisis (in the red, red ink). Line graphs tracing the rise in cases of AIDS could be portrayed in red to convey a sense of urgency. You should avoid using red when presenting financial data unless you want to focus on debts or losses. In our American culture, green is associated with both money (greenbacks) and environmental concerns (Greenpeace). The use of color in Figure 9.8 resonates with the green of U.S. currency and reinforces the compounded effects of early investments. When selecting colors, you should also be aware of cultural differences. For example, in the United States, white is associated with weddings, baptisms, confirmations, and other happy ritual occasions. In Japan, white has an entirely different connotation. There it is a funeral color, associated with sadness.[11]

Combining colors in different ways can convey subtle nuances of meaning. An **analogous color scheme** uses colors that are adjacent on the color wheel, such as green, blue green, and blue. Although this type of color scheme shows the differences among the components represented, it also suggests their connection and compatibility. For example, a pie graph could use analogous colors to represent the students, faculty, and administration of a university. The different colors suggest that these parts are indeed separate, but the analogous color scheme and the inclusion of these parts within a circle imply that they belong together. In this subtle way, the presentation aid itself makes the statement that the components of a university ought to work together.

A **complementary color scheme** uses colors that are opposites on the color wheel, such as red and green. Complementary color schemes suggest tension and opposition among elements in a speech. Because they heighten the sense of drama, they may enliven informative speaking and encourage change in persuasive speaking.

The colors you use for text should always stand out from the background of your aid. Avoid patterned backgrounds that may make the words difficult to read. With poster board, it is best to use a white or cream-colored board and strong primary colors such as red, blue, and green for contrast. Avoid using red letters on transparencies or slides because red tends to bleed into the background. In slides or transparencies, a light background can create glare. Therefore, you might want to use a strong primary color for the background and have the text or other graphic elements printed in white. Color contrast is especially important for computer-generated slides and transparencies because the colors may wash out and appear less distinct when projected than they do when seen on a monitor. Colors like pastel pink, light blue, and pale yellow may not be strong enough for good graphic emphasis in any type of presentation aid.

Speaker's Notes 9.2

PREPARING PRESENTATION AIDS

1. Keep it simple.
2. Be sure all audience members can read the text on your graphics.
3. Balance the visual elements of your aid.
4. Limit the amount of information you include.
5. Provide ample white space.
6. Check for spelling errors.
7. Be consistent in the use of colors and lettering.

A final word of caution concerning color: When you prepare presentation aids on a computer, the colors on your monitor will differ from the final colors when they are printed out on a transparency or slide. Run a sample and project it to see how the final colors will actually look to an audience. If the results are not what you expected, try other colors until you are satisfied.

Making Presentation Aids

To prepare handmade charts, graphs, or other poster aids, begin with a rough draft that allows you to see how your aid will look when it is finished. If you will be making a poster, prepare your draft on newsprint or butcher paper of the same size. With a light pencil, mark off the margins to frame your aid. Divide your planning sheet into four equal sections to help you balance the placement of material. Use a wide-tipped felt market to sketch in your design and words. Now step back to inspect your presentation aid from about the same distance as the back row of your audience. Will these listeners be able to view its contents without straining? Is everything spelled correctly? Is your eye drawn immediately to the most important elements in the poster? Have you positioned your material so that it will be most effective? Does the poster look balanced? Once you have completed a "rough draft" of the aid, construct the final product using stick-on letters and numbers.

Use the exercise "Impromptu Presentation Aids" in Chapter 9 of the IRM to give students practice generating and critiquing rough drafts of aids. Be sure to bring all the materials (i.e. newsprint pages, felt markers, etc.) students will need to work on the aids.

Remember, keep it simple! Are your margins and borders large enough to provide ample white space? Is there anything you can eliminate? If your mock-up looks "busy," make a series of presentation aids instead of just one.

If you use computer-generated graphics to produce slides, transparencies, or handouts, experiment with several different designs. Limit the amount of information on slides and transparencies to six lines per visual and six words per line. Limit the number of slides or transparencies you use. A good rule of thumb is to have *no more than four aids for a six-minute or six aids for ten-minute presentation*. If you use more than this, your speech may become just a voice-over for a slide show.

PowerPoint Presentations

More than 90 percent of all computerized presentations in the United States are created by using the PowerPoint program, which is widely distributed as part of the Microsoft Office software.[12] Because you may well use this program at some time in your professional career, we are supplying these step-by-step guidelines for developing a simple slide presentation using PowerPoint. These directions apply to the software furnished with Office 2000 and Office Millennium editions.

See if your campus computer lab has a PowerPoint presentations specialist on staff. Arrange for your students to meet with this person.

Open the PowerPoint program on your computer. You can access this by using the "Start" button in the bottom left corner of the screen, then opening Programs and clicking PowerPoint. The first screen displayed contains three options for creating a PowerPoint presentation. The AutoContent Wizard provides a fixed set of templates and formats and guides you through the process by asking questions about the type of presentation you plan to make. The Design Template option provides a large selection of slide backgrounds on which you can type your text. These can be viewed on the right of your screen by clicking the button next to the template name. The Blank Presentation option allows you to build your presentation from scratch. Most of the presentation options in the AutoContent Wizard do not match the typical public speaking class assignments, so you should build your presentation using either the Design Template or the Blank Presentation option. Our instructions will take you through working with the Blank Presentation option but are applicable to the Design Template option as well.

FIGURE 9.12
Good Versus Poor PowerPoint Slides

This . . .

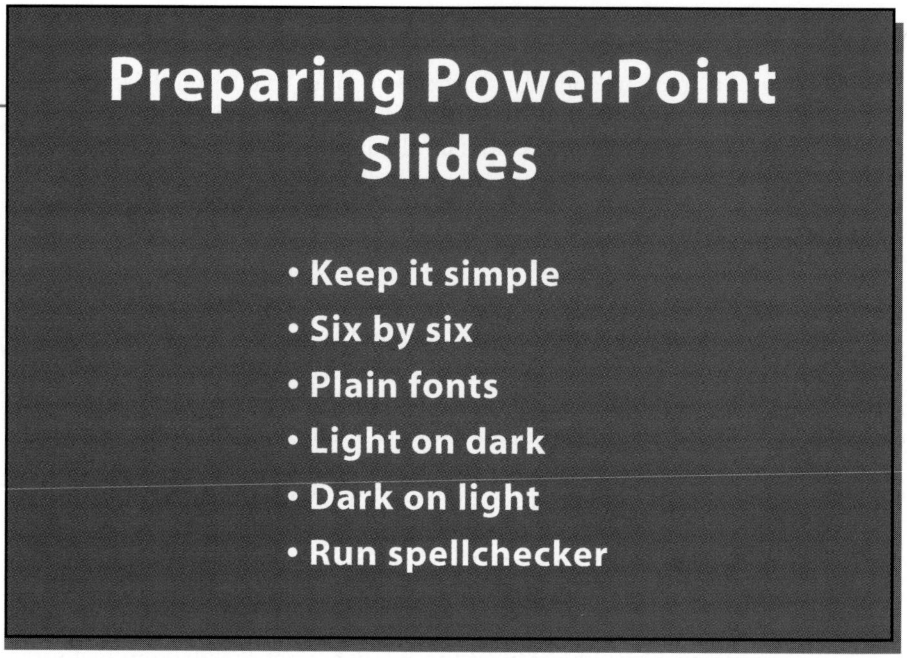

Preparing PowerPoint Slides

- Keep it simple
- Six by six
- Plain fonts
- Light on dark
- Dark on light
- Run spellchecker

NOT This . . .

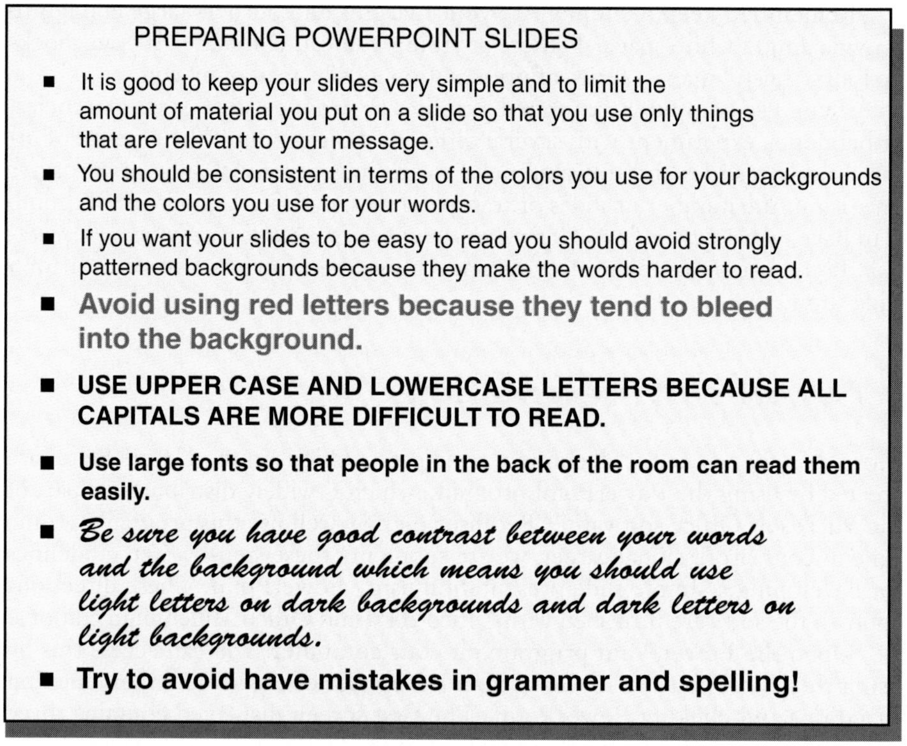

PREPARING POWERPOINT SLIDES

- It is good to keep your slides very simple and to limit the amount of material you put on a slide so that you use only things that are relevant to your message.
- You should be consistent in terms of the colors you use for your backgrounds and the colors you use for your words.
- If you want your slides to be easy to read you should avoid strongly patterned backgrounds because they make the words harder to read.
- Avoid using red letters because they tend to bleed into the background.
- USE UPPER CASE AND LOWERCASE LETTERS BECAUSE ALL CAPITALS ARE MORE DIFFICULT TO READ.
- Use large fonts so that people in the back of the room can read them easily.
- *Be sure you have good contrast between your words and the background which means you should use light letters on dark backgrounds and dark letters on light backgrounds.*
- **Try to avoid have mistakes in grammer and spelling!**

No matter which option you choose, the Office Assistant will appear as an icon (usually an animated paper clip) on your screen. If you get confused or can't remember how to do something, simply click on the icon and a box will appear. Type a question in the space provided, click the "Search" command, and the Office Assistant will provide an answer.

Should you choose the Blank Presentation option, the next screen will provide slide layout options. On this screen you can choose from a title page; a bulleted list; title only; and a variety of chart, graph, and clip art options. Select the bulleted list by clicking on the icon. Now the working box on your screen will show a slide with the appropriate layout. To add background color to your slide, pull down the format menu from the top of your screen, and click on Background. The color selections will appear in the "background fill" box as a pull-down at the bottom. Open this, and several color options will be shown, plus a command for "More Colors," which will display the entire color spectrum available. Choose a strong background color; then click "Apply to All" and each slide you prepare for this presentation will have the same background.

Now you can begin adding text to slide number 1. Add the title of your slide to the title box and the text in the text box. To set the color of the title text, drag and highlight the title; then click the down arrow next to the underlined letter on the lower toolbar on your screen. Click "More Font Colors." Select a font color that contrasts with your background color. Click "OK." Repeat this process with the text material on your slide.

To make additional slides for your presentation, go to the "Common Tasks" command on the top toolbar on your screen. Open this and click "New Slide." The "Layout Options" box will open, and you can then choose the layout you want for this slide. If you prepare a slide and decide you want a different layout, open "Common Tasks" and click on "Slide Layout," then select the option you want. When you have completed all of your slides, save them in a folder on your desktop and make a backup copy on a floppy disk. Once you have prepared the slides, you can open them from your desktop and edit them by changing colors or text.

You can preview your presentation by using the slide sorter view from the View Menu on the toolbar. This shows you all the slides in your presentation. Use the slide sorter to rearrange the order of your slides and to add transitions among them. To change the order of your slides, click on the slide; then drag it to where you want it positioned. Your next step is to open the Slide Show menu on your toolbar. This allows you to view your presentation on your computer monitor. For a speech before an audience, select "Manual Timing" so that you can control the appearance of slides by left-clicking your mouse. You can make the screen go black between slides by hitting the "b" on your keyboard.

If you need help while preparing and previewing your PowerPoint presentation, click on the Office Assistant. PowerPoint 2000 comes with a tutorial on the Office 2000 CD-ROM. For more information and instructions for more advanced presentations with clip art, transitions, and animation, consult one of the online resources listed in InterConnections.LearnMore 9.1, "PowerPoint Presentations."

Using Presentation Aids

As we discussed each of the specific kinds of presentation aids, we offered suggestions on how to use it in presentation. Here we review these suggestions and extract some basic guidelines.

1. Practice using your presentation aid. Integrate it smoothly into your speech by using transitions.
2. Go to the room where you will be speaking to decide where you will place your aid both before and during your speech.
3. Check out any electronic equipment you will use (slide projector, overhead projector, VCR, etc.) in advance of your presentation. Be certain that you can operate it and that it is working properly.
4. Do not display your presentation aid until you are ready to use it. When you have finished with the aid, cover or remove it so that it does not distract your audience.

InterConnections.LearnMore 9.1

POWERPOINT PRESENTATIONS

PowerPointers http://www.powerpointers.com/
A lot of good tips and pointers on using PowerPoint and other presentation software.

PowerPoint Answers
http://www.powerpointanswers.com
A weekly online newsletter with articles, solutions to problems, and resources for PowerPoint users.

PowerPoint in the Classroom
http://www.actden.com/pp/
A simple online tutorial that walks you through the basics of preparing a PowerPoint presentation, incorporating all the bells and whistles.

PowerPoint 97 Tutorial
http://www.wku.edu/~downijr/classes/161/PowerPointManual.htm
An online tutorial for PowerPoint 97; developed and maintained by Professor Joe Downing, Western Kentucky University.

Using PowerPoint
http://www.microsoft.com/office/powerpoint/using/default.htm
Microsoft web site; contains links to tips, tricks, how-to articles, and other online course tutorials.

5. Do not stand directly in front of your presentation aid. Stand to the side of it and maintain eye contact with listeners. You want them to see both you and your presentation aid.
6. When you refer to something on the presentation aid, point to what you are talking about. Don't leave your audience searching for what you are describing.
7. Do not distribute materials during your speech. If you have prepared handouts, distribute them before or after you speak.
8. Do not use too many presentation aids in one speech. Remember, they should enhance your verbal message, not replace it.

In Summary

Presentation aids are tools to enhance the effectiveness of speeches. They can increase comprehension, authenticate a point, add variety, increase your credibility, and help your speech have lasting impact.

Kinds of Presentation Aids. Every speech has at least one presentation aid: the speaker. Your appearance, clothing, and body language must all be in concert with your message and appropriate to the audience and situation. Another form of presentation aid is an object. Unless it is large enough to be seen, small enough to be portable, and strictly under your control, you may have to use a model or a sketch instead.

Visual representations of information, or *graphics*, provide a number of options for presentation aids. Maps can be useful in speeches based on spatial designs. Draw them specifically for your speech so that they contain only the material you wish to emphasize. Graphs can help make complex numerical data more understandable to an audience. *Pie graphs* illustrate the relationships between parts and a whole. *Bar graphs* highlight comparisons and contrasts. *Line graphs* show changes over time. *Mountain graphs* are variations of line graphs that use different colors to fill in the areas.

Charts are visual representations that give form to abstract relationships. *Flow charts* may be used to outline the steps in a process or to show power and authority relationships within an organization. *Sequence charts* that are presented in succession can be especially effective in speeches to emphasize and illustrate various stages in a process. *Textual graphics* are lists of phrases, words, or numbers. They are often presented as *bulleted lists*, *acronyms*, or *columnar data*.

Photographs and pictures can add authenticity to a speech. Photographs provide slice-of-life realism but can also include irrelevant detail. Any photograph used in a speech should be enlarged so that everyone in the audience can see it.

Presentation Media. Speakers may use flip charts, posters, handouts, chalk or marker boards, transparencies, slides, videotapes, audiotapes, and computerized programs to develop presentation aids. Flip charts may be used as spontaneous presentation aids. Handouts can be effective for explaining complex or unfamiliar material but should be distributed either before or after a speech. Chalk and marker boards should be used sparingly to emphasize points or to clarify questions that can arise during the presentation of a speech.

Transparencies and slides help audiences see graphics or pictures more clearly. Transparencies are popular because they are easy to make, inexpensive, and adaptable. Videotapes and audiotapes add variety to a message. They should be used sparingly in presentations because they can easily upstage the speaker.

Most personal computers now have the capacity to generate effective, professional-looking presentation aids, such as transparencies, handouts, or slides. With specialized equipment you can make computer-assisted presentations.

Preparing Presentation Aids. As you plan your presentation aids, follow the basic principles of design and color. The presentation aid must be easy for listeners to see. It should emphasize what the speech emphasizes, excluding all extraneous material. It should seem balanced and pleasing to the eye. Consider using strong colors to add interest and impact.

Using Presentation Aids. Practice using the presentation aid until it seems a natural part of your presentation. Always talk to your audience, not to your presentation aid, and keep the aid out of sight when it is not in use. As you consider the use of presentation aids, be sensitive to their potential ethical impact. Be certain that your presentation aid represents its subject without distortion.

Terms to Know

presentation aids
graphics
pie graph
bar graph
pictographs
line graph
mountain graph
flow chart
sequence charts
textual graphics
bulleted lists
acronym
computer-assisted presentations
analogous color scheme
complementary color scheme

Notes

1. Tad Simons, "Multimedia or Bust," *Presentations*, February 2000, pp. 40–50. *Presentations Online.* http://www.presentations.com.
2. Keven Maney, "PowerPoint Obsession Takes Off," *USA Today*, 12 May 1999. *Technology Archives.* http://www.usatoday.com.
3. Cited in Laurence J. Peter, *Peter's Quotations: Ideas for Our Time* (New York: Bantam, 1979), p. 478.
4. Our thanks for this example go to Professor Mary Katherine McHenry, Northwest Mississippi Community College, Senatobia, Mississippi.
5. Rebecca Ganzel, "Power Pointless," *Presentations*, February 2000, pp. 53–58.
6. Kenneth Brower, "Photography in the Age of Falsification," *Atlantic Monthly*, May 1998, pp. 92–111.
7. Lee Berton, "Deloitte Wants More Women for Top Posts in Accounting," *Wall Street Journal*, 28 Feb. 1993, p. B1.
8. Cornelia Brunner, "Teaching Visual Literacy," *Electronic Learning* (November–December 1994): 16 (2). CompuServe. *Magazine Database Plus* (November 1995).
9. Arthur Goldsmith, "Digitally Altered Photography: The New Image Makers," *Britannica Book of the Year: 1995* (Chicago: Encyclopaedia Britannica: 1995), p. 135.
10. Gloria Borger, "The Story the Pictures Didn't Tell," *U.S. News & World Report*, 22 Feb. 1993, pp. 6–7; and John Leo, "Lapse or TV News Preview?" *The Washington Times*, 3 Mar. 1993, p. G3.
11. Richard Kern, "Making Visual Aids Work for You," *Sales and Marketing Management* (February 1989): 45 (4).
12. Ricky Telg and Tracy Irani, "Getting the Most out of PowerPoint," *Agricultural Education Magazine*, April 2001, p. 11.

10

Using Language Effectively

OUTLINE

THIS CHAPTER WILL HELP YOU

- understand the power of language
- apply standards to use language effectively
- learn ways to magnify the power of words

audience. Her words illustrate the conversational character of effective speeches we discussed in Chapter 1. Moreover, as we discuss in detail in Chapter 11, oral language uses pauses, vocal emphasis, and pitch variations to clarify and reinforce meaning. Such resources are not available in written communication.

In oral communication, time is also important. Jerry Tarver, professor of speech communication at the University of Richmond, emphasizes three significant time differences between spoken and written language.[3] First, he offers "Tarver's Law of Conciseness: *It takes more words per square idea to say something than to write it.*" Because listeners cannot reread words that are spoken, oral language must be simple and speakers often must repeat themselves to be understood. Speakers may need to amplify ideas with examples to ensure that listeners get the point.

Tarver's second time difference concerns *the order in which spoken thoughts develop in a sentence*. His example is excellent:

> **I recently read in a newspaper column a spirited defense of a public figure. The last line of the column was, "For that he should be congratulated, not chastised." Well and good. The reader gobbles up the line in an instant and digests the contrast between congratulations and chastisement. But when we speak the line we feed it to a listener morsel by morsel. And the last two words prove to be rather bland. We need to *hear* "For that he should not be chastised, he should be congratulated." More words; but more important, a different order. . . . In the slower pace of speech, individual words stand out more, and thus *time* accords a special emphasis to the last idea, the climactic idea in the sentence.**
>
> **As a rule, then, the stronger, more impressive idea should be saved for the end. And it will often be the case that the punch comes from a positive rather than a negative thought.[4]**

Tarver's advice to *build up* to your most important point within a sentence repeats a structural principle discussed in Chapter 7—that the main points of a speech often work best when arranged in an order of ascending importance.

Tarver's third effect of time is that "*the rhythm of the syllables is even more important in words written to be heard than in words written to be seen.*" Spoken language can play on the senses like a drum. The beat of the words can embed them in memory and charge them with emotion. At a low point during World War II, when a German invasion of Great Britain seemed imminent, Prime Minister Winston Churchill spoke on radio to the British people in language that seemed to march in military formation. Read the following words aloud to savor their full oral power:

> **We shall not flag nor fail. We shall go on to the end. We shall fight in France and on the seas and oceans; we shall fight with growing confidence and growing strength in the air. We shall defend our island whatever the cost may be; we shall fight on beaches, landing grounds, in fields, in streets and on the hills. We shall never surrender. . . .[5]**

When used in such skillful ways, the spoken word can touch listeners in ways that the written word cannot. There are four ways that effective oral language can influence your audience:

1. It can influence how listeners see subjects.
2. It can influence how listeners feel about those subjects.
3. It can influence how listeners identify with one another.
4. It can influence how listeners act.[6]

Speaker's Notes 10.1

CHARACTERISTICS OF ORAL LANGUAGE

1. Oral language is personal.
2. Oral language is informal.
3. Oral language is colorful.
4. Oral language uses short, simple sentences.
5. Oral language repeats and amplifies ideas.
6. Oral language relies on examples and stories.
7. Oral language emphasizes rhythm.

Understanding these powers of oral language—and how they can be abused as well as used—is essential for both speaker and listener.

The Power to Make Listeners See

Speakers and listeners often see subjects in different ways. The artful use of language, however, can close the gap that separates them. Consider, for example, the problem that confronted one of our students, Scott Champlin. Scott wanted to share an experience he had had in the military so that others would understand what it meant to him. One option was to describe the experience matter-of-factly:

> **While I was parachuting into Panama as part of Operation "Just Cause," I was wounded by a tracer bullet.**

The more he considered that option, the less adequate it seemed. How could he use words to convey the *true sense* of that experience? The depiction he developed allowed listeners to share his leap into danger:

> **The darkness of two o'clock in the morning was penetrated by streaks of red light marking the paths of tracer rounds as they cut their way through the night. Suddenly, I felt something hit me in the right leg with a force that spun me around like a twisted yo-yo at the end of a string.**

ESL: ESL students may have difficulty understanding colloquial language or tuning in to the differences in meaning that changes in rhythm and stress can convey. Ask your non-ESL students to be sensitive to this problem and to watch for feedback from the ESL students showing that they understand.

Here the use of contrast—between "darkness" and "streaks of red light"—paints a vivid word picture. Action verbs such as *penetrated*, *cut*, *knock*, and *spun* enliven the picture. The simile—"like a twisted yo-yo at the end of a string"—brings the picture into sharp focus. Through his artful word choice, Scott was able to share the meaning of his experience.

The power to influence how listeners see things is particularly important when a topic is unfamiliar or unusual. In such cases, your words can become windows that reveal the subject with startling clarity. There can, however, be a negative side to this power of depiction. When listeners don't have a picture of their own to compare with the one revealed by the speaker's words, they are susceptible to deception. Over four hundred years ago, the Renaissance scholar Francis Bacon suggested that the glass in the windows of depiction can be "enchanted." The perspective may be distorted. Words can color or alter things, thus disguising or obscuring reality. The power to make listeners see can also be a power that blinds them.

The Power to Awaken Feelings

Play taped excerpts from the closing arguments of a court case or the final court scene from the film *Inherit the Wind.* Use these to stimulate discussion on how language can arouse feelings.

Language also can influence how listeners feel about things. It can touch their hearts and change their attitudes. This power is ethical when it *supplements* sound reasoning and credible evidence. It is abused if speakers *substitute* appeals to feelings for evidence or reasoning. To arouse emotions, language must overcome the barriers of time, distance, and apathy.

Overcoming Time. Listeners live in the present. This makes it difficult for speakers to awaken feelings about events that lie in the remote past or the distant future. To overcome this obstacle, speakers can use language to make the past and future come alive. Stories that recapture feelings from the past are often told at company meetings to recreate the human dimension of the business and to reestablish corporate heritage and culture. In the following story, the speaker reminds listeners of the legend of Federal Express, a pioneer in overnight delivery:

> **You know, we take a lot for granted. It's hard to remember that Federal Express was once just a fly-by-night dream, a crazy idea in which a few people had invested—not just their time and their money, but their lives and futures. I remember one time early on when things weren't going so well. We were really up against it. Couldn't even make the payroll that week. It looked like we were going to crash. Fred [Smith, founder of the company] was in a deep funk. Never saw him quite like that before or since. "What the hell," he said, and flew off to Las Vegas. The next day he flew back and his face was shining. "We're going to make it," he said. He had won $27,000 at the blackjack table! And we made it. We met the payroll. And then things began to turn around, and Federal Express grew into the giant it is today.[7]**

This story enlivens the past by emphasizing the contrast of emotions—the "deep funk" versus the "shining" face. The use of dialogue—"What the hell," and "We're going to make it!"—re-creates the excitement and brings those feelings into the present. It would not have been as effective had the speaker simply said,

Eloquent language can intensify our feelings about subjects.

"Fred was depressed, but after he got back from Las Vegas he was confident." Such a bare summary would have diminished the emotional power of the scene.

Language can also bring the future close to listeners. Because words can cross the barrier of time, both tradition and a vision of tomorrow can guide us through the present.

Overcoming Distance. The closer anything is to us, the easier it is to develop feelings about it. But what if speakers must discuss faraway people and places? Words can telescope such subjects and bring them close to hand. Let's see how one student used language to reduce the distance between her urban audience and her rural subject:

> **James Johnson has lived in Perry County for eighty-four years. He taught me some important things: why the mist rises on a lake at night, how to make the best wild blackberry jam you've ever put in your mouth, and how to take care of baby rabbits that are abandoned. Today, I want to tell you more about James—and about myself through him.**

By focusing on concrete details of sight, taste, and touch—the mist, the jam, the rabbits—the speaker overcame distance and aroused feelings about a subject that might have otherwise seemed remote.

Overcoming Apathy. We live in an age of communication overkill. Modern audiences are beset with an endless barrage of information, persuasion, and entertainment. Personal images, such as those used by Jesse Jackson at the 1988 Democratic National Convention, allow speakers to reach out and touch even jaded listeners:

> **America's not a blanket woven from one thread, one color, one cloth. When I was a child growing up in Greenville, South Carolina, and grandmother could not afford a blanket, she didn't complain and we did not freeze. Instead, she took pieces of old cloth—patches, wool, silk, gabardine, croakersack on the patches—barely good enough to wipe off your shoes with. But they didn't stay that way very long. With sturdy hands and a strong cord, she sewed them together into a quilt, a thing of beauty and power and culture.**
>
> **Now, Democrats, we must build such a quilt. Farmers, you seek fair prices and you are right, but you cannot stand alone. Your patch is not big enough. Workers, you fight for fair wages. You are right. But your patch, labor, is not big enough. Women, you seek comparable worth and pay equity. You are right. But your patch is not big enough. Women, mothers, who seek Head Start and day care and pre-natal care on the front side of life, rather than jail care and welfare on the back side of life, you're right, but your patch is not big enough. . . .**
>
> **But don't despair. Be as wise as my grandmama. Pool the patches and the pieces together, bound by a common thread. When we form a great quilt of unity and common ground we'll have the power to bring about health care and housing and jobs and education and hope to our nation.[8]**

Jackson's references to his grandmother's loving care aroused latent feelings. The image of a quilt—suggesting the warmth of home and the creation of beauty and value from lowly materials—gave the audience a vision of what they, too, might do. When artfully used, language can overcome the barriers of time, distance, and apathy to make us care about a subject.

The role of language in arousing feeling is also underscored by the contrast between denotative and connotative forms of meaning. The **denotative meaning** of a word is its dictionary definition or generally agreed-on objective usage. For example, the denotative definition of *alcohol* is "a colorless, volatile, flammable liquid, obtained by the fermentation of sugars or starches, which is widely used as a solvent, drug base, explosive, or intoxicating beverage."[9] How different this is from the two connotative definitions offered in this chapter's opening

InterConnections.LearnMore 10.1

LANGUAGE ONLINE

Language: What We Speak
http://www.thymos.com/tat/language.html
An interesting essay exploring the relationship between language and thought; written by Piero Scaruffi, University of California lecturer and author in the area of artificial intelligence.

Verbivore **http://verbivore.com**
Explores the uses and misuses of words in public communication; written and maintained by Richard Lederer, author of *Anguished English*.

The Vocabula Review **http://www.vocabula.com/vocabulareview.htm**
A free monthly online journal devoted to promoting clear, expressive language.

Invite students to translate the opening vignette of this chapter into denotative language. Invite authors of the most interesting translations to read them aloud to the class.

example! **Connotative meaning** invests a subject with emotion. Thus, the "intoxicating beverage" is no longer just a chemical substance but either "the poison scourge" or "the oil of conversation." Connotative language intensifies feelings, whereas denotative language encourages detachment.

The Power to Bring Listeners Together

In many situations, individual action is not enough. It may take people working together to get things done. In addition to arousing strong feelings, Jesse Jackson also reminded listeners that they were part of an important larger group. Only if they acted together—as Democrats rather than as individual interest groups—would they have a chance to win the election.

Ask students to identify heroes, heroines, and enemies common to the cultures represented in the class. Discuss how references to these figures in speeches might unite or divide the audience.

Although words can unite people, they can also drive them apart. Name calling, exclusionary language, and unsupported accusations are invidious dividers. It may take their more positive counterparts to bring people back together. During a 1996 Republican Party primary debate, the contenders attacked and berated each other. Finally, one candidate, Representative Robert Dornan of California, reminded the others that their attacks on each other threatened party unity:

> **I wish the spirit of Ronald Reagan would descend on New Hampshire . . . and [remind us of] his eleventh commandment, that no Republican should speak ill of another. . . . We have to stop tearing at one another. . . . The target is Clinton . . . [and] the moral crisis in the White House. . . . Gentlemen, we're a family here. Let's unify ourselves and make sure we take the White House on November 5th.[10]**

Note that as Dornan pled for unity, he invoked a group hero, Ronald Reagan. He also used the "family" metaphor to counter the division and reminded listeners of a common enemy and shared goal: their desire to defeat President Clinton.

Heroes and enemies, common goals, shared values, and metaphors of inclusion—all can work together to heighten the value of group membership. We discuss these techniques more closely later in this chapter.

The Power to Encourage Action

Even if your listeners share an identity, they still may not be ready to act. What might stand in their way? For one thing, they may not be convinced of the soundness of your proposal. They may not trust you, or they may not think they can do anything about a problem. Finally, they may not be ready to invest the energy or take the risk that action demands.

Your language must convince listeners that action is necessary, that your ideas are sound, and that success is possible. In her speech urging students to act to improve off-campus housing conditions (see Appendix C), Anna Aley painted vivid word-pictures of deplorable off-campus housing. She supported these with both factual examples and her personal experiences. She also reminded listeners that if they acted together, they could bring about change:

Play the video of Anna Aley's speech to demonstrate how language can incite action.

> **What can one student do to change the practices of numerous Manhattan landlords? Nothing, if that student is alone. But just think of what we could accomplish if we got all 13,600 off-campus students involved in this issue! Think what we could accomplish if we got even a fraction of those students involved!**

Anna then proposed specific actions that did not call for great effort or risk. In short, she made commitment as easy as possible. She concluded with an appeal to action:

> **Kansas State students have been putting up with substandard living conditions for too long. It's time we finally got together to do something about this problem. Join the Off-Campus Association. Sign my petition. Let's send a message to these slumlords that we're not going to put up with this anymore. We don't have to live in slums.**

Anna's words expressed both her indignation and the urgency of the problem. Her references to time—"too long" and "it's time"—called for immediate action. Her final appeals to join the association and sign the petition were expressed in short sentences that packed a lot of punch. Her repetition of "slumlords" and "slums" motivated her listeners to transform their indignation into action.

Anna also illustrated another language strategy that is important when you want to move people to action—the ability to depict dramas showing what is at stake and what roles listeners should take.[11] Such scenarios draw clear lines between right and wrong. Be careful, however, not to go overboard with such techniques. Ethical communication requires that you maintain respect for all involved in conflict. As both speaker and listener, be wary of melodramas that offer stark contrasts between good and evil. Such depictions often distort reality.

The Six *C*'s of Language Use

To harness the power of language in your speeches, your words must meet certain standards: clarity, color, concreteness, correctness, conciseness, and cultural sensitivity. We call these the six *C*'s of oral language.

Clarity

Clarity is the first standard, because if your words are not clear, listeners cannot understand your meaning. This may seem obvious, but it is often ignored! To

Ethics Alert! 10.1

THE ETHICAL USE OF POWERFUL LANGUAGE

1. Do not offer listeners distorted depictions of reality.
2. Use emotional words to strengthen reasoning and evidence, not substitute for them.
3. Use language to empower both traditions and visions.
4. Use images to renew appreciation of shared values.
5. Use language to strengthen the ties of community, not divide people.
6. Use language to overcome inertia and inspire listeners to action.
7. Be cautious about melodramatic language that reduces complex issues to good and evil.

Have students discuss the relationship between clarity and simple, direct language. Impress upon them the importance of "eschewing obfuscation!"

be clear, you must yourself understand what you want to say. Next, you must find words that convey your ideas as precisely and as simply as possible. Your voice, face, and gestures should help to reinforce the idea as you present it, a process we shall discuss in the next chapter. Your listeners must be capable of interpreting your words and nonverbal cues. The standard of clarity is met when something closely approximating the idea is reproduced in the minds of these listeners.

One factor that impairs clarity is the use of **jargon**, the technical language that is specific to a profession. Such language is often referred to with an *-ese* at the end, as in "speaking computerese." If you use jargon before an audience that doesn't share that technical vocabulary, you will not be understood. For example, "We expect a positive vorticity advective" may be perfectly understandable to a group of meteorologists, but for most audiences, simply saying "It's going to rain" would be much clearer. Speakers who fall into the jargon trap are so used to using technical language that they forget that others may not grasp it. It does not occur to them that they must translate the jargon into lay language to be understood by general audiences. Adapting technical language so that nonspecialists can understand it can be challenging, but an example in Chapter 6 (page 161), explaining how the OnStar system works in cars, shows how this can be done effectively.

A problem similar to that of jargon is using words that are needlessly overblown. A notorious example occurred when signmakers wanted to tell tourists how to leave the Barnum museum. Rather than drawing an arrow with the word *Exit* above it, they wrote "To the Egress." There's no telling how many visitors left the museum by mistake, thinking that they were going to see that rare creature—a living, breathing "Egress."

Although such misunderstandings may result from innocent incompetence, at other times jargon seems to be purposely befuddling. Some speakers like to satisfy their egos and intimidate others by displaying their technical vocabularies. The parent of a student in Houston received a message from the high school principal regarding a special meeting on a proposed educational program. The message read:

> **Our school's cross-graded, multiethnic, individualized learning program is designed to enhance the concept of an open-ended learning program with emphasis on a continuum of multiethnic, academically enriched learning, using the identified intellectually gifted child as the agent or director of his own learning. Major emphasis is on cross-graded, multiethnic learning with the main objective being to learn respect for the uniqueness of a person.**

FIGURE 10.1
Doublespeak

What They Say	What They Mean
1. Marital discord	*1.* Spouse beating
2. Department of human biodynamics	*2.* Department of physical education
3. Downsizing	*3.* Firing
4. Making a salary adjustment	*4.* Cutting your pay
5. Failed to fulfill wellness potential	*5.* Died
6. Chronologically experienced citizen	*6.* Old codger
7. Initial and pass on	*7.* Let's spread the blame
8. Friendly fire	*8.* We killed our own people
9. Collateral damage	*9.* We killed innocent people

The parent responded:

> **Dear Principal: I have a college degree, speak two foreign languages and know four Indian dialects. I've attended a number of county fairs and three goat ropings, but I haven't the faintest idea as to what you are talking about. Do you?[12]**

Although some people seem to take a strange joy in *not* communicating, others may try to hide the truth behind a smokescreen of technobabble and doublespeak. The former is mindless chatter that hides the lack of actual content, whereas the latter disguises some awkward reality. Public television commentator Bill Moyers warned his audience at the University of Texas against such dangers:

> **If you would . . . serve democracy well, you must first save the language. Save it from the jargon of insiders who talk of the current budget debate in Washington as "megapolicy choices between freeze-feasible base lines." (Sounds more like a baseball game played in the Arctic Circle.) Save it from the smokescreen artists, who speak of "revenue enhancement" and "tax-base erosion control" when they really mean a tax increase. . . . Save it from . . . the official revisionists of reality, who say that the United States did not withdraw our troops from Lebanon, we merely "backloaded our augmentation personnel."[13]**

Fearing the reactions of listeners who actually understand their meaning, such speakers hide behind cloudy technical language.

One way to achieve clarity in oral language is through **amplification**, in which you rephrase ideas to bring them into focus. In effect, you tell listeners something; then you expand and repeat what you are saying. Providing important bits of information or examples that compare and contrast the unfamiliar with the familiar are specific ways to amplify an idea. Note how amplification works in the following speech excerpt, in which each sentence expands and repeats the meaning of the sentence that comes before it:

> **The roadrunner is not just a cartoon character that makes a fool of Wile E. Coyote. It is a member of the cuckoo family and state bird of New Mexico. Still, the cartoon roadrunner and the real roadrunner have much in common. Both are incredibly fast, real roadrunners having been tracked at ground speeds up to 17 miles per hour. Neither takes to the air to chase prey or escape a predator. Both look rather awkward as they run, with strides up to 20 inches long—a real feat for a bird that is only 24 inches long with over half its length in its tail.**

11

Presenting Your Speech

OUTLINE

THIS CHAPTER WILL HELP YOU

- make more effective presentations
- respond to audience feedback
- participate in a question-and-answer session
- improve your voice as an instrument of communication
- understand the dynamics of body language
- prepare for video presentations

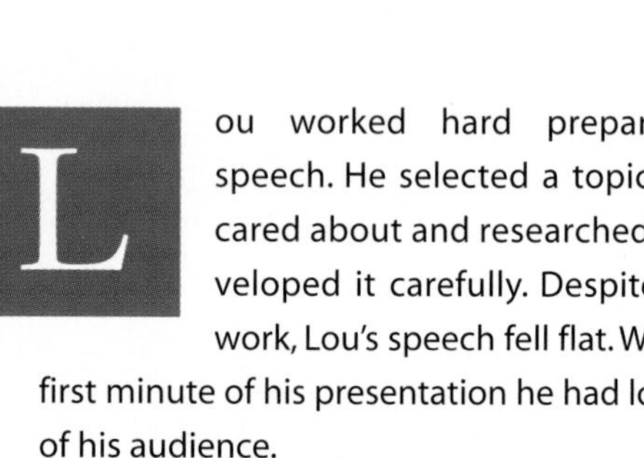

Lou worked hard preparing his speech. He selected a topic that he cared about and researched and developed it carefully. Despite all this work, Lou's speech fell flat. Within the first minute of his presentation he had lost much of his audience.

The trouble began when Lou opened his mouth. His voice did not project energy or enthusiasm. He never varied his pitch or loudness. He looked down at his notes or up at the ceiling, seldom making eye contact with listeners. His soft voice almost lulled the audience to sleep. Lou's presentation suggested that he was not really interested in his topic or in trying to communicate. Little wonder that listeners found their daydreams more interesting and that a potentially worthy speech never had a chance that day.

In this chapter we focus on the **presentation** of a speech. We consider the major ways to present speeches and the factors that make presentations effective or ineffective. We offer advice on responding to audience feedback, handling questions and answers, developing an effective speaking voice, using your body to communicate, and practicing effectively. At the end of the chapter, we indicate how to adapt many of these skills for video presentations.

Developing your ability to present speeches should help you in other settings, such as job interviews, meetings, and even social occasions. Learning how to present yourself as well as your ideas tends to stay with you over the years, providing what Francis Bacon once called "continual letters of recommendation."

There is no gesture that does not speak.

—Montaigne

What Makes a Presentation Effective?

The word *communication* stems from the Latin word *communis*, meaning "common." An effective presentation allows a speaker and audience to hold ideas and feelings in common, even when they come from different cultural backgrounds. Such a presentation makes use of a verbal and nonverbal system of symbols that should work together to create meaning.

At the end of Chapter 12, we reprint the text of a speech first presented at Vanderbilt University by Marie D'Aniello. In her speech Marie traced how friendship evolves from childhood to young adulthood. As she presented this speech, her manner was warm and open, and her face was responsive to audience reactions. *In short, Marie herself seemed the perfect model of a friend!* Her presentation illustrated the harmonious interplay of verbal and nonverbal symbols.

On the other hand, we also remember a student who described her childhood in these terms: "I was always getting into trouble." But as she said these words, she seemed listless; she slouched at the podium, chewed gum, and avoided eye contact. Her passive manner did not reinforce her self-portrait as a boisterous child. Instead, *there was an incongruity between what she said and what she showed*. Whenever verbal and nonverbal symbols seem out of sync, listeners give more credit to the nonverbal message. Yet scholars often give priority to verbal language. Clearly, as these positive and negative examples indicate, verbal language alone cannot invoke the immediacy, the rich totality of human communication.[1]

An effective presentation begins with your attitude. You must be committed to your topic and want to share this commitment. The way you speak should energize your ideas. In brief, *you should want to communicate*. This may seem obvious, but we remember another student in whom this desire to communicate seemed oddly missing. She had done well in high school speaking contests, she told listeners in her first speech, and thought of herself as a good speaker. And in a technical sense, she was right. Her voice was pleasant and expressive, her

An effective presentation makes your ideas come alive while you are speaking.

manner direct and competent. But there was a false note, an overtone of artificiality. In consequence, her listeners gave her a rather chilly reception. It was clear that for her, speaking was an exhibition. *She* was more important than her ideas. Listeners sensed that she had her priorities wrong.

Beyond the right attitude, any good presentation requires certain adjustments. Your presentation must be loud enough to be heard easily in the back of the room where you are speaking. It should not call attention to itself or distract from your message. Consequently, you should avoid pompous pronunciations, artificial vocal patterns, and overly dramatic gestures. Instead, an effective presentation sounds natural and conversational—as though you were talking *with* listeners, not *at* them. This helps reduce the psychological distance between you and your audience.

Immediacy is the term used to describe the closeness between speaker and listeners in successful communication.[2] Communication scholar James McCroskey has written:

> **Immediacy increases the audience's attentiveness; it reduces tension and anxiety for both speaker and audience; it creates greater liking between speaker and audience; and it increases the probability that the speaker's purpose will be accomplished.[3]**

Immediacy relates to the likeableness dimension of ethos, which we discussed in Chapter 2. It encourages listeners to open their minds to you and to be influenced by what you say.[4] How, then, can you encourage immediacy? You can start by reducing actual distance between yourself and listeners. Step out from behind the lectern and move closer to them. Smile at them when appropriate, maintain eye contact, use gestures to clarify and reinforce ideas, and let your voice express your feelings. Even if your heart is pumping, your hands are a little sweaty, and your knees feel a bit wobbly, the self you show to listeners should be a person in control of the situation. Listeners admire and identify with speakers who maintain what Ernest Hemingway once called "grace under pressure."

Your goal should be a speech characterized by an **expanded conversational style**, which we discussed in detail in Chapter 1. An expanded conversational style is direct, spontaneous, colorful, and tuned to the responses of listeners. Such a style, however, is a bit more careful and formal than everyday conversation.

To summarize, *an effective presentation makes your ideas come alive while you are speaking*. It blends nonverbal with verbal symbols so that reason and emotion, heart and head work together to advance your message. The remainder of this chapter will help you move closer to this goal of effective presentation.

Methods of Presentation

In this section we consider the four major methods of speech presentation: impromptu speaking, memorized text presentation, reading from a manuscript, and extemporaneous speaking. We also include suggestions for responding to audience feedback and handling questions and answers.

Impromptu Speaking

Materials for impromptu presentation exercises may be found in Chapter 11 of the IRM.

Impromptu speaking is sometimes called "speaking off the cuff," a phrase that suggests you could put all your notes on the cuff of your shirt. Impromptu

Answering questions gives you a chance to extend and increase the influence of your speech.

Paraphrasing also enables you to steer the question to the type of answer you are prepared to give.

Third, *maintain eye contact with the audience as you answer*. Note that we say "with the audience," not just "with the questioner." Look first at the questioner, then make eye contact with other audience members, returning your gaze to the questioner as you finish your answer. The purpose of a question-and-answer period should be to extend the understanding of the entire audience, not to carry on a private conversation with one person.

Fourth, *defuse hostile questions*. Reword emotional questions in more objective language. For example, if you are asked, "Why do you want to throw our money away on people who are too lazy to work?" you might respond with something like, "I understand your frustration and think what you really want to know is 'Why aren't our current programs helping people break out of the chains of unemployment?'"

Fifth, *don't be afraid to say, "I don't know."* Simply conceding a point or saying "I don't know" can also help defuse a hostile questioner. Roger Ailes, a political media adviser for three U.S. presidents, described how former New York City mayor Ed Koch once used this technique. Koch had spent $300,000 putting bike lanes in Manhattan. Cars were driving in the bike lanes. Cyclists were running over pedestrians. The money seemed wasted. Soon thereafter, when Koch was running for reelection, he appeared on a *Meet the Press*-type of show. This is how the questioning went:

> **One reporter led off with "Mayor Koch, in light of the financial difficulties in New York City, how could you possibly justify wasting three hundred thousand dollars on bike lanes? . . ." Koch smiled and he said, "You're right. It was a terrible idea." He went on. "I thought it would work. It didn't. It was one of the worst mistakes I ever made." And he stopped. Now nobody knew what to do. They had another twenty-six minutes of the program left. They all had prepared questions about the bike lanes, and so the next person feebly asked, "But, Mayor Koch, how could you do this?" And Mayor Koch said, "I already told you, it was stupid. I did a dumb thing. It didn't work." And he stopped again. Now there were twenty-five minutes left and nothing to ask him. It was brilliant.[8]**

Sixth, *keep your answers short and direct.* Don't give another speech.

Seventh, *handle non-questions politely.* If someone starts to give a speech rather than ask a question, wait until he or she pauses for breath and then cut in with something like, "Thank you for your comment" or "I appreciate your remarks. Your question, then, is . . ." or "That's an interesting perspective. Can we have another question?" Don't get caught up in a shouting match. Stay in command of the situation.

Finally, *bring the question-and-answer session to a close.* Call for a final question and, as you complete the answer, summarize your message again to refocus listeners on your central points.

Using Your Voice Effectively

Your voice plays a major role in your communication effectiveness. Consider the following simple sentences:

> I don't believe it.
>
> You did that.
>
> Give me a break.

How many different meanings can you create as you speak these words, just by changing the rhythm, pace, emphasis, pitch, or inflection of your voice?

Your ethos as well as your message can be affected by the quality of your voice. A good speaking voice enhances your image in the ears of listeners. But if you sound tentative, people may think you are not very competent. If you mumble, they may think you are trying to hide something. If you are overly loud or strident, they may find you not very likeable.

> ✱✱ Record a variety of speakers from newscasts and C-SPAN and present them to the class. Discuss how the different voices affect ethos.

How you talk is also part of your identity. Someone who talks in a soft, breathy voice may be thought of as "weak"; another, who speaks in a more forceful manner, may be considered "authoritative." For some speakers, a dialect is part of their ethnicity, a valued part of their personality.[9]

Speaker's Notes 11.1

HANDLING QUESTIONS AND ANSWERS

1. Practice answering tough questions on your topic before an audience of friends.
2. Repeat or paraphrase the question you are asked.
3. Maintain eye contact with the audience as you answer. Don't look at just the person who asks the question.
4. Defuse hostile questions by rewording them in unemotional language.
5. Don't be afraid to say, "I don't know."
6. Keep answers short and to the point.
7. Handle non-questions politely.
8. Bring the question-and-answer session to a close by reemphasizing your message.

Although you may not wish to make radical changes in your speaking voice, minor improvements can produce big dividends. As one voice specialist put it, "Though speech is a human endowment, how well we speak is an individual achievement."[10] With a little effort and practice, most of us can make positive changes. We caution, however, that simple vocal exercises will not fix serious impairments. If you have such a problem, contact the nearest speech pathology clinic for professional help.

The first step in learning to use your voice more effectively is to evaluate how you usually talk. Tape-record yourself while speaking and reading aloud. When you hear yourself, you may say, "Is that really me?" Most tape recorders will slightly distort the way you sound because they do not exactly replicate the spectrum of sounds made by the human voice. Nevertheless, a tape recording gives you an idea of how you may sound to others. As you listen, ask yourself:

- Does my voice convey the meaning I intend?
- Would I want to listen to me if I were in the audience?
- Does my voice present me at my best?

If your answers are negative, you may need to work on pitch, rate, loudness, variety, articulation, enunciation, pronunciation, or dialect. Save your original tape so that you can hear yourself improve as you practice.

Pitch

Pitch is the placement of your voice on the musical scale. Vocal pitches can range from low and deep to high and squeaky. For effective speaking, find a pitch level that is comfortable and that allows maximum flexibility and variety. Each of us has a **habitual pitch**, the level at which we speak most frequently. Additionally, we have an **optimum pitch**, the level that allows us to produce our strongest voice with minimal effort and that permits variation up and down the scale. You can use the following exercise to help determine your optimum pitch:

> **Sing the sound *la* down to the lowest pitch you can produce without feeling strain or having your voice break or become rough. Now count each note as you sing up the scale to the highest tone you can comfortably produce. Most people have a range of approximately sixteen notes. Your optimum pitch will be about one-fourth of the way up your range. For example, if your range extends twelve notes, your optimum pitch would be at the third note up the scale. Again, sing down to your lowest comfortable pitch, and then sing up to your optimum pitch level.[11]**

Tape-record this exercise, and compare your optimum pitch to the habitual pitch revealed during your first recording. If your optimum pitch is within one or two notes of your habitual pitch, then you should not experience vocal problems related to pitch level. If your habitual pitch is much higher or lower than your optimum pitch, you may not have sufficient flexibility to raise or lower the pitch of your voice to communicate changes in meaning and emphasis. You can change your habitual pitch by practicing speaking and reading at your optimum pitch.

Read the following paragraphs from N. Scott Momaday's *The Way to Rainy Mountain* at your optimum pitch level, using pitch changes to provide meaning and feeling. To make the most of your practice, tape-record yourself so you can observe both problems and progress.

> **A single knoll rises out of the plain in Oklahoma, north and west of the Wichita Range. For my people, the Kiowas, it is an old landmark, and they gave it the name Rainy Mountain. The hardest weather in the world is there. Winter**

brings blizzards, hot tornadic winds arise in the spring, and in the summer the prairie is an anvil's edge. The grass turns brittle and brown, and it cracks beneath your feet. There are green belts along the rivers and creeks, linear groves of hickory and pecan, willow, and witch hazel. At a distance in July or August the steaming foliage seems almost to writhe in fire. . . . Loneliness is an aspect of the land. All things in the plain are isolate: there is no confusion of objects in the eye, but one hill or one tree or one man. To look upon that landscape in the early morning, with the sun at your back, is to lose the sense of proportion. Your imagination comes to life, and this, you think, is where Creation was begun.[12]

The purpose of this exercise is to explore the full range of variation around your optimum pitch and to make you conscious of the relationship between pitch and effective communication. Tape yourself reading the passage again, this time exaggerating the pitch variations as you read it. Play back both of the taped readings. If you have a problem with a narrow pitch range, you may discover that exaggerating makes you sound more effective.

When you speak before a group, don't be surprised if your pitch seems higher than usual. Your pitch is sensitive to your emotions and will usually go up when you are under pressure. If pitch is a serious problem, hum your optimum pitch softly to yourself before you begin to speak so that you start out on the right note.

Rate

ESL: Some ESL students may have learned British English. If they have this pronunciation pattern and speak rapidly, it may be difficult for American audiences to understand them. Encourage them to slow down and use the chalkboard to spell out words the audience seems not to understand.

Your **rate**, or the speed at which you speak, helps set the mood of your speech. Serious material calls for a slow, deliberate rate; lighter topics need a faster pace. These variations may involve the duration of syllables, the use of pauses, and the overall speed of presentation.

The rate patterns within a speech produce its **rhythm**. Rhythm is an essential component of all communication.[13] With rhythmic variations you point out what is important and make it easier for listeners to comprehend your message.

Beginners who feel intimidated by the speaking situation often speed up their presentations and run their words together. What this rapid-fire delivery communicates is the speaker's desire to get it over with and sit down! At the other extreme, some speakers become so deliberate that they almost put themselves and their audiences to sleep. Neither extreme lends itself to effective communication.

As we noted in Chapter 3, the typical rate for extemporaneous speaking is about 125 words per minute. You can check your speed by timing your reading of the excerpt from *Rainy Mountain*. If you were reading at the average rate, you would have taken about sixty seconds to complete that material. If you allowed time for pauses between phrases, appropriate for such formal material, your reading may have run slightly longer. If you took less than fifty seconds, you were probably speaking too rapidly or not using pauses effectively.

Student speakers often have difficulty using pauses. Advise them that a pause really isn't as long as it feels while they are speaking. Tape students reading materials from a newspaper, then play the tape back and suggest where they might have used pauses more effectively.

Pausing before or after a word or phrase highlights its importance. Pauses also give your listeners time to contemplate what you have said. They can help build suspense and maintain interest as listeners anticipate what you will say next. Moreover, pauses can clarify the relationships among ideas, phrases, and sentences. They are oral punctuation marks, taking the place of the commas and periods, underlinings and exclamation marks that occur in written communication. For all these good reasons, experienced speakers learn how to use pauses to maximum advantage. Humorist William Price Fox once wrote of Eugene Talmadge, a colorful Georgia governor and fabled stump-speaker, "That rascal knew how to wait. He had the longest pause in the state."[14] Be sure to use pause and vocal emphasis to state your main ideas forcefully.

The lyrical, melodic writing of Kiowa author N. Scott Momaday offers an opportunity to practice reading for vocal improvement. See if you can make your voice convey the meaning of the passage through variations in pitch and rate.

Read the following passage aloud again, using pauses (where indicated by the slash marks) and rate changes (a faster pace is indicated by italic type and a slower pace by capital letters) to enhance its meaning and demonstrate mood changes. This exercise will give you an idea of how pausing and changing rate can emphasize and clarify the flow of ideas:

> **A single knoll rises out of the plain in Oklahoma / north and west of the Wichita Range // For my people / the Kiowas / it is an old landmark / and they gave it the name / Rainy Mountain /// The hardest weather in the world is there // *Winter brings blizzards / hot tornadic winds arise in the spring / and in the summer the prairie is an anvil's edge // The grass turns brittle and brown / and it cracks beneath your feet* // There are green belts along the rivers and creeks / linear groves of hickory and pecan, willow, and witch hazel // At a distance / in July or August / the steaming foliage seems almost to writhe in fire /// LONELINESS IS AN ASPECT OF THE LAND // ALL THINGS IN THE PLAIN ARE ISOLATE /// THERE IS NO CONFUSION OF OBJECTS IN THE EYE // BUT ONE HILL // OR ONE TREE // OR ONE MAN /// To look upon that landscape in the early morning / with the sun at your back / is to lose the sense of proportion // Your imagination comes to life // AND THIS / YOU THINK / IS WHERE CREATION WAS BEGUN.**

Just as pausing can work for you, the wrong use of a pause can be a liability. Some speakers habitually use "ers" and "ums," "wells" and "okays," or "you knows" in the place of pauses without being aware of it. These **vocal distractions** may fill in the silence while the speaker thinks about what to say next, or they may be signs of nervousness. They may also be signals that speakers lack confidence in themselves or their messages. To determine if you have such a habit, tape-record yourself speaking extemporaneously about one of the main points for your next speech. Often simply becoming aware of such vocal distractions is enough to help you control them. Also, don't use "okay," "well," or "you know" as transitions in your speech. Plan more effective transitions (see Chapter 7). Practice your presentation until the ideas flow smoothly. Finally, don't be afraid of the brief strategic silence that comes when you pause. Make silence work for you.

If your natural tendency is to speak too slowly, you can practice developing a faster rate by reading light material aloud. Read the following poem by Charlotte Perkins Gilman in a lively, expressive manner:

There was once an Anthropoidal Ape,
Far smarter than the rest,
And everything that they could do
He always did the best;
So they naturally disliked him,
And they gave him shoulders cool,
And when they had to mention him
They said he was a fool.

Cried this pretentious Ape one day,
"I'm going to be a Man!
And stand upright, and hunt, and fight
And conquer all I can!
I'm going to cut down forest trees,
To make my houses higher!
I'm going to kill the Mastodon!
I'm going to make a fire!"

Loud screamed the Anthropoidal Apes
With laughter wild and gay;
They tried to catch that boastful one,
But he always got away.
So they yelled at him in chorus,
Which he minded not a whit;
And they pelted him with cocoanuts,
Which didn't seem to hit.
And then they gave him reasons
Which they thought of much avail,
To prove how his preposterous
Attempt was sure to fail.
Said the sages, "In the first place
The thing cannot be done!
And, second, if it could be,
It would not be any fun!
And, third, and most conclusive,
And admitting no reply,
You would have to change your nature!
We should like to see you try!"
They chuckled then triumphantly,
These lean and hairy shapes,
For these things passed as arguments
With the Anthropoidal Apes.[15]

Have students read aloud from a popular children's book that requires vocal variety for an effective presentation. Do this as a nongraded, enjoyable activity in class.

If you enjoy this exercise, try reading stories by Dr. Seuss to children. Such tales as *The Cat in the Hat* and *Green Eggs and Ham* should bring out the ham in you! Children normally provide an appreciative audience that encourages lively, colorful, dramatic uses of the voice.

Different cultures have different speech rhythms. In the United States, for example, northerners often speak more rapidly than southerners. These variations in the patterns of speech can create misunderstandings. Californians, who use longer pauses than New Yorkers, may perceive the latter as rude and aggressive. New Yorkers may see Californians as too laid back or as not having much to say.

Such problems can even go beyond simple misunderstanding. Sociologist Ron Scollon reports that Native American Alaskans show deference to authority by slowing their speech and pausing before responding to questions. Unfortunately, non-Native law enforcement officials often interpret these speech customs as signs of antagonism or hostility, and the Native Americans typically receive longer jail sentences than non-Natives.[16] Guard against stereotyping individuals on the basis of what may be culturally based speech rate variations.

Loudness

No presentation can be effective if the audience can't hear you. Nor will your presentation be successful if you overwhelm listeners with a voice that is too loud. When you speak before a group, you usually need to speak louder than you do in general conversation. The size of the room, the presence or absence of a microphone, and background noise may also call for adjustments. Take your cues from audience feedback. If you are not loud enough, you may see listeners leaning forward, straining to hear. If you speak too loudly, they may unconsciously lean back, pulling away from the noise.

You should also be aware that different cultures have different norms and expectations concerning appropriate loudness. For example, in some Mediterranean cultures, a loud voice signifies strength and sincerity, whereas in some Asian and American Indian cultures, a soft voice is associated with good manners and education.[17] When members of your audience come from a variety of cultural and ethnic groups, be especially attentive to feedback on this point.

To speak at the proper loudness, you must have good breath control. If you are breathing improperly, you will not have enough force to project your voice so that you can be heard at the back of a room. Improper breathing can also cause you to run out of breath before you finish a phrase or come to an appropriate pause. To check whether you are breathing properly for speaking, do the following:

Stand with your feet approximately eight inches apart. Place your hands on your lower rib cage, thumbs to the front, fingers to the back. Take a deep breath—in through your nose and out through slightly parted lips. If you are breathing correctly, you should feel your ribs moving up and out as you inhale.

Improper breathing affects more than just the loudness of your speech. If you breathe by raising your shoulders, the muscles in your neck and throat will become tense. This can result in a harsh, strained vocal quality. Moreover, you probably will not take in enough air to sustain your phrasing, and the release of air will be difficult to control. The air and sound will all come out with a rush when you drop your shoulders, leading to unfortunate oral punctuation marks when you don't want or need them. To see if you have a problem, try this exercise:

Take a normal breath and see how long you can count while exhaling. If you cannot reach fifteen without losing volume or feeling the need to breathe, you need to work on extending your breath control. Begin by counting in one breath to a number comfortable for you; then gradually increase the count over successive tries. Do not try to compensate by breathing too deeply. Deep breathing takes too much time and attracts too much attention while you are speaking. Use the longer pauses in your speech to breathe, and make note of your breathing pattern as you practice your speech.

You should vary the loudness of words and phrases in your speech, just as you vary your pitch and your rate of speaking. Changes in loudness are often used to express emotion. The more excited or angry we are, the louder we tend to become. But don't let yourself get caught in the trap of having only two options: loud and louder. Decreasing your volume, slowing your rate, pausing, or dropping your pitch can also express emotion quite effectively. Vanderbilt student speaker Leslie Eason illustrated this dramatically as she introduced her speech on racism. As she read the concluding lines of her poem ("What if I go to Heaven, and then at me they yell, White Angels enter here, Black Angels go to Hell"), Leslie reduced her loudness, lowered her pitch, and slowed her rate. These vocal contrasts had a dramatic impact on listeners.

To acquire more variety in loudness, practice the following exercise recommended by Hillman and Jewell: "First, count to five at a soft volume, as if you were speaking to one person. Then, count to five at medium volume, as if speaking to ten or fifteen people. Finally, count to five, as if speaking to thirty or more people."[18] If you tape-record this exercise, you should be able to hear the clear progression in loudness.

Variety

The importance of vocal variety shows up most in speeches that lack it. Speakers who drone on in a monotone, never varying their pitch, rate, or loudness, send a clear message: they tell us that they have little interest in their topic or in their listeners, or that they fear the situation they are in. Variety can make speeches come to life by adding color and interest. One of the best ways to develop variety is to read aloud materials that demand it to express meaning and feeling. As you read the following selection from *the lives and times of archy and mehitabel*, strive for maximum variation of pitch, rate, and loudness. Incidentally, archy is a cockroach who aspires to be a writer. He leaves typewritten messages for his newspaper-editor mentor, but, because he is a cockroach, he can't type capital letters and never uses punctuation marks. His friend mehitabel, whom he quotes in this message, is an alley cat with grandiose dreams and a dubious reputation.

> **archy what in hell have i done**
> **to deserve all these kittens**
> **life seems to be just one damn litter after another**
> **after all archy i am an artist**
> **this constant parade of kittens**
> **interferes with my career**
> **its not that i am shy on mother love archy**
> **why my heart would bleed if anything happened to them**
> **and i found it out**
> **a tender heart is the cross i bear**
> **but archy the eternal struggle between life and art**
> **is simply wearing me out**[19]

Tape-record yourself while reading this and other favorite poems or dramatic scenes aloud. Compare these practice tapes with your initial self-evaluation tape to see if you have improved in the use of variety in your presentations.

Patterns of Speaking

People often make judgments about others based on their speech patterns. If you slur your words, mispronounce familiar words, or speak with a dialect that sounds unfamiliar to your audience, you may be seen as uneducated or socially inept. When you sound "odd" to your listeners, their attention will be distracted from what you are saying to the way you are saying it. In this section we cover articulation, enunciation, pronunciation, and dialect as they contribute to or detract from speaking effectiveness.

Articulation. **Articulation** refers to the way you produce individual speech sounds. Some people have trouble making certain sounds. For example, they may substitute a *d* for a *th*, saying "dem" instead of "them." Other sounds that are often misarticulated include *s*, *l*, and *r*. Severe articulation problems can interfere with effective communication, especially if the audience cannot understand the speaker or if the variations suggest low social or educational status. Such problems are best treated by a speech pathologist, who retrains the individual to produce the sound in a more acceptable manner.

Enunciation. **Enunciation** refers to the way you pronounce words in context. In casual conversation it is not unusual for people to slur their words—for example, saying "gimme" for "give me." However, careless enunciation causes credibility problems for public speakers. Do you say "Swatuh thought" for "That's what I thought"? "Harya?" for "How are you?"; or "Howjado?" for "How did you do?" These lazy enunciation patterns are not acceptable in public speaking. Check your enunciation patterns on the tape recordings you have made to determine if you have such a problem. If you do, concentrate on careful enunciation as you practice your speech. Be careful, however, to avoid the opposite problem of inflated, pompous, and pretentious enunciation, which can make you sound phony. You should strive to be neither sloppy nor overly precise.

Pronunciation. **Pronunciation** involves saying words correctly. It includes both using the correct sounds and placing the proper accent on syllables. Because written English does not always indicate the correct pronunciation, we may not be sure how to pronounce words that we first encounter in print. For instance, does the word *chiropodist* begin with an *sh*, a *ch*, or a *k* sound?

Have students list words they often mispronounce. Ask them to practice saying the words correctly aloud each day for a week and note whether this carries over into their general conversational practice.

If you are not certain how to pronounce a word, consult a dictionary. An especially useful reference is the *NBC Handbook of Pronunciation*, which contains 21,000 words and proper names that sometimes cause problems.[20] When international stories and new foreign leaders first appear in the news, newspapers frequently indicate the correct pronunciation of their names. Check front-page stories in the *New York Times* for guidance with such words.

In addition to problems pronouncing unfamiliar words, you may find that there are certain words you habitually mispronounce. For example, how do you pronounce the following words?

government	library
February	picture
ask	secretary
nuclear	just
athlete	get

Unless you are careful, you may find yourself slipping into these common mispronunciations:

goverment	liberry
Febuary	pitchur
axe	sekaterry
nuculer	jist
athalete	git

Mispronunciation of such common words can damage your ethos. Most of us know what words we chronically mispronounce and are able to pronounce them correctly when we think about it. The time to think about it is when you are practicing your speech.

Dialect. A **dialect** is a speech pattern typical of a geographic region or ethnic group. Your dialect usually reflects the area of the country where you were raised or lived for any length of time, or your cultural and ethnic identity.[21] In the United States there are three commonly recognized dialects: eastern, southern, and midwestern. Additionally, there are local variations within the broader dialects. For example, in South Carolina, one finds the Gullah dialect from the islands off the coast, the low-country or Charlestonian accent, the Piedmont variation, and the Appalachian twang.[22] And then there's always *"Bah-stahn,"* where you buy a *"lodge budded pup con"* at the movies!

There is no such thing in nature as a superior or inferior dialect. However, there can be occasions when a distinct dialect is a definite disadvantage or advantage. Listeners prefer speech patterns that are familiar to their ears. Audiences may also have stereotyped preconceptions about people who speak with certain dialects. For example, those raised in the South often associate a northeastern dialect with brusqueness and abrasiveness, and midwesterners may associate a southern dialect with slowness of action and mind. Comedian Jeff Foxworthy has noted:

> **A lot of people think everyone in the South is a redneck.... I went to Georgia Tech. I was an engineer at IBM. I just sound stupid. I can't help this, because where I grew up everybody else talked this way. People hear the accent and they want to deduct 100 IQ points.[23]**

You may have to work to overcome such a prejudice against your dialect.

Your dialect should reflect the standard for educated people from your geographic area or ethnic group. You should be concerned about tempering your dialect only if it creates barriers to understanding and identification between you and your audience. Then you may want to work toward softening your dialect so that you lower these barriers for the sake of your message.

Using Your Body to Communicate

Play a videotape of a speech with the sound turned off. See if students can determine the feelings portrayed through the nonverbal language of the speaker.

Communication with your audience begins before you ever open your mouth. Your facial expression, personal appearance, and air of confidence all convey a message. How do you walk to the front of the room to give your speech? Do you move with confidence and purpose, or do you stumble and shuffle? As you begin your speech, do you look listeners directly in the eye, or do you stare at the ceiling as though seeking divine inspiration? This **body language** is a nonverbal message that accompanies your speech. It affects how your audience responds to what you say.[24] For public speaking to be effective, your body language must reinforce your verbal language. If your face is expressionless as you urge your listeners to action, you are sending inconsistent messages. Be sure that your body and words both "say" the same thing. Although we discuss separate types of body language in this section, in practice they all work together and are interpreted as a totality by listeners.[25]

Facial Expression and Eye Contact

> **I knew she was lying the minute she said it. There was guilt written all over her face!**

InterConnections.LearnMore 11.1

NONVERBAL COMMUNICATION

Body Language **http://www.donnellking.com/nvcom.htm**
An introduction to the area of nonverbal communication based on the work of Albert Mehrabian; developed and maintained by Professor Donnell King, Pellissippi State Technical Community College, Knoxville, Tennessee.

Essentials of Nonverbal Communication **http://www3.usal.es/~nonverbal/introduction.htm**
An extensive directory of materials and web sites devoted to the study of nonverbal communication; developed and maintained by Professor Jaume Masip, Department of Social Psychology and Anthropology, University of Salamanca, Spain.

Gestures Around the World **http://www.webofculture.com/worldsmart/gestures.asp**
Want to avoid inadvertently making an obscene gesture in a foreign country? This web site provides information on these as well as other common and useful gestures for travelers; material excerpted from *Gestures: Do's and Taboos of Body Language Around the World*, by Roger Axtell.

Nonverbal Communication **http://digilander.iol.it/linguaggiodelcorpo/nonverb**
An interesting collection of information and links available in English, Italian, and Spanish; a useful online library of resources in proxemics, gestures, facial expressions, and paralinguistics; developed and maintained by Professor Marco Pacori, University of Padova, Italy, and Professor Aleksandra Kostic, University of Nis, Serbia. *Note:* Most, but not all, of the material linked on the home page has been translated into English.

He sure is shifty! Did you see how his eyes darted back and forth? He never did look us straight in the eye!

Most of us believe we can judge people's character, determine their true feelings, and tell whether they are honest from their facial expressions. If there is a conflict between what we see and what we hear, we will usually believe our eyes rather than our ears.

The eyes are the most important element of facial expressiveness. In the mainstream American culture, frequent and sustained eye contact suggests honesty, openness, and respect. We may think of a person's eyes as windows into the self. If you avoid looking at your audience while you are talking, you are drawing the shades on these windows of communication. A lack of eye contact suggests that you do not care about listeners, that you are putting something over on them, or that you are afraid of them. Other cultures view eye contact quite differently. In Japan, downcast eyes may signal attentiveness and agreement. In China, Indonesia, and rural Mexico, people may lower their eyes as a sign of deference. Some Native Americans may find direct eye contact offensive or aggressive.[26]

ESL: Ask ESL students how eye contact is regarded in their culture.

When you reach the podium or lectern, turn, pause, and look at your audience. This signals that you want to communicate and prepares people to listen. During your speech, try to make eye contact with all sectors of your audience. Don't just stare at one or two people. You will make them uncomfortable, and other members of the audience will feel left out. First look at people at the front of the room, then shift your focus to the middle, and finally look at those in the rear. You may find that those sitting in the rear of the room are the most difficult to reach. They may have taken a back seat because they don't want to listen or be involved. You may have to work harder to gain and hold their attention. Eye contact is one way you can reach them.

Start your speech with a smile unless this is inappropriate to your message. A smile signals your goodwill toward listeners and your ease in the speaking situation—qualities that should help your ethos.[27] We noticed that several of our Vanderbilt students combined a smile, a pause, and a nod to certain of their listeners to acknowledge a connection between the point they were making and previous speeches by those listeners. This smile-pause-nod combination illustrates an implied *intertextual signifier*. Such signifiers connect and bridge the various speeches heard by a group. They demonstrate that speakers are aware of the overall communication context in which they are speaking and help listeners make connections as well.

Beyond the initial moment of speaking, your face should reflect and reinforce the meanings of your words. An expressionless face suggests that the speaker is afraid or indifferent. The frozen face may be a mask behind which the speaker hides. The solution lies in selecting a topic that excites you, concentrating on sharing your message, and having the confidence that comes from being well prepared.

You can also try the following exercise:

Utter these statements, using a dull monotone and keeping your face as expressionless as possible:

I am absolutely delighted by your gift.

I don't know when I've ever been this excited.

We don't need to beg for change—we need to demand change.

All this puts me in a very bad mood.

Now repeat them with *exaggerated* vocal variety and facial expression. You may find that your hands and body also want to get involved. Encourage such impulses so that you develop an integrated system of body language.

Movement and Gestures

Most actors learn—often the hard way—that if you want to steal a scene from someone, all you have to do is move around, develop a twitch, or swing a leg. Before long, all eyes will be focused on that movement. This theatrical trick shows that physical movement sometimes can attract more attention than words. All the more reason that your words and gestures should work in harmony and not at cross-purposes! This also means you should avoid random movements, such as pacing back and forth, twirling your hair, rubbing your eyes, or jingling change in your pockets. Once you are aware of such mannerisms, it is easy to control them.

Show videotapes of student speeches that demonstrate good and poor movement and gestures. Discuss the impact of these various behaviors on communication effectiveness.

Your gestures and movement should grow out of your response to your message.[28] They should always appear natural and spontaneous, prompted by your ideas and feelings. They should never look contrived and artificial. For example, you should avoid framing a gesture to fit each word or sequence of words you utter. Perhaps every speech instructor has encountered speakers like the one who stood with arms circled above him as he said, "We need to get *around* this problem." That's not a good way to gesture!

Effective gestures involve three phases: *readiness*, *execution*, and *return*. In the readiness phase you must be prepared for movement. Your hands and body should be in a position that does not inhibit free action. For example, you cannot gesture if your hands are locked behind your back or jammed into your pockets, or if you are grasping the lectern as though it were a life preserver. Instead, let your hands rest in a relaxed position, at your sides, on the lectern, or in front of you, where they can obey easily the impulse to gesture in support of a point you are making. As you execute a gesture, let yourself move naturally and fully. Don't raise your hand halfway, then stop with your arm frozen awkwardly in space. When you have completed a gesture, let your hands return to the relaxed readiness position, where they will be free to move again when the next impulse to gesture arises.

Reducing the physical distance between the speaker and audience can help increase identification.

Do not assume that there is a universal language of gesture. A study of Rwandan culture reveals that Rwandans learn an elaborate code of gestures that is a direct extension of their spoken language.[29] In contrast, our "gesture language" is far less complex and sophisticated. Even more, assuming a universal language of gesture could get you in big trouble with a culturally diverse audience. For example, the American sign for A-OK (thumb and index finger joined in a circle) has an obscene meaning in some cultures, and nodding the head up and down may mean "no" instead of "yes."[30] Management consultant Marc Hequet provides additional insight:

> **The "Hook 'em, Horns!" hand signal, beloved of fans who follow the fortunes of the University of Texas Longhorns college football team, once started a brawl in a crowded Italian nightclub when Texans at separate tables merrily flashed each other the sign—hand raised, middle fingers held down by thumb, index and pinky extended. The innocents didn't know it but in Italy the gesture is referred to as cuckold horns. It means, "Your wife is being unfaithful."[31]**

The Factor of Distance. From **proxemics**, the study of how humans use space during communication, we can derive two additional principles that help explain the effective use of movement during speeches. The first of these principles suggests that *the physical distance between speakers and listeners affects their sense of closeness or immediacy*. Bill Clinton made effective use of this principle during the second of the televised debates of the 1992 presidential campaign. In the town meeting setting of that debate, Clinton actually rose from his seat after one question and approached the audience as he answered it. His movement toward his listeners suggested that he felt a special closeness for that problem and for them. Clinton's body language also enhanced his identification with the live audience and with the larger viewing audience they represented. In contrast, his opponents, President Bush and Ross Perot, were made to seem distant from these audiences.

ESL: Ask ESL students to explain proxemic principles in their countries and discuss how these may vary across cultures.

It follows also that the greater the physical distance between speaker and audience, the harder it is to achieve identification. This problem gets worse when a lectern acts as a physical barrier. Short speakers can almost disappear behind it! If this is a problem, try speaking from either beside or in front of a lectern so that your body language can work for you.

A related but quite different problem arises if you move so close to listeners that you make them feel uncomfortable. If they pull back involuntarily in their chairs, you know you have violated their sense of personal space. A form of this problem occurred during the Gore-Bush presidential debates of 2000. In the third and last of these debates, Gore on several occasions moved aggressively toward Bush's side of the platform as he answered questions. Some viewers felt that Gore had come too close to his opponent; this behavior, they thought, was boorish and inappropriate. For these viewers this behavior reinforced a related bad impression Gore had made during the first debate when he constantly interrupted Bush, sighed and rolled his eyes during Bush's statements, often went overtime during his own answers, and generally seemed not to respect either his opponent or the rules of the debate. Gore's lack of sensitivity to the first law of proxemics as well as to debate etiquette made him look bad to many, especially when he had been expected to dominate the debates. For you the lesson should be clear: you should seek the ideal physical distance—not too distant and not too close—between yourself and listeners to increase your effectiveness.

The Factor of Elevation. The second principle of proxemics suggests that *elevation will also affect the sense of closeness between speakers and listeners*. When you speak, you often stand above your seated listeners in a "power position." Because we tend to associate *above* us with power over us, speakers may find that this arrangement discourages identification. Often they will sit on the edge of the desk in front of the lectern in a more relaxed and less elevated stance. If your message is informal and requires close identification, or if you are especially tall, you might try this approach.

Personal Appearance

Your clothing and grooming affect how you are perceived. General Norman Schwarzkopf, who became a familiar figure on American television as commander of operations for Desert Shield and Desert Storm during the Iraqi conflict of 1991, underscored how important dress can be as he spoke at the University of Richmond:

> **Now, first of all for those of you who don't recognize me, I am the General Schwarzkopf. I said that because for some reason people expect me to be wearing camouflage. If I am not wearing camouflage, I'm not General Schwarzkopf. . . . I work out every other day as you can tell from this magnificent body that stands before you, and at the end of my workout I always go into the steam bath. True story—last summer I walked into the steam bath. I was not wearing camouflage at the time, and there was a man in there, and he turned and looked at me and said, "Did anybody ever tell you that from a distance you look exactly like General Schwarzkopf?" And I thought I'd play along, and I said, "Yes, I hear that a lot." He said, "Yes, it's only when you get up close you realize you're not General Schwarzkopf."[32]**

Few of us have a public identity so closely associated with the way we dress, but nevertheless what we wear is important.[33] How we dress can even influence how we see ourselves and how we behave. A police officer out of uniform may not act as authoritatively as when dressed in blue. A doctor without a white jacket may behave like just another person. You may have a certain type of clothing that makes you feel comfortable and relaxed. You may even have a special "good luck" outfit that raises your confidence.

Your clothing and grooming can affect how you are perceived.

When you are scheduled to speak, dress in a way that puts you at ease and makes you feel good about yourself. Since your speech is a special occasion, you should treat it as such. By dressing a little more formally than you usually do, you emphasize both to yourself and to the audience that your message is important. As we noted in Chapter 9, your appearance can serve as a presentation aid that complements your message. Like any other aid, it should never compete with your words for attention or be distracting. Always dress in good taste for the situation you anticipate.

The Importance of Practice

It takes a lot of practice to sound natural. Although this statement may seem contradictory, it should not be surprising. Speaking before a group is not your typical way of communicating. Even though most people seem spontaneous and relaxed when talking with a small group of friends, something happens when they walk to the front of a room and face a larger audience of less familiar faces. They often freeze or become stilted and awkward. This blocks the natural flow of communication.

The key to overcoming this problem is to practice until you can respond fully to your ideas as you present them. Don't fall into the trap of avoiding practice because it reminds you that you are not confident about your upcoming speech: That makes you a prime candidate for self-fulfilling prophecy![34] Instead, rehearse your speech until your voice, face, and body can express your feelings as well as your thoughts. On the day of your speech, you become a model for your listeners, showing them how they should respond in turn.

To develop an effective extemporaneous style, practice until you feel the speech is part of you. During practice you can actually hear what you have been preparing and try out the words and techniques you have been considering. What looked like a good idea in your outline may not seem to work as well when it comes to life in spoken words. It is better to discover this fact in rehearsal than before an actual audience.

You will probably want privacy the first two or three times you practice. Even then you should try to simulate the conditions under which the speech will be given. Stand up while you practice. Imagine your listeners in front of you.

Many speeches presented on C-SPAN are obviously unrehearsed manuscript presentations. Tape some that are particularly poor with respect to presentation skills and play them to stimulate class discussion.

Speaker's Notes 11.2

PRACTICING FOR PRESENTATION

1. Practice standing up and speaking aloud, if possible in the room where you will be making your presentation.
2. Practice first from your formal outline; then switch to your key-word outline when you feel you have mastered your material.
3. Work on maintaining eye contact with an imaginary audience.
4. Practice integrating your presentation aids into your message.
5. Check the timing of your speech. Add or cut if necessary.
6. Continue practicing until you feel comfortable and confident.
7. Present your speech in a "dress rehearsal" before friends. Make final changes in light of their suggestions.

Picture them responding positively to what you have to say. Address your ideas to them, and visualize your ideas having impact.

If possible, go to your classroom to practice. If this is not possible, find another empty room where the speaking arrangements are similar. Such on-site rehearsal helps you get a better feel for the situation you will face, reducing its strangeness when you make your actual presentation. Begin practicing from your formal outline. Once you feel comfortable, switch to your key-word outline; then practice until the outline transfers from the paper to your head.

Keep material to be read to a minimum. Type or print quotations in large letters so you can see them easily. Put each quotation on a single index card or sheet of paper. If using a lectern, position this material so that you can maintain frequent eye contact while reading. If you will speak beside or in front of the lectern, hold your cards in your hand and raise them when it is time to read. Practice reading your quotation until you can present it naturally while only glancing at your notes. If your speech includes presentation aids, practice handling them until they are smoothly integrated into your presentation. They should seem a natural extension of your verbal message.

During practice, you can serve as your own audience by recording your speech and playing it back. If videotaping equipment is available, arrange to record your speech so that you can see as well as hear yourself. Always try to be the toughest critic you will ever have, but also be a constructive critic. Never put yourself down or give up on yourself. Work on specific points of improvement.

Ethics Alert! 11.1

THE DO'S AND DON'TS OF PRESENTATION

1. Don't use presentation skills to disguise faults of content.
2. Don't judge the characters of others by how they sound.
3. Don't let culturally based variations in eye contact, loudness, or gesture control how you respond to speakers.
4. Don't speak unless you are convinced of the value of your message. Then let your entire body confirm that fact to listeners.

In addition to evaluating yourself, you may find it helpful to ask a friend or friends to listen to your presentation. This outside opinion may be more objective than your self-evaluation, and you will get a feel for speaking to real people rather than to an imagined audience. Seek constructive feedback from your friends by asking them specific questions. Was it easy for them to follow you? Do you have any mannerisms (such as twisting your hair or saying "you know" after every other sentence) that distracted them? Were you speaking loudly and slowly enough? Did your ideas seem clear and soundly supported?

On the day that you are assigned to speak, get to class early enough to look over your outline one last time so that it is fresh in your mind. If you have devoted sufficient time and energy to your preparation and practice, you should feel confident about communicating with your audience.

"Taking the Stage"

As you step to the front of the room at the moment you are asked to speak, you should do so with a certain panache. You should radiate the expectation that you will have something worthy and important to say that listeners should consider carefully. This confidence, this air of leadership, is what communication consultant Judith Humphrey calls "taking the stage."[35] This theatrical metaphor summarizes much of what we have said to this point about preparing for public speaking. Although Humphrey directs her remarks to women in management roles, what she says applies to all public speakers who aspire to influence others in positive ways. Taking the stage, she says, implies six steps.

The first is the *attitude* that every public communication situation is an opportunity to influence, inspire, and motivate others. The second is the *conviction* that what you bring to others will have great value. The third is to create the *character of leadership* as you speak. Humphrey says: "A leader has vision. A leader has a point of view and is not afraid to express it. A leader must also be centered, totally authentic."[36]

Step four is to have a great *script*. You should have a simple, clear, positive message. That leads to step five, which is to use the *language* of leadership. Your words should be forceful and should avoid indirection and self-correction. Don't overuse phrases like "in my opinion" or "maybe I'm wrong but." Don't soften your point or subvert yourself.

Finally, *believe in your views*. As you stand at the lectern, don't shrink into yourself. Expand. Throw an arm over the lectern and stand tall. Stand still and don't fidget. Establish firm eye contact and make strong gestures. Use pause to make your points. "Taking the stage" is your invitation and opportunity to lead others.

In Summary

An effective *presentation* integrates the nonverbal aspects of your voice and body with your words. It is characterized by enthusiasm and naturalness. Your voice and bearing should project your commitment to your message but should not call attention to themselves. You should sound and look spontaneous and natural, not contrived or artificial.

Methods of Presentation. The four major methods of speech presentation are impromptu speaking, memorized presentation, reading from a manuscript, and extemporaneous speaking. In *impromptu speaking* you talk with minimal or no preparation and practice. To present an effective impromptu speech, follow the PREP formula: state your *p*oint, give a *r*eason or *e*xample, and then restate your *p*oint.

Both *memorized* and *manuscript presentations* require that your speech be written out word for word. Be sure that your speech is written in good oral style. An *extemporaneous presentation* requires careful planning, but the wording is spontaneous. Instructors usually require that you present speeches extemporaneously. Extemporaneous speaking allows you to adapt to *feedback* from your audience. Be especially alert for signs that your audience doesn't understand, has lost interest, or disagrees with you; then make adjustments to your message to cope with these problems.

Following any presentation, you may need to answer questions about your material and ideas. Although your responses will be impromptu, you should prepare for questions in advance and plan appropriate responses.

Using Your Voice Effectively. A good speaking voice conveys your meaning fully and clearly. Vocal expressiveness depends on your ability to control your *pitch*, rate, loudness, and variety. Your *habitual pitch* is the level at which you usually speak. Your *optimum pitch* is the level at which you can produce a clear, strong voice with minimal effort. Speaking at your optimum pitch gives your voice flexibility. The *rate* at which you speak can affect the impression you make on listeners. You can control rate to your advantage by using pauses and by changing your pace to match the moods of your material. To speak loudly enough, you need proper breath control. Vary loudness for the sake of emphasis. Vocal variety adds color and interest to a speech, makes a speaker more likeable, and encourages identification between speaker and audience.

Articulation, enunciation, pronunciation, and dialect refer to the unique way you give voice to words. *Articulation* concerns the manner in which you produce individual sounds. *Enunciation* refers to the way you utter words in context. Proper *pronunciation* means that you say words correctly. Your *dialect* may identify the area of the country in which you learned language or your cultural or ethnic background. Occasionally, dialect can create identification and comprehension problems between speaker and audience.

Using Your Body Effectively. You communicate with *body language* as well as with your voice. Eye contact signals listeners that you want to communicate. Your facial expressions should project the meanings of your words. Movement attracts attention; therefore, your movements and gestures must complement your speech, not compete with it. *Proxemics* is the study of how humans use space during communication. Two proxemic principles, distance and elevation, can affect your identification with an audience as you speak. Be sure your grooming and dress are appropriate to the speech occasion and do not detract from your ability to communicate.

The Importance of Practice. You should practice your speech until you have the sequence of main points and supporting materials well established in your mind. It is best to practice your presentation in conditions similar to those in which you will give your speech. Keep citations or other materials that you must read to a minimum. Tape-recording or videotaping can be useful for self-evaluation during rehearsal. All that you do should prepare you for the moment when you "take the stage."

Terms to Know

presentation
immediacy
expanded conversational style
impromptu speaking
PREP formula
memorized text presentation
manuscript presentation
extemporaneous speaking
feedback
pitch
habitual pitch
optimum pitch
rate
rhythm
vocal distractions
articulation
enunciation
pronunciation
dialect
body language
proxemics

Notes

1. Janet Beavin Bavelas, "Redefining Language: Nonverbal Linguistic Acts in Face-to-Face Dialogue," 1992 Aubrey Fisher Memorial Lecture, presented at the University of Utah, October 1992.
2. James C. McCroskey, *An Introduction to Rhetorical Communication*, 3rd ed. (Englewood Cliffs, N.J.: Prentice Hall, 1993), pp. 263–264.
3. Ibid., p. 264.
4. Virginia P. Richmond, James C. McCroskey, and S. K. Payne, *Nonverbal Behavior in Interpersonal Relations*, 2nd ed. (Englewood Cliffs, N.J.: Prentice Hall, 1991), pp. 208–228.
5. Michael Duffy, "Picture of Health," *Time*, 4 Oct. 1993, pp. 28+. *Time Almanac Reference Ed.* CD-ROM. Compact, 1994.
6. "A Letter to Our Readers," *Newsweek*, 4 Oct. 1993, p. 29.
7. These guidelines for handling questions and answers are a compendium of ideas from the following sources: Stephen D. Body, "Nine Steps to a Successful Question-and-Answer Session," *Management Solutions*, May 1988, pp. 16–17; Teresa Brady, "Fielding Abrasive Questions During Presentations," *Supervisory Management*, February 1993, p. 6; J. Donald Ragsdale and Alan L. Mikels, "Effects of Question Periods on a Speaker's Credibility with a Television Audience," *Southern States Communication Journal* 40 (1975): 302–312; Dorothy Sarnoff, *Never Be Nervous Again* (New York: Ballantine, 1987); Laurie Schloff and Marcia Yudkin, *Smart Speaking: Sixty-Second Strategies* (New York: Holt, 1991); and Alan Zaremba, "Q and A: The Other Part of Your Presentation," *Management World*, January–February 1989, pp. 8–10.
8. Roger Ailes, *You Are the Message: Getting What You Want by Being Who You Are* (New York: Doubleday, 1988), p. 170.
9. Howard Giles and Arlene Franklyn-Stokes, "Communicator Characteristics," in *Handbook of International and Intercultural Communication*, ed. Molefi Kete Asante and William B. Gudykunst (Newbury Park, Calif.: Sage, 1989), pp. 117–144.
10. Jon Eisenson, *Voice and Diction: A Program for Improvement* (New York: Macmillan, 1974), p. vii.
11. Adapted from Stewart W. Hyde, *Television and Radio Announcing*, 6th ed. (Boston: Houghton Mifflin, 1991), pp. 80–85.
12. N. Scott Momaday, *The Way to Rainy Mountain* (Albuquerque: University of New Mexico Press, 1969), p. 5.
13. Carole Douglis, "The Beat Goes On: Social Rhythms Underlie All Our Speech and Actions," *Psychology Today*, November 1987, p. 36-41.
14. William Price Fox, "Eugene Talmadge and Sears Roebuck Co.," *Southern Fried Plus Six* (New York: Ballantine Books, 1968), p. 36.
15. Charlotte Perkins Gilman, "Similar Cases," from *In This Our World* (reprinted in Wayland Maxfield Parrish, *Reading Aloud: A Technique in the Interpretation of Literature* (New York: The Ronald Press Company, 1941), pp. 144–145.
16. Cited in Douglis, p. 36 (6).
17. Michael L. Hecht, Peter A. Andersen, and Sidney A. Ribeau, "The Cultural Dimensions of Nonverbal Communication," in *Handbook of International and Intercultural Communication*, pp. 163–185; Larry A. Samovar and Richard E. Porter, *Communication Between Cultures* (Belmont, Calif.: Wadsworth, 1991), pp. 205–206.
18. Ralph Hillman and Delorah Lee Jewell, *Work for Your Voice* (Murfreesboro, Tenn.: Copymatte, 1986), p. 63.
19. Don Marquis, adapted from "mehitabel and her kittens," in *the lives and times of archy and mehitabel.* Copyright ©1927 by Doubleday and Company, Inc. Reprinted by permission of the publisher.
20. *NBC Handbook of Pronunciation*, 4th ed. (New York: Harper, 1991).
21. William B. Gudykunst et al., "Language and Intergroup Communication," in *Handbook of International and Intercultural Communication*, pp. 145–162.
22. Carolanne Griffith-Roberts, "Let's Talk Southern," *Southern Living*, February 1995, p. 82. For a detailed explication of regional dialect variances, see Charles K. Thomas, *An Introduction to the Phonetics of American English*, 2nd ed. (New York: The Ronald Press Co., 1958), pp. 191–260.
23. "Jeff Foxworthy: From Hootenanny to Hoosier," *Satellite TV Week*, 28 July–3 August 1996, p. 1.
24. Samovar and Porter, p. 177.
25. Peter A. Andersen, "Nonverbal Immediacy in Interpersonal Communication," in *Multichannel Integrations of Nonverbal Behavior*, ed. A. W. Siegman and S. Feldstein (Hillsdale, N.J.: Erlbaum, 1985).
26. S. Ishii, "Characteristics of Japanese Nonverbal Communication Behavior," *Communication*, Summer 1973, pp. 163–180; Samovar and Porter, pp. 198–200; "Understanding Culture: Don't Stare at a Navajo," *Psychology Today*, June 1974, p. 107.
27. Research psychologist Carolyn Copper has found that newscasters influence voters when they smile while speaking of candidates, further evidence of the power of facial expression ("A Certain Smile," *Psychology Today*, January–February 1992, p. 20).
28. Charlotte I. Lee and Timothy Gura, *Oral Interpretation*, 8th ed. (Boston: Houghton Mifflin, 1992), pp. 118–119.
29. Edouard Gasarabwe-Laroche, "Meaningful Gestures: Nonverbal Communication in Rwandan Culture," *UNESCO Courier*, September 1993, p. 31–33.

30. Mary Munter, "Cross Cultural Communication for Managers," *Business Horizons*, May–June 1993, p. 69-78. (10). For additional insights into cultural differences in nonverbal communication, see Roger Axtell, *Gestures: The Do's and Taboos of Body Language Around the World* (New York: Wiley, 1991); E. Hall, *Understanding Cultural Differences* (Yarmouth, Me.: Intercultural Press, 1990); J. Mole, *When in Rome . . . A Business Guide to Cultures and Customs in Twelve European Nations* (New York: AMACOM, 1991); D. Ricks, *Big Business Blunders* (Homewood, Ill.: Dow Jones-Irwin, 1983); and C. Storti, *The Art of Crossing Cultures* (Yarmouth, Me.: Intercultural Press, 1990).

31. Marc Hequet, "The Fine Art of Multicultural Meetings," *Training*, July 1993, p. 29 (5).

32. Norman Schwarzkopf, "Leaders for the 21st Century," *Vital Speeches of the Day*, 15 June 1999, p. 519.

33. The literature supporting this conclusion is reviewed by Virginia Kidd, "Do Clothes Make the Officer? How Uniforms Impact Communication: A Review of Literature," presented at the Visual Communication Conference at Pray, Montana, 8 July 2000.

34. Ralph R. Behnke and Chris R. Sawyer, "Public Speaking Procrastination as a Correlate of Public Speaking Communication Apprehension and Self-Perceived Public Speaking Competence," *Communication Research Reports* 16 (1999): 40–47.

35. Judith Humphrey, "Taking the Stage," *Vital Speeches of the Day*, 1 May 2001, pp. 435–438.

36. Ibid., p. 436.

MAKING VIDEO PRESENTATIONS

It is quite likely that at some time in your life you will make a video presentation. You may find yourself speaking live on closed-circuit television, videotaping instructions or training materials at work, using community access cable channels to promote a cause, running for public office, or even appearing on commercial television. Many of these video presentations will utilize a manuscript printed on a teleprompter. At other times you may need to speak impromptu or extemporaneously. With some minor adaptations, the training you receive in this class should serve you well in such situations.[1]

We live in a culture in which the mass media have changed audience expectations. Television especially seems to bring speakers into our homes, giving mass communication more the feeling of personal communication and encouraging a more intimate style of presentation.[2] Because television brings you close to viewers, it magnifies every aspect of your appearance. Therefore, you should dress conservatively, avoiding shiny fabrics, glittery or dangling jewelry, and flashy prints that might "swim" on the screen and distract viewers. You also should not wear white or light pastels because they reflect glare. Ask in advance about the color of the studio backdrop. If you have light hair or if the backdrop will be light, wear dark clothing for contrast. If you have a dark skin tone, request a light or neutral background and consider wearing light-colored clothes.

Both men and women need makeup to achieve a natural look on television. Have powder available to reduce skin shine or hide a five o'clock shadow. Women should use makeup conservatively because the camera will intensify it. Avoid glasses with tinted lenses: they will appear even darker on the screen. Even untinted lenses may cause problems, as they reflect glare from the studio lights. Wear contact lenses if you have them. If you can see well enough to read the monitor without glasses, leave them off.

Television requires a conversational mode of presentation. Your audience may be single individuals or small groups assembled in their homes. Imagine yourself talking with another person in an informal setting. While intimate, however, television is also remote. Since you will have no immediate feedback to help you, your meaning must be instantly clear. Use language that is colorful and concrete so that your audience will remember your material. Use previews and internal summaries to keep viewers on track. You may use visual aids to enhance comprehension, but be sure to confer in advance with studio personnel to be certain your materials will work well in that setting. For example, large poster boards displayed on an easel are more difficult to handle in video presentations than smaller materials. (See related considerations in Chapter 9.)

Vocal variety and facial expressions will become your most important forms of body language. Remember that television will magnify all your movements and vocal changes. Slight head movements and underplayed facial expressions should be enough to reinforce your ideas. Avoid abrupt changes in loudness as a means of vocal emphasis. Rely instead on subtle changes in tempo, pitch, and inflection, and on pauses, to drive your point home.

For most televised presentations, timing is crucial. Five minutes of air time means five minutes, not five minutes and ten seconds. If you run overtime, you will be cut off in midsentence. For this reason television favors manuscript presentations read from a teleprompter. The teleprompter controls timing and preserves a sense of direct eye contact between speakers and listeners. Ask studio personnel how to use the equipment.

Try to rehearse your presentation in the studio with the production personnel. Develop a positive relationship with studio technicians. Your success depends in large part on how well they do their jobs. Provide them with a manuscript marked to show when you will move around or use a visual aid.

Practice speaking from the teleprompter if you will be using one. Use the microphone correctly. Don't blow into it to see if it's working. Remember that the microphone will pick up *all* sounds, including shuffling papers or tapping on a lectern. If you use a stand or hand-held microphone, position it about ten inches below your mouth. The closer the microphone is to your mouth, the more it will pick up unwanted noises like whistled "s" sounds or tongue clicks. Remember that microphones with cords will restrict your movement. If you plan to move about during your presentation, know where the cord is so you won't trip over it.

Don't be put off by distractions as you practice and present your speech. Studio technicians may need to confer with one another while you are speaking. This is a necessary part of their business. They are not being rude or inattentive. Even though they are in the room with you, they are not your audience. Keep your mind on your ideas and your eyes on the camera. The camera may seem strange at first, but think of it as a friendly face waiting to hear what you have to say. Your eye contact with the camera becomes your eye contact with your audience. Be prepared for lighting and voice checks before the actual taping begins. Use this time to run through your introduction. Before you begin your speech and after you finish, always assume that any microphone or camera near you is "live." Don't say or do anything you wouldn't want your audience to hear or see.

Even though the situation is strange, try to relax. If you are standing, stand at ease. If you are sitting, lean slightly forward as if you were talking to someone in the chair next to you. The floor director will give you a countdown before the camera starts to roll. Clear your throat and be ready to start on cue. Begin with a smile, if appropriate, as you make eye contact with the camera. If several cameras are used, a red light on top will tell you which camera is on. During your presentation, the studio personnel may communicate with you using special sign language. The director will tell you what cues they will use.[3]

If you are using a teleprompter script, it will appear directly below or on the lens of the camera. Practice your speech ahead of time until you *almost* have it memorized so that you can glance at the script as a whole. If you have to read it word for word, your eyes may be continually shifting (which will make you look suspicious). If you make a mistake, keep going. Sometimes "mistakes" are improvements. Do not stop unless the director says "cut." If appropriate, smile when you finish and continue looking at the camera to allow time for a fade-out.

NOTES

1. The authors are indebted to Professor Roxanne Gee of the television and film area in the Department of Communication at the University of Memphis for her assistance and suggestions in putting together this advice.
2. Roger Ailes, *You Are the Message: Getting What You Want by Being Who You Are* (New York: Doubleday, 1988), pp. 15–19.
3. Illustrations of major video hand signals may be found in Stewart W. Hyde, *Television and Radio Announcing*, 6th ed. (Boston: Houghton Mifflin, 1991), pp. 80–85.

PART FOUR

Types of Public Speaking

12

Informative Speaking

OUTLINE

THIS CHAPTER WILL HELP YOU

- understand the functions of informative speaking
- apply principles of motivation and attention to help listeners learn
- learn the types of informative speeches and how to design them
- prepare and present informative speeches

In ancient Greek mythology, Prometheus was punished by the other gods for teaching humans how to make fire. These jealous gods knew that people would now be able to keep warm, cook food, use the extended light, and share knowledge as they huddled around their campfires. They would build a civilization and challenge the gods themselves with the power of this new learning. These mythical gods had every right to be angry with Prometheus. He had given the first significant speech of demonstration.

This tale of Prometheus reminds us that information is power. Because we cannot personally experience everything that may be important or interesting to us, we must rely on the knowledge of others to expand our understanding and competence. *Sharing knowledge is the essence of informative speaking.*

Shared information can be important to survival. Early detection and warning systems alert us to storms, and news of medical breakthroughs tell us how to stay healthy. Beyond simply enabling us to live, information helps us to live better. It helps us deal with our world and the people in it. In this chapter we look at the functions of informative communication, suggest ways to help your listeners learn, discuss the major types of informative speeches, and present some basic speech designs that are appropriate to these speeches. Our objective is to help you bring fire to your listeners.

The improvement of understanding is for two ends: first our own increase of knowledge; secondly, to enable us to deliver that knowledge to others.

—John Locke

The Functions of Informative Speaking

Informative speaking is defined by its function. In a single speech you might introduce yourself, provide information, urge action, and celebrate values. *But if your main purpose is to share knowledge, then we call the speech informative.*

There are four reasons why informative speaking is important. First, informative speaking empowers listeners by giving them new ideas and skills. Second, informative speaking can shape listener perceptions. Third, informative speaking helps set the agenda of public concerns. Finally, informative speaking can clarify options for action.

Sharing Information and Ideas

An informative speech *gives to* listeners rather than *asks of* them. The demands on the audience are relatively low. As an informative speaker, you want listeners to pay attention and understand, but you do not try to make them change their behavior. For example, one of our students gave an informative speech on the dangers of prolonged exposure to ultraviolet radiation, but she did not urge her audience to boycott tanning salons. Although informative speaking makes modest demands on the listener, the demands on the speaker are high. Good informative speakers must have a *thorough understanding* of their subject. It is one thing to know something well enough to satisfy yourself. It is quite another to know it well enough to communicate what you know to others.

Our era is sometimes described as the Information Age. Ask students to reflect upon the meaning and significance of this description.

By sharing information, an informative speech reduces ignorance. An informative speech does not simply repeat something the audience already knows. Rather, *the* ***informative value*** *of a speech is measured by how much new and important information or understanding it provides the audience.* As you prepare your informative speech, ask yourself the following questions:

- Is my topic significant enough to merit an informative speech?
- What do my listeners already know about my topic?

Sharing knowledge is the essence of informative speaking.

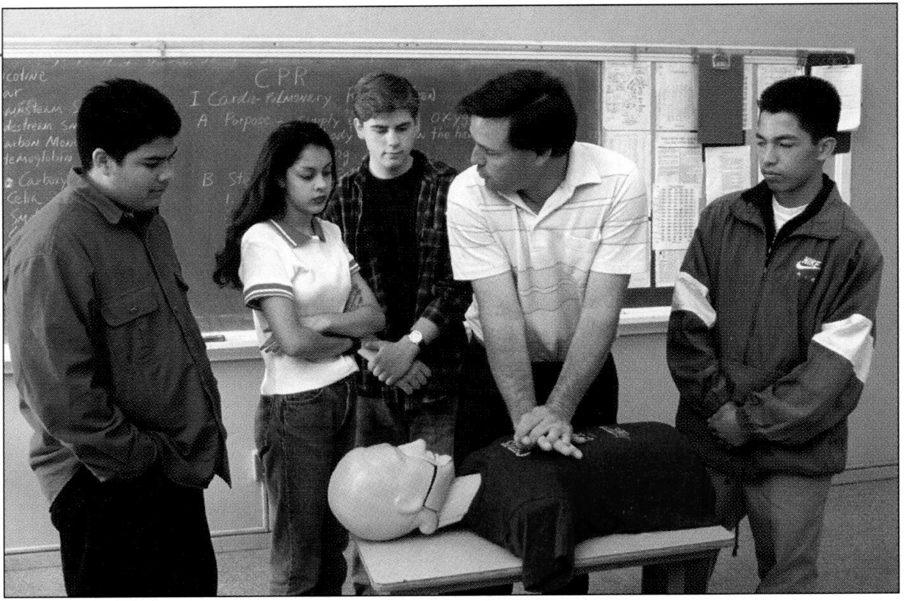

Shared information can be important to survival.

- What more do they need to know?
- Do I understand my topic well enough to help others understand it?

The answers to these questions should help you plan a speech with high informative value.

Emphasize the importance of defining technical terms speakers may take for granted.

In informative speaking, the speaker acts as a teacher. To teach effectively, you must arouse and sustain attention by adapting your message to listeners' interests and needs. You must make your audience aware of how important the new information is. When you have finished, they should feel they have benefited from your message.

Shaping Audience Perceptions

When speakers share information, they also share their points of view. It is virtually impossible to cover everything there is to know about any important subject in a short message. Therefore, although any responsible speaker will strive not to distort the presentation of a subject, the descriptions and explanations offered must be partial. Speakers must be selective about the information they convey, and what they omit may be as important as what they include. When listeners see a subject through the speaker's eyes, they really see an interpretation of it. Moreover, the word-pictures painted by speakers are often colored in subtle ways by their feelings. This selective exposure to a subject can influence the way we respond to it, especially if it is new to us.

This power of informative speaking to influence perceptions serves a **prepersuasive function**, preparing listeners for later persuasive messages. Suppose that you hear *one* of two speeches on teaching as a career. The first, presented by an enthusiastic teacher, describes the personal rewards of teaching and stresses the joy of helping children learn. The other, offered by a teacher suffering from burnout, focuses on discipline problems and administrative red tape. Neither suggests that you should or should not become a teacher. Each provides what he or she *believes* to be an accurate picture. But each creates a totally different predisposition to respond. Depending on which message you hear, you will be primed quite differently for a later persuasive message urging you to become a teacher.

If you have strong feelings about a subject, you must work especially hard *not* to present a distorted perspective. If listeners feel you are blurring the truth or displaying obvious bias, they may dismiss your message as unreliable and lower their estimation of your character and competence.

Setting an Agenda

The amount of information reaching people today can be overwhelming. This flood of information from the mass media serves an **agenda-setting function.**[1] As the media present the "news," they also tell us what we *should* be thinking about. By the amount of coverage allotted to a topic, the media establishes its importance in the public mind.

Informative speaking also performs an agenda-setting role. As it directs our attention to certain subjects, it influences what we feel is important. The informative speech "The 'Monument' at Wounded Knee," which appears in Appendix C, demonstrates this agenda-setting function as it shapes perceptions about our country's policy toward Native Americans. Hearing that speech could predispose listeners both to believe the issue is important and to favor better treatment for this group. As you prepare an informative speech, remember the power you have to establish the importance of your topic in the minds of your listeners. Consider the ethical consequences of your words.

Ask students to go to the library and copy the headline and lead story of the newspaper closest to their home on a recent day. In class discussion, consider how perceptions may be shaped and agendas set by the choice, treatment, and emphasis given to the stories. ESL students can provide an interesting cross-cultural comparison by introducing newspapers from their countries.

Clarifying Options

An informative speech also can reveal and clarify options for action. Information expands our awareness, opens new horizons, and suggests fresh possibilities. Information can also help us discard unworkable options. The better we understand an issue, the more intelligent the choices we can make. For example, what should we know about obesity? Informative speeches may tell us about the consequences of doing something or nothing to correct this condition. They may teach us about the medical soundness of different diets. They may also inform us about the roles of exercise and counseling in weight control. Such information would expand our options for dealing with the problem.

Informative speakers carry a large ethical burden to communicate responsible knowledge of their topics. A responsible informative speech should cover all *major* positions on a topic and present all *vital* information. Although speakers may have strong feelings on a subject, it is unethical to deliberately omit or distort information that is necessary for audience understanding. Similarly, speakers who are unaware of information because they have not done sufficient research are irresponsible. As you prepare your speech, you should seek out material from sources that present different perspectives on your subject. The two speeches on the teaching profession mentioned earlier demonstrate potential ethical abuses of the option-clarifying function of informative speaking. If the speeches are presented as *representative* of teaching as a career, then both speakers are guilty of overgeneralizing from limited personal experience.

Have students watch television newscasts and consider: 1) what informative functions the programs fulfill; 2) whether the programs entertain and persuade as well as inform; and 3) whether the programs are ethical sources of information? Discuss findings in class.

Function	Important When You Are
1. Sharing information and ideas	Introducing new ideas or skills
2. Shaping perceptions	Preparing listeners for later persuasive messages
3. Setting an agenda	Establishing the importance of a topic
4. Clarifying options	Providing a balanced perspective on a subject

FIGURE 12.1
The Functions of Informative Speaking

Ethics Alert! 12.1

THE ETHICS OF INFORMATIVE SPEAKING

1. Be sure you can ethically defend your choice of subjects.
2. Cover all major positions on a subject when there are differing perspectives.
3. Present all information on a topic that is vital for audience understanding.
4. Do not distort information that is necessary for audience understanding.
5. Do sufficient research to speak responsibly on your subject.
6. Do not omit relevant information that is inconsistent with your perspective.
7. Strive to be as objective as possible.

Helping Listeners Learn

The success of an informative speech can be measured in terms of whether and how much the listener learns from the speech. Preparation for a successful informative speech begins by considering how much listeners know initially about

FIGURE 12.2
Audience Considerations for Informative Speeches

Audience Type	Strategies
Interested but uninformed	• Provide basic information in clear, simple language. • Avoid jargon, define technical terms. • Use examples and narratives for amplification. • When communicating complicated information, use analogies, metaphors and/or presentation aids. • Use voice, gestures, and eye contact to reinforce meaning.
Interested and knowledgeable	• Establish your credibility early in the speech. • Acknowledge diverse perspectives on topic. • Go into depth with information and expert testimony. • Offer engaging presentation that keeps focus on content.
Uninterested	• Show listeners what's in it for them. • Keep presentation short and to the point. • Use sufficient examples and narratives to arouse and sustain interest. • Use eye-catching presentation aids and colorful language. • Make a dynamic presentation.
Unsympathetic (toward topic)	• Show respect for listeners and their point of view. • Cite sources the audience will respect. • Present information to enlarge listeners' understanding. • Develop stories and examples to arouse favorable feeling. • Make a warm, engaging presentation.
Distrustful (of speaker)	• Establish your credibility early in the speech. • Rely heavily on factual examples and expert testimony. • Cite sources of information in your presentation. • Be straightforward, business-like, and personable. • Keep good eye contact with listeners.

Visual learners are best served by demonstrations, pictures, and models.

your topic, how interested they may be in it, what preconceptions they may have about it that might help or hinder your purpose, and how they regard you as a speaker. These basic audience considerations can help you select strategies for your presentation. Figure 12.2 charts these audience considerations and directs you to possible strategies.

As an informative speaker, you need to apply basic principles of learning to make your speeches effective. To help your listeners learn and remember your message, you must motivate them by establishing its relevance to their lives, holding their attention throughout your message, and structuring your speech so that it is easily understood. You should also keep in mind that there are different types of intelligences and learning styles.[2] For example, some people are aural learners who learn well through lectures. Others are print learners who learn better when they see things in writing. These people respond well to charts and textual graphics. A third group, visual learners, need something to watch and are best served by demonstrations, pictures, and models. The more you can tap into the sensory modalities that are involved in these various learning styles, the better you can serve the needs of a wider population of listeners.

Ask students to recall their most effective teachers. How did these instructors share knowledge with their classes? What characteristics and techniques of their teaching might serve as models for better informative speeches?

Motivation

To motivate listeners, you must tell them why your message is important to them. In Chapter 4 we discussed motivation as a factor in audience analysis. Now we consider motivation in terms of giving listeners a reason to learn. Ask yourself why listeners would want to know what you have to tell them. Will it help them understand and control the world around them? Will it satisfy their curiosity? Will it improve their health, safety, or general well-being? Will it give them a sense of making a contribution by caring for others? Will it help them establish better relations with family and friends? Will it give them a sense of accomplishment and achievement, thus enhancing their personal growth? Will it contribute to the restoration of moral balance and fairness in the world? Will it provide them with enjoyment? Go back over the motivations discussed in Chapter 4 and determine which of these are most relevant to your topic and your audience. Then frame your speech so that it connects with these needs.

For example, you might relate a speech on how to interview for a job to the needs for control and independence. You could begin by talking about the problem of finding a good job in today's marketplace and provide an example that illustrates how a successful interview can make the difference in who gets hired and who does not. As you preview the body of your speech, you might say, "Today, I'm going to describe four factors that can determine whether you get the job of your dreams. First, . . ." In this case you have given your audience a reason for wanting to listen to the rest of your speech. You have begun the learning process by motivating your listeners.

Attention

Once you have established the importance of your message, you must hold your listeners' attention throughout your speech. In Chapter 7 we discussed how to attract audience attention in the introduction of your speech. Here we focus on how to sustain that interest. You can do so by applying one or more of the six factors that affect attention: *intensity*, *repetition*, *novelty*, *activity*, *contrast*, and *relevance*.

Intensity. An object is intense to the extent that it contrasts with a less intense background. Our eyes are drawn to bright lights, and we are startled by loud noises. In speeches, intense language and vivid images can be used to attract and hold attention. You can emphasize a point by using examples that magnify its importance. You can also achieve intensity through the use of presentation aids and by vocal emphasis and variety. Note how Stephen Huff holds attention through the intensity of his descriptions of the New Madrid earthquakes that struck the southcentral United States in the early nineteenth century:

> **The Indians tell of the night that lasted for a week and the way the "Father of Waters"—the Mississippi River—ran backward. Waterfalls were formed on the river. Islands disappeared. Land that was once in Arkansas ended up in Tennessee. Cracks up to ten feet wide opened and closed in the earth. Geysers squirted sand high into the air. Whole forests sank into the earth as the land turned to quicksand.**

Speakers who gesture sustain attention.

InterConnections.LearnMore 12.1

LEARNING STYLES

Index of Learning Styles **http://www2.ncsu.edu/unity/lockers/users/f/felder/public/ILSpage.html**
Links to learning-style sites and a self-administered, computer-scored quiz that reflects four dimensions of learning: active vs. reflective, sensing vs. intuitive, visual vs. verbal, and sequential vs. global; developed by Professor Emeritus Richard Felder of North Carolina State University.

Multiple Intelligence and Adult Learning **http://www.literacynet.org/diversity/**
Relates information on multiple intelligences to adult learning situations; explanatory articles and links to other sources and programs; developed by Leslie Shelton, director of Project Read: Multiple Intelligence for Adult Literacy and Adult Education.

Seven Perceptual Styles **http://www.learningstyles.org/SevenStylesOverview.htm**
Overview of the seven ways people learn: print, aural, interactive, visual, haptic (touch), kinesthetic, and olfactory; sponsored by the Institute for Learning Styles Research.

Repetition. Repeated sounds, words, or phrases attract and hold attention. Skillful speakers may repeat key words or phrases to emphasize points, help listeners follow the flow of ideas, and embed their messages in audience memory.

As we saw in Chapter 10, repetition underlies alliteration and parallel construction. Alliteration lends vividness to main ideas: "Today, I will discuss how the *M*ississippi River *m*eanders from *M*innesota to the sea." The repetition of the *m* sound catches attention and emphasizes the statement. Similarly, parallel construction establishes a pattern that sticks in the mind. Repeated questions and answers such as "What is our goal? It is to . . ." sustain attention.

Watch videotaped informative speeches and discuss how well the speakers motivate listeners, gain and hold attention, and encourage retention of their messages.

Novelty. We are attracted to anything new or unusual. A novel phrase can fascinate listeners and hold their attention. In a speech on environmental stewardship, Jim Cardoza found a novel way to describe the magnitude of pollution. After reporting that 19 million tons of garbage are picked up each year along the nation's beaches, he concluded: "And that's just the tip of the wasteberg." His invented word, *wasteberg*, reminded listeners of *iceberg* and suggested the vastness of the problem. Some famous novel expressions in American history that have aroused attention for political programs and philosophies are "New Deal," "the New Frontier," and "the Great Society."

Activity. As we noted in Chapter 11, anything that moves attracts attention. Gesturing, approaching the audience to add emphasis to a point, and referring to presentation aids can all add activity. An exciting story or example can also bring a speech to life and attract attention. You can further create a sense of activity by using vivid words, rhythm, and vocal variety. Note the sense of action and urgency in the conclusion of this student's speech:

> **I don't know what you're going to do, but I know what I'm going to do. I'm going to march. I'm going to march down tomorrow and register to vote. There's too much at stake not to. Won't you march with me?**

Contrast. Opposites attract attention. If you work in a noisy environment and it suddenly becomes quiet, the stillness can seem deafening. Similarly, abrupt changes in your pitch or rate of speaking will draw attention. Presenting the pros and cons of a situation creates a sense of conflict and drama that listeners often find arresting. You can also highlight contrasts by speaking of such opposites as life and death, light and dark, or the highs and lows of a situation.

In a speech dramatizing the need to learn more about AIDS, a speaker introduced two or three specific examples with the statement "Let me introduce you to *Death*." Then, as the speech moved to the promise of medical research, she said, "Now let me introduce you to *Life*." This usage combined repetition and contrast to create a dramatic effect.

Surprise is necessary for contrast to be effective. Once people become accustomed to an established pattern, they no longer think about it. They notice any abrupt, dramatic change from the pattern.

Relevance. Things that relate to our specific needs, interests, or concerns hold our attention. Note how Allison McIntyre created relevance for her agenda-setting speech on smoking advertisements by placing a large jar of cigarette butts on the table by the lectern.

> **So you think the cigarette advertisers are losing their fight to recruit smokers at American colleges and universities? Here's what I collected myself in about 45 minutes at noon yesterday, right around the outside of this building. These are our butts. Vanderbilt student butts. Think of all the damaged lungs these represent, right here in this building.**

The striking relevance of her presentation aid made it hard to ignore her speech.

Retention

Even the best information is useless unless your listeners remember and use it. Repetition, relevance, and structural factors can all be used to help your audience remember your message. The more frequently we hear or see anything, the more likely we are to retain it. This is why advertisers bombard us with slogans to keep their product names in our consciousness. These slogans may be repeated in all of their advertisements, regardless of the visuals or narratives presented. The repetition of key words or phrases in a speech also helps the audience remember. In his famous civil rights speech in Washington, D.C., Martin Luther King's repetition of the phrase "I have a dream . . ." became the hallmark of the speech and is now used as its title.

Relevance is also important to retention. Our minds filter incoming information, associating it with things we already know and evaluating it for its potential usefulness. *If you want listeners to remember your message, tell them why and how it relates to their lives.*

Structural factors also affect how well a message is retained. Previews, summaries, and clear transitions can help your audience remember your message. The way you organize your material also affects retention. Suppose you were given the following list of words to memorize:

> **north, man, hat, daffodil, green, tulip, coat, boy, south, red, east, shoes, gardenia, woman, purple, marigold, gloves, girl, yellow, west**

It looks rather difficult, but look what happens when we rearrange the words:

> **north, south, east, west**
>
> **man, boy, woman, girl**
>
> **daffodil, tulip, gardenia, marigold**

Speaker's Notes 12.1

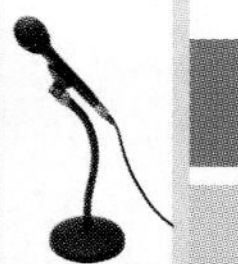

HELPING LISTENERS LEARN

1. Present your material in a fresh and interesting way.
2. Motivate listeners by showing them how they can benefit from your information.
3. Maintain attention with vivid examples and exciting stories.
4. Organize your material clearly to make it easy to remember.
5. Use strategic repetition to embed your ideas in the minds of listeners.
6. Provide previews and summaries to aid retention.

green, red, purple, yellow

hat, coat, shoes, gloves

In the first example, you have what looks like a random list of words. In the second, the words have been organized by categories: Now you have five groups of four related words to remember. Material that is presented in a consistent and orderly fashion is much easier for your audience to retain. In the remainder of this chapter, we look at the major types of informative speeches and the design formats that are most often used to structure informative messages.

Types of Informative Speeches

As we mentioned earlier, the major purpose of an informative speech is to share knowledge in order to expand your listeners' understanding or competence. To meet this challenge, an informative speech will typically describe, demonstrate, or explain its subject. These different procedures divide informative speaking into types. As we discuss them, we will also consider briefings as an important subtype of informative speaking.

Speeches of Description

Often the specific purpose of a speech is to describe a particular activity, object, person, or place. A **speech of description** should give the audience a clear picture of your subject. Effective description relies heavily on the artful use of language. The words must be clear, concrete, and colorful to carry both the substance and feeling of the message. The speech "The 'Monument' at Wounded Knee" in Appendix C provides vivid word-pictures. Thus, the landscape is not simply desolate; it is characterized by "flat, sun-baked fields and an occasional eroded gully." The speaker goes on to describe the monument:

Have students describe a monument or place in their hometown or home country. Focus on how well they use language that is clear, concrete, and colorful. Are listeners left with striking images in their minds?

> **The monument itself rests on a concrete slab to the right of the grave. It's a typical, large, old-fashioned granite cemetery marker, a pillar about six feet high topped with an urn—the kind of gravestone you might see in any**

The speech of demonstration shows the audience how to do something.

> **cemetery with graves from the turn of the century. The inscription tells us that it was erected by the families of those who were killed at Wounded Knee. Weeds grow through the cracks in the concrete at its base.**

The topic, purpose, and materials selected for a descriptive speech should suggest the appropriate design. The "Monument" speech follows a spatial pattern. Other designs that may be used for speeches of description include sequential, chronological, categorical, and comparative designs, which are discussed later in this chapter.

Speeches of Demonstration

The **speech of demonstration** shows the audience how to do something. Dance instructors teach us the Texas two-step. Others may tell us how to access the Internet, or how to prepare for the Law School Admission Test, or even how to build a fire. The tip-off to the speech of demonstration is the phrase *"how to."* What these examples have in common is that they demonstrate a process.

Successful speeches of demonstration empower listeners so that they can perform the process themselves. Jeffrey O'Connor gave his University of New Mexico classmates some vital how-to information as he demonstrated the process of reading a textbook efficiently. He took them through a five-step tour of the process, each step representing a main point of his speech. His presentation, outlined later in this chapter, follows a sequential design.

Another form of speech of demonstration is illustrated by a speech first presented by Suzanne Jones at the University of Memphis. Suzanne took her listeners on a verbal tour of Yellowstone Park, showing them how to access major attractions there. Her speech, which we shall also see outlined later, employs a spatial design.

Many hardware suppliers have videos to demonstrate how to use a tool. Borrow one of these videos from a local store to show in class. Discuss how well the tape works as a speech of demonstration and which of its techniques might be useful in classroom speeches.

Most speeches of demonstration are helped by the use of presentation aids. The aids can take the form of objects that are used in a process, slides that reveal the steps in a process in the order in which they occur, or the speaker's actual performance of the process or activity. If you are preparing a speech of demonstration, review the materials on presentation aids in Chapter 9 to determine what you could use to help your audience better understand your message. When you are demonstrating a process, "show and tell" is usually much more effective than just telling.

Speeches of Explanation

A **speech of explanation** offers information about subjects that are abstract or complicated. Such a speech often makes use of categorical design to break down a complex subject into its parts. It may also favor comparative design to associate the unknown with the known. The speech of explanation may also emphasize causation design to account for the origins of a subject or to predict its future. Katherine Rowan, a communication scholar at Purdue University, suggests that a speech of explanation should

1. set forth the critical features of the subject.
2. compare an example with a nonexample. (Show an instance that *could* be considered an example but is not.)
3. provide additional examples to reinforce what listeners have learned.[3]

In a speech explaining statistical illusions, Stephen Lee noted that when military personnel were added to the figures used to compute unemployment statistics, the rate of unemployment went down. But did the actual number of the unemployed go down? Here is how Stephen explained this problem:

> **Look at what happened to the number. It changed. Look at what happened to the way the number was computed. It changed, too. But what happened to the problem of civilian unemployment, which we all assume this number to represent? It had not changed at all. It all goes back to what Lester T. Thurow said in his basic theory of economics, "A difference is only a difference if it truly makes a difference." Many times a difference in a number does not represent a difference in the real world.[4]**

Speeches of explanation face an even greater challenge when their information runs counter to generally accepted beliefs. Rowan provides an example of how this can work in public safety campaigns:

> **A particularly resilient obstacle to [seat] belt use is the erroneous but prevalent belief that hitting one's head on a windshield while traveling at 30 miles per hour is an experience much like doing so when a car is stationary. . . . If people understood that the experience would be much more similar to falling from a three-story building and hitting the pavement face first, one obstacle to the wearing of seat belts would be easier to overcome.[5]**

As her example indicates, dramatic analogies—such as comparing an auto accident at thirty miles per hour to falling from a building—can help break through our resistance to new ideas that defy folk wisdom. Rowan also recommends that speakers

1. state the prevalent view.
2. acknowledge its apparent legitimacy.
3. demonstrate its inadequacy.
4. show the superiority of the expert view.

The use of strategic comparisons and contrasts can help listeners accept new information and use it in their lives.

Briefings

A **briefing** is a short informative presentation in an organizational setting. Briefings often take place during meetings, as when employees gather at the

Informative presentations are basic to many employee training programs.

beginning of a workday to learn about plans or policy changes.[6] At such a meeting you might be asked to give a status report on a project. Briefings also take place in one-on-one situations, as when you report to your supervisor at work. They can occur as a press briefing, after a crisis or major event occurs.[7] Often a question-and-answer period will follow the briefing.

Although briefings occur frequently in organizations, they are not often done well. Most how-to books on communicating in organizations deplore the lack of brevity, clarity, and directness in presentations.[8] When executives in eighteen organizations were asked, "What makes a poor presentation?" they responded with the following list of descriptions:

- It is poorly organized.
- It is not well delivered.
- It contains too much jargon.
- It is too long.
- It lacks examples or comparisons.[9]

This situation offers you quite an opportunity. Develop the art of the briefing, and you will be valued in your organization. The following rules should guide your preparation:

First, a briefing should be what its name suggests: brief. Cut out any material that is not related directly to your main points. Keep your introduction and conclusions short. Begin with a preview and end with a summary.

Second, organize your ideas before you open your mouth. How can you possibly be organized when you are called on without warning in a meeting to "tell us about your project"? The answer is simple. Prepare in advance (Also, see our guidelines for making an impromptu presentation in Chapter 11). *Never go into any meeting in which there is even the slightest possibility that you might be asked to report without a skeleton outline of a presentation.* Select a simple design and make a key-word outline of points you would cover and the order in which you would cover them. Put this outline on a note card and carry it in your pocket. Your supervisors and colleagues will be impressed with your foresight.

Third, rely heavily on facts and figures, expert testimony, and short examples for supporting materials. Don't drift off into long stories. Use comparison and contrast to make your points clearly and directly.

Speaker's Notes 12.2

PREPARING FOR A BRIEFING

1. Always be prepared to report in a meeting.
2. Keep your remarks short and to the point.
3. Start with a preview and end with a summary.
4. Have no more than three main points.
5. Use facts and figures, expert testimony, and brief examples to support your points.
6. Avoid technical jargon.
7. Present your report with assurance.
8. Be ready to answer tough questions.

Fourth, adapt your language to your audience. If you are an engineer reporting on a project to a group of managers, use the language of management, not the language of engineering. Tell them what they need to know in language they can understand. Relate the subject to what they already know.

Fifth, present your message with confidence. Be sure everyone can see and hear you. Stand up, if necessary. Look listeners in the eye. Speak firmly with an air of assurance. After all, the project is yours, and you are the expert on it.

Finally, be prepared to answer tough questions. Respond forthrightly and honestly. No one likes bad news, but worse news will come if you don't deliver the bad news to those who need to know it *when* they need to know it. Review our suggestions for handling question-and-answer sessions in Chapter 11.

Speech Designs

There are six major design formats that are appropriate for most informative speeches: spatial, sequential, chronological, categorical, comparative, and causation. These designs may also be used in persuasive and ceremonial speeches.

The IRM, Speech Preparation Workbook, and Speech Designer contain outline worksheets, outline checklists, and sample outlines for each of the major design formats. Consult and use these resources to clarify any questions that arise in this section.

Spatial Design

A **spatial design** is appropriate for speeches that develop their topics within a physical setting. Because the order of discussion is based on the nearness of things to one another, the pattern follows the principle of proximity, discussed in Chapter 7. Suppose someone asked you to name the time zones in the United States. If you live in Washington, D.C., you would probably reply, "Eastern, Central, Mountain, and Pacific." If you live in Oregon, you might answer, "Pacific, Mountain, Central, and Eastern."[10] Either answer would follow a spatial pattern, taking where you are as the point of reference.

Most people are familiar with maps and can readily visualize directions. A speech using a spatial design provides listeners with an oral map. Spatial designs are especially useful for speeches of description, so that listeners can visualize clearly the physical relationships of objects to one another. To develop a spatial

A spatial design works in speeches that follow a pattern of places as they develop their topics.

design that is easy for listeners to follow, select a starting point and then take your audience on an *orderly*, systematic journey to a destination. Once you begin a pattern of movement, stay with it to the end of the speech. If you change directions in the middle, the audience may get lost. Be sure to complete the pattern so that you satisfy listeners' desire for closure.

Ask students to present an oral map of their hometowns, pretending that they are offering a tour of major attractions to tourists. Have listeners sketch the outline of the tour. How well do these sketches follow the oral directions? How might these oral maps have produced more accurate sketches?

The body of a speech using a spatial design might have the following general format:

> *Preview:* When you visit Yellowstone, stop first at the South Entrance Visitor's Center, then drive northwest to Old Faithful, north to Mammoth Hot Springs, and then southeast to the Grand Canyon of the Yellowstone.
>
> I. Your first stop should be at the South Entrance Visitor's Center.
>   A. Talk with a park ranger to help plan your trip.
>   B. Attend a lecture or film to orient yourself.
>   C. Pick up materials and maps to make your tour more meaningful.
>
> II. Drive northwest through the Geyser Valley to Old Faithful.
>   A. Hike the boardwalks in the Upper Geyser Basin.
>   B. Join the crowds waiting for Old Faithful to erupt on schedule.
>   C. Have lunch at Old Faithful Inn.
>
> III. Continue north to Mammoth Hot Springs.
>   A. Plan to spend the night at the lodge or in one of the cabins.
>   B. Attend the evening lectures or films on the history of the park.
>
> IV. Drive southeast to the Grand Canyon of the Yellowstone.
>   A. Take in the view from Inspiration Point.
>   B. Hike down the trail for a better view of the waterfalls.

Sequential Design

A spatial design moves listeners through space: a **sequential design** moves them through time. Speeches built on sequential design typically present the steps in a process, especially appropriate to a speech of demonstration. You begin by identifying the necessary steps in the process and the order in which they must take place. These steps become the main points of your speech. In a short presentation, you should have no more than five steps as main points. If you have more, try to cluster some of them into subpoints. It is also helpful to number the steps as you make your presentation.

The following abbreviated outline, developed by Jeffrey O'Connor, illustrates a sequential design:

Preview: The five steps of efficient textbook reading include skimming, reading, rereading, reciting, and reviewing.

I. First, *skim* through the chapter to get the overall picture.
  A. Identify the major ideas from the section headings.
  B. Read any summary statements.
  C. Read any boxed materials.
  D. Make a key-word outline of major topics.

II. Second, *read* the chapter a section at a time.
  A. Make notes in the margins on questions you have.
  B. Look up definitions of unfamiliar words.
  C. Go back and highlight the major ideas.

III. Third, *reread* the chapter.
  A. Fill in your outline with more detail.
  B. Try to answer the questions you wrote in the margin.
  C. Frame questions for your instructor on anything you don't understand.

IV. Fourth, *recite* what you have read.
  A. Use your outline to make an oral presentation to yourself.
  B. Explain the material to someone else.

V. Finally, *review* the material within twenty-four hours.
  A. Review your outline.
  B. Reread the highlighted material.

Presenting the steps in this orderly, sequential way helped Jeffrey "walk and talk" his listeners through the process.

Chronological Design

The **chronological design**, closely related to the sequential design, follows the sequence of important events in the history of a subject. The design provides an interesting option in developing speeches of explanation. You may start with the beginnings of the subject and trace it up to the present through its defining moments. Or, you may start with the present and trace the subject back to its origins. To keep your listeners' attention and to meet time requirements, you must be selective. Choose landmark events as the main points in your message and arrange them in their natural order. A speech on the evolution of the T-shirt using chronological design might be structured as follows:

Preview: The T-shirt began its life as an undergarment, developed into a bearer of messages, and has emerged as high-fashion apparel.

I. The T-shirt originated as an undergarment early in the twentieth century.
  A. The first undershirts with sleeves were designed for sailors, to spare sensitive people the sight of hairy armpits.
  B. They were first sold commercially in the late 1930s.

C. During World War II, T-shirts were used as outerwear in the tropics.

II. After World War II, civilians began using T-shirts as outerwear.
  A. They were comfortable and absorbent.
  B. They were popularized in movies like *Rebel Without a Cause*.
  C. They were easy to care for.

III. T-shirts soon became embellished with pictures and messages.
  A. Children's T-shirts had pictures of cartoon characters.
  B. Adult T-shirt designs were usually related to sports teams.
  C. T-shirts soon were used for "political" statements.
    1. Peace symbols were popular during the 1960s.
    2. Slogans such as "A Woman's Place Is in the House (and in the Senate)" appeared during the 1970s.

IV. Today's T-shirts are unique.
  A. You can customize a message.
  B. You can put your picture on a T-shirt.
  C. You can buy bejeweled T-shirts.

Categorical Design

The **categorical design** is useful to discuss subjects that have natural or customary divisions. Natural divisions may exist within the subject itself, such as

FIGURE 12.3
What Speech Designs to Use When

Design	Use When
Spatial	Your topic can be discussed by how it is positioned in a physical setting or natural environment. It allows you to take your audience on an orderly "oral tour" of your topic.
Sequential	Your topic can be arranged by time. It is useful for describing a process as a series of steps or explaining a subject as a series of developments.
Chronological	Your topic can be discussed as a historical development through certain defining moments.
Categorical	Your topic has natural or customary divisions. Each category becomes a main point for development. It is useful when you need to organize large amounts of material.
Comparative	Your topic is new to your audience, abstract, technical, or simply difficult to comprehend. It helps make material more meaningful by comparing or contrasting it with something the audience already knows and understands.
Causation	Your topic is best understood in terms of its underlying causes or consequences. May be used to account for the present or predict future possibilities.

red, white, and blended wines. Customary divisions represent typical ways of thinking about a subject, such as the four food groups that are essential to a healthy diet. Categories are the mind's way of ordering the world by seeking patterns within it or by supplying patterns to arrange it. Categories help us sort out information so that we can make sense of it. They are especially useful in speeches of explanation.

Each category in the design becomes a main point for development. For a short presentation you should limit the number of categories to four or at most five. Any subject that breaks out into six or more categories will be too complex for most classroom speeches. If you have too many categories, try to cluster some of them as a single main point. If you cannot condense your categories into a manageable number, you should consider other ways to approach your topic.

In her informative speech on child abuse, Amanda Watkins discussed four major categories of child abuse. Following is an abbreviated outline of the body of her speech:

Preview: Four types of child abuse are physical abuse, neglect, sexual abuse, and mental abuse.

I. Physical abuse involves inflicting bodily harm on a child.
  A. This may result from overdiscipline.
  B. There may be no intent to harm the child.
  C. Symptoms may include:
    1. Frequent bruises
    2. Fright in the presence of the abuser
    3. Protest over having to go home
    4. Sudden change in school performance

II. Abusive neglect means failure to provide basic care.
  A. Physical needs, e.g., health care, are neglected.
  B. Truancy represents educational neglect.
  C. Emotional neglect occurs when child is ignored.
  D. Symptoms of neglect may include:
    1. Child is frequently absent from school.
    2. Child is often dirty or smells bad.
    3. Child reports no caregiver at home.

III. Sexual abuse can involve any form of sexual exploitation.
  A. Sexual abuse may be committed by the caregiver.
  B. Sexual abuse is typically underreported because of shame or threats.
  C. Symptoms of sexual abuse may include:
    1. Difficulty walking or sitting
    2. Shying away from any physical contact
    3. Attempting to run away

IV. Mental abuse involves emotional, verbal, and psychological abuse.
  A. This can have serious behavioral or cognitive impact.
  B. Sometimes involves unusual forms of torment
  C. Symptoms of mental abuse may include:
    1. Behavioral withdrawal
    2. Regression to immature behavior
    3. Aggression toward other children

The Student Speeches Video contains several informative speeches and the Guide to the Video Program analyzes their designs. Show one of these speeches in class, then elicit suggestions as to how its design might be improved.

Comparative Design

Ask ESL students to develop a speech in which they compare and contrast a specific custom, law, or practice in this country with its equivalent in their homeland. Have them explain the significance of the cultural similarities and differences they discover.

A **comparative design** is useful when a topic is unfamiliar, abstract, technical, or difficult to understand. It can also help you describe dramatic changes in a subject. Comparative designs aid comprehension by relating the topic to something the audience knows and understands. They can be especially useful in speeches of explanation and briefings. Three basic variations of the comparative design are literal analogy, figurative analogy, and comparison and contrast.

In a **literal analogy**, the subjects compared are drawn from the same field of experience. One student compared the game of rugger as played in his native Sri Lanka to the American game of football. Since both rugger and football are contact sports, the comparison between them was literal.

In a **figurative analogy**, the subjects are drawn from different fields of experience. Paul Ashdown, a professor of journalism at the University of Tennessee, used an extended figurative analogy comparing the World Wide Web to America's "Wild West."[11] Another example of a figurative analogy could relate the body's struggle against infection to a military campaign. In such a design, the speaker might identify the nature of the armies, the ways they fight, and the consequences of defeat and victory. Both literal and figurative analogy designs can be insightful and imaginative, helping listeners see subjects in surprising, revealing ways. But if the comparison seems strained or far-fetched, the speech will collapse and the speaker's ethos will be damaged.

A **comparison and contrast** design points out the similarities and/or differences between subjects or ideas. In this design, each similarity or difference becomes a main point. In the interest of simplicity, you should limit yourself to five or fewer points of similarity and difference in a short presentation. The following example places the emphasis on contrast as it designs the body of a speech:

Preview: Over four decades—from the 1960s to the turn of the century—the women we saw in advertisements changed.

I. The products they advertised changed.
   A. In the 1960s, most women were pitching products in the kitchen or bathroom.
   B. By the year 2000, more women were selling high-ticket items.

II. Women began to appear in different roles.
   A. In the 1960s, most women were shown in domestic (wife/mother) roles.
   B. By the year 2000, more women were shown in professional roles.

III. The apparent ages of women also changed.
   A. In the 1960s, most women in ads appeared to be under thirty.
   B. By the year 2000, older women were well represented in ads.

IV. The attitude toward women in ads also changed.
   A. In the 1960s, most women were portrayed as dumb and dependent.
   B. By the year 2000, more women were portrayed as intelligent and independent.

Causation Design

A **causation design**, often used in speeches of explanation, interprets a subject either as an effect of certain causes or as the cause of certain effects. The speaker usually begins by describing the subject and its importance, then either asks how it came about or what its consequences may be. The major causes or consequences become main points in the body of the speech.

Speeches that use the causation design are subject to one serious drawback—the tendency to oversimplify. Any complex situation will generally have many underlying causes. And any given set of conditions may lead to many different future effects. Be wary of overly simple explanations and overly confident predictions. Such explanations and predictions are one form of faulty reasoning (fallacy), discussed further in Chapter 14.

Martin Lenzini announced at the outset of his informative speech that his research had revealed the existence of a new wonder drug—the aspirin! In his speech based on causation design, Martin discussed aspirin therapy as the cause of many possible consequences.

Preview: A little aspirin could have a large impact on your health.

I. Daily small doses can benefit your heart
- A. Reduces risk of first heart attack by 44%
- B. Lowers chance of second heart attack by 30%
- C. Reduces risk of death during heart attack by 23%

II. Daily doses can also prevent certain cancers
- A. Lowers risk of colon cancer by 40 to 50%
- B. Reduces esophageal cancer by 80 to 90%
- C. Lowers ovarian cancer by 25%

III. Daily doses offer other great possible benefits
- A. Reduces risk of stroke by 25%
- B. Helps the brain by countering dementia and Alzheimer's

IV. Daily doses could also have negative consequences
- A. Can cause serious gastrointestinal bleeding
- B. Takes wounds longer to stop bleeding
- C. Could encourage another kind of stroke
- D. May be of less benefit to women

V. Ask your doctor whether these cause-effect ratios might work for you

Notice that Martin grouped the possible consequences of aspirin therapy into categories within his overall causation design. This mixture of design elements provides a transition into our next topic.

Combined Speech Designs

Although we have presented these designs as simple, basic patterns, effective speeches sometimes combine two or more of them. Combined designs may be appropriate when you want to describe a subject and provide an explanation for it in the same speech. In such speeches, spatial or sequential designs may be linked with categorical or causation designs. The time constraints for most classroom speeches prevent you from developing elaborate, combined designs for most subjects, but occasionally such combinations are both practical and desirable. If you believe that a combined design will work best for your material, first be sure you have time to develop it, and then plan carefully so that you do not confuse listeners as you move from one pattern to another.

Have students analyze the speech at the end of this chapter and other informative speeches in Appendix C in terms of the designs used.

Karen Lovelace wanted her classmates to understand that those who suffer from muscular dystrophy are also victims of insensitivity from their fellow citizens. She used a combined sequential and categorical design to convey her message. In the first part of her speech, she described a day she spent with her wheelchair-bound friend, Donald Morgan. Their day began in his apartment, which is retrofitted so that he can live comfortably. As soon as she and Donald

SAMPLE INFORMATIVE SPEECH

What Friends Are All About

Marie D'Aniello

■ *Marie opens her speech of explanation with a narrative that gains attention by arousing curiosity: What happened in the truck? Why were Cammy and Joe singing? Quickly she shifts that attention to the focus of her speech.*

■ *Throughout her opening, Marie leaves listeners waiting for a direct statement of her purpose. It soon becomes clear that she wants to share ideas and deepen audience understanding. She encourages attention by her interactive orientation: note the frequent use of "we" and how she invites listeners to "think about" their own friendships. She also sold this speech by her warm, vital manner of presentation. She stood in front of the lectern near listeners to encourage identification.*

■ *In her preview, Marie promises to follow a chronological design that will trace "the saga of friendship" to the point of young adulthood. Since this was where her listeners found themselves, the plan offered a then-to-now time pattern. Throughout the speech, she uses simple, clear language to make her points. She has researched her speech diligently, but she needs to establish the credentials of her experts and to document her evidence more carefully.*

It's nine o'clock at night. I'm curled up in the back seat of a new truck and my friends, Cammy and Joe, are in the front singing along with the radio. As I listen to them sing, and I'm lying there, I start to think about my life and all the changes that have occurred in the past year. A year ago I didn't even know who Cammy and Joe were. And now they're two of my dearest friends. It makes me think about friendship and its meaning.

According to Webster's dictionary, to be a friend means that you're someone who someone else feels comfortable with and is fond of. But friendship is so much more than that. According to Plato, true friendship rises out of basic human needs and desires, such as striving for goodness, reaching out to others, and seeking self-understanding. And loving and being loved. Friendship should benefit all who are involved in it and should occur between people who value each other's good qualities. As human beings we need friends in order to survive and grow.

Through our friends we learn who we are, and what we like and don't like. We learn about strengths we never knew we had, weaknesses that maybe we can overcome. Think about your friendships. I'll bet you've learned a great deal and grown a great deal because of them.

If you're like me you probably have one or two really close friends and a lot of great acquaintances. But that's what you need. According to Dr. John Litwac of the University of Massachusetts medical center, people in modern society require a variety of friends to meet their needs. And the variety of friends we need varies over time. In the book *Adult Friendship*, Dr. Litwac says that the friendships we enjoy when we are young differ from those we experience as we grow older. As we develop, so does the complexity and intimacy of our relationships.

In this speech I'm going to take you through the development of friendship, beginning in childhood, and going up through adolescence all the way to young adulthood. I'm going to talk about how we define our friends, the roles that friends play in our lives, and the effect conflicts have on friendship during each stage.

The saga of friendship begins when we are quite young. And the concepts we have of friendship change dramatically over the first decade of life. Psychologists classify childhood as the stage occurring between the ages of 4 and 10. During childhood our friends are those whom we have the most contact with, the children we play with. In childhood that's what friendship is all about. According to Dr. William Rawlings, friendships exist while children are playing together. For example, when I was in kindergarten, I was friends with Michelle when we were playing tag. But the next day I would go and play with others and make friends with them. The friendship vanished until the next time we played together. It had little to do with who Michelle really was. She was simply there and I could play with her.

But when we play as children, we're not only having fun, we're also learning how to assimilate into society and how to develop more lasting friendships. We learn to inhibit our actions, to deal with other people's emotions, and to follow rules. Because we're just starting out and just trying to figure out how everything works, we may run into a lot of conflicts with our friendships during childhood. We may get into silly fights about whose toy is this and whose toy is that, but the fights don't usually last very long and can be resolved fairly easily. Behavior is based on the moment, and the moment turns on what things appear to be.

During childhood, friendship often depends on looks. Maybe that's why some children are so popular and others are ignored. In fact, a study conducted by Dr. William Lipit concluded that children between the ages of 4 to 9 base their descriptions of their friends completely on their looks. That may be sad, but it's just the way it is. Think of this as a phase in the process of growing up.

At the end of childhood, friends become more than just playmates. They're people who share our interests—they're the ones we share our feelings with. Play becomes less, talk becomes more important. Friendship evolves steadily to a new level, called adolescence.

■ *Marie relies especially on examples for her supporting material. In her first main point, she draws on personal experience. In the second main point, she invites listeners to supply examples from their own experience. She uses rhetorical questions to highlight the points and stimulate reflection. She also uses the contrast between play and talk to underscore the difference between the childhood and adolescent phases of friendship.*

I'm sure you remember adolescence. It usually occurs between the ages of 11 and 17. As we live through it, friendship involves revealing and discussing one's personal thoughts and feelings. Just talking can be more important than anything, especially for girls. Boys, male friendships, still involve a good deal of activity, as in organized sports, but even here there is more verbal communication than before. The critical task of adolescence is to develop one's identity, and friends are crucial in that respect. Dr. Graham Allen observes in the book *Friendship* that people in adolescence, more than at any other time in their lives, need to share strong, often confusing emotions. Did you have a best friend in junior high school? A very special friend you would sit and talk with on the phone for hours on end? Well if you did, that's good, that's normal. According to Dr. Allen, that's what you needed.

Think back. Think back to friendship pins, and side ponytails and matching outfits, and sleep-over parties. Think of your first best friend. That person probably knew more about you than anyone in the whole world. She or he was probably your age, in your class, lived near you, and shared your social status. In adolescence we seek out those who are like us because they make us feel more normal. Because the level of intimacy is so much greater in adolescence, the potential for conflict and jealousy also increases. There's so much emotion at stake that an argument in adolescence can easily ruin a friendship. The way we learn to deal with such problems in adolescence prepares us for young adulthood.

Now young adulthood is classified as the stage between 18 and 24, the stage we're all in now. Here at Vanderbilt and I suppose elsewhere, a "friend" can mean many things. Friends can be playmates, confidants, lovers, listeners. Rosemary Adams, writing in the book *Adult Friendship*, tells us that during the college years friends can provide crucial input regarding self-conceptions, career options, and recreational activities. Patterns of friendship vary a lot, and we have many different types of friends. We have party friends. We have classroom friends. And then we have our good, good friends. But you need all of those kinds of friends as you grow older because you are becoming a more complex individual.

■ *In her final main point, Marie continues to engage listeners directly by asking rhetorical questions and by inviting them to consider their own friendships. She also continues to rely heavily on expert testimony, which reflects favorably on her ethos and builds the credibility of her speech. The listener gains the impression that this speech builds on a foundation of responsible knowledge.*

Why do you like your good friends? Do you like them because of what they can do for you? Or do you like them because you can relate to them and share a bond with them? Our friends prevent us from being lonely. In fact 40 percent of college freshmen who reported they felt homesick also reported not having made new friends in college.

Why do some people make friends easily while others struggle to? Researchers speculate that how open and honest you are with others and how much you are willing to give of yourself can affect your forming friendships. Talking and sharing is important because it creates a sense of intimacy. Friendship also depends a great deal on attraction. Whatever attracts you to people is why you like them. Maybe you like people who smile a lot, or maybe you like those who are serious. Maybe you like people who are the complete opposite of you and who possess qualities you wish you had. Or maybe you like people who are just like you, who you feel you know inside and out.

When we're younger, friendships are based on what people appear to be. As we grow older, friendships are based more on what people really are. If you got in a fight with your best friend, would you tell him to hit the road? Chances are you'd probably try to work it out. As we get older, it's easier for us to accept differences in others. Serious betrayals could end friendships. But the researchers I read concluded that the older you get and the older the friendship is, the harder you will work to preserve it because it is all the more precious to you.

■ At this point, Marie reflects on the general meaning of her subject, signaling that she is moving into her conclusion. By citing Plato at the beginning of her speech and concluding with a quotation from Yeats, she dignifies her subject and emphasizes its importance in listeners' lives.

Friendship is hard to define and I think that's probably because it involves your heart and your soul. But out of all the research I've done and all the people I've talked to, no one said that they thought friendship was a bad thing. Of course there are downsides like peer pressure and conflict and sometimes stress, but 91 percent of the college freshmen studied by Dr. Adams felt that the benefits of friendship far outweigh the disadvantages. All I know is that from the day we're born until the day we die, other people affect the way we live. If we're lucky, maybe we'll come to know some of them as friends.

The dynamics of friendship change rapidly throughout our lives. During childhood, friendship is based on play, while in adolescence it turns more on emotion. In young adulthood I think friendship is based on a combination of acceptance, respect, and trust. I remember the words of William Butler Yeats, who said, "Think where man's glory most begins and ends. And say my glory was to have such friends."

WORKS CONSULTED

Blieszner, Rosemary, and Rebecca G. Adams. *Adult Friendship*. Newbury Park: Sage Publications, 1992.

Brenton, Myron. *Friendship*. New York: Stein and Day, 1974.

Cates, Diana Fritz. *Choosing to Feel: Virtue, Friendship and Compassion for Friends*. Notre Dame: University of Notre Dame Press, 1997.

Gilligan, Carol, Nona P. Lyons, and Trudy J. Hammer. *Making Connections: The Relational Worlds of Adolescent Girls at the Emma Willard School*. Cambridge: Harvard University Press, 1990.

Gottman, John M., and Jeffrey G. Parker. *Conversation of Friends: Speculations and Affective Development*. Cambridge: Cambridge University Press, 1986.

Griffiths, Vivienne. *Adolescent Girls and Their Friends*. Aldershot: Avebury, 1995.

Meyer, Luanna H., et al. *Making Friends*. Baltimore: Paul H. Brookes Publishing Co., 1998.

Rawlins, William K. *Friendship Matters*. New York: Aldine de Gruyter, 1992.

Web Sources:

The Friendship Page. http://www.geocities.com/Athens/Acropolis/9761/quofrend.html.

http://www.ozemail.com.

13

Persuasive Speaking

OUTLINE

THIS CHAPTER WILL HELP YOU

- grasp the nature of persuasion
- learn the functions of persuasive messages
- understand how persuasion works
- meet the challenges of persuasive speaking
- select a design for your persuasive speech

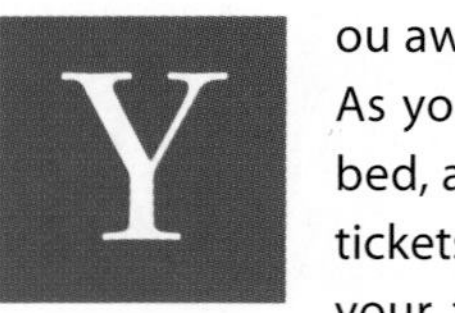

ou awaken to a world of persuasion. As you scramble sleepy-eyed out of bed, a DJ on the clock radio pushes tickets to a rock concert. As you brush your teeth, your roommate tries to convince you that a trip to Florida would be both fun and affordable. As you walk to class, someone hands you a pamphlet protesting the lack of adequate medical care on campus. Throughout your day, ads and pitches of all sorts contend for your attention.

You do your share of persuading too. You convince yourself not to listen to the Florida pitch. On the way back from class you stop to argue with the person handing out brochures about the politics of medical care. You put on your best outfit preparing for a job interview on campus, and you know that if you get the job, you'll constantly have to sell your ideas to others.

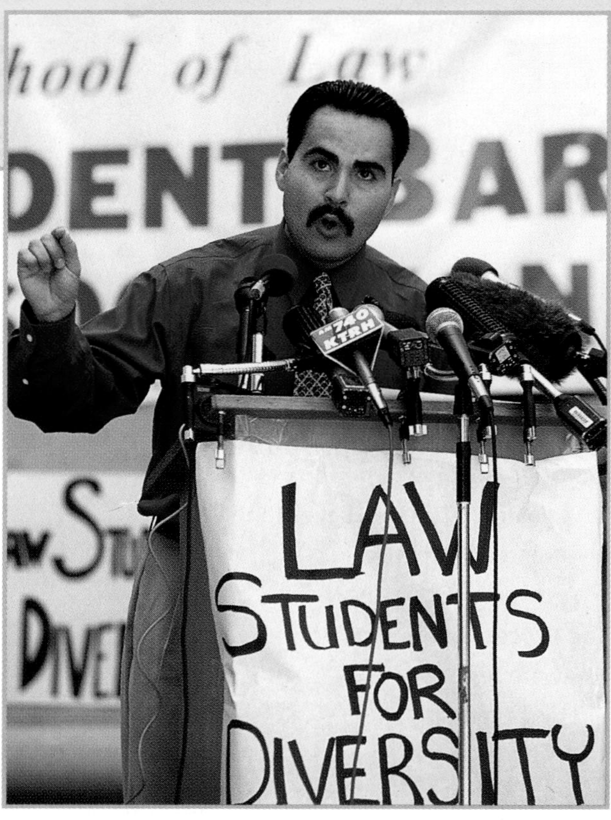

It is clear that in this world of competing interests, values, and agendas, persuasion is unavoidable. To live is to persuade and be persuaded. In such a world, **persuasion** is the art of gaining fair and favorable consideration for our points of view. When we speak, we try to influence how others believe and behave. We may not always succeed—other views may be more persuasive, depending on the listener, the situation, and the merits of the case. But at least we give our ideas the attention they deserve. Persuasion can be ethical or unethical, selfless or selfish, inspiring or degrading. Persuaders may enlighten our minds or prey on our vulnerability. Ethical persuasion, however, calls on sound reasoning and is sensitive to the feelings and needs of listeners. Such persuasion helps us apply the wisdom of the past to the decisions we now must make.

Ask students to keep a log for one day in which they note the times when they either encountered or practiced persuasion. Discuss these in terms of the importance of persuasion in our lives and the various forms that persuasive messages can take.

Beyond its personal importance to us, persuasion is essential to society. The right to persuade and be persuaded is the bedrock of the American political system, guaranteed by the First Amendment to the Constitution. According to the late Supreme Court justice Louis D. Brandeis, "Those who won our independence believed that the final end of the State was to make men [and women] free to develop their faculties; and that in its government the deliberative forces should prevail over the arbitrary."[1] Persuasion in the competing marketplace of ideas, before what one writer has called "the Court of Reason,"[2] is required for these "deliberative forces" to operate.

Deliberation involves the consideration of all sides of an issue before a decision is made. During the debate in the House of Representatives over the impeachment of President Clinton, Rep. Richard Gephardt was asked in the course of a television interview whether the many speeches delivered on the floor of the House had any real

Because there has been implanted in us the power to persuade each other . . . , not only have we escaped the life of the wild beasts but we have come together and founded cities and made laws and invented arts.

—Isocrates

The right to persuade and be persuaded is the bedrock of the American political system.

purpose. Gephardt responded that persuasion is society's alternative to violence. We strongly agree. Our political system is based on the premise that persuasion is more ethical and more practical than force. We should make commitments because we are persuaded, not because we are coerced.

Although you may find the expression of some views to be objectionable, if not downright obnoxious, the freedom to voice unpopular opinions is the very soul of liberty. The English philosopher John Stuart Mill put the matter eloquently:

> If all mankind, minus one, were of the one opinion, and only one person were of the contrary opinion, mankind would be no more justified in silencing that one person, than he, if he had the power, would be justified in silencing mankind.
>
> . . . We can never be sure that the opinion we are endeavoring to stifle is a false opinion; and if we were sure, stifling it would be an evil still.[3]

There are also practical reasons for tolerating opposing opinions. Exposure to different perspectives can produce better decisions.[4] For example, even though Hailey may never agree with Nick's view that we should register guns, his arguments may prompt her to reexamine her thoughts, to understand her convictions better, or perhaps even to modify her position.

Although speaking out on public issues is important, many people shy away from it. They may feel: "What difference can one person make? My words don't carry much weight." Perhaps not, but words make ripples, and ripples can come together to make waves. Just ask Anna Aley, a student at Kansas State University who gave a persuasive speech on substandard student housing. Her classroom speech was later presented in a public forum on campus. The text of her speech, which appears in Appendix C, was reprinted in the local newspaper, which followed it up with investigative reports and a supportive editorial. Brought to the attention of the mayor and city commission, Anna's speech helped promote reforms in the city's rental housing policies. Her words are still reverberating in Manhattan, Kansas.

Perhaps your classroom speech will not have that much impact, but you never know who or what may be changed by it. In this chapter we consider the characteristics of persuasive speaking, the functions of persuasive speeches, the process of persuasion, some of the challenges facing persuasive speakers, and the designs that are appropriate for the structure of these speeches. In the next chapter we will discuss how to fill these designs with persuasive substance in the form of well-developed arguments.

Seven Characteristics of Persuasive Speaking

Have students bring copies of magazine or newspaper "infomercials"—persuasive messages that look like informative messages. Use these as the basis for discussing the differences between information and persuasion.

Seven characteristics define persuasive speaking in contrast with informative speaking:

Informative speeches reveal options; persuasive speeches urge a choice from among options. Informative speakers expand our awareness. For example, an informative speaker might say: "There are three different ways we can deal with the budget deficit. Let me explain these." In contrast, a persuasive speaker would weigh these options and urge support of one of them: "Of the three different ways to deal with the budget deficit, we should choose the following course of action."

Informative speakers function as teachers; persuaders are advocates. The difference is one of passion and engagement. Informative speakers typically discuss a situation in relatively calm and dispassionate tones. Persuasive speakers are more vitally engaged, committed to a cause. This does not necessarily mean that persuaders are loud; the most passionate and intense moments of a speech can be very quiet.

Informative speeches provide supporting material to enlighten listeners; persuasive speeches develop supporting material as evidence to justify advice. An ethical persuasive speech justifies recommendations with good reasons based on responsible knowledge and sensitivity to the best interests of listeners.

Persuasive speeches ask for more audience commitment than do informative speeches. Although there is risk in being exposed to new ideas, more is at stake when listening to a persuasive message. What if a persuasive speaker is mistaken or even dishonest? What if her proposed plan of action is defective? Doing always involves a greater risk than knowing. Your commitment could cost you.

Leadership is more important in persuasive than in informative speeches. Because persuasive speeches involve risk, listeners will weigh the character and competence of speakers more closely. Do they really know what they are talking about? Do they have their listeners' interests at heart? As a persuasive speaker, your ethos will be on public display and will be scrutinized carefully.

Appeals to feelings are more appropriate in persuasive than in informative speeches. Because of the risk involved, listeners may balk at accepting recommendations, even when they are backed up by good reasons. To overcome such inertia, per-

Persuasive speeches can help raise support for worthy causes. Here Sharon Stone speaks out on behalf of Race for the Cure.

Informative Speaking	Persuasive Speaking
1. Reveals options.	1. Urges a choice among options.
2. Speaker acts as teacher.	2. Speaker acts as advocate.
3. Uses supporting material to enlighten listeners.	3. Uses supporting material to justify advice.
4. Asks for little audience commitment.	4. Asks for strong audience commitment.
5. Speaker's leadership less important.	5. Speaker's leadership more important.
6. Fewer appeals to feelings.	6. More appeals to feelings.
7. High ethical obligation.	7. Higher ethical obligation.

FIGURE 13.1
Informative Versus Persuasive Speaking

suaders must often appeal to feelings.[5] This is why persuasive speakers often use emotional appeals to open their speeches. For example, the informative statement "A 10 percent rise in tuition will reduce the student population by about 5 percent next term" might be transformed in the context of a persuasive speech in the following way:

Ask students to bring in examples of print advertisements or descriptions of television commercials that rely primarily on emotional appeals. Discuss the ethics of such advertising techniques.

> **The people who are pushing for the tuition increase don't think a couple of hundred dollars more will have much effect. They think we can handle it. They say that the one in twenty who won't be back doesn't make much difference!**
>
> **Well, let me tell you about my friend Tricia. She's on the Dean's List in chemistry, the pride and hope of her family. Tricia will get a great job when she graduates—if she graduates! But if this increase goes through, Tricia won't be back next term. Her dreams of success will be delayed, perhaps even denied! What do the legislators care about that? What do they care about Tricia's dreams?**
>
> **Perhaps you're in the same boat as Tricia—paddling like mad against the current. But even if you're not, she is one of us, and she needs our help now.**
>
> **Emotional and graphic language, often developed as specific examples, can help people see the human dimension of problems and move them to the right action.**

The ethical obligation for persuasive speeches is greater than that for informative speeches. As Isocrates indicated in the opening quotation, persuasion can be a great blessing to humankind. At their best, persuasive speakers confront us with our obligation to believe and act in socially responsible ways. By describing how they themselves became persuaded, they model how we should deliberate in difficult choice situations. By making intelligence and morality effective in public affairs, they can help the world evolve in more enlightened ways.

For all these reasons, persuasion should not be undertaken lightly. The major differences between informative and persuasive speaking are shown in Figure 13.1.

Major Persuasive Functions

The three major functions that persuasive speeches perform are (1) adjusting listener attitudes, beliefs, and values; (2) urging others to act; and (3) answering opposing views. A persuasive speech may perform all these functions, but it will usually emphasize just one of them.

Adjusting Attitudes, Beliefs, and Values

In Chapter 4 we learned that if speakers are to communicate successfully, they must engage the audience's attitudes, beliefs, and values. At the heart of our **attitudes** are feelings we have developed toward specific kinds of subjects. For example, Cherie's intense dislike for those who practice "ethnic cleansing"—the removal and persecution of entire populations on the basis of religious faith or ethnic affiliation—is her attitude toward them. **Beliefs** are ideas we express about these subjects that may explain our attitudes about them. For example, Cherie's conviction that ethnic cleansing is an especially cruel and aggressive form of intolerance is her belief about that practice. **Values** are underlying general principles of behavior that should justify our beliefs. Cherie's attitude and belief both rise out of her deep value commitment to a world of tolerance in which people respect and appreciate one another's differences.

Ask students to identify three situations that might represent inconsistency among attitudes, beliefs, and values held by many in their classroom audience. How might they frame persuasive speeches that could restore harmony among these elements and expand moral sensitivities concerning these situations?

Ideally, our attitudes, beliefs, and values should be in harmony, creating a coherent spiritual world within us. However, these elements are sometimes undeveloped, disconnected, or even opposed to one another, making for a narrow or confused moral world within listeners. When this is the case, persuasive speakers have the opportunity to create or restore consistency and harmony to the outlooks of listeners. Thus persuasion can perform an important therapeutic and ethical role. For example, if Cherie suspects that her listeners are indifferent to ethnic cleansing, even though they value tolerance strongly, she has the opportunity to arouse and implant an appropriate attitude and belief about that practice through an effective persuasive speech. By providing her audience with compelling information, examples, and stories, and by appealing to their underlying value of tolerance, she can expand the moral universe within them.[6]

In a parallel instance, Sam sensed a disconnection—even a contradiction—among the attitudes, beliefs, and values of many classmates toward capital punishment. He sensed that many of them had an intense hatred for those accused of violent crimes. On the basis of that attitude, they had formed a belief that strongly favored capital punishment. Sam felt that these attitudes and beliefs were inconsistent with the biblical values many of them espoused and with other fundamental values of fairness and respect for life. In the persuasive speech he developed, Sam appealed to these values in an effort to change the attitudes and beliefs of his listeners.

Ethical persuasive speeches often focus on giving listeners good reasons to change or intensify their beliefs. In effect, such persuasion argues that beliefs should express our deeper values and should govern in turn the attitudes we form. Such persuasion helps listeners form strong convictions. Beliefs that rest on our attitudes rather than on our values are often more shallow.

Because values are an integral part of our personality, deep changes in them can have a real impact on how we live. Therefore, speeches that attempt to change values may be perceived as quite radical and extreme. For this reason, such speeches are rare, occurring only in desperate times and situations. During the Vietnam War and the Great Depression, one might well have heard on college campuses persuasive speeches that were critical of American values.

Urging Action

Have students attend a local government meeting (council, zoning board, etc.) and take notes on the proceedings. Ask them to identify whether the speeches they heard addressed attitudes, beliefs, and values, urged action, or contended with opposition.

Persuasive speeches that urge action often follow or build on speeches that address the inner world of audience attitudes, beliefs, and values. Such speeches encourage listeners to act as individuals or as members of a group to put into effect the values, beliefs, and attitudes they profess. Therefore, such speeches bridge the inner spiritual world of listeners and the outer world of action.

When Bonnie Marshall asked audience members to act individually to ensure their right to die with dignity, she was offering such a bridge. She urged listeners to write their state representatives, to draw up a living will, to assign

Speeches that urge action often appeal to audience attitudes, beliefs, and values.

durable power of attorney to a trusted friend or family member, and to let their personal physicians know their wishes. When a persuasive speech urges individual action, listeners must see the necessity for action in personal terms.

When a speech advocates group action, the audience must see itself as having a common identity and purpose—in effect, a shared inner world. As we noted in Chapter 10, the speaker can reinforce group identity by using inclusive pronouns (*we*, *our*, *us*); by telling stories that emphasize group achievements; and by referring to common heroes, opponents, or martyrs. Anna Aley used an effective appeal to group identity as she proposed specific actions:

> **What can one student do to change the practices of numerous Manhattan landlords? Nothing, if that student is alone. But just think of what we could accomplish if we got all 13,600 off-campus students involved in this issue! Think what we could accomplish if we got even a fraction of those students involved!**

By identifying and uniting them as victims of unscrupulous landlords, Anna encouraged her student listeners to act as members of a group.

Speeches advocating action usually involve risk. Therefore, you must present good reasons to overcome your audience's natural caution. The consequences of acting and not acting must be clearly spelled out. Your plan must be practical and reasonable, and your listeners should be able to see themselves enacting it successfully.

Answering Opposing Views

In a world of clashing interests and agendas, in which values may seem in conflict, it is not unusual to hear different points of view on the same subject. This clash of ideas can be instructive, providing listeners with a richer sense of their alternatives. Therefore, unless you decide that the situation calls for the "co-active approach" we shall describe later in this chapter, you should not hesitate from performing the persuasive function of justifying your ideas and criticizing opposing arguments. This verbal "trial by fire," which occurs in the form of **debate** when opponents confront each other directly, can bring listeners closer to the truth of a controversial situation.

When contending with opposition, you refute opposing arguments to clear the way for what you are proposing: "Some say that we cannot afford to land explorers on Mars in the twenty-first century," said Marvin Andrews to his public speaking class. "I say we can't afford not to." Marvin then went on to describe the benefits that might come from such exploration. "But we really have no idea of all the benefits, any more than Queen Isabella could have foreseen the benefits of the voyage of Christopher Columbus. Fortunately, she did not listen to advisers who said his trip would cost too much."

On highly controversial topics such as abortion or gun control, you often can't avoid contentious speeches. If some audience members hold opposing views, your arguments may offend them, make them defensive, or even make them more difficult to persuade. Why, then, would you risk such a speech?

When immediate action is needed, other approaches may take too long to be effective. To secure immediate action, you may have to address opposing beliefs directly and discredit the arguments that support them with indisputable facts and figures or expert testimony. Speeches that contend with opposition may also be the best strategy when your audience is divided in their attitudes toward the topic. In such cases, your target audience will be uncommitted listeners and reasonable opponents. By presenting tactful, carefully documented counterarguments, you may reach some of them. A refutational approach may also help strengthen the resolve of supporters who need assurance that an opposing position can be effectively countered.

Finally, in some situations that are extremely important to you personally, you may want to give a speech of contention as a last-ditch tactic. You may feel that listeners are so strongly entrenched in their opposition that your only hope is to confront them with an argument that shows conclusively why they are mistaken. You hope for a positive delayed effect after their first negative reaction. Or you may even decide that your chances for persuasion are small, but your position deserves to be heard with all the reason and conviction you can muster. You can have your say and feel the better for it.

The Process of Persuasion

Make a transparency of the stages in the persuasive process from the transparency master in Chapter 13 of the IRM. Keep this on the screen during the discussion of this material.

To function effectively as speakers and listeners, we must understand how persuasion works. William J. McGuire, professor of psychology at Yale University, suggests that successful persuasion is a complicated process involving up to twelve phases.[7] For our purposes, these phases may be grouped into five stages: awareness, understanding, agreement, enactment, and integration (see Figure 13.2 on page 355). Familiarity with these stages helps us see that persuasion is not an all-or-nothing proposition. A persuasive message may be successful if it moves people through the process toward a goal.

Awareness

The first stage in the persuasive process is **awareness**. Awareness includes knowing about a problem, paying attention to it, and understanding how it affects our lives. This phase is often called *consciousness raising*. As we noted in Chapter 12, informative speaking can build such awareness and help prepare us for persuasion.[8] Creating awareness is especially important when people do not believe that there actually is a problem. For example, before advocates could change the way females were depicted in children's books, they had to make listeners understand that always showing boys in active roles and girls in passive roles was a serious problem. They had to demonstrate that this could thwart the development of self-esteem or ambition in young girls.[9]

Beyond acquainting listeners with a problem, persuasive messages aimed at building awareness must demonstrate that the problem is important and show listeners how it affects them directly. Joshua Logan's speech "Global Burning," reprinted at the end of this chapter, had the task of raising intense awareness of the environmental threat posed by global warming. Persuasive speakers must raise such awareness before moving on to the next stage in the process.

Understanding

The second phase of the persuasive process is **understanding**. Listeners must grasp what you are telling them. They must be moved by your ideas and know how to carry out your proposals. To provide understanding, Anna Aley used an "inside-outside" approach. She took listeners inside the housing problem in Manhattan by vividly describing her basement apartment. Then she took listeners outside the problem by showing them the total picture of substandard student housing: the number of students involved and the causes of the problem. Ethical persuasion expands our knowledge, demonstrates how some arguments are stronger than others, and provides evidence to support a position.[10]

Finally, the audience must understand how to put the speaker's proposals into effect. In her persuasive speech, reprinted in Appendix C, Bonnie Marshall clearly spelled out the steps she wanted her listeners to take, enumerating these as she presented them.

Agreement

The third stage in the persuasive process is **agreement**. Agreement means that listeners not only accept the speaker's recommendations but remember their

When speakers and audiences celebrate shared beliefs, the result is often a renewed sense of commitment.

reasons for doing so. Agreement can range from small concessions to total acceptance. Lesser degrees of agreement could represent success, especially when listeners have to change their attitudes or risk a great deal by accepting your ideas. During the Vietnam War, classroom speeches attacking or defending our involvement in that conflict were often heard. Feelings about the war ran so high that just to have a speech heard without interruption could be an accomplishment. If a reluctant listener were to nod agreement, or concede, "I guess you have a point," then one could truly claim victory.

Often you achieve agreement by presenting facts and interpretations that make your conclusions seem beyond question. You can help listeners remember their agreement by developing vivid images or interesting stories that embody your message. Although reasoning is important to secure agreement, stories and images will stay with your audience after they have forgotten the details of your argument.

Enactment

The fourth stage in the persuasive process is **enactment**. It is one thing to get listeners to accept what you say. It is quite another to ask them to act on it. If you invite listeners to sign a petition, raise their hands, or voice agreement, you give them a way to enact agreement. By enacting their agreement, listeners make a commitment. The student speaker who mobilized his audience against a proposed tuition increase

- brought a petition to be signed.
- distributed the addresses of local legislators to contact.
- urged listeners to write letters to campus and local newspapers.

He channeled their agreement into constructive action.

Changing agreement to action may require the further use of emotional appeals. Stirring stories and examples, vivid images, and colorful language can arouse sympathy. As she told the story of Harry Smith, who died an agonizing death because he had not signed a living will, Bonnie Marshall moved her listeners to act on behalf of themselves and their loved ones. Anna Aley's concluding story of her neighbor's accident helped motivate her audience to take action against substandard student housing.

Integration

Show a videotape of a student presenting a persuasive speech. Identify the stage(s) of the persuasive process engaged in the speech.

The final stage in the persuasive process is the **integration** of new attitudes and commitments with the listeners' previous beliefs and values. For a persuasive speech to have lasting effect, listeners must see the connection between the attitudes and actions you propose and their important values. Your ideas must fit comfortably within their belief system. As she presented her case for living wills, Bonnie Marshall anchored her appeals in the right to control one's own destiny. Anna Aley tied her attack on housing conditions to the values of fair treatment and safe living conditions. In the second of his two related persuasive speeches, "Cooling the World's Fever," reprinted at the end of Chapter 14, Joshua Logan urged listeners not just to accept his recommendations but to *become* the solution he advocated. He asked for total integration of attitudes, beliefs, values, and actions.

All of us seek consistency between our values and behaviors. For example, it would be inconsistent for us to march against substandard housing on Monday and contribute to a landlord's defense fund on Tuesday. This is why people sometimes seem to agree with a persuasive message, then change their minds. It

FIGURE 13.2
McGuire's Model of the Persuasive Process

dawns on them that this new commitment means that they must rearrange other cherished beliefs and attitudes.

To avoid such a delayed counterreaction, inoculate listeners by anticipating their objections and answering them in the speech. Don't attempt too much persuasion in a single message. Remember that dramatic change may require a campaign of persuasion in which any single speech plays a small but vital role, and be content with what you can accomplish.

To conclude, persuasion can be a complicated process. Any persuasive message must focus on the stage where it can make its most effective contribution: raising awareness; building understanding; seeking agreement; encouraging action; or promoting the integration of beliefs, attitudes, and values. To determine where to focus your persuasive efforts, you must consider the challenges of the specific situation.

The Challenges of Persuasion

The challenges that persuaders face range from confronting a reluctant audience to framing messages that meet the most demanding ethical tests. As you plan a persuasive speech, you need to consider the audience's position on the topic, how listeners might react to you as an advocate, and the situation in which the speech will be presented. At this point, the information and techniques concerning audience analysis that we introduced in Chapter 4 become crucial to success.

Invite a controversial figure from your community to address your class about his or her cause. Have the class analyze the speech and discuss it during the next class period. Focus the discussion on the challenges faced by the speaker and how these were or were not met.

Begin preparing your speech by determining where your listeners stand on the issue. Do they hold varying attitudes about the topic, or are they united? If listeners are divided, you might hope to unify them around your position. If listeners are already united—but in opposition—you might try to divide them and attract some toward your position. Also consider how your listeners might regard you as a speaker on the subject. If you do not have their respect, trust, and goodwill, use supporting testimony from sources they esteem to enhance your ethos and improve your chances for success.

Evaluating the relationships among the audience, the topic, and you as speaker will suggest further strategies for effective persuasion.

Enticing a Reluctant Audience to Listen

If you face an audience that opposes your position, success may be represented by small achievements, such as simply getting thoughtful attention. One way to handle a reluctant audience is to adopt a **co-active approach**, which seeks to

Speaker's Notes 13.1

APPLYING MCGUIRE'S MODEL TO PERSUASIVE SPEECHES

1. Arouse attention with your introduction.
2. Relate your message to your listener's interests and needs.
3. Define complex terms, use concrete examples, and organize your material clearly.
4. Base persuasion on solid supporting material.
5. Include a clear plan of action.
6. Use vivid language to make your message memorable.
7. Ask listeners to make a public commitment.
8. Relate your proposal to your audience's values.

bridge the differences between you and your listeners.[11] The major steps in this approach are as follows:

Have students read the speech by Anna Aley in Appendix C and suggest changes that might be needed if it were to be presented at a luncheon meeting of realtors in Manhattan, KS.

1. *Establish identification and goodwill early in the speech.* Emphasize experiences, background, beliefs, and values that you share with listeners.

2. *Start with areas of agreement before you tackle areas of disagreement.* Otherwise, listeners may simply "turn off and tune out," before you have a chance to state your position.

3. *Emphasize explanation over argument.* By explaining your position more than refuting theirs, you avoid provoking defensive behavior and invite listeners to consider the merits of your case.

4. *Cite authorities that the audience will respect and accept.* If you can find statements by such authorities that are favorable, you can gain "borrowed ethos" for your case. When he spoke before the Harvard Law School Forum, Charlton Heston, president of the National Rifle Association, attempted to disarm a chilly audience by citing his high regard for Dr. Martin Luther King Jr. and mentioning his attendance at King's "I Have a Dream" speech.[12]

5. *Set modest goals for change.* Don't try to push your audience too far too fast. If reluctant listeners have listened to you—if you have raised their awareness and built a basis for understanding—you have accomplished a good deal.

Have students identify a persuasive topic about which they feel strongly. Ask them to find and read at least two articles that oppose their position. Have them identify ideas from these articles that they might incorporate into a multisided presentation before the class. How would they present these ideas?

6. *Make a multisided presentation that compares your position with others in a favorable way.* Show respect for opposing positions and understanding for why others might have supported them. Then reveal how these positions may not merit such support. Your attitude should be not to challenge listeners but to help them see the situation in a new light.

Let's consider how you might apply these steps in a speech against capital punishment before an audience of largely reluctant listeners. You could build identification by pointing out the values you share with the audience, such as "We all respect human life. We all believe in fairness." It might also help to take an indirect approach in which you sketch your reasoning before you announce your purpose.

Persuasive speakers must often entice a reluctant audience to action, remove barriers to commitment, and move listeners to participate.

> **What if I were to tell you that we are condoning unfairness, that we are condemning people to death simply because they are poor and cannot afford a good lawyer? What if I were to show you that we are sanctioning a model of violent behavior in our society that encourages more violence and more victims in return?**

As you present evidence, cite authorities that your audience will respect and accept. "FBI statistics tell us that if you are poor and black, you are three times more likely to be executed for the crime of murder."

Keep your goals modest. Ask only for a fair hearing. Be aware that reluctant listeners may often struggle *not* to give you a fair hearing. Such listeners may distort your message so that it seems to fit what they already believe. Or they may simply deny or dismiss it, saying that it doesn't apply to them. Or they may discredit a source you cite in your speech, believing that any message that relies on *that* source cannot be taken seriously. Remember also that if you propose too much change, you may create a **boomerang effect**, in which the audience reacts by opposing your position even more strongly.[13]

For all these reasons, to hope for a major change on the basis of any single persuasive effort is what McGuire calls the **great expectation fallacy**.[14] Be patient with such listeners. Try to move them a step at a time in the direction you would like them to go. Give them information that may eventually change their minds.

> **I know that many of you may not like to hear what I'm saying, but think about it. If capital punishment does not deter violent crime, if indeed it may encourage more violent crime, isn't it time we put capital punishment itself on trial?**

Finally, make a **multisided presentation**. Acknowledge the arguments in favor of capital punishment, showing that you respect and understand that position, even though you do not accept it.

> **I know that the desire for revenge can be strong. If someone I love had been murdered, I would want the killer's life in return. I wouldn't care if capital punishment wasn't fair. I wouldn't care that it condones brutality. I would just want an eye for an eye. But that doesn't mean you should give it to me. It doesn't mean that society should base its policy on my anger and hatred.**

A multisided approach helps make those you do persuade resistant to later counterattacks, because you show them how to answer such arguments. This is often called the **inoculation effect**, because you "inject" your listeners with a milder form of the arguments they may hear later in more vehement forms.[15]

When you acknowledge and then refute arguments, you also help your credibility in two ways. First, you enhance your trustworthiness by showing respect for your opposition. You suggest that their position deserves consideration, even though you have a better option. Second, you enhance your competence by showing your knowledge of the opposing position—both of the reasons why people may find it attractive and the reasons why it is defective.

After your speech, you should continue to show respect for the audience. Even if some listeners want to argue or heckle, keep your composure. Others may be impressed by your self-control and may be encouraged to rethink their position in light of your example.

There may be times when you and your audience are so far apart that you decide simply to acknowledge your disagreement. You might say that although you do not agree with listeners, you respect their right to their position and hope that they will respect yours. Such openness may help establish the beginnings of trust. Even if audience members do not see you as an ally, they may at least start to see you as an honest, committed opponent and give you a hearing. If you emphasize that you will not be asking them to change their minds but simply asking them to hear you out and to listen to the reasons why you believe as you do, you may be able to have your day in court.

We once heard a student speak against abortion to a class that was sharply divided on that issue. She began with a personal narrative, the story of how her mother had been given a drug that was later found to induce birth defects and was faced with a decision on terminating the pregnancy. The student concluded by saying that if her mother had chosen the abortion route, she would not be there speaking to them that day. She paused, smiled, and said, "Although I know some of you may disagree with my views, I must say I am glad that you are here to listen and that I am here to speak. Think about it." If your reasons are compelling and your evidence is strong, you may soften the opposition and move waverers toward your position.

Do not worry if the change you want does not show up immediately. There often is a delayed reaction to persuasion, a **sleeper effect**, in which change shows up only after listeners have had time to integrate the message into their belief systems.[16] Even if no change is apparent, your message may serve a consciousness-raising function, sensitizing your listeners to the issue and making them more receptive to future persuasion.[17]

Facing a reluctant audience is never easy. But you can't predict what new thoughts your speech might stimulate among listeners or what delayed positive reactions to it there might be.

Removing Barriers to Commitment

Undecided listeners may hesitate because they need more information, because they do not see a connection between their values and interests and the issue at hand, and because they may not feel certain that they can trust your judgment. To deal with these challenges, you should provide needed information, show listeners how your proposal relates to their values or interests, and strengthen your credibility.

Provide Needed Information. Often a missing fact or unanswered question stands in the way of commitment. "I know that many of you agree with me but are asking, 'How much will this cost?'" Anticipating reservations and supplying the necessary information can help move listeners toward your position.

Affirm and Apply Values. Persuasive speeches that threaten audience values are not likely to be effective. You must show listeners that your proposal agrees with their principles. For example, if your listeners resist an educational program for the disadvantaged because they think that people ought to take care of themselves, you may have to show them that your program represents "a hand up, not a handout." Show them that your proposal will lead to other favorable outcomes, such as reductions in crime or unemployment.

As we noted earlier, values are resistant to change. If you can reason from the perspective of your listeners' values, using them as the basis for your arguments, you will create identification and remove a barrier to commitment.

ESL: ESL students may have difficulties determining what values their audience might relate to a given issue. Have ESL students select their persuasive topics early and consult with them on what values might be operative.

Preview the material on expert testimony and evidence from Chapter 14.

Strengthen Your Credibility. When audiences hesitate because they question your credibility, you can "borrow ethos" by citing expert testimony. Call on sources that your listeners trust and respect. Uncommitted audiences will scrutinize both you and your arguments carefully. Reason with such listeners, leading them gradually and carefully to the conclusion you would like them to reach. Provide supporting material each step of the way. Adopt a multisided approach, in which you consider all options fairly, to confirm your ethos as a trustworthy and competent speaker.

When addressing uncommitted listeners, don't overstate your case. Let your personal commitment be evident through your sincerity and conviction, but be careful about using overly strong appeals to guilt or fear. These might backfire, causing listeners to resent and reject both you and your message.[18] It is also important not to push uncommitted listeners too hard. Help them move in the desired direction, but let them take the final step themselves.

Moving from Attitude to Action

Just as opponents may be reluctant to listen, sympathetic audiences may be reluctant to act. It is one thing to agree with a speaker and quite another to accept the inconvenience and risk that action may require. Listeners may believe that the problem does not affect them personally. They may not know what they should do or how they should do it. Or, they may feel that the situation is hopeless.[19] To move people to action, you must give them reasons to act. You may have to remind them of their beliefs, demonstrate the need for involvement, present a clear plan of action, and make it easy for them to comply.

Revitalize Shared Beliefs. When speakers and audiences celebrate shared beliefs, the result is often a renewed sense of commitment. Such occasions may involve telling stories that resurrect heroes and heroines, giving shared beliefs new meaning.[20] At political conventions, Jefferson, Lincoln, Roosevelt, Kennedy, and Reagan are often invoked in speeches. These symbolic heroes can help bridge audience diversity by bringing different factions together.

Speaker's Notes 13.2

ENCOURAGING UNCOMMITTED LISTENERS

1. Provide necessary information.
2. Show how your proposal meets listeners' needs and strengthens their values.
3. Borrow ethos by citing authorities the audience respects.
4. Do not overstate your case or rely too heavily on emotional appeals.

Demonstrate the Need for Involvement. Show your listeners how the quality of their lives depends on action. Demonstrate that the results will be satisfying. It often helps if you can associate the change with a vision of the future. In his final speech, Martin Luther King Jr. said, "I may not get there with you, but I can see the Promised Land." King's vision of the Promised Land helped justify the sacrifice called for in his plan of action.

Have students recall whether the college recruiters they encountered presented clear plans of action as part of the recruitment process. Discuss their experiences and relate these to the material in this section.

Present a Clear Plan of Action. Listeners may exaggerate the difficulty of a proposal or insist that it is impossible. To overcome such resistance, show them how others have been successful using the same approach. Develop examples or narratives that project them completing the project successfully. Stress that "we can do it, and this is how we can do it." A speaker urging classmates to work to defeat a proposed tuition raise said:

> **How many of you are ready to help defeat this plan to raise tuition? Good! I see your heads nodding. Now, if you're willing to sign this petition, hold up your hands. Good! Now, I'm going to pass around this petition, and I want each of you to sign it. If we act together, we can make a difference.**

Be Specific in Your Instructions. Your plan must show listeners what to do and when and how to proceed.

Keep in mind that it may take strong feelings to move people to action. Declare your own commitment and ask listeners to join you. Once people have voiced their commitment, they are more likely to follow through on it.[21]

Make It Easy for Your Audience to Comply. Instead of simply urging listeners to write their congressional representatives, provide them with addresses and telephone numbers, a petition to sign, or preprinted addressed postcards to complete and return.

The Challenge of Ethical Persuasion

Ours is a skeptical and cynical age, made more so by large-scale abuses of communication ethics. Ads assure us that their products will make us sexier or richer, often with no foundation in fact. Persuasive messages disguised as information appear in "infomercials" seen on television. They try to slip into our minds under the radar of critical listening. Public officials may present suspicious statistics, make dubious denials, or dance around questions they don't want to answer directly. Talk show hosts may play fast and loose with facts and

Speaker's Notes 13.3

MOVING PEOPLE TO ACTION

1. Remind listeners of what is at stake.
2. Provide a clear plan of action.
3. Use examples and stories as models for action.
4. Visualize the consequences of acting and not acting.
5. Demonstrate that you practice what you preach.
6. Ask for public commitments.
7. Make it easy for listeners to act.

Ethics Alert! 13.1

GUIDELINES FOR ETHICAL PERSUASION

1. Avoid name calling: attack problems, proposals, and ideas—not people.
2. Be open about your personal interest.
3. Don't adapt to the point of compromising your convictions.
4. Argue from responsible knowledge.
5. Don't try to pass off opinions as facts.
6. Don't use inflammatory language to hide a lack of evidence.
7. Be sure your proposal is in the best interest of your audience.
8. Remember, words can hurt.

use inflammatory language. Little wonder that many people have lost trust in society's major sources of communication.

As a consumer of persuasive messages, you can at least partially protect yourself by applying the thinking skills we discussed in Chapter 3. As a producer of persuasive messages, you can help counter this trend toward unethical communication. Keep three simple questions in mind as you prepare your persuasive speech:[22]

- What is my ethical responsibility to my audience?
- Could I publicly defend the ethics of my message?
- What does this message say about my character?

These questions should light your way through the complexities of ethical persuasion.

As we noted in Chapter 1, an ethical speech is based fundamentally on respect for the audience, responsible knowledge of the topic, and concern for the consequences of your words. The guidelines in Ethics Alert! 13.1 should help you apply these precepts to persuasive messages.

Ask students to bring to class examples of persuasive materials that they believe are unethical. Apply the guidelines listed in Ethics Alert! 13.1 to critique these materials.

Designs for Persuasive Speaking

As you analyze the challenges that confront your persuasive speech, you must also decide how to structure it (see Figure 13.3). Many of the designs used for informative speeches are also appropriate for persuasive speeches. The categorical design can be used to structure a persuasive argument, just as Joshua Logan develops three categories of technological improvement in the solution he offers to global warming (see his speech at the end of Chapter 14). The sequential design can outline the steps in a plan of action to make it seem practical. The comparative design works well for speeches in which you contrast the weaknesses of an opposing argument with the strengths of your own.

In the remainder of this chapter, we look at three designs that are especially suited to persuasive speeches: the problem-solution design, the motivated sequence design, and the refutative design.

Use the "Persuasive Speech Designs" transparency when covering this material.

Refer students to the Speech Designer software or Speech Preparation Workbook for outline worksheets, checklists, and sample outlines for each of these designs.

InterConnections.LearnMore 13.1

PERSUASION

Coercive Persuasion and Attitude Change (Encyclopedia of Sociology, Volume 1) http://www.inlink.com/~dhchase/ofshe.htm
Covers various types of thought reform programs and provides an interesting contrast to the type of ethical persuasive techniques discussed in your text.

Influence at Work http://www.workingpsychology.com/intro.html.
Provides an in-depth but readable introduction to social influence, persuasion, and propaganda; an outstanding web site developed by Kelton Rhoades, Ph.D., consultant and lecturer at the University of Southern California and the Annenberg School for Communication.

Propaganda Analysis http://carmen.artsci.washington.edu/propaganda/home.htm
A discussion of propaganda techniques, with examples from World War II as well as more contemporary applications; prepared by Aaron Delwiche, a graduate student in the School of Communications at the University of Washington.

Problem-Solution Design

The **problem-solution design** first convinces listeners that there is a problem, then shows them how to deal with it. The solution can involve changing attitudes and beliefs or taking action. It is sometimes hard to convince listeners that a problem exists or that it is serious. People have an unfortunate tendency to ignore problems until they reach a critical stage. You can counteract this tendency by vividly depicting the crisis that will surely emerge unless your audience makes a change.

When you prepare a problem-solution speech, do not overwhelm your listeners with details. Cover the most important aspects of the problem, then show

FIGURE 13.3
Selecting Persuasive Speech Designs

Design	Use When
Categorical	• Your topic invites thinking in familiar patterns, such as proving a plan will be safe, inexpensive, and effective. • Can be used to change attitudes or to urge action.
Comparison/ Contrast	• You want to demonstrate why your proposal is superior to another. Especially good for speeches in which you contend with opposing views.
Sequential	• Your speech contains a plan of action that must be carried out in specific order.
Problem-Solution	• Your topic presents a problem that needs to be solved and a solution that will solve it. Good for speeches involving attitudes and urging action.
Motivated-Sequence	• Your topic calls for action as the final phase of a five-step process that also involves, in order, arousing attention, demonstrating need, satisfying need, picturing the results, and calling for action.
Refutative	• You must answer strong opposition on a topic before you can establish your position. The opposing claims become main points for development. Attack weakest points first and avoid personal attacks.

the audience how your solution will work. A problem-solution speech opposing a tuition increase might build on the following general design:

Thesis statement: We must defeat the tuition increase proposal.

I. Problem: The proposal to raise tuition is a disaster!
  A. The increase will create hardships for many students.
    1. Many current students will have to drop out.
    2. New students will be discouraged from enrolling.
  B. The increase will create additional problems for the university and the community.
    1. Decreased attendance means decreased revenue.
    2. Decreased revenue will reduce the university's community services.
    3. Reduced service will mean reduced support from contributors.

II. Solution: Defeat the proposal to raise tuition!
  A. Sign our petition against the tuition increase.
  B. Write letters to your state legislators.
  C. Write a letter to your local newspaper.
  D. Attend our campus rally next Wednesday.

When the problem can be identified clearly and the solution is concrete and simple, the problem-solution design works well in persuasive speeches.

The **stock issues design** is a variation of the problem-solution design. The stock issues design attempts to answer the major questions that a reasonable, careful person would ask before agreeing to a change in policies or procedures.[23] Such questions include:

I. Is there some significant problem?
  A. How did the problem originate?
  B. What caused the problem?
  C. How widespread is the problem?
  D. How long has the problem persisted?
  E. What harms are associated with the problem?
  F. Will these harms continue and grow unless there is change?

II. *What is the solution to this problem?*
  A. Will the solution actually solve the problem?
  B. Is the solution practical?
  C. Would the cost of the solution be reasonable?
  D. Might there be other consequences to the solution?

III. *Who will put the solution into effect?*
  A. Are these people responsible and competent?
  B. What role might listeners play?[24]

Motivated Sequence Design

The **motivated sequence design** is also related to the problem-solution design but is distinctive enough to discuss separately.[25] This design has five steps, beginning with arousing attention and ending with a call for action:

Tape several television commercials and have students identify the persuasive designs used in them. Ask them to reformat one of the commercials into the motivated sequence design.

1. *Arouse attention.* As in any speech, you begin by stimulating interest in your subject. In Chapter 12 we discussed six factors that affect attention: intensity, repetition, novelty, activity, contrast, and relevance. These same techniques may be used to gain attention in persuasive speeches.

2. *Demonstrate a need.* Show your listeners that the situation you wish to change is urgent. Help them see what they can win or lose if they accept or reject your plan for change. To create such understanding, tie your proposal to the basic needs discussed in Chapter 4.

3. *Satisfy the need.* Present a way to satisfy the need you have demonstrated. Set out a plan of action and explain how it would work. Offer examples that show how your plan has worked successfully in other places.

4. *Visualize the results.* Paint verbal pictures that illustrate the positive results listeners can expect. You could show your listeners how their lives will be better when they have enacted your plan. Such a picture of the future can help overcome resistance to action. You could also paint a dire picture of what life could be like if they do not go along with your suggestions. You might even put these positive and negative verbal pictures side by side to strengthen their impact through contrast.

5. *Call for action.* Your call for action may be a challenge, an appeal, or a statement of personal commitment. The call for action should be short and to the point. Give your listeners something specific that they can do right away to start the change. If you can get them to take the first step, the next will come more easily.

Let's look at how this model might work in a brief persuasive speech that appeals to audience motivations for recognition, friendship, and nurturance, using language that activates feelings of sympathy and identification:

1. *Arouse attention*	Have you ever dreamed about being a hero or heroine? Have you ever wished you could do something that would really make a difference in our world? Well, I'm here to tell you how you can if you invest only three hours a week.
2. *Demonstrate a need*	Our community needs volunteers to help children who are lonely and neglected. Big Sisters and Big Brothers of Omaha have a program for these children, but it takes people to make the program work. Last year they had forty-eight student volunteers. This year only thirty have signed up to help. They need at least thirty more. They need you.
3. *Satisfy the need*	Volunteering to be a big brother or a big sister will help keep this vital program going. It will also make you a hero or heroine in the eyes of a child.
4. *Visualize the results*	Maybe you can have an experience that will be as rewarding as mine has been. Last year I worked with ten-year-old Kevin two afternoons a week. He needed help with his homework because his grades were just barely passing. But more than school help, he needed someone who cared about him. The first six weeks, his grades went from D–'s to C–'s, and I took him to a basketball game one weekend. The next six weeks, his grades went up to C's and C+'s, and I took him to a movie. This year Kevin is doing well in school. He's making B's and above in all his courses, but we still meet and work together because I couldn't

bear not to see him. I guess this is a small contribution to humankind, but not to Kevin. When I look in his eyes, I see a glorified reflection of myself.

5. *Call for action* — Won't you make the commitment to become one of the heroines or heroes of our community? Just one or two afternoons a week can make a difference in the life of a child and in our own future. The pay is not good—nothing!—but the rewards are enormous. I've got the applications with me. Let me sign you up now!

If you plan to use the motivated sequence design, first determine where your listeners stand on the issue, and then focus on the steps that will carry persuasion forward. For example, if you are speaking to an audience that is already convinced of the need for a change but lacks a plan to make it work, you could focus on step 3, "Satisfy the need." However, if you are facing an audience that contests the need, your emphasis should be on step 2, "Demonstrate a need."

Bring a grab-bag of small objects (or pictures of objects) to class. Have students select an object and make an impromptu presentation that would sell that object to the class.

Refutative Design

The **refutative design** serves directly the function of answering opposing views. In this design, the speaker raises doubt about a competing position by revealing its inconsistencies and weaknesses. It is often wise to take on your opponent's weakest point first. Your refutation then raises doubt about other opposing arguments. The point of attack may be illogical reasoning or flimsy, insufficient evidence, as we shall discuss further in Chapter 14, or even self-interest and hidden agendas. However, keep the dispute as constructive as you can. Avoid personal attacks unless credibility issues are central and inescapable. Above all, be fair!

ESL: Have ESL students identify topics that are controversial in their cultures and that usually are not openly discussed. What special problems might they have in listening to related speeches? What adjustments might speakers make to minimize these difficulties?

There are five steps in developing an effective refutation. These five steps should be followed in sequence for each point you plan to refute.

1. State the point you are going to refute and explain why it is important.
2. Tell the audience how you are going to refute this point.
3. Present your evidence, using facts and figures, examples, and testimony. Cite sources and authorities that the audience will accept as competent and credible.
4. Spell out the conclusion for the audience. Do not assume that listeners will figure out what the evidence means. Tell them directly.
5. Explain the significance of your refutation—show how it discredits or damages the opposition.

See if you can follow each step in this pattern in the following refutation of an argument opposing sex education in public high schools:

Our well-intentioned friends would have you believe, and this is their biggest concern, that birth-control information increases teenage sexual activity.

I want to share with you some statistical evidence that contradicts this contention—a contention that is simply not supported by the facts.

The latest study on this issue by the Department of Health, Education, and Welfare compared sexual activity rates in sixty high schools across the United States—thirty with sex education programs and thirty without. Their findings show that there are no significant differences in sexual activity rates between these two groups of schools.

Therefore, the argument that access to birth-control information through sex education programs increases sexual activity simply does not hold water. That's typical of the attack on sex education in the schools—to borrow a line from Shakespeare, it's a lot of "sound and fury, signifying nothing."

You can strengthen this design if you follow your refutation by proving a similar point of your own, thus balancing the negative refutation with a positive demonstration. The result supplies the audience with an alternative belief to substitute for the one you have refuted. Use the same five-step sequence to support your position. For example, you might follow the preceding refutation with the following demonstration:

I'm not going to try to tell you that birth-control information reduces sexual activity. But I want to tell you what it does reduce. It reduces teenage pregnancy.

There is reliable evidence that fewer girls become pregnant in high schools with sex education programs. The same study conducted by Health, Education, and Welfare demonstrated that in high schools with sex education programs, the pregnancy rate dropped from one out of every sixty female students to one out of ninety within two years of the program's going into effect.

Therefore, sex education is a good program. It attacks a devastating social problem—the epidemic of children having children.

Any program that reduces unwanted teenage pregnancy is valuable—valuable to the young women involved, valuable to society. We all pay in so many ways for this personal and social tragedy—we should all support a program that works to reduce it. And we should reject the irrational voices that reject the program.

As should now be clear, the study of persuasive speaking is also a study of the arts of effective living. Learning how to use persuasion ethically and effectively, and how to avoid being abused by unethical persuaders, provides skills that are central to successful lives. In the next chapter, we shall learn more about how to fill persuasive designs with the substance of powerful arguments.

In Summary

Persuasion is the art of getting others to consider our point of view fairly and favorably. Persuasion is vital to our political system, which is based on the principle of rule by *deliberation* and choice rather than by force. Groups that have been exposed to different positions usually make better decisions because they are stimulated to examine a situation and to think about their options.

Characteristics of Persuasive Speaking. In contrast with informative speaking, persuasive speaking urges a choice among options and asks for a commitment. Rather than speaking as a teacher, the speaker assumes the role of advocate. Ethical persuasive speaking centers on good reasons based on responsible knowledge. Persuasive speeches rely more on emotional involvement than do informative speeches, and they carry an even heavier ethical burden.

Functions of Persuasive Speeches. Persuasive speeches address the inner world of *attitudes*, *beliefs*, and *values*; urge action in the world around us; and contend with opposing views. While addressing attitudes, beliefs, and values, strive to help listeners find harmony among these elements. Concentrate on adjusting attitudes and beliefs in light of deeper values. Avoid the *great expectation fallacy*, which asks for more change than one could reasonably expect after a single speech. When urging action, ask listeners to act either as individuals or as members of groups. Speeches that emphasize contention usually do not seek to convert opponents, but rather to win over the uncommitted and to influence opinion leaders.

The Process of Persuasion. When persuasion is successful, people listen, learn, agree, and change as a result of what they hear. These behaviors parallel

McGuire's categories of *awareness*, *understanding*, *agreement*, *enactment*, and *integration* of persuasive material. Awareness suggests that we know of a problem, that it commands our serious attention. Understanding implies that we can see the connection between the problem and our lives, and that we know how to carry out the speaker's proposals. Agreement implies our acceptance of a speaker's interpretations and recommendations. Enactment suggests our commitment and readiness to carry out the speaker's ideas. Integration involves consolidating the new attitudes and commitments into our overall belief and value system.

The Challenges of Persuasion. Persuading others can pose many challenges. You may have to entice a reluctant audience to listen, remove barriers that block commitment, move listeners from agreement to action, and be scrupulously ethical. To encourage reluctant listeners, use a *co-active approach* that seeks to bridge differences and to build identification. Remove barriers to commitment by providing vital information, pointing out the relevance to listeners' lives, and building credibility. To move partisan listeners from agreement to action, use vivid language and examples to bring abstract principles to life; prove the need for their involvement; present a clear plan; declare your own commitment as a model; and make it easy for listeners to take the first step into involvement. To be an ethical persuader, be sure that your messages are based on respect for the audience, responsible knowledge of the topic, and concern for the consequences of your words.

Designs for Persuasive Speaking. Three designs in particular serve the needs of persuasive speaking. In a *problem-solution design*, you must first convince the audience that a problem exists, and then advance a solution that corrects it. The *motivated sequence design* has five steps: arousing attention, demonstrating a need, satisfying the need, visualizing results, and calling for action. To use the *refutative design*, state the point you intend to refute, tell how you will refute it, present your evidence, draw a conclusion, and explain the significance of the refutation.

Terms to Know

persuasion
deliberation
attitudes
beliefs
values
debate
awareness
understanding
agreement
enactment
integration
co-active approach
boomerang effect
great expectation fallacy
multisided presentation
inoculation effect
sleeper effect
problem-solution design
stock issues design
motivated sequence design
refutative design

Notes

1. *Whitney v. California*, 274 U.S. 357, 375 (1927).
2. Stephen Edleston Toulmin, *The Uses of Argument* (Cambridge: Cambridge University Press, 1958), p. 8.
3. John Stuart Mill, *On Liberty* (Chicago: Henry Regnery, 1955 [originally published 1859]), p. 24.
4. Charlan Jeanne Nemeth, "Differential Contributions of Majority and Minority Influence," *Psychological Review* 93 (1986): 23–32.
5. Mark A. Hamilton and John E. Hunter, "The Effect of Language Intensity on Receiver Attitudes Toward Message, Source, and Topic," in *Persuasion: Advances Through Meta-Analysis*, ed. M. Allen and R. W. Preiss (Beverly Hills, Calif.: Sage, 1998).
6. For a different view, which depicts persuasion in terms of manipulation and domination, see Sonja K. Foss and Cindy L. Griffin, "Beyond Persuasion: A Proposal for an Invitational Rhetoric," *Communication Monographs* 62 (1995): 2–18.
7. William J. McGuire, "Attitudes and Attitude Change," in *The Handbook of Social Psychology*, ed. Gardner Lindzey and Elliot Aronson (New York: Random House, 1985), vol. 1, pp. 258–261.
8. Roger Brown, *Social Psychology* (New York: Free Press, 1965), pp. 709–763.
9. Gloria Steinem, *Revolution from Within: A Book of Self-Esteem* (Boston: Little, Brown, 1992), p. 120.

10. John C. Reinard, "The Empirical Study of the Persuasive Effects of Evidence: The Status After Fifty Years of Research," *Human Communication Research* 15 (1988): 3–59.

11. Adapted from Herbert W. Simons, *Persuasion: Understanding, Practice, and Analysis,* 2nd ed. (New York: Random House, 1986), p. 138.

12. Charlton Heston, "Winning the Cultural War," *Vital Speeches of the Day,* 1 Apr. 1999, pp. 357–359.

13. N. H. Anderson, "Integration Theory and Attitude Change," *Psychological Review* 78 (1971): 171–206.

14. McGuire, p. 260.

15. Mike Allen, "Meta-Analysis Comparing the Persuasiveness of One-Sided and Two-Sided Messages," *Western Journal of Speech Communication* 55 (1991): 390–404; M. Allen et al., "Testing a Model of Message Sidedness: Three Replications," *Communication Monographs* 56 (1990): 275–291; Jerold L. Hale, Paul A. Mongeau, and Randi M. Thomas, "Cognitive Processing of One- and Two-Sided Persuasive Messages," *Western Journal of Speech Communication* 55 (1991): 380–389; Carl I. Hovland, Arthur A. Lumsdaine, and Fred D. Sheffield, "The Effects of Presenting 'One Side' Versus 'Both Sides' in Changing Opinions on a Controversial Subject," in *Experiments on Mass Communication* (Princeton, N.J.: Princeton University Press, 1949), pp. 201–227; and William J. McGuire, "Inducing Resistance to Persuasion," in *Advances in Experimental Social Psychology,* ed. L. Berkowitz (New York: Academic Press, 1964), pp. 191–229.

16. Mike Allen and James B. Stiff, "Testing Three Models for the Sleeper Effect," *Western Journal of Speech Communication* 53 (1989): 411–426; and T. D. Cook et al., "History of the Sleeper Effect: Some Logical Pitfalls in Accepting the Null Hypothesis," *Psychological Bulletin* 86 (1979): 662–679.

17. M. E. McCombs, "The Agenda-Setting Approach," in *Handbook of Political Communication,* ed. D. D. Nimmo and K. R. Sanders (Beverly Hills, Calif.: Sage, 1981), pp. 121–140.

18. Franklin J. Boster and Paul Mongeau, "Fear-Arousing Persuasive Messages," in *Communication Yearbook* 8, ed. R. Bostrom (Beverly Hills, Calif.: Sage, 1984), pp. 330–377; and Richard E. Petty and Duane T. Wegener, "Attitude Change: Multiple Roles for Persuasion Variables," in *The Handbook of Social Psychology,* 4th ed., ed. Daniel T. Gilbert, Susan T. Fiske, and Gardner Lindzey (Boston: McGraw-Hill, 1998), pp. 353–354.

19. Katherine E. Rowan, "Goals, Obstacles, and Strategies in Risk Communication: A Problem-Solving Approach to Improving Communication About Risks," *Journal of Applied Communication Research* 19 (1991): 322.

20. Michael Osborn, "Rhetorical Depiction," in *Form, Genre, and the Study of Political Discourse,* ed. Herbert W. Simons and Aram A. Aghazarian (Columbia: University of South Carolina Press, 1986), pp. 79–107.

21. R. A. Wicklund and J. W. Brehm, *Perspectives on Cognitive Dissonance* (Hillsdale, N.J.: Erlbaum, 1976).

22. Adapted from Richard L. Johannensen, *Ethics in Communication,* 3rd ed. (Prospect Heights, Ill.: Waveland, 1990), pp. 17–20.

23. J. W. Patterson and David Zarefsky, *Contemporary Debate* (Boston: Houghton Mifflin, 1983).

24. The structure of the stock issues design has been adapted from Charles U. Larson, *Persuasion: Reception and Responsibility,* 8th ed. (Belmont, Calif.: Wadsworth, 1998), pp. 293–295; and Charles S. Mudd and Malcolm O. Sillars, *Public Speaking: Content and Communication* (Prospect Heights, Ill.: Waveland, 1991), pp. 100–102.

25. The motivated sequence design was introduced in Alan Monroe's *Principles and Types of Speech* (New York: Scott, Foresman, 1935) and has been refined in later editions.

Global Burning

Joshua Logan

Ten years ago, five years ago, reasonable people could argue and even disagree over some tough environmental questions: Is there really such a thing as "global warming"? Is the world really getting hotter at a rapid pace? And is it being fanned by humans? Are we really responsible for environmental conditions?

Now there's no more room for argument. Fini. Case closed. The answer to all these questions is YES. This answer has been provided by the United Nations Intergovernmental Panel on Climate Change, reporting during the early part of this year. This authoritative, thousand-page report, which correlates and tests the work of hundreds of environmental scientists from countries all around the globe, concludes that the process of global warming is now in motion and is accelerating. And the fire is fed largely by humans. The United States especially, with about 4 percent of the world's population, accounts for 25 percent of all global warming. We are the ones with our foot on the accelerator.

■ *Joshua Logan presented this first of two related persuasive speeches in his class at the University of Memphis (the second appears at the end of Chapter 14). This first speech focuses on the problem while the second speech emphasizes the solution phase of the underlying persuasive design. Both speeches are characterized by passion and engagement. Josh's evidence justifies his feelings, thus blending reason and emotion.*

Today I want to sketch the dimensions of this problem, and what it might mean for you, your children, and your grandchildren. I will first track the causes of global warming, then trace its recent path and project its future. Sounds like an informative speech, doesn't it? But the most recent Gallup polls—published in April 2001—tell us that the people of the United States are pretty much in denial about global warming: yes, they believe it exists and, yes, they are concerned, but they're not that much concerned. Global warming is something of an abstract, distant problem for them, and they can't see the future all that clearly. That's why this is a problem for persuasion, why this is a challenge for this speech. We must recognize global warming for what it is, the monster we are creating by all our action and inaction. We must become scared—really scared! We must be willing to think green and act green, from the personal everyday decisions we make on disposing trash to the big consumer decisions we make on which cars to buy to the political decisions we make on which candidates to support. We must understand that this hot world is really ready to catch fire—and we must be willing to pay the price to help put the flames out. We must be committed to the proposition that global warming must not become global burning.

■ *Josh announces his purpose and previews his speech. This first speech lays the basis of beliefs and attitudes to justify the program he will present later; it concentrates on arousing awareness, sharing understanding, and securing agreement. The second speech will focus on enactment and integration. The persuasive challenge for this speech is to remove barriers that stand in the way of audience commitment.*

Global warming begins with greenhouse gases—the tons of carbon dioxide that belch out of our smokestacks and our automobile exhausts; the vast clouds of methane gas that rise from our farms and ranches and landfills; the nitrous oxide from fertilizers, cattle feed lots, and chemical products. The world's forests are supposed to absorb much of this industrial and agricultural output, but guess what? We've also been busy cutting the rainforests and clear-cutting our own forests. We're tying nature's hands behind her back at just the wrong moment. So all these deadly gases mix and accumulate in the atmosphere, where they magnify the heat of the sun.

■ *Josh intensifies audience awareness by the use of graphic, concrete words like "belch" and "vast clouds" and by the vivid image of "tying nature's hands behind her back."*

Now let's gain some perspective on where we now stand, because the world has already started to melt. I want to show you a chart that traces the human influence on the atmosphere over the past thousand years. This chart summarizes information tracing the history of the greenhouse gases, according to the

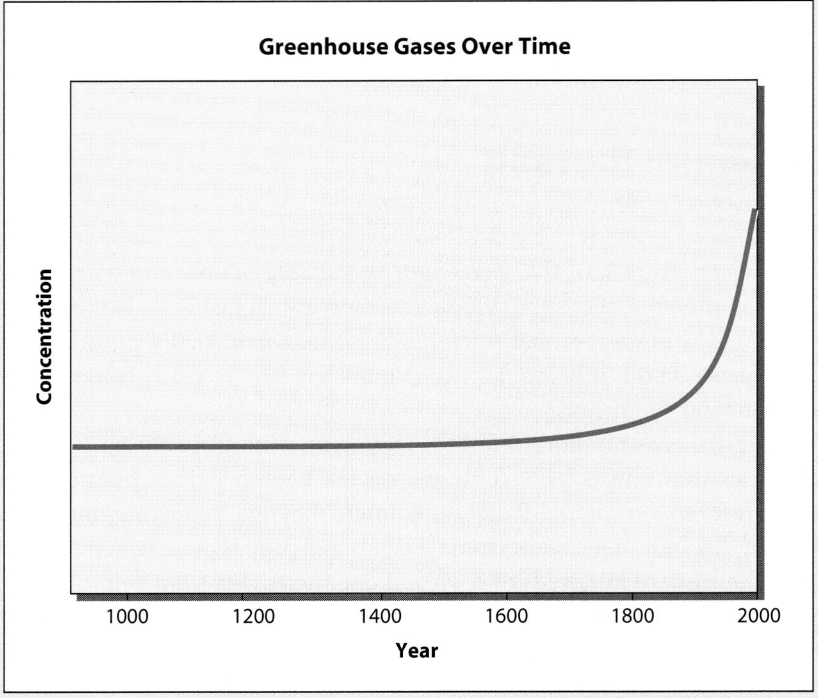

■ *Josh uses a chart to help create perspective concerning the recency and enormity of the problem. His use of contrast is especially effective, and the direct quotation reinforces the authenticity of his evidence. His careful research reinforces his credibility as Josh prepares to present the doomsday scenario that will follow.*

IPCC's *Summary for Policymakers* (page 6). Notice that the bottom border divides the time frame into two-hundred-year periods. The side frame measures the amount of the gas pouring into the atmosphere. Notice that for about eight hundred of these years, this amount is stable and even—almost a straight line. Then as the nineteenth century dawns on the Industrial Revolution, the line begins to climb, at first gradually, then increasingly steep until it almost reaches the vertical during the past half-century. The dry technical language of the summary, speaking to carbon dioxide alone, carries the message of this chart with sharp clarity: "The atmospheric concentration of carbon dioxide (CO_2) has increased by 31 percent since 1750. The present CO_2 concentration has not been exceeded during the past 420,000 years and likely not during the past 20 million years. The current rate of increase is unprecedented during at least the past 20,000 years."

Another of these gases, nitrous oxide, is up 17 percent since 1750, more than in the past thousand years. Finally, methane gas has increased 151 percent—151 percent!—since 1750. The message is the same. We have a problem.

■ *Josh translates a complex situation into a simple word-picture that listeners can grasp. He asks listeners to imagine summer days made ten degrees hotter by global warming. His allusions to the fate of coral reefs and tigers hint at the impact on nature and wildlife. He adds dark humor by advising listeners to visit Miami and New Orleans soon, and he personalizes the picture by suggesting the fate of the barrier islands he loved as a child.*

Now what does all this mean in human terms, especially if this line continues to climb on the charts of the future? For one thing, it's hot, very hot. The decade of the 1990s was the hottest on record, probably reaching back for at least a thousand years. But it won't hold that record for long. The UN congregation of the world's scientists predicts that the earth's surface temperature could rise by as much as ten degrees over the next hundred years. Can you imagine what it will be like to add ten degrees to the average summer day in Memphis? But beyond that, the world's agriculture will be profoundly changed. Fertile lands will become deserts, and vast populations will be forced to relocate.

The story becomes more tragic when we contemplate the fate of the oceans. Some scientists had previously discounted global warming because some of the most dire predictions about rising temperatures had not come true. What they forgot was the capacity of the oceans to absorb heat and smother some of the immediate impact of global warming. But the latest issue of *Science* magazine has published reports that—as they put it—"link a warming trend in the upper 3,000 meters of the world's oceans to global warming caused by human activities." These reports are truly ominous for all living creatures. In particular, they confirm the IPCC predictions that most coral reefs will disappear within thirty to fifty years. And as the oceans continue to warm and melt the great ice shelves in the polar regions, the rise in sea level—perhaps as much as three feet over the next century—will wipe out vast lowland areas such as the Sundarbans in India and Bangladesh, the last, best habitat for the Bengal tiger. Large parts of Florida and Louisiana will surrender to the sea—sell your beach property now and be sure to visit Miami and New Orleans soon! The barrier islands off Mobile Bay, where my parents took me camping as a boy and where I hope to take my own children, will recede into memory. These are just fragments, mere glimpses, of the future global warming has in store for us, our children, and grandchildren.

Josh reassures listeners that the picture he has painted is not inevitable. He also prepares the ground for his next speech, which will complete the problem-solution design of his persuasion.

Well, I hope I have your attention. I hope you're willing to grant that we have a problem, a problem that could well threaten the future of our species. Can we do anything about it? I would like to give you a happy, simple answer to this question, but it is a complex one. It's not like we can just take our foot off the greenhouse accelerator and bring the bus to a halt. Once it is heated, the ocean does not cool quickly. Once they have accumulated, greenhouse gases can linger for generations. But we can do something to change this picture for the better. The future is not an either-or proposition, and we can mitigate some of the worst possibilities. We can cool the fires under global warming to prevent it from becoming global burning. In my next speech I hope to show you how.

WORKS CONSULTED

"Americans Consider Global Warming Real, but Not Alarming." Gallup News Service. 9 Apr. 2001. http://www.gallup.com/poll/Releases/Pr010409.asp (17 Apr. 2001).

"Feeling the Heat." *Time.* 9 Apr. 2001, pp. 22–39.

"Governments Agree: Global Warming Impact Serious." Environment News Service. 19 Feb. 2001. http://ens.lycos.com/ens/feb2001/20011-02-19-01.html (17 Apr. 2001).

"Grim Future Forecast for World's Coastal Areas." Environment News Service. 17 Apr. 2001. http://ens-news.com/ens/apr2001/2001L-04-17-06.html (18 Apr. 2001).

Lazaroff, Cat. "Warming Oceans Attributed to Greenhouse Gases." Environment News Service. 16 Apr. 200l. http://ens.lycos.com/ens/apr2001/2001L-04-16-06.html (17 Apr. 2001).

Petit, Charles W. "Polar Meltdown." *U.S. News & World Report.* 28 Feb. 2000, pp. 65–74.

Shute, Nancy. "The Weather Turns Wild." *U.S. News & World Report.* 5 Feb. 2001, pp. 44–52.

Summary for Policymakers: A Report of Working Group I of the [United Nations] Intergovernmental Panel on Climate Change. January 2001. http://www.usgcrp.gov/ipcc/wg1spm.pdf (17 Apr. 2001).

14

Evidence, Proof, and Argument

OUTLINE

THIS CHAPTER WILL HELP YOU

- transform supporting materials into evidence
- develop evidence into proofs
- arrange proofs into arguments
- recognize and avoid defects of evidence, proofs, and arguments

As he completed his speech, "Cooling the World's Fever," Joshua Logan knew that his persuasive effort had been effective.

Listeners had seemed concerned and attentive as he presented his *evidence.* The dramatic facts and testimony he presented, his striking examples, and the moving stories he related, all had had an impact.

They had nodded in agreement as he developed *proofs* to support his points. His reasoning had led compellingly to his conclusions. He had come across as a credible speaker, demonstrating with every word his concern for listeners and his grasp of his subject. He had spoken in ways that moved listeners, appealing to their social identity and pride as Americans.

By the end of his speech, many of them seemed convinced that his *argument* advocating a solution for global warming was based on a firm grasp of principle and a clear understanding of reality. They were ready to commit to a program that would require far-reaching changes both at the level of government and in their personal lifestyles (see his entire speech at the end of this chapter).

Speech is power: Speech is to persuade.

—Ralph Waldo Emerson

On these three italicized terms—evidence, proof, and argument—rests the fate of any persuasive speech. They provide the substance of persuasion.They might well be represented as expanding circles that share a center. At the core of persuasion, the innermost circle, is evidence, the vital supporting material on which all else depends. The next circle radiating out from this center is proof—the arrangements and interpretations of evidence that appeal to listeners' reasoning, emotions, social identity, and responses to speakers as credible and to their messages as authentic. Finally, the outermost, most inclusive circle of persuasion consists of arguments, which weave evidence and proofs into answers for the most fundamental questions posed by persuasive designs.

In this chapter we discuss these three elements, show how they can be developed and combined to work effectively, explain how to use them ethically, and demonstrate how to avoid mistakes that rob them of their power.

Using Evidence Effectively

Supporting materials used in persuasion are called **evidence**. Consider the following situation: A speaker says, "We should all sign up to be organ donors." A listener asks, "Why?" The speaker replies, "Because I say so." Now consider a different approach, that taken by Paul B. Fowler, a student at Alderson-Broaddus College, as he presented a speech urging his classmates to become organ donors:

> **According to the *Transplant Organ Procurement Foundation Manual*, more than 25,000 kidney transplants have been performed since 1963. Pittsburgh surgeons alone transplant over 100 kidneys per year. However, only 25 percent of kidney patients can receive a kidney from a living family member. Most must wait for several years for an organ from a donor. In the Pittsburgh area alone, over 120 patients are waiting right now for a phone call telling them a kidney has become available. Nationwide, over 5,000 people are waiting.**

The contrast is clear. The person listening to our hypothetical speaker might respond, "You have a right to your opinion, but I have a right to ignore it." Paul's listeners *had* to take his message seriously, even if they did not agree with all his recommendations. The combination of facts and expert testimony lifted his message above personal opinion. His evidence added strength, authority, and objectivity to his speech.

Ask students to find a newspaper article and indicate how its information might be used as evidence, woven into proofs, and developed into arguments in a persuasive speech.

To better understand the power of evidence, we shall consider briefly each type of supporting material identified in Chapter 6 and the ways they work in informative and persuasive speeches.

Facts and Statistics

In informative speeches, facts and statistics enrich our understanding. In persuasive speeches, they encourage us to believe or act in different ways.[1] Facts and figures are especially important during the awareness phase of persuasion to prepare listeners for what will follow. Juli Pardell, arguing for more effective safety regulations in air travel, showed how the judicious use of facts, interlaced with testimony and examples, can create strong evidence:

ESL: Facts and statistics have long been regarded as favored forms of evidence in the United States. Other cultures may place more value on narratives and prestige evidence. Ask your students to consider the validity of these assumptions, being certain to involve ESL students in the discussion. If true, what impact might these differences have on cross-cultural persuasion?

> **The Los Angeles airport deserves special attention. The *Christian Science Monitor* of October 29th this year contends that it "exemplifies the growing congestion that decreases safety margins." Thirty other airports lie within a ninety-mile radius of Los Angeles airport, creating a hubbub of planes in the sky. Within a forty-five-mile radius, 197 planes vie for space in the skies at any given moment. Such overcongestion only increases the chance for planes to crash.**

By the time Juli finished presenting her carefully documented facts, the audience felt she had strong evidence for her case.

Examples

In informative speeches, examples illustrate ideas and create interest. In persuasive speeches, examples can also arouse feelings that make listeners want to act. Factual examples are especially useful. When you can say, "This really happened," you strengthen your position. LaDell Patterson demonstrated the value

Ask students to identify incidents in newscasts that evoked strong feeling as they heard them. Discuss how these events might be used ethically as examples in speeches.

of factual examples in a speech opposing discrimination against women in news organizations. In her speech she cited the experiences of Laura Stepp, a reporter for the *Washington Post*:

> **Ms. Stepp recalled . . . that while a *Washington Post* lawyer was reading one of her stories, she commented that she hoped it would land on the front page because of its importance. His reply to her was, "All you have to do is shake your little fanny and they'll put it on the front page." When she objected, he said he had no idea that the remark was offensive.**

This example, one of many in LaDell's speech, helped move her listeners in favor of the reforms she recommended.

If no single factual example adequately conveys what you want to communicate, a hypothetical example may work better. At the beginning of this book, when we wanted to persuade you of the usefulness of the public speaking course, we invented the hypothetical example of "Mary," a composite person who represented all the successful students we have taught. To be ethical, you must let your listeners know when an example has been fabricated to fit the purposes of your persuasive speech.

Narratives

Have students read or view a recent persuasive speech in which narrative plays a prominent part. In class discussion, ask them: What persuasive work does the narrative perform? How well has the speaker integrated the narrative with other forms of evidence?

In informative speeches, narratives illustrate the meaning of ideas. In persuasive speeches, narratives can carry listeners to the scene of a problem and engage them in a living drama. Kirsten Lientz illustrated these functions when she opened a speech with the following narrative:

> **It's a cold, icy December afternoon. You hear a distant crash, then screams, and finally the unending moan of a car horn fills the silence. You rush the short distance to the scene of the crash, where you find a Ford Bronco overturned with a young woman and two small boys inside. The woman and one of the boys climb from the wreckage unhurt; the other boy, however, is pinned between the dashboard and the roof of the car, unconscious and not breathing. Would you know what to do? Or would you stand there wishing you did? These events are real. Bob Flath saved this child with the skills he acquired at his company's first aid workshop.**

After this dramatic narrative introduction, Kirsten's listeners were prepared to listen to her speech urging them to take the first aid course offered at her university.

Testimony

In informative speeches, testimony adds credibility to the message. In persuasive speeches, testimony can determine whether listeners accept your advice. When you use testimony in a persuasive speech, *you call on experts to support your position*. Introduce these witnesses carefully, emphasizing their credentials. To support her call for air safety improvements Juli Pardell cited eight authoritative sources of information. In his plea for organ donors Paul Fowler cited four reputable books. It was not just Juli or Paul speaking—it was all these sources of testimony together. Expert testimony will be most effective when (1) the audience knows little about the issue because it is new, novel, or complicated; (2) the audience does not feel that the issue affects them directly; and (3) the audience does not have the ability or motivation to independently analyze the situation.[2]

Witnesses who testify *against* their self-interest are called **reluctant witnesses.** They provide some of the most powerful evidence available in persuasion.

Ethics Alert! 14.1

GUIDELINES FOR THE ETHICAL USE OF EVIDENCE

1. Provide evidence from credible sources.
2. Identify your sources of evidence.
3. Use evidence that can be verified by other experts.
4. Acknowledge disagreements among experts.
5. Be sure your evidence is relevant to the issue.
6. Do not withhold any important evidence.
7. Use the most recent evidence available.
8. Use expert testimony to establish facts, prestige testimony to enhance credibility, and lay testimony to create identification.
9. Quote or paraphrase testimony accurately.
10. Be certain your examples and narratives are truly representative of the situation.

For example, Joshua Logan's criticism of President Bush's environmental decisions in the speech reprinted at the end of this chapter was more effective because he spoke as a Republican who had voted for the president.

In ethical persuasive speaking, you should rely mainly on expert testimony. Use prestige or lay testimony as secondary sources of evidence. You can use prestige testimony to stress values you want listeners to embrace. You can use lay testimony to relate an issue to the lives of listeners. Keep in mind that when you quote others, you are associating yourself with them. Be careful with whom you associate!

As you select your evidence, consider different points of view so that you don't simply present one perspective without being aware of others. Gather more research materials than you think you will need so that you have a wide range from which to choose. Be sure you have facts, figures, or expert testimony for each of your main points. Use multiple sources and types of evidence to strengthen your case.

Have students identify misuses of evidence in print advertisements. Discuss the type of evidence misused, the nature of the misuse, and possible reasons for it. What might be the impact on readers?

Proving Your Points

Proofs arrange evidence in persuasive patterns. The nature of proof has been studied since the Golden Age of Greece. In his *Rhetoric* Aristotle suggested that there are three fundamental forms of proof. The first, **logos**, recognizes that we respond to reasoned demonstrations. The second, **pathos**, affirms that we can be touched by appeals to personal feelings such as fear, pity, and anger. The third, **ethos**, recognizes that we respond to the personal qualities of speakers, especially to our perceptions of their competence, character, likeableness, and forcefulness. We are also affected by the credibility of the sources of supporting materials in speeches. In our time the work of many scholars has confirmed the presence of a fourth dimension of proof, **mythos**, suggesting that we respond to appeals to the traditions and values of our culture and to the legends and folktales that embody them.[3]

Ask students to bring in examples of print advertisements that illustrate the four basic forms of proof. Discuss why particular types might have been selected for particular products.

A persuasive speech rarely relies on a single kind of proof. Each type of proof brings its own coloration and strength to the fabric of persuasion. In the

FIGURE 14.1
Weaving the Fabric of Proof

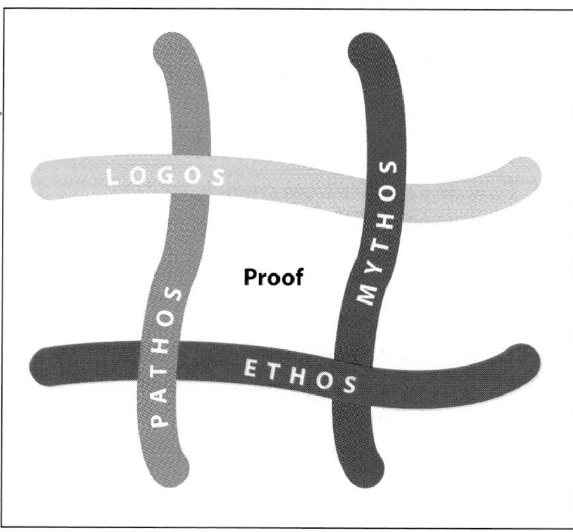

sections that follow, we identify the strengths and qualities of these proofs so that you may weave them effectively into your own persuasive speech.

Appeals to Rationality

Use the "Persuasive Proofs" transparency (the master is in Chapter 14 of the IRM) to reinforce the discussion of this section.

Appeals to our rational nature emphasize the use of facts, statistics, and expert testimony to reach a conclusion. This kind of proof grounds a problem in reality so that listeners know they are dealing with something that is both serious and substantive. Such proofs also interpret the meaning of a situation and guide understanding. The process follows a simple basic pattern:

1. The speaker makes a statement.
2. The speaker offers evidence in support of the statement.
3. The speaker draws a conclusion.

When used in a speech, this simple formula can be quite artful. In a classroom speech on drinking and driving responsibly, Betty Nichols asserted that the sense of security people often feel while riding in cars is a dangerous illusion. To prove this, she presented the following basic facts as evidence:

> **Drunk driving causes 24,000 deaths per year and 65,000 serious injuries.**

Although this evidence is strong, Betty recognized that the facts alone might not be compelling enough to fully support the idea. She would need to interpret them for listeners. Therefore, she added a dramatic contrast to make these figures come to life:

> **Let's compare these numbers with the risk of being a homicide victim. We have a 1 in 150 chance of being murdered, but we have a 1 in 33 chance of being killed or crippled in an alcohol-related accident.**

Notice that as she draws this contrast, Betty weaves into her logos a strand of pathos: listeners begin to see the personal threat involved. This appeal to fear, based on the statistics, becomes even more evident in the following striking conclusion:

> **Therefore our car—which makes us feel so safe, so secure, so powerful—can become our assassin, our coffin.**

When used ethically, appeals to personal feelings can change bad attitudes and advance good causes.

An appeal based on rationality demonstrates the speaker's faith in the audience's intelligence. It implies that if people are offered facts and shown how to interpret them, they will come to the proper conclusion.

Appeals to Feeling

People usually respond strongly when they feel angry, afraid, guilty, excited, or compassionate toward others. When used ethically, appeals to personal feeling can change bad attitudes or advance good causes.[4]

Tape television advertisements that rely primarily on fear appeals. Show them in class and discuss their effectiveness and ethics.

When speakers tell personal stories, emotional appeals can be especially effective. Personal narratives blend the power of feeling with strong credibility. During a congressional debate on handgun control legislation, James Brady, the presidential press secretary who was shot during the assassination attempt on President Reagan, testified before the U.S. Senate Judiciary Subcommittee. Speaking from his wheelchair, he said:

> **There was a day when I walked the halls of this Senate and worked closely with many of you and your staffs. There was a wonderful day when I was fortunate enough to serve the President of the United States in a capacity I had dreamed of all my life. And for a time, I felt that people looked up to me. Today, I can tell you how hard it is to have people speaking down to me. But nothing has been harder than losing the independence and control we all so value in life. I need help getting out of bed, help taking a shower, and help getting dressed.**
>
> **There are some who oppose a simple seven-day waiting period for handgun purchases because it would inconvenience gun buyers. Well, I guess I am paying for their convenience. And I am one of the lucky ones. I survived being shot through the head. Other shooting victims are not as fortunate.[5]**

Often, threads of feeling woven into a proof are the only way to convince people of the human dimensions of a problem or the need for immediate action.

Still, as powerful as emotional proof may be, it should be used with caution. If the appeal to feeling is too obvious, audiences may suspect you are trying to manipulate them. Appeals to negative emotions such as fear or guilt are especially tricky since they can boomerang, causing listeners to discredit both you and your speech. When you use appeals to feeling, support these with facts and figures. In your presentation, let your voice and body language understate rather than overstate the emotional appeal. Don't engage in theatrics!

Appeals Based on Credibility

When you speak, listeners must sense that you are a person of strong conviction and that you know what you are talking about. Your sincerity and personal commitment must be beyond question. Listeners must feel that they can trust you—that you will not distort the truth for personal advantage. Ideally, they will also conclude that you are a likeable person who in turn likes them—that you are a person of goodwill.[6]

Ask students to compile a list of political, cultural, social, literary, scientific, and religious figures, groups, or publications that they respect. Collate these lists of high ethos sources and share them with the class.

Appeals to ethos affirm that listeners are persuaded by the credibility of message sources. As a speaker, you are one such source. The sources of information you cite in your speech are another. Listeners will also evaluate these sources in terms of their competence, character, goodwill, and power. If the evaluation of your sources is positive, audiences will be more inclined to accept your position. Let's look at how Heide Nord used the ethos of her sources to help persuade her listeners to change their attitudes about suntanning. To support the claim "We should avoid prolonged exposure to the sun," Heide emphasized expert testimony supplemented with lay testimony:

> **The most recent *Consumer Report* of the Food and Drug Administration tells us "Prolonged exposure to sunlight without protection is responsible for about 90 percent of skin cancer." The article describes the case of Wendell Scarberry, a skin cancer patient who has had over a hundred surgeries. Wendell talks about the seriousness of the disease and urges us to be careful about sun exposure. "You can't cure skin cancer," he says, "by just having the doc whack it off." Finally, the American Cancer Society in its pamphlet *Fry Now Pay Later* says that skin cancer most often occurs among people who spend a lot of time in the sun, especially if they have been overexposed during their teens or twenties. Well, that's where most of us are right now. The FDA, the American Cancer Society, and Mr. Scarberry form a chorus of credibility, and we need to take their song seriously.**

Heidi's obvious commitment together with the combination of expert and lay testimony made her speech highly credible.

Clearly, proof based on the testimony of reliable, competent, and trustworthy sources is extremely important in persuasive speaking. *Identify your sources and point out why they are qualified to speak on the subject.* It is also helpful if you can say that the testimony is recent. For maximum effect, quote experts directly rather than paraphrasing them.

Appeals to Cultural Identity

Appeals to the values, faith, and feelings that make up our social character can be a powerful source of proof. Such appeals, often expressed in traditional stories, sayings, and symbols, assume that audiences value their membership in a culture and share its heritage. Communication scholar Martha Solomon Watson has noted, "Rhetoric which incorporates mythical elements taps into rich cultural reservoirs."[7]

Appeals to cultural identity often call on patriotism and remind us of our heroes or enemies. They may be based on political narratives, such as the story of George Washington's harsh winter at Valley Forge. They may tell us that ours is "the land of opportunity."[8] Appeals to mythos also may be based on economic legends, such as American stories of success through hard work and thrift that celebrate the rise to power from humble beginnings. These stories justify economic power in our society while assuring the powerless that they too can make it, if only they have "the right stuff." Appeals to cultural identity may also draw on religious narratives. Sacred documents provide a rich storehouse of parables, often used as proof—not just in religious sermons but also in political discourse.[9]

ESL: Ask ESL students to identify the dominant myths of their native cultures and to elaborate on them for the class. Discuss the similarities and differences between these myths and those of the mainstream American culture.

To create the sense of mythos, stories need not be retold in their entirety each time they are invoked. Because they are so familiar, allusions to them may be sufficient. The culturetypes discussed in Chapter 10 are often called into service because they compress myths into a few provocative words. In his speech accepting the Democratic presidential nomination in 1960, John F. Kennedy called on the myth of the American frontier to move Americans to action:

A mini-lecture on myths is available in Chapter 14 of the IRM.

> **The New Frontier of which I speak is not a set of promises—it is a set of challenges. It sums up not what I intend to offer the American people, but what I intend to ask of them.[10]**

This appeal to cultural identity emerged as a central theme of Kennedy's presidency. He didn't need to refer directly to the legends of Daniel Boone and Davy

The Western frontier is a major source of mythos in American speeches. *American Progress*, a painting by American artist John Gast, portrays many icons and ideographs. Which ones can you identify?

Crockett or to the tales of wagons pushing west to meet the dangers and challenges that lay ahead—he was able to conjure up those thoughts in listeners with the phrase "the New Frontier." Allusions to a myth can also be used to refute an exploitative use of the myth. For example, an antismoking billboard we saw in Montana shows two "Marlboro-type" cowboys with the caption, "Bob, I've got emphysema!"

Use the "Mythos and Argument" exercise in Chapter 14 of the IRM.

How can you use appeals to mythos in a classroom speech? Let us look at how Robert Owens used such appeals to urge stronger action against drug traffic in urban slums. Robert wanted to establish that "we must win the battle against drugs on the streets of America." He supported this statement by creating a sense of outrage in listeners over the betrayal of the American Dream in urban America:

> **Read the latest issue of *Time* magazine, and you'll meet an America you never sang about in the songs you learned in school. It's an America in which hope, faith, and dreams are nothing but a bitter memory.**
>
> **They call America a land of hope, but it's hard to hope when your mother is a cocaine addict on Susquehanna Avenue in North Philadelphia.**
>
> **They call America a land of faith, but what faith can you cling to when even God seems to have abandoned the street corners to the junkies and the dealers!**
>
> **They call America a land of dreams, but what kind of dreams can you have when all you hear at night as you lie in bed are the curses and screams of buyers and dealers.**
>
> **We might be able to redeem the hope, the faith, and the dreams Americans like to talk about. But we have to do more than just declare war on drugs. We've got to *go* to war, and we've got to win! If we don't, the crack in the Liberty Bell may only symbolize a deadly drug that is destroying the American spirit all over this land.**

These appeals to a betrayed mythos justified Robert's concluding plea for a broad-based, aggressive campaign to rid America of its drug culture. *The unique function of appeals to cultural identity is to help listeners understand how the speaker's recommendations fit into the total belief and value patterns of their group.* This gives such proof a special role in the persuasive process we discussed in the last chapter. It can help integrate new attitudes and action into the group's culture.

Like appeals to personal feeling, appeals to cultural identity can be a great good or a considerable evil. At its best, such appeals heighten our appreciation of who we are *as a people* and promote consistency between community values and public policy. However, when misused, these appeals can make it seem that there is only one *legitimate* culture. Appeals to cultural identity can abuse those who choose not to conform to the dominant values. Such appeals can tear the social fabric.

Weaving the Fabric of Proof

Speakers must blend the various strands of proof into a convincing demonstration. To fashion such a demonstration, you must (1) determine the type of proof most appropriate to your message and (2) understand how different types of proof can work together.

When audience knowledge of a problem is uncertain, persuasion should emphasize appeals to rationality. If a problem calls for human understanding, appeals to feeling may be needed. If a situation is uncertain or confusing, appeals to credibility rise in importance. If traditions and values are central to a situation, appeals to cultural identity become vital. Cultural appeals can help overcome the differences among people and create a group spirit that is receptive to a message.

Appeals to cultural identity can help listeners understand how the speaker's proposals fit into the belief and value patterns of their group.

Consider again the speech at the end of this chapter. Joshua Logan believed after his first speech (reprinted following Chapter 13) that his listeners accepted the proposition that global warming threatened them and their future. Now he must persuade them that a solution was available and that they could have a meaningful part in it. To establish the credentials of this solution, he must first reestablish his own credibility, that he has done the research necessary to speak as a responsible advocate. As he builds his ethos, he also develops the logos of his case: a detailed factual account of new forms of energy, new energy-efficient products, and new ways to clean up traditional energy sources. His appeals to mythos are indirect: he points to successful efforts by Mexico and China to awaken patriotic regret that the United States had not been more committed to the control of global warming. He concludes by appealing to pathos as he paints a hopeful vision of the family he hopes to have enjoying a threatened place dear to his family's tradition. By combining these various appeals, Joshua weaves a strong fabric of proof, developing a compelling argument that a solution exists that may be equal to the problem.

Speaker's Notes 14.1

WHEN AND HOW TO USE PROOF

1. To increase awareness and understanding, use rational appeals based on facts, statistics, and expert testimony (*logos*).
2. To communicate the human dimensions of a problem, stir listeners with moving examples and stories (*pathos*).
3. To bring faraway and complex problems close to listeners, tell personal stories and introduce expert testimony (*ethos*).
4. To highlight traditions and values, invoke cultural symbols and tell stories that reawaken group identity (*mythos*).

InterConnections.LearnMore 14.1

REASONING

Annual Review of Psychology (1999): Deductive Reasoning **http://www.findarticles.com/cf_0/m0961/1999_Annual/54442295/p1/article.jhtml**
A scholarly review of theory and research on how people reason toward decisions; authored by P. N. Johnson-Laird.

Argumentation and Critical Thinking Tutorial
http://sorrel.humboldt.edu/~act/
An interactive tutorial, with tests developed by Jay VerLinden, professor of Communication at Humboldt State University.

Inductive Reasoning
http://webpages.shepherd.edu/maustin/rhetoric/inductiv.htm
A web site on inductive reasoning with good explanations, examples, and exercises; developed by Professor Michael Austin of Shepherd College.

Mission: Critical **http://www.sjsu.edu/depts/itl/**
An interactive site containing explanations and exercises about the basic concepts of critical thinking; developed by Professor David Mesher for the Institute for Teaching and Learning at San Jose State University.

Forming Arguments

Use the "Argument and Persuasion" transparency (the master is in Chapter 14 of the IRM) as you discuss the material in this section.

The term *argument* can be used in many ways. It can imply a reluctant listener ("He argued with me"), a controversy ("They argued with each other"), or the intellectual content of a persuasive position ("Her argument was as follows"). To avoid confusion, we limit our use of *argument* as follows: ***arguments** are arrangements of proof intended to answer the key questions that arise from persuasive designs.*

In a problem-solution design, there are two key questions:

1. Is there a serious problem?
2. Would the proposed solution solve the problem ethically and effectively?

Therefore, in speeches using such designs there will be two arguments, one proving the existence of a problem, the second defending the proposed solution.

In the refutative design, there may also be two vital questions:

1. Is the attack upon a position justified?
2. Would an alternative be better?

Correspondingly, the speaker will have to build arguments that both validate the attack and prove the superiority of some better position.

In the categorical design, the speaker builds arguments that apply to particular patterns of thinking. For example, if the categories concern whether a plan would be *safe*, *inexpensive*, and *effective*, the speaker must build three arguments that answer these questions.

As they develop arguments, ethical speakers want their work to be judged as sound and persuasive by judicious, critical, and constructive listeners. What these speakers do is to set forth the overall pattern of evidence, proofs, and argument that convinced them. In effect they say to listeners, "See if these considerations don't persuade you as well." Such ethical persuasion invites listeners to inspect the argument and to draw their own conclusions.

Arguments demonstrate various forms of reasoning that address three fundamental questions:

- Is the argument based on generally accepted principles?
- Is the argument based on a careful observation of reality?
- Is the argument based on a similar situation?

Correspondingly, the major patterns of argument are based on reasoning from principle, reasoning from observation, and reasoning from analogy.

Reasoning from Principle

As we absorb the faiths and folkways of our culture, we acquire principles and rules that guide the way we think and live. Such guides often become part of the formal faith of a people. For example "freedom of speech" is written into the Constitution of the United States as a principle of government.

Reasoning from principle may begin by reminding listeners of their political heritage: "We all believe in freedom of speech." Next, it relates a specific issue to that principle: "Melvin would like to speak." Finally, it reaches a conclusion: "We should let Melvin speak." Such reasoning is sometimes called "deductive," because it deduces from some generalized principle a conclusion about a particular relevant case.

Because it begins with shared values, argument based on such reasoning is especially useful for establishing common ground with reluctant audiences. Such argument can also point out inconsistencies between beliefs and behaviors—the gap between what we practice and what we preach. For example, if you can show that the censorship of song lyrics is inconsistent with freedom of speech, then you will have presented a good reason for people to condemn that censorship. We are more likely to change a practice that is inconsistent with cherished principles or values than we are to change the principles or values. Because people like to be consistent and maintain the integrity of their values, argument from principle is a powerful way to change specific attitudes and behaviors.

Occasionally in an argument the principle is unstated, simply assumed, or implied on the faith that listeners themselves will supply and accept it. For example, the unstated principle in Cesar Chavez's "Pesticides Speech," reprinted

To ground his persuasive campaign urging a boycott of grapes, Cesar Chavez argued both from principle and reality, and appealed both to reason and strong feelings.

in Appendix C, might be reconstructed as: "Growers should not poison food to grow more of it." One of the major tasks in understanding arguments is to identify and evaluate such principles so that they don't slip in undetected under our critical guard.

We should also realize that not all people might agree with the items of faith we accept without question. For example, some researchers discovered that if you read the Bill of Rights to people without telling them it is part of the United States Constitution, an alarming percentage would describe it as "radical" or "communistic." Therefore, do not take principles for granted. You may have to defend and explain them to reinforce your listeners' belief in them. A related problem is that people may give lip service to a principle but not be committed to its meaning. As a speaker, you may have to reawaken their faith in the principle.

Another point critical to argument from principle comes when the speaker tries to show that a relevant condition actually exists. For example, Chavez, founder and president of the United Farm Workers union, presented evidence to support his assertion that California growers actually *were* poisoning food—and agricultural workers and consumers as well—in order to grow more. Clearly, the reality of such conditions is often the major point of controversy in a dispute. People may not argue passionately about the *principle* of environmental protection, but allegations about specific cases of pollution are subject to a great deal of dispute. The proofs you offer must establish such claims without question.

Ask students to analyze a persuasive speech in Appendix C to see how evidence, proof, and argument are woven together. Discuss how skillfully this is done and whether there are any obvious defects.

Once the audience accepts the principle, and agrees that you are accurately describing some related condition of reality, then your conclusion should follow: "Yes, the growers have violated their moral obligation and we'd better boycott grapes." Yet, as Aristotle implied in his *Rhetoric*, logic and life may be two different things. When we reason in the real world, we have to account for uncertainty. Because of this uncertainty, British logician Stephen Toulmin recommends that we add qualification as we draw conclusions in real-life arguments.[11]

Qualifiers are words like "probably" or "most likely" or "in most cases." They suggest the degree of confidence we have in the conclusion and acknowledge conditions under which the conclusion might not hold. An example of a qualifier might be, "*Unless* growers can prove they have changed the way they do business, we should join the grape boycott." If you carefully qualify your conclusions, you should come across as a trustworthy persuasive speaker who is not trying to force listeners into an unreasoned commitment. Rather than a sign of weakness, qualifiers can strengthen your credibility before critical listeners.

As you develop a principled pattern of reasoning for your speech, keep these cautions in mind:

1. *Be certain your audience will accept the principles on which your arguments are based.* Remind listeners why they believe as they do. Cite prestigious sources who testify to the importance of such faith. Use appeals to feeling and to cultural identity to reinforce the principles. Use rational appeals to show their practical importance.

2. *Demonstrate the existence of relevant conditions.* This, as we shall see in the next section, is where empirical reasoning joins with principled reasoning to build compelling arguments.

3. *Explain the relationship between principles and conditions.* Don't expect your audience to get the point automatically. Listeners may not see the connection between environmental conditions and their responsibility to maintain the natural beauty of their country. Help them by drawing the point explicitly.

4. *Be certain your reasoning is free from flaws and fallacies.* We discuss such problems of argument in the final section of this chapter.

5. *Be sure your conclusion offers a clear direction for listeners.* Don't leave them foundering without a clear idea as to what you want them to do.

Reasoning from Observation

It should be clear by now that persuaders must base their conclusions on conditions that actually exist. **Reasoning from observation** confirms that an argument is based in reality. Such reasoning is often called **empirical**. It is sometimes called "inductive," in that it draws general conclusions from an inspection of particular related instances.

Discuss how reasoning from observation can be misused to reinforce stereotypes or biased generalizations.

Although reasoning from principle and reasoning from observation may seem to be opposites, they actually work together. Argument that emphasizes the close inspection of reality can reinforce principles so that they are not just items of faith. For example, if we can demonstrate that "free and open discussion actually results in better public decisions," then we bring reality and practicality to the support of the principle of freedom of speech.

Proving the existence of relevant reality conditions is sometimes easy, sometimes difficult. Joshua Logan's argument establishing that "global warming . . . threatens to become 'global burning'"—the problem dimension of his speech which may be found following this chapter—was not that hard. His earlier speech supported his claim, and discussion following that speech suggested that listeners were convinced. Therefore, the major burden of his speech fell now on building an argument supporting his solution.

Discuss and demonstrate further how proofs based on appeals to rationality and emotion can work together to strengthen an argument.

On the other hand, Chavez, who wished his listeners to join in a nationwide boycott of table grapes, faced a different challenge. Many of his listeners might question whether growers were actually using pesticides irresponsibly. To ground his claim, Chavez used rational appeals with striking statistics to establish the severity of the problem in the fields of California.

> **The World Resources Institute reported that over three hundred thousand farm workers are poisoned every year by pesticides. Over half of all reported pesticide-related illnesses involve the cultivation or harvesting of table grapes. They receive *more* restricted-use application permits, which allow growers to spray pesticides known to threaten humans, than *any* other fresh food crop. The General Accounting Office, which does research for the U. S. Congress, determined that *34* of the *76* types of pesticides used *legally* on grapes pose potential human health hazards and could *not be detected* by current multi-residue methods. [The script of the speech supplies the italicized words. They indicate points Chavez particularly wished to emphasize in oral presentations.][12]**

Chavez could bring powerful personal testimony to bear, but realizing that some listeners might suspect him of bias, he used an abundance of expert testimony, including reluctant testimony from sources that might be expected to speak against his position.

> **Even the growers' own magazine, *The California Farmer*, admitted that growers were *illegally* using a very dangerous growth stimulator, called *Fix*, which is quite similar to *Agent Orange*, on the grapes.**

Therefore, he wove into the fabric of his argument the authority of both personal and borrowed credibility. As he pointed out examples of the victims of pesticide poisoning—especially among children—he added the coloration of pathos:

> **This is a very technical problem, with very *human* victims. One young body, Felipe Franco, was born without arms or legs in the agricultural town of**

> **McFarland. His mother worked for the first three months of her pregnancy picking grapes in fields that were sprayed repeatedly with pesticides believed to cause birth defects. . . . *And the children are dying.* They are dying *slow, painful, cruel* deaths in towns called *cancer clusters.* In cancer clusters like McFarland, where the childhood cancer rate is *800 percent* above normal. . . . There are at least *four* other children suffering from cancer and similar diseases which the experts believe were caused by pesticides in the little town of Earlimart, a rate *1200 percent* above normal. In Earlimart, little Jimmy Caudillo died recently from leukemia at the age of three.**
>
> **The grape vineyards of California have become America's Killing Fields.**

What makes this arrangement of proofs empirical is its effort to convince listeners that it pictures reality. This was the critical point in Chavez's argument that a serious problem did indeed exist.

In addition to its special usefulness in problem-solution designs, empirical reasoning also serves refutative designs in speeches that directly confront the opposition. Refutative speeches closely examine opposing positions and criticize specific weaknesses in evidence or proof. They often argue that opponents have presented a distorted or flawed or incomplete picture of reality.

As you incorporate empirical reasoning in your arguments, there are certain things you must consider. First, you must be objective enough to see the situation clearly. Be on guard not to let your biases determine what you see. Remind yourself that it is important to look at an issue from as many perspectives as possible. Second, you must observe a sufficient number of cases. One or two isolated incidents cannot justify an argument. Third, since situations surrounding relevant issues are constantly changing, you must be sure your observations are recent. Fourth, your observations must be truly representative of the situation. The exception does not prove the rule. And, finally, your observations must actually justify your conclusion. They must be relevant to the claim you wish to demonstrate.

Reasoning from Analogy

Ask students to find examples of analogical reasoning at work in current controversies. Are the arguments based on such reasoning effective? Are they valid?

Reasoning from analogy suggests that we can learn how to deal with a problem by considering a similar situation. This related situation becomes a model from which we can draw lessons.

Analogical reasoning can be useful in helping define a problem. It can frame an unfamiliar, abstract, or difficult problem in terms of something that is familiar, concrete, or more easily understood. For example, you might argue analogically, "Just as a wise farmer takes care of her fields to produce good food at harvest, so must we care for the land, air, and water to assure a healthy future for ourselves and our children." Analogical reasoning also can be used to proclaim a vivid

Speaker's Notes 14.2

EVALUATING REASONING FROM OBSERVATION

1. Are your observations objective?
2. Have you read and/or observed enough?
3. Are your observations recent?
4. Are your observations representative of the situation?
5. Do your observations adequately justify your conclusion?

warning: "If we don't deal with global warming, we might well find ourselves on the endangered species list—and not so far into the future! Just like the tiger and the elephant, our habitat is in crisis."

As useful as analogical reasoning can be in building problem arguments, it can be even more useful in developing solution arguments in problem-solution speeches. In these speeches, analogical reasoning suggests that proposals will work (or in refutative designs, that they will *not* work). For example, some of Chavez's opponents might have argued that the grape boycott would be ineffective. Chavez anticipated such argument by emphasizing how previous boycotts had worked. He framed brief but telling analogies for the grape boycott by relating it to the Montgomery bus boycott of the civil rights movement and to previous related successes:

> **I have seen many boycotts succeed. The Reverend Martin Luther King Junior, who so generously supported our first fast, led the way with the bus boycott. And with our first boycott, we were able to get DDT, Aldrin, and Dieldrin banned, in our first contracts with grape growers. Now, even more urgently, we are trying to get deadly pesticides banned.**

In some cases analogical reasoning can be central to the persuasiveness of solutions. For example, in the continuing debate over our nation's drug policy, those who favor legalizing "recreational" drugs frequently base their arguments on an analogy to Prohibition.[13] They claim that the Prohibition amendment caused more problems than it solved because it made drinking an adventure and led to the rise of a criminal empire. They then claim that our efforts to outlaw recreational drugs have had the same result. The reason, they say, is that it is impossible to ban a human desire—that to try to do so simply encourages contempt for the law. Moreover, they assert that legalizing drugs would help put the international drug dealers out of business just as the repeal of Prohibition helped bring about the downfall of the gangsters of the 1930s. Finally, they argue, if drug sales were legal, it would be easier to control the quality of drugs, thus reducing the danger to users (parallel to the health problems associated with bootleg whiskey during Prohibition).

As this example shows, analogical reasoning emphasizes strategic points of comparison between similar situations. People on both sides of an issue will focus on these points, using evidence and proofs to defend or attack them. Opponents to legalizing drugs claim that there are many important differences between drugs and alcohol.[14] They say that alcohol is not as addictive for casual users as heroin or cocaine. They contend that legalization would multiply the drug problem, not reduce it, because it would make drugs more accessible and make them seem acceptable. They further suggest that since many drug abusers are prone to violence, the cost to society would be increased. Thus, the public debate rages on over these crucial points of comparison.

What makes analogical reasoning work? It is similar to empirical reasoning in that it seeks insight through careful observation. Analogy, however, concentrates *on one similar situation* rather than ranging across many. This means that although analogical reasoning may seem more concrete and interesting than some forms of empirical reasoning (such as that based often on statistical evidence), it can also be less reliable. Before you decide to develop an analogy as part of your argument, be sure that the important similarities between the situations outweigh the dissimilarities. If you must strain to make an analogy fit, rely on other forms of reasoning.

One final thing you must consider if you plan to use an analogical argument is the length of time it may take to develop such lines of thought. In a recent speech supporting increased investment in public education, Bob Chase, president of the National Education Association, used an analogy between the importance of publicly funded education and publicly funded fire departments:

> In the nineteenth century, fire was a major public worry in the nation's fast growing cities. An abundance of wood buildings with flammable candles, gas lamps, and open hearths made for a combustible situation. And indeed, some cities suffered terrible fires in which enormous losses of life and property occurred.
>
> Not too surprisingly, private fire fighting companies sprang up in several cities. And they offered property owners the following deal: You pay a monthly or annual fee, and we will come and put out any fire on your property. It was a classic market response to a human need.
>
> Ah, but such an arrangement had a fatal flaw. If your next door neighbor had neglected to purchase fire fighting protection or could not afford to purchase it, his fire went unquenched, and swiftly became a raging inferno that engulfed your property.
>
> So in some cities people then turned to the public sector for a solution, as they often do when confronted with one of these "we-are-all-in-the-same-boat-together" situations. And the modern day public fire department, which we all now take for granted, was born.
>
> It strikes me that ignorance is much like fire. An individual parent can pursue the education of his or her children with great diligence, but end up getting burned because some other parent did not or could not do the same.
>
> Take, for example, the case of a functionally illiterate child. The odds are stacked heavily against the functionally illiterate person. And when that person does not beat the odds, which is often the case, we all end up paying in one way or another. Our prisons, for instance, are full of people who are functionally illiterate. It costs us, on average, \$15,000 a year to keep one person in prison. By contrast, it costs us, on average, \$5,911 a year to educate one K–12 student.[15]

To make this analogy effective, the speaker had to labor to build the basis of comparison, not simply assume the audience would understand it. This obviously took time. Be sure you will have the time to adequately develop such analogical reasoning before you select it as the major pattern for your argument.

The Importance of Defining Terms

The fate of arguments often depends on clear definitions of terms. Have you ever had a heated discussion with someone, only to discover later that the two of you were not even talking about the same things? All persuasive messages should start with definitions of terms so that speakers and listeners can share understanding from the outset. Opening definitions clarify what you mean, re-

Speaker's Notes 14.3

DEVELOPING POWERFUL ARGUMENTS

1. Build arguments around questions reasonable listeners might ask.
2. Justify arguments by evoking accepted principles.
3. Remind listeners of the importance of these principles.
4. Convince listeners that your arguments are based in reality.
5. Create a vivid sense of problem conditions.
6. In analogical reasoning, use a similar situation as a model.
7. Provide clear definitions of basic terms.

InterConnections.LearnMore 14.2

FALLACIES

The Fallacy Files **http://gncurtis.home.texas.net/**
An interactive site containing an extensive collection of fallacies and bad argument, with definitions and examples; well organized and entertaining as well as educational (see especially "Stalking the Wild Fallacy"); developed by Gary N. Curtis, Ph.D., an ontologist with an artificial intelligence company.

Fallacies Leading to Assumptions of Common Sense
http://www.kcmetro.cc.mo.us/longview/ctac/psychology/commonsense4.htm
A look at fallacious assumptions that may underlie arguments based on "common sense"; developed by Professor Matthew Westra, Longview Community College.

Stephen's Guide to the Logical Fallacies
http://datanation.com/fallacies/
The original "fallacies online" web site, with extensive information on critical thinking, logic, and fallacies; developed by Professor Steven Downes for the Institute of Professional Development, University of Alberta.

veal your intentions, and show listeners how you see a subject. When the speaker and audience come from different backgrounds, careful definitions are even more important.

Many problems of definition are based more on disagreements than on misunderstanding. Should alcohol be defined as a drug? Should the fetus be defined as a human being? Such questions lead speakers to *ethical* definitions. In the 1968 Memphis sanitation strike that led to the assassination of Dr. Martin Luther King Jr., the workers marched carrying signs that read, "I Am a Man." This simple-looking statement was actually the tip of an underlying moral argument. The strikers, mostly African Americans, were claiming they were *not* treated like men in social and economic terms. As you develop arguments, keep in mind that definitions can be *the fundamental issues at the heart of controversies*. Define key terms clearly, and support all controversial definitions with evidence and proof.

We often assume that others define things as we do. Ask students to define terms such as sexual harassment, freedom of speech, homosexuality, God's will, etc. Discuss differences in the definitions and how these might affect persuasive efforts.

Avoiding Defective Persuasion

It takes hard work to prepare a persuasive speech—analyzing your audience, researching your topic, planning your strategy, and designing arguments. Do not ruin all this work by committing **fallacies**, or errors of reasoning. Fallacies may crop up in the evidence you use, the proofs you develop, or the reasoning in your arguments. There are also fallacies particular to some of the speech designs discussed in the previous chapter. In this section we identify some of these major errors so that you can guard against them, both as speaker and as listener.

Use the "Find the Fallacy" exercise in Chapter 14 of the IRM.

Defective Evidence

Evidence is defective if the speaker misuses facts, statistics, or testimony.

Misuse of Facts. A major misuse of facts is the **slippery slope** fallacy that assumes that once something happens, it will establish an irreversible trend leading to disaster. The slippery slope fallacy often involves oversimplification and outlandish hyperbole. For example, a prominent religious leader once suggested that feminism was "a socialist, anti-family political movement that encourages women to leave their husbands, kill their children, practice witchcraft, destroy capitalism, and become lesbians."[16]

In an advertisement, the R. J. Reynolds Tobacco Company presented lay testimony by a Florida state employee:

> **The Government is considering a substantial increase in excise taxes as a deterrent to smoking. . . . And restricting smoking in your own home is also under review. . . . I don't think they'll be content with regulating tobacco. There isn't any reason they can't use a similar argument about other products such as meat, cheese, or anything they say we shouldn't consume. When they start regulating they rarely know when to stop.**

In the slippery slope fallacy it is not logic but rather our darkest fears that drive the prediction of events.

A second misuse of evidence involves the **confusion of fact and opinion**. A factual statement is objective and verifiable, such as, "Most Republican governors support the lowering of taxes." An opinion is a personal interpretation of information: a statement of belief, feeling, attitude, or value. Normally, factual and opinion statements stay in their proper places. The problem comes when speakers make impassioned claims based on opinions, such as: "The Republicans have done it now! They're violating our Constitution. They're tossing children out into the cold. They're depriving retired people of their right to a secure old age. These are the *facts* of what they're doing." Opinions can be useful in persuasive speeches when they represent careful interpretations that are supported by evidence. However, treating an opinion as a fact, or a fact as an opinion, is the source of many problems. It can make you seem to claim too much or too little and can raise questions about your competence and ethics.

At one time hunters used to distract their dogs from a trail by dragging a smoked herring across it. In our time, the **red herring** fallacy occurs when persuaders try to draw attention away from the real issues in a dispute, perhaps because they feel vulnerable on those issues or because they see a chance to vilify the opposition. Often the "red herring" they use is some sensational allegation dragged across the trail of the discussion. In the current abortion controversy, some "pro-choice" advocates have discredited their opponents by associating them with terrorists, assassins, and bombers. In return, some "pro-life" advocates have smeared their opposition by suggesting that abortion clinics may be underwritten by "mafia money." Such charges from both sides divert attention from the central issues of the controversy.

Statistical Fallacies. Audiences are often intimidated by numbers. We've all been taught that "figures don't lie" without being reminded that "liars figure." Speakers can exploit this tendency by creating statistical deceptions. For example, consider the **myth of the mean**, the illusion of the average. If you've ever vacationed in the mountains, you know that a stream may have an "average depth" of six inches, yet a person could drown in one of its deep pools. A speaker could tell you not to worry about poverty in Plattsville because the average income is well above the poverty level. Yet this average could be skewed by the fact that a few families are very wealthy, creating an illusion of well-being that is not true for most people. Averages are useful to summarize statistical information, but be sure they do not hide the reality of a situation.

Another statistical fallacy occurs when we offer **flawed statistical comparisons** that start from unequal bases. Suppose you have two salespersons, George and John, working for you. George has just opened a new account, giving him a total of two. John has opened three new accounts for a total of thirteen. George comes to you and asks for a promotion, arguing "My success rate this year is 100 percent, while John's is only 30 percent." George would be guilty of fallacious reasoning, if not bad salesmanship!

Defective Testimony. Testimony can be misused in many different ways. Speakers may omit *when* a statement was made to hide the fact that the testimony is dated. They may leave out important facts about their experts, intimidating us with titles such as "*Dr.* Michael Jones reported that smoking does not harm health." What the speaker *didn't* reveal was that Dr. Jones was a marketing professor who was writing public relations material for the Tobacco Growers Association. Speakers also abuse testimony when they cite words out of context that are not representative of a person's actual position. This can happen when a qualifier is presented as though it represented a concession, misquoting a statement such as "unless the growers are no longer using poisons" as "Ah, hah! He admits—and I quote him—'growers are no longer using poisons.'" As we noted in Chapter 6, prestige and lay testimony can be misused if they replace expert opinion when facts must be established. Finally, the "voice of the people" can be easily misrepresented, depending on *which* people you choose to quote.

Inappropriate Evidence. Other abuses occur when speakers deliberately use one form of evidence when they should be using another. For example, you might use facts and figures when examples would bring us closer to the human truth of a situation. Welfare statistics are sometimes misused in this way. When a speaker talks about poverty in the abstract, it distances listeners from its human reality. George Orwell once complained that such language "falls upon the [truth] like soft snow, blurring the outlines and covering up all the details."[17] On the other hand, speakers may use examples to arouse emotions when what is needed is the dispassionate picture provided by facts and figures. Testimony is abused when it is used to compensate for inadequate facts. Narratives that create mythos may also be used inappropriately. Calling someone a "Robin Hood who steals from the rich to give to the poor" has been used to justify more than one crime.

Ask students to read the "Letters to the Editor" sections of recent newspapers and magazines and to bring in examples of fallacies. Discuss why it may be easier to identify fallacies in arguments you oppose than in those you agree with.

Defective Proof

Any element of proof can be defective. We have already pointed out the danger when appeals to feelings overwhelm judgment and cloud the issue. Speakers might also misuse appeals to cultural identity to promote intolerance, such as, "When are Native Americans going to start being *good* Americans?"

Similarly, speakers may abuse appeals to credibility by attacking the person instead of the argument. This is called an **ad hominem** fallacy. Such persuaders try to avoid issues by calling the opposition derogatory names. For example, during a recent environmental dispute, one side charged that its opponents were "little old ladies in tennis shoes" and "outside agitators." Not to be outdone, the other side labeled their antagonists as "rapists of public parkland."[18] Senator Jennings Randolph, speaking before the U.S. Senate in the not-so-distant past, dismissed arguments in favor of the Equal Rights Amendment for women on grounds they were offered by a "small band of bra-less bubbleheads."[19] Proof by ethos also can be abused when speakers overuse it—when they try to intimidate listeners by citing an overwhelming list of authorities while neglecting to present information or good reasons for accepting their claims.

Finally, speakers neglect their responsibility to prove their points when they merely assert what they have not proved, thereby **begging the question**. Those who "beg the question" usually rely on colorful language to disguise the inadequacy of their proofs so that the words themselves *seem* to establish the conclusion. Some antiabortion advocates may be guilty of this practice when they refer to the fetus as the "unborn *child*" without bothering to address the difficult moral question of when human life actually begins. A similar abuse may occur when the speaker taps into the mythos of the audience without adequate justification or preparation. A conclusion such as, "Be *patriotic!* Support the *American way of life!* Speak out against gun control!" tacked onto a speech without further explanation begs the question because the speaker has not proved that being against gun control is a form of patriotism.

Defective Argument

Major fallacies may infest the basic patterns of reasoning in arguments. It is unethical to commit them purposely—irresponsible to commit them accidentally. In your role as critical listener, be on guard against them at all times.

Errors of Reasoning from Principle. Principled reasoning can only be as good as the underlying premise on which it is built. In the **shaky principle** fallacy, that premise is not sound. *If the principle is faulty, the entire argument may crumble.* We once heard a student begin a line of argument with the following statement of principle: "College athletes are not really here to learn." She was instantly in trouble. When her speech was over, the class assailed her with questions: How did she define *athletes*? Was she talking about intercollegiate or intramural athletes? How about the tennis team? How did she define learning? Was she aware of the negative stereotype at the center of her premise? Wasn't she being unfair, not to mention arrogant? It's safe to say that the speaker did not persuade many people that day. To avoid such a fiasco, be sure that you can defend each word in the principle that underlies your reasoning.

Omitted qualifiers, another fallacy common to reasoning from principle, occurs when a persuader claims too much, in effect confusing probability with certainty. The logic of everyday life is rarely certain. Suppose a friend from the Tau Beta fraternity calls you to set up a blind date. If the principle "Tau Betas are handsome" holds about 90 percent of the time in your experience, and if you are about 90 percent certain that your blind date is a Tau Beta, then your conclusion that your date will be attractive is an assumption qualified by at least two factors of uncertainty. It is better to say: "There is a *good chance* that my date will be handsome." If you point out the uncertainty factor in advance through proper qualification, you may not lose the audience's trust if a prediction does not come true.

Another error common in reasoning from principle is *assuming that if something happens after an event, it was caused by the event.* This **post hoc** fallacy confuses association with causation. It is the basis of many superstitious beliefs. The same people who wear their lucky boots and shirts to ball games may also argue that we should have a tax cut because the last time we had one we avoided war, increased employment, or reduced crime. One of our students fell into the post hoc trap when she argued that low readership of certain books in areas where the books are banned in public schools proves that the bans are effective. There may be many reasons why people don't read books—banning them in school libraries may or may not be among these reasons. It is just as likely that the book bans themselves are simply symptoms of deeper cultural conditions, and that the bans might actually create curiosity about their objects of scorn, resulting in more readership than might otherwise have happened. A speaker must demonstrate that events are causally connected, not just make the assumption based on association.

Finally, a **non sequitur** fallacy occurs when the principle and the observation discussed don't really relate to each other, when the conclusion does not necessarily follow from the relationship between them, or when the evidence presented is irrelevant. Former Speaker of the House Newt Gingrich, lecturing on why men are more suited than women to traditional military combat roles, provided a remarkable example that appears to fit all the conditions of non sequitur reasoning:

> **If combat means living in a ditch, females have biological problems staying in a ditch for 30 days because they get infections. . . . [Moreover,] males are biologically driven to go out and hunt for giraffes.**

Former representative Pat Schroeder responded to this wisdom as follows: "I have been working in a male culture for a very long time, and I haven't met the first one who wants to go out and hunt a giraffe."[20] And then there is the cockeyed non sequitur logic of Marge Schott, an owner of the Cincinnati Reds baseball team. Schott told a Denver radio audience that she would rather see children smoke than take drugs. Her reason? "We smoked a peace pipe with the Indians, right?"[21]

Errors of Reasoning from Observation. A common error in such reasoning is a **hasty generalization** that is based on insufficient or nonrepresentative observations. Suppose a student reasoned: "My big sister in Alpha Chi got a D from Professor Osborn. The guy who sits next to me in history got an F from her. I'm struggling to make a C in her class. Therefore, Professor Osborn is a tough grader." To avoid hasty generalization you would need to know what Professor Osborn's grade distribution looks like over an extended period of time and across courses, plus how her grades compare with other professors teaching the same courses.

Errors of Analogy. A **faulty analogy** occurs when the things compared are dissimilar in some important way. For example, assume that you have transferred from a college with 1,500 students to a university with 15,000 students. You present a speech proposing new campus security measures, arguing that because they worked well at the college, they should also work well at the university. Would such analogical reasoning be valid? That would depend on similarities and dissimilarities between the two schools. Is the size difference important? Are the crime problems similar? Are the schools located in similar settings? Are the students from roughly the same social and economic backgrounds? Dissimilarity on any of these points could raise doubts about the analogy and make your persuasion less convincing.

Fallacies Related to Particular Designs

In addition to fallacies of evidence, proof, and argument, there are at least two major fallacies related to particular persuasive designs. **Either-or thinking**, sometimes called a *false dilemma*, makes listeners think that they have only two mutually exclusive choices. This fallacy is attractive because it is dramatic: it satisfies our need for conflict and simplicity. It occurs in policy issues when one hears statements such as, "It's either jobs or the environment" or "If we pay down the debt, we sacrifice social security." Either-or thinking blinds listeners to other options, such as compromise or creative alternatives not yet considered. Such thinking often infests problem-solution speeches when speakers oversimplify the choices.

People with gardens sometimes make a "straw man" to scare off crows. As the name suggests, the straw is formed into the "likeness" of a man (presumably, a "straw woman" would work as well, as far as the crows are concerned). From this practice comes the **straw man** fallacy, creating a "likeness" of an opponent's view that makes it seem trivial, ridiculous, and easy to refute. As you might suspect, the straw man fallacy appears most often in speeches that contend with opposition. It understates and distorts the position of opponents and is unethical. Reducing the movement in favor of the Equal Rights Amendment for women to "an effort to abolish separate restrooms for men and women" or dismissing affirmative action as "a policy designed to give unfair advantage to minorities" are classic cases. As an ethical persuasive speaker, you have an obligation to represent an opposing position fairly and fully, even as you refute it. Only then will critical listeners respect you and your arguments. The straw man fallacy is an implicit admission of weakness or desperation and can damage what may well be a legitimate case.

Persuasion is constantly threatened by flaws and deception. In a world of competing views, we often see human nature revealed in its petty as well as its finer moments. As you plan and present your arguments or listen to the arguments of others, be on guard against fallacies.

FIGURE 14.2
Gallery of Fallacies

Kind	Nature of the Problem
1. Evidential fallacies	
A. Slippery slope	• Arguing that one bad thing will result in many others
B. Confusing fact with opinion	• Asserting opinions as though they were facts, or discrediting facts as opinions
C. Red herring	• Distracting listeners with sensational, irrelevant material
D. Myth of the mean	• Using an average to hide a problem
E. Flawed statistical comparisons	• Using percentage increases or decreases to distort reality
F. Defective testimony	• Omitting when a statement was made or a speaker's credentials; quoting out of context
G. Inappropriate evidence	• Using facts when examples are needed, or examples when facts are needed, or an intimidating list of authorities as a substitute for information
2. Flawed proofs	
A. Ad hominem	• Attacking the person rather than the point
B. Begging the question	• Assuming as decided what has actually not been proved
3. Defective arguments	
A. Shaky principle	• Basing a line of argument on an unsound assumption
B. Omitted qualifiers	• Confusing probability with certainty by asserting a conclusion without qualification
C. Post hoc	• Assuming because one event follows another, it was caused by it
D. Non sequitur	• Reasoning in which principles and observations are unrelated to each other or to the conclusion drawn
E. Hasty generalization	• Drawing conclusions based on insufficient or nonrepresentative observations
F. Faulty analogy	• Comparing things that are dissimilar in some important way
4. Persuasive design fallacies	
A. Either-or thinking	• Framing choices so that listeners think they have only two options
B. Straw man	• Belittling or trivializing arguments to refute them easily

In Summary

Evidence, proof, and argument provide the substance of persuasion.

Using Evidence Effectively. When used in persuasion, supporting materials become *evidence*. Facts and statistics alert us to a situation we must change. Examples move listeners, creating a favorable emotional atmosphere for the speaker's recommendations. Narratives bring a sense of reality and help listeners identify with the issue. Testimony calls on witnesses to support a position. When you use evidence, strive for recent facts and figures, emphasize factual examples, engage listeners through stories that make your point, and rely primarily on expert testimony.

Proving Your Points. *Proofs* arrange evidence in persuasive patterns. The forms of proof are appeals to our rational nature (*logos*), appeals to feeling (*pathos*), appeals to the credibility of speaker and sources within the speech (*ethos*), and appeals to cultural identity (*mythos*). Appeals to rationality assume that we are thinking creatures who respond to well-reasoned demonstrations. Appeals to feeling affirm that we are creatures of emotion as well. Appeals to credibility recognize that we respond to leadership qualities in speakers and to the authority of their sources of evidence. Appeals to cultural identity relate to our nature as social beings who respond to group traditions and values. To develop sound proof, you must determine what to emphasize in your particular message, and you must be able to combine the strengths of these various forms.

Forming an Argument. An *argument* arranges proofs to answer the key questions suggested in persuasive designs. Arguments are based on underlying forms of reasoning from principle, reasoning from observation, and reasoning from analogy. *Reasoning from principle* begins with a generally accepted principle or rule. *Reasoning from observation* satisfies listeners that the speaker's argument is grounded in reality. *Reasoning from analogy* emphasizes that we can learn about a situation, and how to deal with it, by considering a similar or parallel circumstance. The related situation becomes a model from which we can draw lessons. Arguments depend on clear, persuasive definitions for their effectiveness.

Avoiding Defective Persuasion. Fallacies are errors in reasoning that can damage a persuasive speech. Evidence can be defective when the speaker misuses facts, statistics, and testimony. Common errors include the *slippery slope fallacy*, which assumes that a single instance will establish a trend; the confusion of fact with opinion; and the *red herring*, using irrelevant material to divert attention from the issue. Statistical fallacies include the *myth of the mean*, in which averages create illusions that hide reality, and faulty conclusions based on flawed statistical comparisons. Evidence can also be used inappropriately, featuring facts and figures when the situation calls for examples, examples when the audience needs facts and figures, testimony to hide the weakness of information, or narratives to justify unethical behavior.

Various defects can reduce the value of proof. Speakers misuse proof by credibility when they commit an *ad hominem* fallacy, attacking the person rather than the argument. When speakers merely assert and assume in their conclusion what they have not proved, they commit the fallacy of *begging the question*.

Fallacies are also common in the patterns of argument. If the principle you use as the base of your reasoning is faulty, your entire argument will crumble. Other frequent errors occur when probability is passed off as certainty, and when the speaker confuses association with causation, reasoning that if something happened after an event, it therefore was caused by the event. The latter is called the *post hoc* fallacy. A *non sequitur* fallacy occurs when irrelevant conclusions or evidence are introduced into argument. Empirical reasoning can suffer from a *hasty generalization* drawn from insufficient or nonrepresentative observations. Analogical reasoning is defective when important dissimilarities outweigh similarities.

Either-or thinking can be a special problem in speeches calling for action. This fallacy reduces audience options to only two, one advocated by the speaker, the other undesirable. When speeches that contend with opposition understate, distort, or misrepresent an opposing position for the sake of easy refutation, they commit the *straw man* fallacy.

Terms to Know

evidence
reluctant witnesses
proofs
logos
pathos
ethos
mythos
arguments

reasoning from principle
qualifiers
reasoning from observation
empirical
reasoning from analogy
fallacies
slippery slope
confusion of fact and opinion
red herring
myth of the mean
flawed statistical comparisons
ad hominem
begging the question
shaky principle
omitted qualifiers
post hoc
non sequitur
hasty generalization
faulty analogy
either-or thinking
straw man

Notes

1. Franklin J. Boster et al., "The Persuasive Effects of Statistical Evidence in the Presence of Exemplars," *Communication Studies* 51 (2000): 296–306.
2. Shelly Chaiken, Wendy Wood, and Alice H. Eagly, "Principles of Persuasion," in *Social Psychology: Handbook of Basic Principles*, ed. E. Tory Higgins and Arie W. Kruglanki (New York: Guilford, 1996), pp. 702–742.
3. Representative of this scholarship is Ernest G. Bormann, "Fantasy and Rhetorical Vision: The Rhetorical Criticism of Social Reality," *Quarterly Journal of Speech* 58 (1972): 396–407; Walter F. Fisher, "Narration as a Human Communication Paradigm: The Case of Public Moral Argument," *Communication Monographs* 51 (1984): 1–22; Michael C. McGee, "In Search of 'The People': A Rhetorical Alternative," *Quarterly Journal of Speech* 61 (1975): 235–249; Michael Osborn, "Rhetorical Depiction," in *Form, Genre and the Study of Political Discourse*, ed. Herbert W. Simons and Aram A. Aghazarian (Columbia: University of South Carolina Press, 1986), pp. 79–107; and Janice Hocker Rushing, "The Rhetoric of the American Western Myth," *Communication Monographs* 50 (1983): 14–32.
4. Antonio R. Damasio, *Descartes' Error: Emotion, Reason, and the Human Brain* (New York: Putnam, 1994).
5. From a brochure distributed by Handgun Control, Inc., 1225 Eye Street NW, Washington, DC 20005 (1990).
6. In recent times the importance of "goodwill" to impressions of ethos was discounted by many social scientists. An experimental study that restores the importance of the "goodwill" factor is offered by James C. McCroskey and Mason J. Teven, "Goodwill: A Reexamination of the Construct and its Measurement," *Communication Monographs* 66 (1999): 90–103.
7. Martha Solomon, "The 'Positive Woman's' Journey: A Mythic Analysis of the Rhetoric of STOP ERA," *Quarterly Journal of Speech* 65 (1979): 262–274.
8. Rushing, pp. 14–32.
9. Roderick P. Hart, *The Political Pulpit* (West Lafayette, Ind.: Purdue University Press, 1977).
10. John Fitzgerald Kennedy, "Acceptance Address, 1960," in *The Great Society: A Sourcebook of Speeches*, ed. Glenn R. Capp (Belmont, Calif.: Dickenson, 1969), p. 14.
11. See Toulmin's discussion in *The Uses of Argument* (Cambridge: Cambridge University Press, 1958) and in Stephen Toulmin, Richard Rieke, and Allan Janik, *An Introduction to Reasoning*, 2nd ed. (New York: Macmillan, 1984).
12. Cesar Chavez, "Pesticides Speech," in *Contemporary American Speeches: A Sourcebook of Speech Forms and Principles*, 7th ed., ed. Richard L. Johannesen, R. R. Allen, and Wil A. Linkugel (Dubuque, Iowa: Kendall/Hunt, 1992), pp. 210–213.
13. Lisa M. Ross, "Buckley Says Drug Attack Won't Work," *Commercial Appeal* (Memphis), 14 Sept. 1989, p. B2.
14. Mortimer B. Zuckerman, "The Enemy Within," *U.S. News & World Report*, 11 Sept. 1989, p. 91.
15. Bob Chase, "Education's Brave New World," *Vital Speeches of the Day*, 1 May 1999, pp. 433–437. Used by permission of Vital Speeches, City News Publishing and the National Education Association.
16. Gilbert Cranberg, "Even Sensible Iowa Bows to the Religious Right," *Los Angeles Times*, 17 Aug. 1992, p. B5.
17. George Orwell, *Shooting an Elephant and Other Essays* (London: Secker and Warburg, 1950), p. 97.
18. Michael M. Osborn, "The Abuses of Argument," *Southern Speech Communication Journal* 49 (1983): 1–11.
19. Howard Kahane, *Logic and Contemporary Rhetoric: The Use of Reason in Everyday Life*, 5th ed. (Belmont, Calif.: Wadsworth, 1988) p. 38.
20. *Newsweek*, 30 Jan. 1995, p. 17.
21. *Commercial Appeal* (Memphis), 6 Sept. 1996, p. C1.

Cooling the World's Fever

Joshua Logan

Our world has a fever. And after my last speech, we know the cause of it. Global warming, that threatens to become "global burning." Global burning, that could raise global temperatures by as much as ten degrees by the end of this century. Global burning, that could raise ocean levels by three feet all around the globe. Global burning, that could submerge coastal cities, turn fertile lands into deserts, and destroy vast populations of wildlife. Global burning, that threatens many people, especially those in poor areas of the world, with epidemics of disease and hunger and dislocation. In short, global burning that could disrupt civilization and all life on this planet.

We don't have time to argue anymore over whether global warming or global burning—call it what you will—is a serious problem. We know that it is, thanks to hundreds of scientists around the world whose work has been collected, tested, and reported by the United Nations Intergovernmental Panel on Climate Change. *Time* magazine has summarized the gravity of the problem in light of the IPCC report, "Except for nuclear war or a collision with an asteroid, no force has more potential to damage our planet's web of life than global warming."

Now this is a persuasive speech, and it follows the problem-solution pattern. But I ask a lot more from you than simply *accepting* a solution: I ask that you *become* the solution. I ask for deep changes in attitude and behavior, for your conversion to a new way of environmental living. I know that I ask for a lot, but frankly, there's no other way out of this mess we've made. Whether we are liberal or conservative, Republican or Democrat, Baptist or Episcopalian—global warming confronts us all.

As I said last time, there's no easy or instant way out. It may take a hundred years before the earth benefits from some of the programs we put into place now. But we must begin. So what do you do when you've got a wild fire raging that you want to put out? You take away its fuel supply. What fuels global warming are the greenhouse gases, especially carbon dioxide, methane, and nitrous oxide.

The good news is, there is an emerging technology that could help us rearrange the bleak future I have painted. First, there are promising forms of energy that don't burn fossil fuels. Around the world, wind power is growing at 30 percent a year, with Europe leading the way. Already, this source of energy replaces the work of fifteen coal-fired power plants that would otherwise be belching tons of greenhouse gases into the atmosphere. Sound impractical for us? Just envision a new form of agriculture, wind farms. In North Dakota, farmers who have been earning $50 an acre from wheat are the new pioneers of power. Their wind farms will soon earn up to $2,000 an acre selling wind-generated power. Then of course there's solar power. Last year I enjoyed four days at an eco-resort in Mexico where there was no traditional electrical power. Each afternoon we took showers using hot water that had been warmed by solar power. The same source lighted the large dining room and powered its appliances. No harmful emissions there. Speaking of Mexico, that country is taking the lead in developing geothermal power—energy generated by natural

■ ***Josh summarizes the argument he developed in his speech reprinted at the end of Chapter 13—that global warming is a valid, serious problem. His argument is based on the implied principle that problems created by people can be solved by them. Linked to this is the principle that listeners have a responsibility to future generations not to endanger the planet. His quotation from*** **Time** ***reinforces the gravity of the situation.***

■ ***Josh announces the kind of persuasion he is seeking—in-depth, close to religious conversion. It is not enough that listeners should enact his recommendations or integrate them into their value systems; they must also absorb them into their lifestyles.***

■ ***Josh's argument for his solution relies on an additional set of unstated principles: that a program must be practical and affordable, that listeners must be able to enact its provisions, and that the graver the threat, the more effort and risk listeners should be willing to assume.***

■ ***Josh relies heavily on empirical reasoning from facts and statistics. He uses personal experience to add authenticity. He might have cited his sources of information more frequently to reinforce credibility. He strengthens the design of his problem-solution speech by dividing the discussion of new technology into three categories. This should help audience members remember his message.***

underground heating—and is opening its national power grid to a range of alternative sources for electrical power. I don't even have time to talk about the promising technology of fuel cells that can power buildings and electric cars, or more efficient ways to use traditional forms of energy.

Second, beyond these new forms of energy are also promising new products. Let me introduce you to the Toyota Prius and to the Honda Insight. These are hybrid gas-electric cars that run half the time on a traditional internal combustion engine and the rest of the time on batteries. As *Consumer Reports* describes the Prius, "Power comes from a 1.5 liter gasoline engine and a small electric motor. The Prius can automatically switch between one and other, or run on both, based on conditions. Fuel economy came to 41 mpg in mixed driving. The Prius can seat 5 people comfortably, and is classified as a 'Super Ultra Low Emission Vehicle.'" The Honda did even better: 51 mpg in mixed driving. In fact, these new cars—now priced on the market under $20,000—reduce harmful emissions by 40 percent. Look for even better cars late in this decade: Ford, Chrysler, and Volkswagen have developed prototypes of cars that run very nicely on hydrogen fuel cells—no greenhouse gases!

Third, there are promising new ways to clean up fossil fuel power. British Petroleum has taken the lead in reducing greenhouse emissions from its oil fields and refineries. It and the Ford Motor Company are sponsoring research into what they call "sequestering," stripping harmful residues from greenhouse gases so that they can be stored in abandoned oil and gas wells. Other research programs are exploring how to convert harmful CO_2 gases into minerals to keep them out of the atmosphere.

■ ***Josh asks listeners to combat global warming as citizens and energy consumers. He might have drawn this distinction more clearly. His criticism of President Bush is more effective because he is a Republican who speaks as a "reluctant witness." The appeal to pride he creates by contrasting the words of the president with the actions of China is also effective.***

So there's a great deal of hope out there. What is required is the political will to encourage these new initiatives on a large scale, the same way that the federal government once breathed life and hope into the fledgling airline industry. Here's where you come into the picture. By your votes and your letters, your contributions and your hard work, you can encourage politicians who make global burning a top priority. And once they are elected, we've got to hold their feet to the fire. Let me give just one example. I'm proud to be a Republican—most of the time! I voted for George W. Bush for president, encouraged by his promise to establish mandatory caps on power plant emissions. But once he was elected, President Bush announced there would be no such caps. Moreover, he declared his opposition to the so-called Kyoto Protocol, a worldwide agreement to reduce greenhouse gas emissions. He said, "We will work together, but it's going to be what's in the interest of our country, first and foremost." What's in the interest of our country, first and foremost, is the health and well-being of this and future generations of Americans. Contrast the president's words with the actions of China, which reduced its greenhouse output 17 percent between 1997 and 1999, eliminating more than the entire CO_2 production of Southeast Asia. Surely, if China can do it, so can we.

What we need is a new, green way of thinking and acting. Through our letters to the president, and to our congressmen and senators as well, we've got to help him change his mind and get right on the environment. I urge you to write those letters.

The second thing I would like you to do is to make a personal commitment to change your behaviors. Keep an open mind to the new technologies and the new products like hybrid cars. Factor them into your energy and transportation decisions. Instead of always driving your car, walk or ride a bike. You will discover an added benefit: greater health! Instead of driving alone to work, learn to carpool. You may also make some new friends or deepen old friendships. Let me remind you of another old friend, trees. Trees cleanse the air of CO_2, and they shade our homes, reducing the need for air conditioning in the summer,

How You Can Cool Global Warming

1. Run your dishwasher only when full and use the speed-dry option.
2. Clean or replace air conditioner filters regularly.
3. Set your thermostat lower in winter and higher in summer.
4. Walk, bike, carpool, or use mass transit.
5. Insulate your water heater.
6. Set water heater thermostat below 120°.
7. Install low-flow shower heads.
8. Ask your utility company to conduct a free energy audit of your home.
9. Encourage recycling at school or work.
10. Plant trees next to your home.
11. Wash laundry in cold water.
12. Replace old refrigerators with more energy-efficient models.
13. Reduce garbage by buying reusable products and recycling.
14. Replace standard light bulbs with fluorescent bulbs.
15. When you buy a car, make fuel efficiency a major consideration.
16. When you have your car air conditioner serviced, make sure the coolant is recycled.
17. Install energy-saving windows in your home.
18. Caulk around doors and windows in your home.
19. Insulate all walls and ceilings.
20. If possible, select a utility company that does not produce electricity from fossil fuel sources.

Adapted from *Time*, 9 Apr. 2001, p. 39.

but letting the sun through in the winter. So plant them, and join other green people who are working to encourage the wise management of forests. SOCM—"Save Our Cumberland Mountains"—is such a local group. These dedicated folks helped save Fall Creek Falls from strip mining, and they are working now to discourage the practice of clear-cutting, the large-scale destruction of forests in West Tennessee. I'm proud to belong to SOCM, and I invite you to join us at our next meeting this Thursday, where we are going to plan some serious environmental action.

You can make a difference, even in the small everyday choices you make. At the end of my speech I'm going to give you a list of other green things you can do to help take the red out of global warming. Planting a tree may not sound like much, but magnify every little act by a thousand, and then by a million, and then by a thousand million, as in China. We can make a difference—we must make a difference!

Someday, I hope to take my children, and my grandchildren, to Dauphin Island, Alabama, where they can walk on the sand and swim in the sea and enjoy the wildlife in the Audubon Bird Sanctuary. As I was preparing this speech, I developed an email conversation with Dr. George F. Crozier, executive director of the Sea Lab at Dauphin Island. From that fragile barrier island Dr. Crozier wrote me: "We are incorporating the message of global warming into our educational/outreach efforts in hopes that we can get the public's attention before it is too late." I don't think it's too late. And I hope what I've said in the last two speeches has gained your attention. Together we can cool the fever, and turn down the heat under our planet.

■ ***Josh concludes with a personal vision. His reference to email correspondence with the executive director of the Dauphin Island Sea Lab suggests the extent of his commitment.***

■ ***Josh's list of "Works Consulted" increased considerably over his first speech, reprinted at the end of Chapter 13. You should expand your research accordingly when you develop a topic over several speeches.***

WORKS CONSULTED

"Americans Consider Global Warming Real, but Not Alarming." Gallup News Service. 9 Apr. 2001. http://www.gallup.com/poll/Releases/Pr010409.asp (17 Apr. 2001).

Crozier, George. "Research on Global Warming and Dauphin Island." Email to Joshua Logan. 17 Apr. 2001.

"Feeling the Heat." *Time*. 9 Apr. 2001, pp. 22–39.

Fletcher, Susan R. "Global Climate Change Treaty: The Kyoto Protocol." National Council for Science and the Environment. 6 Mar. 2000. http://www.cnie.org/nle/clim-25.html (19 Apr. 2001).

"Governments Agree: Global Warming Impact Serious." Environment News Service. 19 Feb. 2001. http://ens.lycos.com/ens/feb2001/20011-02-19-01.html (17 Apr. 2001).

"Grim Future Forecast for World's Coastal Areas." Environment News Service. 17 Apr. 2001. http://ens-news.com/ens/apr2001/2001L-04-17-06.html (18 Apr. 2001).

Lazaroff, Cat. "Warming Oceans Attributed to Greenhouse Gases." Environment News Service. 16 Apr. 2001. http://ens.lycos.com/ens/apr2001/2001L-04-16-06.html (17 Apr. 200l).

Lazaroff, Catherine. "New Method Could Reduce Carbon Dioxide Levels Safely." Environment News Service. 31 Aug. 1999. http://ens.lycos.com/ens/aug99/1999L-08-31-07.html (17 Apr. 2001).

Petit, Charles W. "Polar Meltdown." *U.S. News & World Report*. 28 Feb. 2000, pp. 65–74.

Shute, Nancy. "The Weather Turns Wild." *U.S. News & World Report*, 5 Feb. 2001, pp. 44–52.

"Snapshots of the 2001 Cars." *Consumer Reports*, April 2001, pp. 44, 59.

Summary for Policymakers: A Report of Working Group I of the [United Nations] Intergovernmental Panel on Climate Change. January 2001. http://www.usgcrp.gov/ipcc/wg1spm.pdf (17 Apr. 2001).

Summary for Policymakers: Climate Change 2001: Impacts, Adaptation, and Vulnerability. A Report of Working Group II of the [United Nations] Intergovernmental Panel on Climate Change. 13–16 Feb. 2001. http://usgcrp.gov/ipcc/wg2spm.pdf (17 Apr. 2001).

Summary for Policy Makers of the IPCC WG III Third Assessment Report. 28 Feb.–3 Mar.2001. http://www.usgcrp.gov/ipcc/wg3spm.pdf (4 Apr. 2001).

15

Ceremonial Speaking

OUTLINE

THIS CHAPTER WILL HELP YOU

- appreciate the importance of ceremonial speaking
- present speeches of tribute and inspiration
- develop speeches introducing speakers and accepting awards
- prepare a toast or an after-dinner speech
- act as a master of ceremonies

Your college has just concluded an ambitious fund-raising campaign to create scholarships and attract outstanding teachers, artists, and scholars. As the leader of student volunteers who spent many hours soliciting contributions, you have been invited to be master of ceremonies at a banquet celebrating the campaign. At the banquet, you may both present and listen to many kinds of speeches: speeches offering tribute, conferring and accepting awards, introducing other speakers, evoking laughter, and inspiring listeners. They are all part of what we call ceremonial speaking.

There are other occasions when you may be called on to make a ceremonial speech. You may be asked to "say a few words" about a coworker or former teacher who is retiring, to toast a friend's wedding or anniversary, to welcome newcomers to an organization or community, or to present a eulogy for a dear friend or family member.

It is very easy to underestimate the importance of ceremonial speaking. Informative speaking shares knowledge, and persuasive speaking influences attitudes and actions. In comparison, ceremonial speaking, with its occasional moments of humor or inspiration, may not seem that significant. But it can serve a very important purpose.

ESL: Ask ESL students to identify the kinds of ceremonial speeches prominent in their countries. Why are these important there? Do these differ in kind and function with ceremonial speaking in the United States?

[People] who celebrate . . . are fused with each other and fused with all things in nature.

—Ernst Cassirer

Ceremonial speaking stresses the sharing of identities and values that unites people into communities.[1] The philosopher John Dewey observed that people "live in a community in virtue of the things which they have in common; and communication is the way in which they come to possess things in common. What they must have in common . . . are aims, beliefs, aspirations, knowledge—a common understanding."[2] It is ceremonial speaking that celebrates and reinforces our common aims, beliefs, and aspirations.

Rituals and ceremonies are important to all groups because they draw people together.[3] They provide larger-than-life pictures of our identities and ideals.[4] Ceremonial speaking addresses four basic questions: Who are we? Why are we? What have we accomplished? and What can we become together? As it answers these questions, ceremonial speaking provides people with a sense of purpose and helps create an "ordered, meaningful cultural world."[5]

Ceremonial speaking also serves a very practical purpose. As our opening example indicates, ceremonies put the spotlight on the speaker. As you conduct the college's celebration of its fund-raising campaign as master of ceremonies, others will be looking at you and thinking, "Wouldn't he make a good student body president?" or "Wouldn't she be a fine candidate for city council?" From the time of Aristotle, scholars have recognized that ceremonial speaking puts leadership on display.[6]

Ceremonial speaking puts leadership on display.

Ceremonial speeches also establish practical standards for action, advancing the principles that justify arguments and influence behavior.[7] The two student speeches at the end of this chapter illustrate this function. As Leslie Eason paid tribute to Tiger Woods for refusing to accept an identity based on race, she was in effect saying that we should not base our perceptions of ourselves or others on racial criteria. As Ashlie McMillan told the inspiring story of her cousin who is a dwarf, she was also urging her listeners not to let limitations block their own accomplishments. Both implicit messages could serve as principles justifying arguments and influencing behavior.

In this chapter we discuss the techniques and major forms of ceremonial speaking.

Techniques of Ceremonial Speaking

Two techniques, identification and magnification, are vital to the effectiveness of ceremonial speaking.

Identification

Identification occurs when a speech creates the feeling that speaker and listeners share goals, values, emotions, memories, motives, and cultural background. Kenneth Burke, perhaps the most important communication theorist of our time, suggested that identification was the key term of persuasive speaking.[8] Because ritual and ceremony draw people together, identification is also the heart of ceremonial speaking. Speakers promote identification through the use of narrative, the recognition of heroes and heroines, and the renewal of group commitment.

The Use of Narrative. Ceremonial speaking is the time for reliving shared golden moments. For example, if you were preparing a speech for the fundraising celebration, you could recall things that happened during those long evenings when student volunteers were making calls. You might remember moments of discouragement, followed by other moments of triumph when the

Ritual and ceremony can reinforce feelings of identification between speakers and listeners.

contributions were especially large or meaningful. Your story would draw listeners closer together as they remembered emotions they had shared. Stories that evoke humor are especially effective identifiers, because laughter itself is a shared group experience:

> **I don't think that any of us will forget the night that John tripped over a phone cord carrying a tray full of coffee and shorted out the computer network for the phone bank. Although many contributors got "cut off" by the accident, the returned calls netted the highest contributions of any night of the campaign.**

Just be certain your humorous stories don't belittle the people involved.

Ashlie McMillan showed how narrative can advance identification in her tribute to her cousin. In her introduction, she asked listeners to close their eyes and to imagine themselves shrinking. As they imagined miniature versions of themselves, prompted by her skillful use of language, listeners could identify more closely with Tina and the enormous problems she had to confront as a dwarf.

The Recognition of Heroes and Heroines. As you speak of the trials and triumphs of fund raising, you may want to recognize people who made singular contributions. These heroes and heroines can function as role models to inspire future action. As we try to be like them and act like them, the effect again is to draw people together. You must be careful, however, in using this technique. You may leave out someone who deserves recognition and create division rather than identification. Therefore, recognize specific individuals only when they have made truly unusual contributions or when they are representative. You might say, for instance:

> **Let me tell you about Mary Tyrer. She is just one of the many who for the last two months have spent night after night on these phones—talking, coaxing, winning friends for our school, and raising thousands of dollars in contributions. Mary, and all the others like you, we salute you, and promise that we will follow your example in the years to come!**

Renewal of Group Commitment. Ceremonial speaking is a time both for celebrating what has been accomplished and for renewing commitments. Share

InterConnections.LearnMore 15.1

IDENTIFICATION

Kenneth Burke and Identification **http://www.sla.purdue.edu/people/engl/dblakesley/burke/clark.html**
Full text of a paper entitled "Kenneth Burke, Identification, and Rhetorical Criticism," by Professor Gregory Clark of Brigham Young University; presented at the Conference on College Composittion and Communication, March 1997.

The Kenneth Burke Society **http://www-home.cc.duq.edu/~thames/kennethburke/Default.htm**
Information on the life and work of communication theorist Kenneth Burke; contains a discussion section and material on conferences on Burke's work; maintained by Professor Richard Thames, Department of English, Duquesne University.

On Kenneth Burke's Concept of Rhetorical Identification **http://www.libarts.ucok.edu/english/faculty/stein/rhetoric/report/Kenneth_Burke.htm**
A brief explanation of Burke's treatment of identification and consubstantiality; authored by Ricki Higdon.

with your listeners a vision of what the future can be like if their commitment continues. Plead with them not to be satisfied with present accomplishments. Renew their identity as a group moving toward even greater goals.

In his first inaugural address, delivered on the eve of the Civil War, Abraham Lincoln used the technique of identification in an effort to reunite the nation:

Use the activity "The 'Vision' Thing: Presidential Inaugurals and American Renewal," described in Chapter 15 of the IRM, to stimulate discussion of the basic values and visions of American culture as these are shaped and affirmed in ceremonial speaking.

> **I am loath to close. We are not enemies, but friends. We must not be enemies. Though passion may have strained, it must not break our bonds of affection. The mystic chords of memory, stretching from every battle-field, and patriot grave, to every living heart and hearthstone, all over this broad land, will yet swell the chorus of the Union, when again touched, as surely they will be, by the better angels of our nature.**[9]

Magnification

In his *Rhetoric*, Aristotle noted that when you select certain features of a person or event and then dwell on these qualities in your speech of tribute, the effect is to magnify these features until they fill the minds of listeners.[10] These magnified features then characterize the subject in terms of the values they represent. They focus listener attention on what is relevant, honorable, and praiseworthy. We may accordingly identify this vital inspirational technique as **magnification**. For example, imagine that you are preparing a speech honoring Jesse Owens's incredible track and field accomplishments in the 1936 Olympic Games. In your research, you come up with a variety of facts, such as:

Review what classical rhetoricians had to say about ceremonial speaking. The material can be found in the supplement *Classical Origins of Public Speaking*.

- He had a headache the day he won the medal in the long jump.
- He had suffered from racism in America.
- He did not like the food served at the Olympic training camp.
- He won his four gold medals in front of Adolf Hitler, who was preaching the racial superiority of Germans.
- Some of his friends did not want him to run for the United States.
- After his victories, he returned to further discrimination in America.

If you used all this information, your speech might seem aimless. Which of these items should you emphasize, and how should you proceed? To make your

Jesse Owens was both a great Olympic hero and a great inspirational speaker.

selection you need to know what themes are best to develop when you are magnifying the actions of a person. These themes include:

1. Overcoming obstacles
2. Unusual accomplishment
3. Superior performance
4. Pure, unselfish motives
5. Benefit to society

Use the activity "The Celebration of Values Speech," described in Chapter 15 of the IRM, to focus students on the centrality of values in ceremonial speaking. Are different values stressed by the different cultures represented in the class?

As you consider these themes, it becomes clear which items about Jesse Owens you should magnify and how you should go about it. To begin, you would stress that Owens had to overcome obstacles such as racism in America to make the Olympic team. Then you would point out that his accomplishment was unusual, that no one else had ever won four gold medals in Olympic track and field competition. Moreover, the performance was superior, resulting in world records that lasted many years. Because Owens received no material gain from his victories, his motives were pure; his performance was driven solely by personal qualities such as courage, competitiveness, and determination. Finally, you would demonstrate that because his victories repudiated Hitler's racist ideology, causing the Nazi leader public humiliation, Owens's accomplishments benefited our society. The overall effect would be to magnify the meaning of Jesse Owens's great performances both for himself and for his nation.

Ask students to read the ceremonial speeches at the end of this chapter and those in Appendix C. Can they detect the processes of identification and magnification at work? Which of the speeches are most successful in implementing these processes?

In addition to focusing on these basic themes, magnification relies on effective uses of language to create dramatic word-pictures. Metaphor and simile can magnify a subject through creative associations, such as, "He struck like a lightning bolt that day." Parallel structure, the repetition of key words and phrases, can also help magnify a subject and embed it in our minds. For example, if you were to say of Mother Teresa, "Whenever there was hurt, she was there. Whenever there was hunger, she was there. Whenever there was desperation, she was there," you would be magnifying her dedication and selflessness. This technique should make those qualities resonate in the minds of listeners.

Magnification also favors certain speech designs over others. Comparison and contrast designs promote magnification by making selected features stand out. For example, you might contrast the purity of Owens's motives with the crassness of those of today's well-paid athletes. Chronological designs used to relate the history of a situation enhance magnification by dramatizing certain events as stories unfold over time. As Ashlie McMillan sketched incidents in the childhood and adulthood of her cousin, she magnified Tina's developing character. The causation design serves magnification when a person's accomplishments are emphasized as the causes of important effects: Jesse Owens's victories, a speaker might say, refuted Nazi propaganda for many people. Whatever designs ceremonial speeches use, it is important that they build to a conclusion. Speakers should save their best stories, their most telling points, until the end of the speech. Ceremonial speeches must never dwindle to a conclusion.

Types of Ceremonial Speeches

Ceremonial speeches include the speech of tribute (including award presentations, eulogies, and toasts), the acceptance speech, the speech of introduction, the speech of inspiration, and the after-dinner speech (see Figure 15.1). A ceremonial speaker may also serve as a master of ceremonies.

An especially creative form of the ceremonial speaking assignment is "Introducing Your Dream President 2004," an activity described in the IRM.

The Speech of Tribute

Had you developed a speech honoring Jesse Owens's Olympic victories, you would have prepared a **speech of tribute**. The speech of tribute, which may center on a person or an event, recognizes and celebrates accomplishments. For example, you might be called on to honor a former teacher at a retirement ceremony, present an award to someone for an outstanding accomplishment, eulogize a person who has died, or propose a toast to a friend who is getting married.

Speeches of tribute can serve several important purposes. If you have presented a series of speeches on related topics in your class, the speech of tribute

Assign a speech of tribute in which students honor those who had a major impact on their lives. The speech should emphasize vivid and moving images of the person's accomplishments to activate identification and magnification.

FIGURE 15.1
Types of Ceremonial Speeches

Type	Use When
Tributes	You wish to honor a person, group, occasion, or event. Subtypes include award presentations, eulogies, and toasts.
Acceptance	You need to acknowledge an award or honor.
Introductions	You must introduce a featured speaker in a program.
Inspiration	You want to motivate listeners to appreciate and commit to a goal, purpose, or set of values; this may be religious, commercial, political, or social in nature.
After-Dinner	You want to entertain the audience while leaving a message that can guide future behavior. Here, as elsewhere, brevity is golden.
Master of Ceremonies	You must coordinate a program and see that everything runs smoothly. The master of ceremonies sets the mood for the occasion.

gives you a chance to extend your efforts at informing and persuading listeners. For example, Holly Carlson chose the banning of books in the public schools as the topic area for all her speeches. In her informative speech, she demonstrated how books are banned in schools all over the country and listed the books and authors most often targeted. In her persuasive speech she offered a stirring plea for intellectual freedom, urging her listeners to support the right to read and think for themselves. Then for her ceremonial speech, she offered a tribute to one of the most victimized authors, J. D. Salinger. Her tribute to Salinger made her listeners want to read his works themselves. It also dramatized for listeners how hurtful censorship could be. Thus all Holly's speeches were of one fabric, which gave focus and cohesion to her semester's work.

To connect the persuasive and ceremonial assignments, ask students to prepare a speech in which they honor a person or group who has contributed to the cause advanced in their persuasive speech.

Speeches of tribute blend easily with inspirational speeches. As Leslie Eason praised Tiger Woods, she also inspired listeners to apply his example of integrity to their own lives. Ashlie McMillan's tribute to her cousin offered listeners an inspiring model of determination to overcome obstacles to their own achievements.

Praiseworthy accomplishments are usually celebrated for two reasons. First, they are important in themselves: the influence of a teacher may have contributed to the success of many of her former students. Second, they are important as symbols. The planting of the American flag at Iwo Jima during some of the most intense fighting of World War II came to symbolize the fortitude of the entire American war effort; it represented commitment and was more important as a symbol than as an actual event. Indeed, the famous monument commemorating that event has become part of the mythos of America. After the destruction of the World Trade Center in New York, a group of firefighters were photographed raising the American flag over the ruins of the center. That photograph echoed the monument, suggested that the heroic firefighters were like soldiers in a new war, and symbolized the determination of the nation to continue and conquer, even in the face of disaster.

Sometimes the same event may be celebrated for both actual and symbolic reasons. A student speech honoring the raising of $60 million for famine relief celebrated this achievement both as a symbol of global generosity and for the actual help it brought to many starving people. When you plan a speech of tribute, you should consider both the actual and the symbolic values that are represented.

The raising of the American flag at Iwo Jima during World War II became an important cultural symbol for courage and fortitude, themes echoed in the similar photograph of the raising of the flag by firefighters over the wreckage of the World Trade Center.

Developing Speeches of Tribute. As you prepare a speech of tribute, keep the following guidelines in mind. First, *do not exaggerate the tribute*. If you are too lavish with your praise or use too many superlatives, you may embarrass the recipient and make the praise unbelievable. Second, *focus on the person being honored*, not on yourself. Even if you know what effort the accomplishment required because you have done something similar, don't mention that at this time. It will just seem as though you are tooting your own horn when the focus should be on the honoree. Third, *create vivid images of accomplishment*. Speeches of tribute are occasions for illustrating what someone has achieved, the values underlying those achievements, and their consequences. Tell stories that make those accomplishments come to life. Finally, *be sincere*. Speeches of tribute are a time for warmth, pride, and appreciation. Your manner should reflect these qualities as you present the tribute.

When you honor a historical figure, your purpose will usually be to frame present goals in terms of the example you provide. This was the intention of Tommie Albright, Miss Florida Teen 2000 and a student at Daytona Beach Community College, as she spoke at the college's Martin Luther King Jr. Memorial Evening. Notice especially her use of contrast and parallel structure in the following section of her speech (reprinted in full in Appendix C):

> **Martin Luther King had many dreams for us, each with its own challenge to us.**
> **Where he dreamed of peace, we must be peaceful and seek peace.**
> **Where he saw hope, we must provide fulfillment.**
> **Where he dreamed of equality, we must treat each other as equals.**
> **Where he dreamed of brotherhood, we must act as brothers and sisters.**
> **And where he dreamed of justice, we must provide a just society.**[11]

Award Presentations. When you present an award, you often accompany it with a speech of tribute. An **award presentation** recognizes the achievements or contributions of those on whom the award is bestowed. Most award presentations have two main points: they explain the nature of the award, and they applaud what the recipient did to qualify for it.

The elegant use of language is important in ceremonial speaking. Here Toni Morrison accepts the Nobel Prize for Literature.

Unless the award is quite well known, such as an Oscar or Nobel Prize, you should always begin an award presentation by explaining the award:

> **Mary Beth Peterson was a graduate assistant in this department who exemplified the best qualities of a teacher: enthusiasm for her subject, the ability to impart it to others, and a real sense of caring for those whom she taught. After her untimely death, her parents and friends endowed the Mary Beth Peterson Award, offered each year to the graduate assistant in our department who best exemplifies the qualities Mary Beth brought so generously to the classroom.**

The second and most important part of an award presentation involves explaining why the honoree was chosen to receive the award. In talking about the recipient, you should emphasize the uniqueness, superiority, and benefits of his or her achievements. Provide specific examples that illustrate these accomplishments. Finally, you should name the recipient of the award and offer your congratulations and wishes for continued success. The complete text of an award presentation to Olympic track gold medalist Wilma Rudolph may be found in Appendix C.

Eulogies. Earlier we asked you to imagine yourself preparing a speech to honor Jesse Owens. Following his death in 1980, many such speeches were actually presented. A speech of tribute presented on the death of a person is called a **eulogy**. The following comments by Congressman Thomas P. O'Neill Jr., then Speaker of the House, illustrate how some of the major techniques we have discussed can work in a eulogy:

■ *O'Neill's opening highlights the themes of unusual and superior accomplishment. He begins with the actual value of Owens's victories, and then describes their symbolic value.*

> **I rise on the occasion of his passing to join my colleagues in tribute to the greatest American sports hero of this century, Jesse Owens. . . . His performances at the Berlin Olympics earned Jesse Owens the title of America's first superstar. . . .**
>
> **No other athlete symbolized the spirit and motto of the Olympics better than Jesse Owens. "Swifter, higher, stronger" was the credo by which Jesse Owens performed as an athlete and lived as an American. Of his performances in Hitler's Berlin in 1936, Jesse said: "I wasn't running against Hitler, I was running against the world." Owens's view of the Olympics was just that: he was competing against the best athletes in the world without regard to nationality, race, or political view. . . .**
>
> **Jesse Owens proved by his performances that he was the best among the finest the world had to offer, and in setting the world record in the 100-yard dash, he became the "fastest human" even before that epithet was fashionable. . . .**

■ *These comments magnify the values represented by Owens's life and develop the theme of benefit to the community.*

> **In life as well as on the athletic field Jesse Owens was first an American, and second, an internationalist. He loved his country; he loved the opportunity his country gave him to reach the pinnacle of athletic prowess. In his own quiet, unassuming, and modest way—by example, by inspiration, and by performance—he helped other young people to aim for the stars, to develop their God-given potential. . . .**

■ *That Owens remained a patriotic American in the face of racism and indifference magnifies his character.*

> **As the world's first superstar Jesse Owens was not initially overwhelmed by commercial interests and offered the opportunity to become a millionaire overnight. There was no White House reception waiting for him on his return from Berlin, and as Jesse Owens once observed: "I still had to ride in the back of the bus in my hometown in Alabama."**

■ *O'Neill's conclusion emphasizes the symbolic, spiritual values of Owens's life.*

> **Can one individual make a difference? Clearly in the case of Jesse Owens the answer is a resounding affirmative, for his whole life was dedicated to the elimination of poverty, totalitarianism, and racial bigotry; and he did it in his own special and modest way, a spokesman for freedom, an American ambas-**

Noa Ben-Artzi eulogizes her grandfather, Yitzhak Rabin, who was assassinated while serving as Prime Minister of Israel.

> sador of good will to the athletes of the world, and an inspiration to young Americans. . . . Jesse Owens was a champion all the way in a life of dedication to the principles of the American and Olympic spirit.[12]

When presented at memorial services, eulogies should also express the pain of loss and offer comfort.[13] Eulogies presented by family members are usually brief and focus on the personal characteristics of the deceased. At the funeral of the assassinated Israeli prime minister Yitzhak Rabin, many world leaders gave speeches of praise and condolence. Among these luminaries, Noa Ben-Artzi, the prime minister's teenage granddaughter, offered the most moving eulogy:

> You will forgive me, but I do not want to talk about peace today. I want to talk about my grandfather.
>
> Grandfather, you were the pillar of fire before the camp, and now we are just a camp left alone in the dark, and we're so cold. Very few people knew you truly. They can talk about you, but I feel they know nothing about the depth of the pain, the disaster and, yes, this holocaust, for—at least for us, the family and the friends, who are left only as the camp, without you, our pillar of fire.
>
> People greater than I have already eulogized you, but no one knows the caress that you placed on my shoulder and the warm hug that you saved only for us and your half-smile that always told me so much—the same smile that is no more.
>
> I harbor no feelings of revenge because the pain is too great. The ground was taken from under our feet, and we're trying somehow to make something of this void and have not yet succeeded. Grandpa, you were our hero. I want you to know that everything I did, I always saw you before me.
>
> Your appreciation and your love escorted us through every way and road. You never abandoned us, and here you are, my eternal hero, cold and alone, and there's nothing I can do to save you. We love you, Grandfather, forever.[14]

■ *The speaker indicates in her introduction that she will focus on the personal characteristics of the deceased. Note also the use of the enduring metaphors of fire and light and darkness, the biblical allusion, and the connection to the Holocaust, all of which relate Rabin to the mythos of the Jewish people.*

■ *This section reveals the speaker's personal struggle to understand what has happened and to somehow place it meaningfully in her life.*

The importance of sustaining a sense of community is especially critical after the loss of a valued member of the group. Although the eulogy primarily

A toast, a ceremonial speech in miniature, is offered as a tribute to people, as a blessing for their future, or simply in lighthearted enjoyment of the moment.

mourns and honors the person who has died, it also celebrates the values of those who remain and helps them rededicate to what that person stood for.

Ask students to prepare a toast for a classmate who they feel has made the most progress as a speaker or has given a speech they will long remember.

Toasts. A **toast** is a ceremonial speech in miniature, offered as a tribute to people and what they have done, as a blessing for their future, or simply as lighthearted enjoyment of the present moment. You might be asked to toast a coworker who has been promoted or a couple at a wedding reception, or simply to celebrate the beginning of a new year. The occasion may be formal or informal, but the message should always be eloquent. It simply won't do to mutter, "Here's to Tony, he's a great guy!" or "Cheers!" Such a feeble toast is "a gratuitous betrayal—of the occasion, its honoree, and the desire [of the audience] to clink glasses and murmur, 'Hear, hear' in appreciation of a compliment well fashioned."[15]

Whenever you think you might be called on to offer a toast, plan your remarks in advance. Keep your toast brief, and build to a climax. You might toast the "coach of the year" in the following way:

> **I want to offer a toast to a woman who is being recognized tonight as "coach of the year." You talk to the young women in this community, and to many of their parents sitting in this hall, and they'll tell you we should be honoring her as "coach of the century." Friend, confidante, mentor, model, ambassador for the community, and, yes, coach of winning girls' basketball teams year after year, she means so much to so many of us. So here's to Nancy, who will always be our "coach of the year!"**

Because a toast is a speech of celebration, you should refrain from making negative remarks.[16] For example, it would be inappropriate at a wedding reception to say, "Here's to John and Mary. I hope they don't end up in divorce court in a year the way I did!" Although most speeches are best presented extemporaneously, a toast should be memorized. Practice presenting your toast with glass in hand until it flows easily. If you have difficulty memorizing your toast, it is probably too long. Figure 15.2 presents samples of toasts for different occasions.

- May you have warm words on a cold evening, a full moon on a dark night, and a road downhill all the way to your door. (Irish blessing)
- When the roaring flames of your love have burned down to embers, may you find that you've married your best friend. (wedding toast offered by Jeff Brooks, Newton, Mass.)
- As you slide down the bannister of life, may the splinters never point the wrong way.
- May the Good Lord take a liking to you, . . . but not too soon!
- May you have the hindsight to know where you've been, the foresight to know where you're going, and the insight to know when you're going too far.
- As you ramble through life, whatever be your goal, keep your eye upon the doughnut and not upon the hole. (offered by Sid Pettigrew)
- May the road rise to meet you.
  May the wind be always at your back.
  May the sun shine warm upon your face.
  And rains fall soft upon your fields.
  And until we meet again,
  May God hold you in the hollow of His hand. (Irish blessing)

FIGURE 15.2
Sample Toasts

Acceptance Speeches

If you are receiving an award or honor, you may be expected to respond with a **speech of acceptance**. A speech of acceptance should express gratitude for the honor and acknowledge those who made the accomplishment possible. It should remain humble, should focus on the values the award represents, and should use language that matches the dignity of the occasion.

Ask students to prepare the acceptance speech they would love to give for the award they would love to receive.

When Elie Wiesel was awarded the 1986 Nobel Peace Prize, he began his acceptance speech with these remarks: "It is with a profound sense of humility that I accept the honor you have chosen to bestow upon me."[17] (The complete text of Wiesel's acceptance speech may be found in Appendix C). Follow his lead and accept an award with grace and modesty.

In an acceptance speech, you should also give credit where credit is due. If your hometown historical society is awarding you a scholarship, it would be appropriate for you to mention some teachers who prepared you for this moment. You might say something like, "This award belongs as much to Mr. Del Rio as it does to me. He opened my eyes to the importance and relevance of history in our world." When Martin Luther King Jr. accepted his Nobel Peace Prize in 1964, he did so in these words:

> **I accept this prize on behalf of all men who love peace and brotherhood. . . . Most of these people will never make the headlines and their names will not appear in Who's Who. Yet when years have rolled past . . . men and women will know and children will be taught that we have a finer land, a better people, a more noble civilization—because these humble children of God were willing to suffer for righteousness' sake.[18]**

As you accept an award, express your awareness of its deeper meaning. In their acceptance speeches, both Mr. Wiesel and Dr. King stressed the value of freedom and the importance of involvement—of overcoming hatred with loving concern. Finally, be sure the eloquence of your language fits the dignity of the situation. Dr. King relied heavily on an extended movement metaphor in his acceptance speech. He spoke of the "tortuous road" from Montgomery, Alabama,

Speaker's Notes 15.1

MAKING AN ACCEPTANCE SPEECH

1. Be modest.
2. Express your appreciation for the honor.
3. Acknowledge those who made your accomplishment possible.
4. Highlight the values that the award represents.
5. Be sure your language fits the formality of the occasion.

to Oslo, Norway, a road on which, in his words, "millions of Negroes are traveling to find a new sense of dignity." In a similar manner, Mr. Wiesel told the story of a "young Jewish boy discovering the kingdom of night" during the Holocaust. This personal, metaphorical narrative was introduced early in the speech and repeated in the conclusion when Mr. Wiesel remarked, "No one is as capable of gratitude as one who has emerged from the kingdom of night." Although your rhetorical style may not be as eloquent as these Nobel Prize winners, you should make a presentation that befits the dignity of the occasion.

If an award is presented as part of a ceremony involving presentations to more than one person, shorter acceptance speeches may be called for. Wilma Rudolph's brief words of acceptance on the National Sports Awards show were appropriate for that situation.

> **I'm excited. I'll get my breath. I receive this honor, and I dedicate it to the youth of America so they will know that their dreams too can come true. And also to my mother who is eighty-four years old, Blanche Rudolph. Thank you so much for this honor.**

The Speech of Introduction

Ask students to prepare a speech of introduction for the person they most admire, as though that person would then be speaking to the class.

One of the more common types of ceremonial speeches is the **speech of introduction**, in which you introduce a featured speaker to the audience. The importance of this speech can vary, depending on how well the speaker is already known. At times a formal introduction may seem quite unnecessary. For example, when Madonna introduced Muhammad Ali at a gathering of New York sports personalities, she simply said:

> **We are alike in many ways. We have espoused unpopular causes, we are arrogant, we like to have our picture taken, and we are the greatest.**[19]

A good introduction will usually meet three goals: it will make the speaker feel welcome, establish or strengthen the ethos of the speaker, and prepare the audience for the speech that will follow. You make a speaker feel welcome both by what you say and how you say it. Deliver your words of welcome with warmth and sincerity.

As soon as you know you will be introducing a speaker, find out as much as you can about the person. The following guidelines will help build ethos and lay the groundwork for speaker-audience identification:

- Create respect by magnifying the speaker's main accomplishments.
- Don't be too lavish with your praise. An overblown introduction can be embarrassing and distracting. One featured speaker was so overcome by an

Speaker's Notes 15.2

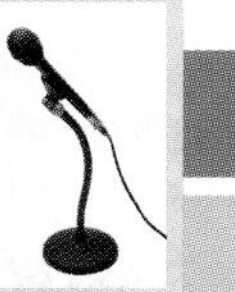

INTRODUCING FEATURED SPEAKERS

1. Be sure you know how to pronounce the speaker's name.
2. Find out what the speaker would like you to emphasize.
3. Focus on those parts of the speaker's background that are relevant to the topic, audience, and occasion.
4. Announce the title of the speech and tune the audience for it.
5. Make the speaker feel welcome. Be warm and gracious.
6. Be brief!

excessive introduction that he responded, "If you do not go to heaven for charity, you will certainly go somewhere else for exaggeration or downright prevarication."[20]

- Mention achievements that are relevant to the speaker's message, the occasion on which the speech is being presented, or the audience that has assembled.
- Be selective! If you try to present too many details and accomplishments, you may take up the speaker's time and make listeners weary. Introducers who drone on too long can create real problems for the speakers who follow.

The final function of an effective introduction is to tune the audience. In Chapter 4 we discussed how preliminary tuning can establish a receptive mood. You tune the audience when you arouse anticipation for the message that will follow. However, this does not mean that you should attempt to preview the speech. Leave that job to the speaker!

The Speech of Inspiration

The **speech of inspiration** arouses an audience to appreciate, commit to, and pursue a goal, purpose, or set of values or beliefs. Speeches of inspiration help listeners see subjects in a new light. Inspirational speeches may be religious, commercial, political, or social. When a sales manager introduces a new product to marketing representatives, pointing up its competitive advantages and its glowing market potential, the speech is both inspirational and persuasive. The marketing reps should feel inspired to push that product with great zeal and enthusiasm. Speeches at political conventions that praise the principles of the party, such as keynote addresses, are inspirational in tone and intent. So also is that great American institution, the commencement address. As different as these speech occasions may seem, they have important points in common.

First, *speeches of inspiration are enthusiastic.* Inspirational speakers accomplish their goals through their personal commitment and energy. Both the speaker and the speech must be active and forceful. Speakers must set an example for their audiences through their behavior both on and off the speaking platform. They must practice what they preach. Their ethos must be consistent with their advice.

Ask students to recall a speech of inspiration they have heard. Why do they remember the speech?

Second, *speeches of inspiration draw on past successes and frustrations to encourage future accomplishment.* At the 1995 Catalyst Awards Dinner, Sheila W. Welling, the president of that organization, evoked vivid memories of what the past was like for women as she urged continued progress toward equality in the workplace in the new millennium:

One hundred years ago, at the dawn of the last millennium, our bustled Victorian great-grandmothers could not run for a bus, let alone for Congress. If the race—as the Victorian poet claimed—went to the swift, women lost. Girdled, corseted, enveloped in yards of gingham and lace, women were balanced precariously on their pedestals.

. . . Women couldn't vote when my mother was born. Every time I think about it, it startles me, even as Edith Wharton wrote her novels, as Helen Keller graduated from Radcliffe with honors, even as women manufactured the arms that led to victory in WWI and the nation's move to global primacy, women still could not vote.[21]

Third, *speeches of inspiration revitalize our appreciation for values or beliefs*. In the later years of his life, when his athletic prowess had faded, Jesse Owens became known as a great inspirational speaker. According to his obituary in the *New York Times*, "The Jesse Owens best remembered by many Americans was a public speaker with the ringing, inspirational delivery of an evangelist. . . . [His speeches] praised the virtues of patriotism, clean living and fair play."[22] In the Owens speech that follows, the ideals of brotherhood and tolerance, as well as fair competition, are stressed. Such speeches can strengthen our sense of mythos, the distinctive code of values underlying our society.

Speeches of Inspiration: An Illustration. In his inspirational speeches to budding athletes, Jesse Owens frequently talked about his Olympic achievements. The following excerpts, taken from a statement protesting America's withdrawal from the 1980 Summer Olympic Games, illustrate his inspirational style. Jesse Owens was unable to deliver this message personally. It was prepared shortly before his death from cancer.

■ *Owens's introduction suggests the larger meaning of his victories and sets the stage for identification.*

What the Berlin games proved . . . was that Hitler's "supermen" could be beaten. Ironically, it was one of his blond, blue-eyed, Aryan athletes who helped do the beating.

I held the world record in the broad jump. Even more than the sprints, it was "my" event. Yet I was one jump from not even making the finals. I fouled on my first try, and playing it safe the second time, I had not jumped far enough.

■ *Note the use of graphic detail to recapture the immediacy of the moment.*

The broad jump preliminaries came before the finals of my other three events and everything, it seemed then, depended on this jump. Fear swept over me and then panic. I walked off alone, trying to gather myself. I dropped to one knee, closed my eyes, and prayed. I felt a hand on my shoulder. I opened my eyes and there stood my arch enemy, Luz Long, the prize athlete Hitler had kept under wraps while he trained for one purpose only: to beat me. Long had broken the Olympic mark in his very first try in the preliminaries.

■ *Owens's use of dialogue helps listeners feel they are sharing the experience.*

"I know about you," he said. "You are like me. You must do it all the way, or you cannot do it. The same that has happened to you today happened to me last year in Cologne. I will tell you what I did then." Luz told me to measure my steps, place my towel 6 inches on back of the takeoff board and jump from there. That way I could give it all I had and be certain not to foul.

As soon as I had qualified, Luz, smiling broadly, came to me and said, "Now we can make each other do our best in the finals."

■ *This narrative leaves open the meaning of Owens's "inside" victory: perhaps it was over self-doubt or over his own stereotype of Germans. Perhaps it was over both.*

And that's what we did in the finals. Luz jumped, and broke his Olympic record. Then I jumped just a bit further and broke Luz's new record. We each had three leaps in all. On his final jump, Luz went almost 26 feet, 5 inches, a mark that seemed impossible to beat. I went just a bit over that, and set an Olympic record that was to last for almost a quarter of a century.

I won that day, but I'm being straight when I say that even before I made that last jump, I knew I had won a victory of a far greater kind—over something inside myself, thanks to Luz.

The instant my record-breaking win was announced, Luz was there, throwing his arms around me and raising my arm to the sky. "Jazze Owenz!" he yelled as loud as he could. More than 100,000 Germans in the stadium joined in. "Jazze Owenz, Jazze Owenz, Jazze Owenz!"

Hitler was there, too, but he was not chanting. He had lost that day. Luz Long was killed in World War II and, although I don't cry often, I wept when I received his last letter—I knew it was his last. In it he asked me to someday find his son, Karl, and to tell him "of how we fought well together, and of the good times, and that any two men can become brothers."

That is what the Olympics are all about. The road to the Olympics does not lead to Moscow. It leads to no city, no country. It goes far beyond Lake Placid or Moscow, ancient Greece or Nazi Germany. The road to the Olympics leads, in the end, to the best within us.[23]

■ ***This scene presents an inspirational model of international competition.***

■ ***Owens shows how individuals can rise above ideologies, as Long's final message invites identification.***

■ ***Owens ends with a metaphor of the "road to the Olympics."***

The After-Dinner Speech

Occasions that celebrate special events or that mark the beginning or end of a course of action often call for an **after-dinner speech**. Political rallies, award banquets, the kickoff for a fund-raising campaign, or the end of the school year may provide the setting for such speaking.

To celebrate the end of the class, hold a special lunch or dinner session. Ask students to prepare brief after-dinner speeches based on the theme, "My most unforgettable moment in this class."

The after-dinner speech is one of the great rituals of American public speaking and public life. In keeping with the nature of the occasion, after-dinner speeches should not be too difficult to digest. Speakers making these presentations usually do not introduce radical ideas that require listeners to rethink their values or that ask for dramatic changes in belief or behavior. Nor are such occasions the time for anger or negativity. They are a time for people to savor who they are, what they have done, or what they wish to do. A good after-dinner speech, however, leaves a message that can act as a vision to guide and inspire future efforts.

The Role of Humor. Humor is an essential ingredient in most after-dinner speeches. In the introduction, humor can place both the speaker and the audience at ease.[24] It can also relieve tension. Enjoying lighter moments can remind us that there is a human element in all situations and that we should not take ourselves too seriously. At least one study has discovered that the use of humorous illustrations helps audiences remember the message of the speech.[25] In addition, humorous stories can create identification by building an "insider's" relationship between speaker and audience that draws them closer together. In sharing humor, the audience becomes a community of listeners.[26]

Ask ESL students to prepare brief speeches on the theme, "Humor in my country," emphasizing examples. Are others in the class able to enjoy the humor? Why or why not?

As we noted in Chapters 6 and 7, however, humor should not be forced on a speech. If you decide to begin with a joke simply because you think a speech should start that way, the humor may seem contrived and flat. Rather, humor must be functional, useful to make a point.

The humor in a speech is best developed out of the immediate situation. Dick Jackman, the director of corporate communications at Sun Company, opened an after-dinner speech at a National Football Foundation awards dinner by warning those in the expensive seats under the big chandelier that it "had been installed by the low bidder some time ago." In her keynote address at the Democratic National Convention in 1988, Texas state treasurer Ann Richards used pointed humor as she took her party to task for not involving women more frequently in major convention roles:

Twelve years ago Barbara Jordan, another Texas woman, . . . made the keynote address to the convention, and two women in 160 years is about par for the course.

But if you give us a chance, we can perform. After all, Ginger Rogers did everything that Fred Astaire did. She just did it backwards and in high heels.[27]

Humor can help relax listeners. Speakers who tell amusing stories about themselves build bonds of identification with an audience.

Humor requires thought, planning, and caution to be effective. If it is not handled well, it can be a disaster. For example, religious humor is usually dangerous, and racist or sexist humor is absolutely forbidden. The first runs the risk of offending some members of the audience and can make the speaker seem intolerant. The second reveals a devastating truth about the speaker's character and can create such negative reactions from the audience that the rest of the speech doesn't stand a chance. In general, avoid any anecdotes that are funny at the expense of others.

Often the best kind of humor centers on speakers themselves. Speakers who tell amusing stories about themselves sometimes rise in the esteem of listeners.[28] When this technique is successful, the stories that seem to put speakers down are actually building them up. A rural politician once told the following story at a dinner on an urban college campus:

> You know, I didn't have good schooling like all of you have. I had to educate myself for public office. Along the way I just tried not to embarrass myself like another fellow from around here once did. This man wanted to run for Congress. So he came up here to your college to present himself to all the students and faculty. He worked real hard on a speech to show them all that he was a man of vision and high intellect.
>
> As he came to the end of his speech, he intoned very solemnly, "If you elect me to the United States Congress, I'll be like that great American bird, the eagle. I'll soar high and see far! I won't be like that other bird that buries its head in the sand, the oyster!" There was a wonderful reaction from the audience to that. So he said it again—said he wasn't going to be no oyster.
>
> Well, I've tried hard not to be an oyster as I represent you, even though I know there's some folks who'd say, "Well, you sure ain't no eagle, either!"[29]

This story, which led into a review of the politician's accomplishments, was warmly appreciated both for its humor and its modesty. It suggests that humor takes time to develop and must be rich in graphic detail to set up its punch line. The story would not have been nearly as effective had the speaker begun with,

"Did you hear the one about the politician who didn't know an ostrich from an oyster?"

Developing an After-Dinner Speech. After-dinner speeches are more difficult to develop than their lightness and short length might suggest. Like any other speech, they must be carefully planned and practiced. They must have an effective introduction that commands attention right away, especially since some audience members may be more interested in talking to table companions than in listening to the speaker. After-dinner speeches should be more than strings of anecdotes to amuse listeners. The stories told must either establish a mood, convey a message, or carry a theme forward. Such speeches should build to a satisfying conclusion that conveys the essence of the message.

Above all, perhaps, after-dinner speeches should be mercifully brief. Long-winded after-dinner speakers can leave the audience fiddling with coffee cups and drawing pictures on napkins. After being subjected to such a speech, Albert Einstein once murmured: "I have just got a new theory of eternity."[30]

Master of Ceremonies

Quite often ceremonial speeches are part of a program of events that must be coordinated with skill and grace if things are to run smoothly. Being the master of ceremonies is no easy task. A speaker who served in such a capacity for a community program once noted:

> **Being an MC was sort of like having to stand up and juggle a dozen oranges in front of an audience. I just kept standing there, fumbling everything and waiting for the whole thing to be over with.[31]**

It takes at least as much careful planning, preparation, and practice to function effectively as a master of ceremonies as it does to make a major presentation. As the **master of ceremonies**, you will be expected to keep the program moving along, introduce participants, and possibly present awards. You will also set the tone or mood for the program.

If at all possible, you should be involved in planning the program from the beginning. Then you will have a better grasp of what is expected of you, what events have been scheduled, what the timetable is, who the featured speakers are, and what special logistics (such as meal service) you might have to deal with. The following guidelines should help you function effectively as a master of ceremonies:[32]

- *Know what is expected of you.* Why were you chosen to emcee the program? Remember, as emcee, you are not the "star" of the program; rather, you are the one who brings it all together and makes it work.
- *Plan a good opener for the program.* Your opening remarks as an emcee are as important as the introduction to a major presentation. You should gain the attention of the audience and prepare them for the program. Be sure that the mood you set with your opener is consistent with the nature of the occasion.
- *Be prepared to introduce the participants.* Be sure you know who they are and can pronounce their names correctly. If you prepare the introductions for them, review the relevant material in this chapter. Find out all you can about them: check Who's Who and local newspaper clipping files, and, if possible, talk to them directly to see what they would like you to emphasize and to determine how you might tune the audience for their speeches.
- *Be sure you know the schedule and timetable so that you can keep the program on track.* Also be sure that the participants get this information. They need to know how much time has been allotted for them to speak. Double-check

this with them before the program and work out some way to cue them in case they should run overtime. If time restrictions are severe (as in a televised program), be ready to edit and adapt your own planned comments.

- *Make certain that any prizes or awards are kept near the podium.* You shouldn't be left fumbling around looking for a plaque or trophy at presentation time.
- *Plan your comments ahead of time.* Develop a key-word outline for each presentation on a running script of the program. Print the name of the person or award in large letters at the top of each outline so that you can keep your place in the program.
- *Practice your presentation.* Although you are not the featured speaker, your words are important (especially to the person whom you will introduce or who will receive the award you will present). Practice your comments the same way you would practice a speech.
- *Make advance arrangements for mealtime logistics.* Speak with the maitre d' before the program to be sure the waiters know the importance of "silent service." If you will be speaking while people are still eating, adapt your message to cope with this distraction by using the attention-gaining techniques discussed in Chapters 7 and 12.
- *Be ready for the inevitable glitches.* Despite your best efforts, Murphy's Law (if anything can go wrong, it will) will surely prevail. Be ready for problems like microphones that don't work or that squeal, trays of dishes being dropped, and people wandering in and out during the course of the program. As you respond to these events, keep your cool and good humor.
- *End the program strongly.* Just as a speech should not dwindle into nothingness, neither should a program. Review the suggestions for speech conclusions in Chapter 7. When ending your presentation, thank those who made the program possible; then leave the audience with something to remember.

The tribute to Wilma Rudolph (the complete text appears in Appendix C) illustrates how one master of ceremonies, Tom Brokaw, performed that role.

As you end this book, we offer our own speech of tribute: this one to you. Public speaking may not have been easy for you. However, it is our hope that you have grown as a person as you have grown as a speaker. Our special wishes, expressed in terms of three underlying metaphors that provide the vision of this book, are that

- You have learned how to overcome the barriers that sometimes separate people and defeat communication.
- You have learned how to build speeches that are both powerful and ethical.
- You have learned how to weave words and evidence into eloquent thoughts and persuasive ideas.

We propose a toast: May you use your new speaking skills to improve the lives and lift the spirits of all who may listen to you.

In Summary

Ceremonial speeches serve important social functions. They place the spotlight on leadership. They reinforce the values that hold people together in a community and give listeners a sense of order and purpose in their lives. They also establish principles that can be applied in later arguments.

Major Techniques of Ceremonial Speaking. Two major techniques of ceremonial speaking are identification and magnification. The first creates close feeling, and the second selects and emphasizes those features of a subject that will convey the speaker's message. Speakers build identification by the use of narratives that remind listeners of shared experiences. Recognizing heroes and heroines also provides ideal models of conduct to draw listeners and speakers closer together. Finally, appeals to group commitment can remind listeners of the values and goals they share. Themes worthy of magnification include overcoming obstacles, achieving unusual goals, performing in a superior manner, having pure motives, and benefiting the community. Eloquent uses of language can also magnify the subjects of ceremonial speeches.

Types of Ceremonial Speeches. Speeches of tribute recognize achievements or commemorate special events, helping listeners appreciate the values these represent. As they describe ideal models of conduct, speeches of tribute also perform an inspirational function. Achievements and events may be significant in themselves or in what they symbolize. Award presentations should explain the nature of the award and what the recipient has done to merit it. Eulogies are speeches of tribute presented on the death of a person or persons. Toasts are ceremonial speeches in miniature that pay tribute, offer blessings, or celebrate the moment.

Speeches of acceptance should begin with an expression of gratitude and an acknowledgment of others who deserve recognition. They should focus on the values that the honor represents. Acceptance speeches often call for more formal language than other speeches and for eloquence that suits the occasion.

Speeches of introduction should welcome the speaker, establish his or her ethos, and tune the audience for the message that will follow. Introductions should focus on information about the speaker that is relevant to the speech topic or the occasion or that has special meaning for the audience.

Speeches of inspiration help listeners appreciate values and make them want to pursue worthy goals. Such speeches often call on stories of past successes. After-dinner speeches should be lighthearted, serving up humor and insight at the same time. Humor should be functional in such speeches, illustrating a point or serving some larger purpose.

The master of ceremonies coordinates a program and sees that things run smoothly. He or she sets the mood of the program, introduces the participants, provides transitions, and sometimes presents awards.

Terms to Know

ceremonial speaking
identification
magnification
speech of tribute
award presentation
eulogy
toast
speech of acceptance
speech of introduction
speech of inspiration
after-dinner speech
master of ceremonies

Notes

1. Celeste Michelle Condit, "The Functions of Epideictic: The Boston Massacre Orations as Exemplar," *Communication Quarterly* 33 (1985): 284–299; Gray Matthews, "Epideictic Rhetoric and Baseball: Nurturing Community Through Controversy," *Southern Communication Journal* 60 (1995): 275–291; Randall Parrish Osborn, "Jimmy Carter's Rhetorical Campaign for the Presidency: An Epideictic of American Renewal," *Southern States Communication Association Convention*, Memphis, March 1996; Ch. Perelman and L. Olbrechts-Tyteca, *The New Rhetoric: A Treatise on Argumentation* (South Bend, Ind.: University of Notre Dame Press, 1971), pp. 47–54; and Richard M. Weaver, *The Ethics of Rhetoric* (Chicago: Henry Regnery, 1953), pp. 164–185.
2. John Dewey, *Democracy and Education* (New York: Macmillan, 1916), p. 4.
3. Bronislaw Malinowski, "The Problem of Meaning in Primitive Languages," in *The Meaning of Meaning: A Study of the Influence of Language upon Thought and of the Science of Symbolism*, 8th ed., edited by C. K. Ogden and I. A. Richards (New York: Harcourt, Brace & World, 1946), p. 315.
4. Michael Osborn, *Orientations to Rhetorical Style* (Chicago: Science Research Associates, 1976), p. 32.
5. James W. Carey, "A Cultural Approach to Communication," *Communication* 2 (1975): 6.

6. Walter H. Beale, "Rhetorical Performance Discourse: A New Theory of Epideictic." *Philosophy and Rhetoric* 11 (1978): 221–246; and Bernard K. Duffy, "The Platonic Functions of Epideictic Rhetoric," *Philosophy and Rhetoric* 16 (1983): 79–93.

7. Christine Oravec, "Observation in Aristotle's Theory of Epideictic," *Philosophy and Rhetoric* 9 (1976): 162–174; and Perelman and Olbrechts-Tyteca.

8. See his discussion in "The Range of Rhetoric," in *A Rhetoric of Motives* (Berkeley and Los Angeles: University of California Press, 1969), pp. 3–43.

9. From *American Speeches*, ed. Wayland Maxfield Parrish and Marie Hochmuth (New York: Longmans, Green, 1954), p. 43.

10. See the discussion in *The Rhetoric of Aristotle*, trans. Lane Cooper (New York: Appleton-Century-Crofts, 1932), I.7, I.9, I.14 (pp. 34–44, 46–55, 78–79).

11. Tommie Albright, "Martin Luther King Jr.'s Legacy for Us," *Vital Speeches of the Day*, 1 Mar. 2000, p. 320.

12. *Congressional Record*, 1 Apr. 1980, pp. 7459–7460.

13. For a more detailed account of the functions of eulogies, see Karen A. Foss, "John Lennon and the Advisory Function of Eulogies," *Central States Speech Journal* 34 (1983): 187–194.

14. "'The Pillar of Fire': Excerpts from the Eulogies at the Funeral Yesterday of Yitzhak Rabin," *Boston Globe*, 7 Nov. 1995, p. A3.

15. Owen Edwards, "What Every Man Should Know: How to Make a Toast," *Esquire*, January 1984, p. 37.

16. The advice that follows is adapted from Jacob M. Braude, *Complete Speaker's and Toastmaster's Library: Definitions and Toasts* (Englewood Cliffs, N.J.: Prentice Hall, 1965), pp. 88–123; and Wendy Lin, "Let's Lift a Glass, Say a Few Words, and Toast 1996," *Memphis Commercial Appeal*, 28 Dec. 1995, p. C3.

17. Elie Wiesel, "Nobel Peace Prize Acceptance Speech," *New York Times*, 11 Dec. 1986, p. A8.

18. Martin Luther King Jr., "Nobel Peace Prize Acceptance Statement," in *The Cry for Freedom: The Struggle for Equality in America*, ed. Frank W. Hale Jr. (New York: Barnes, 1969), pp. 374–377.

19. *Commercial Appeal* [Memphis], 23 Oct. 1995, p. D2.

20. Cited in Morris K. Udall, *Too Funny to Be President* (New York: Holt, 1988), p. 156.

21. Sheila W. Welling, "Working Women: A Century of Change," *Vital Speeches of the Day*, 15 June 1995, pp. 516–517.

22. *Congressional Record*, 1 Apr. 1980, p. 7249.

23. *Congressional Record*, 1 Apr. 1980, p. 7248.

24. Roger Ailes, *You Are the Message* (New York: Doubleday, 1988), pp. 71–74.

25. Robert M. Kaplan and Gregory C. Pascoe, "Humorous Lectures and Humorous Examples: Some Effects upon Comprehension and Retention," *Journal of Educational Psychology* 69 (1977): 61–65.

26. For more on the social function of laughter, see Henri Bergson, *Laughter: An Essay on the Meaning of the Comic*, trans. Cloudsley Brereton and Fred Rothwell (London: Macmillan, 1911).

27. Ann Richards, "Keynote Address," delivered at the Democratic National Convention, Atlanta, Ga., 18 July 1988, *Vital Speeches of the Day*, 15 Aug. 1988, pp. 647–649.

28. Charles R. Gruner, "Advice to the Beginning Speaker on Using Humor—What the Research Tells Us," *Communication Education* 34 (1985): 142–147; and Christie McGuffee Smith and Larry Powell, "The Use of Disparaging Humor by Group Leaders," *Southern Speech Communication Journal* 53 (1988): 279–292.

29. Thanks for this story go to Professor Joseph Riggs, Slippery Rock University.

30. *Washington Post*, 12 Dec. 1978.

31. Cited in Joan Detz, *Can You Say a Few Words?* (New York: St. Martin's, 1991), p. 77.

32. Adapted from Detz, pp. 77–78.

Reach for the Stars!

Ashlie McMillan

Please close your eyes. Imagine now that you are shrinking. Can you feel your hands and feet getting smaller, your arms being pulled in closer to your shoulders? Can you picture your legs now dangling off the edge of your seat as your legs shrink up closer to your hips? Now you are only three feet tall. But don't open your eyes yet. This is your first day of being a diastrophic dwarf.

■ ***In her speech of tribute to her cousin, Ashlie McMillan makes use of both identification and magnification, the major techniques of ceremonial speaking. Her opening asks listeners to imagine themselves as dwarfs. By picturing her cousin in simple, everyday situations, she invites identification with her.***

You wake up and get out of bed, which is quite a drop because the bed is almost as tall as you are. You go to the bathroom to wash your face and brush your teeth, but you must stand on a trash can because the faucet is out of your reach. Now you go back to your dorm room, and you're ready to put on your clothes. But again you can't reach the clothes hanging in your closet because you're too short. You have to struggle to get dressed.

Now you have errands that you must run. But how are you going to do them? If you walk, it will take you a long time because you must take many short steps. And you can't drive a car because you can't reach the pedals, much less see over the steering wheel. Finally you get to the bank. But it takes you about five minutes to get the teller's attention because she can't see you below the counter. Next you go to the grocery store. This takes forever because you can't push a cart. You're forced to use a carry basket and to find people who will reach high items for you. Frustrated yet? Okay, open your eyes.

In 1968 my cousin, Tina McMillan, was born. Today she's in her twenty-ninth year as a diastrophic dwarf. What does that mean? It means that she'll never be taller than three feet. It means that her hands will never be able to bend this way [gestures] because she will never have joints in her fingers or toes. She'll always have club feet, and she had to have a rod put in her spine because all diastrophic dwarfs are plagued with scoliosis.

So what does her dwarfism mean to my cousin? Nothing. When you first meet Tina, you might be a little shocked at how tiny she is. But after a while you forget her physical size because her personality is so large and her spirit is so bright. Today I want to tell you the story of how this small person is reaching for the stars. Her life is a miracle that should teach us never to let obstacles stand in the way of our goals and dreams.

■ ***After introducing her cousin and defining dwarfism, Ashlie begins magnification by selecting incidents that reveal Tina as a spirited, determined fighter who refuses to accept the role of a disabled person. Ashlie's entire speech is built on an inspiring irony: that someone so small in physique should be so large in spirit.***

When my aunt and uncle were told that they were going to have a baby who was a diastrophic dwarf, they prepared themselves. They were ready to tell their child that she would never be able to have a Great Dane dog because it would be three times the size that she was. That she would never be able to ride a horse. That she would never be able to drive a car. And that she might not be able to attend college because the dormitories and other facilities were not built for people three feet tall.

What my aunt and uncle were *not* prepared for was a child with a physical disability who refused to see herself as disabled. I can tell you that growing up with Tina was quite an experience. She was always the ham of the cousins, always the center of attention. I remember going over to her house and playing with her *three* Great Dane dogs in the backyard. I remember every Sunday when my grandpa would take us out to the farm and we would fight over who got to ride the horses. And Tina would even fight my grandfather so she could get up on the horse all by herself. And I remember the day, some time after her sixteenth birthday, that she slid behind the wheel of a car. She had teamed up with some engineers down in Texas to have the pedals extended as well as hand gears made on the steering wheel so that she could drive herself. But perhaps my proudest and fondest memory was watching my cousin walk across the graduation stage at Texas Christian University in 1991. She not only got her degree in English, but she went on to get a master's degree in anthropology from TCU. After she graduated, the university invited her to come back to teach in the English Department. But by this time Tina had a new challenge: She declined the teaching job so that she could enter politics as campaign manager for the mayor of Dallas.

Tina has never stopped challenging the perception that she is disabled. Next April she will be marrying a person of normal stature, and once again she will defy society's assumption that something must be wrong about such a marriage. And then in the fall she plans on attending the University of Texas law school. Want to bet against her there?

■ ***As she nears the conclusion, Ashlie begins to draw lessons from her cousin's life to inspire listeners. The closing sentence suggests an analogy with a point made earlier in the speech: People must stand on dreams as well as boxes to reach distant goals.***

Somehow, against the odds, my cousin has led a normal life. To many people, what she has accomplished might not seem that exceptional. To me, however, she is an inspiration. Whenever I think I've got problems that are too much for me, I think of her and of what she has done, this large and vital person stuffed into such a small body. I think of how she refuses to use her disability as a scapegoat or excuse. And I remember how she does not even consider quitting if something stands in her way. She simply views the obstacle, decides the best way to get around it, and moves on. And although she will lose the ability to walk, probably by the age of forty, I believe that she will still find the way to keep moving toward her goals.

The next time a large obstacle stands in your way, remember Tina, my small cousin who has achieved such noteworthy things. You too may seem too short to grasp your stars, but you never know how far you might reach if you stand upon a dream.

WORKS CONSULTED

Department of Orthopedics, Alfred I. Dupont Institute. Undated. http://gait.aidi.udel.edu (18 Apr. 1998).

Diastrophic Dwarfism. Undated. http://chorus.rad.mcw.edu/doc/01027.html (18 Apr. 1998).

Diastrophic Dysplasia. Undated. http://gasbone.herston.uq.edu.au/~ortho/regsum/genorth108 (18 Apr. 1998).

NORD Research Group. Undated. http://www.stepsn.com/nord/rdb_sum/482.htm (18 Apr. 1998).

Texgene Genetics Network. "Methods of Inheritance." 4 Mar. 1998. http://www.tdh.texas.gov/texgene/inherit.htm (18 Apr. 1998).

A Man for the New Age: Tribute to Tiger Woods

Leslie Eason

You're at the Western Open, where Tiger Woods could be Elvis reincarnated. People clap when he pulls out a club. They clap when he hits the ball. They clap no matter where that ball lands. They clap if he smiles. They clap because he is.

■ Leslie opens by taking her listeners on an imaginary trip to a golf tournament. Her skillful use of language, with its vigorous verbs and simple sentences arranged in parallel structure, fills her speech with color and action.

Not long ago, when not much else was going on and we were tired of O.J. and very much needed a hero, a young man in a red polo shirt materialized out of nowhere doing magical things with a stick in a sport we usually ignored. He was not just good or even outstanding. He was a miracle. His game all but laughed at records set by men twice his age. Nike threw forty million at him. Rolex threw fifty million at him. American Express lined up to give him millions more.

We started having to pay attention to things like the Masters, and Opens, and Invitationals, and other such things that applied to golf. Other people were playing, but he was all we could see, this young god in a red shirt. Suddenly we had to learn a new language—"fore," "eagle," "birdie," "par," and "bogie"—just to keep up with the latest news about him.

■ Leslie makes good use of the principles of tribute. Tiger Woods's sporting accomplishments are unique and exceptional. His attractiveness adds to his status as a hero. More important, his refusal to accept an identity based on race benefits society.

Some people watched him play, and bragged that black people could do just about anything. Then we heard that he was only one-fourth black, and that he did not describe himself as black. Now, in a society that honors the rule that one drop of blood is all it takes to be black, this didn't mean much. We ignored his Thai mother, disregarded the Native American and Chinese and Caucasian he said he had in him, and all we saw was his dark-skinned father, who was always there in the gallery cheering him on.

To us he continued to look a lot like other young black men we knew. Mothers with daughters of a certain age (including my own) said that they wished he was their son-in-law or future son-in-law. Six foot two, a hundred fifty-five pounds, smart—Stanford, remember—clean-cut in his creased khakis, curly hair, gorgeous teeth—gorgeous teeth. Skin the color of what they used to call "suntan" in the Crayola box. And rich—very, very rich.

■ Leslie expresses her own attraction to Tiger through the way she describes him. She uses contrast, with the "gangsta boys," and a striking summary description, "he's prep school and Pepsodent," to etch this description in the minds of listeners.

He's the very opposite of the gangsta boys in the hood—boys who wear their pants hanging below their belt like some people in the penitentiary. Next to them he's prep school and Pepsodent. Some said he put a pretty face on blackness. Others said he couldn't possibly be black.

From the moment the world finally met him at the Nike press conference, people wondered *what*, not *who*, he was. He with the almond eyes, the great-colored skin, the photo-op smile. "What are you?" a reporter asked. He didn't seem quite ready for the question, suggesting he wasn't any one thing, but a lot of everything all rolled up into one. Started going into fractions—one-eighth of this, one-fifth of that, a fourth of something else. Told Oprah he didn't feel comfortable being called black. To describe his ethnicity, he came up with the name *Cablinasian*, combining his Caucasian, Black, Indian, and Asian ethnicities. It seemed both a naive plea for a color-blind, colorless America and a throwback to the quadroon days of old Louisiana when people measured their bloodlines by the teaspoon.

■ Leslie draws two important distinctions in this section. First, the world's way of assigning racial identity underscores what we are, not who we are. Second, Tiger's self-description as "Cablinasian" represents a revolt against the old "one drop is all it takes" rule. These distinctions allow her to conclude that Tiger has transcended the color barrier.

But in actuality, Tiger Woods was something the world needed very much. He transcended the color barrier. Not because he was the first black to do this or do that in golf, but because he refused to be defined by the color of his skin. In the midst of all his fame, fortune, contracts, money, and marriage offers, he had taken the step to destroy the old racist rule, *one drop is all it takes*. He offered instead a new principle: he was an equal representation of all he came from—Caucasian, Black, Indian, and Asian—but that was not *who* he was.

How does all this help Tiger? Well, to some he's considered the best golfer in the world. Not the best black player, but the best player, period. A perfect example of together and the same, instead of separate but equal. How does this help the rest of us? It shows us that race is just a small part of our identity. Our own personal racial equation does not determine who we are or where we're going. Or even what we can do.

You're back at the Western Open. The fan galleries finally look like America—Asian, white, black, Latino, fathers with sons, mothers pushing baby carriages, people who have been playing golf for years, people who didn't know what golf was before Tiger Woods and now want to try it. Everything revolves around Tiger. Even babies go silent when Tiger's about to swing. Once the ball is hit, people resume their conversation and stampede to the next hole to watch him, leaving the next player to struggle by himself.

■ ***In this section Leslie shifts the focus to Tiger's social significance. She dwells on the importance of creating our own identity rather than accepting a prearranged identity based on race. In the process she expands the idea of identity so that it applies more to traits of character and accomplishment.***

So what are we to make of him? His father, Earl Woods, has said that his son would change the course of humanity. You can mark that up to a proud father's hyperbole, but perhaps Tiger has already pointed us in a new direction by his refusal to accept an identity imposed by racist custom. Hopefully one day we will see him as a young man who was simply ahead of his time, instead of viewing him as a naive child trying to escape his heritage.

It's not clear yet who he is, but it's quite clear what he is not. His boundaries are not defined and confined by his complex racial background. Instead, he is what he told us, a complex mixture of heart, talent, dedication, attractiveness of person and personality, and grace under the pressure of constant media attention and tournament competition. The most important ingredient in that mixture is his stubborn refusal to accept the world's ways of limiting identity, and his polite insistence upon leaving himself open to change and growth. He did not inherit a prearranged identity imposed by race; rather, he is responsible for creating who he is and who he will become. Who he is will emerge over time, a product of his character and accomplishments.

■ ***In her brief conclusion, Leslie sketches Tiger against the background of a New Age in which the world must come to accept and appreciate its cultural and racial diversity.***

As we watch him grow and become himself, we can only celebrate what he means for a nation and world that must become more comfortable with its incredible diversity of race and culture. Tiger Woods, you are a man for the New Age, and we salute you!

WORKS CONSULTED

Garrity, John. "You the Kid," *Sports Illustrated*. 9 March 1992. http://www.cnnsi.com/features/1996/sportsman/archive/920309.html (12 Apr. 1998).

Lewis, Andrea. "A Public Course Win—Tiger's Victory Marks a New Stage in Cultural History." *JINN*. 16 Apr. 1997. http://www.pacificnews.org/jinn/stories/3.08/970416-tiger.html (11 Apr. 1998).

Montville, Leigh. "On the Job Training." *Sports Illustrated*. 9 Sept. 1996. http://www.cnnsi.com/features/1996/sportsman/archive/960909.html (12 Apr. 1998).

Reilly, Rick. "Goodness Gracious, He's a Great Ball of Fire." *Sports Illustrated*. 27 Mar. 1995. http://www.cnnsi.com/features/1996/sportsman/archive/950327.html (12 Apr. 1998).

Sirak, Ron. "Golf Owes Charlie Sifford a Great Deal." GolfWeb Library. 24 Feb. 1998. http://services.golfweb.com/library/sirak/charlie980224.html (11 Apr. 1998).

Van Sickle, Gary. "Jackpot!" *Sports Illustrated*. 14 Oct. 1996. http://www.cnnsi.com/features/1996/sportsman/archive/961014.html (10 Apr. 1998).

Appendix A

Communicating in Small Groups

Many of the important communication interactions of your life are conducted in small groups. In school you may be assigned to a team to work on a particular problem relevant to the class. At work you may be assigned to a committee involved in planning a project for the company. In your community there may be problems that can only be solved by people working together.

To understand how group communication functions, we need to consider the nature of a group. Is any gathering of people a group? Not necessarily. For example, a gathering of people waiting for a bus would not be considered a group. To be considered a **group**, a gathering of people must interact with one another over a period of time to reach a goal or goals. Let's suppose that the same people have been meeting at the bus stop every workday for several months. They may chat with one another while waiting for the bus, but this casual interaction is not enough to turn them into a group. Now, suppose that the Metropolitan Transit Organization (MTO) announces in the morning paper that it wants to raise fares from $1.00 to $1.50 each way for the trip from the bus stop to downtown. That morning when the people get together, they begin to discuss with considerable outrage the problem of the increase in fares. One of the people at the bus stop suggests that they all get together at her apartment that evening to come up with a plan to try to get the MTO to reconsider its proposal. When these people get together that evening, they will be interacting as a group. In this appendix we discuss how groups function and how your public communication skills can make you a better participant or leader in groups.

The small-group setting offers both ESL and non-ESL students the chance to practice communication skills under reduced stress. Small-group interaction also helps class members get to know one another. For these reasons, a small-group assignment near the beginning of a term offers special advantages.

Group Problem Solving

When we listen to someone present information or make recommendations, we hear only one version of a problem. That version may be biased, based on self-interest, or it may simply be wrong. When important issues are involved, we need to minimize the risk of such errors. One way to do this is to have a group consider the situation and make recommendations about the problem.

Group problem solving has many advantages over individual efforts. When people from different cultures share their various ways of seeing a problem, they enrich our understanding. We begin to see the world through the eyes of others. This may help us see misconceptions and biases in our own thinking. Listening to others' points of view also can stimulate creative thinking about problems.

ESL: ESL students can often bring new perspectives to the discussion of traditional problems. Encourage these students to contribute to problem-solving discussions.

In well-managed problem-solving groups, people on all sides of an issue have a chance to discuss the similarities and differences of their perspectives.

Through discussion, they may discover some areas of agreement that can help resolve differences. Additionally, small groups of people typically are willing to examine their differences and feel free to explore options for action. Because of these advantages, organizations often use groups to work on important organizational problems. In fact, it is estimated that approximately 20 million meetings take place each day in the United States.[1]

To reduce the possibility of cultural gridlock in mixed ESL and non-ESL groups, encourage leaders to have each participant reflect at the outset upon his or her personal experience with the problem under discussion.

Although working in groups has many advantages, some problems may arise that can make groups less effective. **Cultural gridlock**, the inability to communicate because of profound cultural differences, may occur in groups whose participants come from different backgrounds. For example, people in marketing departments and research-and-development scientists in an organization may bring different expectations to a meeting. Along with these differing expectations, participants from different social backgrounds may bring different perspectives on a problem, agendas, priorities, procedures, ways of communicating, and standards of protocol to meetings. These differences may sidetrack constructive discussions.

Dealing with cultural gridlock is never easy, but the following guidelines will help minimize its impact:

- Allow time for people to get acquainted before starting to work.
- Provide enough room so that people don't feel crowded.
- Distribute an agenda so that people know what to expect.
- Watch for language problems. Summarize discussions. Post key points.
- Avoid using jargon that some participants may not understand.
- Be sensitive to cultural differences in protocol and nonverbal communication.[2]

To heighten sensitivity to the dangers of groupthink, focus on this problem in the evaluation of small group communication. What techniques do groups employ to minimize groupthink?

Another problem groups may encounter is **groupthink**, the development of an uncritical acceptance of group decisions.[3] Groupthink is most likely to occur when groups value interpersonal relationships more than the ability to perform effectively. Other factors that contribute to groupthink include a leader's strong preference for a given decision or the lack of a clear set of procedures for approaching problems. Groupthink is dangerous because outsiders may assume that a group has deliberated carefully and responsibly when it has not.

The problems in decision making that accompany groupthink include (1) incomplete consideration of objectives, (2) poor information retrieval and analysis, and (3) an incomplete consideration of alternative solutions. Dealing with groupthink is difficult, but there are some steps that can guard against it. First, groups need to be aware that groupthink can be a problem. This awareness should include a knowledge of the major symptoms of groupthink:

- Putting pressure on people who argue against what most of the group believe
- Censoring thoughts that differ from group beliefs
- Maintaining an illusion of invulnerability
- Reinforcing an unquestioned belief in the group's moral rightness
- Attempting to rationalize group decisions

Once a group is aware that groupthink is a problem, the leader can take action to minimize its effects. The leader should encourage the group to set standards for investigation and appraisal that discourage uncritical thinking and premature consensus.[4] This suggests that group members must have a systematic way to approach the problem. The following leadership behaviors help reduce groupthink problems:

- Reminding participants to critically evaluate the group's recommendations
- Reserving their own opinions until others have expressed their views
- Assigning the role of the devil's advocate to someone who must ask critical questions about ideas
- Bringing in outsiders to discuss the issues under consideration
- Encouraging creative conflict, wherein the group attacks proposed procedures

Group Problem-Solving Techniques

Group deliberations that are orderly, systematic, and thorough help people reach high-quality decisions. Problem-solving groups can use a variety of methods to achieve their goals.[5]

Reflective Thinking and Problem Solving

The approach recommended for most problem-solving groups is a modification of the reflective thinking technique first proposed by John Dewey in 1910. This systematic approach has five steps: (1) defining the problem, (2) generating possible solutions, (3) evaluating solution options, (4) developing a plan of action, and (5) evaluating the results.

ESL: ESL students may require encouragement to participate actively in group discussions. Give these students special assignments to stimulate their participation. Asking ESL students to report research findings to their groups is one way to encourage them.

Step 1: Defining the Problem. Sometimes the problem assigned to a group is only a symptom of the actual problem. All problem-solving groups should take time to define the problem carefully before looking for a solution. The following guidelines can help define the problem:

- Describe the problem as specifically as possible.
- Explore the causes of the problem.
- Consider the history of the problem.
- Determine who is affected by the problem.
- Obtain enough information to understand the problem.

Step 2: Generating Possible Solutions. Once the problem has been defined, members can work on generating solutions. **Brainstorming** encourages all group members to contribute by producing a large number of possible solutions.[6] It works best with twelve or fewer group members.[7] During brainstorming, members should not attempt to evaluate the solutions or decide what option to follow.[8]

The following rules should govern brainstorming sessions:

Make brainstorming fun by asking students to seek outlandish proposals relating to a problem. These may have limited value in themselves, but can be useful in stimulating creative and critical thinking.

- Present all your ideas, no matter how outrageous they may seem. Keep things playful to encourage creativity. Even an outlandish idea may provide the basis for a workable solution. The more ideas generated, the better.
- Suspend judgment. Allow no one to criticize any suggestion.
- Combine ideas for additional options.

- Don't let seniority or organizational status impede the process. Encourage everyone to participate.

To teach students the value of brainstorming, ask them to compare the effectiveness of problem-solution discussions in which the technique is and is not used.

Brainstorming usually involves a six-step process:

1. The leader asks each member in turn to contribute an idea. If a member does not have an idea, he or she should pass. Stress quantity over quality.
2. A recorder writes down all ideas on a flip chart or marker board so everyone can see them.
3. Brainstorming continues until all members have passed.
4. The suggestions are reviewed for clarification, adding new options, or combining options.
5. The group identifies the most useful ideas.
6. The leader designates someone to receive additional ideas after the meeting. These ideas may be added to the list for consideration during the next phase of the problem-solving process.

There are many variations of brainstorming. When time is short or member status differences may stifle ideas, one alternative may be **electronic brainstorming**, in which participants generate ideas in computer chat groups or via email before meeting face to face.[9] If participants have problems expressing themselves verbally, the leader might try having participants draw pictures that illustrate their ideas.[10]

Step 3: Evaluating Solution Options. Ideally, a group should take a break between generating solutions and evaluating them. During that time, members can gather information on the feasibility of each option and determine if it has been used elsewhere. When the group reconvenes, it should discuss options using the following guidelines:

- Costs of the option
- Probability of success
- Difficulty of enactment
- Time constraints
- Additional benefits to be expected
- Additional problems that might be encountered

Groups should summarize the considerations for each option on a flip chart, then post the summaries so that members can refer to them as they compare options. As options are evaluated, some of them will seem weak and be dropped; others may be strengthened and refined.

The group also may combine options to generate new alternatives. For example, if the group is caught between option A, which promises improved efficiency, and option B, which promises lower cost, it may be possible to combine the best features of each into option C. This approach is similar to the SIL (Successive Integration of Problem Elements) method, developed at the Battelle Memorial Institute, a nonprofit research and development think tank. The SIL method is useful for groups of six or fewer participants. The process includes the following steps:

1. Members independently generate solution options.
2. Two of the members successively read one of their ideas to the group.

3. The group discusses ways to combine the two ideas into one solution.
4. A third member reads an idea that the group attempts to integrate with solution from step 3.
5. The "add an idea" process continues until all of the participants' ideas have been read aloud and the group has tried to integrate them.
6. The process is complete when the group reaches a consensus on a solution.[11]

After each alternative has been considered, members rank the solutions in terms of their acceptability. The option receiving the highest overall rank is the proposed solution.

It is not unusual for participants to become personally caught up with their own solutions. During evaluation, a leader must keep the group focused on ideas and not on participants. Accept differences of opinion and conflict as a natural and necessary part of problem solving. Discussing the strengths of an option before talking about its weaknesses can take some of the heat out of the process.

Step 4: Developing a Plan of Action. Once the group has selected a solution, it must determine how it can be implemented. For example, to improve company morale, a group might recommend a three-step plan: (1) better in-house training programs to increase opportunities for promotion, (2) a pay structure that rewards success in training programs, and (3) increased employee participation in decision making. As the group refines this plan, it should consider what might help or hinder it, the resources needed to enact it, and a timetable for completion.

If the group cannot develop a plan of action for the solution, or if insurmountable obstacles appear, the group should return to step 3 and consider other options.

Step 5: Evaluating Results. Not only must a problem-solving group plan how to implement a solution, it must also determine how to evaluate results once the plan is enacted. The group should establish evaluation criteria for what constitutes success, when results can be expected, and contingency plans to use if the original plan doesn't work. To monitor the ongoing success of a solution, such as the three-part plan to improve morale, the group would have to determine reasonable expectations for each stage in the process. That way, the company could detect and correct problems as they occur, before they damage the plan as a whole. Having a scheduled sequence of expectations also provides a way to determine results while the plan is being enacted, rather than having to wait for the entire project to be completed.

Other Approaches to Group Problem Solving

Although the systematic process described above works well in many situations, there are times when a different approach may be needed. When a group consists of people from different public or private sectors, **collaborative problem solving** may work best.[12] For example, in many urban areas, coalitions of business executives and educators have worked together on plans to train people for jobs in the community. In such situations the problems are usually important and the resources are usually limited. Because there is no established authority structure and because the factions may have different expectations or goals, these coalitions often have problems working together. To be effective, such groups need to spend considerable time defining the problem and exploring each other's perspectives. This should help them recognize their interdependence and begin to really work together. In such groups, the participants must come to see themselves not as members of group A (the executives) or group B (the educators), but as members of group C, the coalition. Leadership is especially difficult in such groups.

One approach that is useful in such situations is **dialogue groups**. According to William Isaacs, director of the Dialogue Project at the Massachusetts Institute of Technology Center for Organizational Learning, "Dialogue is a discipline of collective thinking and inquiry, a process for transforming the quality of conversation, and, in particular, the thinking that lies beneath it."[13] Such groups focus on understanding the different interpretations of the problem that participants bring to the interaction. Their purpose is to establish a conversation between participants from which common ground and mutual trust can emerge.

The role of the facilitator is critical in dialogue groups. According to Edgar Schein of the MIT Center, the facilitator must

1. Seat the group in a circle to create a sense of equality.
2. Introduce the problem.
3. Ask people to share an experience in which dialogue led to "good communication."
4. Ask members to consider what led to good communication.
5. Ask participants to talk about their reactions.
6. Let the conversation flow naturally.
7. Intervene only to clarify problems of communication.
8. Conclude by asking all members to comment however they choose.[14]

The dialogue method is not a substitute for other problem-solving techniques, such as the reflective thinking process presented earlier. Instead, the dialogue method may be used as a precursor because deliberation usually works well only when members understand each other well enough to be "talking the same language." A similar approach may be found in the Kettering Foundation's National Issues Forums.[15]

A similar approach is followed in value-added brainstorming which follows a five-step process.[16] The first step involves listing all ideas about what is causing the problem you are working on. The second step sets out objectives in terms of what you want to accomplish in solving the problem and ties the objectives to the previously listed causes. The third step begins by listing possible sources of models for solutions followed by ideas based on these models. After completing step 3, the leader walks the group through the lists previously generated and asks the members to consider if the ideas generated actually address the problem and if they are feasible to consider further. The fourth step generates ways to turn the feasible ideas into practical plans that can be implemented. The fifth and final step delineates plans for communicating the solution to those who must make it work.

Participating in Small Groups

To be an effective group member you must understand your responsibilities as a group participant. First, you should come to meetings prepared to contribute. You should have read background materials and performed any tasks assigned to you by the group leader. Second, you should be willing to learn from others.

You should try to contribute to the process rather than dominating the discussion. Don't be afraid to admit you are wrong and don't become defensive when challenged. Willingness to change your views is not a sign of weakness, nor is obstinacy a strength. Third, listen constructively. Don't interrupt others. Object if you feel consensus is forming too quickly. You might save the meeting from groupthink.

Analyzing your group communication skills can help you become a more effective group communicator. Use the self-analysis form in Figure A.1 to steer yourself toward more constructive group communication behaviors.

Balance the emphasis on leadership by stressing the importance of good "followership" as well. Ask students to complete the self-evaluation form, "What Kind of Follower Are You?," provided in the IRM.

FIGURE A.1
Group Communication Skills Self-Analysis Form

		Need to Do Less	Doing Fine	Need to Do More
1.	I make my points concisely.	☐	☐	☐
2.	I speak with confidence.	☐	☐	☐
3.	I provide specific examples and details.	☐	☐	☐
4.	I try to integrate ideas that are expressed.	☐	☐	☐
5.	I let others know when I do not understand them.	☐	☐	☐
6.	I let others know when I agree with them.	☐	☐	☐
7.	I let others know tactfully when I disagree with them.	☐	☐	☐
8.	I express my opinions.	☐	☐	☐
9.	I suggest solutions to problems.	☐	☐	☐
10.	I listen to understand.	☐	☐	☐
11.	I try to understand before agreeing or disagreeing.	☐	☐	☐
12.	I ask questions to get more information.	☐	☐	☐
13.	I ask others for their opinions.	☐	☐	☐
14.	I check for group agreement.	☐	☐	☐
15.	I try to minimize tension.	☐	☐	☐
16.	I accept help from others.	☐	☐	☐
17.	I offer help to others.	☐	☐	☐
18.	I let others have their say.	☐	☐	☐
19.	I stand up for myself.	☐	☐	☐
20.	I urge others to speak up.	☐	☐	☐

As you participate in groups, you should also keep in mind the following questions:

- What is happening now in the group?
- What should be happening in the group?
- What can I do to make this come about?

If you notice a difference between what the group is doing and what it *should be* doing to reach its goals, you have the opportunity to demonstrate leadership behavior.

Leadership in Small Groups

Ask students to complete the self-evaluation forms, "What Kind of Leader Are You?" and the "Leadership Potential Questionnaire," both provided in the IRM. Do these forms reveal ways for them to improve?

Interest in leadership is very practical: leaders help get the job done. For over fifty years, social scientists have been studying leadership by analyzing group communication patterns. This research suggests that two basic types of leadership behaviors emerge in most groups. The first is **task leadership behavior**, which directs the activity of the group toward a specified goal. The second is **social leadership behavior**, which helps build and maintain positive relationships among group members.

Task leaders initiate goal-related communication, including both giving and seeking information, opinions, and suggestions. A task leader might say, "We need more information on just how widespread sexual harassment is on campus. Let me tell you what Dean Johnson told me last Friday." Or the task leader might ask, "Gwen, tell us what you found out from the Affirmative Action Office."

Social leaders express agreement, help the group release tension, and behave in a supportive manner. A social leader looks for chances to give compliments: "I think Gwen has made a very important point. You really helped us by finding that out." Sincere compliments help keep members from becoming defensive and help maintain a constructive communication atmosphere. In a healthy communication climate, the two kinds of leadership behavior support each other and keep the group moving toward its goal. When one person combines both styles of leadership, that person is likely to be highly effective.

Leadership has also been discussed in terms of how the leader enacts the task and maintenance functions. An **autocratic leader** makes decisions without consultation, issues orders or gives direction, and controls the members of the group through the use of rewards or punishments. A **participative leader** functions in a more democratic fashion, seeking input from group members and giving them an active role in decision making. A **free-rein leader** leaves members free to decide what to do, how to do it, and when to do it. If you were working in an organization, you would probably say you "worked *for*" an autocratic leader, "worked *with*" a participative leader, and "worked *in spite of*" a free-rein leader.

Currently, work on leadership suggests that leadership styles are either transactional or transformational. **Transactional leadership** takes place in an environment based on power relationships and relies on reward and punishment to accomplish its ends. **Transformational leadership** appeals to "people's higher levels of motivation to contribute to a cause and add to the quality of life on the planet."[17] It carries overtones of stewardship instead of management. Transformational leaders have the following qualities:

- They have a vision of what needs to be done.
- They are empathetic.
- They are trusted.
- They give credit to others.
- They help others develop.
- They share power.
- They are willing to experiment and learn.

In short, transformational leaders lead with both their hearts and their heads. According to John Schuster, a management consultant who specializes in transformational leadership training, "The heart is more difficult to develop. It's easier to get smarter than to become more caring."[18] Recent research suggests that transformational leadership encourages communication from subordinates because they are less intimidated by their superiors and more willing to ask for advice or help.[19]

To understand leadership, you need to consider the major components of **ethos**: competence, integrity, likeableness, and dynamism. An effective leader is competent. This means the leader understands the problem and knows how to steer a group through the problem-solving process. An effective leader has integrity. This means the leader is honest, concerned about the good of the group, and places group success above personal concerns. An effective leader is likeable. This means he or she is friendly and interacts easily with others. Finally, an effective leader is dynamic. Dynamism involves being enthusiastic and energetic.

Don't be intimidated by this idealized portrait of a leader. Most of us have these qualities in varying degrees and can use them when the need for leadership arises. To be an effective leader, remember two basic goals: (1) Cultivate an open leadership style that encourages all sides to air their views, and (2) help others be effective and get the job done.

Planning Meetings

In many situations, meetings seem to be time wasters. This may be because the people who conduct them do not know when to call meetings or how to run them.[20] Meetings should be called when members need to

Have students recall a meeting that ended poorly. What factors of planning and personality might have accounted for the less than desirable outcomes?

- discuss the meaning of information face to face.
- decide on a common course of action.
- establish a plan of action.
- report on the progress of a plan, evaluate its effectiveness, and revise it if needed.

More than just knowing when to call meetings, you need to know how to plan them. The following guidelines should help you plan more effective meetings:

1. *Have a specific purpose for holding a meeting.* Unnecessary meetings waste time. If your goal is simply to increase interaction, plan a social event rather than a meeting.
2. *Prepare an agenda and distribute it to participants before the meeting.* Having an agenda gives members time to prepare and assemble information they might need. Solicit agenda items from participants.
3. *Keep meetings short.* After about an hour, groups grow weary, and the law of diminishing returns sets in. Don't try to do too much in a single meeting.

4. *Keep groups small.* You get more participation and interaction in small groups. In larger groups, people may be reluctant to ask questions or contribute ideas.
5. *Assemble groups that invite open discussions.* In business settings, the presence of someone's supervisor may inhibit interaction. You will get better participation if group members come from the same or near the same working level in the organization.
6. *Plan the site of the meeting.* Arrange for privacy and freedom from interruptions. A circular arrangement contributes to participation because there is no power position. A rectangular table or a lectern and classroom arrangement may inhibit interaction.
7. *Prepare in advance.* Be certain that you have the necessary supplies, such as chalk, a flip chart, markers, note pads, and pencils. If you will use audio-visual equipment, check to be sure it is in working order.

Conducting an Effective Meeting

Group leaders have more responsibilities than other members. Leaders must understand the problem-solving process the group will use so that deliberations can proceed in a constructive way. Leaders should be well informed on the issues involved so that they can answer questions and keep the group moving toward its objective. The following checklist should be helpful in guiding your behavior as a group leader:

- Begin and end the meeting on time.
- Present background information concisely and objectively.
- Lead, don't run, the meeting.
- Be enthusiastic.
- Get conflict out in the open so that it can be dealt with directly.
- Urge all members to participate.
- Keep discussion centered on the issue.
- At the close of a meeting, summarize what the group has accomplished.

As a group leader, you may need to present the group's recommendations to others. In this task, you function mainly as an informative speaker. You should present the recommendations offered by the group, along with the major reasons for making these recommendations. You should also mention reservations that may have surfaced during deliberations. Your job in making this report is not to advocate, but to educate. Later, you may join in any following discussion with persuasive remarks that express your personal convictions on the subject.

Communication Behavior and Group Effectiveness

Research has uncovered certain communication and leadership behaviors that either encourage or thwart group effectiveness.[21] Better group decisions are made when all group members participate fully in the process, members are respectful of each other and leaders are respectful of members, and there are few if any negative socioemotional behaviors in evidence. More specific details of these findings are listed in Figure A.2.

Enhancing Behaviors	Impeding Behaviors
Opinions are sought out.	Members express dislike for others.
Creativity is encouraged.	Members personally attack others.
Participation is encouraged.	Members make sarcastic comments.
Opposing views are encouraged.	Leader sets criteria for solution.
Members provide information.	Leader makes the decision.
Group analyzes suggestions.	Leader intimidates members.
Members listen to one another.	Meeting becomes a gripe session.
Members respect others' ideas.	Disagreements are ignored, not aired.
Members support others' ideas.	Disagreement is discouraged.
Problem is thoroughly researched.	Members pursue personal goals.
Group sets criteria for solution.	
Members are knowledgeable on issue.	
Evidence for suggestions is presented.	
Group focuses on task.	

FIGURE A.2
Behaviors That Enhance or Impede Group Decision Making

Guidelines for Formal Meetings

The larger a group is, the more it needs a formal procedure to conduct meetings. Also, if a meeting involves a controversial subject, it is often wise to have a set of rules to follow. Having clear-cut guidelines helps keep meetings from becoming chaotic and helps ensure fair treatment for all participants. In such situations, many groups choose to operate by **parliamentary procedure**.

Most colleges and universities have a student senate that operates under *Robert's Rules of Order*. Have students attend a senate session and evaluate how the rules were applied during the meeting.

Parliamentary procedure establishes an order of business for a meeting and lays out the way the group initiates discussions and reaches decisions. Under parliamentary procedure, a formal meeting proceeds as follows:

1. The chair calls the meeting to order.
2. The secretary reads the minutes of the previous meeting, which are corrected, if necessary, and approved.
3. Reports from officers and committees are presented.
4. Unfinished business is considered.
5. New business is introduced.
6. Announcements are made.
7. The meeting is adjourned.

Business in formal meetings goes forward by motions, or proposals set before the group. Consider the following scenario. The chair asks: "Is there any new business?" A member responds: "I move that we allot $100 to build a Homecoming float." The member has offered a main motion, which proposes an action. Before the group can discuss the motion, it must be seconded. The purpose of a **second** is to ensure that more than one person wants to see the motion considered. If no one volunteers a second, the chair may ask, "Is there a second?" Typically, another member will respond, "I second the motion." Once a motion is made and seconded, it is open for discussion. It must be passed by majority vote, defeated, or otherwise resolved before the group can move on to other business. With the exception of a few technical motions (such as "I move we take a fifteen-minute recess" or "Point of personal privilege—can we do anything about the heat in this room?"), the main motion remains at the center of group attention until resolved.

Let us assume that as the group discusses the main motion in our example, some members believe the amount of money proposed is insufficient. At this point, another member may say: "I move to amend the motion to provide $150 for the float." The motion to amend gives the group a chance to modify a main motion. It must be seconded and, after discussion, must be resolved by majority vote before discussion goes forward. If the motion to amend passes, then the amended main motion must be considered further.

How does a group make a decision on a motion? There usually is a time when discussion begins to lag. At this point the chair might say, "Do I hear a call for the question?" A motion to "call the question" ends discussion and requires a two-thirds vote for approval. Once the group votes to end discussion, it must then vote to accept or reject the motion. No further discussion can take place until the original or amended original motion is voted on.

Sometimes the discussion of a motion may reveal that the group is confused or sharply divided about an issue. At this point a member may move to "table the motion." This is a way to dispose of a troublesome motion without further divisive or confused discussion. At other times, the discussion of a motion may reveal that the group lacks information to make an intelligent decision. At that point, we might hear from a member: "In light of the uncertainty of costs, I move we postpone further consideration until next week's meeting." The motion to postpone consideration gives the chair a chance to appoint a committee to gather the information needed.

FIGURE A.3
Guide to Parliamentary Procedure

Action	Requires Second	Can Be Debated	Can Be Amended	Vote Required	Function
Main Motion	Yes	Yes	Yes	Majority	Commits group to a specific action or position.
Second	No	No	No	None	Assures that more than one group member wishes to see idea considered.
Move to Amend	Yes	Yes	Yes	Majority	Allows group to modify and improve an existing motion.
Call the Question	Yes	No	No	Two-thirds	Brings discussion to an end and moves to a vote on the motion in question.
Move to Table the Motion	Yes	No	No	Majority	Stops immediate consideration of the motion until a later unspecified time.
Move to Postpone Consideration	Yes	Yes	Yes	Majority	Stops immediate discussion and allows time for the group to obtain more information on the problem.
Move to Adjourn	Yes	No	No	Majority	Formally ends meeting.

These are just some of the important procedures that can help ensure that formal group communication remains fair and constructive. For more information on formal group communication procedures, consult the authoritative *Robert's Rules of Order*.

Notes

1. Scot Ober, *Contemporary Business Communication* (Boston: Houghton Mifflin, 1995), p. 498.
2. Adapted from Marc Hequet, "The Fine Art of Multicultural Meetings," *Training* (July 1993): 29–33.
3. Christopher P. Neck and Charles C. Manz, "From Groupthink to Teamthink: Toward the Creation of Constructive Thought Patterns in Self-Managed Work Teams," *Human Relations* (August 1994): 929–953.
4. L. Janis, *Groupthink: Psychological Studies of Policy Decisions and Fiascoes* (Boston: Houghton Mifflin, 1982), pp. 245–246.
5. For an overview of other methods, see Patricia Hayes Andrews and Richard T. Herschel, *Organizational Communication: Empowerment in a Technological Society* (Boston: Houghton Mifflin, 1996), pp. 213–218.
6. Floyd Hurt, "Better Brainstorming," *Training and Development* (November 1994): 57–59.
7. Ron Zemke, "In Search of Good Ideas," *Training* (January 1993): 46–52.
8. "The Right Way to Brainstorm," *Inc.*, July 1999, p. 93.
9. Gail Kay, "Effective Meetings Through Electronic Brainstorming," *Management Quarterly* (Winter 1994): 15–26; Milam Aiken, Mahesh Vanjami, and James Krosp, "Group Decision Support Systems," *Review of Business* (Spring 1995): 38–42; and Michael C. Kettelhut, "How to Avoid Misusing Electronic Meeting Support," *Planning Review* (July–August 1994): 34–38.
10. Robyn D. Clarke, "For a Better Way to Brainstorm," *Black Enterprise* (January 2000): 114.
11. Zemke.
12. Jacqueline Hood, Jeanne M. Logsdon, and Judith Kenner Thompson, "Collaboration for Social Problem Solving: A Process Model," *Business and Society* (Spring 1993): 1–17.
13. William M. Isaacs, "Taking Flight: Dialogue, Collective Thinking, and Organizational Learning," *Organizational Dynamics* (Autumn 1993): 24–39.
14. Edgar H. Schein, "On Dialogue, Culture, and Organizational Learning." *Organizational Dynamics* (Autumn 1993): 40–51.
15. Michael Osborn and Suzanne Osborn, *Alliance for a Better Public Voice: The Communication Discipline and the National Issues Forums* (Dayton, Ohio: National Issues Forums Institute, 1991).
16. Greg Bachman, "Brainstorming Deluxe," *Training and Development* (January 2000): 15–19.
17. John P. Schuster, "Transforming Your Leadership Style," *Association Management* (January 1994): 39–43.
18. Ibid.
19. Svjetlana Madzar, "Subordinate's Information Inquiry: Exploring the Effect of Perceived Leadership Style and Individual Differences," *Journal of Occupational and Organizational Psychology* (June 2001): 221–232.
20. Much of the material in this section is adapted from Robert D. Ramsey, "Making Meetings Work for You," *Supervision* (February 1994): 14–16; and Becky Jones, Midge Wilker, and Judy Stoner, "A Meeting Primer," *Management Review* (January 1995): 30–32.
21. Michael E. Mayer, "Behaviors Leading to More Effective Decisions in Small Groups Embedded in Organizations," *Communication Reports* (Summer 1988): 123–132.

Appendix B
Handling Communication Apprehension

If you are anxious about speaking in public, you are not alone. Survey after survey places public speaking at or near the top of the list of people's fears.[1] Jerry Seinfeld once observed that since most people prefer death to public speaking, almost anyone would rather be in the coffin than delivering the eulogy at a funeral. For many of us, however, this is no laughing matter.

The National Communication Association recently commissioned the Roper Starch polling organization to conduct a nationwide survey to determine how comfortable and effective people feel communicating in different situations.[2] The study showed that most of us are more comfortable in face-to-face interactions or talking on the phone than we are in giving a speech or speaking up in meetings.

Almost all college students are uncomfortable when they have to address a class. Once when we were team-teaching a public speaking course during the summer session, a student confessed that she attended another college during the regular school year but was taking a required public speaking course with us. If she didn't do well, she simply would not transfer her grade so that it wouldn't spoil her grade point average and keep her out of medical school. Her fears were unfounded. The text of her excellent first speech, "My Three Cultures," has been a staple in all previous editions of our text and may be seen in Appendix C.

USA Today recently opened an article on "stage fright" with the following lines: "Laurence Olivier had it. Carly Simon has it. So does Barbra Streisand. Some Olympic athletes, executives of Fortune 500 companies, tenured professors and high-powered sales people have it."[3] One article directed at computer specialists suggested that "most technical professionals would rather plunge hot needles into their eyes than be forced to stand up and address a room full of people."[4] Most college instructors—even your speech instructor!—may have some communication anxiety, especially during the first meetings of classes, but you probably won't be able to detect it.

Certainly your authors have experienced this problem. As college professors and authors, we have had considerable experience speaking both in and out of the classroom. Being authors of a public speaking text places a special kind of pressure on us. Since we earn our bread and butter telling others how to do something, they expect us to be able to do it ourselves—and do it much better than most other people. Even with all our experience, every time we rise before a new group—a class of undergraduates, a group of graduate students hoping to learn how to teach this course better, our publisher's sales representatives, fellow citizens at community meetings, or professional colleagues at conventions—we feel the burden of this pressure and get the butterflies.

Surprised? Still think that everyone else is more confident than you are? The late Edward R. Murrow, a famous radio and television commentator, once said: "The best speakers know enough to be scared. . . . The only difference between the pros and the novices is that the pros have trained the butterflies to fly in formation."

Steve Raymund, chairman and CEO of Tech Data Corporation (the world's second largest wholesaler of PC products), lists "more confidence to speak in public" as the one thing he would most like to change about himself. His approach to the problem is simple and effective: "If you must conquer it, you must know it. To know it, you have to study it. Then, study it some more."[5] We will follow a similar approach by investigating what communication apprehension is. Our goal is to help you train your own butterflies to fly in formation.

Understanding Communication Apprehension

Earlier we put the words "stage fright" in quotation marks to indicate our reservations about this typical way of describing public speaking fears. "Stage" suggests theatre, and "theatre" suggests performance. *A public speech, we insist, is not a performance, but an interactive communication event.*[6] Those who think of their speeches as performances are also likely to think of themselves as performers. And just as actors don't necessarily believe what they are saying, performers may not think of their speeches as authentic commitments. Their messages may be something they say just for effect. They are also likely to think of audience members as critics and then try to please them rather than communicate with them. To discourage these distorted, even unethical ways of thinking about public communication, we avoid the term "stage fright." Instead, we will use the term***communication apprehension*** to refer to those unpleasant sensations a speaker may experience before or during a presentation. We begin by examining some of the symptoms we generally interpret as communication apprehension, some of the reasons people feel anxious when they stand to speak, and some of the specific things they are concerned about.

Symptoms of Communication Apprehension

It's the night before you are scheduled to make your first oral presentation in class. You turn off the lights and go to bed, but you just can't get comfortable. You toss and turn, get up and plump up your pillow. You try to distract yourself by reciting the alphabet backwards. It doesn't work, so you lie there in the dark worrying. The more you think about your speech, the more anxious, tense, and irritable you become. You notice the sound of music from next door, so you get up, tromp down the hall, burst into the room, and yell, "Will you turn that down! I've got to give a speech tomorrow, so I have to have a good night's sleep!"

Finally, morning comes. You're sitting in class waiting for your turn. You can't listen to the other speeches because you feel miserable. You hear your name called. Your stomach drops. You begin to sweat. Your heart races. Your ears feel hot. Your mouth feels dry. You plod to the podium and look up at the audience. Your knees start to shake. You grab the lectern for support.

Any of these symptoms sound familiar? What you are experiencing is an adrenaline rush. It's the same type of physical reaction you might experience if you suddenly encountered a rattlesnake in the wilderness or a mugger on a dark street. These are the symptoms you usually associate with fear. They make up the "fight or flight" readiness that can help you through a difficult situation. But when it's your turn to speak, neither fight nor flight is appropriate. You've got to give that speech.

Most likely you won't have all these symptoms of communication apprehension, but you may well have some of them. If you didn't, you wouldn't be normal. Moreover, a little bit of communication apprehension is a good thing. It can "psych" you up for your presentation. However, too much communication apprehension can be paralyzing and is cause for real concern. So what does your communication apprehension profile look like? One way to estimate how much communication apprehension you have is to complete the following questionnaire.

A Gauge of Public Speaking Apprehension

Directions: Assume that you have to give a speech within the next few weeks. For each of the statements below, indicate the degree to which the statement applies to you within the context of giving a future speech. Mark whether you strongly agree (SA), agree (A), are undecided (U), disagree (D), or strongly disagree (SD) with each statement. Circle your SA, A, U, D, or SD choices. Do not write in the blanks next to the questions. **Work quickly: just record your first impression.**

	Statement					
____	1. While preparing for the speech, I would feel uncomfortably tense and nervous.	SA_5	A_4	U_3	D_2	SD_1
____	2. I feel uncomfortably tense at the very thought of giving a speech in the near future.	SA_5	A_4	U_3	D_2	SD_1
____	3. My thoughts would become confused and jumbled when I was giving a speech.	SA_5	A_4	U_3	D_2	SD_1
____	4. Right after giving the speech I would feel that I'd had a pleasant experience.	SA_1	A_2	U_3	D_4	SD_5
____	5. I would get anxious when thinking about the speech coming up.	SA_5	A_4	U_3	D_2	SD_1
____	6. I would have no fear of giving the speech.	SA_1	A_2	U_3	D_4	SD_5
____	7. Although I would be nervous just before starting the speech, after starting it I would soon settle down and feel calm and comfortable.	SA_1	A_2	U_3	D_4	SD_5
____	8. I would look forward to giving the speech.	SA_1	A_2	U_3	D_4	SD_5
____	9. As soon as I knew that I would have to give the speech, I would feel myself getting tense.	SA_5	A_4	U_3	D_2	SD_1
____	10. My hands would tremble when I was giving the speech.	SA_5	A_4	U_3	D_2	SD_1
____	11. I would feel relaxed while giving the speech.	SA_1	A_2	U_3	D_4	SD_5
____	12. I would enjoy preparing for the speech.	SA_1	A_2	U_3	D_4	SD_5
____	13. I would be in constant fear of forgetting what I had prepared to say.	SA_5	A_4	U_3	D_2	SD_1
____	14. I would get uncomfortably anxious if someone asked me something that I did not know about my topic.	SA_5	A_4	U_3	D_2	SD_1
____	15. I would face the prospect of giving the speech with confidence.	SA_1	A_2	U_3	D_4	SD_5
____	16. I would feel that I was in complete possession of myself during the speech.	SA_1	A_2	U_3	D_4	SD_5
____	17. My mind would be clear when giving the speech.	SA_1	A_2	U_3	D_4	SD_5
____	18. I would not dread giving the speech.	SA_1	A_2	U_3	D_4	SD_5
____	19. I would perspire too much just before starting the speech.	SA_5	A_4	U_3	D_2	SD_1

____ 20. I would be bothered by a very fast heart rate just as I started the speech. SA_5 A_4 U_3 D_2 SD_1

____ 21. I would experience considerable anxiety at the speech site (room, auditorium, etc.) just before my speech was to start. SA_5 A_4 U_3 D_2 SD_1

____ 22. Certain parts of my body would feel very tense and rigid during the speech. SA_5 A_4 U_3 D_2 SD_1

____ 23. Realizing that only a little time remained in the speech would make me very tense and anxious. SA_5 A_4 U_3 D_2 SD_1

____ 24. While giving the speech I would know that I could control my feelings of tension and stress. SA_1 A_2 U_3 D_4 SD_5

____ 25. I would breathe too fast just before starting the speech. SA_5 A_4 U_3 D_2 SD_1

____ 26. I would feel comfortable and relaxed in the hour or so just before giving the speech. SA_1 A_2 U_3 D_4 SD_5

____ 27. I would do poorly on the speech because I would be anxious. SA_5 A_4 U_3 D_2 SD_1

____ 28. I would feel uncomfortably anxious when first scheduling the date of the speaking assignment. SA_5 A_4 U_3 D_2 SD_1

____ 29. If I were to make a mistake while giving the speech, I would find it hard to concentrate on the parts that followed. SA_5 A_4 U_3 D_2 SD_1

____ 30. During the speech I would experience a feeling of helplessness building up inside me. SA_5 A_4 U_3 D_2 SD_1

____ 31. I would have trouble falling asleep the night before the speech. SA_5 A_4 U_3 D_2 SD_1

____ 32. My heart would beat too fast while I was presenting the speech. SA_5 A_4 U_3 D_2 SD_1

____ 33. I would feel uncomfortably anxious while waiting to give my speech. SA_5 A_4 U_3 D_2 SD_1

____ 34. While giving the speech, I would get so nervous that I would forget facts I really knew. SA_5 A_4 U_3 D_2 SD_1

To determine your score:

1. Fill in the blank next to each item with the NUMBER accompanying the response you circled. BE CAREFUL to enter the CORRECT NUMBER. NOTICE that the numbers printed with the responses are not consistent for every question.
2. Add up the numbers you recorded for the 34 questions. The sum is your public speaking apprehension score.

Interpretation:

34–84	low
85–92	moderately low
93–110	moderate
111–119	moderately high
120+	high

Source: Adapted from James C. McCroskey, "Personal Report of Public Speaking Anxiety," in "Measures of Communication Bound Anxiety," *Speech Monographs* 37 (1970): 276. Used by permission of the National Communication Association.

You may be surprised to find that you didn't score as high on this scale as you thought you would. If your score is higher than 120 on this questionnaire, you should arrange a meeting with your instructor to see if special help is available on campus.

You may have also been surprised when we said that "a little bit of communication apprehension is a good thing." How can this be? The absence of any nervousness could suggest that you don't care about your audience or your message. We recently taught a student who announced to the class that she never had any *stage fright* because she had been very successful in high school forensics and was used to *performing* before a group. She couldn't understand why she was required to take this course. She was indifferent to learning what the course had to offer and indifferent in her preparation. She didn't really listen when others were speaking because she didn't think she could learn anything worth knowing from her classmates. She also didn't listen to her instructors because she felt she already knew all she needed to know about public performances. After all, she had experience and she had been successful. Perhaps because of this attitude, her classroom speeches sounded as though they had been dredged up from her high school forensics files (perhaps they were!). They weren't really tailored to her audience or the assignment. Her delivery was smooth. Her presentations *were* performances in the truest sense of the word. She came across as "showing off." She never connected in any meaningful way with her audience. *She never communicated with them.* That we were never able to teach her the basic meaning of communication—with all its risks and rewards—is one of the failures of our career as educators.

Why Public Speaking Is Frightening

Let's consider some of the reasons why people are not comfortable speaking before a group. Addressing a large number of people face to face is not an everyday occurrence for most of us, and we tend to be somewhat ill at ease in unfamiliar situations. Moreover, you usually will have to speak in public only on important occasions, when a lot depends on how well you express yourself. This element of risk, combined with the feelings of strangeness, can make you nervous.

Additionally, you may be one of those who interpret even the weakest of the symptoms we discussed earlier as signs of fear and then blow them out of proportion. Psychologists refer to this tendency as **anxiety sensitivity**.[7] It is the fear of fear itself. Since such fear can feed on itself until it grows out of control, you must make a real effort not to get too anxious about your anxiety.

It is important to remember that the physical symptoms you may experience before or during speaking are also associated with other types of reactions that we do not usually call "fear." For example, were you ever so excited on Christmas Eve that you couldn't sleep? How did you feel when you heard the first strains of the processional for your high school graduation? What kind of feelings have you had before a big date with a very special person? Did you think of these feelings as "fear" or as "excitement"?

Another factor that contributes to communication apprehension is perfectionism. As a beginning speaker, you may believe that your speech has to be *perfect* to be effective. But no presentation is ever perfect. Even former president Ronald Reagan, who was known as "the great communicator," fumbled some lines and repeated himself at times. It's all right if you make a few mistakes, and besides, your listeners probably won't even notice them unless you call attention to them. So don't fall into the trap of perfectionism.

You may picture the audience as predators lying in wait, ready to pounce on any little mistake you might make, eager to make fun of you as they once might have in grade school. In reality, most audiences—especially college classroom audiences—want speakers to succeed. If you look out in the audience and see someone frowning, it's more likely that that person is worried about his or her own upcoming speech or some personal problem rather than preparing to pounce on you.

You may worry that everyone will know how scared you are. Actually, most listeners won't know this unless you tell them. One time we were taping student speeches in the University of Memphis television studio for a teaching video. We had asked instructors of the basic public speaking course to send us students who had given outstanding speeches in their classes. One young woman began her speech with an excellent interest-arousing introduction. About two minutes into the speech she suddenly stopped, looked at us, and said, "I can't do this! I'm too nervous." With the student's permission, we have used the tape of this episode in many of our classes. We show the speech up until right before she stops. Then we ask class members to estimate how anxious they think this speaker is. Typically they say, "She's not at all nervous." Or, "She's very poised." Then, we start the tape back up and show the segment where she stops. After they get over their surprise, the students get the point.

You may believe that as soon as you stand up to speak, something dreadful is going to happen to you—you'll throw up or pass out. This seldom happens, even with the most communication-apprehensive students. In all our years of teaching, we've never seen a student throw up or pass out in a public speaking class.

A recent survey of the general population identified some specific fears that people have regarding public speaking. The results of this study were reported on page 29. They included shaking, mind going blank, saying something embarrassing, not being able to continue, not making sense, and sounding foolish.

You probably noticed that being graded wasn't on this list. This is because the poll was conducted on a sample of the general adult population, not college students enrolled in a public speaking class. But, since this problem may be weighing on your mind, let's address it first.

If you prepare your speeches solely for the purpose of making a good grade, you likely will not be very successful. *Your main purpose for speaking must be to communicate something of value to your audience*—to provide listeners with new, interesting, or useful information or to convince them to change their way of thinking or behaving. Beyond this, although students often insist that what they are most anxious about is what kind of grade they will get, they are typically just as anxious when making ungraded presentations. Although an ungraded presentation realistically might seem less threatening, the fears associated with communication apprehension usually are not realistic or rational. It is these unrealistic or irrational fears that cause the most problems, so let's examine them one by one.

Shaking. Approximately 80 percent of the people polled indicated that they were afraid that they would tremble or shake while making a presentation. This is the most common specific fear, and it may well be the most common physical reaction. Indeed, as you make your first presentations, your hands may tremble a bit, or your leg muscles may begin to twitch. Is this really all that bad? Chances are you will be more aware of the trembling than anyone in your audience. And, if they do notice it, what will they think? That you're a failure? That you're incompetent? Or, that you—*like them*—are somewhat uncomfortable in front of a group?

Actually, some slight trembling may have a positive effect on how the audience reacts to you. The psychologists have a name for this. They call it "the pratfall effect." When someone in a position of power or authority (as you are when you give a speech) makes a minor mistake, it tends to humanize that person and makes it more likely that people will respond positively. It probably won't affect how competent people think you are, but it may make you seem more likeable.

Is there anything you can do to control your trembling? Probably not as much as you would like. As we noted earlier, fear feeds on itself. The more you think about your trembling and the more you try to control it, the worse it gets.

You stiffen that leg, and it twitches even harder! The best thing to do is to focus on your message and not on your mannerisms. It might also help to use some purposeful physical activity, like gesturing with your hands if they are trembling or walking around from behind the lectern if your leg is twitching. Before you stand to speak, use the relaxation techniques we describe later in this appendix.

Mind Going Blank. The second most common specific fear people reported was that they were afraid their mind would go blank, that they could not remember how they had planned to say something or what they intended to say next. Back in middle school or high school, almost all of us may have had the experience of memorizing a passage for recitation in class—the Gettysburg Address, a scene from Shakespeare, or a poem—and drawing a blank about halfway through our performance. It can be traumatic standing in front of a class of jeering adolescents who just can't wait to make fun of you. Having your mind go blank is one of the major pitfalls of memorized presentations. It is one of the reasons why we do not recommend memorizing your speeches.

An effective speech is presented extemporaneously—prepared and practiced, but not written out and memorized. If you practice your speech using a key-word outline, then keep the outline handy as you present your speech, drawing a blank should not be a major problem for you. Even if you don't say what you had planned to say exactly as you had planned to say it, the audience won't know this unless you tell them. Furthermore, what you say on the spur of the moment may even be *better* than the exact wording you had planned.

Embarrassing Yourself. Whenever you appear before a group to make a presentation, you are putting yourself in the spotlight. The spotlight is bright, and it can show all your wrinkles, and freckles, and anything else you might like to hide. A public speaking student brought home the meaning of this to us several years ago. She also was a cheerleader at Indiana University. One day she came into our office to ask for advice on controlling her communication apprehension. "You're nervous about speaking to twenty-five students!" we exclaimed. "Why, every weekend you're out there in front of sixty thousand people at the stadium!" "That's different," she replied. "Out there I'm not really in the spotlight. Those sixty thousand fans are focused on the game. In this class, the twenty-five students are focused on me talking."

What can you possibly do during a speech that would be all that embarrassing? Tremble in front of people?—we've already discussed that. Forget how you planned to say something?—no big deal. Mispronounce big words or technical terms?—look them up ahead of time. Flub a word?—everyone does this from time to time. Save being embarrassed for the truly ludicrous things that might happen, and keep in mind that you will survive even those.

The first class one of your authors ever taught in college was a large lecture class held in an auditorium—complete with a lectern on a stage. During the first exam a student asked her to cut off the air conditioners that were making such a racket. So she shut off the air conditioner on one side of the stage and was walking across the stage to the other side, not looking where she was going, and tripped over the base of a freestanding chalk board, falling flat on her face in front of two hundred students! Now, that's embarrassing, especially for a first-time graduate student teaching assistant! She wished devoutly that she might crawl through a trap door in the floor, but of course, there was no such convenient escape. To her amazement, however, no one was laughing. The expressions on the faces she could see were ones of concern. She picked herself up, brushed the dirt off her clothes, and muttered something like, "Grace is my middle name!" The students' looks changed from concern to relief when they realized she wasn't hurt, and the incident was forgotten.

Chances are nothing like this will ever happen to you in your public speaking class, but if it does, you will survive it, and you may be even more effective because of it.

Being Unable to Continue Talking. Although almost two-thirds of the people surveyed mentioned being unable to continue talking as a specific concern, it very rarely happens, even to the most anxious of students. This concern is closely related to having your mind go blank, a momentary occurrence that can be handled by having a key-word outline or note cards to refer to.

On rare occasions, a student may experience a panic attack. You're going along presenting your speech, everything is going well, when you suddenly feel overwhelmed with fear for no apparent reason. Not only are you afraid, but you realize that the fear is irrational, and you think perhaps you're "losing it." What you really want to do is drop your notes and bolt for the nearest door. *Don't do it.* It's the worst possible thing you could do. Have courage! Mark Twain once said, "Courage is resistance to fear, mastery of fear, not absence of fear." A panic attack is usually short. It may last only a few seconds, although it may feel to you like it's going on for hours. Keep talking. Look for the friendliest face in the audience and direct your words to that person. Accept your fear for what it is, a temporary aberration. Chances are it will never happen again, but if you are concerned about this possibility, schedule an appointment with your instructor to discuss it.

Not Making Sense and Sounding Foolish. Most speakers who don't make sense and therefore sound foolish do so because they have not adequately prepared for their presentation. This textbook is devoted to helping you prepare and present speeches that make sense and sound intelligent. You will learn how to analyze your listeners and how to adapt your message to their needs and interests. You will learn how to gain responsible knowledge through research and use this material to support your ideas. You will learn how to structure and organize a message for maximum impact and how to use oral language effectively. All of this information will help ensure that you make sense and don't sound foolish.

On the other hand, if you take your assignments lightly, don't adequately prepare and practice your presentations, and then don't make sense and sound foolish . . . well, "that's a whole 'nuther ballgame." You've earned the right to be anxious and to suffer the consequences.

Controlling Communication Apprehension

You've probably heard a lot of advice about how to control communication apprehension. One person says, "Just picture the audience sitting there naked." (Try this, and if you have a rich imagination, the results are apt to be more distracting or amusing than helpful.) Another says, "Just take a really deep breath each time you feel yourself getting anxious." (Do this and you'll start hyperventilating—then you'll really be in trouble.) The people who offer such wisdom usually mean well, but most of the quick-fix techniques simply don't work.

You also may have been told that taking a public speaking class will cure your communication apprehension. One of the biggest myths about a public speaking class is that it can or should rid you of your natural fears. *There is no cure for communication apprehension, but there are things that can help you bring it under control.*

Research shows that the techniques we will discuss here do help and that they work best when used in combination.[8] So try one thing and then another until you find what works best for you.

Relaxation Techniques. A good starting point in learning how to handle your communication apprehension is to master the art of **selective relaxation**. You need to learn how to do this before you start speaking. If you should find yourself up in front of a group with your anxiety growing by leaps and bounds, you can't expect your body to obey when you say to yourself, "Relax!" You have to begin practicing the techniques of relaxation now, long before you stand to speak.

First, find a quiet, comfortable place where you can be by yourself. Sit in a comfortable chair or lie down, close your eyes, and breathe deeply in through your nose and out through your mouth. You should feel yourself beginning to relax.

Once you feel relaxed, begin repeating a prolonged word, a sound that resonates through your nasal cavities—such as the word *one*—each time you exhale. Let your mind drift freely. You should soon feel completely relaxed.

Next, while you are relaxed and breathing deeply, practice selectively tensing and relaxing different muscle groups. Begin by tensing your feet and legs: curl up your toes, tense your arch, tighten your calves, lock your knees, tighten up your thighs. Hold this tension for several seconds and concentrate on how it feels. Not very comfortable, is it? And even with the tension concentrated in the lower part of your body, it's not all that easy to continue your deep breathing. Now, concentrate on breathing deeply again, repeating your special word or sound as you exhale, and consciously letting those muscles relax. Note how this feels. Move on up your body: tense and relax your abdominal muscles, your hand and arm muscles, your neck and head muscles.

After you have done this a number of times, repeating your special word should automatically trigger a relaxation response.

One good thing about this exercise is that once you have mastered the technique, you can practice it unobtrusively in many situations. While you are sitting in class waiting to speak, tense your feet and leg muscles; then relax them. If you find yourself getting nervous while you are speaking, repeat your special word to yourself. The word alone may be enough to help you relax and reduce your apprehension.

Attitude Adjustments. Throughout this chapter we have stressed the importance of thinking of public speaking as an interactive communication event, not a performance. When you adopt a communication orientation to public speaking, your focus is on your message and your audience, not on yourself. You select a topic that involves you so completely that you have little time left to worry about your personal fate. You are entirely focused on your purpose while you are speaking, which is to bring important new information or perspectives to your listeners.

One of the most communication-apprehensive students we ever taught actually left the room in the middle of her first speech to get a drink of water and to try to compose herself. While she was in the hall, we discussed with the class how we might help her. When she came to see us after the speech, we tried to help her focus on her message and her audience. Her second effort was a little better. She stopped during her presentation to try to "pull herself together" but managed to finish without leaving the room. Her third speech (persuasive) was a totally different story. The student worked during the day as a dispatcher for a major interstate trucking firm. She presented a speech urging her classmates to lobby their legislative representatives to vote in favor of a truck safety bill that was pending in Congress. This topic was very important to her, and she made it come alive for us. Her speech was filled with interesting and vital examples of near catastrophes that this legislation would make less likely. She knew her topic. She knew it was important. She got so caught up with the message she had to communicate that she forgot to be anxious. Her classroom audience was spellbound. When she finished, there was a moment of silence while it all sank in, then spontaneous applause. Applause for a speech well given and applause for a speaker who had conquered her personal demons!

Notes

1. The Gallup Organization, "Snakes Top List of American's Fears," 19 Mar. 2001. http://www.gallup.com/poll/releases/pr010319.asp (19 Mar. 2001).

2. National Communication Association, "How Americans Communicate," n.d. http://www.natcom.org/research/Roper/how_americans_communicate.htm (25 June 1999).

3. Nanci Hellmich, "Lifting the Curtain on Stage Fright: Anxiety at Performing Is Normal, but Panic Can Become Paralyzing," *USA Today*, 13 Aug. 1996, p. 6D.

4. Rochelle Garner, "Bore No More," *Computerworld*, 5 Apr. 1999, p. 54.

5. Pedro Pereira, "Top 25 Executives: Steve Raymund," *Computer Reseller News*, 17 Nov. 1997, p. 129.

6. Michael T. Motley, *Overcoming Your Fear of Public Speaking: A Proven Method* (Boston: Houghton Mifflin, 1997).

7. Jennifer D. Mladenka, Chris R. Sawyer, and Ralph R. Behnke, "Anxiety Sensitivity and Speech Trait Anxiety as Predictors of State Anxiety During Public Speaking," *Communication Quarterly* 46 (1998): 417–429.

8. Randolph W. Whitworth and Claudia Cochran, "Evaluation of Integrated Versus Unitary Treatments for Reducing Public Speaking Anxiety," *Communication Education* 45 (1996): 228–235.

Appendix C

Speeches for Analysis

Self-Introductory

Sandra Baltz *My Three Cultures*
Rodney Nishikawa *Free at Last*

Informative

Marge Anderson *Looking Through Our Window: The Value of Indian Culture*
Stephen Huff *The New Madrid Earthquake Area*
Cecile Larson *The "Monument" at Wounded Knee*

Persuasive

Anna Aley *We Don't Have to Live in Slums*
Cesar Chavez *Pesticides Speech*
Bonnie Marshall *Living Wills: Ensuring Your Right to Choose*

Ceremonial

Tommie Albright *Martin Luther King Jr.'s Legacy for Us*
A Tribute to Wilma Rudolph with presentations by Tom Brokaw, Bill Cosby, Gail Devers, Ed Temple, and Wilma Rudolph
Elizabeth Dole *Women in Public Life Commencement Address*
Elie Wiesel *Nobel Peace Prize Acceptance Speech*

My Three Cultures

Sandra Baltz

Sandra Baltz first presented this self-introductory speech many years ago at the University of Memphis. She addressed the themes of cross-culturalism and family values long before these became fashionable. Sandra's deft use of comparison and contrast, and her example of foods illustrating how three cultures can combine harmoniously, are instructive. As her speech developed, she built her ethos as a competent, warm person, highly qualified to give later informative and persuasive speeches on issues involving medical care. Presented at a time when tensions in the Middle East were running high, Sandra's speech served as a gentle reminder that people of goodwill can always find ways to enjoy their differences, and to reaffirm their common membership in the human family.

Several years ago I read a newspaper article in the *Commercial Appeal* in which an American journalist described some of his experiences in the Middle East. He was there a couple of months and had been the guest of several different Arab families. He reported having been very well treated and very well received by everyone that he met there. But it was only later, when he returned home, that he became aware of the intense resentment his hosts held for Americans and our unwelcome involvement in their Middle Eastern affairs. The journalist wrote of feeling somewhat bewildered, if not deceived, by the large discrepancy between his treatment while in the Middle East and the hostile attitude that he learned about later. He labeled this behavior hypocritical. When I reached the end of the article, I was reminded of a phrase spoken often by my mother. "Sandra," she says to me, *"respeta tu casa y a todos los que entran en ella, trata a tus enemigos asi como a tus amigos."*

This is an Arabic proverb, spoken in Spanish, and roughly it translates into "Respect your home and all who enter it, treating even an enemy as a friend." This is a philosophy that I have heard often in my home. With this in mind, it seemed to me that the treatment the American journalist received while in the Middle East was not hypocritical behavior on the part of his hosts. Rather, it was an act of respect for their guest, for themselves, and for their home—indeed, a behavior very typical of the Arabic culture.

Since having read that article several years ago, I have become much more aware of how my life is different because of having a mother who is of Palestinian origin but was born and raised in the Central American country of El Salvador.

One of the most obvious differences is that I was raised bilingually—speaking both Spanish and English. In fact, my first words were in Spanish. Growing up speaking two languages has been both an advantage and a disadvantage for me. One clear advantage is that I received straight A's in my Spanish class at Immaculate Conception High School. Certainly, traveling has been made much easier. During visits to Spain, Mexico, and some of the Central American countries, it has been my experience that people are much more open and much more receptive if you can speak their language. In addition, the subtleties of a culture are easier to grasp and much easier to appreciate.

I hope that knowing a second language will continue to be an asset for me in the future. I am currently pursuing a career in medicine. Perhaps by knowing Spanish I can broaden the area in which I can work and increase the number of people that I might reach.

Now one of the disadvantages of growing up bilingually is that I picked up my mother's accent as well as her language. I must have been about four years old before I realized that our feathered friends in the trees are called "birds" not "beers" and that, in fact, we had a "birdbath" in our backyard, not a "beerbath."

Family reunions also tend to be confusing around my home. Most of my relatives speak either Spanish, English, or Arabic, but rarely any combination of the three. So, as a result, deep and involved conversations are almost impossible. But with a little nodding and smiling, I have found that there really is no language barrier among family and friends.

In all, I must say that being exposed to three very different cultures—Latin, Arabic, and American—has been rewarding for me and has made a difference even in the music I enjoy and the food I eat. It is not unusual in my house to sit down to a meal made up of stuffed grape leaves and refried beans and all topped off with apple pie for dessert.

I am fortunate in having had the opportunity to view more closely what makes Arabic and Latin cultures unique. By understanding and appreciating them I have been able to better understand and appreciate my own American culture. In closing, just let me add some words you often hear spoken in my home—*adios* and *allak konn ma'eck*—goodbye, and may God go with you.

Free at Last

Rodney Nishikawa

Rod Nishikawa presented this sensitive and moving self-introductory speech in his public speaking class at the University of California–Davis. Although most of his classmates were aware of prejudice, Rod's personal narrative—about his first encounter with prejudice as a child—introduced many of them to the Japanese American culture and helped them relate to the problem more closely. Rod's willingness to speak from the heart helped transform his class into a creative, caring community.

Three years ago I presented the valedictory speech at my high school graduation. As I concluded, I borrowed a line from Dr. Martin Luther King's "I Have a Dream" oration: "Free at last, free at last, thank God almighty we're free at last!" The words had only a joyful, humorous place in that speech, but for me personally they were a lie. I was not yet free, and would not be free until I had conquered an ancient enemy, both outside me and within me—that enemy was racial prejudice.

The event in my life that had the greatest effect on me happened over twelve years ago when I was eight years old. I was a shy, naive little boy. I knew I was Japanese, but I didn't consider myself different from my friends, nor did I realize anyone else noticed or even cared. But at least one person did. The "bully" in our class made it a point to remind me by calling me a "Jap." He told me I didn't belong in America, and that I should go back to Japan.

It was hard for me to understand what he meant, because like my parents I was born here in this country. This was my home. I didn't know what to do when I was taunted. All I can remember is going home after school and crying as though my heart were broken. I told my mom that I wished I wasn't Japanese, but that if I did have to be Japanese, why did I have to be born in this country?

Of course my mother knew exactly how I felt. She was about the age I was then when the Japanese attacked Pearl Harbor. She told me how she too had experienced prejudice at school, but that the prejudice she encountered was over a hundred times worse. When my father came home from work, my mom and I told him what had happened. Although my father was understanding, he said that I would never know the meaning of true prejudice because I did not grow up on the West Coast during World War II.

My encounter with the school bully was the beginning of my personal education about prejudice. What I have learned is that prejudice is not a disease that infects only the least educated among us. Rather, it is a bad part of human nature that lies buried deep within all of us. Some people, however, seem to enjoy their prejudice. These people like to feel good by putting others down. But I have also learned how to deal with such problems when they arise. It was the advice from my mother that helped me the most.

My mother explained to me the meaning of the Japanese word *gaman*. *Gaman* means to "bear within" or "bear the burden." It is similar to the American phrase "turn the other cheek," but it means more to "endure" than to "ignore." She told me that when I go back to school, I should practice *gaman*—that even if I am hurt, I should not react with anger or fear, that I should bear the burden within. She said that if I showed anger or fear it would only make things worse, but if I practiced *gaman* things would get better for me. She was right. When I went back to school, I remembered what she had said. I used *gaman*. I bore the burden within. It wasn't easy for an eight-year-old, but I did not show any anger. I did not show any fear to the bully, and eventually he stopped picking on me.

Prejudice has been a bitter teacher in my life, but *gaman* has been an even greater blessing. By learning how to practice it, I feel I have acquired a great deal of inner strength. Whereas Gary [another student in the class] said he is a "competitor," I believe I am a "survivor." I look around my environment, recognize my situation, and cope with it. Because *gaman* has been part of my daily life since I was eight years old, I rarely experience feelings of anger or fear—those negative emotions that can keep a person from really being "free."

Being freed from such negative feelings has also helped me to better understand and accept myself. When I first encountered prejudice, I was ashamed of who I was. I didn't like being different, being a Japanese American. But as I've grown to maturity, I have realized that I'm really proud to be Japanese American: Japanese by blood—with the rich culture and heritage of my ancestors behind me—and American by birth—which makes me equal to anyone in this room because we were all born in this country and we all share the same rights and obligations.

Practicing *gaman* has helped me conquer prejudice. Although my Japanese ancestors might not have spoken as boldly as I have today, I am basically an American, which makes me a little outspoken. Therefore, I can talk to you about racial prejudice and of what it has meant to my life. And because I can talk about it, and share it with you, I am finally, truly, "free at last."

Looking Through Our Window: The Value of Indian Culture

Marge Anderson

This presentation by Marge Anderson, chief executive of the Mille Lacs Band of the Ojibwe, shows that one speech can perform multiple general functions. Anderson both celebrates the values of her culture and persuades listeners to engage in a dialogue, which she defines, citing St. Thomas Aquinas, as "the struggle to learn from each other." The even more fundamental function of her speech is to *inform* her mainstream Minnesota audience of how Native Americans view the world and their relationship to it. From the basis of that understanding, she explains specific accomplishments of her tribe and the rationale behind her people's business decisions. All of us are enriched, she argues, when we are able to look at the world through each other's windows. Therefore, she suggests, her listeners should honor and help preserve the authenticity of the Native American cultural perspective.

Aaniin. Thank you for inviting me here today. When I was asked to speak to you, I was told you are interested in hearing about the improvements we are making on the Mille Lacs Reservation, and about our investment of casino dollars back into our community through schools, health care facilities, and other services. And I do want to talk to you about these things, because they are tremendously important, and I am very proud of them.

But before I do, I want to take a few minutes to talk to you about something else, something I'm not asked about very often. I want to talk to you about what it means to be Indian. About how my people experience the world. About the fundamental way in which our culture differs from yours. And about why you should care about all this.

The differences between Indians and non-Indians have created a lot of controversy lately. Casinos, treaty rights, tribal sovereignty—these issues have stirred such anger and bitterness.

I believe the accusations against us are made out of ignorance. The vast majority of non-Indians do not understand how my people view the world, what we value, what motivates us.

They do not know these things for one simple reason: they've never heard us talk about them. For many years, the only stories that non-Indians heard about my people came from other non-Indians. As a result, the picture you got of us was fanciful, or distorted, or so shadowy, it hardly existed at all.

It's time for Indian voices to tell Indian stories.

Now, I'm sure at least a few of you are wondering, "Why do I need to hear these stories? Why should I care about what Indian people think, and feel, and believe?"

I think the most eloquent answer I can give you comes from the namesake of this university, St. Thomas Aquinas. St. Thomas wrote that dialogue is the struggle to learn from each other. This struggle, he said, is like Jacob wrestling the angel—it leaves one wounded and blessed at the same time.

Indian people know this struggle very well. The wounds we've suffered in our dialogue with non-Indians are well documented; I don't need to give you a laundry list of complaints.

We also know some of the blessings of this struggle. As American Indians, we live in two worlds—ours, and yours. In the 500 years since you first came to our lands, we have struggled to learn how to take the best of what your culture has to offer in arts, science, technology and more, and then weave them into the fabric of our traditional ways.

But for non-Indians, the struggle is new. Now that our people have begun to achieve success, now that we are in business and in the headlines, you are starting to wrestle with understanding us.

Your wounds from this struggle are fresh, and the pain might make it hard for you to see beyond them. But if you try, you'll begin to see the blessings as well—the blessings of what a deepened knowledge of Indian culture can bring to you. I'd like to share a few of those blessings with you today.

Earlier I mentioned that there is a fundamental difference between the way Indians and non-Indians experience the world. This difference goes all the way back to the bible, and Genesis.

In Genesis, the first book of the Old Testament, God creates man in his own image. Then God says, "be fruitful, multiply, fill the earth and conquer it. Be masters of the fish of the sea, the birds of the heaven, and all living animals on the earth."

Masters. Conquer. Nothing, nothing could be further from the way Indian people view the world and our place in it. Here are the words of the great nineteenth century Chief Seattle:

"You are a part of the earth, and the earth is a part of you. You did not weave the web of life, you are merely a strand in it. Whatever you do to the web, you do to yourself."

In our tradition, there is no mastery. There is no conquering. Instead, there is kinship among all creation—humans, animals, birds, plants, even rocks. We are all part of the sacred hoop of the world, and we must all live in harmony with each other if that hoop is to remain unbroken.

When you begin to see the world this way—through Indian eyes—you will begin to understand our view of land, and treaties, very differently. You will begin to understand that when we speak of Father Sun and Mother Earth, these are not new-age catchwords—they are very real terms of respect for very real beings.

And when you understand this, then you will understand that our fight for treaty rights is not just about hunting deer or catching fish. It is about teaching our children to honor Mother Earth and Father Sun. It is about teaching them to respectfully receive the gifts these loving parents offer us in return for the care we give them. And it is about teaching this generation and the generations yet to come about their place in the web of life. Our culture and the fish, our values and the deer, the lessons we learn and the rice we harvest—everything is tied together. You can no more separate one from the other than you can divide a person's spirit from his body.

When you understand how we view the world and our place in it, it's easier to appreciate why our casinos are so important to us. The reason we defend our businesses so fiercely isn't because we want to have something that others don't. The reason is because these businesses allow us to give back to others—to our People, our communities, and the Creator.

I'd like to take a minute and mention just a few of the ways we've already given back:

We've opened new schools, new health care facilities, and new community centers where our children get a better education, where our elders get better medical care, and where our families can gather to socialize and keep our traditions alive.

We've built new ceremonial buildings, and new powwow and celebration grounds.

We've renovated an elderly center, and plan to build three culturally sensitive assisted living facilities for our elders.

We've created programs to teach and preserve our language and cultural traditions.

We've created a Small Business Development Program to help band members start their own businesses.

We've created more than twenty-eight hundred jobs for band members, people from other tribes, and non-Indians.

We've spurred the development of more than one thousand jobs in other local businesses.

We've generated more than fifty million dollars in federal taxes, and more than fifteen million dollars in state taxes through wages paid to employees.

And we've given back more than two million dollars in charitable donations.

The list goes on and on. But rather than flood you with more numbers, I'll tell you a story that sums up how my people view business through the lens of our traditional values.

Last year, the Woodlands National Bank, which is owned and operated by the Mille Lacs Band, was approached by the city of Onamia and asked to forgive a mortgage on a building in the downtown area. The building had been abandoned and was an eyesore on Main Street. The city planned to renovate and sell the building, and return it to the tax rolls.

Although the bank would lose money by forgiving the mortgage, our business leaders could see the wisdom in improving the community. The opportunity to help our neighbors was an opportunity to strengthen the web of life. So we forgave the mortgage.

Now, I know this is not a decision everyone would agree with. Some people feel that in business, you have to look out for number one. But my people feel that in business—and in life—you have to look out for every one.

And this, I believe, is one of the blessings that Indian culture has to offer you and other non-Indians. We have a different perspective on so many things, from caring for the environment, to healing the body, mind and soul.

But if our culture disappears, if the Indian ways are swallowed up by the dominant American culture, no one will be able to learn from them. Not Indian children. Not your children. No one. All that knowledge, all that wisdom, will be lost forever.

The struggle of dialogue will be over. Yes, there will be no more wounds. But there will also be no more blessings.

There is still so much we have to learn from each other, and we have already wasted so much time. Our world grows smaller every day. And every day, more of our unsettling, surprising, wonderful differences vanish. And when that happens, part of us vanishes, too.

I'd like to end with one of my favorite stories. It's a funny little story about Indians and non-Indians, but its message is serious: you can see something differently if you are willing to learn from those around you.

This is the story: Years ago, white settlers came to this area and built the first European-style homes. When Indian People walked by these homes and saw see-through things in the walls, they looked through them to see what the strangers inside were doing. The settlers were shocked, but it makes sense when you think about it: windows are made to be looked through from both sides.

Since then, my people have spent many years looking at the world through your window. I hope today I've given you a reason to look at it through ours.

Mii gwetch.

The New Madrid Earthquake Area

Stephen Huff

Stephen Huff's informative speech skillfully relates his subject to his immediate audience at the outset. He makes excellent use of comparison and contrast, of presentation aids, and of vivid description to make his subject come alive. After first establishing a basis of facts, he builds an imaginary disaster narrative to help his audience understand the magnitude of the problem being discussed. Thus he motivates listeners to take seriously his suggestions for earthquake preparation. A more adequate summary at the end of the speech might have made it even more effective.

How many of you can remember what you were doing around seven o'clock on the evening of October 17th? If you're a sports fan like me, you had probably set out the munchies, popped a cold one, and settled back to watch San Francisco and Oakland battle it out in the World Series. Since the show came on at seven o'clock here in Memphis for its pregame hype, you may not have been paying close attention to the TV—until—until—until both the sound and picture went out because of the Bay Area earthquake.

If you're like me, you probably sat glued to the TV set for the rest of the evening watching the live coverage of that catastrophe. If you're like me, you probably started thinking that Memphis, Tennessee, is in the middle of the New Madrid earthquake area and wondering how likely it would be for a large earthquake to hit here. And if you're like me, you probably asked yourself, "What would I do if a major earthquake hit Memphis?"

As I asked myself these questions, I was surprised to admit that I didn't know very much about the New Madrid earthquake area or the probability of a major quake in Memphis. And I was really upset to discover that I didn't have the foggiest idea of what to do if a quake did hit. So I visited the Center for Earthquake Research and Information here on campus; talked with Dr. Arch Johnston, the director; and read the materials he helped me find. Today, I'd like to share with

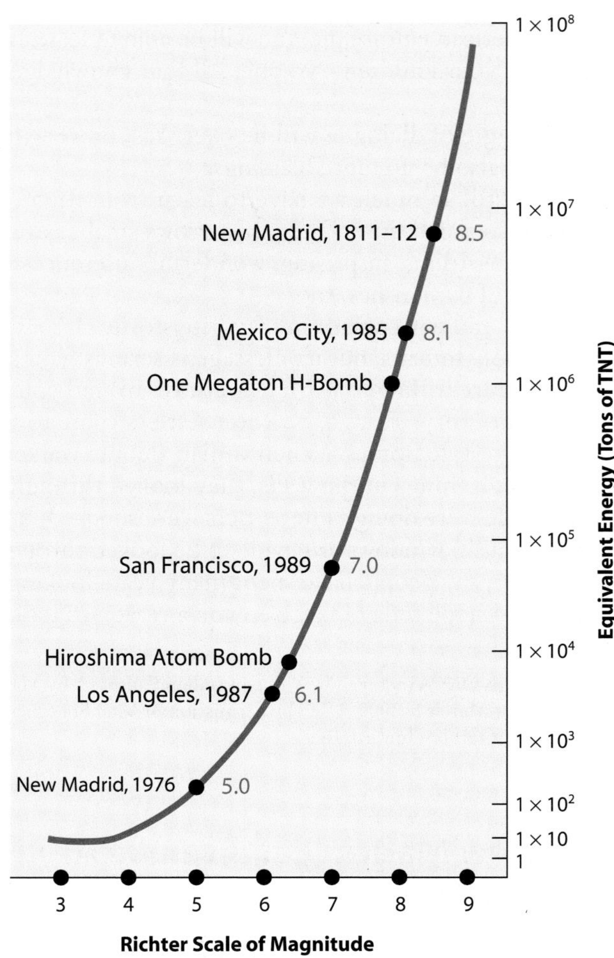

you what I learned about the New Madrid earthquake area, how likely it is that Memphis may be hit by a major quake in the near future, what the effects of such a quake might be, and—most important—what you can do to be prepared.

Let's start with a little history about the New Madrid earthquake area. During the winter of 1811 to 1812, three of the largest earthquakes ever to hit the continental United States occurred in this area. Their estimated magnitudes were 8.6, 8.4, and 8.8 on the Richter scale. [He reveals magnitude chart.] I have drawn this chart to give you some idea of how much energy this involves. To simplify things, I have shown the New Madrid quakes as 8.5. Since a one-point increase in the Richter scale equals a thirtyfold increase in energy release, the energy level of these quakes was over nine hundred times more powerful than the Hiroshima atomic bomb and more than thirty times more powerful than the 7.0 quake that hit San Francisco last October. [He conceals magnitude chart.]

Most of the reports of these early earthquakes come from journals or Indian legends. The Indians tell of the night that lasted for a week and the way the "Father of Waters"—the Mississippi River—ran backwards. Waterfalls were formed on the river. Islands disappeared. Land that was once in Arkansas—on the west bank of the river—ended up in Tennessee—on the east bank of the river. Church bells chimed as far away as New Orleans and Boston. Cracks up to ten feet wide opened and closed in the earth. Geysers squirted sand fifteen feet into the air. Whole forests sank into the earth as the land turned to quicksand. Lakes disappeared and new lakes were formed. Reelfoot Lake—over ten

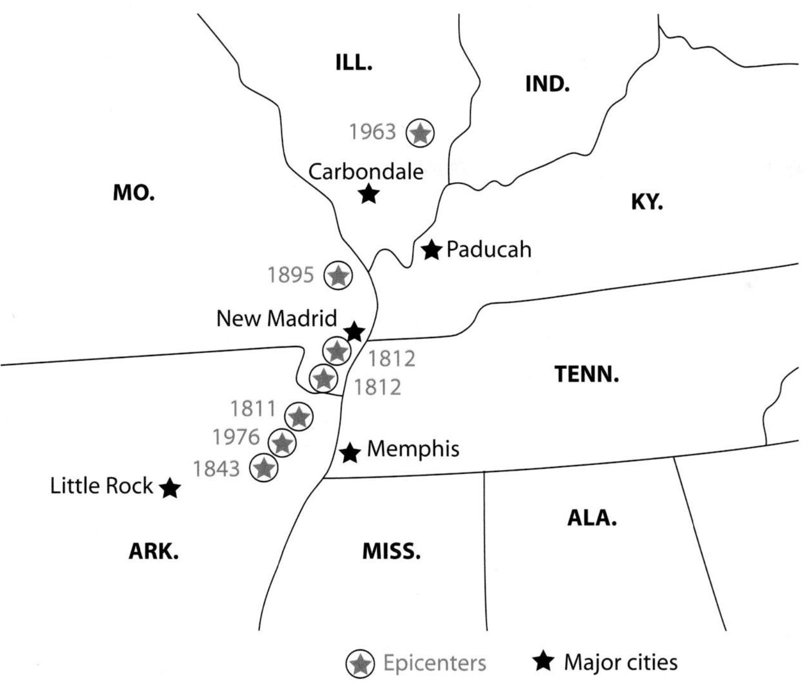

miles long—was formed when the Mississippi River changed its course. No one is certain how many people died from the quakes because the area was sparsely settled with trappers and Indian villages. Memphis was just an outpost village with a few hundred settlers.

[He shows map of epicenters.] As you can see on this map, Memphis itself is not directly on the New Madrid Fault line. The fault extends from around Marked Tree, Arkansas, northeast to near Cairo, Illinois. This continues to be a volatile area of earthquake activity. According to Robert L. Ketter, director of the National Center for Earthquake Engineering Research, between 1974 and 1983 over two thousand quakes were recorded in the area. About 150 earthquakes per year occur in the area, but only about eight of them are large enough for people to notice. The others are picked up on the seismographs at tracking stations. The strongest quake in recent years occurred here in 1976. [He points to location on map.] This measured 5.0 on the Richter scale.

The New Madrid earthquake area is much different from the San Andreas Fault in California. Because of the way the land is formed, the alluvial soil transmits energy more efficiently here than in California. Although the quakes were about the same size, the New Madrid earthquakes affected an area fifteen times larger than the "great quake" that destroyed San Francisco in 1906.

Although scientists cannot predict exactly when another major quake may hit the area, they do know that the *repeat time* for a magnitude-6 New Madrid earthquake is seventy years, plus or minus fifteen years. The last earthquake of this size to hit the area occurred in 1895 north of New Madrid, Missouri. [He points to epicenter on map.] According to Johnston and Nava of the Memphis Earthquake Center, the probability that one with a magnitude of 6.3 will occur somewhere in the fault area by the year 2010 is 40 to 63 percent. By the year 2035 this probability increases to 86 to 97 percent. The probabilities for larger quakes are lower. They estimate the probability of a 7.6 quake within the next fifty years to be from 19 to 29 percent. [He conceals map of epicenters.]

What would happen if an earthquake of 7.6 hit Memphis? Allan and Hoshall, a prominent local engineering firm, prepared a study on this for the Federal Emergency Management Agency. The expected death toll would top 2,400. There would be at least 10,000 casualties. Two hundred thousand residents would be homeless. The city would be without electricity, gas, water, or sewer treatment facilities for weeks. Gas lines would rupture, and fires would sweep through the city. Transportation would be almost impossible, bridges and roads would be destroyed, and emergency supplies would have to be brought in by helicopter. The river bluff, midtown, and land along the Wolfe River would turn to quicksand because of liquification. Buildings there would sink like they did in the Marina area during the San Francisco quake. If the quake hit during daytime hours, at least 600 children would be killed and another 2,400 injured as schools collapsed on them. None of our schools have been built to seismic code specifications.

In fact, very few buildings in Memphis have been built to be earthquake resistant, so it would be difficult to find places to shelter and care for the homeless. The major exceptions are the new hospitals in the suburbs, the Omni Hotel east of the expressway, the Holiday Inn Convention Center, and two or three new office complexes. The only municipal structure built to code is the Criminal Justice Center. The Memphis Pyramid, built by the city and county, which seats over twenty thousand people for the University of Memphis basketball games, was not built to code. I'd hate to be in it if a major quake hit. The prospects are not pretty.

What can we do to prepare ourselves for this possible catastrophe? We can start out by learning what to do if a quake does hit. When I asked myself what I would do, my first reaction was to "get outside." I've since learned that this is not right. The "Earthquake Safety Checklist" published by the Federal Emergency Management Agency and the Red Cross makes a number of suggestions. I've written them out and will distribute them after my speech.

First, when an earthquake hits, if you are inside, stay there. Get in a safe spot: Stand in a doorway, stand next to an inside wall, or get under a large piece of furniture. Stay away from windows, hanging objects, fireplaces, and tall, unsecured furniture until the shaking stops. Do not try to use elevators. If you are outside, get away from buildings, trees, walls, or power lines. If you are in a car, stay in it; pull over and park. Stay away from overpasses and power lines. Do not drive over bridges or overpasses until they have been inspected. If you are in a crowded public place, do not rush for the exit. You may be crushed in the stampede of people.

When the shaking stops, check for gas, water, or electrical damage. Turn off the electricity, gas, and water to your home. Do not use electrical switches—unseen sparks could set off a gas fire. Do not use the telephone unless you must report a severe injury. Check to see that the sewer works before using the toilet. Plug drains to prevent a sewer backup.

There are also some things you can do in advance to be prepared. Accumulate emergency supplies: At home you should have a flashlight, a transistor radio with fresh batteries, a first-aid kit, fire extinguishers, and enough canned or dried food and beverages to last your family for 72 hours. Identify hazards and safe spots in your home—secure tall, heavy furniture; don't hang heavy pictures over your bed; keep flammable liquids in a garage or outside storage area—look around each room and plan where you would go if an earthquake hit. Conduct earthquake drills with your family.

There's one more suggestion that I would like to add. One that is specific to Memphis. Let our local officials know that you are concerned about the lack of preparedness. Urge them to support a building code—at least for public structures—that meets seismic resistance standards.

In preparing this speech, I learned a lot about the potential for earthquakes in Memphis. I hope you have learned something too. I now feel like I know what I should do if an earthquake hits. But I'm not really sure how I would react. Even the experts don't always react "appropriately." In 1971 an earthquake hit the Los Angeles area at about six o'clock in the morning. Charles Richter, the seismologist who developed the Richter scale to measure earthquakes, was in bed at the time. According to his wife, "He jumped up screaming and scared the cat."

Earthquake Preparedness Suggestions

1. If you are inside, stay there. Get in a safe spot: Stand in a doorway, stand next to an inside wall, or get under a large piece of furniture. Stay away from windows, hanging objects, fireplaces, and tall, unsecured furniture until the shaking stops. Do not try to use elevators.
2. If you are outside, get away from buildings, trees, walls, or power lines. If you are in a car, stay in it; pull over and park. Stay away from overpasses and power lines. Do not drive over bridges or overpasses until they have been inspected.
3. If you are in a crowded public place, do not rush for the exit. You may be crushed in the stampede of people.
4. When the shaking stops, check for gas, water, or electrical damage. Turn off the electricity, gas, and water to your home. Do not use electrical switches—unseen sparks could set off a gas fire. Do not use the telephone unless you must report a severe injury. Check to see that the sewer works before using the toilet. Plug drains to prevent sewer backup.

There are also some things you can do in advance to be prepared:

1. Accumulate emergency supplies: At home you should have a flashlight, a transistor radio with fresh batteries, a first-aid kit, fire extinguishers, and enough canned or dried food and beverages to last for 72 hours.
2. Identify hazards and safe spots in your home—secure tall, heavy furniture; don't hang heavy pictures over your bed; keep flammable liquids in a garage or outside storage area—look around each room and plan where you would go if an earthquake hit; conduct earthquake drills with your family.

The "Monument" at Wounded Knee

Cecile Larson

Cecile Larson's classroom speech serves two informative functions. First, it shapes the perceptions of the audience because of the way it describes the "monument" and the perspective it takes on the situation—most of her classmates had had little or no contact with Native Americans, and this might have been their first exposure to this type of information. Second, the speech serves the agenda-setting function in that it creates an awareness of a problem and thus increases the importance of that problem in the minds of the audience. The speech follows a spatial design. Cecile's vivid use of imagery and the skillful contrasts she draws between this "monument" and our "official" monuments create mental pictures that should stay with her listeners long after the words of her speech have been forgotten.

We Americans are big on monuments. We build monuments in memory of our heroes. Washington, Jefferson, and Lincoln live on in our nation's capital. We erect monuments to honor our martyrs. The Minuteman still stands guard at Concord. The flag is ever raised over Iwo Jima. Sometimes we even construct monuments to commemorate victims. In Ashburn Park downtown there is a monument to those who died in the yellow fever epidemics. However, there are some things in our history that we don't memorialize. Perhaps we would just as soon forget what happened. Last summer I visited such a place—the massacre site at Wounded Knee.

In case you have forgotten what happened at Wounded Knee, let me refresh your memory. On December 29, 1890, shortly after Sitting Bull had been murdered by the authorities, about 400 half-frozen, starving, and frightened Indians who had fled the nearby reservation were attacked by the Seventh Cavalry. When the fighting ended, between 200 and 300 Sioux had died—two-thirds of them women and children. Their remains are buried in a common grave at the site of the massacre.

Wounded Knee is located in the Pine Ridge Reservation in southwestern South Dakota—about a three-hour drive from where Presidents Washington, Jefferson, Theodore Roosevelt, and Lincoln are enshrined in the granite face of Mount Rushmore. The reservation is directly south of the Badlands National Park, a magnificently desolate area of wind-eroded buttes and multicolored spires.

We entered the reservation driving south from the Badlands Visitor's Center. The landscape of the Pine Ridge Reservation retains much of the desolation of the Badlands but lacks its magnificence. Flat, sun-baked fields and an occasional eroded gully stretch as far as the eye can see. There are no signs or highway markers to lead the curious tourist to Wounded Knee. Even the *Rand-McNally Atlas* doesn't help you find your way. We got lost three times and had to stop and ask directions.

When we finally arrived at Wounded Knee, there was no official historic marker to tell us what had happened there. Instead there was a large, handmade wooden sign—crudely lettered in white on black. The sign first directed our attention to our left—to the gully where the massacre took place. The mass grave site was to our right—across the road and up a small hill.

Two red-brick columns topped with a wrought-iron arch and a small metal cross form the entrance to the grave site. The column to the right is in bad shape: cinder blocks from the base are missing; the brickwork near the top has deteriorated and tumbled to the ground; graffiti on the columns proclaim an attitude we found repeatedly expressed about the Bureau of Indian Affairs—"The BIA sucks!"

Crumbling concrete steps lead you to the mass grave. The top of the grave is covered with gravel, punctuated by unruly patches of chickweed and crabgrass. These same weeds also grow along the base of the broken chainlink fence that surrounds the grave, the "monument," and a small cemetery.

The "monument" itself rests on a concrete slab to the right of the grave. It's a typical, large, old-fashioned granite cemetery marker, a pillar about six feet high topped with an urn—the kind of gravestone you might see in any cemetery with graves from the turn of the century. The inscription tells us that it was erected by the families of those who were killed at Wounded Knee. Weeds grow through the cracks in the concrete at its base.

There are no granite headstones in the adjacent cemetery, only simple white wooden crosses that tell a story of people who died young. There is no neatly manicured grass. There are no flowers. Only the unrelenting and unforgiving weeds.

Yes, Americans are big on monuments. We build them to memorialize our heroes, to honor our martyrs, and sometimes, even to commemorate victims. But only when it makes us feel good.

We Don't Have to Live in Slums

Anna Aley

Anna Aley was a student as Kansas State University when she presented the following persuasive speech to her public speaking class. Her classmates selected the speech for presentation at a campuswide forum. Anna's speech made such an impression there that the local newspaper printed the text of it and launched an investigation into the community problem Anna revealed. The speech, investigative news stories, and follow-up editorials all created a momentum for change. The mayor responded by establishing a rental inspection program in Manhattan, Kansas. The speech is noteworthy for its vivid language; its effective use of supporting materials, especially narrative; and the deft way in which it focuses listeners on a program of action.

Slumlords—you'd expect them in New York or Chicago, but in Manhattan, Kansas? You'd better believe there are slumlords in Manhattan, and they pose a direct threat to you if you ever plan to rent an off-campus apartment.

I know about slumlords; I rented a basement apartment from one last semester. I guess I first suspected something was wrong when I discovered dead roaches in the refrigerator. I definitely knew something was wrong when I discovered the leaks: the one in the bathroom that kept the bathroom carpet constantly soggy and molding and the one in the kitchen that allowed water from the upstairs neighbor's bathroom to seep into the kitchen cabinets and collect in my dishes.

Then there were the serious problems. The hot water heater and furnace were connected improperly and posed a fire hazard. They were situated next to the only exit. There was no smoke detector or fire extinguisher and no emergency way out—the windows were too small for escape. I was living in an accident waiting to happen—and paying for it.

The worst thing about my ordeal was that I was not an isolated instance; many Kansas State students are living in unsafe housing and paying for it, not only with their money, but their happiness, their grades, their health, and their safety.

We can't be sure how many students are living in substandard housing, housing that does not meet the code specifications required of rental property. We can be sure, however, that a large number of Kansas State students are at risk of being caught in the same situation I was. According to the registrar, approximately 17,800 students are attending Kansas State this semester. Housing claims that 4,200 live in the dorms. This means that approximately 13,600 students live off-campus. Some live in fraternities or sororities, some live at home, but most live in off-campus apartments, as I do.

Many of these 13,600 students share traits that make them likely to settle for substandard housing. For example, many students want to live close to campus. If you've ever driven through the surrounding neighborhoods, you know that much of the available housing is in older houses, houses that were never meant to be divided into separate rental units. Students are also often limited in the amount they can pay for rent; some landlords, such as mine, will use low rent as an excuse not to fix anything and to let the apartment deteriorate. Most importantly, many students are young and, consequently, naive when it comes to selecting an apartment. They don't know the housing codes; but even if they did, they don't know how to check to make sure the apartment is in compliance. Let's face it—how many of us know how to check a hot water heater to make sure it's connected properly?

Adding to the problem of the number of students willing to settle for substandard housing is the number of landlords willing to supply it. Currently, the Consumer Relations Board here at Kansas State has on file student complaints against approximately one hundred landlords. There are surely complaints against many more that have never been formally reported.

There are two main causes of the substandard student housing problem. The first—and most significant—is the simple fact that it is possible for a landlord to lease an apartment that does not meet housing code requirements. The Manhattan Housing Code Inspector will evaluate an apartment, but only after the tenant has given the landlord a written complaint and the landlord has had fourteen days to remedy the situation. In other words, the way things are now, the only way the Housing Code Inspector can evaluate an apartment to see if it's safe to be lived in is if someone has been living in it for at least two weeks!

A second cause of the problem is the fact that campus services designed to help students avoid substandard housing are not well known. The Consumer Relations Board here at Kansas State can help students inspect apartments for safety before they sign a lease, it can provide students with vital information on their rights as tenants, and it can mediate in landlord-tenant disputes. The problem is, many people don't know these services exist. The Consumer Relations Board is not listed in the university catalogue; it is not mentioned in any of the admissions literature. The only places it is mentioned are in alphabetically organized references such as the phone book, but you have to already know it exists to look it up! The Consumer Relations Board does receive money for advertising from the student senate, but it is only enough to run a little two-by-three-inch ad once every month. That is not large enough or frequent enough to be noticed by many who could use these services.

It's clear that we have a problem, but what may not seem so clear is what we can do about it. After all, what can one student do to change the practices of numerous Manhattan landlords? Nothing, if that student is alone. But just think of what we could accomplish if we got all 13,600 off-campus students involved in this issue! Think what we could accomplish if we got even a fraction of those students involved! This is what Wade Whitmer, director of the Consumer Relations Board, is attempting to do. He is reorganizing the Off-Campus Association in an effort to pass a city ordinance requiring landlords to have their apartments inspected for safety before those apartments can be rented out. The Manhattan code inspector has already tried to get just such an ordinance passed, but the only people who showed up at the public forums were known slumlords, who obviously weren't in favor of the proposed ordinance. No one showed up to argue in favor of the ordinance, so the city commissioners figured that no one wanted it and voted it down. If we can get the Off-Campus Association organized and involved, however, the commissioners will see that someone does want the ordinance, and they will be more likely to pass it the next time it is proposed. You can do a great service to your fellow students—and to yourself—by joining the Off-Campus Association.

A second thing you can do to help ensure that no more Kansas State students have to go through what I did is sign my petition asking the student senate to increase the Consumer Relations Board's advertising budget. Let's face it—a service cannot do anybody any good if no one knows about it. The Consumer Relations Board's services are simply too valuable to let go to waste.

An important thing to remember about substandard housing is that it is not only distasteful, it is dangerous. In the end, I was lucky. I got out of my apartment with little more than bad memories. My upstairs neighbor was not so lucky. The main problem with his apartment was that the electrical wiring was done improperly; there were too many outlets for too few circuits, so the fuses were always blowing. On day last November, Jack was at home when a fuse blew—as usual. And, as usual, he went to the fuse box to flip the switch back on. When he touched the switch, it delivered such a shock that it literally threw this guy the size of a football player backwards and down a flight of stairs. He lay there at the bottom, unable to move, for a full hour before his roommate came home and called an ambulance.

Jack was lucky, His back was not broken. But he did rip many of the muscles in his back. Now he has to go to physical therapy, and he is not expected to fully recover.

Kansas State students have been putting up with substandard living conditions for too long. It's time we finally got together to do something about this problem. Join the Off-Campus Association. Sign my petition. Let's send a message to these slumlords that we're not going to put up with this any more. We don't have to live in slums.

WORKS CONSULTED

Kansas State University. *K-State! Campus Living.*

Registrar's Office. Kansas State University. Personal interview. 10 Mar. 1989.

Residential Landlord and Tenant Act, State of Kansas, 1975.

Whitmer, Wade. Director, Consumer Relations Board. Personal interview. 10 Mar. 1989.

Pesticides Speech

Cesar Chavez

Cesar Chavez was the founder and president of the United Farm Workers union, which organized and led national boycotts of table grapes and iceberg lettuce to protest the use of pesticides. The following "generic" speech (dated 1990) was presented to a variety of audiences as Chavez went around the nation speaking to various groups. He would insert names and expand the concluding paragraph depending on the audience. Note the use of statistics in the speech to dramatize the severity of the problem. Consider also how Chavez weaves information and testimony into his message, carefully citing the sources of his information. His citing of "reluctant" testimony from the "growers' own magazine" helps to strengthen his case. Consider also Chavez's use of narratives and analogy to arouse emotion in this speech.

Thank you very much. I am truly honored to be able to speak with you. I would like to thank the many people who made this possible for their kindness and their hospitality (insert names).

Decades ago, the chemical industry promised the growers that pesticides would create vast new wealth and bountiful harvests. Just recently, the experts learned what farm workers, and the truly organic farmers, have known for years. The prestigious National Academy of Sciences recently concluded an exhaustive five-year study, which showed that by using simple, effective organic farming techniques, *instead of pesticides*, the growers could make *more money*, produce *more crops*, and *protect the environment.*

Unfortunately, the growers are not listening. They continue to spray and inject hundreds of millions of pounds of herbicides, fungicides, and insecticides onto our foods.

Most of you know that the United Farm Workers have focused our struggle against pesticides on table grapes. Many people ask me "Why grapes?" The World Resources Institute reported that over three hundred thousand farm workers are poisoned every year by pesticides. Over half of all reported pesticide-related illnesses involve the cultivation or harvesting of table grapes. They receive *more* restricted-use application permits, which allow growers to spray pesticides known to threaten humans, than *any* other fresh food crop. The General Accounting Office, which does research for the U.S. Congress, determined that *34* of the *76* types of pesticides used *legally* on grapes pose potential human health hazards and could *not be detected* by current multi-residue methods.

My friends, grapes are the most dangerous fruit in America. The pesticides sprayed on table grapes are *killing America's children.* These pesticides *soak* the fields, *drift* with the wind, *pollute* the water, and are *eaten* by unwitting consumers. These poisons are designed to kill life, and pose a very real threat to consumers and farm workers alike.

The fields are sprayed with pesticides like captan, a fungicide believed to cause cancer, DNA mutation, and horrible birth defects. Other poisons take a similar toll. Parathion and phosdrin are "*nerve gas*" types of insecticides, which are believed to be responsible for the majority of farm worker poisonings in California. The growers spray sulphites, which can trigger asthmatic attacks, on the grapes. And even the growers' own magazine, *The California Farmer*, admitted that growers were *illegally* using a very dangerous growth stimulator, called *Fix*, which is quite similar to *Agent Orange*, on the grapes.

This is a very technical problem, with very *human* victims. One young boy, Felipe Franco, was born without arms or legs in the agricultural town of McFarland. His mother worked for the first three months of her pregnancy picking grapes in fields that were sprayed repeatedly with pesticides believed to cause birth defects.

My friends, the central valley of California is one of the wealthiest agricultural regions in the world. In its midst are clusters of children dying from cancer.

The children who live in towns like McFarland are surrounded by the grape fields that employ their parents. The children contact the poisons when they play outside, when they drink the water, and when they hug their parents returning from the fields. *And the children are dying.* They are dying *slow, painful, cruel* deaths in towns called *cancer clusters.* In cancer clusters like McFarland, where the childhood cancer rate is *800 percent* above normal.

A few months ago, the parents of a brave little girl in the agricultural community of Earlimart came to the United Farm Workers to ask for our help. Their four-year-old daughter, Natalie Ramirez, has lost one kidney to cancer and is threatened with the loss of another. The Ramirez family knew about our protests in nearby McFarland and thought there might be a similar problem in their home town. Our union members went door to door in Earlimart and found that the Ramirez family's worst fears were true. There are at least *four* other children suffering from cancer and similar diseases, which the experts believe were caused by pesticides in the little town of Earlimart, a rate *1200 percent* above normal. In Earlimart, little Jimmy Caudillo died recently from leukemia at the age of three.

The grape vineyards of California have become America's Killing Fields. These *same* pesticides can be found on the grapes you buy in the store. Study after study, by the California Department of Food and Agriculture, by the Food and Drug Administration, and by objective newspapers, concluded that up to *54 percent* of the sampled grapes contained pesticide residues. Which pesticide did they find the most? *Captan,* the same carcinogenic fungicide that causes birth defects.

My friends, *the suffering must end. So many* children are dying, *so many* babies are born without limbs and vital organs, *so many* workers are dying in the fields.

The growers, the supermarket owners, say that the government can *handle* the problem, can *protect* the workers, can *save* the children. It *should,* but it *won't.* You see, agribusiness is *big business.* It is a *sixteen billion* dollar industry in California alone. Agribusiness contributed very heavily to the successful campaign of Republican governor George Deukmajian. He has rewarded the growers by turning the Agricultural Labor Relations Board into a tool for the growers, run by the growers. The governor even vetoed a bill that would have required growers to warn workers that they were entering recently sprayed fields! And only *one percent* of those growers who *are caught* violating pesticide laws were even fined in California.

President [George Herbert Walker] Bush is a long-time friend of agribusiness. During the last presidential campaign, George Bush ate grapes in a field just *75 miles* from the cemetery where little Jimmy Caudillo and other pesticide victims are buried, in order to show his support for the table grape industry. He recently gave a speech to the Farm Bureau, saying that it was up to the *growers* to restrain the use of dangerous pesticides.

That's like putting *Idi Amin,* or *Adolf Hitler,* in charge of promoting *peace* and *human rights.*

To show you what happens to pesticides supposedly under government control, I'd like to tell you more about captan. Testing to determine the acceptable tolerance levels of captan was done by Bio-Tech Laboratories, later found *guilty* of falsifying the data to the EPA. The tolerance level set was *ten times* the amount allowed in Canada. Later, government agencies tried to ban captan, but were mysteriously stopped several times. Finally, the government banned captan on 42 crops, but *not on grapes.* Even the General Accounting Office found that the government's pesticide testing is wholly inadequate. The government is *not* the answer, it is part of the problem.

The growers and their allies have tried to stop us with *lies,* with *police,* with *intimidation,* with *public relations agencies,* and with *violence.* But *we cannot be stopped.* In our *life and death struggle* for justice, we have turned to the court of last resort: the American people.

At last we are winning. Many supermarket chains have stopped selling or advertising grapes. Millions of consumers are refusing to buy America's most dangerous fruit. Many courageous people have volunteered to help our cause or joined human chains of people who fast, who go without food for days, to support our struggle. As a result, *grape sales keep falling*. We have witnessed truckloads of grapes being dumped because no one would stoop low enough to buy them. As demand drops, so do prices and profits. This sort of economic pressure is the only language the growers understand.

We are winning, but there is still much work to be done. If we are going to beat the greed and power of the growers, we must work *together. Together,* we can end the suffering. *Together,* we can save the children. *Together,* we can bring justice to the killing fields. I hope that you will join our struggle, for it is *your* struggle too. The simple act of boycotting table grapes laced with pesticides is a powerful statement the growers understand. *Please, boycott table grapes.* For your safety, for the workers, *we must act,* and *act together.* (insert additional pitches)

Good night, and God bless you.

Living Wills: Ensuring Your Right to Choose

Bonnie Marshall

Bonnie Marshall was a student at Heidelberg College in Ohio when she made the following persuasive presentation. Her speech is noteworthy for its use of an opening narrative to heighten interest in the problem Bonnie was presenting. The speech is also strong in its use of personal and expert forms of testimony. Clearly, Bonnie had responsible knowledge of her subject. In her conclusion, she makes excellent use of repetition to underscore her message of personal responsibility. She presented the speech with great conviction, and its overall impact led to its selection as a finalist in the Midwest division of the 1991 Houghton Mifflin Public Speaking contest.

Harry Smith was a cranky, obstinate, old farmer. He loved bowling, Glenn Miller music, and Monday night football. He was also dying from cancer of the esophagus, which had metastasized to his lungs. He didn't like doctors, and he liked hospitals and modern medicine even less. Harry used to say that he remembered when three square meals, mom's mustard plaster, and an occasional house call from Doc Jones was all anyone ever needed to stay healthy. Harry didn't want to live in pain, and he hated being dependent on anyone else; yet like so many others, Harry never expressed his wishes to his family. When Harry's cancer became so debilitating that he could no longer speak for himself, his family stepped in to make decisions about his medical care. Since Harry never told them how he felt, his children, out of a sense of guilt over the things they had done and the love they hadn't expressed, refused to let Harry die. He was subjected to ventilators, artificial feedings, and all the wizardry that modern medicine can offer. Harry did die eventually, but only after months of agony with no hope of recovery.

Harry's doctor, my husband, agonized too, over the decisions regarding Harry's care. He knew that the children were acting out of grief and guilt, not for Harry's benefit. Yet because Harry had not documented his wishes, his doctor had no choice but to subject Harry to the senseless torture that he didn't want.

We all know of a similar case that gained national attention. On December 26, 1990, Nancy Cruzan died. The tragic young woman who became the focal point for the right-to-die movement was finally allowed to die after eight long years and a legal battle that reached the hallowed halls of the Supreme Court. Nancy's battle is now over, yet the issue has not been resolved and the need for action is more urgent than ever. Since the Supreme Court ruling on June 25, 1990, public interest in this issue has skyrocketed. From July 1990 to November 1990, the last month statistics were available, the Society for the Right To Die answered 908,000 requests for information. By comparison, in November of 1989, the first month that the Society kept monthly statistics, they answered only 21,000 requests.

Today I would like to explore this problem and propose some solutions that we all can implement.

The *Cruzan* v. *Missouri* decision was significant because it was the first time that the Supreme Court had rendered an opinion on the right-to-die issue. However, the message from the Court is anything but clear and complete. As Justice Sandra Day O'Connor wrote in her concurring opinion, "Today we decide only that one state's practice does not violate the Constitution. . . . The more challenging task of crafting appropriate procedures for safeguarding incompetents' liberty interests is entrusted to the 'laboratory' of the states." So while the Court has for the first time recognized a "constitutionally protected liberty interest in refusing unwanted medical treatment," it has also given the power over this issue back to the states. According to the July 9, 1990, issue of *U.S. News and World Report*, nine states, including Ohio, have no legislation recognizing the legality of living wills. Of the states that do have living will legislation, about one-half do not allow for the withdrawal of nutrition and hydration, even if the will says the patient does not want such treatment, according to Lisa Belken in the June 25th issue of the *New York Times*. Also according to the *Times*, only 33 states have health care proxy laws. Perhaps as a result of all this indecision and inconsistency, desperate patients with terminal illnesses will continue to seek out the "Dr. Deaths" of the medical community, those who, like Dr. Kevorkian of Michigan, are willing to surpass simply allowing the terminally ill to die, to actively bringing about death.

The right-to-die issue may seem far removed from you today, yet the American Medical Association estimates that 80 to 90% of us will die a "managed death." Even today, according to an editorial by Anthony Lewis in the June 29, 1990, *New York Times*, "The problem is far more acute and far-reaching than most of us realize. Almost two million people die in the United States every year, and more than half of those deaths occur when some life-sustaining treatment is ended." The decision to provide, refuse, or withdraw medical treatment should be made individually, personally, with the counsel of family, friends, doctors, and clergy, but certainly not by the state.

More and more, however, these personal decisions are being taken away from patients and their families and instead are being argued and decided in courts of law. Perhaps it began with Karen Ann Quinlan. It certainly continued with Nancy Cruzan, and these decisions could be taken away from you, if we do not act now to ensure that our right to refuse medical treatment is protected. And our right to refuse medical treatment includes the right to refuse artificial nutrition and hydration, just as it includes the right to refuse antibiotics, chemotherapy, surgery, or artificial respiration. According to John Collins Harvey, M.D., Ph.D from the Kennedy Institute of Ethics at Georgetown University, "The administration of food and fluid artificially is a medical technological treatment. . . . Utilizing such medical treatment requires the same kind of medical technological expertise of physicians, nurses, and dietitians as is required in utilizing a respirator for treatment of respiratory failure or employing a renal dialysis machine for the treatment of kidney failure. This medical treatment, however, is ineffective, for it cannot cause dead brain cells to regenerate; it will merely sustain biological life and prolong the patient's dying. Such treatment is considered by many physicians and medical ethicists to be extraordinary." Additionally, the Center for Health Care Ethics of St. Louis University, a Jesuit institution, prepared a brief for the Cruzan case which states that "within the Christian foundation, the withholding and withdrawing of medical treatment, including artificial nutrition and hydration, is acceptable."

So what can we do to protect ourselves and assure that our wishes are carried out? My plan is fourfold. First, we in Ohio must urge our legislators to pass living will legislation. Representative Marc Guthrie, from Newark, Ohio, has drafted a living will bill, House Bill 70. We must urge our legislators to pass this bill, since it is more comprehensive than the Senate version and will better protect our rights on this crucial issue.

Second, we must draw up our own living wills stating our philosophy on terminal care. I propose the use of the Medical Directive, a document created by Drs. Linda and Ezekiel Emanuel. This document details twelve specific treatments that could be offered. You can choose different treatment options based on four possible scenarios. You can indicate either that you desire the treatment, do not want it, are undecided, or want to try the treatment, but discontinue it if there is no improvement. This directive, which also includes space for a personal statement, eliminates much of the ambiguity of generic living wills and provides clearer guidelines to your physician and family.

Third, designate a person to make health care decisions for you should you become incompetent. This person should be familiar with your personal philosophy and feelings about terminal care and be likely to make the same decisions that you yourself would make. You should name this person in a Durable Power of Attorney for Health Care, a legal document that is now recognized in the State of Ohio.

Fourth, have a heart-to-heart talk with your doctor and be sure that he or she understands and supports your wishes on terminal care. Have a copy of your living will and Durable Power of Attorney for Health Care placed in your medical file. Finally, for more information on living wills, you can contact: The Society for the Right To Die, 250 West 57th St., New York, NY 10107, or send $1.00 to the Harvard Medical School Health Letter, 164 Longwood Ave., Fourth Floor, Boston, MA 02115 for a copy of the Emanuels' Medical Directive form.

I am interested in this issue because, through my husband, I have seen patients suffer the effects of not having an advance directive. You need to ask yourself how you feel about terminal care, but regardless of your personal response, we all must choose to protect our rights on this issue. WE must choose to pressure our legislators to adopt living will legislation. WE must choose to draw up our own living wills and health care proxies. And most importantly, WE must choose to discuss this most personal and sensitive issue with our families and loved ones, so that in the absence of a legal document, or even with one, they may confidently make the decisions concerning our life and death that we ourselves would make. Not all patients end up like Nancy Cruzan or Harry Smith. Many people are allowed to quietly slip away from the pain and suffering of life. But that can only happen after the careful, painful deliberation of a grieving family, who can at least take comfort in the fact that they are carrying out their loved one's wishes.

Martin Luther King Jr.'s Legacy for Us

Tommie Albright

Tommie Albright, Miss Florida Teen 2000, presented this inspirational speech of tribute at a Dr. Martin Luther King Jr. Memorial Evening in Daytona Beach, Florida, on January 13, 2000. The evening was sponsored by Daytona Beach Community College, where Ms. Albright was a student. The speech is noteworthy for its eloquence, especially for the way it uses antithesis and parallel construction to achieve the dramatic effects of contrast and repetition. These stylistic techniques and effects are interwoven late in the speech as Albright interprets King's dreams in his own time as calls for action in ours. The speech also reveals an unusual ability to expand ideas to illuminate their larger significance for listeners. We see this trait as Albright develops the theme that "every generation stands on the shoulders of the generation that came before." To prepare her adult listeners for such lofty thoughts coming from such a young person, she acknowledges her youth and limitations at the beginning of the speech with disarming and becoming modesty.

Thank you, Professor Fuqua, for that very kind introduction. I hope you recognize that, as my English Professor and also as the one who invited me to speak here this evening, you must take at least partial responsibility for any faux pas I make.

In all seriousness, though, Professor Fuqua is one of those dream teachers, who inspires and nurtures as she teaches and instructs.

And—along with many other students—I have been really blessed by her brilliant intellect and warm and forgiving nature.

And, I hope she will forgive me for feeling a bit daunted, speaking at this memorable event tonight.

It's daunting because:

Not only am I a teenager speaking before a very intellectual and gifted audience of adults. . . .

But because my words will most likely appear somewhat mundane following those of a sophisticated English professor and coming before those of a practiced preacher.

I suppose I now feel a little like I might feel if our high school football coach came over to our cheerleading squad and sent me into the football game in the middle of all those 200 pound guys.

But, I will do my best.

I have been asked to speak to you this evening with a perspective on Dr. Martin Luther King Jr.'s life, focusing on the present.

And, in doing so, I feel quite fortunate, because I can build on the brilliant review shared with us by Doctor Offiah, who so richly described the work of Dr. King and the impact of the important events of his life on his times.

But, because I am neither a scholar nor a preacher, I can only share with you what I believe is Dr. Martin Luther King's influence on my life and on my times, neither of which are very long in the grand scheme of things.

So, once again, I hope you will bear with me.

Ladies and gentlemen, we young people growing up in America today often look to the celebrated acts and worthy thoughts of others around us upon which to form our own acts and our own thoughts.

Close at hand, I am fortunate to have the thoughts and guidance of a very loving and supportive mother and father and wonderful teachers and professors such as Professor Fuqua here at DBCC.

But when as a young teenager—looking for inspiration and example—beyond my family circle and my classrooms—the life of Martin Luther King Jr. came more naturally to mind than you might imagine.

Outwardly, there is nothing much that links my life directly to Dr. King.

He was a man; I am a woman.

He was black; I am white.

He was a man of the 50s and 60s, which was a generation of turbulent change, and I am a woman of a generation that is yet to be tested.

He was—and still is—one of the most important leaders of the past millennium and I am still a high school and college student, waiting to be tested by life.

But, the fact is that—through his inspired leadership and spellbinding language—Dr. King has become a symbol. . . .

A symbol of calming harmony in a world of angry conflict—for every generation;

A symbol of human understanding in a world of bigoted ignorance—for every generation.

A symbol of tolerance and unity in a world of parochial disharmony—for every generation.

And, therefore, in his teachings and through his leadership principles, Martin Luther King Jr. spoke:

Not just to African Americans, but to all Americans—and especially to me and those of my generation;

And—not just to Americans, but to Europeans, Asians, Africans and all the people of every race and nationality throughout the world.

And not only for harmony and justice in his time, but for harmony and justice in my time and in the time of my children yet to come.

Dr. King's lessons of justice, brotherhood and harmony should have no boundaries of race, nationality or time.

As a white woman in Florida, I am just as much the recipient of his legacy of racial harmony as a black man in Georgia.

Because of Dr. King's Dream, as a white girl attending both an integrated high school and an integrated college, I am blessed by the teaching of brilliant black teachers like Professor Fuqua.

Because of Dr. King's Dream, I now have the friendship of schoolmates I might never have met had it not been for him and the great movement he led for equality and integration.

Because of Dr. King's work, I live in a time of racial harmony, not racial conflict.

So when Dr. Martin Luther King dreamed of the day when "little black boys and black girls will be able to join hands with little white boys and white girls together as sisters and brothers," I believe I was one of the little white girls he dreamed about.

Now no one—least of all me—would say that the total fulfillment of Martin Luther King's Dream of a just society—devoid of bigotry and malice—was realized in his time. . . .

Nor was it realized in your time. . . .

Nor will it be realized in my time.

But, it is our challenge and our responsibility—in our time—to do our very best to follow his teachings and his principles, and to continue the great work he began. . . .

Not only through his nonviolent leadership in the counterculture of the 50s and 60s. . . .

But also through his teachings that every man and woman on this earth has value and deserves respect.

Clearly, Dr. King willed us a legacy to live by—a legacy that is just as vital in our new millennium as it was in his.

In his great ministry of love and brotherhood so brilliantly put forth in his "I Have a Dream" speech Dr. King spoke of his dream of what should be.

It is now the task and responsibility of your generation and my generation to take up his challenge to us of making what should be . . . what is . . . and what will be.

It is now our obligation to make sure that in everything we do, no man's right of life, liberty and the pursuit of happiness is impinged upon.

Dr. King spoke of 1963 as the dawn of the struggle for justice.

It is now our duty to ensure that . . . in our new millennium . . . we continue that struggle for full justice, for all races and nationalities.

Dr. King dreamed of a time when the full meaning of America's creed that all men are created equal would be realized.

It is now up to all of us to make sure that . . . in our time on this earth . . . all men are treated equally.

Dr. King dreamed that one day the sons of former slaves and the sons of former slave owners would be able to sit down at the table of brotherhood.

We have come a long way toward that dream and, today, many of us sit at that table of brotherhood of which Dr. King dreamed. But there are still far too many who do not have a seat at that table. And it is our task to make more room for those who do not yet have a place.

Now, in his ministry and in his famous speech before the Lincoln Memorial, Dr. King was most likely thinking of blacks having a place at the table with whites.

But—in that same spirit—both blacks and whites today must make room for yellows, reds and browns at the table as well.

And there will be many places needed at that table, because, within the next five years, Hispanics will become the largest minority in North America.

Dr. King dreamed of a time when his four little children would not be judged by the color of their skin, but by the content of their character.

So today, it is our obligation to be character conscious and color blind.

And it is just as important that whites and blacks do not judge others by the color of their skin, but by the content of their character as well.

We all should be judged by what we do rather than how we look or how we talk.

And, were he here, I would hope that—in his rich and powerful preacher's voice—Reverend King would say a resounding Amen to that.

Yes—ladies and gentlemen—Martin Luther King had many dreams for us, each with its own challenge to us.

Where he dreamed of peace, we must be peaceful and seek peace.

Where he saw hope, we must provide fulfillment. Where he dreamed of equality, we must treat each other as equals.

Where he dreamed of brotherhood, we must act as brothers and sisters.

And where he dreamed of justice, we must provide a just society.

Let me close my few thoughts with you this evening by saying that Martin Luther King Jr. became famous, not for providing solutions, but for providing challenges and by setting the example.

And, now, each of us must accept his challenge for greater understanding and follow his powerful example.

Each of us, in our time, must fight the good fight for justice and equality.

For it is true that every generation stands on the shoulders of the generation that came before.

Just as Martin Luther King stood on the shoulders of Mahatma Gandhi to see the promised land of brotherhood and non-violent protest. . . .

Your generation must stand on Martin Luther King's shoulders to fulfill the destiny of brotherhood, in your time.

And my generation must stand on your shoulders to fulfill the destiny of brotherhood in our time.

So the higher your generation lifts mine, the higher we can hold the next, and the better off each successive generation thereafter will be.

As a young woman who now walks in your footsteps, all I ask is that you show us the same path of brotherhood and set the same good example that Doctor Martin Luther King Jr. showed and set for you.

I know you have the courage and strength to do so.

And I hope my generation will as well.

Thank you for your time, and good night.

A Tribute to Wilma Rudolph

The following material was presented as part of the National Sports Awards program telecast on NBC, June 23, 1993. The script, transcribed from the telecast of the show and provided by NBC, includes the beginning of the program. Tom Brokaw, NBC Nightly News anchor, was the master of ceremonies. Speeches of tribute were presented by Bill Cosby, entertainer and former college track star; Gail Devers, 1992 Olympic Gold Medal winner in the 100-meter dash; and Ed Temple, Ms. Rudolph's mentor and track coach at Tennessee State University.

Tom Brokaw (Master of Ceremonies): Good evening and welcome. This is such a fitting national celebration because, after all, what would life be without the games that we play? The greatest athletes—the most memorable—are those who give us a sense of exhilaration off the field as well as on. Heywood Hale Broun once said, "Sports don't build character; they reveal it." What you'll share here tonight is the essence of character as revealed by the lives of these great athletes.

Sports are such an important part of our national culture, our language, our fantasies. Well, tonight the National Sports Awards honors those who played their games at the highest level—and lived their lives at the same heights. They lifted us all by their achievements and by their conduct. Four of them are here in Washington with us tonight; one of them, Ted Williams, has been asked by his doctor not to travel, so he's watching from his home. They were all nominated by a panel of leading sports journalists.

The first that we honor tonight is a woman. When she was born, one of twenty-two children in a Tennessee family, no one could have guessed at that time that her story would echo over the decades, or that it would make even a big impression on the 1962 Middle Atlantic Conference High Jump Champion.

Bill Cosby: She was five foot eleven, she was slender, and she had the manner of a duchess, and you know what they called her in Europe? La Gazelle—La Perle Noire—La Chattanooga Choo-Choo. Wouldn't it be nice to be called "La Chattanooga Choo-Choo?"

I had dreams of being a track star, so I have a particularly vivid memory of this woman who broke barriers, broke records, and brought glory to her country at the 1960 Rome Olympics. Very few Olympians have climbed a bigger mountain than the girl from Clarksville, Tennessee—and her story is one of the most powerful and poignant of the modern Olympics. Madame Choo-Choo, I join the nation in saluting you.

When she was four years old, she contracted polio. Watching other children at play was the cruelest hurt of all. She said, "Only my mother gave me the faith to believe I'd ever walk again." She was the twentieth of twenty-two children. The family scrimped to pay for her therapy at the clinic nearly 90 miles away. But in the end it was her own therapy that did it. She threw away the brace, gritted her teeth, and taught herself to walk . . . to run, to throw herself completely into the Burt High School basketball team. Then a visiting coach who saw her play suggested she try something else.

She was naturally blessed with burning speed—and the passion to push it. Long-legged—and glamorous, there had never been a woman runner who looked like *this* and ran like *that.*

The Tennessee Tigerbelles made their international debut at the '56 Olympics. She was sixteen and green, and while the team had won a bronze, she missed her golden moment in the 200. It would be four years before the next Olympics. The girls track team was at the bottom of the budget, so Coach Ed Temple picked up the tab. Going into the Rome Olympics she was among the world's fastest but she remembered her failure in '56 —the narrow margin between gold and bronze.

Coach Temple's home movies—occasionally in focus—show the athletes settling in. Here's Wilma, and her new hat . . . and her new friends. Then it got serious. "From the moment I walked into the stadium," she said, "I blocked out everything. Everything." Her first event was the 100 meters. Eleven seconds flat. She was the fastest woman in the world. Then came the 200—the excruciating demand of speed and stamina. She simply ran away from the rest of the world. Twenty-four flat. An Olympic record. She wasn't done yet. On the last day she ran the anchor leg of the 400-meter relay, and another record fell. It was her third Olympic gold. No American woman had done that in track before.

From out of these Olympic games, Wilma Rudolph entered the company of American heroines. She was honored at every turn. But the greatest reward was in the eyes of her parents. Her hometown set aside old differences. Everyone came out to greet her. That night, for the first time, black and white sat together at the same table. Thirty years ago she gave women a reason to run. She still encourages. She still inspires. It is the simplest, purest athletic endeavor—to run. And oh my—how Wilma could run.

Tom Brokaw: At last summer's Olympic games in Barcelona, we were reminded once again of the power of the human spirit by another American sprinter, gold medal winner Gail Devers.

Gail Devers: I was diagnosed with Graves Disease in 1990, and until I received the proper medication, I had come within two days of having my feet amputated. Long before any of this ever happened, I had heard of a woman named Wilma Rudolph. I read about her in books and I'd watched the Wilma Rudolph stories several times on television and just like Wilma, during my ordeal my first goal was just to walk again. And once I was back on the track running, I thought about her determination.

I knew that she had overcome a very serious illness and still went on to pursue her dream. I felt that if Wilma could do it, I could do it too. Her strong will and her never-give-up attitude had inspired so many of us to keep going despite any obstacles that we may be faced with. And I want to take this opportunity to tell you, Wilma, thank you from the very bottom of my heart. Not just for the example that you've given, not just to me, but to all women in track and field. We love you.

Tom Brokaw: And the man with the movie camera. He has come from Tennessee to present Wilma Rudolph with her award. Her coach and mentor, who retires this fall after forty-two years as coach of the Tennessee State Tigerbelles, Ed Temple, ladies and gentlemen.

Ed Temple: Wilma, you've worked long and hard to achieve these kinds of honors. I've always talked about the adversity that you've had. I tell people that you were able to meet it, to greet it, and defeat it. Wilma, you were an individual who opened up the doors for women's track and field in the United States, and that will always be your greatest legacy. It is an honor for me to be here tonight with you.

Tom Brokaw: And on this occasion the great ones do a great walk, so Wilma Rudolph, will you please come forward so that Gail Devers and Ed Temple can present you the first National Sports Award. Ladies and gentlemen, the object of our attention and affection, Wilma Rudolph.

Wilma Rudolph: I'm excited. I'll get my breath. I receive this honor, and I dedicate it to the youth of America so they will know that their dreams too can come true. And also to my mother who is eighty-four years old, Blanche Rudolph. Thank you so much for this honor.

On June 23, 1993, *The Great Ones: The National Sports Awards* was broadcast on NBC. The program was conceived and produced by George Stevens Jr., Don Mischer, and Michael Stevens, and written by George Stevens Jr. and Brian Brown.

Women in Public Life Commencement Address, Radcliffe College, June 11, 1993

Elizabeth Dole

Elizabeth Hanford Dole received an undergraduate degree from Duke University and a master's degree and law degree from Harvard. Ms. Dole served as the secretary of transportation and the secretary of labor during the Reagan and Bush administrations. More recently she has been president of the American Red Cross. As of this writing, she is being mentioned prominently as a candidate for the United States Senate, representing North Carolina. As secretary of transportation, she instituted campaigns against drunken driving and for automobile safety. As secretary of labor she worked on programs of job training for at-risk youth, job safety regulations, stricter enforcement of child labor laws, and ways to shatter the glass ceiling that often prevents women from advancing in organizations. Ms. Dole's commencement address is a speech of inspiration aimed at getting the female graduates to realize their own potential and value as women. She suggests public service as a viable alternative to the private sector for women. She uses personal examples and narratives to give authenticity to her advice to the young graduates.

I have been asked to share some thoughts this afternoon on women in public policy—an interesting topic, because while there are more women in public leadership roles than in private, there are still relatively few. While there are greater opportunities for women in public leadership than in private, there are still relatively few. While there are greater opportunities for women in government, there obviously remain impediments.

There are many ways to pursue the goal of involving women in shaping public policy. And there are many reasons to pursue this goal. In the first place, it's right. Too many of our number have felt the sting of discrimination. Secondly, women, I believe, have something very special to offer. And, thirdly, our work force is changing. America must be able to welcome women and minorities into its leadership roles if we are to accommodate that change. Sixty-four percent of the new entrants to the work force over the next 10 years will be women. If the public sector is to attract the best and the brightest, it must be able to attract and reward women.

When I was in law school at Harvard, only 24 of the 550 students were women. There were only a few women, at the time, who had made partner in major law firms. The private sector simply was not a strong option. Public policy beckoned as a rewarding alternative—a call to service, a chance to make a positive difference in people's lives.

There are some observations I could offer [women today] which might smooth the way a little. I could summarize them this way: that our greatest obstacle—that we women are women in a world of men—is really an enormous opportunity.

Remember the question Henry Higgins asked in the film *My Fair Lady*, "Why can't a woman be more like a man?" Because I think it's important to learn the correct lesson from our successes, I believe that further gains do not depend on better answers to the question "Why can't a woman be more like a man?" The question we should be asking now is, "Why can't a woman be more like a woman?"

I'd like to quote for you from a recent article in *Life* magazine: "Women," the article asserts, "are more committed than men to cushioning the hard corners of the country, to making it a safer place. Women want stricter law enforcement against drunk driving and illegal firearms and drug dealing. . . . It's not that men don't care about these issues. It's simply that women care more."

I don't know whether that's true. But perhaps our approach is different. Perhaps our involvement in public policy debates provides a leavening influence. Perhaps more women in public service would result in greater focus on cushioning corners for vulnerable Americans. If that's so, then it is doubly important that we women add our voices to the national debates, that we take our places at the tables of power, that we rise to the challenge of leadership when we believe that to be our calling.

So then, why can't a woman be more like a woman? In other words, progress for women in public policy and private life may indeed hinge on our ability to acknowledge and develop our skills and values as women. It may just be that those are the skills and values our country needs most at this moment.

I have been privileged during my years in public service to work with a number of successful women in public policy and I would like to pass along some of their observations, and some of my own, about drawing on our professional female advantages.

The first is to take full advantage of our trumpeted trait of flexibility—in fact to plan for the unexpected, and relish our ability to think on our feet. Rigid guidelines, set agendas, and line reporting responsibilities all help create the illusion of control in the current management environment. But perhaps a knack for flexibility is more important.

Another observation I have is that to succeed in the public arena, women must learn to trust their instincts. It's not just female intuition—it's a cognitive skill that we are perhaps more open to. Estimation skills are now being taught to children as they come up through elementary and secondary schools, and instinct is oftentimes another word for it. It's an ability to take in a great deal of information and quickly reduce it to a rough but generally accurate picture. It's the soft route to hard data.

Yet too often we women allow ourselves to be intimidated into denying our instincts—whether it's a judgment of people, situations, or the heart of the policy question. The women in the audience have probably all had the experience of sitting across the table from someone—a man, let's say, with whom you disagree. Ask yourselves how many times, in this situation, has your reaction been to question your own judgment rather than his—only to find out later that you were right on the money?

Over the ages, we women have perfected to a high art form this trait of second-guessing ourselves. Perhaps it stems from our early constant exposure to society's message that female traits and talents are inferior; but we have to get over it. It takes confidence to trust ourselves, and if we don't have confidence, our voices will be lost if ever they're heard.

The third common denominator I've seen among successful women leaders is a commitment to those who follow. About twenty years ago, a group of us formed an organization called "Executive Women in Government," which still flourishes today. Its purpose is twofold: to help younger women who want to follow into public service by giving them information and advice, and to make it easier for women in policy-making positions to relate to one another across government. Networking—women reaching out to other women—is a way of using our special opportunities to overcome obstacles. I have been helped many times in the stages of my career by women who were ahead of me. As a result, my door is always open to young women who are in need of a mentor, and I would encourage other women to do the same.

The final challenge for women is not to let others define success for us. Our lives are complicated, balancing personal and professional goals, loving our families while searching for individual fulfillment. And every woman must find her own answers—answers that are right for her. Women must allow [themselves], and one another, the freedom to choose. Women across America are discovering that feeling in as many ways as there are women—some through public service, some in the world of business or as lawyers and doctors, and some as wives, mothers, and volunteers. No one can or should tell us where we will find that feeling, or how we will come to define our own success. These are decisions we alone can make for ourselves.

In the fairy tales we were read as children, once having been rescued by the prince, the "female lead" lives happily ever after. That was the theme in Cinderella, Snow White, and Sleeping Beauty. But now perhaps we need to read our daughters a new bedtime story—with a heroine who isn't a princess, but a woman who sees that there are things that need to be changed to make life better for herself and others. A woman who is not a victim, and who doesn't need a rescuer. We need a tale about a woman whose talents and abilities are valued and admired, a woman who uses those talents to succeed. A woman who is committed, who feels passionately about her life's decisions. Such a story would not be a fairy tale—there are thousands of examples. And if each of us continues to ask the right question, "Why can't a woman be more like a woman?" there will be hundreds of thousands more tomorrow.

Nobel Peace Prize Acceptance Speech

Elie Wiesel

Elie Wiesel delivered the following speech in Oslo, Norway, on December 10, 1986, as he accepted the Nobel Peace Prize. The award recognized his lifelong work for human rights, especially his role as "spiritual archivist of the Holocaust." Wiesel's poetic, intensely personal style as a writer carries over into this ceremonial speech of acceptance. He uses narrative very effectively as he flashes back to what he calls the "kingdom of night" and then flashes forward again into the present. The speech's purpose is to spell out and share the values and concerns of a life committed to the rights of oppressed peoples, in which, as he put it so memorably, "every moment is a moment of grace, every hour an offering."

It is with a profound sense of humility that I accept the honor you have chosen to bestow upon me. I know: your choice transcends me. This both frightens and pleases me.

It frightens me because I wonder: do I have the right to represent the multitudes who have perished? Do I have the right to accept this great honor on their behalf? I do not. That would be presumptuous. No one may speak for the dead, no one may interpret their mutilated dreams and visions.

It pleases me because I may say that this honor belongs to all the survivors and their children, and through us, to the Jewish people with whose destiny I have always been identified.

I remember: it happened yesterday or eternities ago. A young Jewish boy discovering the kingdom of night. I remember his bewilderment, I remember his anguish. It all happened so fast. The ghetto. The deportation. The sealed cattle car. The fiery altar upon which the history of our people and the future of mankind were meant to be sacrificed.

I remember: he asked his father: "Can this be true? This is the 20th century, not the Middle Ages. Who would allow such crimes to be committed? How could the world remain silent?"

And now the boy is turning to me: "Tell me," he asks. "What have you done with your life?"

And I tell him that I have tried. That I have tried to keep memory alive, that I have tried to fight those who would forget. Because if we forget, we are guilty, we are accomplices.

And then I explained to him how naive we were, that the world did know and remain silent. And that is why I swore never to be silent whenever and wherever human beings endure suffering and humiliation. We must always take sides. Neutrality helps the oppressor, never the victim. Silence encourages the tormentor, never the tormented.

Sometimes we must interfere. When human lives are endangered, when human dignity is in jeopardy, national borders and sensitivities become irrelevant. Wherever men or women are persecuted because of their race, religion or political views, that place must—at that moment—become the center of our universe.

Of course, since I am a Jew profoundly rooted in my people's memory and tradition, my first response is to Jewish fears, Jewish needs, Jewish crises. For I belong to a traumatized generation, one that experienced the abandonment and solitude of our people. It would be unnatural for me not to make Jewish priorities my own: Israel, Soviet Jewry, Jews in Arab lands.

But there are others as important to me. Apartheid is, in my view as abhorrent as anti-Semitism. To me, Andrei Sakharov's isolation is as much a disgrace as Iosif Begun's imprisonment. As is the denial of Solidarity and its leader Lech Walesa's right to dissent. And Nelson Mandela's interminable imprisonment.

There is so much injustice and suffering crying out for our attention: victims of hunger, or racism and political persecution, writers and poets, prisoners in so many lands governed by the left and by the right. Human rights are being violated on every continent. More people are oppressed than free.

And then, too, there are the Palestinians to whose plight I am sensitive but whose methods I deplore. Violence and terrorism are not the answer. Something must be done about their suffering, and soon. I trust Israel, for I have faith in the Jewish people. Let Israel be given a chance, let hatred and danger be removed from her horizons, and there will be peace in and around the Holy Land.

Yes, I have the faith. Faith in God and even in His creation. Without it no action would be possible. And action is the only remedy to indifference: the most insidious danger of all. Isn't this the meaning of Alfred Nobel's legacy? Wasn't his fear of war a shield against war?

There is much to be done, there is much that can be done. One person—a Raoul Wallenberg, an Albert Schweitzer, one person of integrity, can make a difference, a difference of life and death. As long as one dissident is in prison, our freedom will not be true. As long as one child is hungry, our lives will be filled with anguish and shame.

What all these victims need above all is to know that they are not alone: that we are not forgetting them, that when their voices are stifled we shall lend them ours, that while their freedom depends on ours, the quality of our freedom depends on theirs.

This is what I say to the young Jewish boy wondering what I have done with his years. It is in his name that I speak to you and that I express to you my deepest gratitude. No one is as capable of gratitude as one who has emerged from the kingdom of night.

We know that every moment is a moment of grace, every hour an offering; not to share them would mean to betray them. Our lives no longer belong to us alone; they belong to all those who need us desperately.

Thank you Chairman Aarvik. Thank you members of the Nobel Committee. Thank you people of Norway, for declaring on this singular occasion that our survival has meaning for mankind.

Glossary

acronym A word composed of the initial letters or parts of a series of words.

ad hominem fallacy An attempt to discredit a position by attacking the people who favor it.

after-dinner speech A brief, often humorous, ceremonial speech, presented after a meal, that offers a message without asking for radical changes in attitude or action.

agenda-setting function The work of informative speaking in raising topics to attention and creating a sense of their importance.

agreement The third stage in the persuasive process requires that listeners not only accept the speaker's recommendations but remember their reasons for doing so.

alliteration The repetition of initial consonant sounds in closely-connected words.

amplification The art of developing ideas by finding ways to restate them in a speech.

analogical persuasion Creating a strategic perspective on a subject by relating it to something about which the audience has strong positive or negative feelings.

analogous color scheme Colors adjacent on the color wheel; used in a presentation aid to suggest both differences and close relationships among the components represented.

analogy A connection established between two otherwise dissimilar ideas or things.

antithesis A language technique that combines opposing elements in the same sentence or adjoining sentences.

appreciative phase Phase of listening in which we enjoy the beauty of messages, responding to such factors as the simplicity, balance, and proportion of speeches and the eloquence of their language.

arguments Arrangements of proofs designed to answer key questions that arise in persuasive designs.

articulation The manner in which individual speech sounds are produced.

assimilation The tendency of listeners to interpret the positions of a speaker with whom they agree as closer to their own views than they actually are.

attitudes Feelings we have developed towards specific kinds of subjects.

audience demographics Observable characteristics of listeners, including age, gender, educational level, group affiliations, and sociocultural backgrounds, that the speaker considers when adapting to an audience.

audience dynamics The motivations, attitudes, beliefs, and values that influence the behavior of listeners.

autocratic leader A leader who makes decisions without consultation, issues orders or gives direction, and controls the members of the group through the use of rewards or punishments.

award presentation A speech of tribute that recognizes achievements of the award recipient, explains the nature of the award, and describes why the recipient qualifies for the award.

awareness This first stage in the persuasive process includes knowing about a problem, paying attention to it, and understanding how it affects our lives.

balance Achieving a balance among the major parts of a presentation.

bar graph A kind of graph that shows comparisons and contrasts between two or more items or groups.

begging the question Assuming that an argument has been proved without actually presenting the evidence.

beliefs Ideas we express about subjects that may explain our attitudes towards them.

body The middle part of a speech; used to develop the main ideas.

body language Communication achieved using facial expressions, eye contact, movements, and gestures.

boomerang effect An audience's hostile reaction to a speech advocating too much or too radical change.

brief example A specific instance illustrating a more general idea.

briefing A short, informative presentation given in an organizational setting.

bulleted list A presentation aid that highlights themes by presenting them in a list of brief statements.

call the question A motion that proposes to end the discussion on a motion and to bring it to a vote.

categorical design The use of natural or traditional divisions within a subject as a way of structuring an informative speech.

causation design A pattern for an informative speech that shows how one condition generates, or is generated by, another.

ceremonial speaking (ceremonial speech) Speaking that celebrates special occasions. Common forms are speeches of tribute, inspiration, and introduction, eulogies, toasts, award presentations and acceptances, and after-dinner speeches. Their deeper function is to share identities and reinforce values that unite people into communities.

chronological design Pattern of speech organization that follows a sequence of important events in relating the history of a subject or predicting its future.

claims Conclusions that go beyond factual statements to make judgments about their subjects.

co-active approach A way of approaching reluctant audiences in which the speaker attempts to establish goodwill, emphasizes shared values, and sets modest goals for persuasion.

cognitive restructuring The process of replacing negative thoughts with positive, constructive ones.

collaborative problem solving In group communication, an approach that gathers participants from separate areas of the public or private sectors for their input on a problem.

communication apprehension Anxiety or fear experienced before and during public speaking.

communication environment The setting in which communication occurs, including both physical and psychological factors.

comparative design A pattern for an informative speech that relates an unfamiliar subject to something the audience already knows or understands.

comparison Using supporting material to point out the similarities of an unfamiliar or controversial issue to something the audience already knows or accepts.

comparison and contrast An informative speech design that points out similarities and differences between subjects or ideas.

competence The speaker's appearance of being informed, intelligent, and well-prepared.

complementary color scheme Colors opposite one another on the color wheel; used in a presentation aid to suggest tension and opposition among various elements.

comprehensive phase Phase of listening in which we focus on, understand, and interpret spoken messages.

computer-assisted presentation The use of commercial presentation software to join audio, visual, textual, graphic, and animated components.

confusion of fact and opinion A misuse of evidence in persuasive speaking in which personal opinions are offered as though they were objective facts, or facts are dismissed as though they were mere opinion.

connotative meaning The emotional, subjective, personal meaning that certain words can evoke in listeners.

constructive listening The role of the listener in the creation of meaning. Involves discovering the speaker's intention, tracing out the implications and consequences of the message, and applying the message to one's life.

contrast Using supporting materials to emphasize difference between two things.

contrast effect A tendency by listeners to distort the positions of a speaker with whom they disagree and to interpret those positions as even more distant from their own opinions than they actually are.

coordination The requirement that statements equal in importance be placed on the same level in an outline.

critical listening The careful analysis and evaluation of message content.

critique An evaluation of a speech.

cultural gridlock Occurs when the cultural differences in a group are so profound that the varying agendas, priorities, customs, and procedures create tensions that block constructive discussion.

cultural sensitivity The respectful, appreciative awareness of the diversity within an audience.

culturetypes Terms that express the values and goals of a group's culture.

debate The clash of opposing ideas, evaluations, and policy proposals on a subject of concern.

decoding process The process by which the listener determines the meaning of the speaker's message and decides the speaker's intent.

deductive reasoning A form of thinking that begins with a generally accepted truth, connects an issue with that truth, and draws a conclusion based on the connection.

definition A translation of an unfamiliar word into understandable terms.

deliberation Allowing all sides to express their opinions before a decision is made.

demagogues Political speakers who try to inflame feelings without regard to the accuracy or adequacy of their claims in order to promote their own agendas.

denotative meaning The dictionary definition or objective meaning of a word.

descriptions Word pictures that help listeners visualize information by evoking vivid, concrete images in their minds.

dialect A speech pattern associated with an area of the country or with a cultural or ethnic background.

dialogue group A group assembled to explore the underlying assumptions of a problem but not necessarily to solve it.

direct quotation Repeating the exact words of another to support a point.

discriminative phase Phase of listening in which we detect the vital sounds of spoken communication.

disinformation Communication that offers what appears to be information, but that actually deceives listeners and impedes their understanding.

dynamism The impact made on listeners when they perceive a speaker as confident, decisive, and enthusiastic.

egocentrism Holding the view that one's own experiences and thoughts are the norm.

either-or thinking A fallacy that occurs when the speaker informs listeners that they are restricted to two options, only one of which is desirable.

electronic brainstorming A group technique in which participants generate ideas in computer chat groups or by email.

empathic phase Phase of listening in which we suspend judgment, allow speakers to be heard, and try to see things from their points of view.

empirical A form of thinking that emphasizes the close inspection of reality.

enactment The fourth stage of the persuasive process in which listeners take appropriate action as the result of their agreement.

encoding process The process by which the speaker combines words, tones, and gestures to convey thought and feelings to the audience.

enduring metaphors Metaphors of unusual power and popularity that are based on experience that lasts across time and that crosses many cultural boundaries.

enunciation The manner in which individual words are articulated and pronounced in context.

ethics The moral dimension of human conduct, governing how we treat others and wish to be treated in return.

ethnocentrism The tendency of any nation, race, religion, or organized group to believe that its way of looking at and doing things is right and that other perspectives have less value.

ethos Those characteristics that make a speaker appear honest, credible, and appealing; a kind of proof created by a speaker's own favorable impression and by association with credible testimony.

eulogy A speech of tribute presented upon a person's death.

evidence Supporting materials used in persuasive speeches, including facts and figures, examples, narratives, and testimony.

examples Verbal illustrations of the speaker's points.

expanded conversational style A presentational quality that, while more formal than everyday conversation, preserves its directness and spontaneity.

expert testimony Information derived from authorities within a field.

explanations A combination of facts and statistics to clarify a topic or process mentioned in a speech.

extemporaneous presentation (extemporaneous speaking) A form of presentation in which a speech, although carefully prepared and practiced, is not written out or memorized.

extended example A detailed illustration that allows a speaker to build impressions.

facts and statistics Items of information that can be used to illustrate and prove points made by the speaker. When expressed numerically, such information appears in statistics.

factual example An illustration based on something that actually happened or that really exists.

fallacies Errors in reasoning that make persuasion unreliable.

faulty analogy A comparison drawn between things that are dissimilar in some important way.

feedback The audience's immediate response to a speaker.

figurative analogy A comparison made between things that belong to different fields.

figurative language The use of words in certain surprising and unusual ways in order to magnify the power of their meaning.

filtering Listening to only part of a message, the part the listener wants to hear.

flawed statistical comparisons Statistical reasoning that offers fallacious conclusions by comparing unequal and unlike situations.

flow chart A visual method of representing power and responsibility relationships.

formal outline The final outline in a process leading from the first rough ideas for a speech to the finished product.

free-rein leader A leader who leaves members free to decide what, how, and when to act, offering no guidance.

gender stereotyping Generalizations based on oversimplified or outmoded assumptions about gender and gender roles.

general purpose (general function) The speaker's overall intention to inform or persuade listeners, or to celebrate some person or occasion.

good form A primary principle of structure, based on simplicity, symmetry, and orderliness.

graphics Visual representations of information.

great expectation fallacy The mistaken idea that major change can be accomplished by a single persuasive effort.

groupthink Occurs when a single, uncritical frame of mind dominates group thinking and prevents the full, objective analysis of specific problems.

habitual pitch The level at which people speak most frequently.

hasty generalization An error of inductive reasoning in which a claim is made based on insufficient or nonrepresentative information.

hypothetical example A representation of reality, usually a synthesis of actual people, situations, or events.

identification The close involvement of subject, speaker, and listener.

ideographs Words that convey in a compressed way a group's basic, political faith or system of beliefs.

immediacy A quality of successful communication achieved when the speaker and audience experience a sense of closeness.

impromptu speaking A talk delivered with minimal or no preparation.

information cards Records of facts and ideas obtained from an article or book used in research.

informative speech Speech aimed at extending understanding.

informative value A measure of how much new and important information or understanding a speech conveys to an audience.

inoculation effect Preparing an audience for an opposing argument by answering it before listeners have been exposed to it.

integration Final stage of the persuasive process in which listeners must connect new attitudes and commitments with previous beliefs and values to ensure lasting change.

integrity The quality of being ethical, honest, and dependable.

interference Any physical noise or psychological distraction that impedes the hearing of a speech.

internal summary Reminding listeners of major points already presented in a speech before proceeding to new ideas.

introduction The first part of a speech, intended to gain the audience's attention and to prepare them for the rest of the presentation.

inversion Changing the normal order of words to make statements memorable and emphatic.

jargon Technical language related to a specific field that may be incomprehensible to a general audience.

key-word outline An abbreviated version of a formal outline, used in presenting a speech.

lay testimony Information that is derived from the first-hand experience of ordinary citizens.

likeableness The quality of radiating goodness and good-will and inspiring audience affection in return.

line graph A visual representation of changes across time; especially useful for indicating trends of growth or decline.

listener A person who interprets the message offered by the speaker to construct its meaning.

literal analogy A comparison made between subjects within the same field.

logos A form of proof that makes rational appeals based on facts and figures and expert testimony.

magnification A speaker's selecting and emphasizing certain qualities of a subject to stress the values they represent.

main motion A proposal that would commit a group to some specific action or declaration.

main points The most prominent ideas of the speaker's message, and a speech's principal points of focus.

malapropisms Language errors that occur when a word is confused with another word that sounds like it.

manuscript presentation A speech read from a manuscript.

marking Adding a gender reference when none is needed—e.g., "a woman doctor."

master of ceremonies A person who coordinates an event or program, sets its mood, introduces participants, provides transitions, and may also present awards.

maxims Brief and particularly apt sayings.

memorized text presentations Speeches that are committed to memory and delivered word for word.

message The fabric of words, illustrations, voice, and body language that conveys the idea of the speech.

metaphor A figure of speech in which anticipated words are replaced by new, surprising language in order to create a new perspective. (7, 10)

mirror questions Questions that repeat part of a previous response to encourage further discussion.

motion Formal proposal for group consideration.

motivated sequence design A persuasive speech design that proceeds by arousing attention, demonstrating a need, satisfying the need, visualizing results, and calling for action.

motivation Internal forces that impel action and direct human behavior toward specific goals.

mountain graph A variation of a line graph in which different colors are used to fill in the areas above and below the line(s).

move to amend A parliamentary move that offers the opportunity to modify a motion presently under discussion.

multisided presentation A speech in which the speaker's position is compared favorably to other positions.

myth of the mean The deceptive use of statistical averages in speeches.

mythos A form of proof that connects a subject to the culture and tradition of a group through the use of narratives.

narrative A story used to illustrate some important truth about a speaker's topic.

non sequitur fallacy A deductive error occurring when conclusions are drawn improperly from the premises that precede them.

onomatopoeia The use of words that sound like the subjects they signify.

opinions Expressions of personal attitude or belief offered without supporting material.

optimum pitch The level at which people can produce their strongest voice with minimal effort and that allows variation up and down the musical scale.

order A consistent pattern used to develop a speech.

parallel construction Wording an outline's main points in the same way to emphasize their importance and to help the audience remember them.

paraphrase A summary of something said or written.

parliamentary procedure A set of formal rules that establishes an order of business for meetings and encourages the orderly, fair, and full consideration of proposals during group deliberation.

participative leader A leader who seeks input from group members and gives them an active role in decision making.

pathos Proof relying on appeals to personal motives and emotions.

personification A figure of speech in which nonhuman or abstract subjects are given human qualities.

persuasion The art of convincing others to give favorable attention to our point of view.

persuasive speech Speech intended to influence the attitudes or actions of listeners.

pictographs On a chart, a visual image symbolizing the information it represents.

pie graph A circle graph that shows the size of a subject's parts in relation to each other and to the whole.

pitch The position of a human voice on the musical scale.

plagiarism Presenting the ideas and words of others without crediting them as sources.

post hoc fallacy A deductive error in which one event is assumed to be the cause of another simply because the first preceded the second.

postpone consideration (move to postpone consideration) A motion that defers discussion until some specified time when necessary information will be available.

precision Using information that is closely and carefully related to the specific purpose and context of a speech; particularly important when a topic varies widely in application.

preliminary tuning effect The effect of previous speeches or other situational factors in predisposing an audience to respond positively or negatively to a speech.

prepersuasive function The way in which informative speaking shapes listeners' perceptions, preparing them for later persuasive speeches on a topic.

PREP formula An outlining technique for an impromptu speech: state a point, give a reason or example, and restate the point.

presentation The act of offering a speech to an audience, integrating the skills of nonverbal communication, especially body language, with the speech content.

presentation aids Supplemental materials used to enhance the effectiveness and clarity of a presentation.

prestige testimony Information coming from a person who is highly regarded, but not necessarily an expert on a topic.

preview The part of the introduction that identifies the main points to be developed in the body of the speech and presents an overview of the speech to follow.

principle of closure The need for a satisfactory end or conclusion to a speech.

principle of proximity The idea that things occurring together in time or space should be presented in the order in which they normally happen.

principle of similarity The principle that like things should be grouped together.

probes Questions that ask an expert to elaborate on a response.

problem-solution design A persuasive speech pattern in which listeners are first persuaded that they have a problem and then are shown how to solve it.

pronunciation The use of correct sounds and of proper stress or accent on syllables in saying words.

proof An interpretation of evidence that provides a good reason for listeners to agree with the speaker.

proxemics The study of how human beings use space during communication.

qualifiers Words that suggest the degree of confidence a speaker has in the conclusion of his or her argument.

quoting out of context An unethical use of a quotation that changes or distorts the original speaker's meaning or intent by not including parts of the quote.

rate The speed at which words are uttered.

reasoning from analogy Argumentative reasoning that is based upon similar or parallel situations, in which one situation becomes a model from which to draw conclusions about the other.

reasoning from observation Argumentative reasoning that is based upon the close inspection of reality. Such reasoning, sometimes called empirical or inductive, often uses factual and statistical evidence and expert testimony.

reasoning from principle Argumentative reasoning that is based upon shared principles, values, and rules. Such reasoning, sometimes called deductive, often makes use of narratives, appeals to cultural identity (mythos), and prestige testimony.

receiver apprehension Fear of misinterpreting, inadequately processing and/or not being able to adjust psychologically to messages sent by others.

recency Ensuring that the information in a speech is the latest that can be provided.

red herring fallacy The use of irrelevant material to divert attention.

refutative design A persuasive speech design in which the speaker tries to raise doubts about, damage, or destroy an opposing position.

reinforcer A comment or action that encourages further communication from someone being interviewed.

reliability The trustworthiness of information critical to the credibility of a speech.

reluctant testimony Highly credible form of supporting material in which sources of evidence speak against their apparent self-interest.

reluctant witnesses Those who offer reluctant testimony; i.e., they speak against their apparent self-interest.

research overview A listing of the main sources of information that could be used in a speech and of the major ideas from each source.

responsible knowledge An understanding of the major features, issues, experts, latest developments, and local applications relevant to a topic.

rhetorical questions Questions that have a self-evident answer, or that provoke curiosity that the speech then proceeds to satisfy.

rhythm Rate patterns of vocal presentation within a speech.

Robert's Rules of Order The authoritative, traditional "bible" of parliamentary procedure.

second A motion must receive a "second" before group discussion can proceed; ensures that more than one member wishes to have the motion considered.

self-awareness inventory A series of questions that a speaker can ask to develop an approach to a speech of introduction.

sequence chart Visual illustrations of the different stages of a process.

sequential design A pattern for an informative speech that presents the steps involved in the process being demonstrated.

sexism Allowing gender stereotypes to control interactions with members of the opposite sex.

sexist language The use of masculine nouns and pronouns when the intended reference is to both sexes, or the use of derogatory, emotional, trigger words when referring to women.

simile A language tool that clarifies something abstract by comparing it with something concrete; usually introduced by "as" or "like."

simplicity A desirable quality of speech structure; suggests that a speech have a limited number of main points and that they be short and direct.

skills training Developing abilities and attitudes that help speakers control and transform communication apprehension into a positive factor.

slang The language of the street; informal, colorful expressions that may be widely used, but are not accepted in standard usage, and may be inappropriate on some occasions.

sleeper effect A delayed reaction to persuasion.

slippery slope fallacy The assumption that once something happens, an inevitable trend is established that will lead to disastrous results.

social leadership behavior Occurs when leaders focus upon building and maintaining positive, productive relationships among group members.

source cards Records kept of the author, title, place and date of publication, and page references for each research source.

source citation Parenthetical reference in a speech outline to sources listed in full under Works Consulted.

spatial design A pattern for an informative speech that orders the main points as they occur in physical space.

specific purpose The speaker's particular goal or the response that the speaker wishes to evoke.

speech of acceptance A ceremonial speech expressing gratitude for an honor and acknowledging those who made the accomplishment possible.

speech of demonstration An informative speech aimed at showing the audience how to do something or how something works.

speech of description An informative speech that creates word pictures to help the audience understand a subject.

speech of explanation A speech that is intended to inform the audience about abstract and complex subjects, such as concepts or programs.

speech of inspiration A ceremonial speech directed at awakening or reawakening an audience to a goal, purpose, or set of values.

speech of introduction A ceremonial speech in which a featured speaker is introduced to the audience.

speech of tribute A ceremonial speech that recognizes the achievements of individuals or groups or commemorates special events.

stereotypes Generalized pictures of a race, gender, or group that supposedly represent its essential characteristics. (1, 4)

stock issues design A persuasive speech pattern that attempts to answer the major general questions a reasonable person would ask before agreeing to a change in policies or procedures.

stories Accounts of actions or incidents that demonstrate points the speaker is making. See also narrative.

straw man fallacy Understating, distorting, or otherwise misrepresenting the position of opponents for the sake of refutation.

subordination The requirement that material in an outline descend in importance from main points to subpoints to sub-subpoints to sub-sub-subpoints.

subpoint The major division within a speech's main points.

substance A quality possessed by a speech when it has an important message, a careful plan of development, and adequate facts, examples, and testimony.

sub-subpoints Divisions of subpoints within a speech.

summary statement The speaker's reinterpretation of the speech's main idea at the end of a presentation.

supporting materials The facts and figures, testimony, examples, and narratives that constitute the building blocks of successful speeches.

symbolic racism An indirect form of racism that employs code words and subtle, unspoken contrast to suggest that one race is superior to another.

table the motion (move to table the motion) Suspends indefinitely the discussion of a motion.

task leadership behavior A leadership emphasis that directs the attention and activity of a group towards a specified goal.

testimonial Lay testimony used to endorse a person, practice, or institution.

testimony Citing the observations, opinions, or conclusions of other people or institutions to clarify, support, and strengthen a presentation.

textual graphics Visual presentation of key words in a speech using a chalkboard, poster board, flip chart, transparency, slide, or handout.

thesis statement The speech's central idea. (2, 5)

thoroughness Providing complete and accurate information about a topic.

toast A short speech of tribute, usually offered at celebration dinners or meetings.

topic area inventory chart A means of determining possible speech topics by listing topics you find interesting and subjects your audience finds interesting, and then matching them.

transaction The process by which we discover who we are as we communicate with others.

transactional leadership A leadership style based on power relationships that relies on reward and punishment to achieve its ends.

transformation The dynamic, positive effect of successful, ethical communication on the identities of the speaker and listener and on public knowledge.

transformational leadership A leadership style based on mutual respect and stewardship rather than on control.

transitions Connecting elements used in speeches. (2, 7)

trigger words Words that arouse such powerful feelings that they interfere with the ability to listen critically and constructively.

understanding This second phase in the persuasive process requires that listeners must grasp the meaning of the speaker's message.

universal human values Eight values identified by the Institute for Global Ethics that transcend cultural differences: love, truthfulness, fairness, freedom, unity, tolerance, responsibility, and respect for life.

values Underlying principles or standards of desirable or ideal behavior that should justify our beliefs and attitudes.

verbatim Using the exact words of a source.

verifier A statement by an interviewer confirming the meaning of what has just been said by the person being interviewed.

visualization The process of systematically picturing oneself succeeding as a speaker and practicing a speech with that image in mind.

vocal distractions Filler words, such as "er," "um," and "you know," used in the place of a pause.

working outline A tentative plan showing the pattern of a speech's major parts, their relative importance, and the way they fit together.

works cited A form of bibliography provided at the end of a formal outline that lists just those sources of supporting material actually used in the speech.

works consulted A form of bibliography provided at the end of a formal outline that lists all sources of research considered in the preparation of the speech.

Photo Credits

Chapter 1 **1:** © Frank Siteman/PhotoEdit. **4:** © Don Klumpp/Getty Images. **8:** © AP/Wide World Photos. **10:** © R.W. Jones/CORBIS. **14:** © Bob Daemmrich/The Image Works. **23:** © Dick Blume/The Image Works.

Chapter 2 **28:** © B. Stitzer/PhotoEdit. **31:** © Bob Daemmrich/Stock Boston. **35:** ©Ron Fehling/Masterfile. **39:** © 2003 PhotoDisc, Inc. **43:** © M. Granitsas/The Image Works.

Chapter 3 **56:** © Seth Resnick/Stock Boston. **60:** © Loren Santow. **62:** © Paula Lerner. **66:** © Michael Newman/PhotoEdit. **69:** © Bob Daemmrich/The Image Works. **73:** © Erik Freeland/Corbis SABA.

Chapter 4 **83:** © LWA—Dann Tardif/The Stock Market. **86:** © Bob Daemmrich/The Image Works. **87:** © Bonnie Kamin/The Image Works. **89:** © Mark Ludak/The Image Works. **95:** © Richard B. Levine. **99:** © AP/Wide World Photos. **107:** © Jonathan Nourok/PhotoEdit.

Chapter 5 **120:** © Rob Crandall/Stock Boston. **123:** © G&M David de Lossy/Getty Images. **124:** © Chris Tagaki. **134:** © David Young-Wolff/PhotoEdit. **140:** © James Marshall/The Image Works.

Chapter 6 **156:** © David Young-Wolff/PhotoEdit. **163:** © AP/Wide World Photos. **165:** © Martin Simon/Corbis SABA. **172:** © Bob Winsett/CORBIS.

Chapter 7 **182:** © Richard Pasley/Stock Boston. **187:** © Charles Gupton/Stock Boston. **194:** © Asahi Shimbum. **196:** © AP/Wide World Photos. **202:** © David Young-Wolff/PhotoEdit.

Chapter 8 **208:** © Jennifer Waddell. **225:** © Joel Gordon Photography, 1992.

Chapter 9 **231:** © Eyewire, Inc. **234:** © AP/Wide World Photos. **236:** © Michael Newman/PhotoEdit. **237:** © Comstock Inc. **244:** Kiser/Glacier National Park Archives; © Dan Fagre/U.S. Geological Survey. **248:** © Dan Bosler/Getty Images.

Chapter 10 **260:** © Billy E. Barnes/Stock Boston. **261:** © David Young-Wolff/PhotoEdit. **264:** © Flip Schulke/CORBIS. **270:** © L. Dematteis/The Image Works. **275:** © Jeff Greenberg/PhotoEdit. **279:** © Jonathan Nourok/Getty Images.

Chapter 11 **286:** © Richard B. Levine. **287:** © Joel Gordon Photography, 1993. **289:** © AP/Wide World Photos. **293:** © Joel Gordon Photography, 1992. **295:** © G&M David de Lossy/Getty Images. **299:** © Chris Mooney/BWP Studios. **307:** © Richard B. Levine. **309:** © AP/Wide World Photos.

Chapter 12 **318:** © AP/Wide World Photos. **320:** © Bob Daemmrich/Stock Boston. **321:** © Bob Daemmrich/Stock Boston. **322:** © Michael Newman/PhotoEdit. **325:** © Shmuel Thaler/Jeroboam. **326:** © Al Campanie/Syracuse Newspapers/The Image Works. **330:** © Bob Stern/The Image Works. **332:** © Paul S. Howell/Getty Images. **334:** © Bob Mahoney/The Image Bank.

Chapter 13 **346:** © Bob Daemmrich/The Image Works; © AP/Wide World Photos. **348:** © Patsy Lynch/CORBIS. **351:** © Paula Bronstein/Getty Images. **353:** © Andrew Yates Productions/Getty Images. **357:** © Jonathan Nourok/PhotoEdit.

Chapter 14 **374:** © James Lemass/Getty Images. **379:** © Joel Gordon, 1993. **381:** "American Progress," by John Gast, 1872, oil on canvas, Autry Museum of American Heritage, Los Angeles. **383:** © Suzanne Dunn/Syracuse Newspapers/The Image Works. **385:** © Bettmann/CORBIS.

Chapter 15 **404:** © Richard B. Levine; © Bob Daemmrich/Stock Boston. **406:** © Bruce Henderson/Stock Boston. **408:** © Hulton-Deutsch Collection/CORBIS; © James Burke/TimePix. **410:** © Alan Goldstein/Folio; © Thomas E. Franklin/Corbis SABA. **411:** © Pressens Bild AB/Getty Images. **413:** © AP/Wide World Photos. **414:** © David Young-Wolff/PhotoEdit. **420:** © Bob Daemmrich/The Image Works.

Index